MW00355717

DICTIONARY OF AMERICAN HAND TOOLS

A Pictorial Synopsis

Other books by Alvin Sellens

THE STANLEY PLANE A History and Descriptive Inventory

WOODWORKING PLANES A Descriptive Register of Wooden Planes

STANLEY FOLDING RULES A History and Descriptive Inventory

SELLENS OF KANSAS A Genealogy of a Pioneer Family

DICTIONARY
OF
AMERICAN HAND TOOLS

A Pictorial Synopsis

Compiled
by
ALVIN SELLENS

4880 Lower Valley Road, Atglen, PA 19310 USA

Copyright © 2002 by Alvin Sellens

Library of Congress Cataloging-in-Publication Data:

Sellens, Alvin.
Dictionary of American hand tools: a pictorial synopsis/compiled by Alvin Sellens.
p.   cm.
ISBN 978-0-7643-1592-3 (hardcover)
1. Tools--United States--Dictionaries. I. Title.
TJ1195.S42 2002
621.9'08'0973--dc21   89-70210
2002001108

All rights reserved. No part of this work may be reproduced or used in any form or by any means—graphic, electronic, or mechanical, including photocopying or information storage and retrieval systems—without written permission from the publisher.
The scanning, uploading and distribution of this book or any part thereof via the Internet or via any other means without the permission of the publisher is illegal and punishable by law. Please purchase only authorized editions and do not participate in or encourage the electronic piracy of copyrighted materials.
"Schiffer," "Schiffer Publishing Ltd. & Design," and the "Design of pen and inkwell" are registered trademarks of Schiffer Publishing Ltd.

ISBN: 978-0-7643-1592-3
Printed in China

Schiffer Books are available at special discounts for bulk purchases for sales promotions or premiums. Special editions, including personalized covers, corporate imprints, and excerpts can be created in large quantities for special needs. For more information contact the publisher:

Published by Schiffer Publishing Ltd.
4880 Lower Valley Road
Atglen, PA 19310
Phone: (610) 593-1777; Fax: (610) 593-2002
E-mail: Info@schifferbooks.com

For the largest selection of fine reference books on this and related subjects, please visit our website at
www.schifferbooks.com
We are always looking for people to write books on new and related subjects. If you have an idea for a book, please contact us at proposals@schifferbooks.com

CONTENTS

PREFACE

This volume contains an illustration, description and purpose of practically every variety of American hand tool. The intent is to facilitate easy and rapid identification of any tool.

Most of the illustrations were taken from American trade catalogues. Photography, sketches and other sources were used for illustrations only when American trade literature was not available. Names and size data were also generally drawn from trade literature. Sizes are usually the combined limits from several catalogues. Usage of the tool is specified along with the associated craft where possible.

Emphasis is placed upon use of the correct tool names as used by the original makers, sellers and users. It is recognized that the term "Correct Name" is a relative expression. The names of tools have changed in some cases over a period of years and spellings of certain words have also undergone revision. Even guttural variations and slang terms must be considered as correct if there is evidence of widespread usage. Application of a descriptive name to a common tool to relate to a specific trade was a common practice. Needless to say, any given tool may have more than one correct name.

Tools addressed in this volume were made prior to the American entry into World War II in 1941.

The term "American Hand Tools", as used here-in, includes any tool made and offered for sale in North America in addition to any imported tool known to have been used in America. It is well known that tools were imported in quantity from England during the early years of American industrial expansion. However, in many cases there are marked differences between English and American names for identical items. Every effort has been made to utilize only the American names.

Data is assembled for convenience of tool identification. The names of many tools are transposed to allow items of like nature to be grouped together. Each illustration is clearly captioned with the most common name of the tool. Other names are shown under the preceding entry. Cross referencing is provided. Tools unique to many common crafts are listed for reference.

TOOLS LISTED BY TRADE

Listings of tools used in the following trades are included in their normal alphabetical sequence:

Bee Keeper
Blacksmith
Book Binder
Brick Mason
Cabinet Maker (Joiner)
Carpenter
Carver (Wood)
Caulker (Ship)
Cement Worker
Coach Maker (Carriage Maker)
Coal Miner
Comb Maker
Cooper
Currier
Electrotyper and Printer
Farmer
Farrier
Garden and Lawn Keeper
Ice Harvester (Ice Industry)
Jeweler
Logging (Lumbering)
Moulder (Casting)
Pattern Maker
Piano Maker (Piano Tuner)
Plasterer
Plumber
Railroad Construction
Saddle and Harness Maker (Trimmer)
Ship Builder
Shoe Maker (Shoe Cobbler)
Slater
Stone Cutter
Stone Mason
Stone Quarryman
Tanner
Taxidermist
Tinsmith (Tinner)
Turpentine Harvester
Upholsterer
Watch and Clock Repairman
Wheelwright

ACKNOWLEDGMENTS

The author gratefully acknowledges the assistance and support of the persons listed below. Each of these individuals generously shared their knowledge, provided specific material, loaned reference books or allowed photography of tools for which suitable illustrations could not be located.

Ron Baird	Fairgrove, Missouri
Ken Bassett	Tacoma, Washington
Roger Daniels	Fayette, Missouri
Robert K. Ginder	Atwood, Illinois
Will Gordon	Bull Shoals, Arkansas
Frank Gray	Kansas City, Kansas
Bill Hinz	Partridge, Kansas
Robert Hunn	Augusta, Kansas
Lex Jones	Augusta, Kansas
Norman Kamb	Dallas, Texas
Lysle Machin	Russell, Kansas
Edward R. Mark	McLean, Virginia
E. A. Olson	Lincoln, Nebraska
Herold Parkes	Kansas City, Kansas
Ivan Risley	Kansas City, Missouri
Elliot Sayward	Levittown, New York
Roger K. Smith	Athol, Massachusetts
Philip E. Stanley	Westborough, Massachusetts
Mark Sutterby	Udall, Kansas
R. T. Whalen	Baltimore, Maryland
Philip Whitby	Englewood, Colorado

Assistance is also acknowledged from many un-named persons who generated or shared the data obtained from my files. Much of this information was gathered many years before a book was anticipated. Sources of some of these scattered data were never recorded.

Information was drawn freely from the many fine books available regarding tools and crafts of America. Those books listed in the bibliography were especially useful and enlightening. Illustrations were taken primarily from American trade catalogues. These catalogues are not listed in detail but are acknowledged as being the indispensible part of the information required to compile this book.

Financial support for preparation of the manuscript was provided by the Grants-in-Aid Program of The Early American Industries Association, Charles F. Hummel, Chairman.

ALPHABETICAL LISTING OF TOOLS

A

Tool names starting with the letter A, including multiple listings of :

ADZE
ANVIL
ANVIL TOOL
APRON
AWL
AXE
AXE, BROAD

ACID BRUSH. A type of coarse brush. See *Brush, Acid*.

ADDICE. See *Adze*. Addice is an obsolete spelling.

ADJUSTABLE SCREW CLAMP. See *Clamp, Carriage Makers' Adjustable* and *Clamp, Quick*.

ADJUSTABLE WRENCH. See *Wrench, Adjustable*.

ADVERTISING HAMMER. A type of long-handled hammer. See *Hammer, Bill Posters'*.

ADZ. See *Adze*. Adz is an obsolete spelling.

ADZE. An impact cutting tool used for hewing and smoothing of a timber. The adze consists of a cutting edge fixed at right angles to a handle. The bit is curved back toward the handle to facilitate control of the tool during use. The cutting edge is beveled on the side adjacent to the handle. The handle is normally removed for sharpening. The adze is an ancient tool form and was used in America prior to the usage of metal implements. Knight's American Mechanical Dictionary pictures a stone adze used by the Chalam Indians for hollowing out log canoes. See also *Hammer Attachment*.

ADZE, BOWL. Also called CHAIR MAKERS' ADZE and HOLLOWING ADZE. A small one-handed adze with the bit curved back toward the handle in both planes. The bowl adze is used to hollow out a small workpiece such as a bowl or chair seat. This tool was a specialty device and was not carried by the major tool and hardware houses. Most of them are either homemade or blacksmith made. Bowl adzes have been widely imported from Europe for tool collectors rather than for use by craftsmen.

Bowl Adze

ADZE, CANOE. See *Adze, Gutter*.

ADZE, CARPENTERS'. Also called FOOT ADZE, HOUSE ADZE and HOUSE CARPENTERS' ADZE. An adze used for smoothing a large surface such as a framing timber or a floor. The poll is flat and could be used for driving pegs or light nails. The conventional usage of this tool is a chipping or smoothing action roughly between the feet of the user. Inasmuch as the cutting edge was kept extremely sharp, an unsteady hand or a glancing blow could easily result in injury to the user's foot. The colloquial term FOOT ADZE served as a reminder of the potential danger. Width of the cutting edge is 3 to 5 inches. The most common width is 4 inches. The eye is square or rectangular and is tapered such that the handle can be removed through the eye. This tool is normally considered to be a two-handed implement; however, the smallest size could be procured with a short handle suitable for use with one hand. The carpenters' adze was listed by one supplier as being available with a spike or spur in place of the flat poll. However, the spiked adze was generally listed as a ship builders' tool. See *Adze, Ship Carpenters'*.

Bowl Adze

Full Head
or Flat Head

Half Head,
Half Flat Head
or Square Head

Carpenter's Adze

ADZE, CHAIR MAKERS'. See *Adze, Bowl*.

ADZE, CONNECTICUT HAND. See *Adze, Hand*.

ADZE, COOPERS'. A one-handed adze used by a cooper for a variety of tasks including leveling the end of a barrel and cutting the chime. A stout hammer face, provided opposite the cutting edge, allows the adze to be used for hoop driving and most of the other pounding tasks required by the cooper. The adze was often used in place of a hammer. A unique feature of the coopers' adze is the metal bolt through the entire length of the handle. This internal reinforcement makes the handle practically indestructible from general use. Width of the cutting edge is 2 to 3 1/2 inches.

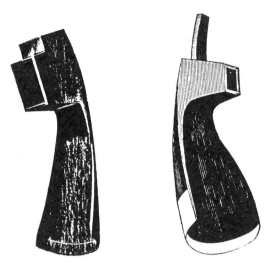

Flat Head   Spike Head

Gutter Adze

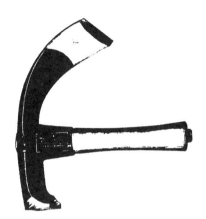

Coopers' Adze

ADZE, COOPERS' TUB. A small coopers' adze weighing from 1 1/2 to 2 pounds. This tool was intended for use in tub or keg work.

ADZE, DOUBLE BIT. Also called RAILROAD ADZE and TIE ADZE. An adze having two cutting bits rather than one bit and a poll. Cutting width is 2 to 4 inches. This adze was intended primarily for use in railroad construction work. See also *Adze, Tie*.

ADZE, HAMMER HEAD. Also called SCOTCH PATTERN ADZE. A tool similar to a Ship Carpenters' Adze except that this type of adze has a small hammer head on the end of the spike. See *Adze, Ship Carpenters'*.

Hammer Head Adze

ADZE, HAND. Also called CONNECTICUT HAND ADZE and STIRRUP ADZE. A one-handed adze, with a straight cutting edge, having the iron attached with a collar and wedge. The hand adze has a short handle curved back very close to the cutting edge. The handle is often enclosed. See illustration. The hand adze has been widely imported from Europe for tool collectors.

Double Bit Adze

ADZE, FOOT. See *Adze, Carpenters'*.

ADZE, GUTTER. Also called CANOE ADZE and SPOUT ADZE. A two-handed adze with the bit and cutting edge formed into a hollow curve approaching a half circle. This tool was used to hollow out wooden gutters, troughs, spouts and similar long workpieces.

Hand Adze

Hand Adze

ADZE, HOUSE. See *Adze, Carpenters'*.

ADZE, HOUSE CARPENTERS'. See *Adze, Carpenters'*.

ADZE, HOLLOWING. See *Adze, Bowl*.

ADZE, ICE. A tool used to smooth blocks of ice during the various cutting and storing phases of the ice harvest. One particular use was to smooth the layers as ice was being packed into the ice house. Width of cutting edge is approximately 6 1/4 inches.

Ice Adze

ADZE, LIPPED. See *Adze, Ship Carpenters' Lipped*. LIPPED ADZE is a short name for Ship Carpenters' Lipped Adze.

ADZE, RAILROAD. Also called TRACK ADZE. This tool is similar to a Carpenters' Adze except that the railroad adze is of heavier construction and generally has a wider cutting edge. Width of the cutting edge is 4 to 8 inches. The primary usage of the railroad adze is to pare down a railroad crosstie or bridge timber when repairing or building a roadbed. See also *Adze, Double Bit* and *Adze, Tie*.

Flat Head
or Full Head

Square Head
or Half Flat Head

Railroad Adze

ADZE, SCOTCH PATTERN. See *Adze, Hammer Head*.

ADZE, SHIP. See *Adze, Ship Carpenters'*.

ADZE, SHIP CARPENTERS'. Also called SHIP ADZE. A two-handed adze similar to the Carpenters' Adze except generally lighter weight and having a tapered spike in place of the flat poll. Used extensively in the ship building trade for smoothing decks as well as for cutting both curved and straight framing timbers. The spike, called a spur in some catalogues, is approximately three inches long and squared on the end. It was used to drive nails down below the surface of the decking. The nails were driven deep enough to avoid interference when smoothing the surface and to avoid future interference with cleaning the deck and moving cargo. The ship carpenters' adze was available with cutting edges of 4 to 6 inches. One supplier listed this tool as being available with a flat head in place of a spike.

Ship Carpenters' Adze

ADZE, SHIP CARPENTERS' LIPPED. Also called LIPPED ADZE. A two-handed adze similar to the Ship Carpenters' Adze except that the edges of the cutting bit are turned up. The turned up edges reduce tearing at the edges of the cut and allow the cut to be smoothly terminated as might be required at a bulkhead or stanchion. These tools were listed with cutting edges of 4 1/2 to 6 inches.

Ship Carpenters' Lipped Adze

ADZE, SPANISH ROUND EYE. A spiked adze with a round eye for insertion of the handle. Width of cut is 5 to 6 inches. This tool was produced in America primarily for export but was also offered for sale internally.

Spanish Round Eye Adze

ADZE, SPOUT. See *Adze, Gutter.*

ADZE, STIRRUP. The term "Stirrup" is derived from the D-shaped metal strap used for attachment of the handle. See *Adze, Hand.*

ADZE, TIE. An adze with two narrow cutting bits. This tool was intended for use in railroad construction and repair. Overall length from the tip of one cutting edge to the other is approximately 20 inches.

Tie Adze

ADZE, TRACK. See *Adze, Railroad.*

ADZE AXE. A narrow-bit adze in combination with an axe bit. The shank of the adze bit is curved back toward the handle rather than being almost straight as in the axe mattock. The cutting edge of the adze bit is either curved, as illustrated, or straight across. This tool has an axe-handle type eye.

Adze Axe

ADZE HAMMER. A type of hammer with the peen shaped like a rudimentary adze bit. See *Hammer, Adze.*

ADZE HANDLE. The common adze handle, generally made from hickory or ash, has a graceful double curve that brings the cutting edge of the adze parallel to the floor at a point just ahead of the user's feet. Length is 32 to 36 inches. A common length is 34 inches. The Ship Carpenters' Adze Handle listed by some suppliers was shaped slightly different than the handle of the Carpenters' Adze. See illustration.

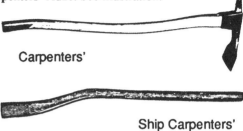

Carpenters'

Ship Carpenters'

Adze Handle

AGATE BURNISHER. See *Burnishing Tool, Agate.*

AGRICULTURAL FORGE. An inexpensive Blacksmiths' Forge. See *Forge, Agricultural.*

AGRICULTURAL WRENCH. A type of screw wrench. See *Wrench, Agricultural.*

ALCOHOL TORCH. See *Torch, Alcohol.*

ALFALFA FORK. See *Fork, Hay.*

ALLEN WRENCH. See *Wrench, Socket Set Screw.*

ALLIGATOR WRENCH. See *Wrench, Alligator.*

ALUMINUM LEVEL. See *Level, Aluminum.*

ALUMINUM PLANE. See *Plane, Aluminum.*

AMATEURS' BENCH. A small wood-working bench. See *Bench, Amateurs'.*

AMATEURS' PLANE. See *Plane, Amateurs'.*

AMPOULE FILE. See *File, Glass Cutting.*

ANGLE BENDER. See *Bending Machine.*

ANGLE BORER. See *Boring Tool, Angular Borer* and *Boring Tool, Bit Brace, Corner.*

ANGLE BRACE. See *Boring Tool, Angular Borer* and *Boring Tool, Bit Brace, Corner.*

ANGLE DIVIDER. An adjustable mechanical device used to bisect or transfer an angle. This tool is useful for such tasks as fitting trim and mouldings into irregular corners. Also used for layout of multi-sided figures.

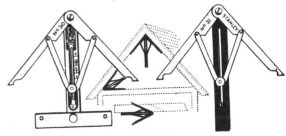

Angle Divider

ANGLE FLOAT. See *Float, Plasterers'*.

ANGLE GAUGE. A set of thin metal gauges used to determine the degree of an angle.

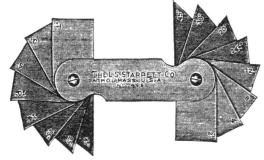

Angle Gauge

ANGLE JAW TONGS. See *Tongs, Angle Jaw*.

ANGLE PADDLE. Also called PLASTERERS' PADDLE. A plasterers' tool used for final smoothing and touchup of a curved surface such as a corner moulding. Width is 3 to 3 1/4 inches and length is about 8 inches. The illustrated tool is made of maple.

Angle Paddle

ANGLE PEEN HAMMER. See *Hammer, Angle Peen*.

ANGLE PLANE. See *Plane, Chamfer*.

ANGLE TOOL. See *Cement Tool, Outside*.

ANGLE TROWEL. See *Trowel, Plasterers' Angle*.

ANGLE WRENCH. See *Wrench, Adjustable*.

ANGULAR BIT BRACE. See *Boring Tool, Angular Borer* and *Boring Tool, Bit Brace, Corner*.

ANGULAR BIT HOLDER. See *Boring Tool, Angular Borer* and *Boring Tool, Bit Brace, Corner*.

ANGULAR BIT STOCK. See *Boring Tool, Angular Borer* and *Boring Tool, Bit Brace, Corner*.

ANGULAR BORER. See *Boring Tool, Angular Borer*.

ANGULAR FILE. See *File, Knife*.

ANGULAR SWAGE. A type of blacksmiths' swage. See *Anvil Tool, Swage*.

ANIMAL MARKER. See *Ear Marker*.

ANNULAR BIT. A boring tool that will cut a circular groove or hole without destroying the inner part of the circle. See *Boring Tool, Bit, Barrel Saw* and *Boring Tool, Bit, Hole Saw*.

ANNULAR SAW. See *Boring Tool, Bit, Barrel Saw* and *Boring Tool, Bit, Hole Saw*.

ANTI-RATTLER TONGS. See *Tongs, Anti-Rattler*.

ANVIL. A block of metal, usually iron, on which a workpiece is positioned for hammering or shaping. An anvil usually has a flat work surface in contrast to the mandrel which has a curved surface.

ANVIL, BAND SAW. An anvil used in straightening and tensioning a band saw blade. Weight is 70 to 260 pounds.

Band Saw Anvil

ANVIL, BENCH. A small general-purpose anvil intended for mounting on a work bench. Weight is 6 to 25 pounds.

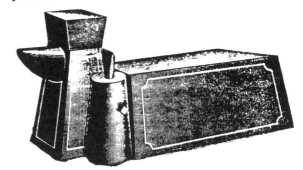

Bench Anvil

ANVIL, BLACKSMITHS'. A heavy iron block with a hardened or applied steel top face suitable for use by a blacksmith in working hot metal. A blacksmiths' anvil has a rounded projecting horn on one end and a square hole, called a hardie hole, in the top face for insertion of various anvil tools. In addition to the hardie hole, most blacksmiths' anvils have a small round hole in the top face called a pritchel hole. This hole allows a small punch to completely penetrate the workpiece thus making a clean hole. The small flat area at the base of the horn, called the table, is made of unhardened metal. This table can be used as backing for a cutting tool without risking damage to the tool. See the illustration for names of the various parts of a blacksmiths' anvil.

Anvils were made with both wrought and cast iron bodies. Both types generally have a steel face welded to the body. The wrought varieties are considered to be superior and are higher in price. Wrought anvils were advertised as being stronger and tougher than cast iron types and one supplier advertised that wrought anvils would ring. Early wrought anvils were forged in two pieces and welded together at the waist. Later catalogues contained the boast that certain makes of anvils were forged from a single block.

Cast anvils were often made in two pieces. The horn was covered or pointed with steel and then welded to the body. The least expensive line of cast anvils, the so-called FARMERS ANVILS, had neither a steel face nor a steel covered horn. The cast blocks of these inexpensive anvils were ground flat on top and case hardened. Needless to say, they were intolerant of abuse and chipped easily with rough usage. The professional full-time blacksmith generally worked with a wrought iron anvil weighing 200 to 300 pounds. Farm shops, garages and other such shops requiring an anvil for intermittent duty were more apt to include a cast anvil of 150 pounds or less. Anything above 350 pounds was intended for some special heavy-duty application. Anvils weighing from 1/2 pound to 800 pounds were listed by some suppliers. The sizes below 80 pounds were sometimes called MINIMS.

Many smiths were proud of the rhythmic ring of their anvils and considered the sound as a sort of professional trademark. Some makers of cast anvils apparently tried to downgrade this idea by advertising that their anvils did not reverberate and that therefore more energy was transmitted to the workpiece. Without joining the argument over which was best, most of us who have pounded iron would agree that dull hammer thuds issuing from the blacksmith shop leaves something to be desired.

A unique code consisting of a three digit number is used to specify weight of an anvil. The first number signifies the hundredweights (originally 112 pounds). The second number means the number of additional quarters of a hundredweight and the third number is the number of additional pounds. The number 135 on an anvil would denote 112 pounds plus 84 (3 times 28) plus 5, or a total of 201 pounds.

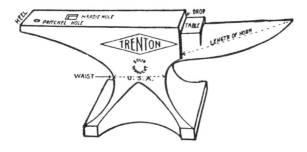

Parts of an Anvil

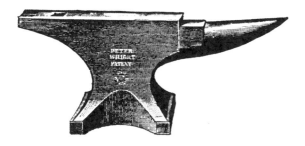

Blacksmiths' Anvil

ANVIL, CLINCH. Also called CLINCH BLOCK. A small iron block used for holding against the head of a horse shoe nail while the nail is being clinched with a hammer. The block prevents the nail from backing out thus loosening the shoe.

Clinch Anvil

ANVIL, CLIPHORN. See *Anvil, Farriers'*.

ANVIL, COMBINATION. An anvil made in combination with another tool. Several varieties of anvil-vise and anvil-vise-drill combinations have been noted. Some examples are illustrated.

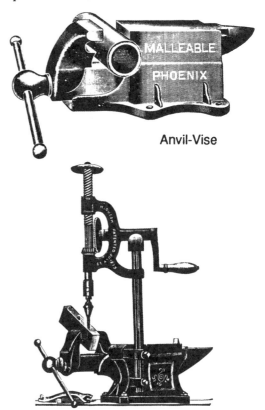

Anvil-Vise

Anvil-Vise-Drill

Combination Anvil

ANVIL, COOPERS'. A small anvil or stake used by a cooper when punching and riveting metal barrel hoops. The anvil is set upright in a heavy wooden block or stump. Weight of a coopers' anvil is 15 to 50 pounds. The type with the horn was also called BEAK HORN, BEAK IRON,

BECK IRON, BICK IRON, BICK IRON STAKE and COOPERS BEAK HORN. Beck and Bick are probably both shortened versions of the term "Bickern".

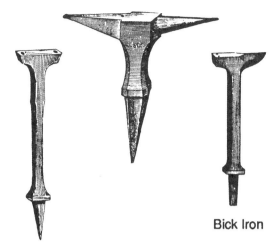

Bick Iron

Coopers' Anvil

ANVIL, CURTAIN FASTENER. Also called RIVETING ANVIL. An anvil used for installing the snap fasteners in buggy side windows and curtains. A coach makers' or trimmers' tool.

Curtain Fastener Anvil

ANVIL, CUTLERS'. An anvil used to assemble or repair knives.

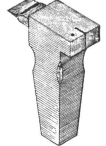

Cutlers' Anvil

ANVIL, DENGEL. See *Anvil, Scythe.*

ANVIL, DOUBLE BICK. Also called DOUBLE HORN ANVIL and DOUBLE PIKED ANVIL. A variety of anvil having two horns. The illustrated anvil has one horn rounded on top as on a common Blacksmith Anvil and the other horn is flattened on top. Weights from 84 to 350 pounds were available. Diderot shows a double bick anvil in his illustration of a spur makers' shop.

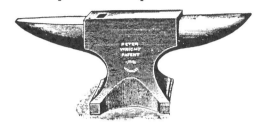

Double Bick Anvil

ANVIL, DOUBLE HORN. See *Anvil, Double Bick.*

ANVIL, DOUBLE PIKED. See *Anvil, Double Bick.*

ANVIL, FARMERS'. An inexpensive anvil intended for use by farmers and for other light duty applications. The farmers' anvil is generally the same shape as the Blacksmiths' Anvil. See illustrations under *Anvil, Blacksmiths'.*

ANVIL, FARRIERS'. Also called CLIPHORN ANVIL, FARRIERS' CLIPHORN ANVIL and HORSE SHOERS' ANVIL. A special type of anvil suitable for use in forming horseshoes. The farriers' anvil is similar to the Blacksmiths' Anvil except for the addition of a small nib or clip horn that projects from one side of the anvil table. The clip horn extends approximately 1 1/4 inches and is used for drawing the positioning clips often used on shoes for draft horses. A farriers' anvil has a main surface that is somewhat narrower than that of the blacksmith anvil and some have two pritchel holes of different sizes. A common size of a farriers' anvil is 150 pounds but weights from 80 to 400 pounds were listed. They were available in either wrought or cast iron and generally were made with a steel face. See also *Farriers' Hoof Rest.*

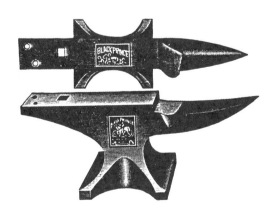

Farriers' Anvil

ANVIL, FARRIERS' CLIPHORN. See *Anvil, Farriers'.*

ANVIL, FARRIERS' COMBINATION. A combination anvil and foot-operated vise suitable for use by a farrier when making and fitting horse shoes.

Farriers' Combination Anvil

ANVIL, HARNESS MAKERS'. A small anvil suitable for use by harness and saddle makers. Weight is about 11 pounds. The illustrated anvil can be used while positioned on the foot or on either side. The holes and slots are intended to facilitate various types of riveting, punching and swaging associated with harness making.

Harness Makers' Anvil

ANVIL, HORSESHOERS'. See *Anvil, Farriers'.*

ANVIL, JEWELERS'. Also called JEWELERS' STAKE. A very small anvil or stake used for making and repairing jewelry. Maximum length of the horn-type anvil is 4 to 5 inches. The face of the square anvil is 1/2 to 2 inches on each side. An anvil similar to the illustrated horn-type was called a *BICK IRON* by one supplier.

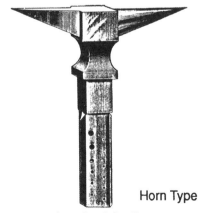

Horn Type

Jewelers' Anvil

Rotary

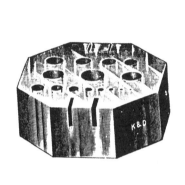

Block   Square

Jewelers' Anvil

ANVIL, KNEE. An anvil that can be positioned on the knee while in use. Used for harness repair and for similar light tasks. The striking surface of the illustrated tool is 1 1/2 inches in diameter. A similar tool with a concave striking surface was used for cracking nuts.

Knee Anvil

ANVIL, LAP. Also called KNEE ANVIL and LAP IRON. A small anvil intended to rest on and between the knees. This tool is used for working leather or for similar light pounding. One particular use was for beating and compacting heavy leather for use as shoe soles. See *Hammer, Shoe Makers' Beating Out.* The illustrated tool has a 3 3/4 inch diameter face.

8

Knee Anvil

ANVIL, LATHE. An anvil used for supporting a shaft or pipe for straightening. It can be used upright, as shown in the illustration, for removal of a gear from a shaft or spindle.

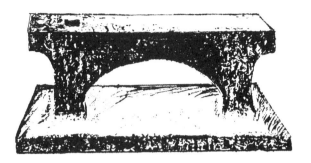

Oilfield Anvil

ANVIL, OPTICAL RIVETING. An anvil used to assemble and repair eye glasses.

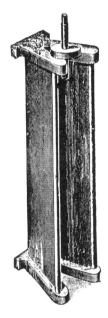

Lathe Anvil

ANVIL, NAIL MAKERS'. A type of anvil used by a nail maker when pointing and heading nails by hand. This anvil was sometimes supported by a low bench or stand such that the nail maker could sit down while at work.

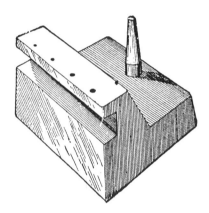

Optical Riveting Anvil

ANVIL, PLOW. A hand-held tool used as a backing bar when sharpening a plow share point or heading a rivet. It can also be used in a swage block or wooden stand. The illustrated tool has a 3 inch diameter face and a round tapered shank. Weight is 4 to 4 1/2 pounds.

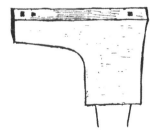

Nail Makers' Anvil

ANVIL, OILFIELD. A large anvil used in the oil fields for sharpening drill bits. This type of anvil has a wide rectangular face with a hardie hole but does not have a horn. A common size is 350 pounds.

Plow Anvil

ANVIL, PLOW MAKERS'. A tool similar to the Blacksmiths' Anvil except for the unique shape of the table. The horn is set approximately two inches below the face and the table is angled. Weight is 190 to 200 pounds.

Plow Makers' Anvil

ANVIL, RIVETING. See *Anvil, Curtain Fastener*.

ANVIL, ROPE CLAMP. An anvil used to close a split metal loop around one or more strands of rope when making a rope halter. The anvil is fastened in a vise during use.

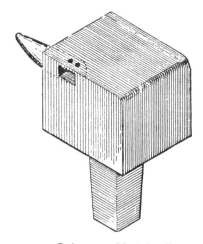

Scissorsmiths' Anvil

ANVIL, SCYTHE. Also called DENGEL ANVIL and DENGEL STOCK. A small sharpening anvil that could be carried to the field by the workman. Weight is 1 to 1 1/4 pounds. The anvil was pounded into any convenient stump or log for rigidity during use. It is normally used with a dengel hammer.

Rope Clamp Anvil

ANVIL, SAW. See *Swage Bar*.

ANVIL, SAW MAKERS'. A simple rectangular anvil used by a saw maker for tensioning a large saw blade. The top surface of the saw makers' anvil is ground to a precision flatness. Weight is 50 to 380 pounds. A common size is 110 pounds.

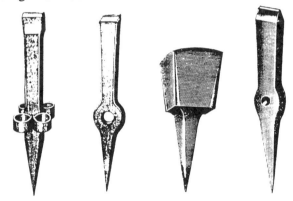

Scythe Anvil

ANVIL, SNAP FASTENER. See *Anvil, Curtain Fastener*.

ANVIL, STOVEPIPE. See *Mandrel, Stovepipe*.

ANVIL CUTTER. See *Anvil Tool, Cutter*.

ANVIL TOOLS. The family of cutting and forming tools used in conjunction with the anvil are called Anvil Tools. These items consist of BOTTOM TOOLS which rest in the hardie hole of the anvil and TOP TOOLS which are hand-held. Anvil tools are made of tough steel with the faces hardened sufficiently to minimize deforming during repeated usage with either hot or cold workpieces.

Saw Makers' Anvil

ANVIL, SCISSORSMITHS'. A small anvil used to repair and assemble scissors. This type of device was often used by the itinerant scissors and knife sharpener.

Each bottom tool has a square shank which fits loosely into the hardie hole of the anvil and a flat shoulder that rests on the anvil surface. A loose fit is required to allow rapid changing of tools even though the tool may have expanded from being in contact with a hot workpiece. The tools are made for use with hardie holes of various sizes. The most common sizes of shanks are made to fit 3/4 inch and one inch square holes. Usage of a bottom tool consists of placing the workpiece on the tool and striking it with a hand hammer or sledge. These tools can be used by a smith working alone and doing his own forging with a hand hammer. Large workpieces that require handling with both hands are worked in the same manner except that the hammer or sledge is wielded by the helper.

Top tools are intended to be held in place on the workpiece and struck with the hand hammer or sledge. These tools generally have a round or oval eye in which a short wooden handle is fitted. They could be procured with or without handles. Top tools were also made by some suppliers with a recessed waist instead of an eye. A withe of hazel or a heavy gauge wire could be twisted around the narrow waist of the tool and brought out to form a handle. See illustration. The smith uses the handle to place the top tool on the workpiece in the proper position to be struck by a sledge or hammer wielded by the helper. The handle serves the dual purpose of allowing the hand to be kept a distance from the heat of the workpiece and helps to minimize the risk of injury should the helper fumble the sledge. Length of the handle varies from 13 inches for small tools to 20 inches or more for large heavy tools. A buggy spoke was often used as a readily available replacement for a broken handle.

Wood Handle

Wire Handle

Top Tools

When a top tool is used for repeated operations on a hot workpiece, it is necessary to cool the tool periodically by dipping it into the slake tub. Such cooling is necessary to avoid drawing the temper of the tool. Bottom tools are less susceptible to this type of overheating inasmuch as they are in intimate contact with the large mass of the anvil. Top tools are of little use to the smith working alone except when working with very small items not requiring hand support. Holding fixtures and moveable props are sometimes used to support the workpiece but are not adaptable for general use.

Hand-held tools without handles, such as small punches and chisels, are also called "Anvil Tools" by some suppliers. These tools are listed in normal alphabetical sequence.

ANVIL TOOL, ANGULAR SWAGE. See *Anvil Tool, Swage.*

ANVIL TOOL, BACKING OUT PUNCH. A top tool with a straight shank used to drive out a tight-fitting pin or rivet. Sometimes listed as a steel workers' tool. Sizes from 1/4 inch to 1 inch diameter were listed.

Backing Out Punch

ANVIL TOOL, BENDING FORK. A bottom tool used in bending a long rod or bar. The heated workpiece is placed between the prongs of the bending fork and pulled or pushed to form the degree of bend desired.

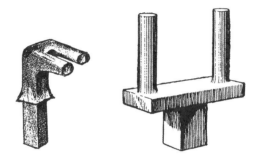

Bending Fork

ANVIL TOOL, BOBBING. See *Anvil Tool, Countersink.*

ANVIL TOOL, BOBBING PUNCH. See *Anvil Tool, Countersink.*

ANVIL TOOL, CALK SWAGE. See *Anvil Tool, Toe Calk Die.*

ANVIL TOOL, CENTER PUNCH. A top tool used to mark a center on an iron workpiece to facilitate a subsequent drilling operation. Similar to the Countersink except that this tool has a thinner taper at the point.

Center Punch

ANVIL TOOL, CHANNEL SWAGE. Also called TIRE CHANNEL SWAGE. A tool used for joining the ends of a tire channel to fit a buggy wheel. A channel-shaped tire was sometimes fitted to a wheel to provide a seat for installing a solid rubber tire. The unique shape of the swage allowed the channel to be welded and smoothed without distorting the tire.

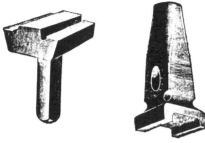

Channel Swage

ANVIL TOOL, CLIP SWAGE. A farriers' tool used to finish the clips on a horse shoe.

Clip Swage

ANVIL TOOL, COLD CHISEL. See *Anvil Tool, Cold Cutter.*

ANVIL TOOL, COLD CUTTER. Also called COLD CHISEL and COLD SET. A top tool used to cut cold metal. The cutter is positioned on the workpiece and struck with a hand hammer or sledge with sufficient force to make a deep crease. The remainder of the metal is then broken at the crease. A hardie is normally used for this type of cutting when a helper is not available. For deep cuts, the workpiece is creased simultaneously on both sides by using a hardie on the bottom and a cold cutter on the top. Note the relatively blunt taper of this tool compared to the hot cutter. Size refers to the length of the cutting edge. Sizes from one inch to two inches were listed. See also *Chisel, Track.*

Cold Cutter

ANVIL TOOL, COLD SET. See *Anvil Tool, Cold Cutter.*

ANVIL TOOL, COLLAR SWAGE. See *Anvil Tool, Swage.*

ANVIL TOOL, COUNTERSINK. Also called BOBBING PUNCH and BOBBING TOOL. A top tool used to dimple hot iron thus providing space for a recessed rivet head or bolt head. This type of tool was available in several sizes.

Countersink

ANVIL TOOL, CREASER. A farriers' tool used to make a crease along each side of a horse shoe to accommodate the nail heads. The creaser also provides a break in the smooth surface of the shoe which increases side traction. The tool is positioned on the shoe and struck with the hand hammer or sledge with sufficient force to crease the hot metal.

Creaser

ANVIL TOOL, CUPPING. An anvil tool used to form a spherical object. The top and bottom tools may be used together or separately to forge a rounded shape. Used extensively for making decorative knobs on grill work and metal fencing.

Cupping Tool

ANVIL TOOL, CUTTER. Also called ANVIL CUTTER. A metal-cutting shears that is operated by a blow from a hammer. Information is from *Knight's American Mechanical Dictionary.*

Anvil Cutter

ANVIL TOOL, CUTTING BLOCK. A bottom tool, made of mild or unhardened steel, used on the anvil as a cutting surface when the workpiece cannot be positioned on the anvil table.

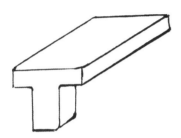

Cutting Block

ANVIL TOOL, DOLLY. A tool used for sharpening a rock drill. Several patterns were made to match the points of various standard drills. The dolly is hammered against the end of the heated rock drill thus straightening and sharpening the points.

Dolly

ANVIL TOOL, DRILL SPREADER. Also called DRILL SWAGE. These are special-purpose anvil tools used to straighten and sharpen the points of a rock drill. The faces are intended to crease and form the heated drill rather than to cut the metal.

Drill Spreader

ANVIL TOOL, DRILL SWAGE. See *Anvil Tool, Drill Spreader.*

ANVIL TOOL, FERRULE. A bottom tool used in forming and welding ferrules and other small bands. Height is approximately 8 inches.

Ferrule Tool

ANVIL TOOL, FLATTER. A top tool used on hot metal to smooth out hammer marks or other irregularities in the surface. The flatter is positioned on the workpiece and struck with a hand hammer or sledge. Flatters have been noted with squared, rounded and beveled edges. A rounded edge is useful for working close to a fillet. Sizes from 1 inch to 4 1/2 inches across were available. Octagonal flatters were also available.

Flatter

ANVIL TOOL, FOOT. A tool used to smooth out hammer marks in hot metal. This tool is essentially an offset flatter for use on a bent workpiece. See also *Anvil Tool, Flatter.*

Foot Tool

ANVIL TOOL, FORE PUNCH. See *Anvil Tool, Nail Punch.*

ANVIL TOOL, FULLER. A tool used to groove hot metal thereby drawing it out to a greater length. The fuller is useful for lengthening a bar, strap or rod without spreading it appreciably in the lateral direction. It can also be used for forming a neck or groove in a workpiece. The bottom fuller rests in the hardie hole of the anvil and the top fuller is held with a short handle. They can be used singly or as a pair. Size refers to the diameter of the curvature of the working surface. Sizes from 1/4 inch to 3 inches were listed. The Round Faced Fuller, shown in the illustration, was used for spreading the metal in both directions or for local thinning of the workpiece. This variety was not listed by most suppliers. The Offset Fuller is made with the extended side flush with the side of the anvil. This allows a crooked workpiece to be fullered by positioning the crook down over the side of the anvil.

Bottom Fuller   Top Fuller

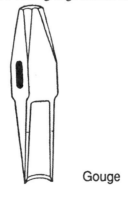

Round Faced Fuller   Offset Fuller

Fuller

ANVIL TOOL, GOUGE. Also called GOUGE CHISEL. A hot cutter with a curved cutting edge similar to a gouge.

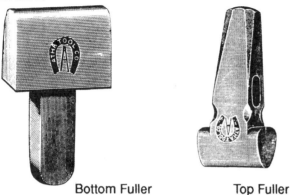

Gouge

ANVIL TOOL, HARDIE. Also called HARDY. A bottom tool used to cut hot or cold metal. The workpiece is positioned on the hardie and struck with a hammer or sledge with sufficient force to make a deep crease. The remainder of the metal is then broken at the crease. A larger workpiece might be creased on two or more sides before being broken. In order to avoid damage to the cutting edge of the hardie, the hammer blows are never sufficiently hard to completely sever the workpiece. The toe hardies, shown in the illustration, are farriers' tools used in the forming of horse shoes.

Common Hardie   Farriers' or Toe Hardie

Hardie

ANVIL TOOL, HARDY. See *Anvil Tool, Hardie.*

ANVIL TOOL, HARROW TOOTH. Also called HARROW TOOL. A special-purpose swage used to make or sharpen a tooth for a drag harrow.

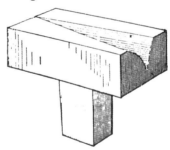

Harrow Tooth Tool

ANVIL TOOL, HEEL FORMER. A farriers' tool used for making uniform heels on horse shoes. The several indentations accommodate different sizes of shoes.

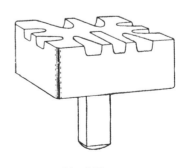

Heel Former

ANVIL TOOL, HORSESHOE CALK SWAGE. See *Anvil Tool, Toe Calk Swage.*

ANVIL TOOL, HOT CUTTER. Also called HOT CHISEL, HOT SET and SPLITTING CHISEL. A top tool used to cut hot metal. This tool is similar to a cold cutter except that the hot cutter has a thinner taper in the shank above the cutting edge. See *Anvil Tool, Cold Cutter.* Size refers to the length of the cutting edge. Sizes from one inch to two inches were listed. See also *Anvil Tool, Gouge.*

Hot Cutter

ANVIL TOOL, LANDSLIDE HOLDER. See *Anvil Tool, Plow Iron.*

ANVIL TOOL, NAIL PUNCH. Also called FORE PUNCH. A top tool used to punch nail holes in a horse shoe. The hand-held version of this tool is called a Pritchel.

Nail Punch

ANVIL TOOL, NUT SWAGE. See *Anvil Tool, Swage.*

ANVIL TOOL, PLOW HOLDER. See *Anvil Tool, Plow Iron.*

ANVIL TOOL, PLOW IRON. Also called LANDSLIDE HOLDER and PLOW HOLDER. A tool used for holding the landslide while welding the plow point. The tool is bolted to the hardy hole of the anvil to prevent movement while in use.

ANVIL TOOL, PUNCH. Also called ROUND EYE PUNCH. A top tool used for making a hole in hot metal. The punch is driven half-way through the metal against the face of the anvil. The workpiece is then turned over and the punch is driven completely through and into the hardie or pritchel hole. The punch is tapered such that it

Plow Iron

spreads the metal after the initial hole is punched out. Removing a large section of metal rather than spreading is thought to needlessly weaken the workpiece. Size refers to the width of the punch at the point. Sizes from 1/4 to one inch were listed. Oval-shaped punches of the same sizes were also available. See also *Anvil Tool, Backing Out Punch* and *Anvil Tool, Center Punch.*

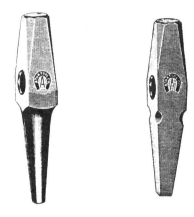

Punch

ANVIL TOOL, PUNCHING BLOCK. A bottom tool with one or more small holes to allow a punch to completely penetrate the workpiece. This tool is especially useful when the anvil does not have a pritchel hole.

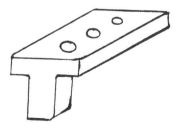

Punching Block

ANVIL TOOL, RIVET BUSTER. See *Anvil Tool, Side Chisel.*

ANVIL TOOL, RIVET SET. Also called BUTTON HEAD RIVET SET, BUTTON HEAD SET, CONICAL RIVET SNAP, RIVET SET HAMMER and RIVET SNAP. A tool used to form the head of a large rivet. This tool is sometimes listed as a bridge builders' tool or a steel workers' tool.

Rivet Set

ANVIL TOOL, RIVET SNAP. See *Anvil Tool, Rivet Set.*

ANVIL TOOL, ROUND EYE PUNCH. See *Anvil Tool, Punch.*

ANVIL TOOL, ROUND PUNCH. See *Anvil Tool, Punch.*

ANVIL TOOL, SADDLE. A bottom tool used for working a forked piece such as an open-end wrench. This tool is shaped so that one portion of the workpiece can extend underneath the forging surface.

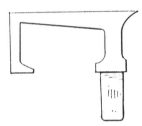

Saddle Tool

ANVIL TOOL, SET HAMMER. A top tool used to smooth (set down) and flatten hot metal. It serves the same general purpose as the flatter but the set hammer is normally uniform from top to bottom and is therefore much stronger and heavier than a flatter of comparable size. It is useful for squaring up the inside of a bend or against a shoulder. The set hammer is placed on the workpiece and struck with a hand hammer or sledge rather than being used as a hammer as the name implies. The common set hammer has sharp square edges as shown in the illustration. A less common variety was made with rounded edges for use in setting down metal adjacent to a fillet. Sizes from 3/4 to 3 inches square were listed; however, most set hammers are 1 1/2 to 2 inches square.

ANVIL TOOL, SIDE CHISEL. Also called RIVET BUSTER and SIDE SET. A tool used for close work such as cutting off a pin or a rivet head flush with a surface. Length of cut is approximately 1 1/2 inches. See also *Anvil Tool, Cold Cutter.* This tool is listed as a bridge builders' tool, steel workers' tool and track tool by various suppliers.

ANVIL TOOL, SIDE SET. See *Anvil Tool, Side Chisel.*

Set Hammer   Side Chisel

ANVIL TOOL, SOW. A holding fixture used on the anvil when shaping or sharpening four-pointed rock drills. Width of the slot is 3/8 to 3/4 inches.

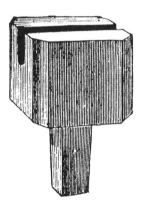

Sow

ANVIL TOOL, SPRING SWAGE. See *Anvil Tool, Swage.*

ANVIL TOOL, SQUARE CHISEL. A top tool used to clean up the corners of a square hole. The illustrated tool is home-made.

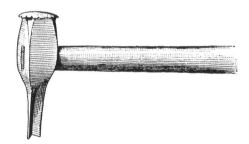

Square Chisel

ANVIL TOOL, SQUARE PUNCH. See *Anvil Tool, Punch.*

ANVIL TOOL, SWAGE. A tool used to form heated metal. The hot metal is hammered into the swage cavity thus forming it into the shape of the swage. A typical usage would be to form a round end on a square bar. The bottom swage rests in the hardie hole of the anvil and the top swage is held with a short handle. They can be used singly or as a pair. The most common type of swage has a semi-circular cavity. Size refers to the diameter of the working recess. Sizes from 1/4 inch to 4 1/2 inches were listed. The Collar Swages, shown in the illustration, are used when welding or forming a collar on a rod. Forming the shoulders of such a piece is almost impossible without this type of tool. A matched top and bottom pair could be used for final forming of a complete collar. The Spring Swage is a form of a combined top and bottom tool used for light work. The Nut Swage is a specialized tool used for forming or finishing six-sided nuts and bolt heads. This tool was also called an ANGULAR SWAGE.

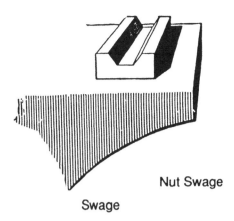

Nut Swage

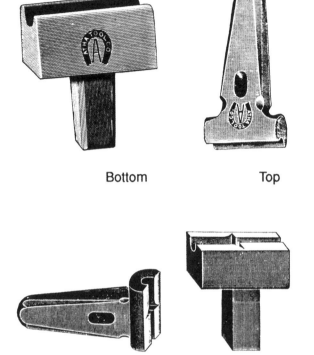

Bottom Top

Collar Swage

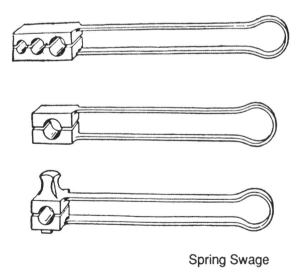

Spring Swage

Swage

Swage

ANVIL TOOL, TIRE CHANNEL SWAGE. See *Anvil Tool, Channel Swage.*

ANVIL TOOL, TIRE SET. A tool used when forging a wagon tire joint. The concave surface was used when finishing the weld to avoid creating a flat spot on the tire.

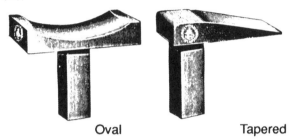

Oval Tapered

Tire Set

ANVIL TOOL, TOE CALK DIE. Also called CALK SWAGE, HORSESHOE CALK SWAGE and WELDING DIE. This tool is a special-purpose swage used to sharpen horse shoe toe calks. The calks required frequent sharpening when used on ice or frozen ground. Two sizes were listed.

Toe Calk Die

ANVIL TOOL, TOE HARDIE. See *Anvil Tool, Hardie.*

ANVIL TOOL, WELDING DIE. See *Anvil Tool, Toe Calk Die.*

ANVIL VISE. See *Anvil, Combination.*

APRON. A protective article of clothing worn over the fore part of the body. An apron usually has strings that can be tied around the waist.

APRON, BLACKSMITHS'. Also called LUMBERMANS' APRON. A heavy leather apron worn by the blacksmith as protection against the heat of the workpiece and of the forge. The apron also serves as a shield against the hot sparks created as the workpiece is hammered on the anvil. Some blacksmiths' aprons were listed as being made of muleskin.

Blacksmiths' Apron

APRON, BUTCHERS'. A water-proof apron worn by a butcher, carriage washer, fish packer, fisherman, meat packer or tanner. Length is approximately 54 inches.

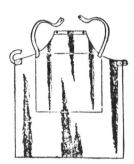

Butchers' Apron

APRON, CARPENTERS'. An apron worn by a carpenter that serves the dual purpose of clothing protection and providing for handy carriage of small tools and nails. These aprons were often used as give-away advertising pieces by lumber yards and hardware stores.

Carpenters' Apron

APRON, COOPERS'. A half-apron similar in shape to the Blacksmiths' Apron but usually made of striped ticking material or canvas. See illustration under *Apron, Blacksmiths'*.

APRON, LUMBERMANS'. See *Apron, Blacksmiths'*.

APRON, NAIL. Also called **WAIST-TYPE CARPENTERS' APRON.** A short apron, worn by a carpenter, consisting of one or more open pockets to provide for carriage of

and access to nails. Special pockets for a rule and a pencil were sometimes included.

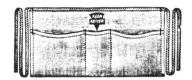

Nail Apron

APRON, SHOP. A long apron worn primarily for protection of the clothing. The self-conscious model in the illustration is Gerry Sellens wearing the shop apron obtained by the author for use during high school shop class.

Gerry Sellens

Shop Apron

APRON, WEAVERS'. A leather apron intended for use in a textile mill. Size of the illustrated apron is 15 by 18 inches. The apron served to assure that the weavers' clothing did not extend forward as he worked at the machine. A pair of shears was generally tucked under the waistband.

ARCH PUNCH. See *Punch, Leather.*

ARCHIMEDES DRILL. See *Boring Tool, Archimedes Drill.*

ARCHIMEDES SCREW DRIVER. See *Screw Driver, Archimedes.*

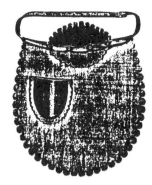

Weavers' Apron

ARCHITECTS' RULE. See *Rule, Architects'*.

ARCHITRAVE MOULDING PLANE. See *Plane, Moulding*.

ARKANSAS STONE. A type of stone used for sharpening a cutting edge. See *Sharpening Stone*.

ARM BOARD. See *Pommel and Raising Board*.

ARM STAKE. A curriers' tool with a dull rounded blade used for final finishing of a hide when extra smoothness was required. The tool was pushed with the armpit and shoulder to massage a hide held taut between one hand and a stationary clamp. The process was called "Staking".

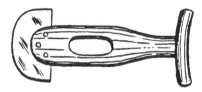

Arm Stake

ARMORERS' BIT BRACE. See *Boring Tool, Bit Brace, Armorers'*.

ASPARAGUS CHISEL. A garden or agricultural tool. See *Chisel, Asparagus*.

ASPARAGUS GOUGE. A garden or agricultural tool. See *Gouge, Asparagus*.

ASPARAGUS KNIFE. A garden or agricultural tool. See *Knife, Asparagus*.

ASPHALT AXE. See *Axe, Asphalt*.

ASPHALT CUTTER. See *Axe, Asphalt*.

Asphalt Mattock. See *Mattock, Asphalt*.

ASPHALT PATCHING HOE. See *Hoe, Asphalt Patching*.

ASPHALT RAKE. See *Rake, Asphalt*.

ASTRAGAL MOULDING PLANE. See *Plane, Moulding, Astragal*.

ASTRAGAL TOOL. See *Turning Tool, Astragal*.

ASTRIGAL. See *Plane, Moulding, Astragal*. Astrigal is an incorrect spelling.

AUGER. See *Boring Tool, Auger* and *Boring Tool, Bit, Auger*.

AUGER, HOLLOW. See *Hollow Auger*.

AUGER, PUMP. See *Boring Tool, Pump Auger*.

AUGER, PUMP LOG. See *Boring Tool, Pump Auger*.

AUGER, SPOKE. See *Hollow Auger*.

AUGER BIT. See *Boring Tool, Bit, Auger*.

AUGER BIT FILE. See *File, Auger Bit*.

AUGER BIT GUIDES. A set of graduated metal cylinders each with a center hole sized to accept an auger bit lead screw. The guides will keep a bit centered thereby allowing an existing hole to be re-bored or counter-bored.

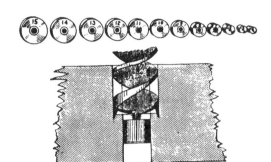

Auger Bit Guides

AUGER BIT HANDLE. A wrench used to rotate a bit or reamer. See *Wrench, Bit*.

AUGER GAUGE. See *Bit Gauge*.

AUGER HANDLE. See *Boring Tool, Auger Handle*.

AUSTRIAN STAVE AXE. A type of bearded axe. See *Axe, Stave*.

AUTO BALL PEEN HAMMER. See *Hammer, Ball Peen, Auto*.

AUTO TIRE LOCK. See *Lock, Auto Tire*.

AUTO TOOL WRENCH. A combination wrench used in early automobiles. See *Wrench, Auto Tool*.

AUTOMATIC DRILL. See *Boring Tool, Archimedes Drill* and *Boring Tool, Push Drill*.

AUTOMATIC HAND DRILL. See *Boring Tool, Push Drill*.

AUTOMATIC PUNCH. A type of leather punch. See *Punch, Leather*.

AUTOMATIC SCREW DRIVER. See *Screw Driver, Push*.

AUTOMOBILE MALLET. See *Mallet, Rubber*.

AUTOMOBILE RIM WRENCH. See *Wrench, Automobile Rim*.

AUTOMOBILE WRENCH. See *Wrench, Automobile*.

AWL. A pointed hand tool used for scribing a line or for piercing semi-rigid material such as leather. This type of tool generally makes a hole by spreading the material rather than cutting. The awl is an ancient tool form used by the American Indians before the coming of white settlers.

AWL, BELT. An awl used for making the lacing holes in webbed or leather belting material. The belt awl is heavier and stronger than the Harness Awl and Thong Awl. The patented awl shown in the illustration has a cutting edge that can be used for opening the hole. Also called THONG AWL by some suppliers.

Lathrops' Patent

Belt Awl

AWL, BRAD. An short awl, generally with a chisel-shaped point, used for making a starting hole for a brad or wood screw. The brad awl is pressed into the wood with the chisel point across the grain and twisted back and forth to make the hole. These awls were sometimes sold without handles.

Stickney Patent

Shouldered

Common

Brad Awl

AWL, CANE SEATING. See *Awl, Seat.*

AWL, CARPET. Also called UPHOLSTERERS' AWL. An awl used for opening holes in a carpet for sewing. Overall

length is 7 1/2 to 8 1/2 inches. This tool is somewhat heavier than the Seat Awl.

Carpet Awl

AWL, COLLAR. An awl used for piercing and sewing leather horse collars. Length of blade is approximately 6 inches. Similar to the Drawing Awl.

Collar Awl

AWL, DRAWING. An awl with an eye close to the pointed end. The eye was used to draw a cord or leather thong back through the material being worked.

Drawing Awl

AWL, HARNESS. Also called SADDLERS' AWL. A diamond-shaped awl for use in working heavy leather. The diamond shape is said to make a hole that is less apt to tear out. Pulling the stitching thread into one corner of the diamond shaped hole results in a neat seam.

Harness Awl

AWL, ICE. See *Ice Pick.*

AWL, LACING. A saddle makers' tool used to open holes in heavy leather for insertion of lacing. Cross section of the lacing awl is a half-round shape.

Lacing Awl

AWL, LOCK STITCH. Also called SEWING AWL. A stitching awl intended for use in repair of leather, canvas and other heavy material. The common stitching awl is a patented device with a built-in spool for holding the thread.

Lock Stitch Awl

AWL, MARKING. See *Awl, Scratch.*

AWL, PAD. See *Awl, Seat.*

AWL, PEG. A rigid awl with a short blade used to make starting holes for boot or shoe pegs.

Common

Shouldered

Peg Awl

AWL, RING. A type of marking device. See Awl, *Scratch.*

AWL, ROUND. See *Awl, Seat.*

AWL, SADDLERS'. See *Awl, Harness.*

AWL, SADDLERS' STRINGING. Also called STRINGING AWL. An awl used for lacing with heavy thongs.

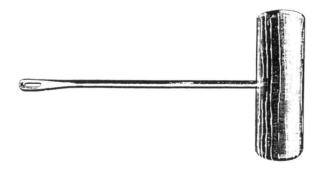

Saddlers' Stringing Awl

AWL, SCRATCH. Also called MARKING AWL, RING AWL, SCRIBE and SCRIBER. An awl used for scribing a line. Some examples are illustrated. The home made awl shown in the illustration consists of a solid iron ball welded to a section of pitchfork tine.

Socket Type

Common Type

Ship Carpenters'

Machinists'

Ring

Home Made

Scratch Awl

AWL, SEAT. Also called CANE SEATING AWL, PAD AWL, ROUND AWL, STABBING AWL and UPHOLSTERERS' AWL. A thin round awl used for opening and enlarging holes in upholstery material, leather and heavy cloth. The seat awl was also used in the application of cane seating material. The blade is approximately four inches long. The tool was available with and without a shoulder. The process of hand stitching the upper of a shoe was called "Stabbing".

Seat Awl

AWL, SEWING. A curved awl used to make the holes in heavy material for receipt of the sewing needle. See also *Awl, Lock Stitch.*

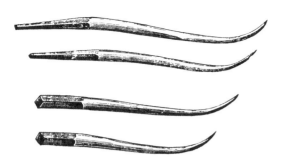

Sewing Awl

AWL, SHIP CARPENTERS'. See *Awl, Scratch.*

AWL, SHOULDERED. An awl with a bolster to provide increased strength and increased resistance to splitting of the handle. See *Awl, Brad* and *Awl Peg.*

AWL, STABBING. A shoe makers' name for a seat awl. See *Awl, Seat.*

AWL, STRINGING. See *Awl, Saddlers' Stringing.*

AWL, STRIP. A shoe makers' or saddle makers' tool. A cutting device used to plow a shallow groove for recessing of stitches.

Strip Awl

AWL, THONG. A diamond shaped awl used by saddle and harness makers. Length of blade is approximately 3 1/2 inches. Similar to the common Harness Awl except heavier. See also *Awl, Belt.*

Thong Awl

AWL, TINNERS'. A strong awl used for piercing light sheet metal and for enlarging an existing hole in thin metal.

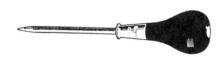

Tinners' Awl

AWL, UPHOLSTERERS'. See *Awl, Carpet* and *Awl, Seat.*

AWL HAFT. Also called AWL HANDLE. A replaceable handle for an awl. Hafts were bought separately for several types of awls. Most of the hafts were easily removable and would fit several sizes of awls. Inasmuch as some types of awls were easily broken, a replaceable haft was economical as well as being convenient.

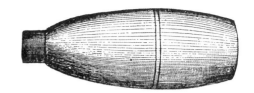

Brad Awl Haft

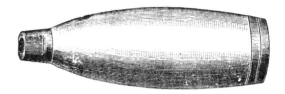

Peg Awl Haft

Sewing Awl Haft

Sewing Awl Haft

Sewing Awl Haft

Awl Haft

AWL HANDLE. See *Awl Haft.*

AX. See *Axe.* Ax is an obsolete spelling.

AXE. An impact cutting tool consisting of a cutting edge or edges fixed parallel to a handle. Used for hewing or chopping. An axe is generally a two-handed tool as differentiated from a hatchet which is a smaller tool intended for use with one hand. The terms Axe and Hatchet are used interchangeably for some of the smaller axes. See also *Hatchet.* The axe is one of the basic tool groups and was used in America prior to the use of metal implements.

AXE, ADZE. A type of adze. See *Adze Axe.*

AXE, ASPHALT. Also called ASPHALT CUTTER. A tool, with heavy cutting edges, used to remove a section of asphalt when repairing a road or driveway. The cutting edge is about 2 1/2 inches wide.

Asphalt Axe

AXE, BEARDED. An axe with the cutting edge extending a distance from the eye in the direction of the handle. A small bearded axe, beveled on one side only, is sometimes called a COACH MAKERS' AXE, COACH MAKERS' SIDE AXE, WHEELERS' AXE or WHEEL- WRIGHTS' AXE. The larger bearded axes are generally beveled on both sides and were apparently used for felling. See also *Axe, Stave*.

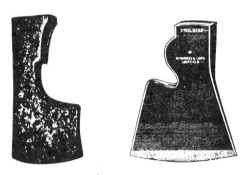

Bearded Axe

AXE, BENCH. A common name for the Broad Hatchet. See *Hatchet, Broad*.

AXE, BOAT. See *Axe, Single Bit*, boat pattern.

AXE, BOOMING. See *Axe, Single Bit*, booming pattern.

AXE, BOY SCOUT. Also called BOY SCOUT HATCHET and SCOUT AXE. A small axe suitable to be carried by a boy scout on a camping trip. Weight is about 1 1/4 pounds and length of the handle is 13 to 14 1/2 inches. The boy scout axe is often sold with a sheath. See *Axe Sheath*.

Boy Scout Axe

AXE, BOYS. A small single bit axe with a 22 to 30 inch handle. Weight is 1 3/4 to 3 1/4 pounds. A common weight is 2 1/4 pounds. This type axe was made in several of the patterns shown under *Axe, Single Bit*.

Boys Axe

AXE, BOYS' Camp. See *Hatchet, Camp*.

AXE, BROAD. A hewing axe having a long cutting edge. See also *Axe, Last Block* and *Axe, Sleeper*.

AXE, BROAD, COMMON. Also called HEWING AXE. A two-handed broad axe intended for squaring up a timber such as might be used in a log house or as a railroad cross-tie. Length of the cutting edge is 5 to 16 inches. A common size is 12 inches. The cutting edge is normally beveled on one side only. A broad axe handle is curved outward in the direction of the cutting edge bevel and is often curved upward in the direction of the poll. The curved handle provides hand clearance between the handle and the workpiece and allows the workman to stand beside the timber being hewed. The handle can be fitted into either end to make the axe suitable for either right or left hand usage. Several patterns of broad axes, as illustrated, were listed by more than one supplier. They were all available in the same general range of sizes except that the New England Pattern was listed in narrow widths only. The New England Pattern was also available with the cutting edge beveled on both sides and may have doubled as a felling axe.

Australian Pattern

Common Broad Axe

California Pattern

New England Pattern

Canada Pattern or Canadian

New Orleans Pattern

Kelly Standard Pattern

New York Pattern

Michigan Pattern

Ohio Pattern

Common Broad Axe

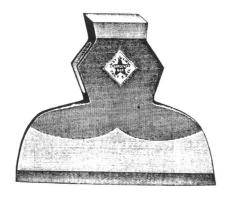

Pennsylvania Pattern

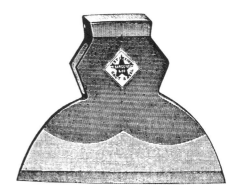

Western Pattern

Pittsburg Pattern

Yankee Pattern

Common Broad Axe

AXE, BROAD, COOPERS'. A wide-bitted axe used by the cooper for initial dressing of staves and heading pieces. The coopers' broad axe has a short one-handed handle. The eye is slightly offset from the cutting edge allowing a straight handle to be used. This axe is often referred to as a COOPERS' AXE or a COOPERS' SIDE AXE. The cutting edge is 7 1/2 to 11 1/2 inches long.

Ramsey Pattern

Coopers' Broad Axe

AXE, BROAD, EUROPEAN PATTERN. A large one-handed axe having the cutting edge extending both forward and aft of the eye and with the forward extension coming to a point. Cutting edge lengths up to 16 inches have been noted. This type axe is beveled on one side only. Both right and left hand varieties were available. These axes are light-weight and are equipped with short offset handles for one-handed use. European pattern axes have been imported in large quantities for tool collectors. Some were made in the United States; however, most of

Watauga-Canada Pattern

Common Broad Axe

these axes seen in American tool collections are of European origin. This type axe is often called Goosewing because the shape is thought to resemble the wing of a goose. The term "Goosewing" is widely used by collectors and tool dealers; however, available evidence indicates that the term was never used by the makers or original sellers of the axes.

European Pattern Broad Axe

AXE, BROAD, SHIP CARPENTERS'. Also called KENT AXE, SHIP AXE, SHIP CARPENTERS' AXE and SHIP PATTERN BROAD AXE. A variety of wide bitted axe favored by Ship Carpenters. The bit shank is somewhat longer and the cutting edge is shorter than in most Common Broad Axes. Length of the cutting edge is 5 to 7 1/2 inches.

Ship Carpenters' Broad Axe

AXE, BROAD, TURPENTINE. A broad axe used to score the bark when tapping a turpentine tree. Similar to a Common Broad Axe except that the turpentine axe has a concave curvature of the cutting edge. The curved cutting edge will make a wide slash in the bark of a tree with one blow of the axe. Length of the cutting edge is 14 to 14 1/2 inches.

Turpentine Broad Axe

AXE, BUSH. A two-handed tool used for cutting bushes and small trees when clearing land for agricultural use. This tool combines the features of an axe and a bush hook. Weight of the illustrated bush axe is four pounds.

Bush Axe

AXE, BULL. See *Axe, Pole*.

AXE, CAMP. See *Axe, Campers'*.

AXE, CAMPERS'. Also called CAMP AXE and HALF AXE. A 1 1/2 to 2 3/4 pound axe with a 24 inch handle. This axe is suitable for light tasks such as cutting wood for a camp fire or sharpening tent stakes.

Campers' Axe

AXE, CHISEL. See *Axe, Mortising Chisel*.

AXE, CHOPPING. Also called LOPPING AXE. A term used by timber workers to denote a light Single Bit Axe. A chopping axe was often employed to lop off small branches and clean up the log. The larger single bit axe and the double bit axe were used for notching and other heavy work. See *Axe, Single Bit*.

AXE, CLOG MAKERS'. Also called SABOT MAKERS' AXE. A side axe used for roughing out the blocks when making a wooden shoe. The illustrated tool is probably of French origin.

Clog Makers' Axe

AXE, COACH MAKERS'. See *Axe, Bearded.*

AXE, COACH MAKERS' SIDE. See *Axe, Bearded.*

AXE, COAL. See *Axe, Coal Miners'.*

AXE, COAL MINERS'. Also called COAL AXE, MINERS' AXE, THREE-QUARTER AXE and TIMBERERS' AXE. A single bit axe with a short handle. Used for cutting and notching the timbers in a mine. Weight is 3 to 5 pounds and length of the handle is 20 to 28 inches.

Coal Miners' Axe

AXE, COOPERS'. See *Axe, Broad, Coopers'.*

AXE, COOPERS' SIDE. See *Axe, Broad, Coopers'.*

AXE, CRUISERS'. See *Axe, Double Bit.*

AXE, DOCK. See *Axe, Single Bit*, dock pattern.

AXE, DOCK BUILDERS'. See *Axe, Single Bit*, dock pattern.

AXE, DOUBLE BIT. A two-handed axe having two cutting bits. The bits are usually identical. Weight is 3 to 6 pounds.

It is generally considered that use of the double bit axe as a craftsmans tool is an American innovation. It has been theorized that the two cutting edges grew out of the Yankee urge to do things faster. Having two bits instead of one would allow a greater time span between sharpenings. The wood cutter generally favors one bit and keeps it honed to perfection while letting the other bit deteriorate somewhat. The dull side is used to trim close to the ground and for similar uses where the honed edge might be damaged. Many users of the double bit axe consider that the balance and therefore the striking accuracy is superior to that of the single bit axes. The double bit did not come into general use until late in the 19th century. It is noted that the 1877 *Douglas Axe Catalogue* contained only one double bit axe.

Several patterns of double bit axes were available. See illustrations. The Combination Pattern Axe, as illustrated, has an Ohio Pattern bit on one side and a Full Wedge Pattern on the other. Other combinations of bits

could be special ordered. One supplier listed a small double bit axe weighing 2 1/2 pounds called a CRUISERS' AXE or TIMBER CRUISERS' AXE.

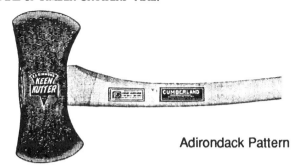

Adirondack Pattern

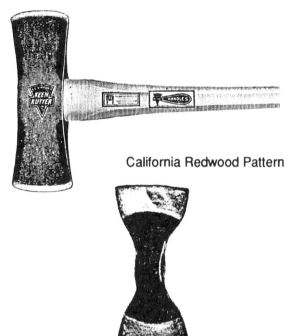

California Redwood Pattern

Bow Tie or Butterfly Pattern

Reversible or Half Peeling Pattern
Double Bit Axe

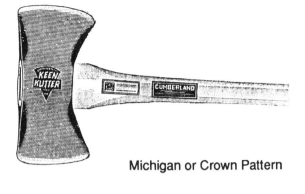

Michigan or Crown Pattern

Combination Pattern   **Delaware Pattern**

Michigan Pattern, Narrow

**Falling Pattern
or California Falling**   **Humbolt Pattern
or Redwood**

Ohio Pattern   **Pacific Coast Pattern
or Puget Sound Falling**

Lippincott Pattern   **Maine Pattern**

**California Pattern
or Full Peeling**

Double Bit Axe

Swamping Pattern

Wedge Pattern
or Half Wedge

Yankee Pattern

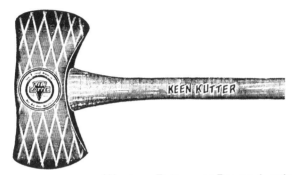

Western Pattern or Pennsylvania

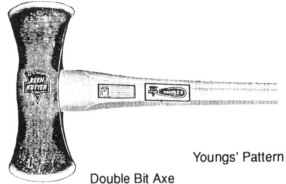

Youngs' Pattern

Double Bit Axe

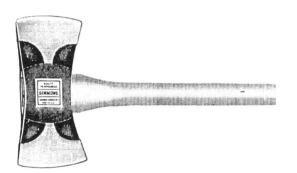

Western Pattern, Hollow Bevel

AXE, FAMILY. See *Axe, House.*

AXE, FELLING. An axe used for cutting trees. The felling axe has the cutting edge beveled on both sides. *Mercer* indicates that the axe, rather than the saw, was used exclusively for felling trees prior to the 1880 time period. See *Axe, Bearded; Axe, Double Bit* and *Axe, Single Bit.*

AXE, FIRE ENGINE. See *Axe, Firemans'.*

AXE, FIREMANS'. Also called FIRE ENGINE AXE. An axe used by fire fighters for general prying and chopping. These axes generally weigh from 3 1/2 to 8 pounds and have a 4 1/2 to 6 inch cutting edge. Firemans' axes were available in several patterns as illustrated. One type was also available with a flat head in place of the ripping spike.

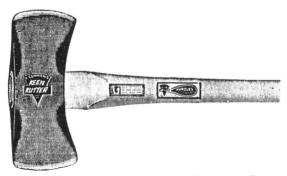

Wisconsin Pattern

Double Bit Axe

Hunts' Pattern

Underhill Pattern

Firemans' Axe

Lippincott Pattern

Firemans' Axe

AXE, FREIGHTERS'. A 2 ³/₄ pound axe with a 30 to 32 inch handle.

Freighters' Axe

AXE, GOOSEWING. See *Axe, Broad, European Pattern.*

AXE, HALF. See *Axe, Campers'.*

AXE, HAND. Any small one-handed axe was often called a Hand Axe. See *Hatchet.*

AXE, HEWING. This term is usually used to refer to an axe that is beveled on one side only. Hewing a timber normally means to flatten the side or to make the timber thinner. A felling axe is occasionally referred to as a Hewing Axe. See *Axe, Broad.*

AXE, HOUSE. Also called FAMILY AXE and QUARTER AXE. A small axe recommended for use around the house to accomplish tasks such as splitting kindling and sharpening stakes. Weight is 2 to 3 ¹/₂ pounds and handle length is 18 to 20 inches. The house axe was made in several of the patterns shown under *Axe, Single Bit.*

House Axe

AXE, HUNTERS'. Also called AXE PATTERN HATCHET, HUNTERS' HATCHET, SPORTSMANS' AXE and SPORTSMANS' HATCHET. A 1 ¹/₄ to 2 ¹/₄ pound axe with a 13 to 20 inch handle. Width of cut is 2 ³/₄ to 4 inches. The hunters' axe was made in several of the patterns shown under *Axe, Single Bit.*

Hunters' Axe

AXE, ICE. A narrow axe used to cut and dress blocks of ice. The curved hook opposite the cutting edge was used to maneuver a block of ice into the desired position. Weight is 2 ³/₄ to 4 ¹/₂ pounds. Cutting width is approximately 2 ³/₄ inches. These axes were made in several patterns as illustrated. See also *Hatchet, Ice.*

Boston Pattern

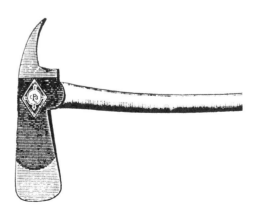

Chicago Pattern

Ice Axe

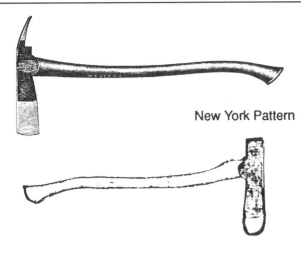

New York Pattern

Philadelphia Pattern

Ice Axe

AXE, INDIAN. A stone axe of the type used by American Indians prior to the general availability of metal tools. The wooden handle is held to the recessed waist of the axe head by rawhide thongs.

Indian Axe

AXE, JEDDING. See *Cavel*.

AXE, KENT. An axe of the general shape of the Ship Carpenters' Broad Axe was sometimes listed as a kent axe. One variety of the kent axe is beveled on both sides and was used for felling. See *Axe, Broad, Ship Carpenters'*.

AXE, KILLING. See *Axe, Pole*.

AXE, LAST BLOCK. Also called LAST BLOCK CHIPPING AXE. A small broad axe with a single bevel used for rough shaping of a wooden boot or shoe last.

Last Block Axe

AXE, LOPPING. See *Axe, Chopping*.

AXE, MARKING. Also called STAMP AXE. An axe, with raised characters on the poll, used for marking logs or timbers. Logs were marked to show ownership should they become mixed with other logs on the way to the mill. This type axe was available with letters, numbers, symbols or any combination.

Marking Axe

AXE, MAULING. A single bit axe with a hardened poll that could be used for driving spikes or wedges. See *Axe, Single Bit*, rafting pattern.

AXE, MINERS'. See *Axe, Coal Miners'*.

AXE, MORTISING. See *Axe, Post*.

AXE, MORTISING CHISEL. Also called CHISEL AXE. A mortising tool commonly used in Continental Europe but not sold extensively in the United States. The right angle handgrip is formed as an integral part of the cutting bit. An additional length of handle is not required.

Mortising Chisel Axe

AXE, POLE. Also called BULL AXE and KILLING AXE. An axe used for felling cattle in a slaughter house. The animal was hit between the eyes with the poll of the axe thus stunning it for slaughter.

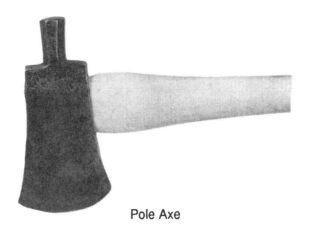

Pole Axe

AXE, POLL. This is a seldom-used name for a single bit axe. See *Axe, Single Bit.*

AXE, POST. Also called MORTISING AXE. An axe having a long narrow bit with the cutting edge beveled on both sides. The purpose of this tool is to cut a deep mortise for rough joinery such as might be used in fitting a brace into a corner post.

Post Axe

AXE, QUARTER. See *Axe, House.*

AXE, RAFTING. See *Axe, Single Bit*, rafting pattern.

AXE, SAFETY. A hatchet with a metallic guard that can be closed over the cutting edge. See *Hatchet, Guarded.*

AXE, SAFETY POCKET. See *Hatchet, Guarded.*

AXE, SCORING. See *Axe, Single Bit*, scoring pattern.

AXE, SCOUT. See *Axe, Boy Scout.*

AXE, SHIP. See *Axe, Broad, Ship Carpenters'.*

AXE, SHIP CARPENTERS'. See *Axe, Broad, Ship Carpenters'.*

AXE, SIDE. An axe having the cutting edge beveled on one side only. The term is usually used to refer to a one-handed axe such as a Coopers' Broad Axe. See *Axe, Bearded; Axe, Broad, Coopers'; Axe, Broad, European Pattern* and *Axe, Stave.*

AXE, SINGLE BIT. An axe having one bit only. The cutting edge is generally beveled on both sides. The standard single bit axe is a two-handed general-purpose tool used for felling, wood cutting, trimming and most other chopping tasks. The poll opposite the cutting bit serves primarily for purposes of weight and balance but is sometimes hardened to accommodate occasional use as a light maul. A few varieties were listed as having a laid-on steel face as shown by the Dock Pattern illustration. The Rafting Pattern axe is also listed as being suitable for use as a maul. Each pattern of axe was made in several sizes from 2 to 8 pounds except for the Cedar Pattern which was offered in the 2 1/2 pound size only. The nominal weight is approximately 4 1/2 pounds. These tools could be procured with handles of various lengths or without handles. The differences between patterns consist of small variations in width, length, thickness and shape. From appearance of the illustrations, some of the patterns are almost identical. It is doubtful if these differences in patterns were distinguishable in all cases even by the users. The Michigan and Yankee are the patterns commonly listed in later catalogues. The African and Spanish Pattern axes were produced primarily for export but were offered for sale internally. The Home-Made axe illustration shows the general shape of many early smith-made axes.

Many of the patterns shown were available in both the plain and beveled styles. See Bevel illustration.

See also Axe, *Bearded ; Axe, Boy Scout; Axe, Boys; Axe, Broad; Axe, Campers'; Axe, Coal Miners'; Axe, Firemans'; Axe, Freighters'; Axe, House; Axe, Hunters'; Axe, Ice; Axe, Miners'; Axe, Mortising Chisel; Axe, Pole; Axe, Post; Axe, Side* and *Axe, Stave.*

No Bevel   Common Bevel

Phantom Bevel   Hollow Bevel

Types of Bevel

Adirondack Pattern   African Pattern

Single Bit Axe

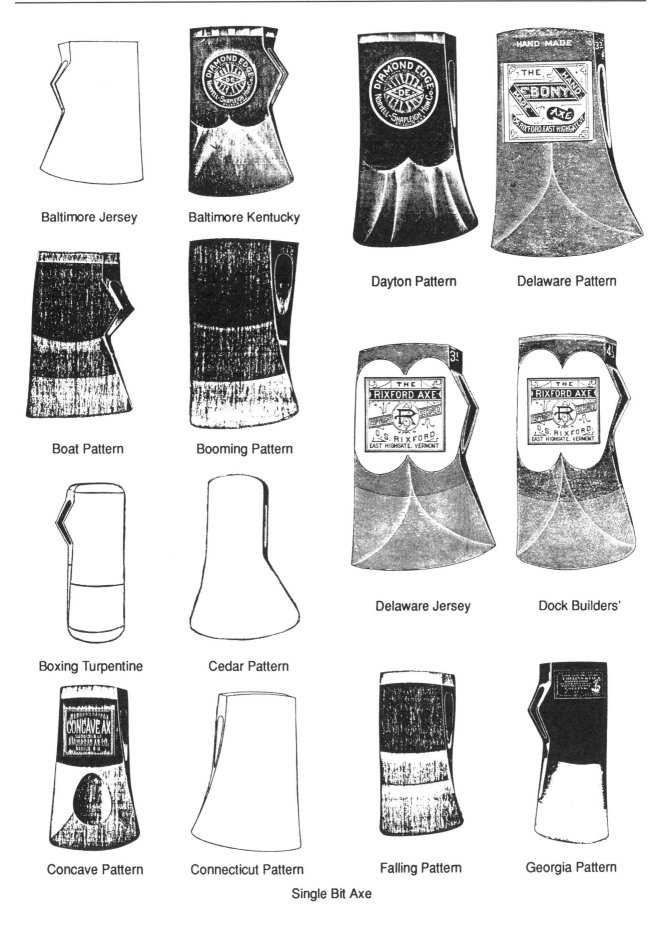

Baltimore Jersey

Baltimore Kentucky

Dayton Pattern

Delaware Pattern

Boat Pattern

Booming Pattern

Delaware Jersey

Dock Builders'

Boxing Turpentine

Cedar Pattern

Concave Pattern

Connecticut Pattern

Falling Pattern

Georgia Pattern

Single Bit Axe

Hagan Jersey Pattern

Half Wedge Pattern

Kentucky Pattern

Long Island Pattern

Home Made

Hooser Pattern
or Zeek

Jersey Pattern
or Baltimore Jersey

Lumberman Pattern

Maine Pattern

Jersey Oval Head

Kennebec Pattern

Michigan Pattern

Moses Weld Pattern

Single Bit Axe

New England Pattern

North Carolina Pattern

Rafting Pattern or Mauling

North Western Pattern

Ohio Pattern
or Western Crown

Rockaway Pattern   Rockaway Jersey Pattern

Ohio Heavy Poll

Ohio Jersey Pattern

Scoring Pattern

Philadelphia Jersey Pattern

Spanish Pattern
Round Head

Single Bit Axe

35

Round Eye
Spanish Pattern, de Tumba(Falling Axe)

Flat Head

Western Pattern

Western Crown Pattern

Wisconsin Pattern

Tillinghast Pattern

Turpentine Pattern

Yankee Pattern

Yankee Wide Bit

Single Bit Axe

Virginia Pattern   Wedge Pattern or Full Wedge

AXE, SLATERS'. Also called SAX, SAXE, SLATE CLEAVER, SLATE CUTTERS' TRIMMER, SLATE TRIMMER and ZAX. A one-handed tool with a long cutting edge on one side and a sharp spike opposite the cutting edge. This tool was used to trim and punch holes in roofing slates. The cutting edge is approximately 16 inches long. The handle is often leather-filled to reduce the shock on the hand during use.

West Virginia
Pattern

Single Bit Axe

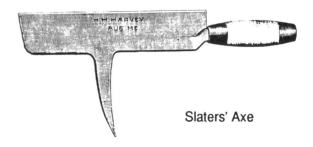

Slaters' Axe

AXE, SLEEPER. A small broad axe used for hewing sleepers. A sleeper is a heavy transverse beam used for support of a temporary building or platform. Length of the cutting edge of the sleeper axe is 6 to 8 inches.

Sleeper Axe

AXE, SPORTSMANS'. See *Axe, Hunters'*.

AXE, STAMP. See *Axe, Marking*.

AXE, STAVE. Also called AUSTRIAN STAVE AXE. These unique bearded axes were listed in an American catalogue of 1910. Sizes were not stated.

Stave Axe

AXE, STONE. Also called GRANITE PEEN HAMMER, PEEN HAMMER and STONE CUTTERS' PEEN HAMMER. A double-bitted tool used by a mason for cutting and dressing stone. Weight is 3 to 18 pounds. See also *Axe, Indian*.

Tooth Type   Straight Peen

Butterfly Peen

Stone Axe

AXE, THREE-QUARTER. See *Axe, Coal Miners'*.

AXE, TOMMY. A tool used for handling and sorting pulp wood.

Tommy Axe

AXE, TOOTH. See *Axe, Stone*.

AXE, TRADE. A crude axe used extensively in the northeast part of the United States for trading with the Indians. These axes are characterized by a round eye formed by wrapping the metal around a mandrel and hammer welding it back into the shank. The bit is wider than the eye and has a uniform taper. The early trade axes have bits 8 to 9 inches long. They were used for felling and general chopping. Smaller axes of the same pattern were later used by the Indians as weapons and as belt axes by the hunters and trappers of the era. The trade axe was the fore-runner of the tomahawk.

Trade Axe

AXE, TURPENTINE. See *Axe, Broad, Turpentine; Axe, Single Bit*, boxing turpentine pattern and *Axe, Single Bit*, turpentine pattern.

AXE, WEDGE. A blunt axe, with a very thick poll, used for finishing a split started with wedges. The poll is 2 to 2 1/2 inches thick. The wedge axe is the fore-runner of the common wood choppers' maul. *Mercer* calls this tool a HOLZAXT and SLEDGE AXE.

Wedge Axe

AXE, WHEELERS'. A bearded axe used by a wheelwright for rough shaping of wagon wheel spokes and for the outside of the felloes. See illustration under *Axe, Bearded*.

AXE BOX. A special wood box used for shipment and storage of an axe. One supplier put up each axe in a patented wedge-shaped box, as illustrated, to prevent them "From getting shopworn and being handled by the public".

Axe Box

AXE HANDLE. Handles for axes are generally made of hickory or ash. Hickory is superior for the purpose because of its ability to withstand repeated shocks without breaking. Broad axe handles were generally curved upward as shown in the illustration and were also curved slightly outboard in the direction of the cutting bevel. One supplier listed broad axe handles as being reversible; however, it is doubtful that a handle curved in two planes could be satisfactorily reversed. Broad axe handles were generally made by the user and were curved to suit his own taste. When the author tried to buy a broad axe handle in the ozarks many years ago, he was told that the only way to get a good one was to cut a hickory tree and have at it. Double bit axe handles are symetrical in order to allow convenient use of either bit. Nominal length is 36 inches. They were available in lengths from 32 to 36 inches.

Single bit axe handles are generally curved as shown in illustration (c). Early handles for this type axe were straight per illustration (d). The first mass production of curved handles has been attributed to Aaron and Obert Blanchard starting in 1853. Apparently, curved handles rapidly became standard. It is noted that a general catalogue dated 1865 offered only curved handles for single bit axes. Standard single bit handles were available in lengths from 28 to 42 inches. The nominal length is 36 inches.

Broad Axe Handle

Double Bit Axe Handle

Axe Handle

(c) Single Bit Axe Handle or Fawn Foot

(d) Single Bit Axe HAndle

Axe Handle

AXE HANDLE HOOKAROON. See *Hookaroon.*

AXE HANDLE SHIELD. A steel shield used to protect the axe handle from splintering adjacent to the head.

Axe Handle Shield

AXE MATTOCK. Also called PULASKI. A cutting tool with an axe bit on one side and a mattock bit on the other. This tool was originally designed for fighting forest fires. However, it was found useful for cutting turf and tree roots and was later offered as a farm tool.

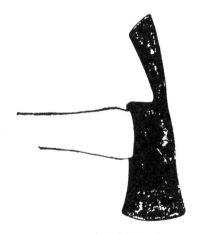

Axe Mattock

AXE PATTERN HATCHET. See *Axe, Hunters'.*

AXE SHEATH. Also called HATCHET CASE and HATCHET SHEATH. A leather sheath used to cover the head of a small axe such as a Boy Scout Axe or Hunters' Axe. The sheath often has a belt loop to facilitate carrying the axe. The leather covering protects both the axe edge and the bearer.

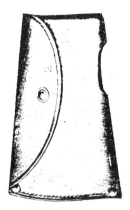

Axe Sheath

AXE STONE. See *Sharpening Stone, Axe.*

AXLE CUTTER. A patented tool designed for cutting back the nut shoulder on wagon and carriage axles that have become worn. The shoulder is cut back with this device and then threaded with a common die. The illustrated tool is Young's Patent dated August 17, 1880.

Axle Cutter

AXLE GAUGE. A tool used to measure the set of the end spindles of a wagon or buggy axle. Each spindle must be slanted slightly downward to account for dish of the wheel. The ideal amount of slant results in the bottom spoke of the wheel being plumb when the wagon is on level ground. In addition, the spindle is slanted slightly forward to give the wheel sufficient "Gather" to make it track straight. Most axle gauges were home made and many were quite crude. In many cases the gauge served only to assure that the two ends of the axle were slanted the same amount. The commercial gauges were generally equipped with calibrated dials and various adjustment features.

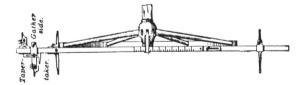

Carleton's Patent

Wills' Patent

Axle Gauge

Axle Gauge

AXLE NUT HOLDER. See *Wrench, Axle Nut Holder.*

AXLE SETTER. A tool used to bend a wagon or buggy axle spindle. It was generally required to adjust the spindles when installing a new axle or new wheels. The ends of the axles were bent slightly downward and forward to account for the amount of dish in the wheels. This tool could also be used to straighten an axle that had been inadvertently bent. The illustrated tool was advertised as being suitable for bending axles up to 1 1/4 inches in diameter at any point and in any direction. Other models were available that would set larger axles.

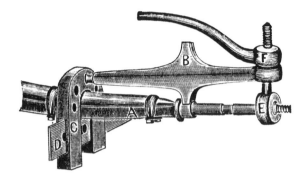

Axle Setter

B

Tool names starting with the letter B, including multiple listings of:
- Bar
- Beading Tool
- Bellows
- Bench
- Boring Tool
- Boring Tool, Bit
- Boring Tool, Bit Brace
- Broom
- Brush
- Burnishing Tool

Included also are listings of the tools used by the:
- Bee Keeper
- Blacksmith
- Book Binder
- Brick Mason

Babbitt File. See *File, Babbitt*.

Babbitt Float. See *File, Babbitt*.

Babbitt Ladle. See *Ladle, Melting*.

Back Check Plane. See *Plane, Sash Filletster*.

Back Filletster. See *Plane, Sash Filletster*.

Back Ogee. See *Plane, Moulding, Reverse Ogee*.

Back Saw. See *Saw, Back*.

Back Tool. See *Bookbinding Tool, Embossing Roll*.

Background Tool. See *Leather Tool, Stippling*.

Backing Boards. See *Bookbinding Tool, Backing Boards*.

Backing Hammer. A book binders' hammer. See *Hammer, Backing*.

Backing Knife. See *Drawing Knife, Coopers'*.

Backing Out Punch. See *Anvil Tool, Backing Out Punch* and *Punch, Backing Out*.

Badger Plane. See *Plane, Badger*.

Bag Frame Stuffer. See *Leather Tool, Bag Frame Stuffer*.

Bag Hook. See *Hook, Bag*.

Bag Punch. See *Leather Tool, Bag Punch*.

Bag Punch Gauge. See *Leather Tool, Bag Punch Gauge*.

Bakers' Rasp. See *Rasp, Bread*.

Balance Wheel File. See *File, Watch Makers'*.

Bale Hook. See *Hook, Bale*.

Bale Tie Cutter. See *Knife, Bale Tie Cutter*.

Bale Tie Snips. Also called Cotton Bale Snips. A tool used for cutting the metal ties from bales prior to processing the baled material. See also *Band Cutter*.

Bale Tie Snips

Baler Fork. See *Fork, Baler*.

Baler Press Fork. See *Fork, Baler*.

Ball. See *Engravers' Ball*.

Ball Bit Brace. A variety of bit brace. See *Boring Tool, Bit Brace, Gentlemans'*.

Ball Bolt Wrench. See *Wrench, Ball Bolt*.

Ball Gauge. Also called Radius Gauge. A gauge used by a die sinker to check cutter diameter. Sizes of the indentations are 1/8 to 1 inch diameter.

Ball Gauge

Ball Peen Hammer. See *Hammer, Ball Peen*.

Ball Point. A tool used to form a seat for a divider leg when scribing a circle around a hole. It can be used on a divider, compass or trammel. These tools were sold in sets of 4 in sizes from 1/2 to 1 9/16 inches in diameter.

Ball Point

BALL STAKE. See *Stake, Ball*.

BALLAST FORK. See *Fork, Stone*.

BALLING GUN. A device used to administer medicine to a horse. The gun is used to place a medicine ball deep in the throat such that the horse is forced to swallow. The trigger on the gun releases the ball.

Balling Gun

BALLING IRON. A tool used to hold the mouth of a horse in the open position for insertion of medication with the balling gun. See *Balling Gun*.

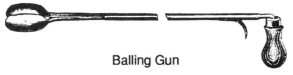

Balling Iron

BANANA KNIFE. See *Knife, Banana*.

BAND CUTTER. Also called WIRE BAND CUTTER. A device used to cut and remove wire ties from bundles of grain before threshing. The band cutter snips the wire and grasps one end so that it can be pulled free from the bundle.

Band Cutter

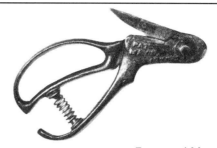

Patented May 8, 1878

Band Cutter

BAND JAW TONGS. See *Tongs, Band Jaw*.

BAND KNIFE. See *Knife, Band*.

BAND MOULDING. See *Plane, Moulding*.

BAND OGEE. See *Plane, Moulding, Grecian Ogee*.

BAND SAW. A saw that uses a flexible blade made in the form of an endless belt. See *Saw, Foot and Hand Power*.

BAND SAW ANVIL. See *Anvil, Band Saw*.

BAND SAW BRAZING VISE. See *Vise, Band Saw Brazing*.

BAND SAW CLAMP. See *Vise, Band Saw Brazing*.

BAND SAW FILE. See *File, Band Saw*.

BAND SAW FILING VISE. See *Vise, Band Saw Filing*.

BAND SAW VISE. See *Vise, Band Saw Brazing* and *Vise, Band Saw Filing*.

BAND SETTER. A tool used to size and smooth the end of a carriage or wagon wheel hub for installation of the band.

Band Setter

BAND TONGS. See *Tongs, Band Jaw*.

BANDAGE KNIFE. See *Knife, Bandage*.

BANDING PLANE. See *Plane, Banding*.

BANKERS' SHEARS. See *Shears, Desk*.

BAR. A piece of metal, long in proportion to its width, intended to be used for prying, separating or packing.

BAR, BREAKING. See *Bar, Ice*.

BAR, CAULKING. See *Bar, Ice*.

BAR, CAR STARTING. Also called CAR MOVER and STARTING BAR. A heavy pry bar used to start a railroad car when moving the car by hand.

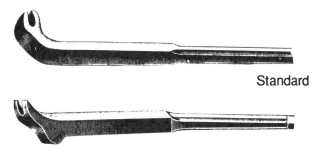

Car Starting Bar

BAR, CARPENTERS' PRYING. See *Bar, Wrecking*.

BAR, CARPENTERS' RIPPING. See *Bar, Wrecking*.

BAR, CLAW. A heavy steel bar used to pull a railroad spike. Length is approximately 5 feet. See also *Bar, Shackle*.

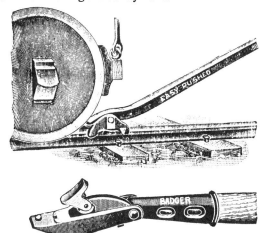

Standard

With Heel

Goose Neck

Claw Bar

BAR, CROW. A steel tool used for digging post holes and for general-purpose prying. Available in lengths up to 7 feet. One type is also called PINCH BAR. The types having wedge and diamond points are also called LINE BAR, LINING BAR and RAILROAD LINE BAR.

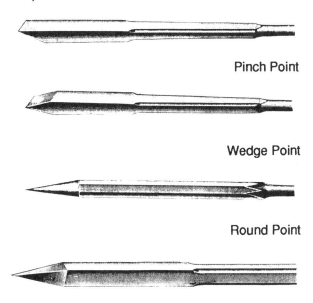

Pinch Point

Wedge Point

Round Point

Diamond Point

Crow Bar

BAR, DIGGING AND TAMPING. Also called DIGGING BAR. A general-purpose tool used in construction work. Length is approximately 6 feet.

Digging and Tamping Bar

BAR, FLAGGING. Also called PAVERS' BAR. A tool used for positioning and spacing of flagstones. Length is 4 to 5 feet.

Flagging Bar

BAR, FORK. See *Bar, Ice*.

BAR, HOUSE. See *Bar, Ice*.

BAR, ICE. A tool used in the ice harvesting and storage industry. The various types of bars were used for splitting out, breaking, moving and manipulating large blocks of ice. These bars are 4 to 5 feet long. See also *Fork, Splitting*.

Breaking Bar

Ice Bar

43

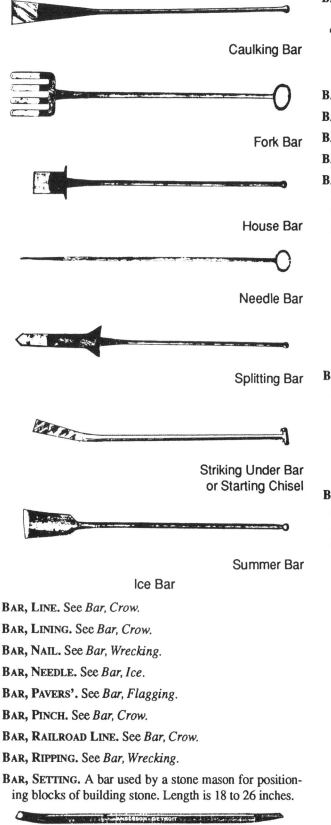

Caulking Bar

Fork Bar

House Bar

Needle Bar

Splitting Bar

Striking Under Bar
or Starting Chisel

Summer Bar

Ice Bar

BAR, LINE. See *Bar, Crow.*

BAR, LINING. See *Bar, Crow.*

BAR, NAIL. See *Bar, Wrecking.*

BAR, NEEDLE. See *Bar, Ice.*

BAR, PAVERS'. See *Bar, Flagging.*

BAR, PINCH. See *Bar, Crow.*

BAR, RAILROAD LINE. See *Bar, Crow.*

BAR, RIPPING. See *Bar, Wrecking.*

BAR, SETTING. A bar used by a stone mason for positioning blocks of building stone. Length is 18 to 26 inches.

Setting Bar

BAR, SHACKLE. A tool used to pull a railroad spike.

Shackle Bar

BAR, SPLITTING. See *Bar, Ice* and *Fork, Splitting.*

BAR, STARTING. See *Bar, Car Starting.*

BAR, STRIKING UNDER. See *Bar, Ice.*

BAR, SUMMER. See *Bar, Ice.*

BAR, TAMPING. Also called RAILROAD TAMPING BAR. A heavy iron bar with a blunt end used to pack loose earth when setting a post or timber. Some tamping bars have two blunt ends. Length is approximately 5 1/2 feet.

Tamping Bar

BAR, TIMBER. A light bar used as a lever when unloading logs from a wagon or railroad car.

Timber Bar

BAR, WRECKING. Also called CARPENTERS' PRYING BAR, CARPENTER' RIPPING BAR, NAIL BAR and RIPPING BAR. A bar used by a carpenter or house wrecker to loosen boards and pull nails.

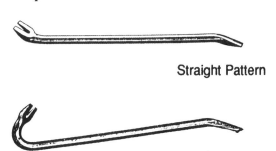

Straight Pattern

Gooseneck Pattern

Corner Pattern

Wrecking Bar

BAR CHISEL. See *Chisel, Ice.*

BAR CLAMP. See *Clamp, Bar*.

BAR FOLDING MACHINE. See *Tinsmiths' Machine, Folding*.

BAR LETTERING PALLET. See *Bookbinding Tool, Lettering Pallet*.

BAR TONGS. See *Tongs, Blacksmiths'*.

BARB WIRE CUTTER. A tool developed during World War I for use in cutting barbed wire entanglements. Overall length of the illustrated tool is 15 inches.

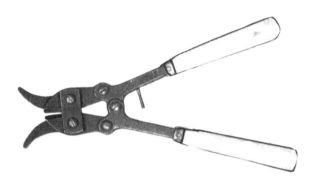

Barb Wire Cutter

BARB WIRE LIFTER. A device that will grasp the inside of a reel of barb wire allowing the reel to be lifted and carried by two men. Lifting a roll of barb wire without a tool is a sticky task.

Barb Wire Lifter

BARK SPUD. Also called PEELING IRON. A tool used to remove bark from a tree trunk. Overall length is approximately 30 inches except for the western cedar spud which is somewhat longer. When removing bark from a tree, the trunk is first girdled in two places and the bark is slit lengthwise between the girdles with a hatchet. The bark spud is then used like a chisel to separate the bark from the wood.

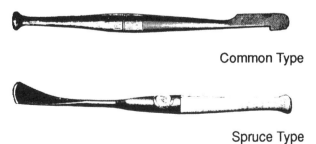

Common Type

Spruce Type

Bark Spud

Western Cedar Type

Bark Spud

BARLEY FORK. See *Fork, Barley*.

BARN FORK. See *Fork, Coal*.

BARREL BRUSH. See *Brush, Barrel*.

BARREL CART. See *Cart, Barrel*.

BARREL DRIFT. See *Drift Pin*.

BARREL FORGE. See *Forge, Bridge Builders'*.

BARREL HATCHET. See *Hatchet, Barreling*.

BARREL HEAD CUTTER. See *Head Cutter*.

BARREL HEADER. A tool used to pry or force the head into a wooden barrel. The header shown in illustration (b) was also listed as a FRUIT PRESS.

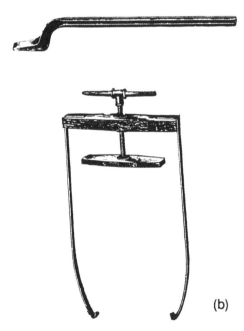

(b)

Barrel Header

BARREL SAW. See *Boring Tool, Bit, Barrel Saw*.

BARREL SET-UP FORM. A jig used to start the initial assembly of the staves for a wooden barrel. The assembly procedure is called "Raising" a barrel.

BARREL TRUCK. A wheel barrow used to transport a barrel. The clamp on the handle adjusts to grasp the lip at the top of the barrel. See also *Cart, Barrel*.

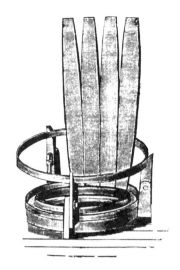

Barrel Set-Up Form

Barrel Truck

BARRELING HATCHET. See *Hatchet, Barreling.*

BARRETTE FILE. See *File, Barrette.*

BARROW. See *Wheel Barrow.*

BASE KNIFE. See *Knife, Paper Hangers' Casing.*

BASE MOULDING PLANe. See *Plane, Moulding.*

BASE PLANE. See *Plane, Moulding.*

BASE WHEEL. See *Knife, Paper Hangers' Casing.*

BASE AND BAND PLANE. See *Plane, Moulding.*

BASIN WRENCH. See *Wrench, Basin.*

BASKET SHAVE. A basket makers' tool. See *Plane, Basket Shave.*

BASTARD FILE. A medium-coarse file. See *File, Bastard.*

BATHTUB STAKE. See *Stake, Bathtub.*

BATTERY CLAMP TOOL. A tool used to clean the inside of terminal clamp of a lead-acid battery and to spread the clamp for installation.

Battery Clamp Tool

BATTERY PLIERS. See *Pliers, Battery.*

BATTERY WRENCH. See *Wrench, Battery.*

BEAD MOULDING PLANE. Any woodworking plane used to form a salient bead. See *Plane, Beading; Plane, Car Beading; Plane, Moulding, Center Bead; Plane, Moulding, Side Bead;* and *Plane, Moulding, Torus Bead.*

BEAD PLANE. Any woodworking plane used to form a salient bead. See *Plane, Beading; Plane, Car Beading; Plane, Moulding, Center Bead; Plane, Moulding, Side Bead;* and *Plane, Moulding, Torus Bead.*

BEAD SAW. See *Saw, Bead.*

BEAD TOOL. See *Turning Tool, Astragal.*

BEADER. See *Beading Tool, Carriage Makers'; Beading Tool, Wood* and *Leather Tool, Beader.*

BEADER CHUCK. See *Leather Tool, Beader Chuck.*

BEADING MACHINE. See *Tinsmiths' Machine, Beading.*

BEADING PLANE. See *Plane, Beading.*

BEADING TOOL. Any of a number of hand tools used to raise or form a bead on a workpiece.

BEADING TOOL, BOILER. Also called FLUE BEADING TOOL and TUBE BEADING TOOL. A tool used to crimp and expand the end of a boiler smokestack or tube.

Boiler Beading Tool

BEADING TOOL, CARRIAGE MAKERS'. A draw tool used to strike a small bead along the edge of a straight or curved workpiece. The illustrated tool has two irons to facilitate beading both sides of the workpiece or to allow working from either direction.

Carriage Makers' Beading Tool

BEADING TOOL, FLUE. See *Beading Tool, Boiler.*

BEADING TOOL, LATHE. See *Turning Tool, Astragal* and *Turning Tool, Beading.*

BEADING TOOL, LEATHER. See *Leather Tool, Beader.*

BEADING TOOL, MASONS'. See *Tuck Pointer.*

BEADING TOOL, TINNERS'. See *Tinsmiths' Machine, Beading.*

BEADING TOOL, TUBE. See *Beading Tool, Boiler.*

BEADING TOOL, TURNING. See *Turning Tool, Astragal* and *Turning Tool, Beading.*

BEADING TOOL, WOOD. Also called HAND BEADER. A hand tool used for striking a bead in wood. The short sole allows the tool to be used along a curved edge. Most of these tools use a scraping action to form the profile rather than a cutting or shaving action. See also *Beading Tool, Carriage Makers'.*

Windsor Beader

Wooden Beader

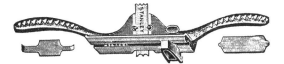

Wood Beading Tool

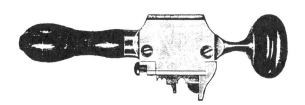

Wood Beading Tool

BEAK HORN. An anvil or stake on which the beak is a predominant feature. See *Anvil, Coopers'* and *Stake, Beakhorn.*

BEAK IRON. An anvil or stake on which the beak is a predominant feature. See *Anvil, Coopers'.*

BEAKHORN STAKE. See *Stake, Beakhorn.*

BEAM. See *Tanners' Beam.*

BEAM BORER. See *Boring Tool, Boring Machine.*

BEAM COMPASS. See *Trammel Points.*

BEAM KNIFE. See *Knife, Curriers'.*

BEAM SCALE. See *Scales, Steelyard.*

BEARING SCRAPER. See *Scraper, Bearing.*

BEARDED AXE. See *Axe, Bearded.*

BEATING HAMMER. A book binders' hammer. See *Hammer, Beating.*

BEATING IRON. See *Maul, Basket Makers'.*

BEATING OUT HAMMER. See *Hammer, Shoe Makers' Beating Out.*

BECK IRON. See *Anvil, Coopers'.*

BEDBUG GUN. A very small spray gun used to spread insecticide powder. The flexible leather top allows the can to act as a bellows. Capacity of the illustrated gun is one ounce.

Bedbug Gun

BED BOLT WRENCH. See *Wrench, Bed Key.*

BED KEY. See *Wrench, Bed Key.*

BED MOULDING PLANE. See *Plane, Moulding.*

BEE HIVE SCRAPER. See *Scraper, Bee Hive.*

BEE KEEPERS' TOOLS. The special-purpose bee keepers' tools listed below can be found in normal alphabetical sequence. These tools may also have been used for other purposes.
BEE SMOKER
BEE VEIL

BRUSH, BEE
KNIFE, UNCAPPING
SCRAPER, BEE HIVE
SWARM CATCHER
TOOL BOX, BEE KEEPER

BEE SMOKER. A device used to emit smoke while working with bees. The bellows provide a forced draft. The smoke tranquilizes the bees allowing the beekeeper to work with the hive with less danger to himself and to the bees.

Bee Smoker

BEE VEIL. A protective veil used to keep bees away from the head and neck while doing routine hive work.

Bee Veil

BEET FORK. See *Fork, Vegetable.*

BEET HOE. See *Hoe, Farm.*

BEET KNIFE. See *Knife, Beet.*

BEET TOPPING KNIFE. See *Knife, Beet.*

BEETLE. Also called CIRCUS BEETLE and CIRCUS MAUL. A heavy two-handed wooden maul used for driving wooden wedges, framing dowels and tent stakes. The beetle is usually made of elm and reinforced with iron bands similar to a wagon hub. Size is 6 to 8 inches in diameter. See also *Hawsing Beetle.*

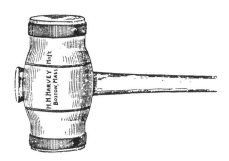

Beetle

BELAYING PIN. A pin around which a line is tied or snubbed. Used aboard boats and ships. These tools are usually made of strong wood such as hickory or locust but are sometimes made of metal. Overall length is 11 to 20 inches.

Belaying Pin

BELECTION MOULDING PLANE. See *Plane, Moulding, Bolection* and *Plane, Moulding, Nosing.* Belection is an incorrect spelling.

BELL CENTERING PUNCH. See *Punch, Bell Centering.*

BELL CENTERING TOOL. See *Punch, Bell Centering.*

BELL HANGERS' AUGER. See *Boring Tool, Bell Hangers'.*

BELL HANGERS' BIT. See *Boring Tool, Bit, Bell Hangers'.*

BELL HANGERS' DRILL. See *Boring Tool, Bell Hangers.*

BELL HANGERS' GIMLET. See *Boring Tool, Bell Hangers'* and *Boring Tool, Bit, Bell Hangers'.*

BELL HANGERS' PLIERS. See *Pliers, Bell Hangers'* and *Pliers, Bottlers'.*

BELLOWS. A device for directing a stream of air by alternately drawing air into a cavity and expelling it through an orifice.

BELLOWS, BLACKSMITHS'. A large bellows used for intensifying a forge fire. Size refers to the width of the bellows across the widest part. Sizes from 18 inches to 50 inches were listed. A common size is 36 inches. The bellows were normally mounted overhead close to the forge with a small air pipe routed down and under the forge. They were operated by pulling on a rope or thong located near the forge. Quite often a D handle was attached to the pull rope and dangled just above the smiths head. In some cases a second D handle or stirrup close to the floor allowed the bellows to be pumped with the foot when both hands were busy with other tasks. By the end of the nineteenth century, blacksmith bellows were largely obsoleted by the smaller and less expensive rotary blowers.

Blacksmiths' Bellows

BELLOWS, FOOT. Also called FOOT BLOWER. Any of several varieties of small bellows worked with the foot. This type of bellows are used for blow pipes, melting furnaces, dental work and for general-purpose work requiring small quantities of forced air.

Foot Bellows

BELLOWS, HAND. A hand-operated bellows used to direct a small quantity of air. Width is 6 to 12 inches. They are used to operate a lab burner, assist in starting a fire in a stove or fireplace or to remove dust from an appliance such as a piano.

Hand Bellows

BELLOWS, MOULDERS'. A medium-size bellows intended for use in a foundry. Width is 7 to 17 inches. The Facing Bellows are used to to coat the inside of the mould with blacking and the Sprinkling Bellows are used to dampen the mould prior to pouring. The common type bellows are also used in machine shops to remove dust from motors.

Facing Bellows

Moulders' Bellows

Sprinkling Bellows

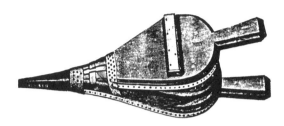

Common Type Bellows

Moulders' Bellows

BELLOWS, PIANO. A bellows used to remove dust and debris from a piano. Length of the cylinder is 16 to 18 inches.

Piano Bellows

BELLOWS, SULPHUR. Also called POWDER GUN. A bellows adapted to spreading dry insecticide on vines and other vegetation. This type bellows was also used by painters for blowing sand. Width is 6 to 10 inches.

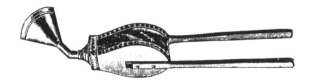

Sulphur Bellows

BELT AWL. See *Awl, Belt.*

BELT BORER. See *Punch, Belt.*

BELT CLAMP. See *Clamp, Belt.*

BELT CUTTER. A tool used to cut the holes in a flat leather belt for insertion of belt studs.

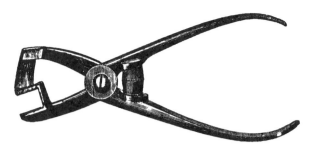

Belt Cutter

BELT GAUGE. A gauge used to indicate the lacing and pin size required for a given thickness of flat belt. The illustrated tool is a brass plate about 3 1/2 inches in diameter and 1/4 inch thick.

Belt Gauge

BELT GROOVER. A tool used to groove a leather belt such that the lacing on the pulley side will be flush with the belt surface. Overall length is about 6 inches.

Belt Groover

BELT HOLE PROTECTION PUNCH. See *Punch, Belt Hole Protector.*

BELT KNIFE. See *Knife, Leather.*

BELT HAMMER. See *Hammer, Belt.*

BELT LACER. A device for fastening alligator-type lacing to a flat belt. One type, see illustration, uses the jaws of an ordinary vise to provide the crimping pressure.

Belt Lacer

Belt Lacer

BELT MAKERS' PLANE. See *Plane, Belt Makers'.*

BELT MAKERS' SHAVE. See *Spoke Shave, Carriage Makers' Panel.*

BELT MARKER. A tool used to point off the positions on a belt where the lacing holes are to be punched. Overall length is approximately 5 1/2 inches.

Belt Marker

BELT PRESS. A belt makers' tool used for flattening and setting a finished splice.

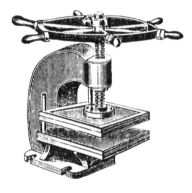

Belt Press

BELT PUNCH. See *Punch, Belt.*

BELT PUNCH KNIFE. See *Knife, Belt Punch.*

BELT SQUARE. See *Square, Belt.*

BELTING SHEARS. See *Shears, Belting.*

BENCH. A long work surface of the proper height to accommodate the intended task.

BENCH, AMATEURS'. A small work bench with two vises similar to a Cabinet Makers' Bench. Length is 3 1/2 to 4 feet. See illustration under *Bench, Cabinet Makers'.*

BENCH, CABINET MAKERS'. Also called CARPENTERS' BENCH and JOINERS' BENCH. A woodworkers' bench having a front vise and a tail vise. This type of bench normally has a tool well at the back. Holes along the front edge are provided for insertion of bench stops. Length is 4 1/2 to 10 feet. A common length is 7 feet.

Cabinet Makers' Bench

BENCH, CARPENTERS'. See *Bench, Cabinet Makers'*.

BENCH, CARVERS'. See *Bench, Wood Carvers'*.

BENCH, JEWELERS'. A bench intended for use by a jewelry maker. The pull-out lap tray has a seamless metal insert to catch the filings and scrap for salvage.

Jewelers' Bench

BENCH, JOINERS'. See *Bench, Cabinet Makers'*.

BENCH, MANUAL TRAINING. A bench intended for use in a woodworking school. One type, see illustration, has a vise on both sides and is intended to be used simultaneously by two students.

BENCH, SHAVING. Also called COOPERS' SHAVING BENCH and SHAVING HORSE. A bench with a foot-operated clamp for holding the workpiece while using a drawing knife. This type of tool was used extensively by coopers and shingle makers.

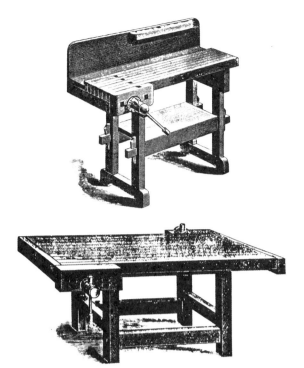

Manual Training Bench

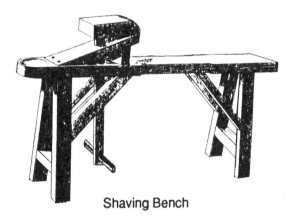

Shaving Bench

BENCH, SPOKE. Also called SPOKE TENONER. A bench used in a wheelwright shop when cutting tenons on wagon and buggy wheel spokes. Several cutters were furnished with the bench to work tenons of various sizes. A felloe boring attachment was also available.

Spoke Bench

51

BENCH, WATCH MAKERS'. A high bench of a type favored by watch makers and repairmen. The top has a lip to prevent the small parts from rolling off. A multitude of small drawers is a characteristic of the watch makers' bench.

Watch Makers' Bench

BENCH, WOOD CARVERS'. Also called CARVERS' BENCH. A small woodworking bench. The illustrated bench top is 39 inches long.

Wood Carvers' Bench

BENCH ANVIL. See *Anvil, Bench*.

BENCH AXE. See *Hatchet, Broad*.

BENCH BLOCK. See *Bookbinding Tool, Bench Block*.

BENCH BRACKET. A bracket used to stabilize one end of a board while the other end is clamped in the front vise of a cabinet makers' bench. The illustrated bracket mounts in a hole in the front of the bench.

Bench Bracket

BENCH BRUSH. See *Brush, Brick Layers' Dust*.

BENCH CLAMP. See *Clamp, Bench*.

BENCH DOG. See *Clamp, Bench*.

BENCH DRILL. See *Boring Tool, Bench Drill*.

BENCH FORGE. A small forge. See *Forge, Bench*.

BENCH HACK SAW. See *Saw, Bench*.

BENCH HATCHET. See *Hatchet, Broad*.

BENCH HOOK. A wooden tool used on the bench to assist in holding a small workpiece while performing an operation such as planing. See also *Bench Stop* and *Hook, Sail Makers'*.

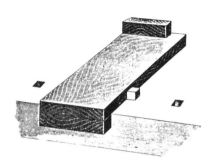

Bench Hook

BENCH KEY. A watch makers' tool. See *Wrench, Sleeve*.

BENCH LEVEL. See *Level, Straight Edge*.

BENCH PIN. A wooden block that fits into a mortise in the front of a jewelers' bench. The block provides either a flat or a sloped surface to support a workpiece for filing and cutting.

Bench Pin

BENCH PLANE. See *Plane, Bench*.

BENCH PLATE. A heavy iron plate with holes of various sizes to accept tinsmith tools. The bench plate is normally set into a low work bench or secured to the top of a special bench plate stand. Sizes from 18 to 94 pounds were listed.

Bench Plate

Bench Plate

Bench Stop

BENCH RAMMER. A sand casting tool. See *Rammer, Bench.*

BENCH RULE. See *Rule, Manual Training* and *Rule School.*

BENCH SAW. See *Saw, Bench* and *Saw, Joiner.*

BENCH SCREW. A threaded pair used to make or repair the vise for a Cabinet Makers' or Manual Training Bench.

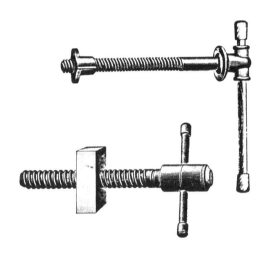

Bench Screw

BENCH SCREW DRIVER. See *Screw Driver, Bench.*

BENCH SHEARS. See *Shears, Bench* and *Tinsmiths' Machine, Shears.*

BENCH STOP. Also called BENCH HOOK. A device extending above the surface of the bench to block movement of the workpiece. Various stops were available that could be quickly raised above the bench surface for use or stowed flush with the surface when not in use. Other types are intended to fit into conveniently located holes in the bench surface and are removed when not required.

Bench Stop

BENCH VISE. See *Vise, Bench.*

BENDING BLOCK. Also called RING BENDING BLOCK. A small swage block used by a jeweler for shaping a ring section. The illustration shows a bending block and associated punch.

Bending Block

BENDING FORK. See *Anvil Tool, Bending Fork.*

BENDING IRON. Also called BENDING PIN. A plumbers' tool used for flaring a hole in a lead pipe or conduit and for smoothing an elbow in a lead pipe. Length is about 12 inches.

Bending Iron

BENDING MACHINE. Also called METAL BENDER. A hand-operated machine used to bend a metal rod or strap. This type of machine was often used in wagon or buggy repair shops and in sheet metal shops.

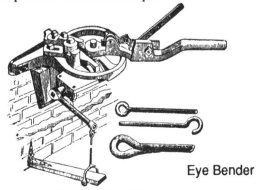

Eye Bender

Bending Machine

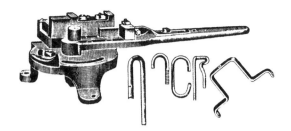

Angle or U Bender

Bending Machine

BENDING PIN. See *Bending Iron*.

BENDING SPRING. Also called PIPE BENDING SPRING. A tool used for bending a lead pipe or light conduit without collapsing the sidewalls. The spring is placed inside the pipe while the bend is being made. It can be easily removed by rotating the end of the spring thus tending to reduce the spring diameter. Size is 1 to 2 inches in diameter.

Bending Spring

BENDING TOOL. A hand tool used by a blacksmith for bending a heated rod or bar. The forks of the tool are placed astride the workpiece and the handle of the tool is then moved sidewise to impart the desired bend. See also *Anvil Tool, Bending Fork*.

Bending Tool

BENT CHISEL. See *Chisel, Bent*.

BENT CRUCIBLE TONGS. See *Tongs, Crucible*.

BENT GOUGE. See *Gouge, Bent*.

BENT GRAVER. See *Graver*.

BENT GROOVING CHISEL. See *Chisel, Bent Grooving*.

BENT NECK GOUGE. See *Gouge, Bent*.

BENT RASP. See *Rasp, Bent*.

BENT TONGS. See *Tongs, Blacksmiths'*.

BEVEL. A wooden tool used to transfer an angle. A wing nut is generally used to allow the bevel to be quickly adjusted and locked into position. This type of tool is often home made. Lengths up to 2 feet have been noted. As a descriptive term, "Bevel" is generally considered to be any angle other than 90 degrees. See also *Rule, Ship Carpenters' Bevel* and *Sliding T Bevel*.

Bevel

BEVEL CREASER. See *Leather Tool, Creaser*.

BEVEL EDGE SQUARE STAKE. See *Stake, Bevel Edge Square*.

BEVEL SQUARE. See *Square, Combination*.

BEVEL TICKLER. See *Leather Tool, Tickler*.

BEVEL TOOL. A type of turning tool. See *Turning Tool, Bevel*.

BEVELED CHISEL. See *Chisel, Beveled*.

BEVELER. See *Leather Tool, Beveler*.

BEVELING Machine. See *Leather Tool, Beveling Machine*.

BEVELING PLANE. See *Plane, Beveling*.

BEZEL TOOL. Also called WATCH CASE BEZEL TOOL. A tool used to recut a watch case bezel or to undercut the rim that holds the bezel.

Bezel Tool

BICK IRON. See *Anvil, Coopers'* and *Anvil, Jewelers'*.

BICK IRON STAKE. See *Anvil, Coopers'*.

BICYCLE BRUSH. See *Brush, Bicycle*.

BICYCLE OILER. See *Pocket Oiler*.

BICYCLE TIRE PLUG PLIERS. See *Pliers, Tire Plug*.

BICYCLE WRENCH. See *Wrench, Bicycle*.

BILECTION. See *Plane, Moulding, Bolection* and *Plane, Moulding, Nosing*. Bilection is an incorrect spelling of Bolection.

BILL. See *Hook, Bill*.

BILL HOOK. See *Hook, Bill*.

BILL POSTERS' HAMMER. See *Hammer, Bill Posters'*.

BILLIARD SCREW DRIVER. See *Screw Driver Bit*.

BINDING TRIMMER. See *Leather Tool, Trimmer*.

BIRD STUFFING FORCEPS. See *Forceps, Taxidermists'*.

BISSONNETTE. See *Leather Tool, Edger*.

BIT. See *Boring Tool, Bit* and sub-headings thereof. The term "Bit" is also used for the cutting side of an axe or hatchet head and for a plane iron.

BIT BRACE. See *Boring Tool, Bit Brace* and sub-headings thereof.

BIT BRACE WRENCH. See *Wrench, Socket.*

BIT EXTENSION. See *Boring Tool, Bit Extension.*

BIT GAUGE. Also called AUGER GAUGE and BORING GAUGE. A device that can be attached to a bit to gauge and limit the depth of the hole being drilled.

Garrett's Patent June 14, 1881

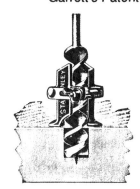

Bit Gauge

BIT HANDLE. See *Wrench, Bit.*

BIT HOLDER. See *Boring Tool, Bit Extension.*

BIT STOCK. See *Boring Tool, Bit Brace* and sub-headings thereof.

BIT STOCK DRILL. See *Boring Tool, Bit, Twist Drill* and *Boring Tool, Hand Drill.*

BIT WRENCH. See *Wrench, Bit.*

BIT AND SQUARE LEVEL. See *Level, Bit and Square.*

BLACK LEAD BRUSH. See *Brush, Electrotypers'.*

BLACKING BRUSH. See *Brush, Tanners' Blacking.*

BLACKSMITHS' CROSS PEEN HAMMER. See *Hammer, Blacksmiths'.*

BLACKSMITHS' DRILL. See *Boring Tool, Post Drill* and *Boring Tool, Tire Drill.*

BLACKSMITHS' HAND HAMMER. See *Hammer, Blacksmiths'.*

BLACKSMITHS' LEG VISE. See *Vise, Post.*

BLACKSMITHS' MANDREL. See *Cone.*

BLACKSMITHS' TOOLS. The special-purpose blacksmiths' tools listed below can be found in normal alphabetical sequence. These tools may also have been used for other purposes. Inasmuch as the blacksmith did a wide variety of tasks, other tools were commonly included in a blacksmith shop. See also *Farriers' Tools* and *Wheelwrights' Tools.*

ANVIL, BLACKSMITHS'
ANVIL, PLOW
ANVIL, PLOWMAKERS'
ANVIL TOOL
ANVIL TOOL, BACKING OUT PUNCH
ANVIL TOOL, BENDING FORK
ANVIL TOOL, CENTER PUNCH
ANVIL TOOL, COLD CUTTER
ANVIL TOOL, COUNTERSINK
ANVIL TOOL, CUPPING
ANVIL TOOL, CUTTER
ANVIL TOOL, DOLLY
ANVIL TOOL, DRILL SPREADER
ANVIL TOOL, FLATTER
ANVIL TOOL, FERRULE
ANVIL TOOL, FOOT
ANVIL TOOL, FULLER
ANVIL TOOL, GOUGE
ANVIL TOOL, HARDIE
ANVIL TOOL, HARROW TOOTH
ANVIL TOOL, HOT CUTTER
ANVIL TOOL, PLOW IRON
ANVIL TOOL, PUNCH
ANVIL TOOL, RIVET SET
ANVIL TOOL, SADDLE
ANVIL TOOL, SET HAMMER
ANVIL TOOL, SIDE CHISEL
ANVIL TOOL, SOW
ANVIL TOOL, SQUARE CHISEL
ANVIL TOOL, SWAGE
APRON, BLACKSMITHS'
AWL, SCRATCH
BELLOWS, BLACKSMITHS'
BENDING TOOL
BLOWER
BOLT HEADER
BOLT HEADING MACHINE
BORING TOOL, BIT, MACHINE
BORING TOOL, BIT, TWIST DRILL
BORING TOOL, BIT BRACE, BLACKSMITHS'
BORING TOOL, POST DRILL
CHISEL, COLD
CLAMP, PLOW POINT
CONE
FIRE TOOLS, BLACKSMITHS'
FORGE, BLACKSMITHS'

GRIND STONE, PEDAL
HAMMER, BLACKSMITHS'
HAMMER, FOOT POWER
HAMMER, SHOULDER PEEN
HAMMER, STRAIGHT PEEN
LEVELING BLOCK
NAIL HEADER
NIPPERS, BLACKSMITHS'
PINCERS, FARRIERS'
PUNCH, HAND
ROD CUTTER
RULE, BLACKSMITHS'
SHEARS, METAL
SLEDGE, BLACKSMITHS'
SLEDGE, DOUBLE FACE
SWAGE BLOCK
SWINGING MONKEY
TAP AND DIE
TONGS, ANGLE JAW
TONGS, BAND JAW
TONGS, BLACKSMITHS'
TONGS, BRAZING
TONGS, CHAIN
TONGS, RIVET
TUYERE IRON
VISE, POST

BLANK HAMMER. A book binders' hammer. See *Hammer, Backing*.

BLANK ROLL. See *Bookbinding Tool, Embossing Roll*.

BLAST BURNER. See *Torch, Gasoline*.

BLASTING TOOLS. See *Coal Miners' Blasting Tools*.

BLEEDER. A spring-loaded device used to cut a small slit in the skin for the purpose of removing blood. At one time it was thought that bleeding was a sure cure for many of the common ailments. See also *Flem* and *Leather Tool, Bleeder*.

Bleeder

BLIND NAIL PLANE. See *Plane, Chisel Gauge*.

BLIND NAIL TOOL. See *Chisel, Chip Nailing* and *Plane, Chisel Gauge*.

BLIND SLAT CHISEL. See *Chisel, Blind Slat*.

BLINDMANS' RULE. See *Rule, Blindmans'*.

BLOCK HEATER. Metal blocks used to clamp-up horn and tortoise shell comb blanks for heating prior to cutting the teeth. Heating was used to soften and straighten the

blanks. The heat was provided by circulating steam through each block.

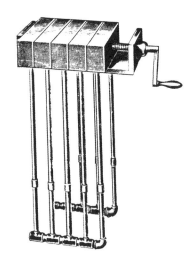

Block Heater

BLOCK HOOK. A hook used to wedge a barrel stave against the top of a block while backing or hollowing with the drawing knife. The hook is sharpened and driven into a block or stump.

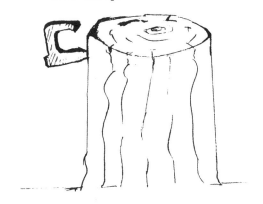

Block Hook

BLOCK KNIFE. See *Knife, Block*.

BLOCK MAKERS' GOUGE. See *Gouge, Block Makers'*.

BLOCK PLANE. See *Plane, Block*.

BLOCK SCRAPER. See *Scraper, Butcher Block*.

BLOCK SHAVE. See *Spoke Shave, Carriage Makers' Panel*.

BLOCKING HAMMER. See *Hammer, Electrotype Finishers'*.

BLOCK MAKERS' TRIMMING HAMMER. See *Hammer, Pavers' Side*.

BLOODSTONE. See *Burnishing Tool, Bloodstone*.

BLOW PIPE. See *Glass Blow Pipe* and *Torch, Alcohol*.

BLOW TUBE. See *Glass Blow Pipe*.

BLOW TORCH. See *Torch, Gasoline*.

BLOWER. A rotary device used to generate and direct a stream of air to a blacksmith forge fire. Free-standing blowers of many sizes and types were available for connection to the permanent masonry forges preferred by professional blacksmiths. The most common type of blower has a rotary crank handle as shown in the illustration. A counterweight on the handle was sometimes used to give a flywheel effect and thereby provide air for a short period after the smith released the handle. Another type of blower was operated with a spring-loaded lever.

A twelve inch diameter blower was the standard size but smaller and larger ones were available. A 16 inch model sold by one supplier was said to have the same capacity as a 50 inch bellows. The 10 inch size was listed as being adequate for a rural shop. Belt driven bellows were sometimes used in large commercial shops. In these large shops, a central blower operated continuously and provided air to several forges. Regulation was obtained by a damper at each forge. One maker stated that an 18 inch blower would provide air to 4 fires. Most of the small portable forges were equipped with an attached blower and ducting. See also *Bellows, Blacksmiths'*.

Blower

BLOWHORN STAKE. See *Stake, Blowhorn*.

BOARD. A piece of sawed lumber of considerable width and length. Usually less than two inches thick.

BOARD MATCH PLANE. See *Plane, Match*.

BOARD MEASURE. See *Rule, Board Measure*.

BOARD RULE. See *Rule, Board Measure* and *Rule, Board Stick*.

BOARD STICK. See *Rule, Board Stick*.

BOASTER. See *Stone Cutters' Tool, Chisel*.

BOASTING CHISEL. See *Stone Cutters' Tool, Chisel*.

BOAT AXE. See *Axe, Single Bit*, boat pattern.

BOAT CLAMP. See *Clamp, Carriage Makers'*.

BOAT CLAMP SCREW. See *Clamp, Ship Carpenters'*.

BOAT HOOK. See *Hook, Boat*.

BOB. A suspended weight. See *Plumb Bob*.

BOBBIN. An egg-shaped block of wood used by a plumber for straightening and rounding a lead pipe. One or more bobbins were driven through the pipe to press out large dents or kinks. Also used in combination with a drift plug to smooth straight sections of pipe.

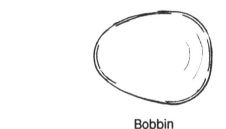

Bobbin

BOBBING PUNCH. See *Anvil Tool, Countersink*.

BOBBING TOOL. See *Anvil Tool, Countersink*.

BODKIN. A pointed tool used for spreading a hole during interweaving of cloth, rope or basket material. Also used by a book binder for making the holes for sewing. The blade is 4 to 10 inches long.

Bodkin

BODY CLAMP. A type of C clamp. See *Clamp, C*.

BOG HOE. See *Hoe, Farm*.

BOG SPADE. See *Spade*.

BOILER BEADING TOOL. See *Beading Tool, Boiler*.

BOILER CLAMP. See *Clamp, C*.

BOILER DRILL. See *Boring Tool, Ratchet*.

BOILER EXPANDER. A tinsmiths' tool used to spread the

body of a wash boiler and hold it in position while the bottom is being double seamed or soldered.

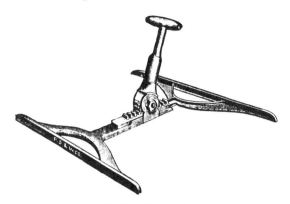

Boiler Expander

BOILER MAKERS' HAMMER. See *Hammer, Boiler Makers'*; *Hammer, Boiler Riveting* and *Hammer, Scaling*.

BOILER MAKERS' MAUL. See *Maul, Boiler Makers'*.

BOILER PICK. See *Pick, Boiler*.

BOLECTION MOULDING PLANE. See *Plane, Moulding, Bolection* and *Plane, Moulding, Nosing*.

BOLT CLIPPER. Also called BOLT CUTTER, BOLT TRIMMER and RIVET CLIPPER. A compound-action cutting tool used to cut bolts, metal rods and chain links. Available from 12 to 42 inches long. The 36 inch clipper was advertised as being capable of cutting a 5/8 inch bolt.

Bolt Clipper

BOLT CUTTER. See *Bolt Clipper*.

BOLT DIE. See *Tap and Die*.

BOLT GRIPPER. A complicated tool intended to grip the head of a carriage or plow bolt to prevent rotation when removing a rusted nut. The two claws can be separately adjusted against the sides of the bolt. The plunger is then cranked down to press against the end or head of the bolt. Patented in 1891.

BOLT HEADER. Also called BOLT HEADING TOOL and HEADING TOOL. A tool used by a blacksmith to form the head on a bolt. Headers for bolt sizes from 1/4 inch to 1 1/4 inches were available. The majority of the headers noted were made by the user and many are quite crude. The illustrated plow bolt header was made from a buggy axle. Home made headers have been noting with coun-

tersunk slots and irregular shapes to allow for making non-standard bolt heads. For many years after standard bolts were readily available in large stores, the small-town blacksmith was often called upon to make a bolt that was needed immediately. A set of bolt headers was common equipment in a blacksmith shop.

Bolt Gripper

Plow Bolt Header

Bolt Header

BOLT HEADING MACHINE. A foot-operated vise incorporating a set of heading dies of various sizes. An adjustable stop provides a means of gauging and controlling the length of the bolt. See also *Vise, Farriers'*.

Bolt Heading Machine

BOLT HEADING TOOL. See *Bolt Header.*

BOLT HOLDER. See *Tire Bolt Holder.*

BOLT REAMER. See *Boring Tool, Bit, Reamer.*

BOLT TAP. See *Tap and Die.*

BOLT THREADER. See *Bolt and Nut Threader.*

BOLT TONGS. See *Tongs, Blacksmiths'.*

BOLT TRIMMER. See *Bolt Clipper.*

BOLT AND NUT THREADER. Also called BOLT THREADER AND NUT TAPPER. A crank-operated machine used to thread a bolt or nut.

Bolt and Nut Threader

BONE CHISEL. See *Chisel, Bone* and *Chisel, Guarded.*

BONE CUTTER. See *Grinding Mill.*

BONE DRILL. See *Boring Tool, Bit Brace, Orthopedic; Boring Tool, Bone Drill* and *Boring Tool, Cranial.*

BONE GOUGE. See *Gouge, Bone.*

BONE FOLDER. A book binders' tool consisting of a flat piece of bone with dull rounded edges. Length is about 6 1/2 inches. This tool is used by a book binder to crease the heavy end sheets and to hold the partially assembled book in place while the glue is brushed on. It is also used as a general-purpose print shop tool for folding and creasing.

Bone Folder

BONE MILL. See *Grinding Mill.*

BONE REAMER. See *Boring Tool, Bone Reamer.*

BONE SAW. A surgical tool. See *Saw, Bone.*

BONING KNIFE. See *Knife, Butchers'.*

BONING STICKS. See *Winding Sticks.*

BOOKBINDING TOOL. Any tool used in hand binding of a book including the decoration and marking of the leather cover.

BOOKBINDING TOOL, BACKING BOARDS. A pair of rigid boards used to hold the pages or sections of a book in position while in the press. The illustrated boards are made of wood with steel facing.

Backing Boards

BOOKBINDING TOOL, BENCH BLOCK. A flat iron block 10 to 20 inches long and up to two inches thick. The bench block is used to provide a firm surface for skiving the edges of the leather to be used as a book cover.

Bench Block

BOOKBINDING TOOL, CREASER. A hand tool used to make decorative lines on a leather book cover. Single, double and triple line creasers were available that would make lines of various widths and spacings. Creasers are generally made of polished steel.

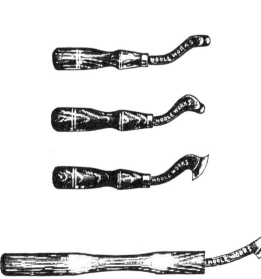

Creaser

BOOKBINDING TOOL, EMBOSSING ROLL. Also called BACK TOOL, BLANK ROLL, and GILDING ROLL. A bronze roller used to make a decorative design and to apply gold leaf to the leather cover of a book. These rolls are generally 3 1/2 to 4 1/2 inches in diameter and are fitted with 16 inch wooden handles. The user grasps the roll with one or both hands and rests the handle on his shoulder during use. They are heated prior to use. These tools often have a notch ground into the roll surface to provide a precise starting point for the impression. The rolls that make straight lines only are sometimes called FILLET ROLLS.

Embossing Roll

BOOKBINDING TOOL, FORMING IRON. A rigid iron block used to form and check the rounded spine of a book. Length is approximately 20 inches.

Forming Iron

BOOKBINDING TOOL, GOLD CUSHION. A rigid leather-covered cushion used as a base for pieces of gold leaf ready to be applied. The illustrated cushion and storage box is 8 by 16 inches.

Gold Cushion

BOOKBINDING TOOL, HAND PALLET. A bronze tool used for embossing a short length of design on a leather book cover. Various designs, the same as used on the embossing rolls, were available. See *Bookbinding Tool, Embossing Roll.* The hand pallet is used in confined areas such as on the spine of the book. Length of the illustrated tool is 3 1/4 inches.

Hand Pallet

BOOKBINDING TOOL, HAND STAMP. A bronze tool similar to the Hand Pallet except having a small decorative pattern. See *Bookbinding Tool, Hand Pallet.* These stamps were often used to make the corners or fillers for a book cover design. They are heated during use.

Hand Stamp

BOOKBINDING TOOL, LETTERING PALLET. Also called BAR LETTERING PALLET. An hand tool capable of clamping and holding a series of individual letter stamps. The lettering pallet is used in a manner similar to the hand pallet. See *Bookbinding Tool, Hand Pallet.* Inside length is 2 1/4 to 7 inches.

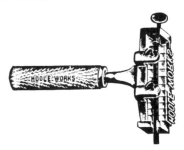

Lettering Pallet

BOOKBINDING TOOL, POLISHER. A steel rubbing and smoothing tool used on a leather book covering to smooth and even the surface prior to tooling.

Polisher

BOOKBINDING TOOL, PRESS. The standing press is used for flattening and glueing the book pages and sections during the binding process. The lying press is used primarily for intermediate functions such as trimming. The sewing press serves to position the pages and bands for stitching.

Lying or Cutting Press
Bookbinding Press

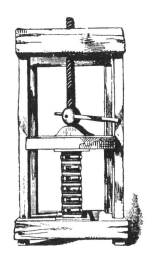

Standing Press

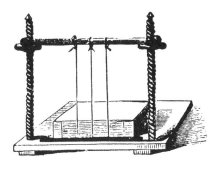

Sewing Press or Sewing Frame

Bookbinding Press

BOOKBINDING TOOL, PRESS PALLET. A pallet used to clamp-up large design stamps for a book cover. The illustrated tool has a solid brass frame and a steel bottom.

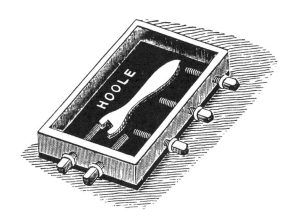

Press Pallet

BOOKBINDING TOOL, RUBBER. A steel rubbing and smoothing tool used on a book cover.

Book Rubber

BOOK PRESS. See *Copying Press*.

BOOK BINDERS' TOOLS. The special-purpose book binders' tools listed below can be found in normal alphabetical sequence. These tools may also have been used for other purposes.

BODKIN
BONE FOLDER
BOOKBINDING TOOL, BACKING BOARDS
BOOKBINDING TOOL, BENCH BLOCK
BOOKBINDING TOOL, CREASER
BOOKBINDING TOOL, EMBOSSING ROLL
BOOKBINDING TOOL, FORMING IRON
BOOKBINDING TOOL, GOLD CUSHION
BOOKBINDING TOOL, HAND PALLET
BOOKBINDING TOOL, HAND STAMP
BOOKBINDING TOOL, LETTERING PALLET
BOOKBINDING TOOL, POLISHER
BOOKBINDING TOOL, PRESS
BOOKBINDING TOOL, PRESS PALLET
BOOKBINDING TOOL, RUBBER
BURNISHING TOOL, AGATE
BURNISHING TOOL, BLOODSTONE
BURNISHING TOOL, BOOK BINDERS'
COPYING PRESS
HAMMER, BACKING
HAMMER, BEATING
HAMMER, GOLD BEATING
KNIFE, BOOK BINDERS'
KNIFE, GOLD
NIPPERS, BAND
PLANE, BOOK BINDERS' PLOW
SEWING KEY

BOOK CASE PLANE. See *Plane, Shelf Rail*.

BOOM AUGER. See *Boring Tool, Boom Auger*.

BOOMING AXE. See *Axe, Single Bit*, booming pattern.

BOOT CALK TOOL. Also called BOOT CALK WRENCH. A tool used to insert calks into the heels of a lumberman's boots. This type of calk was also used by ice harvest workers.

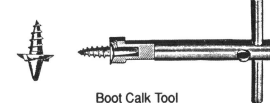

Boot Calk Tool

Boot Calk Wrench. See *Boot Calk Tool.*

Borax Box. A box for holding and spreading soldering flux. Powdered borax or other flux was sprinkled evenly over the workpiece by rubbing a rod or bar over the notches on the spout of the box.

Borax Box

Border Tool. See *Cement Tool, Rounding.*

Bordering Tool. See *Gun Stock Tool.*

Bore Gauge. A flat gauge used to determine the bore of a shotgun or rifle. One side is calibrated for standard sizes of shotguns and the other side for rifles or handguns.

Bore Gauge

Borer, Belt. See *Punch, Belt.*

Borer, Bung. See *Boring Tool, Bung Borer.*

Borer, Hub. See *Hub Boxing Machine.*

Borer, Tap. See *Boring Tool, Tap Borer.*

Boring Bit. See *Boring Tool, Bit.*

Boring Gauge. See *Bit Gauge.*

Boring Machine. See *Boring Tool, Boring Machine.*

Boring Tool. Any tool used for making or enlarging a hole by use of rotary motion. Boring tools and the handles or mechanisms for holding the tools are included under the general heading of Boring Tool. See also *Hole Cutter* and *Washer Cutter.*

Boring Tool, Angular Borer. Also called an Angular Bit Brace, Angular Bit Holder, Angular Bit Stock and Angular Borer. An adjustable bit-holding attachment used for boring a hole at an angle with the bit brace.

Angular Borer

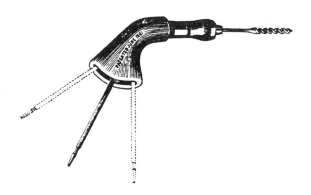

Angular Borer

Boring Tool, Archimedes Drill. Also called Automatic Drill, Reciprocating Drill and Spiral Drill. A drill in which the bit is attached to the end of a spiral shaft. The bit is caused to rotate first in one direction and then in the other by moving a nut up and down the spiral.

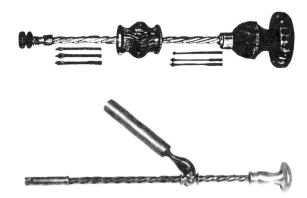

Archimedes Drill

Boring Tool, Auger. A tool for boring a deep hole 1/4 inch or larger in diameter and using a T handle for rotational leverage. The term "Auger" is generally used in reference to a boring tool having a pod or spiral cavity for collection and/or discharge of shavings. See *Boring Tool, Bit, Auger* for a description of the general features of spiral augers. Augers of the shell and spoon design are ancient tools and have been in use for several hundred years.

The origin of the spiral auger is somewhat obscure but is generally considered to be an American invention. *Knight* attributes the invention to Lilley in the early 1800s. The 1809 patent of E. L'Hommedieu formalized the design showing a center lead screw and two cutting lips. Refinements were developed in rapid succession including the cutting nib or knicker, single and double twist types and the curved cutting lip. The types of augers are shown under other boring tool headings.

Boring Tool, Auger Handle. A straight cross-bar type handle for use with an auger. Some handles were made to be readily detached and were intended for use with several augers. Other handles were permanently or semi-permanently attached. Normal length of the handle is about 18 inches.

Bell Hangers' Auger

Common Handle

BORING TOOL, BELL HANGERS' GIMLET. See *Boring Tool, Bell Hangers'* and *Boring Tool, Bit, Bell Hangers'*.

BORING TOOL, BENCH DRILL. A crank-operated drill made for attachment to the top of a work bench.

Peck's Patent Handle

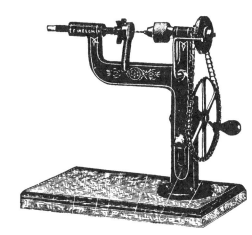

Pratt's Patent Handle

Jewelers' Bench Drill

Ratchet Type Handle

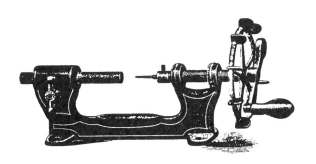

Auger Handle

BORING TOOL, AUTOMATIC DRILL. See *Boring Tool, Archimedes* and *Boring Tool, Push Drill*.

BORING TOOL, AUTOMATIC HAND DRILL. See *Boring Tool, Push Drill*.

BORING TOOL, BEAM BORER. See *Boring Tool, Boring Machine*.

BORING TOOL, BELL HANGERS'. Also called BELL HANGERS' AUGER and BELL HANGERS' DRILL. A long thin auger or gimlet, with a T handle, used for drilling through a wall or floor for the purpose of routing a bell wire. These tools were available from 3/16 to 3/8 inches in diameter and up to 36 inches long. See also *Boring Tool, Bit, Bell Hangers'*.

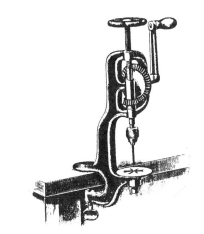

Bench Drill

BORING TOOL, BIT. Also called AUGER, BORING BIT and DRILL. A boring tool made with a shank for interchangeable use in a bit brace, breast drill, hand drill or other device whereby it can be made to rotate.

BORING TOOL, BIT, ANDREWS' PATTERN. A spiral bit on which the curved lip is said to provide a drawing cut for ease of boring and smoothness of the hole. Size is 1/4 to 1 inch.

Andrews' Pattern Bit

BORING TOOL, BIT, AUGER. A bit for making holes 3/16 to 2 inches in diameter. The term "Auger" is generally used in reference to a boring tool having a hollow or spiral cavity for collection and/or discharge of shavings. Spiral augers can be generally categorized as Single Twist, Double Twist and Solid Center as shown in illustration (a); Coarse Lead Screw, Fine Lead Screw and No Lead Screw as shown in illustration (b); Two Cutting Nibs, One Cutting Nib and No Cutting Nib as shown in illustration (c); One Cutting Lip, Two Cutting Lips and Two Curved Cutting Lips as shown in illustration (d); and combinations of the above. The specific types of auger bits are shown under other boring tool headings.

Single Twist

Double Twist

Solid Center

(a)

Auger and Auger Bit Types

Coarse	Fine	None
	(b)	Lead Screws

Two	One	None
	(c)	Cutting Nibs

One	Two	Curved
	(d)	Cutting Lips

Auger and Auger Bit Types

BORING TOOL, BIT, BARREL SAW. A machine bit used primarily to bore the leg supports for tables and chairs. Sizes are 1 to 2 inches in diameter.

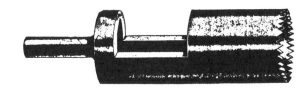

Barrel Saw

BORING TOOL, BIT, BELL HANGERS'. A long bit used for drilling through a wall or floor for the purpose of stringing bell wire. Sizes are 3/16 to 1 1/8 inches in diameter and up to three feet long. The smaller sizes are often of the gimlet type and are called BELL HANGERS' GIMLETS.

Gimlet

Bell Hangers' Bit

Twist Type

Bell Hangers' Bit

BORING TOOL, BIT, BORING MACHINE. A bit intended for use in a hand-operated boring machine. See *Boring Tool, Boring Machine*. Sizes are 1/2 to 2 inches in diameter.

Boring Machine Bit

BORING TOOL, BIT, BRICK. See *Boring Tool, Bit, Marble*.

BORING TOOL, BIT, BROACH. Also called ENGLISH REAMER. A tool used to enlarge a hole or cutout by reaming action. The illustrated broach is a tapered five-sided tool with a tang suitable for use with a handle or in a bit brace. Similar tools having from 3 to 8 sides have been noted. The small sizes used by a jeweler are often held in a pin vise. A narrow tapered file with coarse cutting teeth was also called a broach by some suppliers.

Broach Bit

BORING TOOL, BIT, BRUSH. A small bit used for drilling the holes for setting bristles or fibres in a brush. Wire gauge sizes 1 through 20 were available.

Brush Bit

BORING TOOL, BIT, CAR. Also called CAR BUILDERS' BIT. A long auger bit with a 9 to 12 inch twist is known as a car bit. These bits were available in any of the several patterns and in sizes from 1/4 to 1 inch. The name was derived from the usage of these bits in building railroad cars.

Car Bit

BORING TOOL, BIT, CAR BUILDERS'. See *Boring Tool, Bit, Car*.

BORING TOOL, BIT, CARPENTERS'. The common 7 to 11 inch auger bits were often listed as carpenters' bits or as carpenters' auger bits. They were available singly or in sets and in a variety of types and patterns. See illustrations under other *Boring Tool, Bit* headings. Sizes were generally 1/4 inch to one inch in diameter with larger sizes available separately. The size marked on the bit is 16ths of an inch. Thus a set was generally 13 bits numbered 4 through 16 inclusive.

BORING TOOL, BIT, CASTER. A special bit used for installing casters and chair tips on furniture.

For Stem Tips

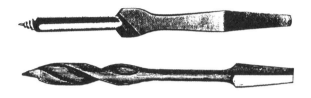

For Philadelphia Casters

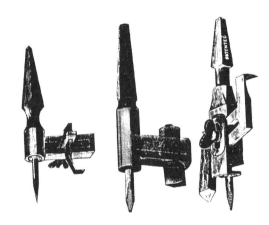

For Socket Casters

Caster Bit

BORING TOOL, BIT, CENTER. Also called GERMAN CENTER BIT. A flat bit with a spike center. Sizes are 3/16 to 3 inches. Two spurs, as shown in the illustration, were often used on bits larger than 2 inches.

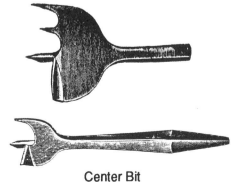

Center Bit

BORING TOOL, BIT, CHAIR. A short bit used by a chair maker for drilling holes for the rungs and back slats. Sizes are 1/8 to 1 inch. These bits are often permanently seated in a bit brace. The chair maker would have a set of braces each with a different size bit. The user would sometimes file a notch on the back of the bit to indicate the proper depth of the hole. The bits that are tapered evenly back toward the shank are called a bulbous type.

Chair Bit

BORING TOOL, BIT, COOKS' PATTERN. A double twist bit with curved cutting lips. Sizes are 3/16 to 2 inches. This type of bit is especially useful for reboring and for starting a hole at an angle to the surface.

Cook's Pattern Bit

BORING TOOL, BIT, COUNTERBORE. A bit capable of boring a shallow hole coincident with a smaller hole. Many of the woodworking counterbore tools are intended to drill a screw hole and make the counterbore of the proper size for insertion of a plug to conceal the screw.

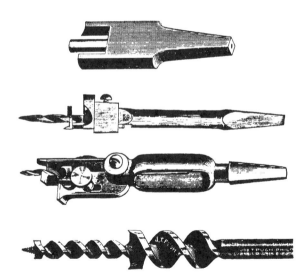

Counterbore Bit

BORING TOOL, BIT, COUNTERSINK. A bit used to countersink a hole to accommodate the head of a common wood screw. Some types of countersink bits are intended to cut either wood or metal and some will drill deep enough to countersink the screw head completely below the surface.

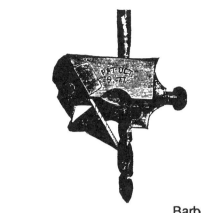

Barber's Patent

Davis Patent

Acme

Shepardson's Patent

Smith's Patent

Clark's Patent

Wheeler's Patent

Countersink Bit

Snail

Rose

Lightning

For Metal

For Metal

Billings' Patent

Humphries' Patent

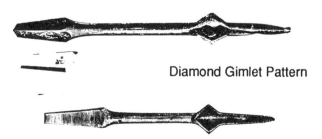

Diamond Gimlet Pattern

Countersink Bit

BORING TOOL, BIT, DOUBLE TWIST. See *Boring Tool, Bit, Auger,* illustration (a).

BORING TOOL, BIT, DOWEL. Also called COOPERS' DOWELING BIT and DOWELING BIT. A short rigid bit suitable for drilling dowel holes. These bits were available in either the single or double twist type and in sizes of 3/16 to 1 inch. Length is approximately 5 1/2 inches overall. See also *Boring Tool, Bit, Spoon.*

Dowel Bit

BORING TOOL, BIT, DRILL. See *Boring Tool, Bit, Twist Drill.*

BORING TOOL, BIT, DUCK BILL. See *Boring Tool, Bit, Spoon.*

BORING TOOL, BIT, ELECTRICIANS'. An extra-long bit used for drilling through walls and sills for routing electrical circuits. Sizes are 3/16 to 1 inch in diameter and up to 36 inches long. One supplier listed an Electricians' bit that appeared to be an extra long version of the single nib Irwin Pattern bit. See *Boring Tool, Bit, Irwin Pattern.*

Electricians' Bit

BORING TOOL, BIT, EXPANSIVE. A bit that is adjustable for drilling holes of different diameters. Several varieties were available. Some examples are shown.

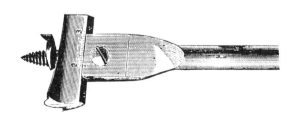

Blake's Patent

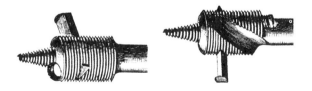

Clark's Patent

Expansive Bit

Derby

Ives' Patent

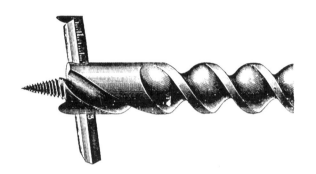

Swan's Patent

Expansive Bit

BORING TOOL, BIT, FLAT. Also called FLAT DRILL and METAL DRILL. The flat bit was used extensively with small hand drills and push braces and was sometimes called a drill point. The larger sizes, up to 5/8 inches, were generally capable of drilling metal as well as wood. See also *Boring Tool, Bit, Pipe* and *Boring Tool, Bit, Ratchet.*

Drill Point

Flat Bit

BORING TOOL, BIT, FORD PATTERN. A bit similar to the common Ship Auger Bit but designed to force the chips inward rather than against the side of the hole. Sizes are 3/16 to 1 1/2 inches.

Ford Pattern Bit

BORING TOOL, BIT, FORSTNER. A bit valued for its capability of drilling a hole with a flat bottom. The Forstner bit will start on a slanted surface at any angle with the wood. It was patented in 1874 and is still being made under the same name. Sizes are 1/4 to 3 inches.

Forstner Pattern Bit

BORING TOOL, BIT, GAS FITTERS'. A long spiral bit used to route gas lines through walls and floors. Available in sizes to accommodate the standard size gas lines. Both single and double twist types were used for this application.

BORING TOOL, BIT, GIMLET. A bit commonly used for drilling holes smaller than 1/4 inch in diameter and for making starting holes for wood screws. Gimlet bits up to 1/2 inch in diameter have been noted. The small sizes were sometimes listed as SPRIG BITS or SPRIG GIMLETS. Sprig is an old name for a small nail without a head.

German Pattern

American Pattern

Double Cut

Holt's Patent

Gimlet Bit

BORING TOOL, BIT, GOUGE. A bit shaped like a hollow half circle. Similar to a Shell Bit except that the end of the gouge bit is almost straight across. See illustration. Some suppliers used the names GOUGE BIT, POD BIT and SHELL BIT interchangeably.

Gouge Bit

BORING TOOL, BIT, HOLE SAW. Also called HOLLOW MILL SAW. A bit brace tool used to cut a large hole through a thin workpiece. The circular cutting element has teeth like a saw. See also *Boring Tool, Bit, Barrel Saw.*

Hole Saw

BORING TOOL, BIT, IRWIN PATTERN. Also called COMMON AUGER BIT and SOLID CENTER BIT. The solid center auger, see *Boring Tool, Bit, Auger,* illustration (a), is commonly called the Irwin Pattern. This common type of bit was available singly and in sets from 3/16 inch to 1 1/2 inches in diameter.

Single Lip

Double Lip

Irwin Pattern Bit

BORING TOOL, BIT, JENNINGS PATTERN. Also called DOUBLE TWIST AUGER. The double twist auger with two cutting lips and two nibs, see *Boring Tool, Bit, Auger,* illustration (a), is known as the Jennings or Russell Jennings Pattern. These bits were available singly and in sets from 3/16 to 2 inches in diameter.

Jennings Pattern Bit

BORING TOOL, BIT, KEY LEAD. A piano repairmans' tool used for drilling a hole for a tuning pin. This tool is a short bit similar to the Gouge Bit. Available in three sizes.

Key Lead Bit

BORING TOOL, BIT, MACHINE. A wood-cutting bit used in bench or post drills. Sizes up to 1 1/2 inches in diameter were available. See also *Boring Tool, Bit, Mortise.*

Machine Bit

BORING TOOL, BIT, MARBLE. Also called BRICK BIT and MARBLE DRILL. A scraping tool used for drilling brick, marble or stone.

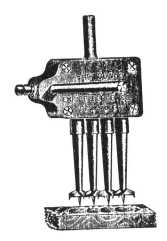

Marble Bit

BORING TOOL, BIT, MORTISE. Also called MACHINE BIT and PULLEY MORTISING BIT. A boring device having 3 or 4 bits that are operated from one shaft. Used for rapid drilling of a mortise. This type tool was used extensively for installing sash cord pulleys. Bit sizes are 7/8 and 1 inch.

Mortise Bit

BORING TOOL, BIT, NOSE. A bit similar to the Shell Bit except that the nose is turned inward to form a cutting lip.

Nose Bit

BORING TOOL, BIT, NOSING. See *Boring Tool, Bit, Nose.*

BORING TOOL, BIT, PIPE. A flat bit intended for drilling a hole in a lead pipe. Sizes are 1/8 to 2 1/2 inches in diameter.

Pipe Bit

BORING TOOL, BIT, PIPE REAMER. See *Boring Tool, Pipe Reamer.*

BORING TOOL, BIT, POD. See *Boring Tool, Bit, Gouge; Boring Tool, Bit, Shell* and *Boring Tool, Bit, Spoon.*

BORING TOOL, BIT, QUILL. See *Boring Tool, Bit, Shell.*

BORING TOOL, BIT, RATCHET. Also called RATCHET DRILL BIT. A flat metal-cutting bit intended for use in a ratchet drill. Sizes are 3/16 to 1 1/2 inches.

Ratchet Drill Bit

BORING TOOL, BIT, REAMER. A bit used to enlarge or taper an existing hole. See also *Boring Tool, Pipe Reamer* and *Broach.*

Bolt Reamer Bit

Half Round

Square

Octagon

Center Reamer

Reamer Bit

Taper Reamer

Reamer Bit

BORING TOOL, BIT, RIM. A bit used to drill and counterbore a wooden bicycle rim.

Rim Bit

BORING TOOL, BIT, RUSSELL JENNINGS. See *Boring Tool, Bit, Jennings Pattern.*

BORING TOOL, BIT, SHELL. A bit shaped essentially like a hollow half circle. The same as a Gouge Bit except that the end of the shell bit is somewhat pointed. These bits were used extensively for boring small holes but lacked an adequate self centering feature. A lead screw was added as a variation but failed to become popular. This type bit was sometimes listed as a POD BIT because of the center cavity or pod for collecting the shavings. Sizes are 1/8 to 1/2 inch. The common type was also called LIP BIT and QUILL BIT.

Common Type

With Lead Screw

Shell Bit

BORING TOOL, BIT, SHIP. Also called SHIP AUGER and SHIP AUGER BIT. Single twist augers of the standard 8 to 10 inch length are generally called Ship Bits. It is said that this is the best type of bit for drilling hardwood. The variety without a lead screw is superior for drilling a straight hole in a thick workpiece. Sizes are 1/4 inch to 2 1/8 inches.

Ship Bit

BORING TOOL, BIT, SHIP AUGER CAR. Also called SHIP AUGER PATTERN CAR BIT. A car bit of the single twist pattern. See *Boring Tool, Bit, Car.* This type of car bit was said to be designed for rough work. Sizes are 1/4 to 1 1/4 inches.

Ship Auger Car Bit

BORING TOOL, BIT, SNELLS' PATENT. Sizes are 3/16 to 1 inch.

Ship Pattern

Double Twist

Snell's Patent Bit

BORING TOOL, BIT, SOLID CENTER. See *Boring Tool, Bit, Auger,* illustration (a) and *Boring Tool, Bit, Irwin Pattern.*

BORING TOOL, BIT, SOLID LIP. A obscure type of spiral auger bit with the cutting lip joined to the second twist. This type of bit is useful for starting a hole at an angle to the surface of the workpiece.

Solid Lip Bit

BORING TOOL, BIT, SPOON. Also called DOWEL BIT and DUCK BILL BIT. A bit similar in appearance to the Shell Bit except that the cutting edge is closed over like the end of a spoon. This is not a common variety of bit and is often mistaken for the more common Shell Bit. Sizes are 1/16 to 1 inch in diameter. These bits were sometimes listed as POD BITS.

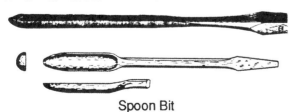

Spoon Bit

BORING TOOL, BIT, SPRIG. See *Boring Tool, Bit, Gimlet.*

BORING TOOL, BIT, SQUARE HOLE. A bit said to be capable of drilling a square hole in soft wood. Sizes are 3/8 to 1 inch.

Square Hole Bit

BORING TOOL, BIT, STORAGE BATTERY. A bit intended for use in drilling the links and terminals of a lead-acid storage battery.

Storage Battery Bit

BORING TOOL, BIT, SUGAR TREE. A spiral bit, with a very short twist, used for tapping a maple tree. Sizes are 3/8 to 3/4 inches.

Sugar Tree Bit

BORING TOOL, BIT, SYRACUSE. See *Boring Tool, Bit, Twist Drill.*

BORING TOOL, BIT, TAPER. A bit used to bore a tapered hole such as might be required in a lathe tool handle. Sizes are 1/2 to 1 inch at the large end.

Taper Bit

BORING TOOL, BIT, TWIST DRILL. Also called BIT STOCK DRILL and DRILL BIT. This type bit is the forerunner of the high speed twist drills found in every modern shop. The blacksmiths' drill bit shown in the illustration was made for cutting soft iron at low speeds and is easily damaged if used with modern equipment at high speeds. The round shank types were available in sizes from 1/16 to 2 inches in diameter and those with bit brace type shanks were available up to 1/2 inch.

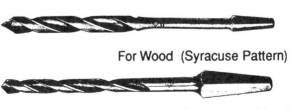

For Wood (Syracuse Pattern)

For Wood or Metal

Twist Drill Bit

Blacksmiths' Drill

Twist Drill Bit

BORING TOOL, BIT BRACE. Also called BIT STOCK, BRACE, CRANK BRACE, DRILL BRACE, DRILL STOCK and HAND BRACE. A hand tool with provisions for holding a bit and for causing the bit to rotate by means of a cranking motion of an eccentric.

BORING TOOL, BIT BRACE, ARMORERS'. A bit brace made of brass or similar non-sparking material. This tool was intended for use around armories or gas works where sparks would be undesirable.

Armorers' Bit Brace

BORING TOOL, BIT BRACE, BLACKSMITHS'. A solid iron bit brace intended for use in a blacksmith shop. The brace, of the type shown in illustration (a), is made of solid metal approximately one inch in diameter. The center sleeve is made of steel, copper or brass and will rotate on the shaft if adequately greased. The pad is dimpled to allow use with a beam having a centering pin. Illustration (b) is an example of a blacksmith-made brace intended for use with a beam. Illustration (c) shows a bit brace under a hand beam. The smith pulls down on the beam with one hand while rotating the brace with the other hand. See also *Boring Tool, Post Drill.*

(a)

Blacksmiths' Bit Brace

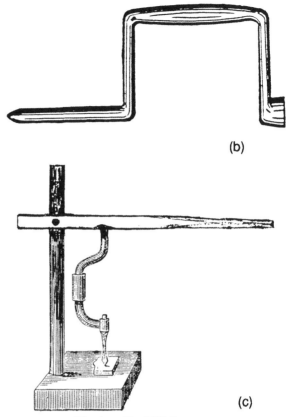

(b)

(c)

Blacksmiths' Bit Brace

BORING TOOL, BIT BRACE, CAGE HEAD. A bit brace having two or more metal ribs supporting the pad. This type of brace was generally made by the user.

Cage Head Bit Brace

BORING TOOL, BIT BRACE, CARPENTERS'. A common metal bit brace with a wooden pad is often listed as a carpenters' bit brace or a carpenters' brace. These braces were made in many sizes and patterns. Some examples are illustrated. The Spofford Pattern brace was also available with a metal pad.

Armstrong's Double Grip

Carpenters' Bit Brace

Backus' Patent

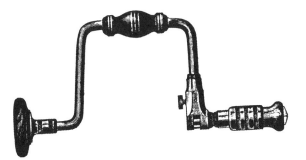

Bolen's Patent

Barber's Patent

Spofford's Patent

Carpenters' Bit Brace

BORING TOOL, BIT BRACE, CHAIR MAKERS'. A wooden brace with a short bit permanently attached and having no pad or a very small pad. The braces without a pad were intended for use with a breast plate. The illustrated breast plate has a strap that fastens around the chest of the user. Some plates have two straps. The chairmakers' brace has been imported from Europe in large quantities for tool collectors.

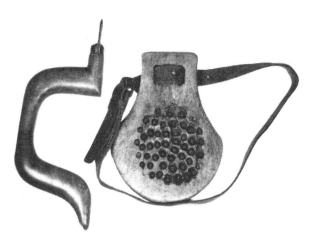

Chair Makers' Bit Brace

BORING TOOL, BIT BRACE, COMBINATION. A bit brace having the combined functions of more than one type of brace. The type illustrated will serve either as a regular bit brace, breast drill or corner brace.

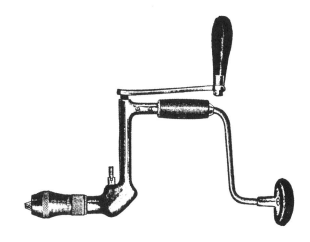

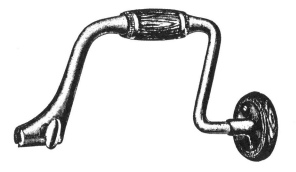

Combination Bit Brace

BORING TOOL, BIT BRACE, COOPERS'. A wooden brace with a short bit permanently attached. This type of brace was used for drilling the dowel holes in the head pieces of a wooden barrel. The coopers' brace normally has a large pad and is used with the pad against the operators' stomach or chest.

Coopers' Bit Brace

BORING TOOL, BIT BRACE, CORNER. Also called ANGLE BRACE. A bit brace intended for use in drilling a hole near a wall or corner where the full sweep of a normal brace is not possible. This type of brace was used extensively by electricians when wiring completed houses and was sometimes known as an ELECTRICIANS' BIT BRACE. See also *Boring Tool, Ratchet*.

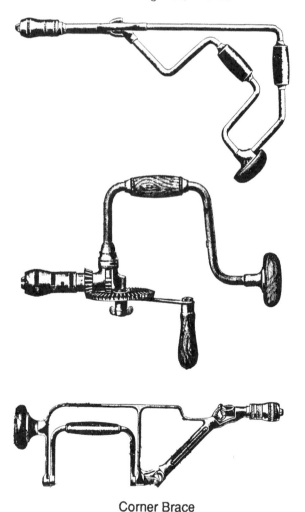

Corner Brace

BORING TOOL, BIT BRACE, GENTLEMAN'S. Also called BALL BIT BRACE. A small bit brace with a ball-shaped handle on the sweep. Intended for light work.

Gentleman's Bit Brace

BORING TOOL, BIT BRACE, ORTHOPEDIC. Also called BONE DRILL and CRANIAL DRILL. A bit brace used in bone surgery. A burr and a typical drill bit are included in the illustration. Overall length of the bit brace is approximately 9 inches. Generally made of stainless steel or steel with heavy plating.

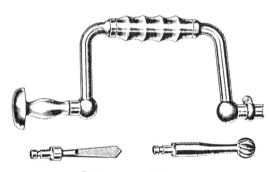

Orthopedic Bit Brace

BORING TOOL, BIT BRACE, PRIMITIVE. A term widely used by tool collectors to identify the wooden bit braces having removeable bit pads rather than removeable bits. Many of these braces are home made and are quite primitive in construction. Available evidence indicates that the term "Primitive" was not used by the makers of these tools. The bit pad in illustration (b) is released by pressing on the spring lever at the rear of the pad. The pad has a square shank with a notch. Other types have screw-in pads, various types of notched pads and pads retained by friction only.

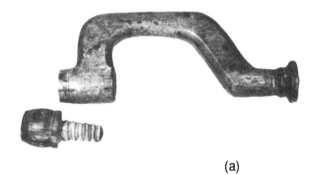

(a)

Primitive Bit Brace

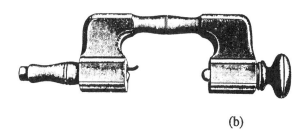

(b)

Primitive Bit Brace

BORING TOOL, BIT BRACE, RATCHET. See *Boring Tool, Bit Brace, Carpenters'*.

BORING TOOL, BIT BRACE, SHEFFIELD. A type of wooden bit brace having a spring-loaded bit release lever in the cast head. Each bit is notched to mate with a tang on the bit release lever. A Sheffield type brace having brass reinforcing strips inlaid on each side is called a Plated Brace. Most braces of this type were made in England.

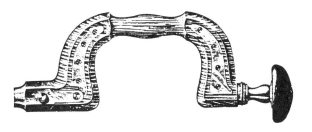

Plated

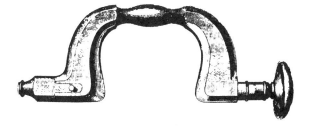

Plain

Sheffield Bit Brace

BORING TOOL, BIT BRACE, SPRING LATCH. A metal bit brace having a spring-loaded bit retention latch that mates with a notch in the bit. Both metal and wooden breast pads were available. Some references refer to the metal pad variety as a COACH MAKERS' BRACE.

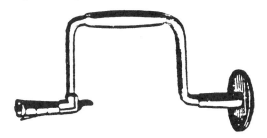

Spring Latch Bit Brace

BORING TOOL, BIT BRACE, THUMB SCREW. An inexpensive bit brace using a common thumb screw to retain the bit. This type of brace was included in many boys tool sets and was generally used in toy tool boxes. It is essentially an inexpensive version of the Gentleman's Bit Brace.

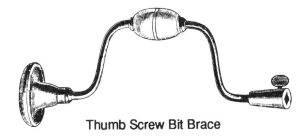

Thumb Screw Bit Brace

BORING TOOL, BIT BRACE, WIMBLE. Also called DOUBLE CRANK BRACE. A two-handed bit brace said to allow fast boring of deep holes. Used for boring holes in large bridge timbers and for similar tasks.

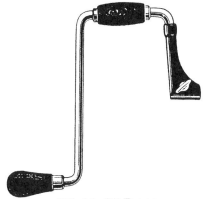

Wimble Bit Brace

BORING TOOL, BIT EXTENSION. Also called BIT HOLDER. A tool that allows a bit to be extended into a cavity or congested area. Length is 23 to 30 inches.

Bit Extension

BORING TOOL, BIT HOLDER. See *Boring Tool, Bit Extension*.

BORING TOOL, BIT STOCK. See *Boring Tool, Bit Brace*.

BORING TOOL, BOILER DRILL. See *Boring Tool, Ratchet*.

BORING TOOL, BONE DRILL. An orthopedic surgeons' tool used to make a hole in a bone for insertion of a wire or pin.

Bone Drill

BORING TOOL, BONE REAMER. An orthopedic surgeons' tool used to make or enlarge a hole in a bone for insertion of a wire or pin.

Bone Reamer

BORING TOOL, BOOM AUGER. A large auger used in the ship yards. Size is 2 to 5 inches in diameter. This tool was listed with and without a ring for insertion of the handle. A Boom Auger is another name for a large nut or ring auger. See *Boring Tool, Nut Auger* and *Boring Tool, Ring Auger*.

BORING TOOL, BORING MACHINE. Also called BEAM BORER. A machine used to drill holes in wooden planks and beams. The operator holds the drill in position by sitting on the bottom plate. The upright of some machines will adjust to allow drilling at a fixed angle to the surface of the workpiece and some will fold flat to facilitate storage and transportation. Bits from 1/2 to 2 inches in diameter were available.

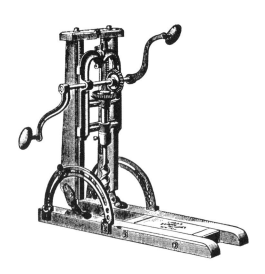

Boring Machine

BORING TOOL, BOW DRILL. A drill that is made to rotate by movement of a bow across a spool attached to the bit. The bow drill was used to drill small holes particularly in hard brittle material such as shell or stone. The illustrated item was listed as a PIANO MAKERS' DRILL STOCK. Bows were made of wood, steel or whalebone. The bow drill is the oldest form of mechanical drilling device that has been documented.

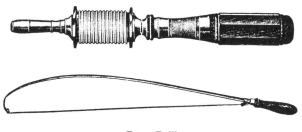

Bow Drill

BORING TOOL, BRACE. See *Boring Tool, Bit Brace*.

BORING TOOL, BRACE CHUCK. An adapter chuck that will allow use of a round-shank bit in a common bit brace intended for use with a square-shank bits.

Brace Chuck

BORING TOOL, BREAST DRILL. Also called BREAST AUGER and DRILL STOCK. A drill with a large pad which allows the drilling pressure to be applied by the chest or stomach of the operator. See also *Boring Tool, Coal Auger*.

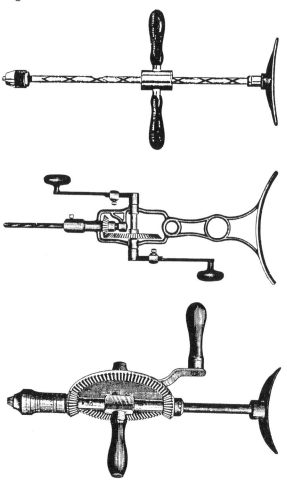

Breast Drill

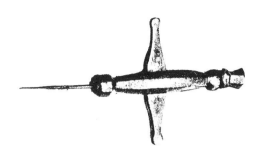

Breast Drill

BORING TOOL, BRIDGE AUGER. A long-handled boring tool used for railroad bridge work and for similar heavy construction. This type of tool often consists of a ship bit welded to a long metal handle. See also *Boring Tool, Nut Auger* and *Boring Tool Ship Auger.*

Bridge Auger

BORING TOOL, BUNG BORER. Also called BUNG HOLE BORER, BUNG HOLE REAMER, and TAP BORER. A tool used to bore or ream the bung or tap hole in a barrel. Sizes from 5/8 to 4 inches in diameter were available. See also *Boring Tool, Tap Borer.*

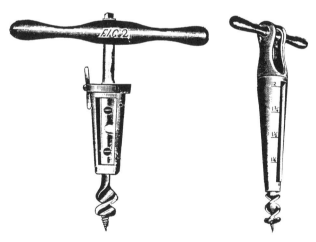

Bung Borer

BORING TOOL, BURRING REAMER. See *Boring Tool, Pipe Reamer.*

BORING TOOL, CARPENTERS' AUGER. See *Boring Tool, Nut Auger.*

BORING TOOL, CHAIN DRILL. A device that utilizes the rotary motion of the bit brace to tighten a chain thus feeding the drill into the workpiece. This type drill was used extensively for drilling into pipe or round bar. The chain served to steady the workpiece in addition to providing a constant pressure on the drill. Illustration (a) is an attachment used with a bit brace. Illustration (b) is a self contained chain drill that is also called RATCHET CHAIN DRILL.

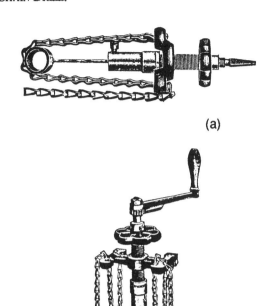

(a)

(b)

Chain Drill

BORING TOOL, COAL AUGER. A bit with a unique tip designed for boring in coal or slate.

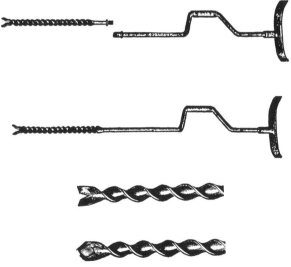

Coal Auger

BORING TOOL, COAL MINERS'. Also called POST DRILL. A miners' drilling machine that is supported by the top and bottom of the mine shaft. See also *Boring Tool, Roof Auger.*

Coal Miners' Drill

BORING TOOL, CRANIAL. Also called TREPHINE. A surgical instrument used for cutting out a circular section of the skull.

Cranial Drill

BORING TOOL, CRANIAL DRILL. See *Boring Tool, Cranial* and *Boring Tool, Bit Brace, Orthopedic.*

BORING TOOL, CRANK DRILL. The Sanford' Patent drill was intended for drilling or countersinking metal. It was used for machine repair or assembly work. The Rusby Patent drill has a chuck that will grasp a tapered shank. It is suitable for use with either wood or metal bits. This drill has a unique feature that allows the chuck to be extended an additional 8 inches for drilling in a cavity or other restricted area.

BORING TOOL, DRILL BRACE. See *Boring Tool, Bit Brace.*

BORING TOOL, DRILL STOCK. See *Boring Tool, Bit Brace.*

BORING TOOL, DRILLING MACHINE. A device used primarily in machine repair work. It can be clamped to any convenient bracket and the head adjusted to work in

any direction. Advertised by the supplier as an IMPROVED PATENT UNIVERSAL ANGULAR AND RATCHET DRILLING MACHINE.

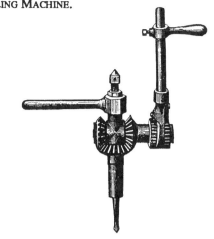

Sanford's Patent

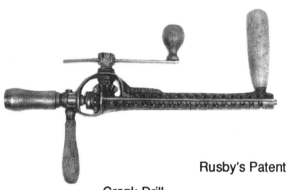

Rusby's Patent

Crank Drill

Drilling Machine

BORING TOOL, DRILLING POST. A clamp or fixture used to keep the ratchet drill at a constant angle with the workpiece. Sometimes called an OLD MAN.

BORING TOOL, EARTH AUGER. Also called WELL AUGER. A tool for drilling in soil. The Chisel Bit Auger was listed as being suitable for drilling clay and hardpan. The Pod Auger is used to take a core sample. The Spiral Auger is used to loosen and remove stones. Sizes from 1/2 to 6 inches in diameter were listed.

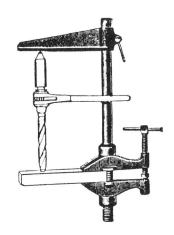

Drilling Post

Chisel Bit

Horizontal Drill

Pod

Pod

Ribbon

Spiral

Twist

Earth Auger

BORING TOOL, EGGBEATER DRILL. See *Boring Tool, Hand Drill*.

BORING TOOL, EXTENSION. See *Boring Tool, Bit Extension*.

BORING TOOL, EYE AUGER. See *Boring Tool, Ring Auger*.

BORING TOOL, FARMERS' AUGER. See *Boring Tool, Nut Auger*.

BORING TOOL, GAS FITTERS' AUGER. A long T-handled auger of the proper size for routing a standard gas line. Sizes to match 1/4 to 2 1/2 inch pipes were listed.

Gas Fitters' Auger

BORING TOOL, GIMLET. Also called HANDLED GIMLET, SCREW POINT GIMLET and TWIST GIMLET. A small T-handled boring tool used to drill a hole in a thin workpiece or to make a starting hole for a nail or screw. Standard sizes are 1/16 to 1/2 inch. Those tools intended for making starting holes for given sized nails were called NAIL GIMLETS, SPIKE GIMLETS or SPRIG GIMLETS and were sometimes listed the same as the corresponding nail sizes. Sizes of 8 to 30 penny were available. See *Boring Tool, Bit, Gimlet* for other types of points.

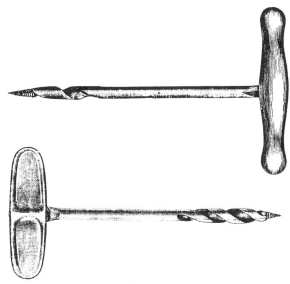

Gimlet

BORING TOOL, HAMMER HEAD. A tool used to drill a piano hammer head and butt at a fixed angle.

BORING TOOL, HAND DRILL. Also called BIT STOCK DRILL and GEARED BRACE. A drill used for boring small holes. The small size is sometimes called an EGGBEATER DRILL because of the resemblance to a kitchen egg beater.

Hammer Head Drill

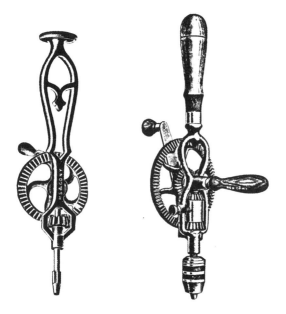

Hand Drill

BORING TOOL, HANDLED. A small boring tool, with a fixed T-handle, used for drilling holes up to 3/8 inches in diameter. See also *Boring Tool, Gimlet.*

Handled Boring Tool

BORING TOOL, HORIZONTAL DRILL. See *Boring Tool, Tire Drill.*

BORING TOOL, HUB. See *Boring Tool, Hub Reamer* and *Hub Boxing Machine.*

BORING TOOL, HUB REAMER. A large tapered reamer, with a T handle, used to enlarge and taper the hole in a wagon hub. Many of the larger reamers have a hook at the end on which a weight can be suspended. The weight serves to increase the downward pressure on the reamer and to assist in maintaining it in the vertical position.

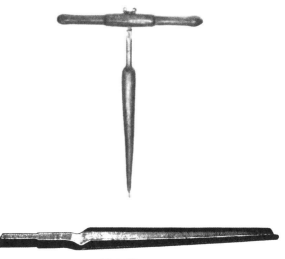

Hub Reamer

BORING TOOL, ICE AUGER. Any of several varieties of augers suitable for drilling in ice. The ice auger is generally lighter in construction than a wood auger and may have a spike rather than a lead screw. Size is 1 1/2 to 5 inches in diameter. A light T-handled auger similar to a farmers' nut auger is often listed as an ice auger. Many of the T-handled augers larger than 2 1/2 inches in diameter were intended for use in ice rather than for wood. See illustration under *Boring Tool, Nut Auger.*

Ice Auger

BORING TOOL, JEWELERS' STOCK. Also called BROACH LATHE. A jewelers' drill intended to be driven by a bow. The drill is held in a vise during use.

Jewelers' Stock

BORING TOOL, LENS DRILL. A tool used by an optician for drilling a hole in glass. Also suitable for use by jewelers and for other light duty applications.

Lens Drill

BORING TOOL, MEASURING PUMP AUGER. A three inch auger used to cut a hole in the head of a barrel for insertion of a measuring pump.

Measuring Pump Auger

BORING TOOL, MILLWRIGHTS' AUGER. An tool similar to the common nut auger but with a longer twist. Sizes are 1/2 to 2 inches in diameter. One supplier listed an overall length of 26 inches.

Millwrights' Auger

BORING TOOL, NAIL GIMLET. See *Boring Tool, Gimlet.*

BORING TOOL, NOSE AUGER. A T-handled auger having a cutting lip on the nose. See *Boring Tool, Bit, Nose.*

BORING TOOL, NUT AUGER. Also called BOOM AUGER and ICE AUGER. A T-handled auger with the handle retained by use of a nut. These augers normally have a 7 to 9 inch twist. Sizes are 3/8 to 5 inches in diameter. The Farmers' Auger is generally listed with a short twist. A long variety of nut auger was sometimes listed as a BRIDGE AUGER.

Nut Auger · Farmers'

Carpenters'

Nut Auger

BORING TOOL, PIPE REAMER. Also called BURRING REAMER. A tool used for removing burrs from inside the end of a pipe after the pipe is cut to length.

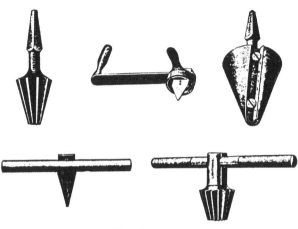

Pipe Reamer

BORING TOOL, POD AUGER. Any of a number of different styles of boring instruments having a pod or cavity to receive the chips. American trade catalogues often used the term "Pod" in connection with illustrations of Gouge, Nose, Shell or Spoon Augers. See also *Boring Tool, Earth Auger.*

BORING TOOL, POST AUGER. A long auger with a short twist. Size is 2 to 3 inches in diameter.

Post Auger

BORING TOOL, POST DRILL. Also called BLACKSMITHS' DRILL, DRILL PRESS and UPRIGHT DRILL. A hand-operated drill intended to be attached to a post or wall. This type of drill was a standard fixture in small blacksmith shops and in repair shops of all kinds.

BORING TOOL, POST HOLE AUGER. A tool used for drilling holes in the earth for setting fence posts. Size is 4 to 12 inches in diameter. A similar tool is used to drill shallow wells. Sections of metal pipe are used to lengthen the handle as required.

BORING TOOL, PUMP AUGER. Also called PUMP LOG AUGER. An auger used to drill a lengthwise hole in a log for use as a pump or water pipe. This tool has sectioned extensions of various lengths to accommodate drilling a long section of pipe. Sizes are 1 ½ to 4 inches in diameter.

Post Drill

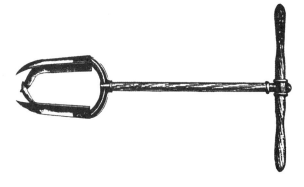

Post Hole Auger

Pump Auger

BORING TOOL, PUMP DRILL. An ancient form of drill that is made to rotate by up and down motion of a crossbar. Except for the small pump drills used by jewelers, these tools were generally made by the user. Illustration (b) shows a crude home-made drill that uses a rounded stone as a flywheel.

BORING TOOL, PUMP REAMER. Also called PUMP RIMMER. A large reamer used to increase the size of the hole in a pump log or wooden pipe after use of the pump auger. Sizes are 2 to 5 ½ inches in diameter.

BORING TOOL, PUSH DRILL. Also called AUTOMATIC DRILL and AUTOMATIC HAND DRILL. A drill bit holder, employing a spiral shaft, in which the bit is made to rotate when the handle is pushed.

(b)

Pump Drill

Pump Reamer

Push Drill

BORING TOOL, RAFTING AUGER. An extra-long ring auger with a 12 to 14 inch twist. Sizes are 1 ¼ to 4 inches. Rafting augers were available in both double and single twist patterns. See illustration under *Boring Tool, Ring Auger.*

BORING TOOL, RATCHET. Also called BOILER DRILL, CORNER RATCHET BORER and RATCHET DRILL. A type of bit brace used to drill a hole in a restricted area such as in a corner. The tool shown in illustration (a) was particularly recommended for use by boiler makers and bridge builders. See also *Boring Tool, Bit Brace, Corner.*

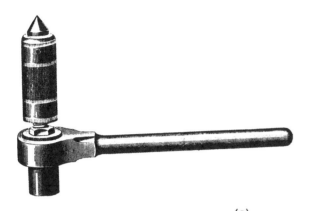

(a)

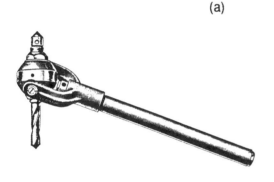

Universal

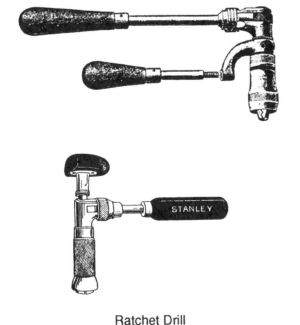

Ratchet Drill

BORING TOOL, RATCHET EXTENSION. A bit brace extension having a ratchet mechanism. This tool was used to gain the advantage of a ratchet without discarding the plain non-ratcheting bit brace.

Ratchet Extension

BORING TOOL, RECIPROCATING. See *Boring Tool, Archimedes Drill* and *Boring Tool, Push Drill.*

BORING TOOL, RING AUGER. Also called EYE AUGER. A heavy-duty auger with an integral iron ring for insertion of a cross-bar handle. Ring augers were available in single and double twist patterns and in sizes from 3/8 to 4 inches in diameter. See also *Boring Tool, Rafting Auger.* A ring auger with a long twist was sometimes called a CUBAN AUGER.

Ring Auger

BORING TOOL, ROOF AUGER. A tool intended for boring an overhead hole in a horizontal mine shaft.

Roof Auger

83

BORING TOOL, SET AUGER. A tool used in ship building. Same as a Treenail Auger except that the twist of a set auger is only one half as long. See illustration under *Boring Tool, Treenail Auger.*

BORING TOOL, SHIP AUGER. Also called SHIP CARPENTERS' AUGER and SINGLE TWIST AUGER. An eccentric or T-handled auger having a single twist. See *Boring Tool, Bit,* illustration (a). Size is 1/4 to 4 1/2 inches in diameter.

L' Hommedieu's Patent

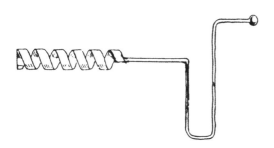

Ship Auger

BORING TOOL, SHIP TREENAIL AUGER. See *Boring Tool, Treenail Auger.*

BORING TOOL, SILL BORER. Also called JOIST TOOL. A crank-operated tool used for boring small holes in a sill or a similar restricted area. This tool was used primarily by electricians and gas fitters.

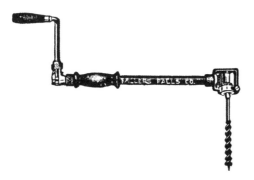

Sill Borer

BORING TOOL, SPIKE GIMLET. See *Boring Tool, Gimlet.*

BORING TOOL, SPIRAL. See *Boring Tool, Archimedes Drill* and *Boring Tool, Push Drill*

BORING TOOL, SPOON AUGER. A T-handled auger with a cutting edge like a spoon bit. See illustration under *Boring Tool, Bit, Spoon.* See also *Clog Makers' Tools.*

BORING TOOL, SPRIG. See *Boring Tool, Gimlet.*

BORING TOOL, T-HANDLED. Any of several varieties of boring tools rotated by use of a long two-handed cross bar. Several varieties of T augers are shown under other boring tool headings.

BORING TOOL, TAP BORER. A tool used to bore or scrape a hole in a thin workpiece. The plumbers' tap borer is used to bore and ream holes in lead pipe. This tool is sharpened to scrape rather than cut. The plumbers' tap borer is similar to one type of coopers' tool, also called tap borer, used to cut or ream the tap hole in the head of a barrel. A coopers' tap borer often has a lead screw which allows it to cut the initial hole as well as to ream. Size is 3/4 to 3 inches in diameter. The coopers' tap borer was also called BUNG BORER.

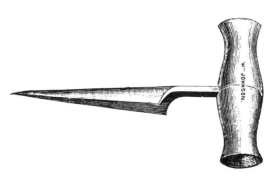

Plumber' (New York Pattern)

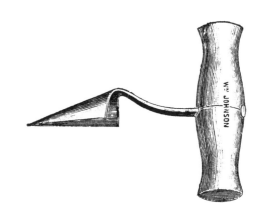

Plumbers' (Philadelphia Pattern)

Coopers' (Ring Tap)

Tap Borer

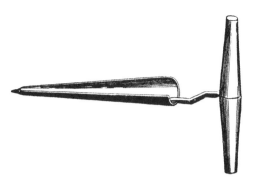

Coopers'

Tap Borer

BORING TOOL, TIRE DRILL. A device used to drill a wagon tire and felloe for installation of a tire bolt. Illustration (a) shows a typical tire drill made for bolting to the top of a bench. Other similar items were intended to be clamped in a vise during use. The post drill shown in illustration (b) has an optional attachment for mounting a wheel such that it would rotate at a convenient height underneath the drill spindle. The bench-top device was also called BLACKSMITHS' DRILL, HORIZONTAL BLACKSMITHS' DRILL and HORIZONTAL DRILL.

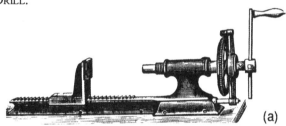

(a)

(b)

Tire Drill

BORING TOOL, TRACK DRILL. A device used to drill a railroad rail for installation of a splice plate.

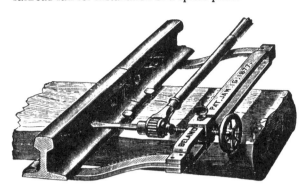

Track Drill

BORING TOOL, TREENAIL AUGER. Also called SHIP TREENAIL AUGER. A ship builders' tool used to drill the holes for wooden pegs. Size of the illustrated tool was listed as 1/2 to 1 1/2 inches in diameter. Length of the twist is 11 to 20 inches. Other types of augers were also used for this purpose.

Treenail Auger

BORING TOOL, WELL AUGER. See *Boring Tool, Earth Auger* and *Boring Tool, Post Hole Auger*.

BOSS FORMER. See *Tinsmiths' Machine, Boss Former*.

BOSSING MALLET. See *Mallet, Bossing*.

BOSSING STICK. A plumbers' tool used to shape lead. The varying contour of this tool makes it useful for beating or pressing sheet lead into precise shapes. Bossing sticks are normally made of dense wood such as boxwood, dogwood, hickory or lignum vitae.

Bossing Stick

BOTTLERS' PLIERS. See *Pliers, Bottlers'*.

BOTTOM KNIFE. See *Clog Makers' Tools*.

BOTTOM STAKE. See *Stake, Bottom*.

BOTTOM TOOL. See *Anvil Tools* and *Tap and Die*.

BOTTOM WHEEL. See *Shoe Makers' Tool, Bottom Wheel*.

BOTTOMING SAW. A comb makers' tool. See *Saw, Bottoming*.

BOTTOMING TAP. See *Tap and Die*.

BOUNCER. See *Leather Tool, Bouncer*.

BOUND MALLET. See *Mallet, Ring*.

BOW COMPASS. See *Compass, Bow*.

BOW DRILL. See *Boring Tool, Bow Drill*.

BOW FILE. See *Riffler*.

BOW PLIERS. A jewelers' tool. See *Pliers, Bow*.

BOW SAW. See *Saw, Turning*.

BOW TIE AXE. See *Axe, Double Bit*, bow tie pattern.

BOWL ADZE. See *Adze, Bowl*.

BOWL SHAVE. A small cutting tool, with a curved bottom, used to shave a surface such as the inside of a bowl or a chair seat. The illustrated tool cuts on the push stroke.

Bowl Shave

BOX CAR SEAL. A device used to crimp a lead box car seal. The tool crimps the seal and imprints an identifying name or logo.

Box Car Seal

BOX CHISEL. See *Chisel, Box*.

BOX END WRENCH. See *Wrench, Box*.

BOX HAMMER. A large nail hammer. See *Hammer, Boxing*.

BOX HATCHET. See *Hatchet, Barreling* and *Hatchet, Box*.

BOX HOOK. See *Hook, Box*.

BOX LOOP EDGER. See *Leather Tool, Box Loop Edger*.

BOX OPENER. A prying tool used to open a wooden box or crate. See also *Chisel, Box*.

Box Opener

BOX PRESS. See *Wheel Box Press*.

BOX SCRAPER. See *Scraper, Box*.

BOX VISE. See *Vise, Post*.

BOX WHEEL. See *Shoe Makers' Tool, Box Wheel*.

BOX WRENCH. See *Wrench, Box*.

BOXING HAMMER. See *Hammer, Boxing* and *Hammer, Bursting*.

BOXING MACHINE. See *Hub Boxing Machine*.

BOXING TURPENTINE AXE. See *Axe, Single Bit*, boxing turpentine pattern.

BOXWOOD RULE. See *Rule, Boxwood*.

BOY SCOUT AXE. See *Axe, Boy Scout*.

BOY SCOUT HATCHET. See *Axe, Boy Scout*.

BOYS' AXE. See *Axe, Boys'*.

BOYS' CAMP AXE. See *Hatchet, Camp*.

BOYS' SMOOTH PLANE. See *Plane, Smooth, Boys'*.

BRACE. See *Boring Tool, Bit Brace*.

BRACE CHUCK. See *Boring Tool, Brace Chuck*.

BRACE SOCKET WRENCH. See *Wrench, Socket*.

BRACE WRENCH. See *Wrench, Socket*.

BRACELET MANDREL. See *Mandrel, Jewelers'*.

BRACKET SAW. See *Saw, Bracket*.

BRAD. A small nail whose head has a projection on one side only. The meaning of the term has now been expanded to include the entire group of nails generally called finishing nails.

BRAD AWL. See *Awl, Brad*.

BRAD HAMMER. See *Hammer, Brad*.

BRAD PUNCH. See *Punch, Brad*.

BRAD SETTER. See *Punch, Brad*.

BRAKE. See *Tinsmiths' Machine, Brake* and *Willow Brake*.

BRASS BOUND LEVEL. See *Level, Brass Bound*.

BRASS BOUND RULE. See *Rule, Brass Bound*.

BRASS FILE. See *File, Brass*.

BRASS HAMMER. See *Hammer, Soft Faced*.

BRASS RULE. See *Rule, Blacksmiths'*.

BRAZING CLAMP. See *Vise, Band Saw Brazing.*

BRAZING TONGS. See *Vise, Band Saw Brazing.*

BRAZING TORCH. See *Torch, Brazing.*

BRAZING VISE. See *Vise, Band Saw Brazing.*

BREAD RASP. A bakers' tool. See *Rasp, Bread.*

BREAKING BAR. See *Bar, Ice.*

BREAKING HAMMER. A stone workers' tool. See *Hammer, Bursting.*

BREAST AUGER. See *Boring Tool, Breast Drill.*

BREAST DRILL. See *Boring Tool, Breast Drill.*

BRICK AXE. See *Skutch.*

BRICK BIT. See *Boring Tool, Bit, Marble.*

BRICK CHISEL. See *Chisel, Brick.*

BRICK CLEANER. Also called BRICK SET and CHIPPING CHISEL. A hand tool used to chip mortar from used bricks.

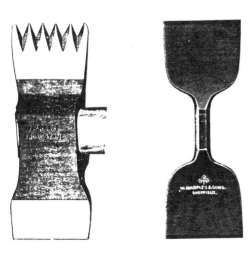

Hatchet Type

Brick Cleaner

BRICK CUTTER. See *Chisel, Brick.*

BRICK DRILL. A tool used to pound a hole through plaster or through a brick wall. The hole is formed by rotating the drill between blows from a hammer. The hollow type is also called PIPE DRILL. See also *Star Drill.*

Brick Drill

BRICK HAMMER. See *Hammer, Brick Layers'.*

BRICK JOINTER. See *Tuck Pointer.*

BRICK LAYERS' SKUTCH. See *Skutch.*

BRICK MASONS' TOOLS. Also called BRICK LAYERS' TOOLS. The special-purpose brick masons' tools listed below can be found in normal alphabetical sequence. These tools may also have been used for other purposes. Many of them are also suitable for use by the Stone Mason.

BORING TOOL, BIT, MARBLE
BRICK CLEANER
BRICK DRILL
BRUSH, ACID
BRUSH, BRICK LAYERS' DUST
BRUSH, BRICK STRIPER
CHISEL, BRICK
CHISEL, PLUGGING
CLAMP, BRICK
HAMMER, BRICK LAYERS'
HOD
HOE, MORTAR
JOINT FILLER
JOINT RAKER
LEVEL, MASONS'
PLUMB BOB
SAND SCREEN
SKUTCH
STAR DRILL
TONGS, BRICK
TOOL BAG
TROWEL, BRICK
TROWEL, POINTING
TUCK POINTER

BRICK SET. See *Brick Cleaner* and *Chisel, Brick.*

BRICK SHOVEL. See *Shovel, Brick.*

BRIDGE AUGER. See *Boring Tool, Bridge Auger.*

BRIDGE BUILDERS' CHISEL. See *Chisel, Track.*

BRIDGE BUILDERS' FORGE. See *Forge, Bridge Builders'.*

BRIDGE BUILDERS' HAMMER. See *Hammer, Boiler Riveting* and *Hammer, Bridge Builders'.*

BRIDGE BUILDERS' RABBET. See *Plane, Rabbet.*

BRIDGE BUILDERS' SQUARE. See *Square, Bridge Builders'.*

BRIDLE TAPE INSERTER. See *Piano Tool, Bridle Tape Inserter.*

BROACH. See *Boring Tool, Bit, Broach.*

BROACH HOLDER. See *Vise, Pin.*

BROACH LATHE. See *Boring Tool, Jewelers' Stock.*

BROAD. See *Turning Tool, Metal.*

BROAD AXE. See *Axe, Broad.*

BROAD AXE HANDLE. See *Axe Handle.*

BROAD HATCHET. See *Hatchet, Broad.*

BROAD TOOL. One size of stone chisel. See *Stone Cutters' Tool, Chisel.*

BROOM. A coarse brush, generally with a long handle, used for sweeping loose debris.

BROOM, RAILROAD TRACK. A broom used to remove snow and small obstructions from a railway track.

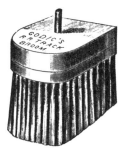

Railroad Track Broom

BROOM, STABLE. A broom used for cleaning a horse stable. Width is approximately 12 inches.

Stable Broom

BROOM, STREET. A street cleaners' tool. Width is approximately 16 inches.

Street Broom

BROOM, SWITCH. A wire broom intended for use on railway and street car switches. The end of the handle has a chisel for removing ice.

Switch Broom

BROOM, WAREHOUSE. A heavy broom intended for sweeping a large area such as a warehouse or mill.

Warehouse or Mill Broom

BROOM, WHIST. A general-purpose hand brush made of broom corn.

Whist Broom

BROOM CLIPPER. A device intended for clipping a finished broom to square up the head. This tool is similar to the Feed Cutter.

Broom Clipper

BROOM CORN KNIFE. See *Knife, Broom Corn.*

BROOM KNIFE. See *Knife, Broom Corn.*

BROOM MAKERS' HAMMER. See *Hammer, Broom Makers'.*

BROOM MAKERS' PRESS. See *Vise, Broom Makers'.*

BROOM MAKERS' VISE. See *Vise, Broom Makers'.*

BROOM NEEDLE. A broom makers' tool used for stitching a household or warehouse broom. Overall length is 6 to 7 inches.

Broom Needle

BROOM POUNDER. See *Hammer, Broom Makers'.*

BROOM RAKE. See *Rake, Leaf.*

BROWNING TROWEL. See *Trowel, Plasterers' Browning.*

BRUSH. A tool, generally for use with one hand, consisting of flexible bristles set into a handle. Used for scrubbing, smoothing, sweeping or for spreading a liquid.

BRUSH, ACID. Also called TUCK POINTERS' BRUSH. A coarse brush used to spread acid on old concrete or mortar prior to patching.

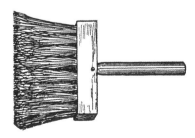

Acid Brush

BRUSH, BARREL. A curved brush used for cleaning barrels and kegs.

Barrel Brush

BRUSH, BEE. A horsehair brush used for removing the bees as honey is being taken from the hive.

Bee Brush

BRUSH, BICYCLE. A stiff brush used when cleaning and repairing a bicycle. Overall length is about 10 1/2 inches.

Bicycle Brush

BRUSH, BRICK LAYERS' DUST. Also called BENCH BRUSH, COUNTER BRUSH and MOULDERS' DUSTER. A thick brush used to remove the dust from the base or the top layer of bricks prior to laying the mortar. Also used by moulders and as a general-purpose cleaning tool. Overall length is about 14 inches.

Brick Layers' Dust Brush

BRUSH, BRICK STRIPER. A stiff brush used for painting or coating the mortar between courses of bricks. Length is 2 to 4 inches.

Brick Striping Brush

BRUSH, BUTCHER BLOCK. A very coarse brush used to scrape a butchers' chopping block or bench. This brush is made with flat steel wire.

Butcher Block Brush

BRUSH, BUTTON. A brush used to clean around the buttons on upholstered furniture. Advertised by one supplier as tool for maintaining carriages.

Button Brush

BRUSH, CALCIMINE. Also called KALSOMINE BRUSH. A wide brush used to apply calcimine to walls and ceilings. Width is 6 to 8 inches. Calcimine is a wash with a whiting base similar to whitewash.

Calcimine Brush

BRUSH, CARD. A brush used to clean the cards in a textile mill machine. Length of the illustrated tool is 19 inches.

Card Brush

BRUSH, CASTING. See *Brush, Stucco Dash* and *Brush, Wire.*

BRUSH, CLOCK. A brush used for cleaning the parts of a large clock. Overall length is 11 inches.

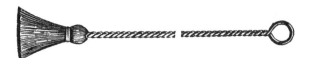

Clock Brush

BRUSH, COUNTER. See *Brush, Brick Layers' Dust.*

BRUSH, CUSPIDOR. Advertised as being made of palmetto fibre. The illustrated brush is 5 inches in diameter.

Cuspidor Brush

BRUSH, DAMPING. A brush used by a furrier for dampening the leather side of a skin and for glazing a fur.

Damping Brush

BRUSH, ELECTROTYPERS'. A print shop tool.

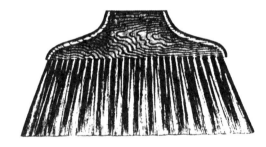

Coating Brush

Black Lead Brush

Electrotypers' Brush

BRUSH, FILE. See *File Cleaner.*

BRUSH, FLUE. See *Brush, Tube.*

BRUSH, GEAR. A flat brush with stiff bristles used for cleaning and oiling gears. Width is about 1 inch.

Gear Brush

BRUSH, GLUE. A short round brush with stiff bristles used for spreading hot glue. Sizes listed are 1/2 to 4 inches in diameter.

Glue Brush

BRUSH, HORSE. A brush used for grooming a horse.

Horse Brush

BRUSH, KALSOMINE. See *Brush, Calcimine*.

BRUSH, KEG. A brewers' brush used for cleaning the inside of a beer keg. The bristles of the illustrated brush are made of kitool, rice root and tampico.

Keg Brush

BRUSH, LOOM DUSTER. A soft brush similar to the Brick Layers' Dust Brush. A textile mill tool.

Loom Dust Brush

BRUSH, MARKING. Also called CHINA MARKING BRUSH. A brush used for lettering signs and for making decorative designs.

BRUSH, MOTTLING. A brush with extra-short camels hair bristles. Width is 1 to 4 inches.

Marking Brush

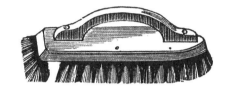

Mottling Brush

BRUSH, MOULDERS'. A brush intended for use in cleaning casting patterns. See also *Brush, Brick Layers' Dust*.

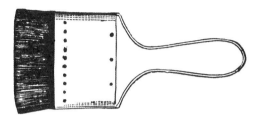

Hard

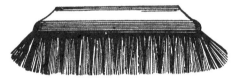

Soft

Moulders' Brush

BRUSH, PAINT. A flat brush used for general-purpose painting. The brush used for painting large surfaces was often listed as a Wall Brush. See also *Brush, Marking; Brush, Sash* and *Brush, Striping*.

Paint Brush

BRUSH, PAINTERS' DUST. A brush used to dust door frames and similar surfaces prior to painting. This tool has thick 3 1/2 to 4 inch bristles.

Painters' Dust Brush

BRUSH, PAPER HANGERS'. A wide brush used when hanging wall paper. Width of the Smoothing Brush is 10 to 12 inches. The Paste Brush is 6 to 8 inches wide.

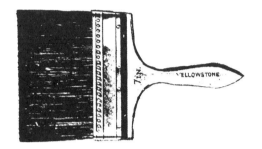

Paste Brush

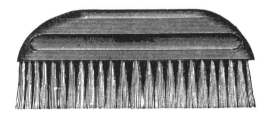

Smoothing Brush

Paper Hangers' Brush

BRUSH, PLASTERERS' FINISHING. A coarse brush used to damp finish the final coat of plaster. Width is approximately 8 1/2 inches.

Plasterers' Finishing Brush

BRUSH, PLATE CLEANING. A brush, made of fine spun metal, used to clean half tone and electrotype plates.

Plate Cleaning Brush

BRUSH, ROOF. A coarse brush used for coating a roof. Also used on decks and sides of vessels. The handle is approximately 4 feet long.

Roof Brush

BRUSH, SASH. Also called SASH TOOL. A brush used for painting window sash.

Sash Brush

BRUSH, SCRATCH. A steel or brass wire brush used by watch-case makers. See also *Brush, Wire*.

Scratch Brush

BRUSH, SHIP SEAM. A brush used to clean seams and joints of a ship prior to caulking or tarring.

Ship Seam Brush

BRUSH, SILVERSMITHS'. A brush used by a silversmith to clean and burnish new silver objects.

End Brush

Silversmiths' Brush

Cup Brush

Goblet Brush

Silversmiths' Brush

BRUSH, STENCIL. A round brush used for inking stencils. Diameter is 7/16 to 1 1/2 inches.

Stencil Brush

BRUSH, STIPPLING. A stiff brush used to impart a stipple effect to a plastered ceiling. Length is 8 to 9 inches. The brush is pushed against the surface to produce the desired surface finish.

Stippling Brush

BRUSH, STRIPING. A paint brush used for making stripes.

Dagger

Pencil

Striping Brush

Sword

Striping Brush

BRUSH, STUCCO DASH. Also called CASTING BRUSH and STUCCO BRUSH. A stiff brush made of heavy fibre. Overall length of the brush and handle is 14 to 18 inches.

Stucco Dash Brush

BRUSH, SUEDE. A very soft wire brush used on suede leather.

Swede Brush

BRUSH, SWING. A brass or soft steel brush used to impart a frosted or satin finish on gold, silver or plated ware.

Swing Brush

BRUSH, TANNERS' BLACKING. Also called BLACKENING BRUSH. A brush used to apply the blacking to the back of a finished hide. Tanners' blacking is a solution of sulphate of iron used as a dye and sealer.

BRUSH, TUBE. Also called FLUE BRUSH. A brush used for cleaning the tubes and flues of a steam engine or other boiler.

Tanners' Blacking Brush

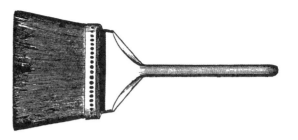

Tube Brush

Whitewash Brush

BRUSH, VARNISH. A paint brush recommended for applying varnish.

Oval

Window Brush

BRUSH, WIRE. A general-purpose brush used for cleaning scale or other foreign material from a workpiece. Wire brushes were made in a wide variety of sizes and shapes. Some examples are illustrated.

Flat Chisel Point

Varnish Brush

BRUSH, WALL. See *Brush, Paint.*

BRUSH, WATCH. A soft brush used when cleaning a watch or clock.

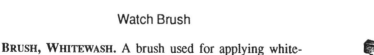

Watch Brush

BRUSH, WHITEWASH. A brush used for applying whitewash to a large surface such as a fence or wall. Width is 6 1/2 to 10 1/2 inches.

BRUSH, WINDOW. A brush specially adapted for cleaning windows.

Casting Brush

Handled Scratch Brush

Wire Brush

BRUSH BIT. See *Boring Tool, Bit, Brush.*

BUCK. See *Saw, Buck.*

BUCK SAW. See *Saw, Buck.*

BUCKET. See *Fire Bucket.*

BUCKET STAVE GAUGE. A gauge used to check for proper bevel on the edges of a stave for a small coopered container such as a bucket or churn. The pegs in the device are adjusted to match the radius of the proposed container. When a stave is placed against the pegs, the beveled edges should match the angle of the gauge legs to assure proper fit after assembly.

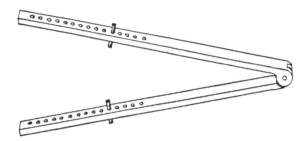

Bucket Stave Gauge

BUCKLE LOOP PUNCH. See *Punch, Buckle Loop.*

BUCKLE TONGUE PUNCH. See *Leather Tool, Buckle Tongue Punch.*

BUDDING KNIFE. See *Knife, Budding.*

BUFF. A jewelers' polishing tool. These tools generally have a soft felt surface.

Ring Buff

Setting Buff

Thimble Buff

Buff

BUFFER. A farriers' tool used to unclinch the nails when removing a shoe. A shoeing hammer is used to drive the buffer under the clinch thus cutting off or straightening

the end of the clinched nail. The illustrated tool has a nail punch on one end that is useful for cleaning or widening nail holes in the shoe.

Buffer

BUFFER STEEL. See *Shoe Makers' Tool, Buffer Steel.*

BUFFING WHEEL. A wheel consisting of layers of heavy cloth sewed together. This type of wheel, along with various buffing compounds, is used to clean and shine metal.

Buffing Wheel

BUGGY JACK. See *Jack, Wagon.*

BUGGY WHIP. See *Whip.*

BUGGY WRENCH. See *Wrench, Buggy.*

BUHL SAW. See *Saw, Bracket.*

BUILDERS' IRON. A tool used by an electrotype builder to melt strips of wax for building up a mould. The illustration shows a builders' iron and a gas stove used to heat the iron for use. Self-contained irons, heated by gas or electricity, were also available.

Iron

Stove

Builders' Iron

BUILDERS' KNIFE. See *Knife, Electrotype Builders'*.

BULB EXPANDER. A laboratory tool that will stretch rubber tubing and bulbs to facilitate attachment to pipettes or glass tubes.

Bulb Expander

BULB TROWEL. See *Trowel, Garden*.

BULL AXE. See *Axe, Pole*.

BULL LADLE. See *Ladle, Foundry*.

BULL LEADER. A device used to lead or control a bull. The snap shown in illustration (a) is intended to be attached to an existing ring in the nose of the animal. The rigid handle keeps the bull at a distance from the handler. The device shown in illustration (b) connects directly to the nose.

(a) Bull Snap

(b)

Bull Leader

BULL PLANE. See *Plane, Bull* and *Plane, Smooth*.

BULL PUNCH. See *Trocar*.

BULL SETT. A granite cutters' tool.

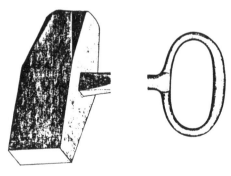

Bull Sett

BULL SNAP. See *Bull Leader*.

BULL TROCAR. See *Trocar*.

BULLDOG PINCERS. A shoe makers' tool. See *Pincers, Bulldog*.

BULLET STAKE. See *Stake, Ball*.

BULLNOSE PLANE. See *Plane, Bullnose*.

BULLNOSE RABBET. See *Plane, Bullnose Rabbet*.

BUMPING HAMMER. See *Hammer, Raising*.

BUNDLE FORK. See *Fork, Bundle*.

BUNG BORER. See *Boring Tool, Bung Borer*.

BUNG BURNER. An iron that is heated and used to sear the inside of the bung hole of a barrel. Some coopers believed that searing the raw edge of the hole would lengthen the life of the barrel by delaying the start of decay. This type of tool was also used to sear the edge of drain holes in the bottom of carriages and the center hole in wagon wheel hubs.

Bung Burner

BUNG CHISEL. See *Chisel, Bung*.

BUNG HOLE BORER. See *Boring Tool, Bung Borer*.

BUNG HOLE REAMER. See *Boring Tool, Bung Borer*.

BUNG PICK. See *Pick, Bung*.

BUNG STARTER. Also called BUNG FLOGGER and FLOGGER. A wooden mallet, with a flexible handle, used to hit the side of a barrel adjacent to the bung hole thus loosening the bung. Length of the handle is approximately 30 inches. The head of the mallet is made of a hard wood such as apple or maple and the handle is generally made of hickory.

Bung Starter

BUR. See *Setting Bur*.

BUR CHISEL. See *Chisel, Corner*.

BURIN. A variety of graving tool. See *Graver*.

BURLING IRON. A tool used by a weaver to pick knots and loose threads from the cloth. The process is called "Burling" or "Picking".

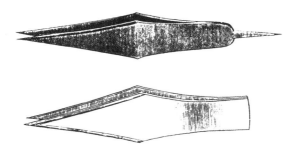

Burling Iron

BURNER PLIERS. See *Pliers, Gas.*

BURNING IRON. See *Bung Burner.*

BURNISHER. See *Burnishing Tool.*

BURNISHING TOOL. A tool with an extra-smooth face or edge used to rub and glaze the surface of a workpiece.

BURNISHING TOOL, AGATE. A fine burnishing tool with an agate tip used by book binders, picture frame gilders, jewelers and silversmiths. Several sizes and shapes of tips were available.

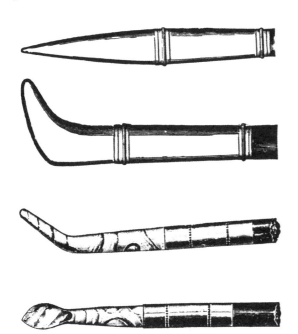

Agate Burnishing Tool

BURNISHING TOOL, BLOODSTONE. A fine burnishing tool used by book binders, jewelers and silversmiths. One supplier stated that 60 different shapes were carried in stock.

BURNISHING TOOL, BOOK BINDERS'. Also called BOOKBINDING BURNISHER. A tool used to smooth and burnish the gold leaf used in the impressions on a book cover and on the edges of a book. These tools are made of steel, agate, flint or bloodstone. See *Burnishing Tool, Agate* and *Burnishing Tool, Bloodstone.*

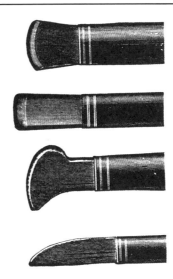

Bloodstone Burnishing Tool

BURNISHING TOOL, ELECTROTYPE FINISHERS'. A tool used to burnish the joints of the completed electrotype. Made of polished steel.

Electrotype Burnishing Tool

BURNISHING TOOL, HEEL. See *Shoe Makers' Tool, Burnisher.*

BURNISHING TOOL, JEWELERS'. A steel tool used by a jeweler to turn and smooth soft metal.

Case or Plate Burnisher

Bent Oval

Spear

Jewelers' Burnishing Tool

97

Spoon

Straight Oval

Jewelers' Burnishing Tool

BURNISHING TOOL, LEATHER. See *Leather Tool, Bouncer* and *Leather Tool, Slicker*.

BURNISHING TOOL, SCRAPER. Also called CABINET BURNISHER, CABINET MAKERS' BURNISHER, SCRAPER STEEL and TURNING STEEL. A tool used to turn the edge of a scraper blade. The tool is rubbed along the squared edge of a scraper blade thus turning the edge and forming a sharp scraping surface. Oval, round and square varieties were available.

Scraper Burnishing Tool

BURNISHING TOOL, SHOE MAKERS'. See *Shoe Makers' Tool, Burnisher* and *Shoe Makers' Tool, Long Stick*.

BURNISHING TOOL, SILVERSMITHS'. Also called PEWTERERS' BURNISHER. A tool used to burnish and form silver or pewter. Made of highly polished steel. Overall length is 8 1/2 to 11 1/2 inches.

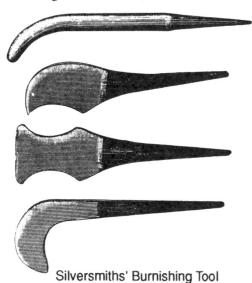

Silversmiths' Burnishing Tool

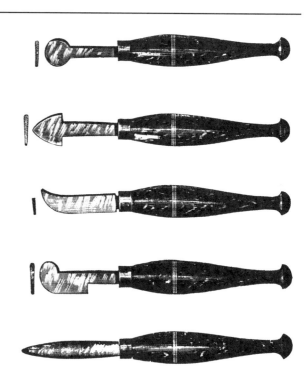

Silversmiths' Burnishing Tool

BURR STONE PICK. See *Pick, Mill*.

BURRING MACHINE. See *Tinsmiths' Machine, Burring*.

BURRING REAMER. See *Boring Tool, Pipe Reamer*.

BURRING TOOL. See *Boring Tool, Pipe Reamer*.

BURSTING HAMMER. See *Hammer, Bursting*.

BURSTING SLEDGE. See *Sledge, Bursting*.

BUSH AXE. See *Axe, Bush*.

BUSH CHISEL. A stone workers' tool. See *Chisel, Bush*.

BUSH HAMMER. A stone workers' tool. See *Hammer, Bush*.

BUSH HOOK. See *Hook, Bush*.

BUSH SCYTHE. See *Scythe*.

BUSH WRENCH. A coopers' tool. See *Wrench, Bush*.

BUTCHER BLOCK BRUSH. See *Brush, Butcher Block*.

BUTCHER BLOCK PLANE. See *Plane, Butcher Block*.

BUTCHER BLOCK SCRAPER. See *Scraper, Butcher Block*.

BUTCHER SAW. See *Saw, Butcher*.

BUTCHER SAW PUNCH. See *Punch, Saw*.

BUTCHERS' APRON. See *Apron, Butchers'*.

BUTCHERS' BLOCK. Also called MEAT BLOCK. A freestanding meat cutting block used in a butcher shop. The top is usually end grain hard maple. Round and square shapes were available. The illustrated block was offered in sizes of two to four feet in diameter.

Butchers' Block

BUTCHERS' CLEAVER. See *Cleaver.*

BUTCHERS' KNIFE. See *Knife, Butchers'.*

BUTCHERS' STEEL. A tool used for sharpening a butcher knife. Length of the blade is 10 to 12 inches.

Butchers' Steel

BUTT CHISEL. See *Chisel, Butt.*

BUTT FELT INSERTER. See *Piano Tool, Butt Felt Inserter.*

BUTT GAUGE. A tool used for measuring and marking the location of butt hinges on a door or jamb. This tool will also indicate the proper depth of cut to match the thickness of the butt.

Fulton's Patent

Butt Gauge

Reeves' Patent

Butt Gauge

BUTT GAUGE MORTISER. A device used to cut the ends of the mortise for a butt hinge and to serve as a guide for the vertical cut.

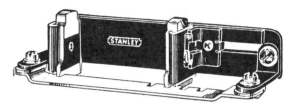

Butt Gauge Mortiser

BUTT MORTISER. A device used to cut the mortise for a butt hinge.

Butt Mortiser

BUTT AND RABBET GAUGE. A marking gauge used for hanging doors, mortising and for general marking tasks. Generally used with a push stroke. The illustrated tool has a brass shaft and a rosewood body.

Butt and Rabbet Gauge

BUTTER FORK. See *Fork, Butter.*

BUTTER KNIFE. See *Knife, Butter.*

BUTTER PACKER. A tool used to pack butter into a tub or cask for shipment. Also used for handling and packing lard.

Butter and Lard Spade

Butter Spade

Butter Paddle

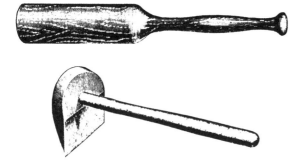

Butter Packer

BUTTER SAMPLER. See *Sampler, Cheese.*

BUTTER SPADE. See *Butter Packer.*

BUTTER TONGS. See *Tongs, Butter.*

BUTTER TROWEL. See *Trowel, Butter.*

BUTTER WORKER. Also called BUTTER TABLE. A unique machine used to work butter as required to remove the buttermilk and water. Size of the table is 3 to 4 feet in diameter. Several varieties of roller-type butter workers have been noted.

BUTTERESS. See *Butteris.* Butteress is a variation in spelling.

BUTTERFLY AXE. See *Axe, Double Bit,* bow tie pattern.

Butter Worker

BUTTERFLY PEEN HAMMER. See *Axe, Stone.*

BUTTERIS. Also called BUTTERESS and BUTTRESS. A farriers' tool used for trimming the inside of the hoof and for smoothing the bottom surface. The pad of the butteris is positioned against the farriers' shoulder and pressure is applied by moving the shoulder forward. The butteris is used by some farriers for part of the functions normally accomplished with the hoof knife.

French Style

Butteris

BUTTON BRUSH. See *Brush, Button.*

BUTTON FASTENER. A device used to install a shoe button. One type of shoe button has a clip with two wire prongs that are crimped over when the button is installed. Installation is similar to that of a modern paper staple.

Button Fastener

BUTTON GAUGE. See *Rule, Button Gauge*.

BUTTON HEAD RIVET SET. See *Anvil Tool, Rivet Set*.

BUTTON HEAD SET. See *Anvil Tool, Rivet Set*.

BUTTON HOLE CHISEL. See *Chisel, Button Hole*.

BUTTON HOLE CUTTER. A tool used to cut the initial slit for forming a button hole.

Chisel Type

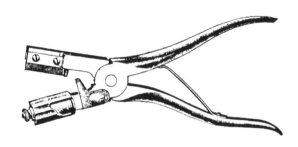

Plier Type

Shoe Makers'

Button Hole Cutter

BUTTON HOLE PLIERS. See *Button Hole Cutter*.

BUTTON MACHINE. A device used by a shoe maker to crimp metal buttons and snaps on leather.

Button Machine

BUTTON NEEDLE. A tool used for tying buttons in old lazy-backs or in carriage linings that are fastened to the wood. The needle implants a special fastener clip into the lining; the button is then tied to the clip.

Button Needle

BUTTON SLICK. See *Moulders' Hand Tool*.

BUTTRESS. See *Butteris*. Buttress is a variation in spelling.

C

Tool names starting with the letter C including multiple
  listings of:
  CALIPER
  CART
  CARVING TOOL
  CAULKING TOOL
  CEMENT TOOL
  CHISEL
  CLAMP
  COMBINATION TOOL
  COMPASS
  CRAYON

Included also are listings of the tools used by the:
  CABINET MAKER (JOINER)
  CARPENTER
  CARVER (WOOD)
  CAULKER (SHIP CAULKER)
  CEMENT WORKER
  COACH MAKER (CARRIAGE MAKER)
  COAL MINER
  COMB MAKER
  COOPER
  CURRIER

CABBAGE CORER. A tool intended for use in removing the
core from a head of cabbage.

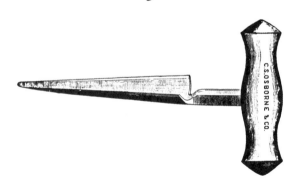

Cabbage Corer

CABBAGE POT. An iron pot used for reducing scrap metal
to a solid ball. The pot has a hole in the bottom so that
the solidified mass can be punched out. The illustrated
pot is 10 inches in diameter.

CABINET. See *Tool Cabinet*.

CABINET FILE. See *File, Wood*.

CABINET MAKERS' BURNISHER. See *Burnishing Tool,
Scraper*.

Cabbage Pot

CABINET MAKERS' CHISEL. See *Chisel, Firmer*.

CABINET MAKERS' EDGE PLANE. See *Plane, Edge*.

CABINET MAKERS' TOOLS. Also called FINISH CARPEN-
TERS' TOOLS and JOINERS' TOOLS. The special-purpose
cabinet makers' tools listed below can be found in nor-
mal alphabetical sequence. These tools may also have
used for other purposes.
  ANGLE DIVIDER
  APRON, SHOP
  AUGER BIT GUIDES
  AWL, BRAD
  AWL, SCRATCH
  AWL HAFT
  BEADING TOOL, WOOD
  BENCH, CABINET MAKERS'
  BENCH BRACKET
  BENCH HOOK
  BENCH SCREW
  BENCH STOP
  BEVEL
  BIT GAUGE
  BORING TOOL, BIT
  BORING TOOL, BIT BRACE
  BORING TOOL, BREAST DRILL
  BURNISHING TOOL, SCRAPER
  BUTT GAUGE
  BUTT GAUGE MORTISER
  BUTT MORTISER
  BUTT AND RABBET GAUGE
  CHISEL, BUTT
  CHISEL, CHIP NAILING

CHISEL, CORNER
CHISEL, DRAWER LOCK
CHISEL, FIRMER
CHISEL, LOCK MORTISING
CHISEL, MORTISING
CHISEL, NOTCHING
CHISEL, PARING
CHISEL GRINDER
CHISEL HANDLE
CLAMP, BAR
CLAMP, BENCH
CLAMP, CABINET MAKERS'
CLAMP, CARRIAGE MAKERS'
CLAMP, CARRIAGE MAKERS' ADJUSTABLE
CLAMP, CORNER
CLAMP, DOOR
CLAMP, HAND SCREW
CLAMP, MITER
CLAMP, PIPE
CLAMP, WOODEN
CLAMP HORSE
COMPASS, PENCIL
CORNERING TOOL
CUTTING GAUGE
DRAWING KNIFE
FILE, TAPER
FILE, WOOD
FILE HANDLE
GAINING TOOL
GLUE BRUSH
GLUE POT
GOUGE, BENT
GOUGE, FIRMER
GOUGE, PARING
HAMMER, JOINERS'
HAMMER, NAIL
LEVEL, CARPENTERS'
MALLET, CHISEL
MARKING GAUGE
MITER BOX
MITER JACK
MITER MACHINE
MITER PLANER
MITER TEMPLATE
MITER TRIMMER
MORTISING GAUGE
MORTISING MACHINE
NAIL SET
PANEL GAUGE
PENCIL, CARPENTERS'
PITCH ADJUSTER
PLANE, BADGER
PLANE, BEADING
PLANE, BENCH
PLANE, BLOCK

PLANE, BULLNOSE RABBET
PLANE, CABINET MAKERS'
PLANE, CASE MAKERS'
PLANE, CHAMFER
PLANE, CHISEL GAUGE
PLANE, COPING
PLANE, CORNER ROUNDING
PLANE, DADO
PLANE, DOOR
PLANE, DOOR TRIM
PLANE, DOUBLE COPING
PLANE, DOVETAIL
PLANE, EDGE
PLANE, EDGE TRIMMING
PLANE, FILLETSTER
PLANE, FLOOR
PLANE, FLUTING
PLANE, HAND RAIL
PLANE, LOW ANGLE
PLANE, MATCH
PLANE, MITER
PLANE, MOULDING
PLANE, NOSING
PLANE, PANEL PLOW
PLANE, RABBET
PLANE, RAISING
PLANE, RIPPING
PLANE, SASH
PLANE, SASH FILLETSTER
PLANE, SCRAPER
PLANE, SHOULDER
PLANE, SHOOT BOARD, WOOD
PLANE, SIDE RABBET
PLANE, TABLE
PLANE, TOOTHING
PLUMB BOB
RASP, WOOD
ROUTER
ROUTER, CABINET MAKERS'
RULE
SASH PULLEY DRIVER
SAW, BACK
SAW, CABINET
SAW, DOVETAIL
SAW, FLOOR
SAW, FOOT AND HAND POWERED
SAW, HAND
SAW, JOINER
SAW, MITER BOX
SAW, MOULDING
SAW, STAIR
SAW FILING GUIDE
SAW JOINTER
SAW SET
SCRAPER, CABINET

SCRAPER, COACH MAKERS'
SCREW DRIVER
SLIDING T BEVEL
SLITTING GAUGE
SPOKE SHAVE
SQUARE, MITER
SQUARE, STEEL
SQUARE, TRY
STAIR BUILDERS' GAUGE
STAIR GAUGE
TOOL CHEST, CABINET MAKERS'
VISE, COACH MAKERS'
VISE, SAW
VISE, TAIL
VISE, WOOD WORKERS'

CABINET OGEE. See *Plane, Moulding, Cabinet Ogee.*

CABINET RASP. See *Rasp, Wood.*

CABLE SHEATH KNIFE. See *Knife, Cable Sheath.*

CAGE HEAD BRACE. See *Boring Tool, Bit Brace, Cage Head.*

CALCIMINE BRUSH. See *Brush, Calcimine.*

CALCULATING RULE. See *Rule, Calculating.*

CALENDER SCRAPER. See *Scraper, Calender.*

CALF FEEDER. A milk pail with a large nipple used for feeding a calf. The illustrated pail can be suspended from a barn door or rail by use of the attached bracket.

Calf Feeder

CALIPER. A measuring device, with two adjustable legs, used to determine or transfer a dimension of an irregular object.

CALIPER, COMBINATION. Also called COMBINATION DIVIDERS and EXTENSION DIVIDERS. A combination tool, having replaceable legs, for use as an inside caliper, outside caliper and divider.

CALIPER, DANCING MASTER. Also called FANCY CALIPER. A caliper with the legs fashioned to resemble the legs and feet of a dancer.

CALIPER, DOUBLE. Also called DOUBLE JOINT CALIPER. A caliper having two sets of measuring legs of different sizes.

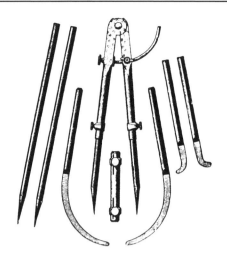

Combination Caliper

Dancing Master Caliper

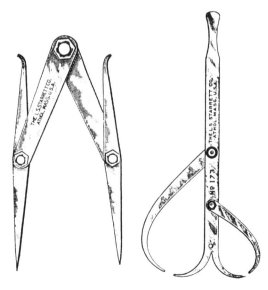

Double Caliper

Double Caliper

CALIPER, DOUBLE JOINT. See *Caliper, Double.*

CALIPER, DUPLICATING. A home made wooden caliper used by an instrument maker. Overall length is about 12 inches.

Duplicating Caliper

CALIPER, ELECTROTYPE FINISHERS'. A caliper, with sharp feelers, used to scale the depth of a cut or impression. Length is 9 to 12 inches.

Electrotype Finishers' Caliper

CALIPER, FANCY. A caliper with feelers made to resemble hands or some other whimsical shape. Length is approximately 2 1/2 inches. See also *Caliper, Dancing Master.*

Fancy Caliper

CALIPER, FIRM JOINT. Also called PLAIN CALIPER. A caliper having the joint pin sufficiently tight to retain the setting while transferring or scaling a measurement.

Length of legs are 4 to 36 inches. A large outside caliper of this type was also listed as a granite carvers' tool.

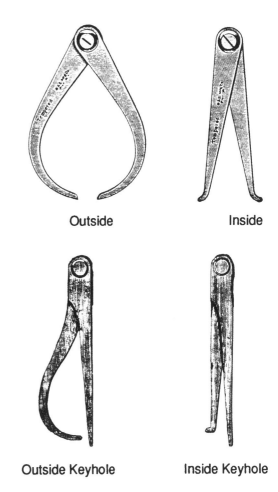

Outside   Inside

Outside Keyhole   Inside Keyhole

Hermaphrodite

Firm Joint Caliper

CALIPER, GRANITE CARVERS'. See *Caliper, Firm Joint.*

CALIPER, HERMAPHRODITE. See *Caliper, Firm Joint.*

CALIPER, INSIDE. See *Caliper, Combination; Caliper, Double; Caliper, Firm Joint; Caliper, Self Registering* and *Caliper, Spring.*

CALIPER, KEYHOLE. See *Caliper, Firm Joint* and *Caliper, Spring*.

CALIPER, LOG. A large caliper, generally made of wood, used to measure the diameter of a log. The beam, as shown in illustration (a), is often imprinted with a board-foot table. The tool shown in illustration (c) is a woodcutters' tool calibrated in cords.

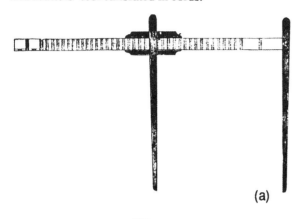

(a)

(c)

Log Caliper

CALIPER, NAVY. Also called DOUBLE S CALIPER. Length of the illustrated tool is 2 1/2 inches.

Navy Caliper

CALIPER, OUTSIDE. See *Caliper, Combination; Caliper, Double; Caliper, Firm Joint; Caliper, Self Registering; Caliper, Spring* and *Caliper, Wing*.

CALIPER, REGISTER. See *Caliper, Self Registering*.

CALIPER, SELF REGISTERING. Also called REGISTER CALIPER. A caliper having a scale to allow direct reading of the setting.

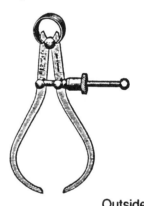 

Outside   Inside

Self Registering Caliper

CALIPER, SPRING. A caliper with a spring-tempered top bow. The spring pulls the caliper legs outward as the adjustment nut is loosened.

Outside   Inside

Keyhole

Spring Caliper

CALIPER, WALKING WHEEL. A lumbering tool used for measuring a log. The caliper measures the diameter. The length is determined by counting the revolutions of the wheel as it is walked down the log. The distance between adjacent spokes of the illustrated tool is 6 inches. The beam has a board-foot table.

Walking Wheel Caliper

CALIPER, WING. Also called WINGED CALIPER. A caliper with a curved adjustment guide and a thumb screw for locking the adjustment. Length of the legs are 6 to 12 inches.

Wing Caliper

CALIPER CHISEL. See *Turning Tool, Sizer.*

CALIPER RULE. See *Rule, Caliper.*

CALK EXTRACTOR. A tool used to remove ice calks from a horse shoe.

Calk Extractor

CALK SWAGE. See *Anvil Tool, Toe Calk Die.*

CALK WRENCH. See *Boot Calk Tool.*

CALKING TOOL. See *Caulking Tool.* Calking is a variation in spelling.

CALLIPER. See *Caliper.* Calliper is a variation in spelling.

CAMERA LEVEL. A small level. See *Level, Cross Test.*

CAMP AXE. See *Axe, Campers'.*

CAMP HATCHET. See *Hatchet, Camp.*

CAMPBELL TOOL. See *Rule Attachment.*

CAMPERS' AXE. See *Axe, Campers'.*

CANDLE HOLDER. A miners' tool. This device can be hooked over a lateral plank or pressed into the sidewall for support.

Candle Holder

CANDLE MOULD STAKE. See *Stake, Candle Mould.*

CANDY PRESS. A roller-type device used to press candy into individual pieces. The illustrated machine has several interchangeable brass rollers each with a different pattern.

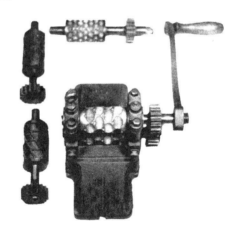

Candy Press

CANE HOE. See *Hoe, Farm.*

CANE KNIFE. See *Knife, Cane.*

CANE SEATING AWL. See *Awl, Seat.*

CANOE ADZE. See *Adze, Gutter.*

CANT DOG. A lumbering tool. See *Peavey.*

CANT FILE. See *File, Cant Saw.*

CANT HOOK. Also called MILL HOOK. A tool used for rolling and turning logs. The cant hook is similar to the Peavey except that the shaft is blunt rather than having a spike at the end. The stock is usually made of maple or hickory and is 2 1/2 to 6 feet long. The illustration shows a Hog Nosed variety of cant hook. The Crow Foot type has two small spikes in place of the turned-over nose. The cant hook was patented in 1856. See also *Landing Hook*.

Cant Hook

CANT HOOK, ICE. A cant hook used to manipulate blocks of ice. The handle is approximately 4 feet long.

Ice Cant Hook

CANT SAW FILE. See *File, Cant Saw*.

CAP CRIMPER. See *Pliers, Cap Crimping*.

CAP MAKERS' KNIFE. See *Knife, Cap Makers'*.

CAP SCREW WRENCH. See *Wrench, Set Screw*.

CAPE CHISEL. See *Chisel, Cape*.

CAPEN CHISEL. See *Chisel, Cape*.

CAPPING PLANE. See *Plane, Hand Rail*.

CAR BEADING PLANE. See *Plane, Car Beading*.

CAR BIT. A long auger bit. See *Boring Tool, Bit, Car*.

CAR BUILDERS' BIT. See *Boring Tool, Bit, Car*.

CAR BUILDERS' HATCHET. See *Hatchet, Half*.

CAR BUILDERS' WRENCH. See *Wrench, Construction*.

CAR HOOK. See *Hook, Ice*.

CAR ICING HOOK. See *Hook, Ice*.

CAR MOVER. See *Bar, Car Starting*.

CAR STARTING BAR. See *Bar, Car Starting*.

CAR WRENCH. See *Wrench, S*.

CARBIDE LAMP. Also called DRIVERS' LIGHT, MINERS' LAMP, MINERS' LIGHT and MINERS' PIT LAMP. A small lamp that uses dry carbide and water for fuel. The lamp is worn on the cap or may be fastened to a vehicle to serve as a driving light. The top tank contains water which is allowed to drip into a container of carbide to produce an inflammable gas. The lamp must be maintained upright to assure constant dripping of the water.

CARBON PLIERS. See *Pliers, Carbon*.

CARBON SCRAPER. See *Scraper, Carbon*.

Carbide Lamp

CARBORUNDUM RUBBING BRICK. See *Rubbing Brick*

CARD BRUSH. See *Brush, Card*.

CARD CLEANER. A comb used to clean the cards in a textile mill machine.

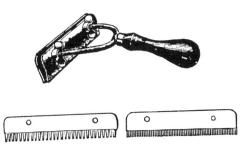

Card Cleaner

CARD HAMMER. See *Hammer, Card* and *Hammer, Saddlers'*.

CARD PLANE. See *Plane, Card*.

CARD SCRAPER. See *Scraper, Card*.

CARD SHEET MARKER. A textile mill tool.

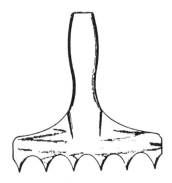

Card Sheet Marker

CARD STRETCHER. A textile mill tool used for redrawing or taking blisters out of card clothing.

CARD STRICKLE. A tool used in a textile mill to sharpen and level the teeth of a card.

CARD TOOTH PULLER. A textile mill tool used to straighten or remove a damaged card tooth.

Card Stretcher

Card Strickle

Card Tooth Puller

CARPENTERS' AUGER. See *Boring Tool, Nut Auger*.

CARPENTERS' CLAMP. See *Clamp, Bar*.

CARPENTERS' PRYING BAR. See *Bar, Wrecking*.

CARPENTERS' RIPPING BAR. See *Bar, Wrecking*.

CARPENTERS' SQUARE. See *Square, Steel*.

CARPENTERS' TOOL BOX. See Tool *Case, Carpenters'* and *Tool Chest, Carpenters'*.

CARPENTERS' TOOLS. The special-purpose carpenters' tools listed below can be found in normal alphabetical sequence. These tools may also have been used for other purposes.

ADZE, CARPENTERS'
ADZE, GUTTER
ANGLE DIVIDER
APRON, CARPENTERS'
APRON, NAIL
AWL, SCRATCH
BAR, WRECKING
BEVEL
BORING TOOL, ANGULAR BORER
BORING TOOL, AUGER HANDLE
BORING TOOL, BIT
BORING TOOL, BIT BRACE
BORING TOOL, BIT EXTENSION
BORING TOOL, BORING MACHINE

BORING TOOL, BREAST DRILL
BORING TOOL, NUT AUGER
BORING TOOL, SILL BORER
CHALK LINE
CHALK LINE REEL
CHALK LINE SPOOL
CHISEL, CORNER
CHISEL, FLOOR
CHISEL, FRAMING
CHISEL, MORTISING
CHISEL, RIPPING
CHISEL, WRECKING
CHISEL GRINDER
CHISEL HANDLE
CLAMP, BAR
CLAMP, FLOORING
CLAMP, PIPE
CLAPBOARD GAUGE
CLAPBOARD GAUGE, WOODEN
CLAPBOARD MARKER
COMPASS, PENCIL
DRAWING KNIFE, CARPENTERS'
DRAWING KNIFE, FOLDING HANDLE
FILE, TAPER
FILE HANDLE
FLOOR JACK
GOUGE, FRAMING
HAMMER, NAIL
HAMMER, NAIL HEADING
HAMMER, RIPPING
HATCHET, BROAD
HATCHET, SHINGLING
LEVEL, CARPENTERS'
LEVEL, LINE
MALLET, CHISEL
MARKING GAUGE
NAIL PULLER
NAIL SET
PENCIL, CARPENTERS'
PINCERS, CARPENTERS'
PITCH ADJUSTER
PLANE, BENCH
PLANE, BLOCK
PLANE, FLOOR
PLANE, FURRING
PLANE, GUTTER
PLANE, MATCH
PLANE, RABBET
PLANE, SCRUB
PLUMB BOB
PREACHER
RIPPER, CARPENTERS' STAGING
RIPPER, SLATERS'
RULE
SAW, DOCKING

Saw, Hand
Saw Filing Guide
Saw Jointer
Saw Set
Screw Driver
Slick, Carpenters'
Sliding T Bevel
Spoke Shave
Square, Protractor
Square, Steel
Square, Try
Tool Case, Carpenters'
Tool Chest, Carpenters'
Vise, Saw

CARPET AWL. See *Awl, Carpet*.

CARPET CLAMP. See *Clamp, Carpet Sewers'*.

CARPET HAMMER. See *Hammer, Upholsterers'*.

CARPET LAYERS' HAMMER. See *Hammer, Upholsterers'*.

CARPET PRESS. A metal weight used to hold one edge of a carpet in place while working on the opposite edge. Weight is 15 to 50 pounds.

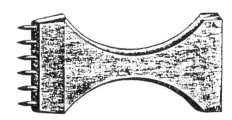

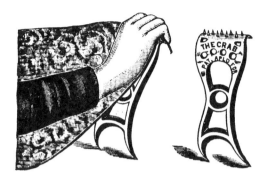

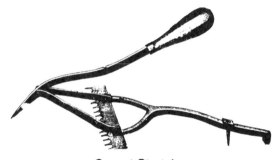

Carpet Stretcher

Carpet Press

CARPET SEWERS' CLAMP. See *Clamp, Carpet Sewers'*.

CARPET STRETCHER. Also called WEBBING STRETCHER. A tool used to stretch carpet or other fabric for nailing. The straining fork was listed as a carpet stretcher but was specially recommended for smaller tasks such as stretching upholstery.

Straining Fork

Handled

Carpet Stretcher

CARPET VISE. See *Vise, Carpet*.

CARRIAGE IRONERS' HAMMER. See *Hammer, Carriage Ironers'*.

CARRIAGE KNOB WRENCH. See *Wrench, Carriage Knob*.

CARRIAGE MAKERS' BEADING TOOL. See *Beading Tool, Carriage Makers'*.

CARRIAGE MAKERS' BODY KNIFE. See *Drawing Knife, Carriage Body*.

CARRIAGE MAKERS' CLAMP. See *Clamp, Carriage Makers'* and *Clamp, Carriage Makers' Adjustable*.

CARRIAGE MAKERS' DRAWING KNIFE. See *Drawing Knife, Carriage Makers'*.

CARRIAGE MAKERS' JARVIS. See *Jarvis*.

CARRIAGE MAKERS' MOULDING TOOL. See *Moulding Tool, Carriage Makers'*.

CARRIAGE MAKERS' PANEL SHAVE. See *Spoke Shave, Carriage Makers' Panel*.

CARRIAGE MAKERS' PLANE. See *Plane, Carriage Makers'*.

CARRIAGE MAKERS' PLOW PLANE. See *Plane, Carriage Makers' Plow* and *Plane, Panel Plow, Carriage Makers*.

CARRIAGE MAKERS' PLUG CUTTER. See *Plug Cutter*.

CARRIAGE MAKERS' RABBET. See *Plane, Carriage Makers'*.

CARRIAGE MAKERS' ROUTER. See *Router, Carriage Makers'*.

CARRIAGE MAKERS' SPOKE SHAVE. See *Spoke Shave, Carriage Makers'*.

CARRIAGE MAKERS' TOOLS. See *Coach Makers' Tools*.

CARRIAGE ROUTER KNIFE. See *Drawing Knife, Carriage Router*.

CARRIAGE WRENCH. See *Wrench, Buggy*.

CART. A push-type vehicle used for transporting freight or other heavy objects. See also *Wheel Barrow*.

CART, BARREL. A cart used for transporting a wooden barrel. See also *Barrel Truck*.

Barrel Cart

CART, HAND. A general-purpose cart with high wheels.

Hand Cart

CART, WALL PAPER. A cart especially adapted for transporting rolls of wallpaper in a factory or warehouse.

CARTING GRAB SKIPPER. See *Grab Skipper*.

CARVERS' BENCH. See *Bench, Wood Carvers'*.

CARVERS' CLAMP. See *Clamp, Bench*.

CARVERS' MARKER. See *Carving Tool, Marker*.

CARVERS' PUNCH. See *Carving Tool, Marker*.

Wall Paper Cart

CARVERS' SCREW. Also called WOOD CARVERS' SCREW. A screw device used to hold the workpiece firmly to the bench while the carving is in process. The pointed end of the tool is screwed into waste material at the bottom of the carving and the other end is inserted into a hole in the bench. The wing nut is then tightened below the bench and holds the carving block in position.

Carvers' Screw

CARVERS' TOOLS. Wood carving was an important trade when furniture was decorated with hand carved mouldings and designs. The hand work gradually gave way to machine carvings and machine carving was obsoleted by changes in furniture design. Hand carving in the 20th century has been practiced primarily as a hobby. The special-purpose wood carvers' tools listed below can be found in normal alphabetical sequence. These tools may also have been used for other purposes.

BENCH, WOOD CARVERS'
CARVERS' SCREW
CARVING TOOL, CHISEL
CARVING TOOL, GOUGE
CARVING TOOL, MACARONI
CARVING TOOL, MARKER
CARVING TOOL, PARTING
CARVING TOOL, VEINER
CARVING TOOL HANDLE
CLAMP, BENCH
KNIFE, CARVERS'
MALLET, CARVERS'
RIFFLER
SHARPENING STONE, CARVING TOOL
VISE, WOOD CARVERS'

CARVING POINT. See *Stone Cutters' Tool, Point*.

CARVING CHISEL. See *Carving Tool, Chisel* and *Stone Cutters' Tool, Point.*

CARVING TOOL. A hand tool used for carving and shaping of a solid material. The term is usually used to denote a wood-carving tool unless otherwise stated. The common types of wood carving tools were each made in several types and several sizes. One supplier listed 343 different Addis wood carving tools in stock at one time. When sold in sets, the set generally included 12 or less tools.

CARVING TOOL, CHISEL. A carving tool with a straight cutting edge on the end. A wide variety of widths were available.

Straight

Skew or Corner

Fishtail

Bent or Short Bent

Bent Curved or Corner

Carving Chisel

CARVING TOOL, GOUGE. A carving tool with a curved cutting edge at the end. The degree of curve is called "Sweep".

Straight

Fishtail

Carving Gouge

Back Bent

Short Bent or Front Bent

Long Bent

Carving Gouge

CARVING TOOL, LEATHER. See *Leather Tool, Carving.*

CARVING TOOL, MACARONI. A carving tool that cuts a groove with a square bottom. Width is 1/8 to 3/8 inches.

Macaroni Tool

CARVING TOOL, MARKER. Also called CARVERS' MARKER, CARVERS' PUNCH and MATTING TOOL. A tool used to impart a fixed design to a wood carving. It is generally used to create a background pattern. The marker is struck with a mallet to imprint the design on the wood.

Carving Marker

CARVING TOOL, PARTING. A V shaped carving tool used to cut a deep groove in the workpiece or to separate the carving from the excess stock.

Straight

Parting Tool

Short Bent or Front Bent

Long Bent or Bent

Parting Tool

CARVING TOOL, PLASTER. See *Plasterers' Ornamental Tools*.

CARVING TOOL, PUNCH. See *Carving Tool, Marker*.

CARVING TOOL, SADDLERS'. See *Leather Tool, Carving*.

CARVING TOOL, VEINER. Also called VEINING TOOL. A carving tool similar to a Gouge with a deep U shape.

Veiner

CARVING TOOL HANDLE. A handle for the common variety of wood carving tool. Carving tools were often sold without handles. The craftsman would made or procure handles to suit his particular grip.

Carving Tool Handle

CARVING TOOL STONE. See *Sharpening Stone, Carving Tool*.

CASE HAMMER. See *Hammer, Case*.

CASE HOOK. See *Hook, Box*.

CASE MAKERS' PLANE. See *Plane, Case Makers'*.

CASE OPENER. Also called WATCH CASE OPENER. A tool, with dull rounded edges, used to open the back of a watch case.

Case Opener

CASE STAKE. See *Stake, Watch Case*.

CASEMENT PLANE. See *Plane, Moulding, Quarter Round*.

CASING KNIFE. See *Knife, Paper Hangers' Casing*.

CASING MOULDING PLANE. See *Plane, Moulding, Quarter Round*.

CASING WHEEL. See *Knife, Paper Hangers' Casing*.

CASING WRENCH. See *Wrench, Casing*.

CASTER BIT. See *Boring Tool, Bit, Caster*.

CASTING BRUSH. See *Brush, Stucco Dash* and *Brush, Wire*.

CATTLE BRANDER. See *Ear Marker*.

CATTLE LEADER. See *Bull Leader*.

CATTLE MARKER. See *Ear Marker*.

CATTLE PROD. A spiked pole used by stockmen and packing house workers to goad cattle up a loading chute or along an aisle. The handle is 6 to 6 1/2 feet long.

Cattle Prod

CATTLE PUNCH. See *Ear Marker*.

CAULKERS' TOOLS. The special-purpose ship caulking tools listed below can be found in normal alphabetical sequence. These tools may also have been used for other purposes.
  Caulking Tool, Ship
  Hawsing Beetle
  Hawsing Iron
  Mallet, Caulking
  Reaming Iron

CAULKING BAR. See *Bar, Ice*.

CAULKING CHISEL. See *Caulking Tool*.

CAULKING HAMMER. See *Hammer, Caulking*.

CAULKING IRON. See *Caulking Tool*.

CAULKING TOOL. Also called CAULKING CHISEL and CAULKING IRON. A blunt chisel used to drive caulking material into a seam or cavity. See also *Chincing Iron*.

CAULKING TOOL, CEILING DROP. Also called CEILING IRON. OVERALL length is approximately 15 inches.

113

Ceiling Drop Tool

CAULKING TOOL, COOPERS'. See *Chincing Iron*.

CAULKING TOOL, PLUMBERS'. Also called CAULKING CHISEL and CAULKING TOOL. A tool used by a plumber or steam fitter to drive caulking material into the cavity around a pipe or shaft.

Common Iron

Corner Tool

Curved Stub

Gasket Chisel

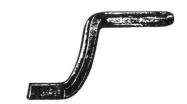

Offset Tool

Packing Chisel or Spring

Picking Iron

Plumbers' Caulking Tool

Right Angle Tool

S Iron

Spreading Iron

Throat Iron

Upright Iron

Yarning Iron

Plumbers' Caulking Tool

CAULKING TOOL, SHIP. A metal tool used to drive caulking material into the seams of a wooden or metal-clad ship. The Caulking or Making Iron was the most common type; it was available in thicknesses of 1/16 to 1/4 inches and in various widths.

CAVEL. Also called JEDDING AXE. A small Stone Masons' Axe having a flat face and a pointed peen.

CAVETTO. See *Plane, Moulding, Cove*.

CAVIL. See *Cavel*. Cavil is a variation in spelling.

114

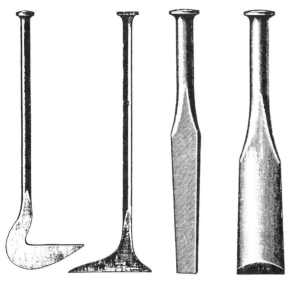

Reef Hook   Boot Iron   Spike Iron   Sharp or Butt Iron

Caulking or   Crooked or   Dumb or   Clearing or
Making Iron   Bent Iron   Deck Iron   Reefing Iron

Ship Caulking Tool

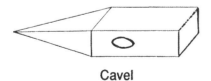

Cavel

C CLAMP. See *Clamp, C.*

CEILING DROP TOOL. See *Caulking Tool, Ceiling Drop.*

CEILING IRON. See *Caulking Tool, Ceiling Drop.*

CELLULOID FILE. See *File, Celluloid.*

CEMENT ROLLER. See *Cement Tool, Roller.*

CEMENT SAMPLER. See *Sampler, Cement.*

CEMENT TOOL. Also called GRANITOID TOOL. Any of

several tools used for smoothing and finishing concrete was usually listed as a cement tool.

CEMENT TOOL, CENTER KNIFE. See *Cement Tool, Jointer.*

CEMENT TOOL, CIRCLE EDGER. See *Cement Tool, Edger.*

CEMENT TOOL, CORNER. See *Cement Tool, Inside.*

CEMENT TOOL, CORRUGATING. A tool used to a create a grooved non-slip surface on concrete.

Corrugating Tool

CEMENT TOOL, CURBING. Also called CURB EDGER, CURBING EDGER, EDGER and ROUND CORNER TROWEL. A tool used to smooth a sharply curved surface such as a curb. Available in bronze or iron.

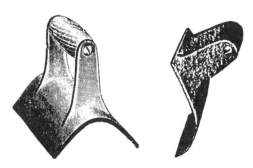

Curbing Tool

CEMENT TOOL, DRIVEWAY GROOVER. A tool used to make or smooth the large grooves between sections of concrete in a surface such as a driveway. Length is approximately 6 1/2 inches.

Round

V Type

Driveway Groover

CEMENT TOOL, DRIVEWAY ROLLER. See *Cement Tool, Roller.*

CEMENT TOOL, EDGER. Also called CURB EDGER and CURBING TOOL. A tool used to make a small break at the edge of a concrete surface. Patterns were available to make a concave, convex, square or bevel edge. Available in bronze or iron.

Bevel

Circle or Radius Edger

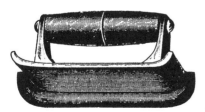

Concave

Cement Edger

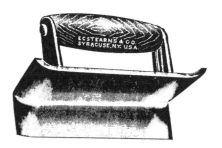

Square

Roller Type

Handled

Cement Edger

CEMENT TOOL, FLOAT. A tool with a flat bottom used for the final smoothing action of a concrete surface.

Cement Float

CEMENT TOOL, GUTTER. Also called CURB-GUTTER TOOL and ROUND CORNER TROWEL. A tool used to smooth a concave surface.

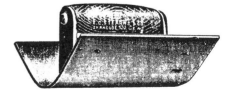

Gutter Tool

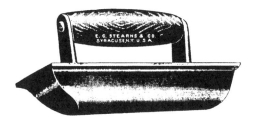

Gutter Tool

CEMENT TOOL, INDENTATION ROLLER. See *Cement Tool, Roller*.

CEMENT TOOL, INSIDE. Also called CORNER TOOL, CORNER TROWEL, CORNERING TOOL and INSIDE SQUARE ANGLE TOOL. A cement tool used to smooth a square inside corner. Available with either a square point or with a small radii.

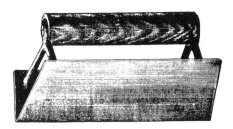

Inside Tool

CEMENT TOOL, JOINTER. Also called CENTER KNIFE, GROOVER, SIDEWALK CREASER and SIDEWALK GROOVER. A tool used to smooth the joint between two concrete surfaces. Available in bronze or iron.

Roller Type

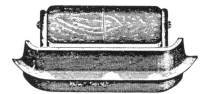

Cement Jointer

Half Jointer

Sidewalk

V Type

Cement Jointer

CEMENT TOOL, OUTSIDE. Also called ANGLE TOOL, OUTSIDE SQUARE ANGLE TOOL, SQUARE EDGER and STEP FINISHING TOOL. A cement tool used to smooth an outside 90 degree angle such as a step or rail. Useful for applying a surface finish and for patching either new or old work.

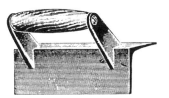

Outside Tool

CEMENT TOOL, ROLLER. Also called INDENTATION ROLLER and SIDEWALK ROLLER. A roller used to provide a non-slip surface to a sidewalk or similar concrete area. Size is 6 to 12 inches long. Available in bronze or iron.

CEMENT TOOL, ROUNDING. Also called BORDER TOOL. A specific variety of edger that forms a curved drop.

CEMENT TOOL, SIDEWALK GROOVER. See *Cement Tool, Jointer*.

CEMENT TOOL, STEP. A tool used to finish the outside edge of an overhanging step. Available in bronze or iron.

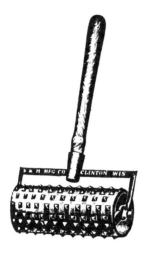

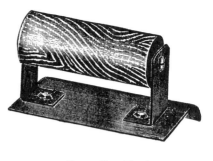

Rounding Tool

Dot Roller

Step or Step Nosing Tool

CEMENT WORKERS' TOOLS. The special-purpose cement tools listed below can be found in normal alphabetical sequence. These tools may also have been used for other purposes.

CEMENT TOOL, CORRUGATING
CEMENT TOOL, CURBING
CEMENT TOOL, DRIVEWAY GROOVER
CEMENT TOOL, EDGER
CEMENT TOOL, FLOAT
CEMENT TOOL, GUTTER
CEMENT TOOL, INSIDE
CEMENT TOOL, JOINTER
CEMENT TOOL, OUTSIDE
CEMENT TOOL, ROLLER
CEMENT TOOL, ROUNDING
CEMENT TOOL, STEP
CHISEL, CONCRETE
CLAMP, DOG
HOE, MORTAR
TAMPER
TROWEL, CEMENT

Driveway Roller

CENTER BEAD MOULDING PLANE. See *Plane, Moulding, Center Bead.*

CENTER BIT. See *Boring Tool, Bit, Center.*

CENTER FINDER. A device used to accurately locate the center of a round, square, oval or rectangular workpiece. The illustrated tool was patented July 3, 1906.

CENTER GAUGE. A tool used to measure the number of threads per inch on taps and screws. A chart on one side shows the proper size of tap drill to be used for a given size screw.

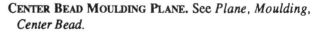

Line Roller

Cement Roller

118

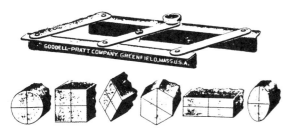

Center Finder

Center Gauge

CENTER KEY. See *Drill Drift*.

CENTER KNIFE. See *Cement Tool, Jointer*.

CENTER PUNCH. See *Anvil Tool, Center Punch* and *Punch, Center*.

CENTER SQUARE. See *Square, Center*.

CENTERING PUNCH. See *Punch, Bell Centering*.

CENTERING TOOL. See *Punch, Bell Centering*.

CENTRE. See *Center*. Centre is a variation in spelling.

CHAIN DETACHER. A holding fixture used for detaching the links on all sizes of square-link farm machinery chain.

Chain Detacher

CHAIN DRILL. See *Boring Tool, Chain Drill*.

CHAIN DRILLING ATTACHMENT. See *Boring Tool, Chain Drill*.

CHAIN HOOK. See *Hook, Chain*.

CHAIN NOSE PLIERS. See *Pliers, Chain*.

CHAIN PIPE WRENCH. See *Wrench, Chain Pipe*.

CHAIN PLIERS. See *Pliers, Chain*.

CHAIN PUNCH. See *Punch, Chain*.

CHAIN SAW. See *Saw, Chain*.

CHAIN TONGS. See *Tongs, Chain* and *Wrench, Chain Pipe*.

CHAIN VISE. A type of post vise. See *Vise, Chain*.

CHAIR BIT. See *Boring Tool, Bit, Chair*.

CHAIR MAKERS' ADZE. See *Adze, Bowl*.

CHAIR MAKERS' BIT BRACE. See *Boring Tool, Bit Brace, Chair Makers'*.

CHAIR MAKERS' SPOKE SHAVE. See *Spoke Shave, Chair Makers'*.

CHAIR SEAT SHAVE. See *Spoke Shave, Chair Makers'*.

CHALK. See *Crayon, Chalk*.

CHALK LINE. Also called MASONS' LINE. A string used to mark a straight line between two points several feet apart. With chalk applied to a line, the line is stretched between the points and snapped against the surface to be marked. Chalk is thereby transferred leaving a temporary mark. Often used for marking a coarse when laying shingles. Cotton, sea grass and linen chalk lines were available in various sizes and lengths. The illustrated container was advertised as a self-chalking line. It contained 50 yards of line and a quantity of powdered chalk.

Chalk Line

CHALK LINE REEL. A spindle-type device used for storage and rapid unwinding of a chalk line. These devices are generally home made in a wide variety of sizes and shapes.

Chalk Line Reel

CHALK LINE SPOOL. Also called CHALK LINE REEL. A wooden spool, about 3 1/2 inches long, used for storing chalk line. Usually made of durable wood such as apple, beech, laurel or boxwood. Some spools have a hole through the center for insertion of a scratch awl. The awl could be pressed into a wood surface to hold the chalk line in position for use. Spools were available with and without the awl and the line.

Chalk Line Spool

CHAMFER FROG. A device used to center a beer keg chamfer knife for repetitive work on containers of identical size.

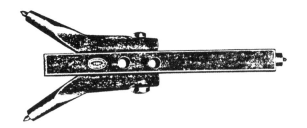

Chamfer Frog

CHAMFER GAUGE. See *Drawing Knife Chamfer Guides.*

CHAMFER GUIDES. See *Drawing Knife Chamfer Guides.*

CHAMFER KNIFE. See *Knife, Chamfer.*

CHAMFER PLANE. See *Plane, Chamfer.*

CHAMFER SHAVE. See *Spoke Shave, Chamfer.*

CHAMFER TOOL. See *Cornering Tool* and *Leather Tool, Chamfer.*

CHAMFERER. See *Drawing Knife Chamfer Guides.*

CHAMFERING SHAVE. See *Spoke Shave, Chamfer.*

CHAMPAGNE NIPPERS. See *Nippers, Champagne.*

CHAMPAGNE PLIERS. See *Pliers, Bottlers'.*

CHAMPER KNIFE. See *Knife, Chamfer.* Champer is a variation in spelling.

CHAMPFERING KNIFE. See *Knife, Chamfer.* Champfering a variation in spelling.

CHANNEL CHISEL. See *Chisel, Channel.*

CHANNEL CUTTER. See *Shoe Makers' Tool, Channel Cutter.*

CHANNEL GOUGE. See *Shoe Makers' Tool, Channel Gouge.*

CHANNEL OPENER. See *Shoe Makers' Tool, Channel Opener.*

CHANNEL SWAGE. See *Anvil Tool, Channel Swage.*

CHANNELER. See *Leather Tool, Channeler.*

CHARIOT PLANE. See *Plane, Chariot.*

CHASER. See *Chisel, Electrotype Trimmer.*

CHASING HAMMER. See *Hammer, Chasing.*

CHASING TOOL. Also called **CHASING PUNCH.** A tool used to imprint thin metal. Used primarily for background work on bronze and copper. This tool is also suitable for use on leather. See also *Screw Chaser.*

Chasing Tool

CHECK NUT WRENCH. See *Wrench, Check Nut.*

CHECKERING FILE. See *File, Chequering.*

CHECKERING TOOL. See *File, Chequering* and *Gun Stock Tool.*

CHECKING CHISEL. See *Chisel, Checking.*

CHECKING TOOL. See *Leather Tool, Checking.*

CHEESE KNIFE. See *Knife, Butter* and *Knife, Cheese.*

CHEESE SAMPLER. See *Sampler, Cheese.*

CHEESE TRIER. See *Sampler, Cheese.*

CHEQUERING FILE. See *File, Chequering.*

CHEST. See *Tool Chest.*

CHICKEN HOUSE SCRAPER. See *Scraper, Chicken House.*

CHICKEN PUNCH. See *Punch, Poultry.*

CHICKEN STICKING KNIFE. See *Knife, Poultry Killing.*

CHIME MAUL. See *Maul, Chime.*

CHINA MARKING BRUSH. See *Brush, Marking.*

CHINCING IRON. Also called **COOPERS' CAULKING IRON** and **COOPERS' CAULKING TOOL.** A tool used to insert flag or reed into the joints of a wooden barrel to prevent the barrel from leaking. Length is approximately 4 1/2 inches.

Chincing Iron

CHIP CARVING KNIFE. See *Knife, Carvers'.*

CHIP NAILING CHISEL. See *Chisel, Chip Nailing.*

CHIPPING CHISEL. See *Brick Cleaner; Chisel, Chipping* and *Chisel, Cold.*

CHIPPING HAMMER. See *Hammer, Chipping.*

CHIPPING KNIFE. See *Knife, Chipping.*

CHIPPING TOOL. See *Glass Chipping Tool.*

CHISEL. A hand tool with a straight cutting edge at the end of a blade; used to cut, pare or separate solid material such as metal or wood. Used by striking or by applying pressure to the end of the tool.

CHISEL, ASPARAGUS. A chisel-shaped tool used to cut asparagus. Asparagus is cut slightly below the surface of the ground.

Asparagus Chisel

CHISEL, BAR. See *Chisel, Ice.*

CHISEL, BENT. Also called CRANKED CHISEL and OFFSET CHISEL. A chisel having the handle offset in the direction of the beveled edge. The offset allows hand clearance with the chisel blade flat on the workpiece. Bent chisels are often considered to be pattern makers' tools.

Bent Chisel

CHISEL, BENT GROOVING. A metal-cutting tool used to cut an oil groove in a bearing.

Bent Grooving Chisel

CHISEL, BEVELED. A wood chisel with the blade beveled the entire length of each side. A wide bevel makes the chisel easier to sharpen and somewhat lighter than the flat variety. See illustration under *Chisel, Butt.*

CHISEL, BLIND SLAT. A hollow chisel used to cut the mortises in a blind stile for insertion of the slats.

Blind Slat Chisel

CHISEL, BOASTING. See *Stone Cutters' Tool, Chisel.*

CHISEL, BONE. A medical tool used in bone surgery. Length is 7 to 8 1/2 inches. Usually made of stainless steel or heavily plated. See also *Chisel, Guarded.*

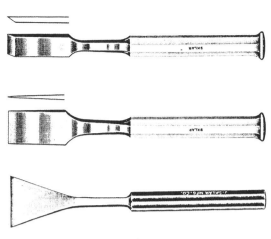

Bone Chisel

CHISEL, BOX. Also called BOX OPENER and CRATE OPENER. A prying tool with a chisel-like edge used for opening wooden boxes. Available in a variety of types from 6 to 18 inches long. See also *Box Opener.*

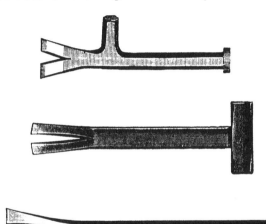

Box Chisel

CHISEL, BRICK. Also called BRICK CUTTER and BRICK LAYERS' CHISEL. A chisel used to cut and trim brick. Cutting width is 2 1/2 to 5 inches. The brick chisel is available with either one or both sides beveled. Some suppliers indicated that a BRICK SET is beveled on one side only and a BRICK CHISEL is beveled on both sides.

Set

Brick Chisel

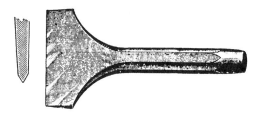

Chisel

Brick Chisel

CHISEL, BRIDGE BUILDERS'. See *Chisel, Track.*

CHISEL, BUNG. A narrow chisel used to pry the bung from a barrel.

Bung Chisel

CHISEL, BUSH. Also called GRANITE BUSH CHISEL. A stone cutters' chisel having several replaceable cutting edges. Size is 1/4 to 11/16 inches thick.

Bush Chisel

CHISEL, BUTT. Also called POCKET CHISEL. A short wood chisel suitable for installing butts and for other close work. Blade length is 2 1/2 to 3 1/2 inches. Butt chisels were available from 1/8 to 2 inches wide and with beveled or plain blades. Both tang and socket handles were available. The socket butt is generally longer than the tang variety.

Tang Type

Socket Type

Butt Chisel

CHISEL, BUTTON HOLE. A chisel, with a cutting edge of 3/8 to 1 inch, used to cut the slit for making a button hole. See also *Button Hole Cutter.*

CHISEL, CABINET MAKERS'. See *Chisel, Firmer.*

CHISEL, CAULKING. See *Caulking Tool, Plumber.*

Button Hole Chisel

CHISEL, CAPE. Also called CAPEN CHISEL. A metal-cutting chisel having a long tapered shank. Width of the cutting edge is 1/8 to 1 inch. Useful for cutting a keyway or for clipping off a rivet head.

Cape Chisel

CHISEL, CAPEN. See *Chisel, Cape.*

CHISEL, CARVING. See *Carving Tool, Chisel.*

CHISEL, CHANNEL. A tool used to remove pieces of glass and fabric from a channel-shaped frame. Used by a glazier when replacing a broken glass.

Channel Chisel

CHISEL, CHEEKING. A skewed chisel said to have been used for cutting the inside edges of the mouth of a bench plane. Right and left hand varieties are illustrated. This shape of tool was probably obtained by reworking a common firmer chisel.

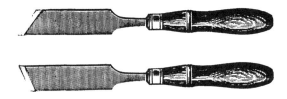

Cheeking Chisel

CHISEL, CHIP NAILING. Also called BLIND NAIL TOOL. A curved 1/4 inch wood chisel used to raise a chip for the purpose of concealing a nail. The chip is glued down on top of the nail thus hiding the nail head from view. See also *Plane, Chisel Gauge.*

Chip Nailing Chisel

CHISEL, CHIPPING. A tool used for removing scale or residue from a rough casting and for similar tasks. The cutting edge is slightly concave. Length is 5 to 8 inches. See also *Brick Cleaner* and *Chisel, Cold.*

Chipping Chisel

CHISEL, CLAPBOARD. A wide all-metal chisel used for splitting out clapboards.

Clapboard Chisel

CHISEL, COACH MAKERS. A variety of firmer chisel. See *Chisel, Firmer.*

CHISEL, COLD. Also called HAND COLD CHISEL. A chisel with a blunt cutting edge shaped and tempered for cutting cold metal. Width of cut is 3/16 to 1 1/4 inches. The cutting edge is beveled to a total angle of about 65 degrees. See also *Anvil Tool, Cold Cutter; Chisel, Rivet Buster* and *Chisel, Track.*

Cold Chisel

CHISEL, CONCRETE. A chisel intended for use in breaking old concrete and for trimming new work. Length is 12 to 18 inches.

Concrete Chisel

CHISEL, CORNER. Also called BUR CHISEL. A chisel with two cutting edges set at right angles to each other. This tool is useful for cleaning out the corners of a mortise. Width of cut is 1/2 to 1 1/2 inches on each side.

Corner Chisel

CHISEL, CRANKED. See *Chisel, Bent.*

CHISEL, DECK. Also called SHIP CARPENTERS' CHISEL. A heavy-duty chisel with the handle slightly offset to allow the tool to be used for paring and smoothing a large surface. Width of the cutting edge is 1 to 4 inches.

Deck Chisel

CHISEL, DIAMOND NOSE. See *Chisel, Diamond Point.*

CHISEL, DIAMOND POINT. Also called DIAMOND NOSE CHISEL. A metal-cutting chisel used to cut a V shaped oil groove in a bearing and for similar tasks. The point is sharpened to the shape of a diamond. Width across the points is 1/8 to 7/8 inches.

Diamond Point Chisel

CHISEL, DRAWER LOCK. A chisel with the cutting edge offset 90 degrees to the handle. Used to cut the mortise for installing a lock in furniture.

Drawer Lock Chisel

CHISEL, ELECTROTYPE FINISHERS'. A tool used to make the final corrections and cleanup of the plate. Made in several sizes to match the sizes of type.

Electrotype Finishers' Chisel

CHISEL, ELECTROTYPE TRIMMER. Also called CHASER and HAND TRIMMER. A chisel used to shave high spots in electrotype half tones and zincs. Width is 1/2 to 5/8 inches.

Electrotype Trimming Chisel

CHISEL, FILE CUTTERS'. Also called FILE MAKERS' CHISEL. A chisel used for cutting a file by hand. Several sizes were available for making files of different widths and degrees of coarseness. The chisel selected for cutting each file was slightly wider than the file blank being worked. The chisel was moved along the file blank primarily by feel and was struck once with a special hammer at each position. It was held 2 to 15 degrees from the vertical away from the user. A small file with fine teeth required the least slope. The blank was smoothed and greased prior to cutting to facilitate movement of the chisel.

File Cutters' Chisel

CHISEL, FILE MAKERS'. See *Chisel, File Cutters'*.

CHISEL, FIRMER. A medium-duty wood chisel such as might be used in a cabinet shop. Width is 1/16 to 3 inches. The length of a one inch standard type firmer chisel is 5 1/2 to 6 1/2 inches. Firmer chisels were available with either tang or socket type handles and with beveled or plain blades. The socket type is somewhat heavier and longer than the tang variety. The regular or standard type firmer was called CABINET MAKERS' CHISEL and CABINET MAKERS' FIRMER CHISEL by some suppliers. COACH MAKERS' FIRMER CHISELS were offered by some dealers in either tang or socket configuration. They are essentially the same as the regular firmer chisel except for a slight increase in length and weight. MILLWRIGHTS' FIRMERS were offered in lengths of 8 to 10 inches.

Socket Type

Tang Type

Firmer Chisel

Coach Makers'

Millwrights'

Firmer Chisel

CHISEL, FLOOR. A thin metal chisel used to trim flooring boards. Length is 12 to 24 inches and cutting width is 1 to 2 1/2 inches.

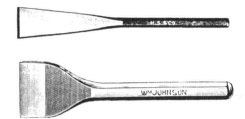

Floor Chisel

CHISEL, FRAMING. Also called SOCKET FRAMING CHISEL. A heavy-duty socket chisel suitable for use by a framing carpenter. An iron ring on the handle allows use of a heavy mallet for making deep cuts. Width of blade is 1/4 to 3 inches. The standard framing chisel blade is 7 to 8 inches long. Lengths up to 10 inches were listed for MILLWRIGHTS FRAMING CHISELS.

Standard

Millwrights'

Framing Chisel

CHISEL, GASKET. See *Caulking Tool, Plumbers*.

CHISEL, GLAZIERS'. A short chisel intended for cleaning old putty from window sashes. Width is 1 1/2 to 2 inches.

Glaziers' Chisel

Glaziers' Chisel

CHISEL, GRANITE. See *Stone Cutters' Tool, Chisel.*

CHISEL, GUARDED. A chisel listed by a supplier of surgical tools as a post-mortem tool. Length is 11 inches. The illustrated tool is made of stainless steel.

Guarded Chisel

CHISEL, HALF ROUND NOSE. Also called HALF ROUND GOUGE. A chisel capable of grooving soft metal. Used for such tasks as gouging out an oil groove in a bronze bearing. Width is 1/8 to 7/8 inches.

Half Round Nose Chisel

CHISEL, HOT. See *Anvil Tool, Hot Cutter.*

CHISEL, ICE. Also called BAR CHISEL, ICE PACKING CHISEL, ICE SPLITTING CHISEL, SEPARATING CHISEL, SIDEWALK SOCKET CHISEL and SPLITTING CHISEL. A wide chisel, of light design, used primarily in the ice industry for breaking out blocks of ice and for trimming the blocks during the storage process. Also used for breaking blocks of ice loose from the floor and for straightening and spacing the blocks for storage. Also listed as being suitable for scraping ice from steps and sidewalks. One variety of ice chisel has a socket and was used with a 3 1/2 foot wooden handle. Another type has an integral iron handle and was available with handles up to 6 feet long. Blade width is 2 1/2 to 5 inches.

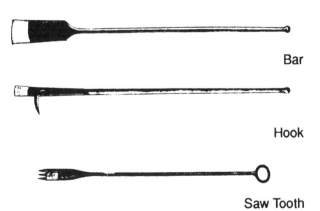

Bar

Hook

Saw Tooth

Ice Chisel

Splitting

Ice Chisel

CHISEL, KEY LIFTING. A tool used for removing a half-moon key. Length is 6 to 6 1/2 inches.

Key Lifting Chisel

CHISEL, KEY SEATING. Also called KEYWAY SEATING CHISEL. A metal-cutting chisel used to deepen or clean out a keyway slot. Width of cut is 1/4 to 3/4 inches.

Key Seating Chisel

CHISEL, KEYWAY SEATING. See *Chisel, Key Seating.*

CHISEL, LANTERN. A tinners' tool used for cutting holes in circular work. Sizes listed are 1/4 to 2 inches wide and 4 1/2 to 5 1/2 inches long.

Lantern Chisel

CHISEL, LATHE. See *Turning Tool, Chisel.*

CHISEL, LOCK MORTISING. Also called LOCK MORTISING TOOL. A bent chisel especially adapted for cleaning out a lock mortise.

Lock Mortising Chisel

CHISEL, MARBLE. See *Stone Cutters' Tool, Chisel.*

CHISEL, MILLWRIGHTS. A wood chisel with an extra long blade. See *Chisel, Firmer* and *Chisel, Framing.*

CHISEL, MORTISING. A narrow chisel with a thick blade used for cutting a deep mortise. The heavy blade allows the chisel to be used as a lever against the side of the mortise. Both socket and tang type handles were available. Width is 1/16 to 3/4 inches.

Mortising Chisel

CHISEL, NOTCHING. A thin wedge-shaped chisel without a distinct bevel on either side. Intended for use by a stair builder. Width is 1 to 2 inches.

Notching Chisel

CHISEL, OFFSET. An offset metal chisel used by an electrician or plumber for cutting and prying adjacent to a wall. Especially recommended for removing baseboards and mouldings. Length is approximately 11 inches. See also *Chisel, Bent.*

Offset Chisel

CHISEL, PACKING. See *Caulking Tool, Plumbers'* and *Chisel, Ice.*

CHISEL, PARING. A chisel with a long blade used for paring and final fitting of the workpiece. This tool is often listed as a LONG THIN PARING CHISEL. Blade length is 8 to 8 1/2 inches. Both tang and socket handles were listed; however, the paring chisel normally has a tang handle and is used by pushing rather than with a mallet. Paring chisels are generally considered to be pattern makers' tools. See also *Chisel, Bent.*

Paring Chisel

CHISEL, PAVEMENT. See *Chisel, Wall Joint.*

CHISEL, PIANO MAKERS'. A piano repairmans' tool listed as a shimming, scraping and burning chisel. Width of the illustrated tool is one inch.

Piano Makers' Chisel

CHISEL, PITCHING. See *Stone Cutters' Tool, Pitching.*

CHISEL, PLOW. A trimming tool that cuts with a shoulder rather than with a sharp edge. Length is approximately 8 inches.

Plow Chisel

CHISEL, PLUGGING. A tool used to clean mortar from brick joints and to remove a brick from a wall. Width of the cutting edge is 1/8 to 1 inch.

Plugging Chisel

CHISEL, PLUMBERS'. Also called HAMMER HEAD CHISEL, METAL WOOD CHISEL, STEEL WOOD CHISEL and WOOD CHISEL. An all-metal wood chisel intended for use by a plumber or for other rough tasks. Width is 1/2 to 2 inches. Overall length is 10 to 14 inches.

Plumbers' Chisel

CHISEL, POCKET. A short general-purpose chisel that is the same length or slightly longer than a butt chisel. Width is 1/8 to 2 inches. Length of blade is approximately 4 1/2 inches. See also *Chisel, Butt.*

Pocket Chisel

CHISEL, RAILROAD TRACK. See *Chisel, Track.*

CHISEL, RIPPING. Also called WRECKING CHISEL. An all-metal chisel tempered to cut metal or wood. Used by a plumber or electrician for cutting and prying. Width is 1/2 to 2 inches and overall length is 11 to 18 inches.

CHISEL, RIVET BUSTER. Also called SIDE CHISEL. A variety of cold chisel used to cut the heads from rivets. Length is 9 to 12 inches.

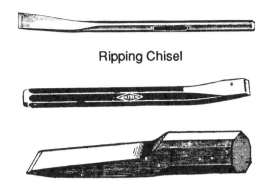

Ripping Chisel

Rivet Buster

CHISEL, ROUND NOSE. A tool used for cutting an oil groove in a bearing and for similar tasks. Diameter of the cutting edge is 1/8 to 7/8 inches.

Round Nose Chisel

CHISEL, SEPARATING. See *Chisel, Ice*.

CHISEL, SHANK. See *Chisel, Tang*.

CHISEL, SHIP CARPENTERS'. See *Chisel, Deck* and *Chisel, Slice*.

CHISEL, SIDE. See *Anvil Tool, Side Chisel* and *Chisel, Rivet Buster*.

CHISEL, SLICE. A Bent Chisel listed with ship builders' tools. Width was not stated. This may be the same tool listed as a Deck Chisel listed in later catalogues.

Slice Chisel

CHISEL, SOCKET. A chisel in which the handle fits into a conic cavity formed as part of the chisel blade. A socket-type chisel is considerably more rugged than the tang type and is therefore adapted to heavy tasks. See illustration under *Chisel, Firmer*.

CHISEL, SOCKET BUTT. A butt chisel with a socket type handle. See *Chisel, Butt*.

CHISEL, SOCKET FIRMER. A firmer chisel with a socket type handle. See *Chisel, Firmer*.

CHISEL, SOCKET FRAMING. See *Chisel, Framing*.

CHISEL, SPLITTING. See *Anvil Tool, Hot Cutter; Chisel, Ice; Stone Cutters' Tool, Splitter* and *Stone Cutters' Tool, Splitting Chisel*.

CHISEL, STARTING. See *Bar, Ice*.

CHISEL, STONE. See *Stone Cutters' Tool, Chisel*.

CHISEL, TANG. A chisel in which the handle is retained by being fitted over a tapered spike. Some suppliers referred to the tang as a shank. See illustration under *Chisel, Firmer*. Unlike the turning tool, the tang chisel has a bolster to serve as stop for the handle.

CHISEL, TANGED BUTT. A butt chisel with a tang-type handle. See *Chisel, Butt*.

CHISEL, THONGING. See *Punch, Lace*.

CHISEL, TOOTH. See *Stone Cutters' Tool, Tooth Chisel*.

CHISEL, TRACK. Also called BRIDGE BUILDERS' CHISEL and RAILROAD TRACK CHISEL. This tool is a large cold cutter, weighing 4 to 6 pounds, used in railroad construction and repair. Both straight and cross peen types were available. See also *Anvil Tool, Cold Cutter*.

Track Chisel

CHISEL, TURNING. See *Turning Tool, Chisel*.

CHISEL, WALL JOINT. Also called PAVEMENT CHISEL. A tool used by a stone paver to position a block. Length is 11 to 15 inches and width is 1/4 to 1/2 inches at the point.

Wall Joint Chisel

CHISEL, WIRE. A tinsmiths' tool used for cutting and crimping wire. Width is 1/4 to 2 inches and length is approximately 4 1/2 inches.

Wire Chisel

CHISEL, WOOD. The term "Wood Chisel" is used in a general sense to mean any of the several types of chisels intended for cutting wood. See also *Chisel, Plumbers'*.

CHISEL, WRECKING. See *Chisel, Ripping*.

CHISEL, YARNING. See *Caulking Tool, Plumbers'*.

CHISEL ATTACHMENT. Also called BUTT CHISEL ATTACHMENT. A gadget that is supposed to facilitate cutting the recess for a butt hinge. The device consists of an attachment clamp, which serves as a stop, and a spur cutter. The illustrated tool was patented in 1907. It is shown attached to a firmer chisel.

Chisel Attachment

CHISEL AXE. See *Axe, Mortising Chisel.*

CHISEL BIT AUGER. See *Boring Tool, Earth Auger.*

CHISEL GAUGE. See *Plane, Chisel Gauge.*

CHISEL GRINDER. Also called GRINDING HOLDER. A device used to hold a chisel or plane iron at a fixed angle while grinding or honing. The angle is adjustable.

Chisel Grinder

CHISEL HANDLE. A handle for a wood chisel. A leather tipped handle is generally used when the chisel is intended to be used with a mallet. A handle with a metal ring is installed for heavy-duty applications. Inasmuch as chisel handles were easily damaged and required frequent replacement, they were stock items in every hardware store.

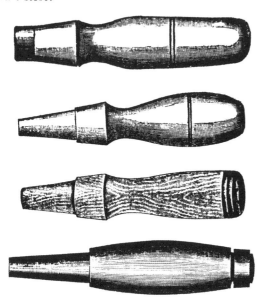

Chisel Handle

CHISEL HOLDER. Also called COLD CHISEL HOLDER. A device used to hold a chisel in the upright position thus leaving both hands free to manipulate the workpiece and the hammer. Intended to be clamped in a vise for use.

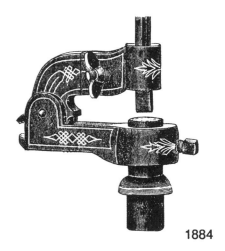

1884

Chisel Holder

CHISEL MALLET. See *Mallet, Chisel.*

CHISEL PEEN HAMMER. See *Hammer, Belt.*

CHISEL POINT FILE. See *File, Tooth Pointing.*

CHOPPING AXE. See *Axe, Chopping.*

CHUCK. See *Boring Tool, Brace Chuck* and *Clamp, Watch Case.*

CHUTE BOARD. See Plane, Shoot Board. Chute is a variation in spelling.

CIDER MILL. Also called CIDER PRESS. A mill used to grind and press apples to extract the juice for making cider. The illustrated mill was advertised as having a capacity of 3 to 6 barrels per day.

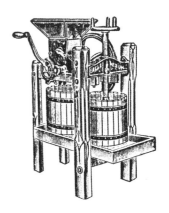

Cider Mill

CIDER PRESS. See *Cider Mill.*

CIGAR BOX HAMMER. See *Hammer, Brad.*

CIGAR BOX OPENER. A tool used in a cigar store for opening a cigar box and removing the nail. Openers were made in a multitude of patterns and were often used as give-a-way advertising items. Some examples are illustrated.

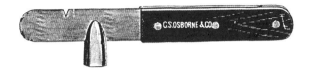

Cigar Box Opener

CIGAR KNIFE. See *Knife, Cigar Makers'*.

CIGAR LIGHTER PLANE. See *Plane, Spill*.

CIGAR MAKERS' KNIFE. See *Knife, Cigar Makers'*.

CIRCLE CUTTER. See *Washer Cutter*.

CIRCLE EDGER. See *Cement Tool, Edger*.

CIRCLE FACE PLANE. See *Plane, Carriage Makers'* and *Plane, Circular*.

CIRCULAR CLAW HAMMER. See *Hammer, Circular Claw*.

CIRCULAR LEVEL. See *Level, Circular*.

CIRCULAR PLANE. See *Plane, Carriage Makers'* and *Plane, Circular*.

CIRCULAR SAW. See *Saw, Foot and Hand Powered*.

CIRCULAR SAW VISE. See *Vise, Circular Saw*.

CIRCULAR SHEARS. See *Tinsmiths' Machine, Circular Shears*.

CIRCULAR SPOKE SHAVE. See *Spoke Shave, Circular*.

CIRCUMFERENCE RULE. See *Rule, Circumference*.

CIRCUS BEETLE. See *Beetle*.

CIRCUS MAUL. See *Beetle*.

CLAM HOOK. See *Hook, Clam*.

CLAM KNIFE. See *Knife, Clam*.

CLAMMING MARKER. See *Shoe Makers' Tool, Clamming Marker*.

CLAMP. A device used to temporarily hold or press two or more work pieces together. See also *Drill Block; Leather Tool, Strap Holder and Tire Clamp*.

CLAMP, BAND SAW. See *Vise, Band Saw Brazing*.

CLAMP, BAR. Also called CARPENTERS' CLAMP, DOOR CLAMP, FURNITURE CLAMP and JOINERS' CLAMP. A long clamp with one jaw fastened to the end of a bar and the other jaw adjustable in increments along the length of the bar. Several sizes were available with openings up to 10 feet.

Steel Bar

Wooden Bar

Bar Clamp

CLAMP, BELT. A clamp used to hold the ends of a flat belt in position for lacing. Several sizes were available for use with belts up to 36 inches wide.

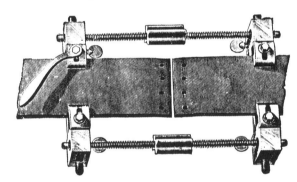

Belt Clamp

CLAMP, BENCH. Also called BENCH DOG, CARVERS' CLAMP, HOLD-DOWN and HOLDFAST. A clamp used to hold a workpiece stationary to the top of the bench.

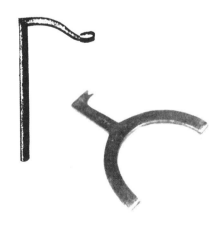

Bench Clamp

Bench Clamp

CLAMP, BOAT. See *Clamp, Carriage Makers'*.

CLAMP, BODY. See *Clamp, C*.

CLAMP, BOILER. See *Clamp, C*.

CLAMP, BRAZING. See *Vise, Band Saw Brazing*.

CLAMP, BRICK. A clamp used to handle bricks. The illustrated clamp can be adjusted to grasp from 4 to 12 bricks.

Brick Clamp

CLAMP, C. A clamp shaped like the letter C as shown in the illustration. The name is also applied to any of the various clamps shaped to resemble a letter C. See also *Clamp, Carriage Makers'*.

Body Clamp

Bridge Clamp

C Clamp

Boiler or Stem Fitters' Clamp

Deep Throat Clamp

Machinists' Clamp

C Clamp

CLAMP, CABINET. See *Clamp, Cabinet Makers'* and *Clamp, Carriage Makers'*.

CLAMP, CABINET MAKERS'. Also called CABINET CLAMP, DOOR CLAMP, DOOR FRAME CLAMP, GLUE CLAMP and PIANO MAKERS' CLAMP. A clamp similar to the Bar Clamp except lighter in construction and generally shorter. Length is 2 1/2 to 8 feet.

Cabinet Makers' Clamp

CLAMP, CARPET SEWERS'. A clamp used to hold the edges of carpet together for sewing. Overall length of the illustrated clamp is 5 inches.

Carpet Sewers' Clamp

CLAMP, CARRIAGE MAKERS'. Also called BOAT CLAMP, C CLAMP, CABINET CLAMP, CARRIAGE CLAMP and SCREW CLAMP. A C shaped clamp with a 2 to 12 inch opening and generally having a wing nut for tightening. This type of clamp is a general-purpose device used by practically every craftsman.

Carriage Makers' Clamp

CLAMP, CARRIAGE MAKERS' ADJUSTABLE. Also called ADJUSTABLE SCREW CLAMP. A Carriage Makers' Clamp that is adjustable along a ribbed iron bar. Size of opening is 4 to 72 inches.

Carriage Makers' Adjustable Clamp

CLAMP, CARVERS'. See *Clamp, Bench*.

CLAMP, CLOSED END. A variety of Hand Screw Clamp having only one screw. This clamp has a leather strap fastened across one end which serves as a fixed stop in place of a second screw.

Closed End Clamp

CLAMP, CLOTH CUTTERS'. An adjustable clamp used to hold a stack of cloth in alignment. Maximum length of opening is 2 1/4 inches.

Cloth Cutters' Clamp

CLAMP, COLUMN. An adjustable clamp especially adapted to holding staved columns and tanks during assembly.

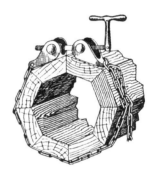

Column Clamp

CLAMP, CORN SHOCK. See *Clamp, Fodder*.

CLAMP, CORNER. A clamp with a bifurcated jaw. Length of the opening is 6 to 9 inches.

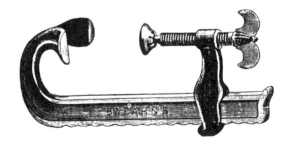

Corner Clamp

CLAMP, DOG. A tool used for clamping concrete forms. Length of opening is 22 to 48 inches.

CLAMP, DOOR. A clamp used to hold a door on edge. See also *Clamp, Bar* and *Clamp, Cabinet Makers'*.

CLAMP, ECCENTRIC. A clamp that is tightened by movement of an eccentric arm. The illustrated clamp is adjustable along an iron bar. Length of opening is 2 to 96 inches.

Dog Clamp

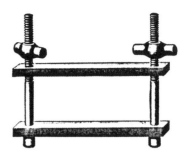

Flask Clamp

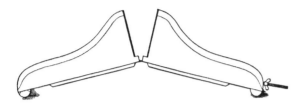

Door Clamp

Eccentric Clamp

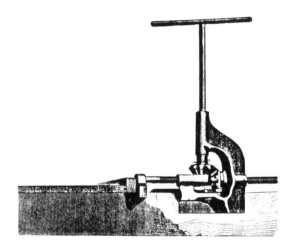

Peoples' Patent

CLAMP, EXTENSION. A clamp that pushes two objects apart rather than compressing. The illustrated tool is home made.

Extension Clamp

CLAMP, FILING. See *Vise, Saw*.

CLAMP, FLASK. A tool used in foundry work for holding sand casting frames in position. See also *Flask*.

CLAMP, FLOORING. A clamp used to press a warped or crooked flooring board into proper alignment for nailing. See also *Floor Jack*.

Flooring Clamp

CLAMP, FODDER. Also called CORN SHOCK CLAMP, FODDER SQUEEZER and ROPE CLAMP. A device used to compress and hold a bundle or shock of fodder for tying. Illustration (b) is a home made corn shock squeezer consisting of two pieces of hardwood mortised together and sharpened on three ends. A length of 1/2 inch rope is attached.

Fodder Clamp

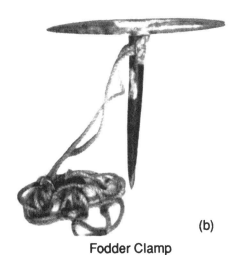

(b)

Fodder Clamp

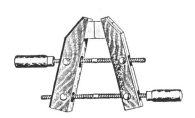

Jorgensen Patent

CLAMP, FURNITURE. See *Clamp, Bar.*

CLAMP, HAND SCREW. A double-screw type clamp used extensively in woodworking and for other general purpose tasks. The later variety has steel nuts inserted loosely in the jaws such that the nut can swivel and allow the clamp to be easily tightened on an angular workpiece. Length of jaws is 4 to 24 inches. See also *Clamp, Wooden.*

Metal

Hand Screw

CLAMP, HANDLE. A device used to clamp an extension to the handle of a ceiling brush or window cleaning tool.

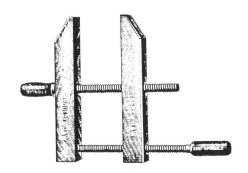

Handle Clamp

CLAMP, HOOK END. See *Clamp, Ship Carpenters'.*

CLAMP, IVORY. A clamp used when repairing the keys of a piano.

Wooden

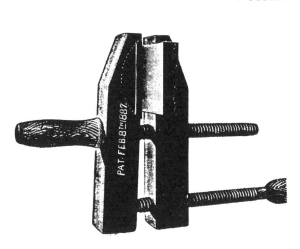

Self Adjusting

Hand Screw

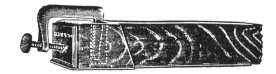

Ivory Clamp

CLAMP, JOINERS'. See *Clamp, Bar.*

133

CLAMP, JOINT. An adjustable two-element clamp used to draw up and hold joints of all kinds.

Joint Clamp

CLAMP, KEY SEAT. Also called KEY SEAT RULE BLOCKS. A pair of small clamps intended for use with a steel rule to form a key seat straight edge. Used for marking parallel lines on a cylindrical shaft.

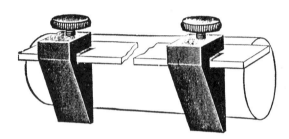

Key Seat Clamp

CLAMP, LEVER. See *Shoe Makers' Tool, Lever Clamp*.

CLAMP, MACHINISTS'. See *Clamp, C* and *Clamp, Parallel*.

CLAMP, MEASURING BAR. A pair of clamps used to make an adjustable measuring rod from two 1 by 1/2 inch wooden bars. Also used to form an extendable trammel point beam.

Measuring Bar Clamp

CLAMP, MITER. A clamp used to hold two corners of a picture frame in alignment for nailing and glueing. The clamp shown in illustration (a) was patented July 11, 1899.

CLAMP, PARALLEL. A rigid clamp with all sides parallel or perpendicular to each other. Intended for use by a machinist. Length of opening is 1 to 6 inches.

(a)

Miter Clamp

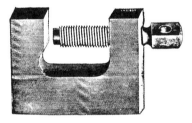

Parallel Clamp

CLAMP, PIPE. Clamp fixtures that will fit on a standard galvanized pipe. Length of opening is governed only by the length of pipe used. Size is adjustable by sliding one of the fixtures along the pipe.

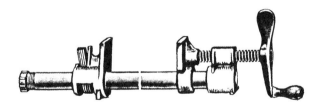

Pipe Clamp

CLAMP, PLANK SCREW. A self-holding clamp used for planking and sealing a ship.

CLAMP, PLOW POINT. A clamp that will hold a plow point to the share for welding.

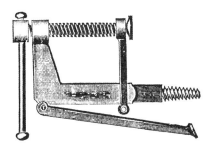

Plank Screw Clamp

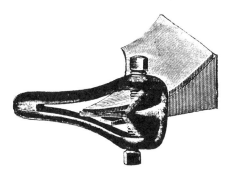

Plow Point Clamp

CLAMP, POOL CUE. A metal clamp used to hold the tip of a pool cue in place while the glue is drying. Overall length is approximately 5 1/4 inches. The illustrated tool was patented July 1, 1884.

Pool Cue Clamp

CLAMP, QUICK. Also called ADJUSTABLE SCREW CLAMP and SELF LOCKING CLAMP. A variation of the Bar Clamp used for boat building, pattern making and general purpose work. Length of opening is 2 1/2 to 96 inches.

Quick Clamp

CLAMP, QUILTING FRAME. Also called QUILT CLAMP and QUILT FRAME CLAMP. An inexpensive C clamp, with a coarse thread, used to hold the corners of a quilting frame. Width of opening is 2 1/2 to 3 inches.

CLAMP, RIM. A wheelwrights' tool used to hold a felloe or rim in place on a spoke while working the adjacent spoke into position. It can also be used to press the felloe

onto the spoke tenon. The loop encircles the hub of the wheel and the handscrew is tightened to bear on the felloe.

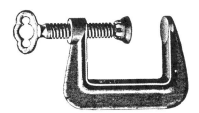

Quilting Frame Clamp

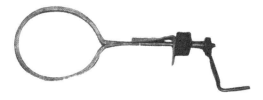

Rim Clamp

CLAMP, RING. Also called RING HOLDER. A jewelers' clamp used for holding a ring.

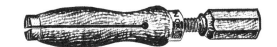

Ring Clamp

CLAMP, RIVETING. A boiler makers' or steel workers' tool used for holding a plate or other member in place while starting the rivet pattern.

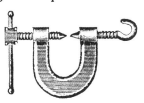

Riveting Clamp

CLAMP, ROPE. Also called RIGGERS' SCREW. A clamp used for holding a rope while the end is being bound or woven. See also *Fodder Clamp*.

Lobster Claw

Rope Clamp

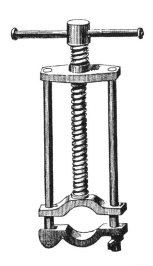

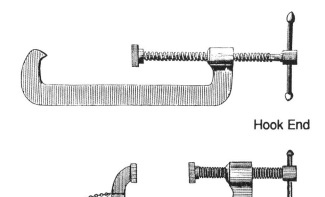

Hook End

Sliding Jaw

For Wire Rigging

Rope Clamp

Ship Carpenters' Clamp

CLAMP, RULE. A device used to clamp two steel rules together to obtain additional length. The illustrated clamp will work with rules of different widths.

CLAMP, SPLICING. See *Splicing Clamp*.

CLAMP, STEAM FITTERS'. See *Clamp, C*.

CLAMP, TEST TUBE. A clamp used in a laboratory to grasp a test tube.

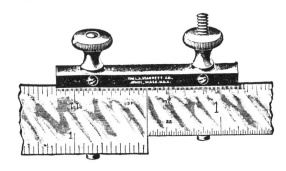

Rule Clamp

Stoddard's Patent

CLAMP, SAW. See *Vise, Saw*.

CLAMP, SCREW. See *Clamp, Carriage Makers'*.

CLAMP, SHACKLE. A clamp used for installing shaft rubbers on a buggy. Hard rubber shims were often used to reduce the clicking noise of the shaft hangers.

Wooden

Test Tube Clamp

CLAMP, TIRE BOLT. See *Tire Bolt Holder*.

CLAMP, TOOL MAKERS'. A steel clamp intended for use in precision machine work. This clamp is rigidly constructed and has extra-fine screw threads. Length of opening is 5/8 to 2 3/8 inches.

Shackle Clamp

CLAMP, SHIP CARPENTERS'. Also called BOAT CLAMP SCREW, HOOK END CLAMP and SHIP CLAMP SCREW. A shallow screw-type clamp with a 6 to 36 inch opening.

Tool Makers' Clamp

CLAMP, TRAP. Also called TRAP SETTER. A clamp used to depress one spring of a steel trap while the other spring is being set. Two clamps are used on large traps.

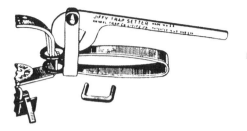

Trap Clamp

CLAMP, TUBING. Also called PINCH COCK. A clamp used in a laboratory to close off a rubber tube.

Day's Patent

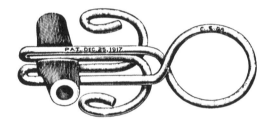

Mohr's Patent

Tubing Clamp

CLAMP, VIOLIN. A clamp used in the assembly of a wooden musical instrument.

Straight

Violin Clamp

Curved

Violin Clamp

CLAMP, WAGON TIRE. A device for holding the ends of a wagon tire together while being hammer welded.

Wagon Tire Clamp

CLAMP, WATCH CASE. Also called CHUCK and WATCH CASE CHUCK. A clamp intended for use by a watch case engraver.

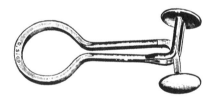

Watch Case Clamp

CLAMP, WOODEN. Essentially a wooden C Clamp. Also called HAND SCREW and WOOD VISE. Size is 4 3/4 to 20 inches.

Wooden Clamp

CLAMP HORSE. Also called TRESTLE CLAMP. A saw horse with an integral cabinet makers' clamp. Used in pairs for assembling a door or edge joining long boards.

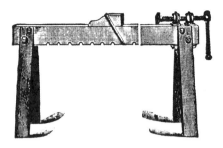

Clamp Horse

CLAMPING HANDLE. A clamp that will grip a steel tape at any point. Used when necessary to apply tension to a tape.

Clamping Handle

CLAMPING TOOL. A device used for clamping or crimping a metal stay to support the side curtains of a carriage. The curtain material is placed over a small rod and a metal strip is crimped around both the rod and the material.

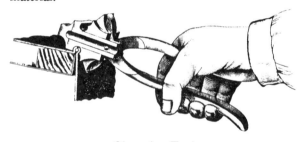

Clamping Tool

CLAPBOARD CHISEL. See *Chisel, Clapboard.*

CLAPBOARD GAUGE. Also called CLAPBOARD HOLDER, CLAPBOARD SLIDING GAUGE and SIDING GAUGE. A device used to obtain a gauged width of board to the weather when installing clapboards or lap siding. Usually used in pairs to position both ends of the board.

Clapboard Gauge

CLAPBOARD GAUGE, WOODEN. A gauge used to keep the courses straight when installing clapboards. One catalogue referred to this tool as a FLOOR GAUGE.

Wooden Clapboard Gauge

CLAPBOARD HOLDER. See *Clapboard Gauge.*

CLAPBOARD MARKER. Also called SIDING MARKER and WEATHER BOARD MARKER. A device used to scribe a cutoff line when installing a clapboard. The marker is placed astride the siding board and against the upright. Movement of the marker will then scribe a line.

Clapboard Marker

CLAPBOARD SLICK. See *Slick, Clapboard.*

CLAPBOARD SLIDING GAUGE. See *Clapboard Gauge.*

CLAW. See *Clamp, Rope; Nail Claw* and *Tack Claw.*

CLAW BAR. See *Bar, Claw.*

CLAW HAMMER. See *Hammer, Nail.*

CLAW HATCHET. See *Hatchet, Claw.*

CLAW JACK. See *Jack, Lifting.*

CLAW TOOL. See *Tack Claw.*

CLAY PICK. See *Pick, Railroad.*

CLEARANCE PUNCH. See *Punch, Pin.*

CLEATER. See *Roofing Cleater and Nailer.*

CLEAVE. Also called CLEAVER. A basket makers' tool used to rive willow basket splits. This tool is usually made of boxwood or horn. Both three and four section cleaves have been noted. A similar tool made of iron, called a *Splitter,* is used by a cooper.

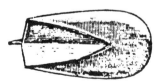

Cleave

CLEAVER. Also called BUTCHERS' CLEAVER, MEAT CLEAVER and SAUSAGE MEAT CHOPPER. A butchers' tool used to chop meat and bone. See also *Cleave* and *Ice Cleaver*.

Cleaver

CLEVIS TONGS. See *Tongs, Band Jaw*.

CLINCH ANVIL. See *Anvil, Clinch*.

CLINCH BLOCK. See *Anvil, Clinch*.

CLINCH TONGS. See *Tongs, Clinch*.

CLINKER HOOK. See *Fire Tools, Furnace*.

CLINKER TONGS. See *Tongs, Clinker*.

CLIP. See *Trimmers' Clip*.

CLIP SWAGE. See *Anvil Tool, Clip Swage*.

CLIPHORN ANVIL. See *Anvil, Farriers'*.

CLIPPER. Also called FETLOCK CLIPPER and HORSE CLIPPER. A tool used for clipping the hair from horses and dogs. See also *Orange Clipper*.

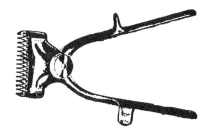

Clipper

CLOCK BRUSH. See *Brush, Clock*.

CLOCK HAND REMOVER. See *Hand Puller*.

CLOCK HOLE CLOSING PUNCH. See *Punch, Hole Closing*.

CLOCK KEY. Also called BENCH CLOCK KEY and CLOCK LET DOWN KEY. A tool with a socket-type end to match a clock spring shaft. The tool is used to let the main spring unwind slowly after the pawl is released. Single and double-end types were available.

Clock Key

CLOCK MAKERS' FILE. See *File, Watch Makers'*.

CLOCK SCREW DRIVER. See *Screw Driver, Clock*.

CLOG MAKERS' AXE. See *Axe, Clog Makers'*.

CLOG MAKERS' TOOLS. Also called SABOT MAKERS' TOOLS and WOODEN SHOE TOOLS. Special-purpose tools used to hollow out the inside of a wooden shoe. The illustrated tools are associated with shoes made entirely of wood rather than the typical English clog having only the sole made of wood. The clog maker used a block knife and a small axe as standard tools for shaping the outside of the shoe.

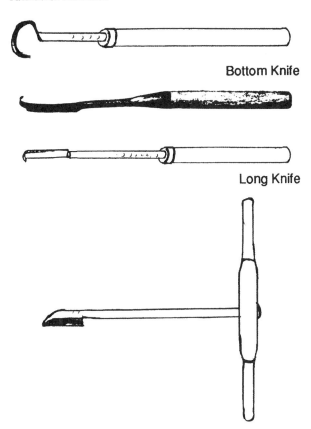

Bottom Knife

Long Knife

Boring Tool, Spoon Auger
or Hollowing Tool

Clog Makers' Tools

CLOTH CUTTERS' CLAMP. See *Clamp, Cloth Cutters'*.

CLOTH CUTTING MACHINE. A device used to cut a roll of cloth or upholstery material.

CLOTH KNIFE. See *Knife, Cloth*.

CLUB. See *Froe Club*.

CLUSTER BEAD PLANE. See *Plane, Moulding, Reeding*.

COACH MAKERS' ROUTER. See *Router, Carriage Makers'*.

COACH MAKERS' SIDE AXE. See *Axe, Bearded*.

COACH MAKERS' SPOKE SHAVE. See *Spoke Shave, Carriage Makers'* and *Spoke Shave, Carriage Makers' Panel*.

Cloth Cutting Machine

COACH MAKERS' TOOLS. Also called CARRIAGE MAKERS' TOOLS. The special-purpose coach makers' tools listed below can be found in normal alphabetical sequence. These tools may also have been used for other purposes.

AXE, BEARDED
BEADING TOOL, CARRIAGE MAKERS'
BORING TOOL, BIT
BORING TOOL, BIT BRACE, SPRING LATCH
BUNG BURNER
CHISEL, FIRMER
CHISEL, MORTISING
CLAMP, CARRIAGE MAKERS'
CLAMP, CARRIAGE MAKERS' ADJUSTABLE
CLAMP, SHACKLE
CLAMP, WOODEN
CLAMPING TOOL
DRAWING KNIFE, CARRIAGE BODY
DRAWING KNIFE, CARRIAGE MAKERS'
DRAWING KNIFE, CARRIAGE ROUTER
GLUE BRUSH
GLUE POT
GOUGE, FIRMER
HAMMER, CARRIAGE IRONERS'
JARVIS
JIGGER, COACH MAKERS'
MALLET, CHISEL
MARKING GAUGE
MORTISING GAUGE
MOULDING TOOL, CARRIAGE MAKERS'
PLANE, CARRIAGE MAKERS'
PLANE, CARRIAGE MAKERS' PLOW
PLANE, PANEL PLOW
PLANE, PANEL PLOW, CARRIAGE MAKERS'
PLANE, PANEL PLOW, CURVED
PLUG CUTTER
RASP, WOOD
ROUTER, CARRIAGE MAKERS'
SAW, HAND
SCRAPER, COACH MAKERS'
SPOKE SHAVE, CARRIAGE MAKERS'
SPOKE SHAVE, CARRIAGE MAKERS' PANEL
SQUARE, TRY
THILL COUPLER
TOOL CHEST, CABINET MAKERS'
VISE, COACH MAKERS'
WASHER CUTTER
WRENCH, BUGGY

COAL AUGER. See *Boring Tool, Coal Auger.*

COAL AXE. See *Axe, Coal Miners'.*

COAL MINERS' BLASTING TOOLS. Tools used for blasting in a mine. The tamper and the needle, as illustrated, are made of pure copper to meet the requirements of mining safety laws pertaining to use of spark producing apparatus adjacent to explosives. The needle penetrates the main charge to assure adequate coupling with the fuse.

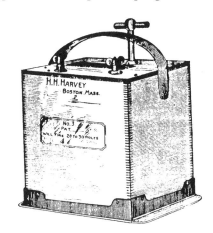

Blasting Battery

Drill

Spoon

Tamping Bar

Coal Miners' Blasting Tools

Needle or Pricker

Coal Miners' Blasting Tools

COAL MINERS' TOOLS. The special-purpose coal mining tools listed below can be found in normal alphabetical sequence. These tools may also have been used for other purposes.

AXE, COAL MINERS'
BORING TOOL, COAL AUGER
BORING TOOL, COAL MINERS'
BORING TOOL, ROOF AUGER
CARBIDE LIGHT
COAL MINERS' BLASTING TOOLS
FORK, COAL
HATCHET, COAL MINERS' TRACK
PICK, COAL
SHOVEL, COAL MINERS'
SHOVEL, SCOOP
SLEDGE, COAL
WEDGE, COAL

COAL TONGS. See *Tongs, Coal*.

COATING BRUSH. See *Brush, Electrotypers'*.

COBBLE RAMMER. See *Rammer, Sand*.

COBBLERS' HAMMER. See *Hammer, Shoe Makers'*.

COBBLERS' TOOLS. See *Shoe Tools*.

COCK BEAD. See *Plane, Moulding, Cock Bead*.

COFFEE MILL. See *Grinding Mill*.

COFFEE SAMPLER. See *Sampler, Grain*.

COFFEE TRIER. See *Sampler, Grain*.

COFFIN SHAPED PLANE. See *Plane, Smooth*.

COIL FILE. See *File, Magneto*.

COKE FORK. See *Fork, Coal*.

COKE SCOOP. See *Shovel, Scoop*.

COKE SHOVEL. A type of scoop shovel. See *Shovel, Scoop*.

COKE TROWEL. See *Trowel, Coke*.

COLD CUTTER. See *Anvil Tool, Cold Cutter*.

COLD CHISEL. See *Anvil Tool, Cold Cutter* and *Chisel, Cold*.

COLD CHISEL HOLDER. See *Chisel Holder*.

COLD SET. See *Anvil Tool, Cold Cutter*.

COLLAR AWL. See *Awl, Collar*.

COLLAR BLOCK. See *Horse Collar Tool, Collar Block*.

COLLAR MEASURE. See *Horse Collar Tool, Measuring Yoke*.

COLLAR PALM. See *Sewing Palm*.

COLLAR ROD. See *Horse Collar Tool, Stuffing Rod*.

COLLAR STUFFER. See *Horse Collar Tool, Stuffing Rod*.

COLLAR SWAGE. See *Anvil Tool, Swage*.

COLLAR TOOL. See *Horse Collar Tool*.

COLLICE. See *Shoe Makers' Tool, Collice*.

COLTED LONG STICK. See *Shoe Makers' Tool, Long Stick*.

COLUMN CLAMP. See *Clamp, Column*.

COMB. See *Card Cleaner, Curry Comb, Mane Comb, Weavers' Comb* and *Wool Comb*.

COMB MAKERS' TOOLS. The special-purpose comb makers' tools listed below can be found in normal alphabetical sequence. These tools may also have been used for other purposes.

BLOCK HEATER
ENGRAVING STAND
GRAILLE
KNIFE, COMB MAKERS'
POLKA MACHINE
QUANNET
SAW, BOTTOMING
SHAVE, COMB MAKERS'
SLASHING MACHINE
STONE SETTER
TONGS, COMB MAKERS'
WELDING PRESS

COMBINATION BRACE. See *Screw Driver Brace*.

COMBINATION DIVIDERS. See *Caliper, Combination*.

COMBINATION TOOL. Any tool that is intended to accomplish more than one type of task.

COMBINATION TOOL, HOUSEHOLD. A multiple-purpose tool listed as a can opener, cork screw, glass cutter, knife sharpener and tack hammer.

Household Combination Tool

COMBINATION TOOL, ODD JOBS. A tool advertised as being suitable for use as a a beam compass, depth gauge, inside compass, marking gauge, mitre level, mitre square, mortise gauge, plumb, scratch awl, spirit level and try square. Odd Jobs is a trademarked name of *Stanley Tools*.

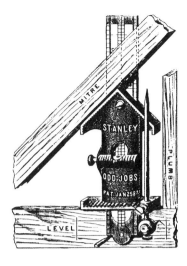

Odd Jobs

COMBINATION TOOLS. The combination tools listed below can be found in normal alphabetical sequence.

ANVIL, COMBINATION
ANVIL, FARRIERS' COMBINATION
BORING TOOL, BIT BRACE, COMBINATION
CALIPER, COMBINATION
COMBINATION TOOL, HOUSEHOLD
COMBINATION TOOL, ODD JOBS
FENCE TOOL, COMBINATION
HAMMER, COMBINATION
HAMMER, TACK
LACE CUTTER, COMBINATION
LEVEL, COMBINATION
PLANE, BEADING
PLANE, COMBINATION
PLANE, MATCH
PLIERS, COMBINATION
PLIERS, SLIP JOINT
RULE, COMBINATION
SAW, COMBINATION
SCREW DRIVER, COMBINATION
SQUARE, COMBINATION
VISE, COMBINATION
WRENCH, AUTO TOOL
WRENCH, COMBINATION
WRENCH, CRANK

COME ALONG. A tool used to grip wire and to provide a convenient hand hold or method of attachment. Used for stringing and stretching all types of wire.

Come Along

COMMANDER. A basket makers' tool used to bend or straighten a basket split. This tool consists of a metal bar with a fork on one end and a narrow loop on the other. It is essentially a small version of the Blacksmiths' Bending Tool. See also *Maul, Basket Makers'*.

Commander

COMMON AUGER BIT. See *Boring Tool, Bit, Irwin Pattern*.

COMPASS. An adjustable device for scribing an arc or circle. Called DIVIDERS by some suppliers. Unlike the dividers, the compass generally does not have a means of precision adjustment. See also *Dip Compass, Dividers* and *Scriber*.

COMPASS, BOW. Also called COOPERS' BOW COMPASS. A compass in which the two legs are made of a single piece of wood.

Bow Compass

COMPASS, CLUB. A common metal compass having one leg formed in the shape of a cone. This configuration allows a circle or arc to be drawn about a hole. See illustration of the cone-type leg under *Dividers, Parallel*.

COMPASS, COOPERS'. A large compass used by a cooper to scribe the barrel head outline onto the workpiece. See illustrations under *Compass, Bow* and *Compass, Wing*.

COMPASS, GENERAL-PURPOSE. A common compass used for metal layout, woodwork and for similar tasks. Length of legs are 3 to 8 inches.

General-Purpose Compass

COMPASS, LEATHER. Also called SADDLERS' COMPASS. A sturdy compass with legs 3 to 12 inches long. Used to scribe an arc or lay out a pattern on leather. One variety of leather compass has a sharpened hook on one leg that will cut a shallow groove in the workpiece.

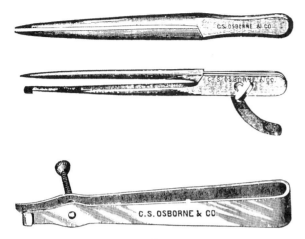

Leather Compass

COMPASS, PENCIL. Also called PENCIL DIVIDERS. A compass with one leg fashioned to hold a common lead pencil. Used for layout of scrollwork patterns and for similar work. Also used as a desk tool for school work.

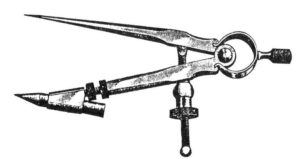

Pencil Compass

COMPASS, SADDLERS'. See *Compass, Leather.*

COMPASS, WING. Also called WINGED DIVIDERS. A compass having a curved guide attached to one leg. The adjustment can be secured with a set screw in the opposite leg. Length of legs are 6 to 12 inches.

Wing Compass

COMPASS PLANE. See *Plane, Carriage Makers'* and *Plane, Circular.*

COMPASS SAW. See *Saw, Compass.*

COMPLEX MOULDING PLANE. See *Plane, Moulding, Complex.*

COMPOSING STICK. A metal tray used by a typesetter to assemble one line or segment of individual type elements.

Composing Stick

CONCHO CUTTER. See *Leather Tool, Concho Cutter.*

CONCRETE BUSH HAMMER. See *Hammer, Bush.*

CONCRETE CHISEL. See *Chisel, Concrete.*

CONCRETE TOOL. See *Cement Workers' Tools.*

CONDUCTOR STAKE. A tinsmiths' tool. See *Stake, Conductors'*

CONDUCTORS' PUNCH. See *Punch, Conductors'.*

CONE. Also called BLACKSMITHS' MANDREL and TAPER MANDREL. A large mandrel used by a blacksmith when forging loops or rings. Sizes from 55 to 450 pounds and 30 to 58 inches tall were available. One type of cone is slotted as shown in the illustration. The slot provides space for grasping the workpiece with tongs and also provides space for the eye when a ring with an eyebolt is being forged. See also *Organ Tuners' Cone.*

Cone

CONICAL RIVET SNAP. See *Anvil Tool, Rivet Set.*

CONNECTICUT HAND ADZE. See *Adze, Hand.*

CONSTRUCTION WRENCH. See *Wrench, Construction.*

CONTOUR MARKER. See *Moulding Former.*

CONTRACTORS' PICK. See *Pick, Contractors'.*

COOPERS' AXE. See *Axe, Broad, Coopers'.*

COOPERS' BEAK HORN. See *Anvil, Coopers'.*

COOPERS' BOW COMPASS. See *Compass, Bow.*

COOPERS' CAULKING IRON. See *Chincing Iron*.

COOPERS' CAULKING TOOL. See *Chincing Iron*.

COOPERS' DRIVER. See *Hoop Driver*.

COOPERS' HATCHET. See *Hatchet, Barreling*.

COOPERS' SAW. See *Saw, Cabinet*.

COOPERS' SHAVE. See *In-Shave*.

COOPERS' SIDE AXE. See *Axe, Broad, Coopers'*.

COOPERS' STAVE KNIFE. See *Drawing Knife, Coopers'*.

COOPERS' TOOLS. The special-purpose coopers' tools listed below can be found in normal alphabetical sequence. These tools may also have been used for other purposes.

ADZE, COOPERS'
ADZE, COOPERS' TUB
ANVIL, COOPERS'
APRON, COOPERS'
AXE, BROAD, COOPERS'
BARREL HEADER
BARREL SET-UP FORM
BENCH, SHAVING
BLOCK HOOK
BORING TOOL, BIT, DOWEL
BORING TOOL, BIT BRACE, COOPERS'
BORING TOOL, BUNG BORER
BORING TOOL, TAP BORER
BUNG BURNER
CHAMFER FROG
CHINCING IRON
COMPASS, BOW
COMPASS, COOPERS'
CRESSET
CRIPPLE
DOWEL FORMER
DOWELING MACHINE
DOWNSHAVE
DRAWING KNIFE, COOPERS'
FLAGGING IRON
FROE
FROE CLUB
HAMMER, COOPERS'
HAMMER, HOOP SET
HATCHET, BARRELING
HEAD CUTTER
HEAD FLOAT
HOOP DOG
HOOP DRIVER
IN-SHAVE
JIGGER, COOPERS'
JUMPER
KNIFE, CHAMFER
MALLET, RUBBER
MAUL, CHIME
PICK, BUNG

PINCERS, CARPENTERS'
PLANE, COOPERS' JOINTER
PLANE, CROZE
PLANE, HOWEL
PLANE, LEVELING
PLANE, ROUNDING
PUNCH, COOPERS'
RAISING IRON
RIVET SET
ROUND SHAVE
SAW, CABINET
SAW, TURNING
SCORP
SCRAPER, COOPERS'
SPLITTER
SPOKE SHAVE, COOPERS'
TONGS, ANGLE JAW
TRUSS HOOP
VISE, COOPERS'
WRENCH, BUSH

COPE. See *Flask*.

COPING PLANE. See *Plane, Coping* and *Plane, Double Coping*.

COPING SAW. See *Saw, Coping*.

COPPER HAMMER. See *Hammer, Soft Faced*.

COPPER TONGS. See *Tongs, Copper*.

COPPER WORKERS' HAMMER. See *Hammer, Coppersmiths'*.

COPPERING HAMMER. See *Hammer, Coppering*.

COPPERING PUNCH. See *Punch, Coppering*.

COPPERSMITHS' HAMMER. See *Hammer, Coppersmiths'*.

COPPERSMITHS' MALLET. See *Mallet, Coppersmiths'*.

COPPERSMITHS' SQUARE STAKE. See *Stake, Coppersmiths'*.

COPPERSMITHS' STAKE. See *Stake, Coppersmiths'*.

COPYING PRESS. Also called BOOK PRESS, LETTER PRESS and STANDING PRESS. A press used when duplicating a letter or other printed matter.

Copying Press

144

COPYING WHEEL. See *Pouncing Wheel* and *Tracing Wheel.*

CORD WHEEL. See *Shoe Makers' Tool, Cord Wheel.*

CORDAGE RULE. See *Rule, Cordage.*

CORDWAINERS' TOOLS. See *Shoe Tools.*

COREBOX PLANE. See *Plane, Corebox.*

CORING KNIFE. See *Knife, Coring.*

CORK BORER. See *Cork Cutter.*

CORK BORING MACHINE. A laboratory device used to bore a hole in a cork for insertion of a tube.

Cork Boring Machine

CORK CUTTER. Also called **CORK BORER.** A tool consisting of a hollow brass tube sharpened on one end. The cork cutter was used in drug stores and similar establishments to make small corks. They were usually sold in a set comprised of 6 or 8 cutters of different sizes. The set includes a rod to push the completed cork from the cutter.

Cork Cuttter

CORK CUTTER SHARPENER. Also called **CORK BORER SHARPENER.** A tool consisting of a solid cone and an attached knife blade. The brass cork cutter is pushed over the end of the cone and rotated against the knife blade. The taper of the cone allows cork cutters of various sizes to be sharpened.

CORK CUTTERS' KNIFE. See *Knife, Cork Cutters'.*

CORK DRIVER. See *Corker.*

CORK FLOAT. See *Float, Plasterers'.*

Cork Cutter Sharpener

CORK GAUGE. A gauge used to determine the proper size of cork or rubber stopper.

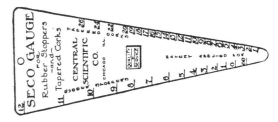

Cork Gauge

CORK MEASURE. See *Rule, Cork Measure.*

CORK PRESSER. A device used to press and taper a cork to the desired size. The cork is inserted between the wheel and the curved plate. As the handle is pushed down, the cork is rolled between the two corrugated surfaces thus being beveled and pressed as desired.

Cork Presser

CORK SQUEEZER. A drug store tool used to compress and soften a small cork.

Cork Squeezer

CORKER. Also called **CORK DRIVER** and **HAND CORKER.** A tapered device used to compress a cork and insert it into a beer keg.

CORN CUTTER. See *Knife, Corn.*

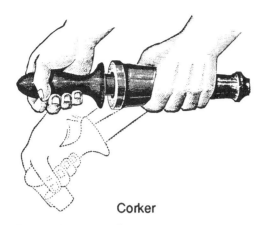

Corker

Corn Planter

CORN HOOK. See *Knife, Corn.*

CORN HUSKER. A tool used to split the husk when removing an ear of corn from the stalk. Numerous types of huskers were available. Some examples are illustrated.

Home Made Peg

Pin or Peg

Hook

Corn Husker

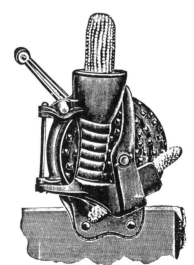

CORN KNIFE. See *Knife, Corn.*

CORN PLANTER. A hand-operated device used to drop grains of corn into loose soil. The point of the planter is pressed into the earth and the handles pulled apart to release either one or two grains of seed corn. Some planters were equipped with attachments to plant pumpkins and broom corn.

CORN SHELLER. A device or machine used to remove dry corn from the cob. Illustrations (c) and (d) shellers consists of hinged metal hand grips with ridges on the inside. The device is folded around the ear and rotated to loosen the grains from the cob.

(c)

Corn Sheller

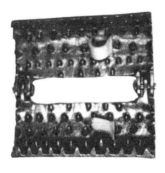

Corn Sheller

CORN SHOCK CLAMP. See *Clamp, Fodder.*

CORN TOPPER. See *Knife, Corn Topping.*

CORN TOPPING KNIFE. See *Knife, Corn Topping.*

CORNER BLOCK. A brick layers' tool. Used in pairs to hold a horizontal line taut along a wall. One block is set astride each end of the wall. and the line is stretched between the blocks.

Corner Block

CORNER BRACE. See *Boring Tool, Bit Brace, Corner.*

CORNER CHISEL. See *Chisel, Corner.*

CORNER CLAMP. See *Clamp, Corner.*

CORNER KNIFE. See *Knife, Paper Hangers' Casing.*

CORNER RATCHET BORER. See *Boring Tool, Ratchet.*

CORNER ROUNDING PLANE. See *Plane, Corner Rounding.*

CORNER TOOL. See *Cement Tool, Inside.*

CORNER TROWEL. See *Cement Tool, Inside* and *Trowel, Plasterers' Corner.*

CORNERING TOOL. Also called CHAMFER TOOL. A cutting tool used to make a small chamfer on the corner of a wooden workpiece. The tool is placed on the corner and drawn along the workpiece at a fixed angle to the surface. See also *Cement Tool, Inside.*

Cornering Tool

Cornering Tool

CORNICE BRAKE. See *Tinsmiths' Machine, Brake.*

CORNICE HAMMER. See *Hammer, Cornice.*

CORNICE OGEE. See *Plane, Moulding, Cabinet Ogee.*

CORNICE PLANE. See *Plane, Moulding, Cornice.*

CORRUGATING TOOL. See *Cement Tool, Corrugating.*

CORSET KNIFE. See *Knife, Corset.*

COT INSTALLING MACHINE. A tool used when installing a cot on the roll of a carding machine. A textile mill tool.

Drawing-On

Pushing-On

Cot Installing Machine

COT SCARFER. See *Knife, Cot Scarfer.*

COTTER FILE. See *File, Cotter.*

COTTER PIN EXTRACTOR. See *Cotter Pin Lifter.*

COTTER PIN LIFTER. Also called COTTER PIN EXTRACTOR. A tool used as a lever to remove a cotter pin. Length is 6 to 9 inches.

Cotter Pin Lifter

COTTER PIN PLIERS. See *Pliers, Cotter Pin.*

COTTON BALE SNIPS. See *Bale Tie Snips.*

COTTON GIMLET. See *Sampler, Cotton.*

COTTON HOE. See *Hoe, Farm.*

COTTON HOOK. A type of bale hook. See *Hook, Bale.*

COTTON JACK. See *Jack, Lifting*.

COTTON SAMPLER. See *Sampler, Cotton*.

COTTON SAMPLING KNIFE. See *Knife, Cotton Sampling*.

COTTON SCREW. A type of jack. See *Jack, Lifting*.

COTTON SEED FORK. See *Fork, Cotton Seed*.

COTTON STAPLE RULE. See *Rule, Cotton Staple*.

COUNTER. See *Tally Register*.

COUNTER BRUSH. See *Brush, Brick Layers' Dust*.

COUNTERBORE. See *Boring Tool, Bit, Counterbore*.

COUNTERSINK. See *Anvil Tool, Countersink; Boring Tool, Bit, Countersink* and *Leather Tool, Countersink*.

COVE AND BEAD MOULDING PLANE. See *Plane, Moulding, Cove*.

COVE MOULDING PLANE. See *Plane, Moulding, Cove*.

COVETTA MOULDING PLANE. See *Plane, Moulding, Cove*.

COW HOBBLE. See *Cow Kickers*.

COW KICKERS. A device intended to prevent a cow from kicking while being milked. It consists of two wide hooks linked with a chain. The illustrated device has an extra clip to hold the tail.

Cow Kickers

CRADLE. A farm tool used for harvesting grain. See *Grain Cradle*.

CRANBERRY HOE. See *Hoe, Farm*.

CRANDAL. See *Hammer, Crandall*. Crandal is an incorrect variation in spelling.

CRANDALL. See *Hammer, Crandall*.

CRANDLE. See *Hammer, Crandall*. Crandle is a variation in spelling.

CRANIAL DRILL. See *Boring Tool, Bit Brace, Orthopedic* and *Boring Tool, Cranial*.

CRANK DRILL. See *Boring Tool, Crank Drill*.

CRANK WRENCH. See *Wrench, Crank*.

CRANKED CHISEL. See *Chisel, Bent*.

CRANKED GOUGE. See *Gouge, Bent*.

CRATE OPENER. See *Chisel, Box*.

CRAYON. A marking device made of chalk, soap, resin, wax or gum.

CRAYON, CHALK. Also called RAILROAD CHALK CRAYON. A large white or blue crayon used by railroad workers, machinists and miners. Diameter is 1 inch and length is approximately 4 inches.

Chalk Crayon

CRAYON, LUMBER. Also called TIMBER CRAYON. A crayon suitable for marking on rough lumber.

Lumber Crayon

CRAYON, METAL. A crayon made of soapstone or other material that is suitable for marking on iron.

Soapstone Pencil

Metal Crayon

CREAM SEPARATOR. A machine used to separate cream from whole milk. Centrifugal action removes the cream and allows it run out one spout while the milk runs out of the other. Thicker cream can be obtained by more rapid turning of the handle.

CREASER. See *Anvil Tool, Creaser; Bone Folder; Bookbinding Tool, Creaser; Leather Tool, Creaser* and *Seam Rubber*.

CREASING HORN STAKE. See *Stake, Creasing Horn*.

CREASING MACHINE. See *Leather Machine, Creasing* and *Tinsmiths' Machine, Grooving*.

CREASING STAKE. See *Stake, Creasing*.

CREEPERS. See *Ice Creepers*.

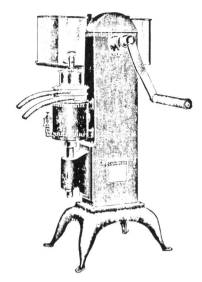

Cream Separator

Cripple

CRESCENT WRENCH. See *Wrench, Adjustable.*

CRESSET. An open fire pot used to heat the staves of a barrel during assembly. A small fire of chips or coal is kindled inside the cresset and a partially assembled barrel is placed down over the entire device. The fire heats the staves sufficiently to allow them to be bent into the final shape of the barrel.

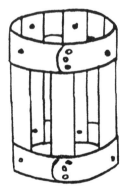

Cresset

CRIMPING MACHINE. See *Tinsmiths' Machine, Crimping* and *Tinsmiths' Machine, Stovepipe Crimper.*

CRIMPING SCREW. See *Shoe Makers' Tool, Crimping Screw.*

CRINGLE FID. See *Fid.*

CRIPPLE. A frame used to hold a beer keg while cutting the chamfer.

CRIPPLER. See *Raising Board.*

CROCHET FILE. See *File, Crochet.*

CROOKED KNIFE. See *Knife, Crooked.*

CROSS CUT SAW. See *Saw, Cross Cut.*

CROSS CUT FILE. See *File, Cross Cut.*

CROSS FILE. See *File, Crossing.*

CROSS JOINT TROWEL. See *Trowel, Cross Joint.*

CROSS PEEN HAMMER. See *Hammer, Blacksmiths'* and *Hammer, Cross Peen.*

CROSS PEEN SLEDGE. See *Sledge, Blacksmiths'.*

CROSS RIM WRENCH. See *Wrench, Cross Rim.*

CROSS TEST LEVEL. See *Level, Combination* and *Level, Cross Test.*

CROSSING FILE. See *File, Crossing.*

CROTCH EDGER. See *Leather Tool, Edger.*

CROTCH TONGS. See *Tongs, Blacksmiths'.*

CROW BAR. See *Bar, Crow.*

CROWS. See *Plane, Croze.* Crows is a variation in spelling.

CROWS STOCK. See *Plane, Croze.*

CROW'S FOOT. See *Wrench, Crow's Foot.*

CROWN MOULDING PLANE. See *Plane, Moulding, Cornice.*

CROWN SPLITTER. See *Leather Tool, Crown Splitter.*

CROZE. See *Plane, Croze.*

CRUCIBLE TONGS. See *Tongs, Crucible.*

CRUISERS' AXE. A small double bit axe. See *Axe, Double Bit.*

CUBAN AUGER. See *Boring Tool, Ring Auger.*

CULTIVATING HOE. See *Hoe, Farm.*

CUPOLA PICK. See *Pick, Cupola.*

CUPPING TOOL. See *Anvil Tool, Cupping.*

CURB EDGER. See *Cement Tool, Curbing* and *Cement Tool, Edger.*

CURB-GUTTER TOOL. See *Cement Tool, Gutter.*

CURBING TOOL. See Cement *Tool, Curbing* and *Cement Tool, Edger.*

CURD CUTTER. Also called CURD KNIFE and WHEY KNIFE. A slicing device used to cut and break cheese curd into small pieces to hasten drainage of the whey.

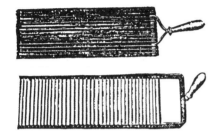

Curd Cutter

CURD RAKE. See *Rake, Curd.*

CURRIERS' BEAM. A bench upon which the currier spreads the tanned hide to be worked. The beam board or actual work surface is 5 1/2 to 6 inches wide and is usually made of a hard wood such as lignum vitae.

Curriers' Beam

CURRIERS' SLICKER. A smoothing tool used to finish a tanned hide. The function of the STEEL SLICKER is to remove inequalities in thickness and to help stretch the hide. The BRASS SLICKER is used to smooth the hair side after it has been scoured with an abrasive. The GLASS SLICKER is used to spread and smooth the sizing material. A similar tool with a stone or iron edge is used to smooth and flatten any coarse grain as the tanning process is nearing completion.

Brass Slicker

Glass Slicker

Steel Slicker
or Stretching Iron

Curriers' Slicker

CURRIERS' TOOLS. The special-purpose curriers' tools listed below can be found in normal alphabetical sequence. These tools may also have been used for other purposes.

   ARM STAKE
   CURRIERS' BEAM
   CURRIERS' SLICKER
   FINGER STEEL
   KNIFE, CURRIERS'
   KNIFE, MOON
   POMMEL
   RAISING BOARD

CURRY COMB. A comb used to groom a horse.

Curry Comb

Curry Comb

CURTAIN FASTENER ANVIL. See *Anvil, Curtain Fastener.*

CURVED LIP TONGS. See *Tongs, Blacksmiths'.*

CURVED SCRAPER. See *Scraper, Moulding.*

CUSPIDOR BRUSH. See *Brush, Cuspidor.*

CUT AND THRUST. A name occasionally applied to a Dado Plane. See *Plane, Dado.*

CUTTING BLOCK. See *Anvil Tool, Cutting Block.*

CUTTING CREASER. See *Leather Tool, Creaser.*

CUTTING DIE. See *Leather Tool, Cutting Die.*

CUTTING GAUGE. A tool used to cut strips of veneer parallel with the edge of a cutting board. See also *Slitting Gauge*

Cutting Gauge

CUTTING NIPPERS. See *Nippers, End Cutting; Nippers, Tinsmiths' Cutting* and *Nippers, Wire.*

CUTTING PICK. See *Pick, Cutting.*

CUTTING PLIERS. See *Pliers, Wire Cutting.*

CUTTING PUNCH. See *Punch, Grommet.*

CYLINDER SCRAPER. See *Scraper, Carbon.*

CYLINDER WRENCH. See *Wrench, Cylinder.*

CYMA MOULDING PLANE. See *Plane, Moulding, Ogee* and *Plane, Moulding, Reverse Ogee.*

D

Tool names starting with the letter D including multiple listings of:
Dividers
Drawing Knife

DABBER. See *Engravers' Dabber.*

DADO PLANE. See *Plane, Dado.*

DAMPING BRUSH. See *Brush, Damping.*

DANCING MASTER CALIPER. See *Caliper, Dancing Master.*

DANDELION CUTTER. See *Knife, Asparagus.*

DANDELION DIGGER. Also called WEED DIGGER. A tool intended for use in removing dandelions. It consists of a straight metal fork set into a short wooden handle. The swell in the handle is used as a fulcrum to provide leverage.

Dandelion Digger

DANDELION RAKE. See *Rake, Dandelion.*

DANGEL. See *Dengel.* Dangel is a variation in spelling.

DAPPING DIE. Also called DAPPING DIE BLOCK. A type of small swage block used by a jeweler or watch maker. Width is 1 1/2 to 3 inches square. Made of brass or iron.

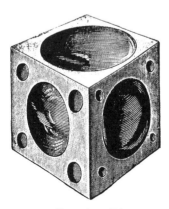

Dappintg Die

DAPPING DIE BLOCK. See *Dapping Die.*

DARBY. Also called PLASTERERS' DARBY and Plasterers' FLOAT. A flexible plasterers' tool used for smoothing of a newly plastered surface. Often used on ceilings. Length is 36 to 44 inches.

Darby

DECK CHISEL. See *Chisel, Deck.*

DECK SCRAPER. See *Scraper, Ship.*

DEHORNING GOUGE. A tool used for gouging out the matter from the roots of the horns of old cattle after the horns have been cut off.

Dehorning Gouge

DEHORNING OUT-CUTTER. A tool used for cutting the hair and hide away from the base of the horn in young cattle.

Dehorning Out-Cutter

DEHORNING SAW. See *Saw, Dehorning.*

DEHORNING SHEARS. See *Shears, Dehorning.*

DENGEL ANVIL. See *Anvil, Scythe.*

DENGEL HAMMER. See *Hammer, Dengel.*

DENGEL OUTFIT. A tool used to produce a sharp hammered edge on a scythe. The scythe is positioned in the notch and the top of the tool is struck with a hammer. A dengeledge approximately 1/8 inch wide is produced. The tool was said to be capable of producing a perfect edge in the hands of a novice.

DENGEL STOCK. See *Anvil, Scythe.*

DENT BALL. See *Dummy.*

Dengel Outfit

DENT REMOVING HAMMER. See *Hammer, Instrument Repair.*

DERRICK HATCHET. See *Hatchet, Rig Builders'.*

DESK RULE. See *Rule, School.*

DESK SHEARS. See *Shears, Desk.*

DEVIL'S CLAW. A tool for handling chain. See *Hook, Chain.*

DIAGONAL PLIERS. See *Pliers, Diagonal.*

DIAMOND GAUGE. See *Stone Size Gauge.*

DIAMOND NOSE CHISEL. See *Chisel, Diamond Point.*

DIAMOND POINT CHISEL. See *Chisel, Diamond Point* and *Turning Tool, Spear Point.*

DIAMOND POINT DRIVER. See *Sash Point Driver.*

DIAMOND SHOVEL. See *Shovel, Diamond.*

DIBBLE. A conical shaped tool used to make the hole for planting seedlings. Often made of solid metal or metal with a wooden handle. Home made varieties are sometimes made entirely of wood.

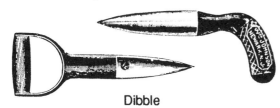

Dibble

DIE. See *Tap and Die.*

DIE SINKERS' FILE. See *File, Die Sinkers'.*

DIE STOCK. See *Tap and Die.*

DIGGING AND TAMPING BAR. See *Bar, Digging and Tamping.*

DIGGING BAR. See *Bar, Digging and Tamping.*

DIGGING HOE. See *Hook, Potato.*

DIGGING HOOK. See *Hook, Potato.*

DINK. See *Leather Tool, Cutting Die.*

DIP COMPASS. Also called DIPPING NEEDLE and MINERS' DIP COMPASS. A magnetic compass intended to be used in a mine to locate the highest concentration of iron ore and to determine the pitch of the stratum. The compass is held by the bale while in use. The illustrated tool was patented November 2, 1880.

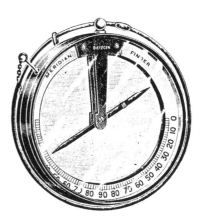

Dip Compass

DIPPER. A turpentine harvesting tool. See *Turpentine Dipper.*

DIPPING NEEDLE. See *Dip Compass.*

DIRT PICK. See *Pick, Dirt* and *Pick, Railroad.*

DIRT RAMMER. See *Tamper.*

DIRT SHOVEL. See *Shovel, Round Point.*

DIRT TAMPER. See *Tamper.*

DISC SHARPENER. An agricultural machine used to sharpen a disc or plow coulter. The illustrated tool has provisions for rotating both the sharpening stone and the disc.

Disc Sharpener

DITCH KNIFE. See *Knife, Ditch.*

DIVIDERS. A tool used to divide or transfer a measurement. A divider has a means of locking the setting and usually has a means of precision adjustment.

DIVIDERS, GENERAL PURPOSE. Length of legs are 5 to 24 inches. This tool was made in a variety of shapes and sizes. Some general types are illustrated. This device was listed as a compass by some suppliers. See also *Compass* and *Caliper.*

Spring

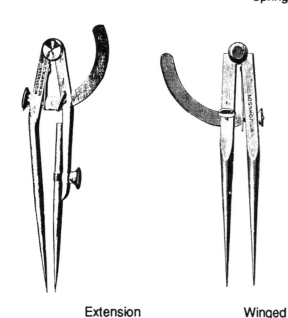

Extension   Winged

General Purpose Dividers

DIVIDERS, COMBINATION. See *Caliper, Combination.*

DIVIDERS, PENCIL. See *Compass, Pencil.*

DIVIDERS, PARALLEL. A machinists' divider in which the legs remain parallel at any adjustment point. The vernier adjustment of the illustrated tool was patented February 23, 1886.

DOCK AXE. See *Axe, Single Bit,* dock pattern.

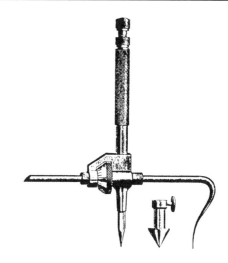

Parallel Dividers

DOCK BUILDERS' AXE. See *Axe, Single Bit,* dock pattern.

DOCK CUTTER. A tool used to cut the tap root of a dock plant several inches below the surface of the ground.

Dock Cutter

DOCKING SAW. See *Saw, Docking.*

DOG. A general term often used to refer to a device in which a hook is used to grasp and hold. See *Clamp, Bench; Clamp, Dog; Hoop Dog; Logging Dog; Pinch Dog; Plank Puller; Spoke Dog* and *Tire Dog.*

DOG CLAMP. See *Clamp, Dog.*

DOG HEAD HAMMER. See *Hammer, Saw.*

DOG TAIL. See *Moulders' Hand Tool.*

DOG WRENCH. See *Wrench, Lathe Dog.*

DOLLY. See *Anvil Tool, Dolly* and *Riveting Dolly.*

DOOR CLAMP. See *Clamp, Bar; Clamp, Cabinet Makers'* and *Clamp, Door.*

DOOR FRAME CLAMP. See *Clamp, Cabinet Makers'.*

DOOR MOULDING PLANE. See *Plane, Moulding, Door.*

DOOR PLANE. See *Plane, Door.*

DOOR SPRING WRENCH. See *Wrench, Door Spring.*

DOOR TRIM PLANE. See *Plane, Door Trim.*

DOT ROLLER. A type of cement roller. See *Cement Tool, Roller.*

DOUBLE BEAD PLANE. See *Plane, Moulding, Reeding.*

DOUBLE BICK ANVIL. See *Anvil, Double Bick.*

DOUBLE BIT ADZE. See *Adze, Double Bit.*

DOUBLE BIT AXE. See *Axe, Double Bit.*

DOUBLE BIT HATCHET. See *Hatchet, Double Bit.*

DOUBLE CALIPER. See *Caliper, Double.*

DOUBLE CLAW HAMMER. See *Hammer, Double Claw.*

DOUBLE COPING PLANE. See *Plane, Double Coping.*

DOUBLE CRANK BRACE. See *Boring Tool, Bit Brace, Wimble.*

DOUBLE END BLOCK PLANE. See *Plane, Block.*

DOUBLE END MATCH PLANE. See *Plane, Match.*

DOUBLE FACE HAMMER. See *Hammer, Double Face.*

DOUBLE FACE SLEDGE. See *Sledge, Double Face.*

DOUBLE FACE TURNING HAMMER. A type of farriers' forging hammer. See *Hammer, Farriers' Rounding.*

DOUBLE HORN ANVIL. See *Anvil, Double Bick.*

DOUBLE JOINT CALIPER. See *Caliper, Double.*

DOUBLE PICK-UP TONGS. See *Tongs, Blacksmiths'.*

DOUBLE PIKED ANVIL. See *Anvil, Double Bick.*

DOUBLE RAZEE PLANE. See *Plane, Double Razee.*

DOUBLE ROOFING SEAMER. See *Roofing Double Seamer.*

DOUBLE ROOFING TONGS. See *Tongs, Double Seamer.*

DOUBLE S CALIPER. See *Caliper, Navy.*

DOUBLE SEAM STAKE. See *Stake, Double Seam.*

DOUBLE SEAMER. See *Roofing Double Seamer.*

DOUBLE SEAMER TONGS. See *Tongs, Double Seamer.*

DOUBLE SEAMING MACHINE. See *Tinsmiths' Machine, Double Seaming.*

DOUBLE SPOKE SHAVE. See *Spoke Shave, General Purpose.*

DOUBLE TWIST AUGER. See *Boring Tool, Bit, Auger* and *Boring Tool, Bit, Jennings Pattern.*

DOUBLETREE PIN HAMMER. See *Hammer, Doubletree Pin.*

DOVETAIL PLANE. See *Plane, Dovetail.*

DOVETAIL SAW. See *Saw, Dovetail.*

DOWEL BIT. See *Boring Tool, Bit, Dowel.*

DOWEL CUTTER. See *Dowel Former.*

DOWEL FORM. See *Dowel Former.*

DOWEL FORMER. Also called DOWEL CUTTER and DOWEL FORM. A tool consisting of a sharpened metal tube attached to a firm base. A square strip of wood is centered on the tool and driven through to form a round dowel. This type of tool was often used by a cooper for making head dowels.

DOWEL POINTER. Also called DOWEL TRIMMER. A small bit brace tool used to point the end of a dowel. Larger versions of this tool are called *Spoke Pointers.*

Dowel Former

Dowel Pointer

DOWEL TRIMMER. See *Dowel Pointer.*

DOWEL TURNER. See *Turning Tool, Dowel.*

DOWEL TURNING MACHINE. A hand-operated machine used for cutting a long dowel from a square strip of wood. Several sizes of interchangeable cutters were available.

Dowel Turning Machine

DOWELING BIT. See *Boring Tool, Bit, Dowel.*

DOWELING BOX. A cutting tool used to form a dowel from a square strip of wood. This type of tool usually has from 2 to 4 for cutters for making dowels of various sizes. It is similar in function to the Rounder.

Doweling Box

DOWELING JIG. A patented device used to properly position a bit for drilling matching dowel holes in two workpieces to be joined.

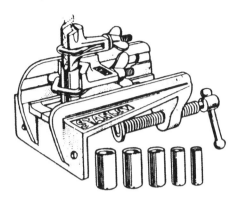

Doweling Jig

DOWELING MACHINE. A hand cranked machine capable of drilling two holes simultaneously in a one inch board. Intended for drilling the matching dowel holes required to join the heading pieces of a barrel. A coopers' tool.

Doweling Machine

DOWNSHAVE. A coopers' tool used to smooth the outside of a barrel. The tool is pushed downward with both hands while leaning over the end of the barrel.

Downshave

DRAFTING RULE. See *Rule, Architects'* and *Rule, Drafting.*

DRAG. See *Flask.*

DRAG SHOE. Also called WAGON DRAG. A metal-clad shoe used as a brake for a horse drawn wagon or heavy coach. The shoe was chained to the wagon carriage where it could be placed under a rear wheel thus preventing the wheel from turning. The sliding shoe would act as a brake to slow the wagon on a down slope.

Drag Shoe

DRAG TONGS. See *Tongs, Ice.*

DRAIN CLEANER. A long-handled tool used to clean drainage tiles and ditches.

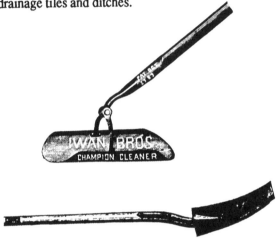

Drain Cleaner

DRAW BENCH. A device used for drawing large quantities of wire or rod. A draw plate is mounted solidly to the bench. The crank provides a steady force to draw the metal through the plate. See *Draw Plate.*

Draw Bench

DRAW GAUGE. An adjustable tool used to cut strips of leather. Five sizes were offered with the adjustable slides from 4 to 8 inches long. Handles were made of brass with rosewood fill, iron with wood fill and solid iron.

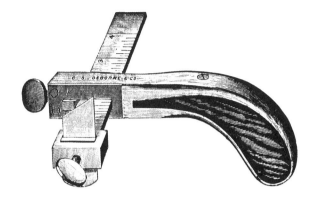

Draw Gauge

DRAW KNIFE. See *Drawing Knife*.

DRAW KNIFE CHAMFER GAUGE. See *Drawing Knife Chamfer Guides*.

DRAW PIN. See *Moulders' Hand Tool*.

DRAW PLATE. A rigid steel plate, with a series of precision holes, used for drawing soft metal. These plates are suitable for use with a drawing bench when large quantities of material are involved and can be used in a vise if desired. Plates having square, round, oval, knife shaped and half-round holes were available. The illustrated plate is approximately 3/16 inches thick and 6 1/2 inches long. See also *Leather Tool, Drawing Plate*.

Draw Plate

DRAW SHAVE. See *Spoke Shave*.

DRAW TOOL. See *Electrotype Finishers' Tool, Draw*.

DRAW TONGS. See *Tongs, Draw*.

DRAWER LOCK CHISEL. See *Chisel, Drawer Lock*.

DRAWING AWL. See *Awl, Drawing*.

DRAWING KNIFE. A wood-cutting knife, with two side handles, used to cut while being drawn toward the user. See also *Shave, Comb Makers'*.

DRAWING KNIFE, CARPENTERS'. A medium weight drawing knife with a straight blade. Cutting length is 6 to 20 inches. See also *Drawing Knife, Folding Handle*.

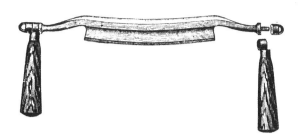

Adjustable Handle

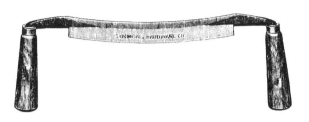

Carpenters' Drawing Knive

DRAWING KNIFE, CARRIAGE BODY. Also called CARRIAGE MAKERS' BODY KNIFE, CARRIAGE MAKERS' RABBET KNIFE and RABBET KNIFE. A type of routing tool in the form of a drawing knife. The illustrated tool was furnished with 3 interchangeable blades from 1/2 to 1 1/2 inches wide.

Carriage Body Knife

DRAWING KNIFE, CARRIAGE MAKERS'. Also called COACH MAKERS' DRAWING KNIFE. A drawing knife with a thin narrow blade. Cutting length is 6 to 12 inches and the blade is 3/4 to 1 inch wide. Some suppliers specify a difference between a carriage makers' and a coach makers' drawing knife. See illustration. Other suppliers' used the two names interchangeably.

Carriage Makers'   Carpenters'   Coach Makers'

Cross Sectional View

Carriage Makers' Drawing Knife

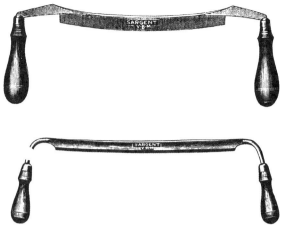

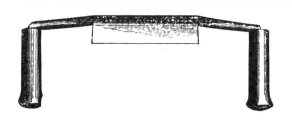

Backing Knife

Carriage Makers' Drawing Knife

DRAWING KNIFE, CARRIAGE MAKERS' BODY. See *Drawing Knife, Carriage Body.*

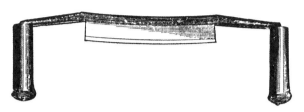

Heading Knife

DRAWING KNIFE, CARRIAGE ROUTER. Also called RABBET KNIFE and WAGON MAKERS' KNIFE. A type of wide routing knife used for cutting a shallow groove. Overall length is 6 to 16 inches.

Carriage Router Knife

Hollowing Knife

DRAWING KNIFE, COACH MAKERS'. See *Drawing Knife, Carriage Makers'.*

DRAWING KNIFE, COOPERS'. Any of the several drawing knives used by the cooper. The BACKING KNIFE was used to remove wood from the outside (back) of barrel stave. This knife was usually straight but occasionally has a slight curve to cut a convex shape. The BENT KNIFE was listed as a combination hollowing and backing knife. The HEADING KNIFE cuts the chamfer on the barrel head. The HOLLOWING KNIFE is severely curved to cut the inside surface of the stave. The HOOP and PARING KNIVES were used to thin and shape wooden barrel hoops. The paring knife is a light version of the hoop knife used for final finishing. The SHAVE-UP KNIFE is a long-handled tool used for rough trimming of the outside surface of the barrel. The STAVE KNIFE has a heavy blade suitable for removing large amounts of wood during preliminary dressing of the stave.

Hoop Knife

Paring Knife

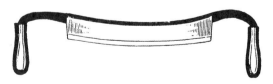

Bent Knife

Coopers' Drawing Knife

Shave-Up Knife

Coopers' Drawing Knife

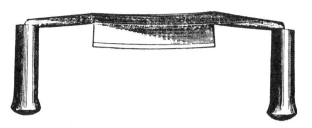

Stave Knife

Coopers' Drawing Knife

DRAWING KNIFE, FOLDING HANDLE. A Carpenters' Drawing Knife having handles that fold over the cutting edge. The folding feature reduces the size to facilitate storage and also protects the cutting edge while stored in a tool chest.

Folding Handle Drawing Knife

DRAWING KNIFE, LINEMAN'S. A heavy knife with a straight cutting edge. Cutting length is 10 to 14 inches.

Lineman's Drawing Knife

DRAWING KNIFE, PONY. A small drawing knife having a 4 inch cutting edge.

Pony Drawing Knife

DRAWING KNIFE, RIB SHAVE. A drawing knife used by a butcher for taking out a pork loin and trimming off the back fat.

Rib Shave Drawing Knife

DRAWING KNIFE, SHINGLE. Also called PEELING KNIFE and SHINGLE SHAVE. A heavy drawing knife with a straight cutting edge and raised handles. Used to thin and trim shingles and for peeling poles. Cutting length is 8 to 18 inches. Width of the blade is up to 1 3/4 inches. Similar to a Wagon Makers' Drawing Knife but generally heavier.

Shingle Knife

DRAWING KNIFE, STAVE MAKERS'. A drawing knife used for coarse dressing of rough barrel staves.

Stave Makers' Knife

DRAWING KNIFE, TIMBER. Also called TIMBER SHAVE. A heavy knife used for peeling poles and other similar applications. The cutting edge is approximately 14 inches long and 2 1/2 inches wide.

Timber Knife

DRAWING KNIFE, WAGON MAKERS'. A heavy drawing knife with a straight cutting edge and straight or drooped handles. Similar to a Carpenters' Drawing Knife except that the wagon makers' knife has a wider and heavier blade. Cutting length is 6 to 12 inches.

Wagon Makers' Knife

DRAWING KNIFE CHAMFER GUIDES. Also called DRAWING KNIFE CHAMFERERS and CHAMFER GAUGE. A pair of stops that can be clamped to a drawing knife to serve as guides when chamfering the corner of a workpiece.

Chamfer Guides

DRAWING PLATE. See *Leather Tool, Drawing Plate.*

DRAWING PLIERS. See *Tongs, Draw.*

DRAWING TOOL. See *Leather Tool, Modeling.*

DRESSER. Also called LEAD BEATER, LEAD DRESSER and PLUMBERS' DRESSER. A tool used by a plumber to beat or press sheet lead or lead pipe into the desired shape. Also used by linemen when installing lead sheathing over cable splices. The dresser is usually flat on the bottom and 1 3/4 to 2 inches wide. Dressers with V shaped bottoms have been noted. Overall length is 13 to 14 inches. Made of a hard durable wood such as beechwood, dogwood or lignum vitae.

Dresser

DRIFT PIN. Also called BARREL DRIFT. A steel pin or punch used to temporarily align two members having coincident holes. When forced into the holes, the uniform taper of the drift pin will force alignment of the two pieces. Size refers to the largest diameter of the pin. Sizes from 7/16 to 1 1/16 inches were listed. This tool was also listed as a STONE CUTTERS' BREAKING WEDGE.

Drift Pin

DRIFT PLUG. A cylindrical wooden pin used to remove the dents from lead pipe. One or both ends of the plug are tapered. Usually made of dogwood or lignum vitae. Lead pipe was often dented or partially collapsed during shipment. The pipe was hammered back into the original shape as a drift plug was forced through the pipe opening. The process was called "Drifting".

Drift Plug

DRIFT PUNCH. See *Punch, Drift.*

DRIFTING PICK. See *Pick, Drifting.*

DRILL. See *Boring Tool, Bit, Twist Drill* and *Star Drill.*

DRILL BIT. See *Boring Tool, Bit, Twist Drill.*

DRILL BLOCK. A machinists' tool used to hold a rod or pipe for drilling. The illustration shows a drill block and associated clamp. The blocks are used in pairs to support a long workpiece.

Drill Block

DRILL BRACE. See *Boring Tool, Bit Brace.*

DRILL CHUCK. An adjustable chuck used to grasp the round shank of a small drill or other cutter. The illustrated tool was recommended for use in a blacksmiths' drill. See also *Boring Tool, Brace Chuck.*

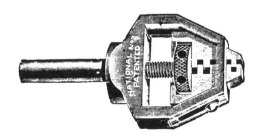

Drill Chuck

DRILL DRIFT. Also called CENTER KEY. A metal wedge used to force a drill from a tapered chuck. The combination drill drift and impact hammer shown in illustration (b) allows the drift to be used with one hand leaving the other hand free to catch the tool as it drops from the chuck.

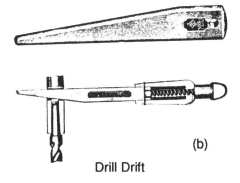

(b)

Drill Drift

DRILL FILE. See *File, Joint.*

DRILL GAUGE. See *Wire Gauge.*

DRILL POINT. See *Boring Tool, Bit, Flat.*

DRILL POINT GAUGE. A tool used to gauge the cutting angle of a twist drill bit. The main bevel of the gauge is 59 degrees. A second bevel of 41 degrees is used for gauging the correct cutting angle of a countersink.

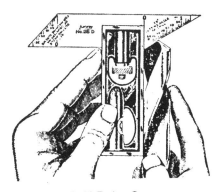

Drill Point Gauge

DRILL PRESS. See *Boring Tool, Post Drill.*

DRILL PRESS VISE. See *Vise, Drill.*

DRILL SEEDER. See *Garden Planter.*

DRILL SHARPENING HAMMER. See *Hammer, Sharpening.*

DRILL SPREADER. See *Anvil Tool, Drill Spreader.*

DRILL STOCK. See *Boring Tool, Bit Brace* and *Boring Tool, Breast Drill.*

DRILL SWAGE. See *Anvil Tool, Drill Spreader.*

DRILL VISE. See *Vise, Drill.*

DRILLING HAMMER. See *Hammer, Striking.*

DRILLING MACHINE. See *Boring Tool, Drilling Machine.*

DRILLING POST. See *Boring Tool, Drilling Post.*

DRIVE PUNCH. See *Punch, Leather* and *Punch, Pin.*

DRIVERS' LIGHT. See *Carbide Lamp.*

DRIVEWAY GROOVER. See *Cement Tool, Driveway Groover.*

DRIVEWAY ROLLER. See *Cement Tool, Roller.*

DRIVING HAMMER. See *Hammer, Farriers' Shoeing.*

DRIVING HOOK. See *Peavey.*

DRIVING PUNCH. See *Punch, Driving.*

DROVE. See *Stone Cutters' Tool, Chisel.*

DRUG MILL. A type of grinding machine. See *Grinding Mill.*

DRY POINT. See *Electrotype Finishers' Tool, Point.*

DUCK BILL BIT. See *Boring Tool, Bit, Spoon.*

DUCK BILL PLIERS. See *Pliers, Stockinger.*

DUMMY. Also called PLUMBERS' DUMMY. A plumbers' tool used to straighten the dents in lead pipe. The tool consists of a bent iron rod with a ball on one end. The ball is placed inside the pipe and levered outward to push out a dent or flat. A similar tool called a Dent Ball is used to remove the dents from brass musical instruments. Sets of brass and steel dent balls having diameters of 1/4 to 2 1/2 inches have been noted. The balls are threaded to allow attachment to handles of various lengths and shapes.

Dummy

DUST BRUSH. See *Brush, Brick Layers' Dust* and *Brush, Painters' Dust.*

DUST FORK. See *Fork, Coal.*

DUSTER. A moulders' tool used to spray dust on a casting form. The illustrated tool has an 18 inch cylinder. See also *Bellows, Moulders'.*

Duster

DUTCH PLANE. A plasterers' smoothing tool made entirely of wood. The tool is rounded on one edge and flat on the other. Length is 20 to 22 1/2 inches and width is 3/8 to 1 1/2 inches.

Dutch Plane

E

Tool names starting with the letter E including a multiple listing of:
Electrotype Finishers' Tool

Included also is a listing of the tools used by the:
Electrotyper and Printer

EAR MARKER. Also called ANIMAL MARKER, CATTLE BRANDER, CATTLE MARKER, CATTLE PUNCH, EAR PUNCH, HOG MARKER and STOCK MARKER. A tool used to mark hogs or cattle by punching a hole in the ear. Different shaped dies were available. See also *Hog Snouter.*

Ear Marker

EAR PUNCH. See *Ear Marker.*

EARTH AUGER. See *Boring Tool, Earth Auger.*

EASY OUT. See *Screw Extractor.*

EAVES TROUGH CLOSING FORM. A special-purpose sheet metal mandrel used for closing the end of an eaves trough. Also used for closing the ends of a trough for use as a chicken feeder or waterer.

Eave Trough Closing Form

ECCENTRIC CLAMP. See *Clamp, Eccentric.*

EDGE CHANNELER. See *Leather Tool, Channeler.*

EDGE PLAIN. See *Shoe Makers' Tool, Edge Shave.*

EDGE PLANE. See *Plane, Edge* and *Shoe Makers' Tool, Edge Shave.*

EDGE SHAVE. See *Shoe Makers' Tool, Edge Shave.*

EDGE TOOL. Any of a variety of cutting tools for wood such as chisels, planes and gouges. See also *Leather Tool, Edger.*

EDGE TRIMMING PLANE. See *Plane, Edge Trimming.*

EDGER. Any of several tools used to cut or form along an edge. See *Cement Tool, Edger; Leather Tool, Edger; Side Edger* and *Turf Edger.*

EDGING-UP TONGS. See *Tongs, Ice.*

EDITORS' SHEARS. See *Shears, Desk.*

EGG CRATE. A wooden case used by egg producers to gather, store and transport eggs.

Egg Crate

EGG GRADER. An adjustable balance used to determine whether or not an egg exceeds a minimum weight. The catalogue description states that hatching eggs should weigh 23 ounces to the dozen.

Egg Grader

EGG SLICK. See *Moulders' Hand Tool.*

EGG TESTER. A metal pendulum on a thread that was advertised as being capable of indicating whether or not an egg was fertile. While being held over the egg, a circular motion of the pendulum would indicate a fertile egg. A back and forth motion was a negative indication.

162

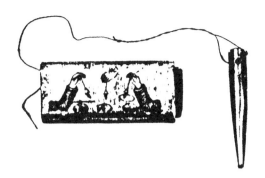

Egg Tester

EGGBEATER DRILL. See *Boring Tool, Hand Drill.*

ELBOW EDGING MACHINE. See *Tinsmiths' Machine, Elbow Edging.*

ELECTRIC LEVEL. A type of spirit level. See *Level, Electric.*

ELECTRICIANS' BIT BRACE. See *Boring Tool, Bit Brace, Corner.*

ELECTRICIANS' DRILL BIT. See *Boring Tool, Bit, Electricians'.*

ELECTRICIANS' LEVEL. See *Level, Electricians'.*

ELECTROTYPE FINISHERS' TOOL. A specialized tool used to prepare and correct electrotype and stereotype plates. The allied tools of the photo engraver are also included in this general category.

ELECTROTYPE FINISHERS' TOOL, DRAW. A tool used for cutting a border around a halftone and for defining an outline. The tool cuts while being pulled along a straight edge. Also available with replaceable cutting edges having different widths.

Draw Tool

ELECTROTYPE FINISHERS' TOOL, DRY POINT. See *Electrotype Finishers' Tool, Point.*

ELECTROTYPE FINISHERS' TOOL, HALFTONE COMB. Also called **HALFTONE RAKE.** A tool used to soften harsh edges of a halftone. The comb is grooved to match the various sizes of screens used to make the halftone.

Halftone Comb

ELECTROTYPE FINISHERS' TOOL, LINING GAUGE. A print shop tool.

Lining Gauge

ELECTROTYPE FINISHERS' TOOL, POINT. Also called **DRY POINT.** An etching and correcting tool with a sharp point on both ends. The illustrated tool has a cork handle.

Finishers' Point

ELECTROTYPE FINISHERS' TOOL, RAISING. A tool used for raising a dot or letter on a halftone or zinc. This tool can also be used for stippling.

Raising Tool

ELECTROTYPE FINISHERS' TOOL, ROULETTE. A roller-type tool used to lighten up printing plates and to soften harsh edges. The tool has serrations on the roller to match the standard lines on a halftone. Similar tools were available for stippling and making diagonal lines.

Roulette Tool

ELECTROTYPE FINISHERS' TOOL, SMASHER. Size is 1/4 to 1 1/2 inches square.

Smasher

ELECTROTYPE FINISHERS' TOOL, TYPE HIGH GAUGE. A tool used by a pressman or compositor for gauging the thickness of zinc plates, electrotype plates and base mounts.

Type High Gauge

ELECTROTYPERS' AND PRINTERS' TOOLS. The special-purpose electrotypers' and printers' tools listed below can be found in normal alphabetical sequence. These tools may also have been used for other purposes.

BRUSH, ELECTROTYPERS'
BRUSH, PLATE CLEANING
BUILDERS' IRON
BURNISHING TOOL, ELECTROTYPE FINISHERS'
CALIPER, ELECTROTYPE FINISHERS'
CHISEL, ELECTROTYPE FINISHERS'
CHISEL, ELECTROTYPE TRIMMER
ELECTROTYPE FINISHERS' TOOL, DRAW
ELECTROTYPE FINISHERS' TOOL, HALFTONE COMB
ELECTROTYPE FINISHERS' TOOL, LINING GAUGE
ELECTROTYPE FINISHERS' TOOL, POINT
ELECTROTYPE FINISHERS' TOOL, RAISING
ELECTROTYPE FINISHERS' TOOL, ROULETTE
ELECTROTYPE FINISHERS' TOOL, SMASHER
ELECTROTYPE FINISHERS' TOOL, TYPE HIGH GAUGE
ETCHING NEEDLE
HAMMER, ELECTROTYPE FINISHERS'
HAMMER, HALFTONE SOFTENING
KNIFE, ELECTROTYPE BUILDERS'
KNIFE, INK
LINING TOOL
PLANE, SHOOT BOARD, LEAD
PLANE, STEREOTYPE
PLANER
PROOF PLANER
PUNCH, ELECTROTYPE FINISHERS'
PUNCH, HALFTONE SOFTENING
QUOIN
SAW, ELECTROTYPE FINISHERS'
SCRAPER, ELECTROTYPE FINISHERS'
SKIMMER

ELEVATOR FORK. An ice harvest tool. See *Fork, Elevator.*

EMBOSSING MACHINE. See *Leather Machine, Embossing.*

EMBOSSING ROLL. See *Bookbinding Tool, Embossing Roll.*

EMBOSSING WHEEL CARRIAGE. See *Leather Tool, Embossing Wheel Carriage.*

EMERY WHEEL DRESSER. See *Grinding Wheel Dresser.*

END CUTTING NIPPERS. See *Nippers, End Cutting.*

END WRENCH. See *Wrench, End.*

ENGINEERS' DOUBLE FACED HAMMER. See *Hammer, Double Face.*

ENGINEERS' HAMMER. See *Hammer, Ball Peen* and *Hammer, Blacksmiths'.*

ENGINEERS' HATCHET. See *Hatchet, Engineers'.*

ENGINEERS' RULE. See *Rule, Engineers'.*

ENGINEERS' WRENCH. See *Wrench, Combination* and *Wrench, Open End.*

ENGLISH REAMER. See *Boring Tool, Bit, Broach.*

ENGRAVERS' BALL. A clamping device used for grasping and holding an item while it is being engraved. The ball is placed on the leather ring-shaped pad allowing it to be freely rotated and swiveled. This tool is also used by die sinkers and watch case makers.

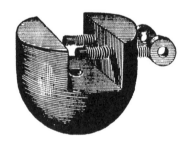

Ball

Pad

Engravers' Ball

ENGRAVERS' BLOCK. A sophisticated version of the engravers' ball. The workpiece is clamped between the jaws of the tool or between pins extending from the jaws. See *Engravers' Ball*.

Engravers' Block

ENGRAVERS' CHUCK. A special-purpose device used to hold a workpiece while engraving. The illustrated chucks are representative of the several sizes and shapes available.

Ring or Coin Holder

Engravers' Chuck

ENGRAVERS' DABBER. A soft pad used to dab dye or ink on a workpiece during the engraving process. Made of hard wood and covered with kid leather. Dye is used to highlight the completed cuts to assure an even design. Ink is dabbed on a woodcut in order to take a quick proof of the design.

Engravers' Dabber

ENGRAVERS' PENCIL. See *Pencil, Engravers'*.

ENGRAVERS' STAND. An adjustable revolving stand used by a comb maker. The illustrated stand is 6 1/2 inches in diameter.

Engravers' Stand

ENGRAVERS' TABLE. A small revolving table used by an engraver for resting the workpiece or the chuck.

Engravers' Table

ENGRAVING TOOL. See *Graver*.

ENSILAGE FORK. See *Fork, Coal*.

165

ENTERING FILE. See *File, Warding.*

EQUALING FILE. See *File, Equaling.*

ERASER. See *Ink Eraser.*

ESCAPEMENT FILE. See *File, Escapement.*

ETCHING NEEDLE. See *Etching Tool.*

ETCHING TOOL. Also called ETCHING NEEDLE. A pointed tool used for very fine etching of a metal printing plate.

Diamond Point

Steel Point

Etching Tool

EUROPEAN PATTERN BROAD AXE. See *Axe, Broad, European Pattern.*

EXPANDER. A tinners' tool. See *Boiler Expander.*

EXPANSION PLIERS. See *Pliers, Expansion.*

EXPANSIVE BIT. See *Boring Tool, Bit, Expansive.*

EXPANSIVE HOLLOW AUGER. See *Hollow Auger.*

EXPLODING WEDGE. See *Wedge, Exploding.*

EXTENSION BIT. See *Boring Tool, Bit Extension.*

EXTENSION DIVIDERS. See *Caliper, Combination.*

EXTENSION KNIFE. See *Knife, Extension Blade.*

EXTENSION RULE. See *Rule, Extension.*

EXTRACTOR. See *Screw Extractor* and *Spoke Extractor.*

EYE AUGER. See *Boring Tool, Ring Auger.*

EYE GLASS RULE. See *Rule, Eye Glass.*

EYE GLASS SCREW DRIVER. See *Screw Driver, Eye Glass.*

EYELET PUNCH. See *Punch, Eyelet.*

EYELET REMOVER. A tool used to remove shoe eyelets and hooks without damaging the shoe material.

Eyelet Remover

EYELET SET. A tool used to swage eyelets into leather or canvas. Several sizes were available to accommodate different sizes of eyelets. Eyelets are used to provide strong tying and lacing points.

Eyelet Set

F

Tool names starting with the letter F including multiple listings of:

FILE
FIRE TOOLS
FLOAT
FORCEPS
FORGE
FORK

Included also is a listing of the tools used by the:

FARMER
FARRIER

FACE HAMMER. See *Hammer, Stone.*

FAMILY AXE. See *Axe, House.*

FAMILY GRIND STONE. See *Grind Stone, Family.*

FANCY CALIPER. See *Caliper, Dancing Master* and *Caliper, Fancy.*

FANCY PLANE. See *Plane, Fancy.*

FANCY WOOD PLANE. See *Plane, Fancy.*

FARM TOOLS. The special-purpose farm tools listed below can be found in normal alphabetical sequence. These tools may also have been used for other purposes.

ANVIL, FARMERS'
ANVIL, SCYTHE
AXE, BUSH
AXE MATTOCK
BAND CUTTER
BAR, CROW
BELLOWS, SULPHUR
BORING TOOL, NUT AUGER
BORING TOOL, POST HOLE AUGER
BROOM, STABLE
BRUSH, HORSE
BULL LEADER
CALF FEEDER
CHAIN DETACHER
CLAMP, FODDER
CLIPPER
CORN HUSKER
CORN PLANTER
CORN SHELLER
COW KICKERS
CURRY COMB
DEHORNING GOUGE
DEHORNING OUT-CUTTER
DENGEL OUTFIT

DIBBLE
DISC SHARPENER
DOCK CUTTER
EAR MARKER
EGG CRATE
EGG TESTER
FEED CUTTER
FENCE TOOL
FENCE TOOL, COMBINATION
FLAIL
FORCEPS, PIG
FORGE, AGRICULTURAL
FORK, BALER
FORK, BARLEY
FORK, BUNDLE
FORK, COAL
FORK, HAY
FORK, HEADER
FORK, SHAVING
FORK, STABLE
FORK, VEGETABLE
FRUIT PICKER
GRAFTING FROE
GRAIN CRADLE
GRAIN SCOOP
GRAIN SICKLE
GRASS HOOK
GREASE GUN
GRIND STONE, PEDAL
GRIND STONE, SICKLE
HAMMER, DENGEL
HAY THIEF
HOE, FARM
HOE, GRUB
HOE, PLANTERS'
HOE, SCUFFLE
HOE, STABLE
HOG CATCHER
HOG HOLDER
HOG RINGER
HOG SNOUTER
HOOK, BALE
HOOK, BILL
HOOK, BUSH
HOOK, HOP
HOOK, POTATO
KNIFE, ASPARAGUS
KNIFE, BALE TIE CUTTER

KNIFE, BEET
KNIFE, BLOCK
KNIFE, BROOM CORN
KNIFE, BUDDING
KNIFE, CANE
KNIFE, CORN
KNIFE, CORN TOPPING
KNIFE, DITCH
KNIFE, HAY
KNIFE, HEDGE
KNIFE, LETTUCE
KNIFE, MAIZE
KNIFE, PRUNING
KNIFE, SEED POTATO
KNIFE, SOD
KNIFE, STRAW
LANTERN
MATTOCK
MAUL, POST
ORANGE CLIPPER
PICK, DIRT
PICK MATTOCK
PLIERS, WIRE
PLOW BOLT HOLDER
POST HOLE DIGGER
PUNCH, POULTRY
RAKE, HAY
SAW, BUCK
SAW, DEHORNING
SAW, ICE
SAW, PRUNING
SCYTHE
SCYTHE RIFLE
SEED STRIPPER
SEEDER
SHEARS, DEHORNING
SHEARS, GRAPE
SHEARS, HORSE
SHEARS, PRUNING
SHEARS, SHEEP
SHOVEL, SCOOP
SLEDGE, FARMERS'
SPADE
SPRAYER
STAKE PUNCH
STRAW AND HAY CUTTER
TACKLE BLOCK
TOBACCO SPEAR
TOBACCO SPUD
TONGS, HOG
TRANSPLANTER
VISE, FARMERS'
WIRE COILER
WIRE CRIMPER
WIRE CUTTER

WIRE SPLICING TOOL
WIRE STRETCHER
WRENCH, AGRICULTURAL
WRENCH, CYLINDER
WRENCH, FARMERS'

FARMERS' AUGER. See *Boring Tool, Nut Auger.*

FARMERS' FORGE. See *Forge, Agricultural.*

FARRIERS' CLIPHORN ANVIL. See *Anvil, Farriers'.*

FARRIERS' HOOF REST. Also called FARRIERS' ANVIL. A stand upon which the farrier can place a horse hoof for final dressing of the toe after the shoe has been nailed on. The rest is about 20 inches high.

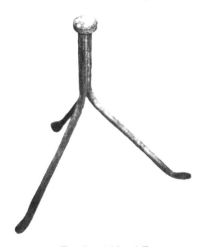

Farriers' Hoof Rest

FARRIERS' TOOLS. The special-purpose farriers' tools listed below can be found in normal alphabetical sequence. These tools may also have been used for other purposes.

ANVIL, CLINCH
ANVIL, FARRIERS'
ANVIL, FARRIERS' COMBINATION
ANVIL TOOL, CLIP SWAGE
ANVIL TOOL, CREASER
ANVIL TOOL, HARDIE
ANVIL TOOL, HEEL FORMER
ANVIL TOOL, NAIL PUNCH
ANVIL TOOL, TOE CALK DIE
BUFFER
BUTTERIS
FARRIERS' HOOF REST
FOOT ADJUSTER
FORGE, FARRIERS'
HAMMER, FARRIERS' FITTING
HAMMER, FARRIERS' ROUNDING
HAMMER, FARRIERS' SHARPENING
HAMMER, FARRIERS' SHOEING
HAMMER, FARRIERS' TURNING
HOOF PARER
HOOF TESTER
HOOF TRIMMER

HOOK, HOOF
KNIFE, FARRIERS'
NIPPERS, FARRIERS'
NIPPERS, HOOF
PINCERS, FARRIERS'
PRITCHEL
RASP, HORSE
RASP, HOT
SHARPENING STONE, HORSE SHOERS' KNIFE
SHOE SPREADER
SHOEING RACK
SLEDGE, TURNING
SOLE KNIFE
TOE KNIFE
TONGS, CLINCH
TONGS, FARRIERS'
TOOL BOX, FARRIERS'
TWITCH
VISE, FARRIERS'

FEATHER EDGE FILE. See *File, Feather Edge.*

FEATHER KNIFE. See *Knife, Feather.*

FEED CUTTER. Also called STRAW CUTTER. A farm tool used to chop fodder and to remove the seed heads from cane. The knife could be purchased separately. See also *Block Knife* and *Straw and Hay Cutter.*

Feed Cutter

FELLING AXE. See *Axe, Felling.*

FELLOE. Also called FELLY. A segment of the outside wooden rim of a wagon wheel into which the spokes are inserted. When half of the perimeter of the wheel is made from a single piece of wood, it was called a rim rather than a felloe.

FELLOE OILER. See *Wheel Oiler.*

FELLOE RASP. See *Rasp, Wood.*

FELLOE SAW. See *Saw, Felloe.*

FELLOW. See *Felloe.* Fellow is a variation in spelling.

FELLY. See *Felloe.* Felly is a common variation in spelling.

FELT KNIFE. See *Knife, Felt.*

FELT PICKER. See *Piano Tool, Felt Picker.*

FELT SCISSORS. See *Piano Tool, Felt Scissors.*

FELT SPADE. See *Piano Tool, Felt Spade.*

FENCE PLIERS. See *Pliers, Fence.*

FENCE TOOL. Any of a number of tools used to cut, splice, twist or stretch wire. The illustrated tool is 17 inches long. See also *Pliers, Fence.*

Fence Tool

FENCE TOOL, COMBINATION. A combined wire cutter, hammer, hatchet, staple puller and screw driver. It is said that a tool of this type was often carried by cowboys to facilitate minor on-the-spot fence repair.

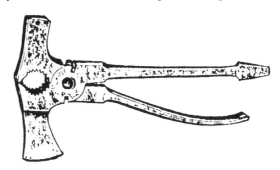

Combination Fence Tool

FERRULE TOOL. See *Anvil Tool, Ferrule.*

FETLOCK CLIPPER. See *Clipper.*

FIBRE BOARD PLANE. See *Plane, Fibre Board.*

FIBRE MALLET. See *Mallet, Fibre.*

FID. A cone-shaped tool used to separate the strands when splicing a rope. Usually made of a dense wood such as lignum vitae or hickory. The hand-held fid is 6 to 24 inches long. The free-standing variety is 30 to 40 inches long. The Cringle Fid was also used to shape the eye in a boltrope. See also *Marlin Spike.*

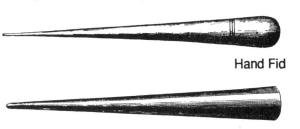

Hand Fid

Cringle or Standing Fid

Fid

FILE. An abraiding tool with roughened surfaces used to remove surface material from a solid such as metal or wood. Files are classified as to single (mill) cut and double cut. Single cut files have ridges cut in one direction only and double cut means that the file has two rows of ridges that are crossed. The edges are generally single cut. Saw files and files intended for use on soft metal are generally single cut. Machinists' files are usually double cut. The cuts of a file are classified as Rough, Coarse, Bastard (Regular), Second Cut (Fine), Smooth and Dead Smooth (Super Fine or Finishing). See illustration of file cuts. When a file is not cut on one or more side, these sides are said to be "Safe". A "Bellied" file is slightly convex in both planes on one or both sides. Each of the many common type files were offered in several lengths. An enormous variety of files were available when cut, type and length were considered. The Nicholson File Company, in an 1893 advertisement, stated that 3000 varieties of files and rasps were kept in stock.

It has been reported that hand-cut files were produced in America as early as 1698 but files were generally imported prior to about 1820. The first practical file cutting machine in America was put into operation in 1862 in Pawtucket, RI. Within a few years of that date, practically all files were machine cut. However, a few special purpose files were being hand cut as late as the 1920s.

Sections of files of comparable length are shown in the cross section illustration.

All files have a tang handle unless noted in the individual description.

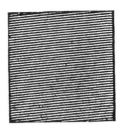

Smooth

Single File Cut

Rough

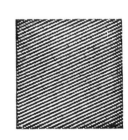

Middle or Coarse

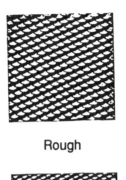

Bastard

Second or Fine

Smooth

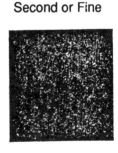

Dead Smooth

Double File Cuts

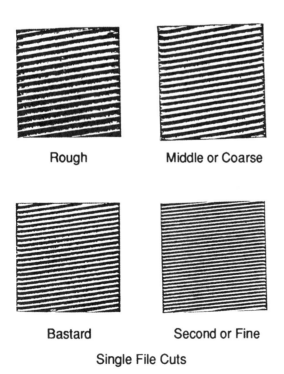

Rough

Middle or Coarse

Bastard

Second or Fine

Single File Cuts

Flat

Mill

Warding

Pillar

File Cross Sections

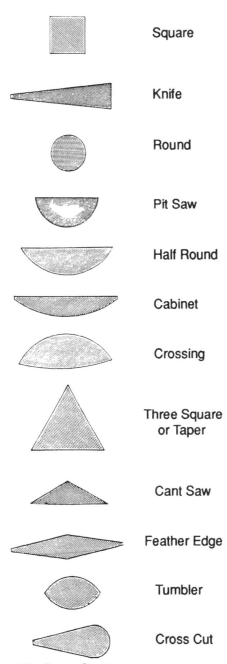

Square

Knife

Round

Pit Saw

Half Round

Cabinet

Crossing

Three Square
or Taper

Cant Saw

Feather Edge

Tumbler

Cross Cut

File Cross Sections

FILE, AMPOULE. See *File, Glass Cutting*.

FILE, ANGULAR. See *File, Knife* and *File, Warding*.

FILE, AUGER BIT. A file made especially for sharpening the cutting edges of an auger bit. One end cuts on the flat sides only and the other end cuts only on the edges.

Auger Bit File

FILE, BABBITT. Also called BABBITT FLOAT and LEAD FLOAT. A half round or flat file with an open single cut

that is not prone to clog when filing babbitt, lead and other soft metal. Length is 8 to 18 inches.

Babbit File

FILE, BALANCE WHEEL. See *File, Watch Makers'*.

FILE, BAND SAW. A triangular-shaped file with blunt edges. The edges are serrated in order to round the gullets between the teeth of the saw. Length is 3 to 14 inches. Both blunt and taper varieties were available.

Blunt

Taper

Band Saw File

FILE, BARRETTE. A Swiss-Pattern file that cuts on the wide side only. Length is 2 to 12 inches.

Barrette File

FILE, BASTARD. "Bastard" is one of the standard classifications of roughness and refers to a standard file that is slightly to the coarse side of medium. This is one of the most common varieties of files. One reference states that the name was derived because the bastard file was originally a non-standard cut between coarse and fine. See illustration under *File*.

FILE, BLUNT. Any of the several varieties of files having only a slight taper.

FILE, BRASS. A flat file having an open double cut that is not prone to clog when working brass. Also used for other soft metal.

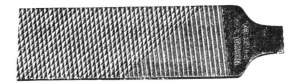

Brass File

171

FILE, CABINET. See *File, Wood.*

FILE, CANT. See *File, Cant Saw.*

FILE, CANT SAW. Also called CANT FILE and LIGHTNING FILE. A single-cut file used for sharpening back saws and cross cut saws with M shaped teeth. Also used for filing an inner angle such as that of a square bolt hole or an open-end wrench. Length is 4 to 12 inches.

Blunt

Taper

Cant Saw File

FILE, CELLULOID. A file used to work celluloid and hard rubber. Length is 4 1/2 to 9 inches.

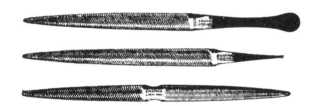

Celluloid File

FILE, CHECKERING. See *File, Chequering.*

FILE, CHEQUERING. A small file used for making decorative grooves on a gun stock. A similar file has been noted that has an offset rib for use as follower. The follower is placed in the preceding groove to assure equal spacing.

Chequering File

FILE, CHISEL POINT. See *File, Tooth Pointing.*

FILE, CHISEL TOOTH. See *File, Tooth Pointing.*

FILE, CLOCK MAKER. See *File, Watch Maker.*

FILE, COIL. See *File, Magneto.*

FILE, COTTER. A pointed pillar file. Length is 3 to 12 inches.

FILE, CROCHET. A tapered file with both edges rounded. Length is 2 to 10 inches.

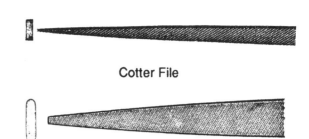

Cotter File

Crochet File

FILE, CROSS. See *File, Crossing.*

FILE, CROSS CUT. Also called GREAT AMERICAN FILE. A file used to sharpen the common cross-cut timber saw. Length is 4 to 12 inches.

Cross Cut File

FILE, CROSSING. Also called CROSS FILE, OVAL FILE and SHADBELLY FILE. Length is 2 to 18 inches. Also available in a blunt pattern.

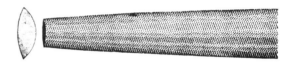

Crossing File

FILE, DIE SINKERS'. A small thin file with a tang handle. Normally sold in sets of 12 different cross sections. Length is about 3 1/2 inches.

FILE, DRILL. See *File, Joint.*

FILE, EQUALING. An very thin flat file used by watch and clock makers to cut equal spaces between gear teeth. Length is 3 to 12 inches. This type of file has a constant thickness from tip to tang.

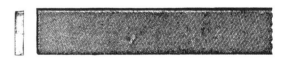

Equaling File

FILE, ESCAPEMENT. Also called WATCH FILE. A small file used by watch and clock makers. These short square-handled files were normally sold in sets containing the common cross sections. Length is approximately 5 1/2 inches. See also *File, Watch Makers'.*

FILE, FEATHER EDGE. Also called CURRY COMB FILE. Used for filing the sear spring in a gun and for cutting the notches in a curry comb. Length is 4 to 18 inches.

172

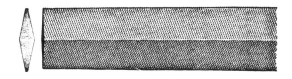

Feather Edge File

FILE, FINISHING. A name used by some suppliers to denote a smooth or dead smooth variety of file.

FILE, FLAT. A general-purpose file with a rectangular cross section. Length is 2 to 20 inches. See also *File, Hand* and *File, Wood.*

Regular

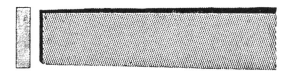

Blunt, Hand or Potance

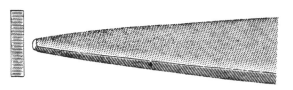

Tapered

Flat File

FILE, FLOAT CUT. See *Float, Plane Makers'* and *Float, Wood.*

FILE, FORK. A flat file with two rounded edges. Length is 4 to 6 inches.

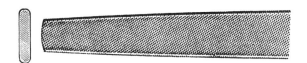

Fork File

FILE, FRAME SAW. See *File, Pit Saw.*

FILE, FRETWORK. A family of small round-handled files intended for smoothing the curved edges of wooden fretwork cutouts. Length is 2 1/2 to 3 inches. These files are generally sold in sets consisting of six or more with different cross sections.

FILE, GIN SAW. A single-cut file used for sharpening the raker saws in a cotton gin. Length is 3 1/2 to 8 inches.

Gin Saw File

FILE, GLASS CUTTING. Also called AMPOULE FILE. A tool used in a laboratory for cutting glass tubes and vials.

Glass Cutting File

FILE, GREAT AMERICAN. See *File, Cross Cut.*

FILE, HALF ROUND. A common type of file made in a variety of tapers. Length is 2 to 20 inches. See also *File, Wood.*

Blunt

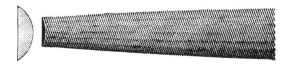

Taper

Half Round File

FILE, HAND. A blunt file that is rectangular in cross section. It is generally safe on one edge. Some suppliers indicate that a hand file is slightly thicker than the common flat file. See illustration under *File, Flat.*

FILE, HOOK TOOTH. A file with a shallow half-round shape on one side. It is used for sharpening a circular saw. Length is 6 to 12 inches.

Hook Tooth File

FILE, HORSE TOOTH. Also called HORSE MOUTH RASP, HORSE TOOTH FLOAT, HORSE TOOTH RASP and INCISOR TOOTH FILE. A tool used to smooth the edges of a horses tooth. The serrated portion of the jointed file, see illustration, is approximately 1 by 3 1/4 inches. The file portion is often replaceable. The cut of a horse tooth file is fairly smooth. A similar tool having a coarse rasp-like file is probably a shoe makers' tool.

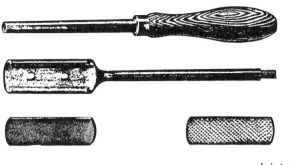

Jointed

Offset

Straight

Horse Tooth File

FILE, IVORY. Also called IVORY FLOAT. A tool used by a piano maker to trim and dress ivory. Length is 6 to 12 inches.

Ivory File

FILE, JOINT. Also called DRILL FILE. A file with serrations on the edges only. The square-edged type is used extensively for filing drills. Length is 3 to 6 inches.

Square Edge

Round Edge

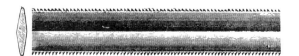

Watch Case

Joint File

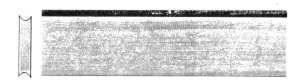

Hollow Edge

Joint File

FILE, KNIFE. Also called ANGULAR FILE. A tool used by a gunsmith for filing the inner angles of the sear and for general-purpose tasks of a similar nature. Length is 2 to 14 inches. Also made in a blunt pattern.

Knife File

FILE, LATHE. A single-cut file intended for lathe work. This file is cut at a very high angle.

Lathe File

FILE, LEAD. See *File, Babbitt.*

FILE, LIGHTNING. Similar to a Cant Saw File except somewhat thicker in cross section. See illustration under *File, Cant Saw.*

FILE, MAGNETO. Also called COIL FILE, PLATINUM FILE and PLATINUM POINT FILE. A small thin file, with a chisel point, used to clean and brighten magneto ignition and spark plug points. The chisel edge is used to facilitate spreading the spring-loaded points.

Magneto File

FILE, MARBLE. See *File, Marble Cutters'.*

FILE, MARBLE CUTTERS'. Also called MARBLE FILE. A file used by a marble cutter to smooth and shape the edges of a workpiece. These files were available in either flat or half-round patterns.

Marble Cutters' File

FILE, MILL. A flat single-cut file of rectangular cross section similar to the Flat File except slightly thinner. These files were used for sharpening mill saws and for general-purpose work. Length is 4 to 20 inches. They were commonly available with and without safe edges and with either one or both edges rounded. Available in blunt and narrow-point varieties.

Mill File

FILE, NEEDLE. A short thin file intended for general-purpose tasks requiring a tool with a small cross-section. These files were normally sold in sets of 6 to 12 with each file having a different cross section. Overall length, including the round handle, is 4 3/4 to 6 1/4 inches.

FILE, OVAL. See *File, Crossing*.

FILE, PILLAR. Similar to a Flat File but somewhat narrower. Length is 2 to 20 inches. A pillar file usually has one safe edge.

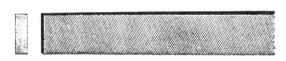

Regular

Narrow

Extra Narrow

Pillar File

FILE, PIPPIN. Length is 2 to 10 inches.

Pippin File

FILE, PIT SAW. Also called FRAME SAW FILE. A single-cut file with a semi-circular cross section used for sharpening a pit or frame saw. Length is 4 to 12 inches.

Pit Saw File

FILE, PIVOT. See *File, Watch Makers'*.

FILE, PLANER KNIFE. A flat double-ended file having a thin rectangular cross section. Used for sharpening a planer knife without removing the knife from the machine. The planer knife file does not have a tang. Length is 8 to 12 inches and width is approximately one inch.

Planer Knife File

FILE, PLATINUM. See *File, Magneto*.

FILE, POTANCE. A flat file with parallel sides. See *File, Flat*.

FILE, RAT TAIL. See *File, Round*.

FILE, RATCHET. See *File, Watch Makers'*.

FILE, REAPER. A single-cut file used to sharpen mowing and reaping machine knives. The beveled edges are safe. Length is 7 to 10 inches. A cross-sectional view is shown.

Reaper File

FILE, RIFFLER. See *Riffler*.

FILE, ROLLER. A machine-driven file specially adapted for filing the flutes of feed rollers in cotton spinning machinery. The roller file is single-cut. Length is 4 inches.

Roller File

FILE, ROUND. Also called GULLETING FILE, RAT TAIL FILE and ROUND GULLETING FILE. A round general-purpose file, usually tapered. Length is 2 to 20 inches. Used for enlarging a round hole, smoothing a curved section or for gulleting a saw. Gulleting deepens the recesses between the teeth of a saw thus increasing the effective length of the teeth.

175

Tapered or Rat Tail

Blunt or Gulleting

Round File

FILE, ROUND EDGE. See *File, Joint.*

FILE, ROUND EDGE JOINT. See *File, Joint.*

FILE, ROUND GULLETING. See *File, Round.*

FILE, ROUNDING OFF. A thin file used by a machinist or pattern maker. Often used for rounding the teeth after cutting a gear. This file has serrations on the flat side only. Length is 3 to 5 inches.

Rounding Off File

FILE, SAFETY. A general-purpose file made without a tang in order to be safely carried in the pocket. Length of the illustrated file is 8 inches.

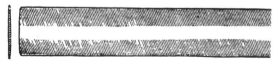

Safety File

FILE, SAW. See *File, Taper.*

FILE, SCREW HEAD. A thin file with sharply defined serrations on the edges. Used to cut the slot in the head of a screw. This file was available either double ended or with a tang. Length is 2 to 4 inches.

Screw Head File

FILE, SECOND CUT. "Second Cut" is one of the standard classifications of file roughness and denotes a file that is slightly to the coarse side of smooth. This is one of the most common types of files. See illustration under *File.*

FILE, SHADBELLY. See *File, Crossing.*

FILE, SHEAR TOOTH. An open single-cut file listed as being capable of doing quick work on soft steel, iron, brass castings, wood and marble. Especially suitable for lathe work. Length is 8 to 12 inches.

Shear Tooth File

FILE, SLIM TAPER. See *File, Taper.*

FILE, SLITTING. A file having a narrow diamond-shaped cross section. Used to cut a slit or notch. Length is 2 to 12 inches.

Slitting File

FILE, SQUARE. A general-purpose file having a square cross section. Used for enlarging a square or rectangular hole. Length is 2 to 20 inches. The blunt variety was also made with a bellied shape and with one or both sides safe.

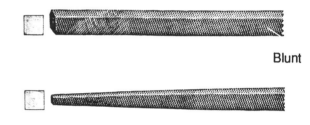

Blunt

Taper

Square File

FILE, SQUARE EDGE. See *File, Joint.*

FILE, STAVE SAW. A file used for sharpening a cylinder saw. Two shapes are illustrated. Length is 6 to 12 inches.

Stave Saw File

FILE, TAPER. Also called SAW FILE. A file, generally single-cut, with a triangular cross section. Length is 2 to 20 inches. Used primarily for sharpening hand saws. A Slim Taper variety was available for use on saws having extra-fine teeth. The edges of a taper file are slightly rounded to avoid cutting a sharp nick at the base of the saw tooth.

Slim

Taper File

Regular

Double Ender or Reversible

Taper File

FILE, THREE SQUARE. A double-cut file similar to the Taper File except that all three edges of the three square are brought out to sharp points. The edges are not serrated. These files are generally tapered to a fine point but a Blunt variety was available. Used primarily for filing taps and for cleaning out sharp angles. Length is 4 to 20 inches.

Three Square File

FILE, TOOTH POINTING. Also called CHISEL POINT FILE and CHISEL TOOTH FILE. A special-purpose file used for sharpening the points of inserted teeth in a circular saw. Length is 8 to 10 inches.

Tooth Pointing File

FILE, TOPPING. A flat file rounded on both edges. Similar to one version of the Stave Saw File except made of heavier stock. See illustration under *File, Stave Saw*.

FILE, TUMBLER. A double-cut file used for shaping the tumblers in a gun lock. Length is 4 to 18 inches.

Tumbler File

FILE, WAGON MAKERS'. A flat file with a coarse single cut intended for use on hardwood. This coarse cut is sometimes called a FLOAT CUT.

Wagon Makers' File

FILE, WARDING. Also called ENTERING FILE. An extra-thin file used by a locksmith for filing the wards in keys and for similar general-purpose tasks. Length is 2 to 20 inches.

Warding File

FILE, WATCH. See *File, Escapement* and *File, Watch Makers'*.

FILE, WATCH MAKERS'. Also called CLOCK MAKERS' FILE. A small file having a unique shape required for use by a watch or clock maker. Length is 3 to 4 inches. See also *File, Equaling* and *File, Escapement*.

Balance Wheel, Blunt

Balance Wheel, Taper

Escape Wheel

Pivot

Ratchet

Watch Makers' File

FILE, WOOD. A general-purpose tool used for dressing wood. Length is 6 to 18 inches.

Flat

Wood File

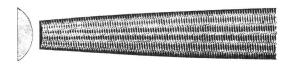

Half Round

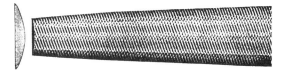

Cabinet

Wood File

FILE, WOOD CARVERS'. See *Riffler*.

FILE BRUSH. See *File Cleaner*.

FILE CARD. See *File Cleaner*.

FILE CLEANER. Also called FILE BRUSH, FILE CARD and FILE CLEANING CARD. A brush with short stiff bristles used to clean the debris from the teeth of a file. Overall length is approximately 8 1/2 inches.

File Cleaner

FILE CLEANING CARD. See *File Cleaner*.

FILE CUTTERS' CHISEL. See *Chisel, File Cutters'*.

FILE CUTTERS' HAMMER. See *Hammer, File Cutters'*.

FILE HANDLE. A handle made to fit the tang of a standard file. Various shapes of wooden and metal handles were available.

File Handle

FILE HOLDER. A device that can be attached to a common file to stabilize the file during use. See also *Saw File Holder*.

For Taper File

Austin's Patent

File Holder

FILE MAKERS' CHISEL. See *Chisel, File Cutters'*.

FILE MAKERS' HAMMER. See *Hammer, File Cutters'*.

FILE STUBS. This tool consists of short sections of the common varieties of files along with a holder. These stubs are suitable for use in congested areas not accessible to a standard file. The illustrated tool uses file sections two inches long.

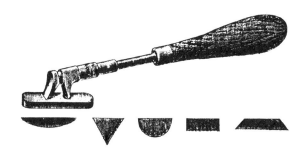

File Stubs

FILING CLAMP. See *Vise, Saw*.

FILING GUIDE. See *Saw Filing Guide*.

FILING PLATE. Also called JOINT WIRE FILING PLATE. A jewelers' tool used for holding a joint wire during filing or smoothing. A joint wire is a hollow tubular wire sometimes used as a spindle for a shaft or as a conduit for another wire.

Filing Plate

FILING VISE. See *Vise, Band Saw Filing* and *Vise, Saw.*

FILLET GAUGE. Also called Radius Gauge. A set of gauges used to determine the radii of a fillet or corner.

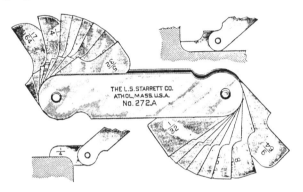

Fillet Gauge

FILLET ROLL. See *Bookbinding Tool, Embossing Roll.*

FILLET TOOL. Also called WAXING IRON. A pattern makers' tool used for applying pre-formed wood or leather fillets. The ball-shaped end of the tool is used to press and smooth the fillet into a sharp corner. This tool can also be heated and used to apply beeswax to form a fillet.

Fillet Tool

FILLETSTER. See *Plane, Filletster* and *Plane, Sash Filletster.*

FILLISTER. See *Plane, Filletster.* Fillister is a variation in spelling.

FINGER STEEL. A small turning steel user by a currier to provide frequent touch-ups to the knife. Overall length is approximately 5 inches. It is said that the currier kept the finger steel between his fingers continuously while using the knife.

Finger Steel

FINISHING BRUSH. See *Brush, Plasterers' Finishing.*

FINISHING FILE. See *File, Finishing.*

FINISHING TROWEL. See *Trowel, Moulders'* and *Trowel, Plasterers' Finishing.*

FINISHING WHEEL. See *Leather Tool, Overstitch Wheel.*

FIRE BUCKET. Also called FIRE PAIL. A 12 to 14 quart bucket intended to contain sand or water for use in case of fire. The bucket is hung on a special hook at a strategic location in the shop. The bottom of the bucket is shaped such that the bucket cannot be set down without spilling and is therefore less apt to be used for general tasks.

Fire Bucket

FIRE ENGINE AXE. See *Axe, Firemans'.*

FIRE HOOK. See *Hook, Fire.*

FIRE POKER. See *Fire Tools.*

FIRE PAIL. See *Fire Bucket.*

FIRE POT. A gasoline heater used for melting lead. The cast iron melting pot is set on top of the heater until ready for use. A plumbers' tool.

Fire Pot

FIRE RAKE. See *Rake, Fire.*

FIRE SET. See *Fire Tools, Blacksmiths'.*

FIRE TOOLS. Hand tools used to tend a fire.

FIRE TOOLS, BLACKSMITHS'. Also called FIRE SET. Small fire tools used in a blacksmiths' forge. Many of these tools were made by the smith for his own use. The commercial items were generally sold in packages of three and were listed as a FIRE SET. Length is 22 to 25 inches.

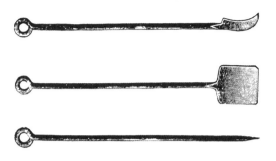

Blacksmiths' Fire Tools

FIRE TOOLS, FURNACE. Tools used for firing a boiler room or moulders' furnace. Length is 6 to 12 feet.

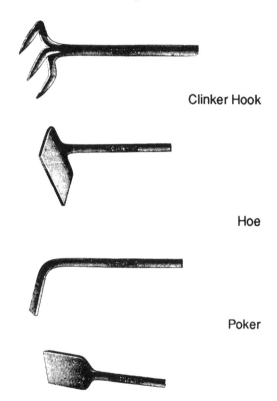

Clinker Hook

Hoe

Poker

Slice Bar

Furnace Fire Tools

FIREMANS' AXE. See *Axe, Firemans'*.

FIREMANS' HATCHET. See *Hatchet, Firemans'*.

FIREMANS' WALL PICK. See *Pick, Poll*.

FIRING IRON. See *Searing Iron*.

FIRM JOINT CALIPER. See *Caliper, Firm Joint*.

FIRMER CHISEL. See *Chisel, Firmer*.

FIRMER GOUGE. See *Gouge, Firmer*.

FISH FORK. See *Fork, Fish*.

FISH KNIFE. See *Knife, Fish*.

FISH SCALER. A fish packers' tool used for rapid removal of scales. The scaler has dull serrations or knobs rather than sharp ridges as would be used for a rasp or file. Numerous varieties of this type tool were offered.

Fish Scaler

FITTERS' CLAMP. See *Clamp, C*.

FITTING HAMMER. See *Hammer, Farriers' Fitting*.

FITTING UP WRENCH. See *Wrench, Construction*.

FLAG IRON. See *Flagging Iron*.

FLAGGING BAR. See *Bar, Flagging*.

FLAGGING IRON. Also called COOPERS' FLAGGING IRON and FLAG IRON. A Y-shaped tool used to spread the staves of a tight barrel for insertion of flagging or calking material. Length is about 20 inches. Flagging is used between the staves to prevent the barrel from leaking. With the chime hoop removed, the forked end of the flagging iron is placed over the end of two staves. It is then used as lever to separate the staves.

Flagging Iron

FLAIL. Also called THRESHING FLAIL. A tool consisting of a heavy wooden swingle attached to a handle with a rope or thong. Used to thresh out small lots of grain, buckwheat or beans. The illustrated tool has a 22 1/2 inch swingle and a 5 1/2 foot handle. A flail is usually made of some durable wood such as black locust.

Flail

FLANGE. See *Moulders' Hand Tool*.

FLANGE WRENCH. See *Wrench, Flange*.

FLANGED HAMMER. See *Hammer, Tinners' Flanged*.

FLASK. The box or frame in which the sand is tamped around a casting pattern. The top portion is called the COPE and the bottom is the DRAG. A cam-operated flask clamp is also shown in the illustration.

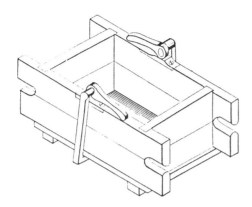

Flask

FLASK CLAMP. See *Clamp, Flask*.

FLAT BIT. See *Boring Tool, Bit, Flat* and *Boring Tool, Bit, Pipe*.

FLAT DRILL. See *Boring Tool, Bit, Flat* and *Boring Tool, Bit, Pipe*.

FLAT FILE. See *File, Flat*.

FLAT NOSE PLIERS. See *Pliers, Flat Nose*.

FLAT SCREW DRIVER. See *Screw Driver, Flat*.

FLATTER. See *Anvil Tool, Flatter*.

FLEAM. See *Flem*. Fleam is a variation in spelling.

FLEM. Also called HORSE FLEM. A knife-like tool used by a veterinarian to lance a boil or to open an infection.

Flem

FLESH FORK. See *Fork, Flesh*.

FLESHING KNIFE. See *Knife, Fleshing*.

FLOAT. The term "Float" or "Float Cut" is generally used to designate a coarse single-cut file with the serrations at a low angle. See also *File, Horse Tooth; File, Wagon Makers'* and *Head Float*.

FLOAT, CEMENT. See *Cement Tool, Float*.

FLOAT, IVORY. See *File, Ivory*.

FLOAT, LEAD. See *File, Babbitt*.

FLOAT, PLANE MAKERS'. A coarse file used to clean out the throat when making a wooden plane.

Plane Makers' Float

FLOAT, PLASTERERS'. A plasterers' smoothing tool. The face is made of wood, metal or cork. Length is 10 to 18 inches. See also *Darby*.

Wooden

Cork

Angle

Plasterers' Float

FLOAT, WOOD. Also called WOOD WORKERS' FLOAT. A general-purpose wood working tool used for rapid removal of excess stock. Length is 12 to 14 inches.

Wood Float

FLOGGER. See *Bung Starter*.

FLOGGING HAMMER. See *Hammer, Flogging.*

FLOOR CHISEL. See *Chisel, Floor.*

FLOOR CLAMP. See *Floor Jack.*

FLOOR GAUGE. See *Clapboard Gauge, Wooden.*

FLOOR GROOVER. An electric linemans' tool used to make a groove in a subfloor board or in an overhead beam for routing of electrical wiring. Length is 11 inches overall. Similar to one variety of TIMBER SCRIBE.

Floor Groover

FLOOR JACK. Also called FLOOR CLAMP. A device used to apply pressure to a floor board when laying a floor. The operator steps on the device causing spikes to grip the subfloor while a cam applies side pressure to the floor board. The device shown in the illustration was patented June 24, 1890. See also *Clamp, Flooring.*

Floor Jack

FLOOR LAYERS' HAMMER. See *Hammer, Flooring.*

FLOOR PLANE. See *Plane, Floor.*

FLOOR SAW. See *Saw, Floor.*

FLOOR SCRAPER. See *Scraper, Floor.*

FLOOR SHAVER. An ice harvest tool. See *Ice Shaver.*

FLOORING CLAMP. See *Clamp, Flooring.*

FLOORING HAMMER. See *Hammer, Flooring.*

FLOORING HATCHET. See *Hatchet, Flooring.*

FLOORING SAW. See *Saw, Floor.*

FLORAL FORK. See *Fork, Garden.*

FLOUR AUGER. See *Sampler, Cement.*

FLOUR SAMPLER. See *Sampler, Cement.*

FLOUR TESTER. Also called FLOUR SLICK. A paddle-shaped tool made of polished spring steel. Length is about 6 inches. The tester, with a thin layer of flour, is flashed in a hot oven. The evenness of browning is used as a criterion of the quality of the flour.

Flour Tester

FLUE BEADING TOOL. See *Beading Tool, Boiler.*

FLUE BRUSH. See *Brush, Tube.*

FLUE CLEANER. See *Scraper, Flue.*

FLUTE. See *Moulders' Hand Tool.*

FLUTING PLANE. See *Plane, Fluting.*

FLUTING GOUGE. A wood carving tool with a deep sweep. See *Carving Tool.*

FLUTING TOOL. See *Gun Stock Tool* and *Moulders' Hand Tool.*

FLY CUTTER. See *Washer Cutter.*

FODDER CLAMP. See *Clamp, Fodder.*

FODDER SQUEEZER. See *Clamp, Fodder.*

FOG HORN. A horn used on a ship to give warning of approach in a fog. The illustrated horn is made of tin with a wooden mouthpiece. Length is 24 to 40 inches.

Fog Horn

FOLDING HANDLE DRAW KNIFE. See *Drawing Knife, Folding Handle.*

FOLDING MACHINE. See *Tinsmiths' Machine, Folding.*

FOLDING RULE. See *Rule, Folding.*

FOLDING SAWING MACHINE. See *Sawing Machine.*

FOOT ADJUSTER. Also called HOOF LEVELER. A farriers' tool used to measure the angle of a hoof with respect to the ground. This tool is usually made of brass.

Foot Adjuster

FOOT ADZE. "Foot Adze" is a colloquial term. See *Adze, Carpenters'*.

FOOT BELLOWS. See *Bellows, Foot*.

FOOT BLOWER. See *Bellows, Foot*.

FOOT POWER. See *Foot Power Wheel*.

FOOT POWER HAMMER. See *Hammer, Foot Power*.

FOOT POWER WHEEL. Also called FOOT POWER, FOOT WHEEL and LATHE WHEEL. A foot-operated flywheel used to provide smooth uninterrupted power to a device such as a jewelers' lathe or jewelers' buffer.

Foot Power Wheel

FOOT POWERED LATHE. See *Lathe, Foot Powered*.

FOOT POWERED SAW. See *Saw, Foot and Hand Powered*.

FOOT TOOL. See *Anvil Tool, Foot*.

FOOT VISE. See *Vise, Farriers'*.

FOOT WHEEL. See *Foot Power Wheel*.

FORCEPS. A tool or instrument for grasping an object. The term is normally used when referring to a delicate or precision instrument.

FORCEPS, PIG. A tool used to assist during farrowing. Overall length is approximately 17 inches. These forceps have dull rounded corrugations to allow grasping the animal without injury.

Pig Forceps

FORCEPS, TAXIDERMISTS'. A tool used by a taxidermist for inserting the stuffing material into a bird or small animal. Length is approximately 12 inches.

Taxidermists' Forceps

FORE AUGER. A tool used to cut down the end of a large spoke such that it can be pointed with common spoke pointer. The illustrated auger will work spokes up to 1 inch square. This tool was not intended to cut the complete tenon inasmuch as it does not have provisions for cutting a square shoulder.

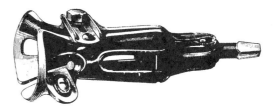

Fore Auger

FORE PLANE. See *Plane, Fore*.

FORE PUNCH. See *Anvil Tool, Nail Punch* and *Pritchel*.

FORGE. A surface upon which a fire is built for the purpose of heating metal to a working temperature. A forge has a built-in source of forced air or provisions for connecting an outside source. The supplier catalogues were not always consistent in nomenclature and recommended usage of the many varieties of forges. Some general types are illustrated.

FORGE, AGRICULTURAL. Also called FARMERS' FORGE. A small portable forge intended for use by farmers and for other light duty applications such as repair work. An 18 to 22 inch fire box was a common size.

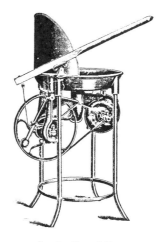

Agricultural Forge

FORGE, BENCH. A forge small enough to set on a workbench. This type of forge was often used by miners and prospectors. The illustration shows a portable bench forge along with a shipping case.

FORGE, BLACKSMITHS'. A forge suitable for heating a large variety of workpieces such as might be forged in a blacksmith shop. Many of the larger shops used a built-in forge of masonry construction. A typical forge listed by one supplier had a 28 by 40 inch firepan. Illustration

(b) shows two Queen's Patent Forges 30 and 36 inches in diameter.

Bench Forge

(b)
Blacksmiths' Forge

FORGE, BRIDGE BUILDERS'. Also called BARREL FORGE. A portable forge in which the mechanism is protected by an iron drum. Suitable for use by bridge builders, railroad repairmen and tank builders.

Bridge Builders' Forge

FORGE, FARMERS'. See *Forge, Agricultural*.

FORGE, FARRIERS'. A forge intended for use only with short workpieces such as horse shoes. Three sides of the forge were often enclosed thus allowing close control of the fire and of the smoke. This type of forge construction would be especially convenient if the work was being done in an open shed or drive-through shop. The farriers' forge is generally smaller than the Blacksmiths' Forge.

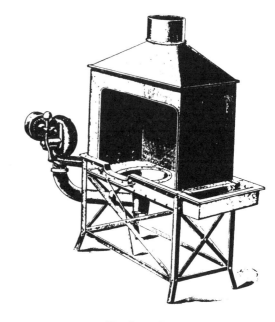

Farriers' Forge

FORGE, MACHINISTS'. See *Forge, Tool Makers'*.

FORGE, RIVET. A small forge used by a boiler maker or bridge builder to heat rivets. A common size is 18 inches in diameter.

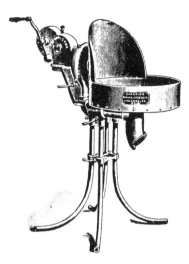

Rivet Forge

FORGE, TOOL MAKERS'. Also called MACHINISTS' FORGE. A medium sized forge often used in machine shops. A common hearth size is 24 by 24 inches.

Tool Makers' Forge

FORGE BLOWER. See *Blower, Blacksmiths'*.

FORGING HAMMER. See *Hammer, Forging*.

FORGING TONGS. See *Tongs, Farriers'*.

FORK. An implement consisting of a handle with two or more prongs or tines on one end. Used for digging, guiding, lifting or pitching.

FORK, BALER. Also called BALER PRESS FORK. A short-handled fork with straight tines used by the platform man to feed a stationary hay baler. Length of tines is about 4 inches.

FORK, BALLAST. See *Fork, Stone*.

Baler Fork

FORK, BARLEY. A large fork with oval tines used to handle barley. This type of fork has a stop at the root of the tines to facilitate increased loading of the fork.

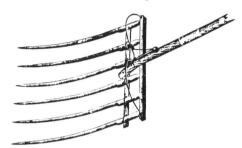

Barley Fork

FORK, BARN. See *Fork, Coal*.

FORK, BEET. See *Fork, Vegetable*.

FORK, BENDING. See *Anvil Tool, Bending Fork*.

FORK, BUNDLE. Also called PITCH FORK. A two or three tined fork used to pitch bundles of grain. Bundles from the reaper were pitched from the ground to a wagon, from the wagon to a stack and from the stack to the separator.

Bundle Fork

FORK, BUTTER. A wooden fork used to lift butter from the churn. Width is about 5 inches.

Butter Fork

FORK, COAL. Also called BARN FORK, COKE FORK, DUST FORK, ENSILAGE FORK, KAFFIR CORN FORK, SILO FORK, TANBARK FORK and TANNERS' FORK. A large fork with blunt tines intended to be used for handling a variety of loose material including coal. Forks of this shape with 6 to 18 tines were listed. Width is 11 1/2 to 20 1/2 inches.

Coal Fork

FORK, COTTON SEED. A large fork with closely spaced diamond shaped tines used for handling cotton seed hulls. Also listed as a SAWDUST SCOOP. A similar scoop with wider-spaced tines was listed as a CHAFF FORK.

Cotton Seed Fork

FORK, ELEVATOR. An ice harvest tool used to guide a block of ice onto the elevator. Length of the handle is 6 to 7 feet.

Elevator Fork

FORK, ENSILAGE. See *Fork, Coal.*

FORK, FISH. A one-pronged device used to handle fish and packing house scraps. Two-tined fish forks were also listed.

Fish Fork

FORK, FLESH. A butchers' tool used for handling pieces of cut meat. Overall length is 18 to 36 inches.

Flesh Fork

FORK, FLORAL. See *Fork, Garden.*

FORK, GARDEN. Also called SPADING FORK and WEEDING FORK. A small hand tool used for weeding and loosening the soil in a flower bed.

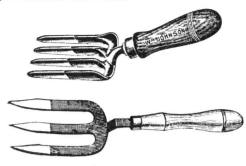

Garden Fork

FORK, HAY. Also called ALFALFA FORK and PITCH FORK. A two to four tined fork used for handling loose hay.

Hay Fork

FORK, HEADER. A four-tined fork with long tines used to handle grain heads clipped by the horse-drawn headers of the 1920 era. The heads were handled with a large fork inasmuch as they were light weight and did not bind together well. Similar to one variety of Hay Fork except that the header fork is larger.

Header Fork

FORK, MANURE. See *Fork, Shaving.*

FORK, POTATO. See *Fork, Spading.*

FORK, RAIL. A tool used to maneuver a railroad rail. Length is approximately 34 inches.

Rail Fork

FORK, RAISING. See *Raising Fork.*

FORK, SHAVING. A 4 to 6 tined fork used for handling shavings at a planing mill. Forks of this general shape and size were also listed as MANURE FORKS, MILL

FORKS, PULP FORKS and STREET FORKS. A fork of this type, with 8 to 12 tines, was listed as a SLUICE FORK.

Shaving Fork

FORK, SPADING. Also called POTATO DIGGER. A fork used for loosening the soil in small garden or flower plots and for digging potatoes.

Spading Fork

FORK, SPLITTING. Also called ICE BREAKER and SPLITTING BAR. A heavy fork used in the plow groove for breaking floats or large sheets of ice from the ice field. Weight is 14 to 18 pounds. The handle is 4 to 5 feet long.

Splitting Fork

FORK, STABLE. A wooden fork used for light tasks such as forking hay to the horses.

Stable Fork

FORK, STONE. Also called BALLAST FORK. A fork with heavy square tines used to handle stone or ballast. Shaped essentially like the Coal Fork except that the stone fork has shorter tines. Width is 8 1/2 to 13 inches. Forks of this size and general shape were also listed as ASPHALT FORKS and PHOSPHATE FORKS.

Stone Fork

FORK, STRAINING. See *Carpet Stretcher*.

FORK, TANNERS'. See *Fork, Coal*.

FORK, VEGETABLE. Also called BEET FORK and VEGETABLE SCOOP. A fork with round or broad oval tines having ball-shaped points. The beet fork has widely spaced tines.

Vegetable Fork

FORK, WEEDING. See *Fork, Garden*.

FORK BAR. See *Bar, Ice*.

FORK FILE. See *File, Fork*.

FORKSTAFF. See *Plane, Forkstaff*.

FORMER. A foot-powered machine, with interchangeable cutters, used for making wooden mouldings and for fluting. A powered machine having this function has become known as a shaper. See also *Moulding Former*.

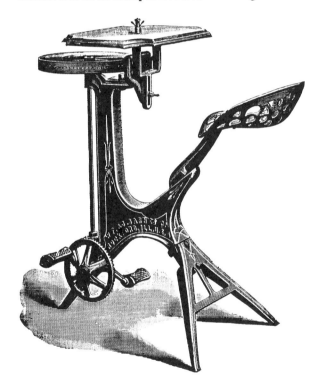

Former

FORMING IRON. See *Bookbinding Tool, Forming Iron*.

FORMING MACHINE. See *Tinsmiths' Machine, Pipe Former*.

FORSTNER BIT. See *Boring Tool, Bit, Forstner*.

FORWARDING STICK. See *Rule, Forwarding Stick*.

FOUNDRY RIDDLE. See *Riddle*.

FRAME OPENER PLIERS. See *Pliers, Frame Opener*.

FRAME SAW. See *Saw, Cabinet* and *Saw, Felloe*.

FRAME SAW FILE. See *File, Pit Saw*.

FRAMED PIT SAW. A type of pit saw. See *Saw, Pit*.

FRAMING CHISEL. See *Chisel, Framing*.

FRAMING GOUGE. See *Gouge, Framing*.

FRAMING HAMMER. A large nail hammer. See *Hammer, Boxing*.

FRAMING SAW. See *Saw, Docking*.

FRAMING SQUARE. See *Square, Steel*.

FRAMING TOOL. A combination tool used for laying out rafters.

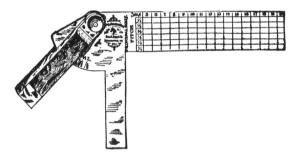

Topp's Patent

Framing Tool

FREIGHT HOOK. See *Hook, Box*.

FREIGHTERS' AXE. See *Axe, Freighters'*.

FRET SAW. See *Saw, Bracket*.

FRETWORK FILE. See *File, Fretwork*.

FROE. Also called COOPERS' FROE and STAVE FROE. A tool used for splitting out shingles and barrel staves. The working edge is kept fairly sharp for entering the wood but is intended to split rather than cut. The froe is placed along the grain of the workpiece and struck with the froe club. After the split is started, the froe is twisted to complete the separation of the shingle or stave. Cutting length is 5 to 24 inches. The handle is 12 to 16 inches long and extends straight up from the eye. Numerous examples of froes have been noted that have curved blades. These tools were probably home made attempts to facilitate making barrel staves. It is doubtful if any curved froe was satisfactory.

Froe

Froe

FROE CLUB. Also called FROE MALLET. A wooden mallet used for striking the back side of the froe. Froe clubs were often made by the user and are generally crude.

Froe Club

FROE MALLET. See *Froe Club*.

FROG. See *Chamfer Frog*.

FRONT CUTTING PLIERS. See *Nippers, End Cutting*.

FROST WEDGE. See *Wedge, Frost*.

FROSTING TOOL. See *Stone Cutters' Tool, Frosting*.

FROW. See *Froe*. Frow is a variation in spelling.

FRUIT AUGER. Also called FRUIT LIFTER and SUGAR DEVIL. A grocery store tool used to loosen dried fruit that is caked in the barrel. Also used for breaking up sugar that has hardened in the barrel. The illustrated tool was patented July 7, 1875.

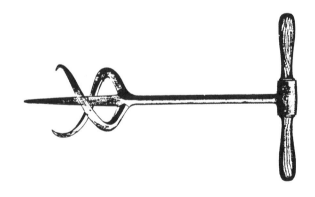

Fruit Auger

FRUIT BOX HATCHET. See *Hatchet, Box*.

FRUIT LIFTER. See *Fruit Auger*.

FRUIT PICKER. A rake-type device with a canvas bag attached that will allow fruit to be picked from a high branch of the tree. Any length of handle can be attached.

Fruit Picker

FRUIT PRESS. A press used to extract the juice from fruit and berries. See also *Barrel Header*.

Fruit Press

FUDGE WHEEL. See *Shoe Makers' Tool, Fudge Wheel*.

FULLER. See *Anvil Tool, Fuller*.

FULLERS' TEASEL. See *Teasel*.

FURNACE SCOOP. See *Shovel, Scoop*.

FURNACE TOOLS. See *Fire Tools, Furnace*.

FURNITURE CLAMP. See *Clamp, Bar*.

FURNITURE HANDLE WRENCH. See *Wrench, Furniture Handle*.

FURRIERS' DAMPING BRUSH. See *Brush, Damping*.

FURRIERS' KNIFE. See *Knife, Furriers'*.

FURRING PLANE. See *Plane, Furring*.

FURROWING PICK. See *Pick, Mill*.

FUSE CUTTER. A tool used to cut a dynamite fuse to length and crimp the cap to the end. Length of the illustrated tool is 5 1/2 inches.

Fuse Cutter

FUTTOCK SAW. See *Saw, Futtock*.

G

Tool names starting with the letter G including multiple listings of:
- GAUGE
- GOUGE
- GRIND STONE

Included also is a listing of tools used by the:
- GARDENER AND LAWN KEEPER

GAD TONGS. See *Tongs, Blacksmiths'*.

GAGE. See *Gauge*. Gage is a variation in spelling.

GAINING TOOL. Also called HAND GAINING TOOL. A tool used to cut a small groove in a straight or curved workpiece. Width of cutter is 1/8 to 1/4 inches.

Gaining Tool

GAMBREL. A tool used by a fur trapper to support a small animal for skinning.

Gambrel

GARDEN CULTIVATOR. A pull-type device used for loosening the soil in a garden. See also *Garden Plow*.

Garden Cultivator

GARDEN PLANTER. Also called DRILL SEEDER and ROW PLANTER. A device used to plant corn and other row crops in a garden.

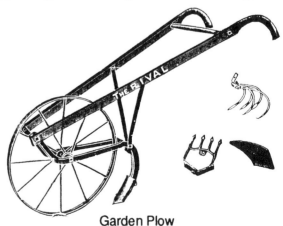

Garden Planter

GARDEN PLOW. Also called GARDEN CULTIVATOR. A push-type tilling and cultivating machine for use in a garden.

Garden Plow

GARDEN PULVERIZER. A garden weeding and tilling tool. Width of the illustrated tool is 7 1/2 inches. The sharp points are useful for breaking up clods or a crusted surface.

Garden Pulverizer

GARDEN SEEDER. A tool used for planting small vegetable or flower seeds. Several interchangeable discs were available for planting seeds of various sizes.

Garden Seeder

GARDEN AND LAWN TOOLS. The special-purpose garden and lawn tools listed below can be found in normal alphabetical sequence. These tools may also have been used for other purposes.

CHISEL, ASPARAGUS
DANDELION DIGGER
DIBBLE
FORK, GARDEN
FORK, SPADING
GARDEN CULTIVATOR
GARDEN PLANTER
GARDEN PLOW
GARDEN PULVERIZER
GARDEN SEEDER
GOUGE, ASPARAGUS
GRASS HOOK
HOE, GARDEN
HOE, SCUFFLE
HOE RAKE
KNIFE, ASPARAGUS
KNIFE, PRUNING
LAWN EDGE TRIMMER
LAWN MOWER
LAWN MOWER SHARPENER
LAWN ROLLER
POTATO PLANTER
RAKE, DANDELION
RAKE, GARDEN
RAKE, LEAF
SHEARS, BORDER
SHEARS, GRASS
SHEARS, HEDGE
SHEARS, PRUNING
SOD LIFTER
SPIKE TAMPER
SPRAYER
STAKE PUNCH
TROWEL, GARDEN
TURF EDGER
WEED DIGGER
WEEDER
WHEEL BARROW

GAS BURNER CLEANER. A file-type device used for removing carbon deposits from a gas burner.

Gas Burner Cleaner

GAS BURNER PLIERS. See *Pliers, Gas.*

GAS FITTERS' AUGER. See *Boring Tool, Gas Fitters' Auger.*

GAS FITTERS' BIT. See *Boring Tool, Bit, Gas Fitters'.*

GAS PIPE PLIERS. See *Pliers, Gas.*

GAS PLIERS. See *Pliers, Gas.*

GAS RETORT SCOOP. A unique scoop used for charging a gas retort. The body of the scoop is 8 feet long.

Gas Retort Scoop

GAS TROWEL. See *Trowel, Gas.*

GASKET CHISEL. See *Caulking Tool, Plumbers'.*

GASKET CUTTER. See *Washer Cutter.*

GASOLINE TORCH. See *Torch, Gasoline* and *Torch, Soldering.*

GAUGE. A tool used to measure, compare, mark or to cut to a precise standard. The special-purpose gauges listed below can be found in normal alphabetical sequence. These tools may also have been used for other purposes.

ANGLE GAUGE
AXLE GAUGE

191

BALL GAUGE
BELT GAUGE
BIT GAUGE
BORE GAUGE
BUCKET STAVE GAUGE
BUTT GAUGE
BUTT AND RABBET GAUGE
CENTER GAUGE
CLAPBOARD GAUGE
CLAPBOARD GAUGE, WOODEN
CORK GAUGE
CUTTING GAUGE
DRAW GAUGE
DRILL POINT GAUGE
ELECTROTYPE FINISHERS' TOOL, LINING GAUGE
ELECTROTYPE FINISHERS' TOOL, TYPE HIGH GAUGE
FILLET GAUGE
FOOT ADJUSTER
GAUGE STANDARD
GEAR TOOTH GAUGE
GLASS GAUGE
GOLD TESTING NEEDLES
HOLE GAUGE
HORSE COLLAR TOOL, MEASURING YOKE
HUB BOXING GAUGE
JOINTER GAUGE
JOURNAL GAUGE
KNITTING NEEDLE GAUGE
LEATHER TOOL, BAG PUNCH GAUGE
LEATHER TOOL, ROUND PUNCH GAUGE
LEATHER TOOL, TRACE PUNCH GAUGE
LUMBER GAUGE
MAINSPRING GAUGE
MARKING GAUGE
MORTISING GAUGE
NUT AND WASHER GAUGE
PANEL GAUGE
PAPER GAUGE
PIANO TOOL, TUNING PIN GAUGE
PLANE, CHISEL GAUGE
RING SIZER
RING STICK
ROPE GAUGE
RULE
RULE GAUGE
SAW GAUGE
SAW SET GAUGE
SAW TENSION GAUGE
SAW TOOTH GAUGE
SHEET METAL GAUGE
SHINGLE GAUGE
SHOE MAKERS' TOOL, SOLE GAUGE
SLITTING GAUGE
SPHEROMETER
STAIR BUILDERS' GAUGE

STAIR GAUGE
STONE SIZE GAUGE
TAPER GAUGE
THREAD GAUGE
TIRE MEASURING WHEEL
TRACK GAUGE
TURNING GAUGE
WHEEL GAUGE
WIRE GAUGE

GAUGE GLASS CUTTER. See *Glass Cutter.*

GAUGE HAND PULLER. See *Hand Puller.*

GAUGE STANDARD. A precision device used to check a fixed machinists' gauge for accuracy.

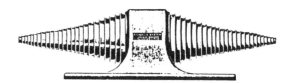

Gauge Standard

GAUGERS' MARKING IRON. See *Timber Scribe.*

GAUGING ROD. See *Rule, Gauging Rod.*

GAUGING TROWEL. See *Trowel, Gauging.*

GEAR BRUSH. See *Brush, Gear.*

GEAR PULLER. See *Wheel Puller.*

GEAR TOOTH GAUGE. A tool used to gauge the proper depth for cutting gear teeth. A separate gauge is required for each pitch.

Gear Tooth Gauge

GEARED BRACE. See *Boring Tool, Hand Drill.*

GENTLEMAN'S BIT BRACE. See *Boring Tool, Bit Brace, Gentleman's.*

GERMAN CENTER BIT. See *Boring Tool, Bit, Center.*

GERMAN PATTERN PLANE. A type of bench plane. See *Plane, Horn.*

GIG SADDLERS' TRIMMER. See *Leather Tool, Trimmer.*

GILDING ROLL. See *Bookbinding Tool, Embossing Roll.*

GIMLET. See *Boring Tool, Bell Hangers'; Boring Tool, Bit, Bell Hangers'; Boring Tool, Bit, Gimlet; Boring Tool, Gimlet; Sampler, Cement* and *Sampler, Cotton.*

GIMLET BIT. See *Boring Tool, Bit, Gimlet.*

GIMPER. A silversmiths' tool used for cutting out the corners of a metal plate that is to be bent into a three dimensional shape. This tool was made in several sizes and patterns. Typical cuts are shown in the illustration.

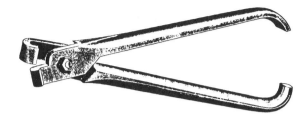

Gimper

GIN SAW FILE. See *File, Gin Saw*.

GIRDLE WRENCH. See *Wrench, Girdle*.

GLASS BLOW PIPE. Also called BLOW TUBE, PONTIL, PONTY and PUNTY. A glass blowers' tool consisting of a hollow iron pipe flared on one end. Length is up to five feet.

Glass Blow Pipe

GLASS BLOWERS' TONGS. See *Tongs, Glass Blowers'*.

GLASS CHIPPING TOOL. A tool used to produce decorative chipping around the edges of glass nameplates, signs and similar items.

Glass Chipping Tool

GLASS CUTTER. A tool used to scratch glass thus providing a track on which the glass can be broken. The tool consists of a hardened wheel or a diamond point set at the end of a rigid handle. It is generally used by being drawn along a straight edge. A glass cutter often includes a series of notches to fit over various thicknesses of glass to aid in applying a constant pressure to a narrow edge for breaking.

Glass Cutter

Diamond Point

Gauge Glass or Tube

Circle

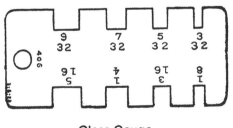

Circle

Glass Cutter

GLASS CUTTERS' RULE. See *Rule, Glass Cutters'*.

GLASS CUTTERS' SQUARE. See *Square, Glass Cutters'*.

GLASS CUTTING FILE. See *File, Glass Cutting*.

GLASS FILE. See *File, Glass Cutting*.

GLASS GAUGE. A tool used to determine the thickness of a sheet of glass.

Glass Gauge

GLASS PLIERS. See *Pliers, Glass*.

GLASS ROLLER PLIERS. See *Pliers, Glass Roller*.

GLASS SLICKER. See *Curriers' Slicker* and *Leather Tool, Slicker*.

GLASS TAPPER. A glass cutters' tool used to tap glass to induce breaking. The tool consists of a 3/4 inch brass knob on the end of a 6 1/2 to 9 inch handle.

Glass Tapper

GLASS TONGS. See *Tongs, Glass.*

GLASS TUBE CUTTER. See *Glass Cutter.*

GLAZIERS' CHISEL. See *Chisel, Glaziers'.*

GLAZIERS' HAMMER. See *Hammer, Glaziers'.*

GLAZIERS' KNIFE. See *Knife, Putty.*

GLUE BRUSH. See *Brush, Glue.*

GLUE CLAMP. See *Clamp, Cabinet Makers'.*

GLUE POT. A double iron pot in which sheet or flake glue is melted. The outside pot is kept filled with water to avoid overheating the glue. Some pots are tinned inside to provide a smooth surface. Sizes up to four quarts were available. The better quality pots are equipped with a lid.

The glue pot was a necessary tool for every cabinet maker and carriage maker prior to the use of liquid glue. Clean and freshly melted glue was required to produce a quality job. The pot had to be cleaned out each day in hot weather and every two days in mild weather to prevent spoilage of the glue.

Common Type   Self Heating

Glue Pot

GLUE SCRAPER. See *Scraper, Cabinet.*

GLUT. See *Wedge, Wood Splitting.*

GOBLET BRUSH. See *Brush, Silversmiths'.*

GOLD BEATING HAMMER. See *Hammer, Gold Beating.*

GOLD CUSHION. See *Bookbinding Tool, Gold Cushion.*

GOLD KNIFE. See *Knife, Gold.*

GOLD PAN. A washing pan for gold used by a prospector or miner. Dirt, gravel and water is taken into the pan and swirled until the gold sinks to the bottom. Swirling of the pan is continued until most of the dirt and gravel is thrown over the rim and only the gold remains.

Horn Type

Gold Pan

GOLD TESTING NEEDLES. A set of gauges used to estimate the quality of a sample of gold.

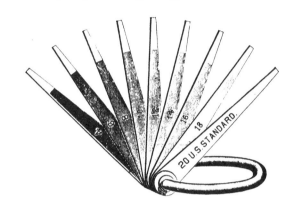

Gold Testing Needles

GONIOMETER. An instrument for measuring plane angles. One supplier listed the illustrated tool as an ARM PROTRACTOR AND GONIOMETER. It was patented July 31, 1900. Recommended as being particularly suitable for measuring the outside angles of a crystal.

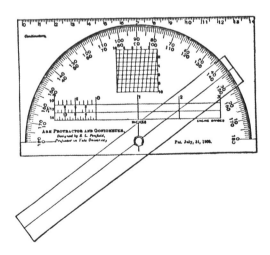

Goniometer

GOOSEWING AXE. See *Axe, Broad, European Pattern.*

GOTHIC BEAD. See *Plane, Moulding, Gothic Bead.*

GOUGE. A hand tool with a curved cutting edge at the end of a blade, used to cut or pare solid material such as metal or wood. See also *Anvil Tool, Gouge*.

GOUGE, ASPARAGUS. A gouge-shaped tool used to cut asparagus below the surface of the ground. Width is 7/8 to 1 inch.

Asparagus Gouge

GOUGE, BENT. Also called BENT NECK GOUGE, BENT SHANK GOUGE, CRANKED GOUGE and OFFSET GOUGE. A gouge having the handle offset in the direction of the concave side of the cutting edge. The offset allows hand clearance with the gouge blade flat on the workpiece.

Bent Gouge

GOUGE, BENT NECK. See *Gouge, Bent*.

GOUGE, BENT SHANK. See *Gouge, Bent*.

GOUGE, BLOCK MAKERS'. A heavy gouge with a deep curvature. Used for making wooden pulleys. Width is 3/4 to 2 1/2 inches.

Block Makers' Gouge

GOUGE, BONE. A medical tool used in bone surgery. Usually made of stainless steel or heavily plated.

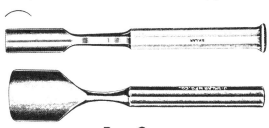

Bone Gouge

GOUGE, CARVING. See *Carving Tool, Gouge*.

GOUGE, COACH MAKERS'. A variety of firmer gouge. See *Gouge, Firmer*.

GOUGE, CRANKED. See *Gouge, Bent*.

GOUGE, FIRMER. A medium-duty gouge such as might be used in a cabinet shop. Width is 1/8 to 3 inches. The regular or standard one inch firmer has a blade length of 5 1/2 to 7 inches. Firmer gouges were available with either socket or tang handles and with the cutting edge

beveled either inside or outside. The COACH MAKERS' FIRMER GOUGE is slightly longer and heavier than the regular type. MILLWRIGHTS' FIRMER GOUGES were offered with blades from 8 to 10 inches long. See also *Gouge, Framing*.

Regular Socket

Coach Makers' Tang

Millwrights'

Firmer Gouge

GOUGE, FRAMING. A heavy-duty socket gouge suitable for use by a framing carpenter. The handle has an iron ring at the end to allow use of a mallet for making deep cuts. Cutting width is 1/4 to 3 inches. The regular framing gouge has a blade length of 7 1/2 to 8 inches. Lengths up to 10 inches were listed for MILLWRIGHTS' FRAMING GOUGES. This tool was sometimes listed as a HEAVY SOCKET FIRMER GOUGE.

Framing Gouge

GOUGE, HALF ROUND NOSE. See *Chisel, Half Round Nose*.

GOUGE, HAMMER HEAD. See *Gouge, Plumbers'*.

GOUGE, LATHE. See *Turning Tool, Gouge*.

GOUGE, MILLWRIGHTS'. A gouge with an extra long blade. See *Gouge, Firmer* and *Gouge, Framing*.

GOUGE, OFFSET. See *Gouge, Bent*.

GOUGE, PARING. A gouge with a thin blade used for paring and final fitting of the workpiece. Width is 1/8 to 2 inches and length of the blade is 8 to 9 inches. Both tang and socket types were listed but the paring gouge normally has a tang handle. This type of gouge is often made with an inside bevel. The paring gouge is generally considered to be a pattern makers' tool.

Paring Gouge

Paring Gouge

GOUGE, PLUMBERS'. Also called HAMMER HEAD GOUGE. An all-metal gouge intended for use by a plumber or for similar tasks. Cutting width is 1/2 to 1 inch.

Plumbers' Gouge

GOUGE, SLICE. A gouge with a unique bend. Listed as a ship builders' tool.

Slice Gouge

GOUGE, SOCKET FIRMER. See *Gouge, Firmer*.

GOUGE, TURNING. See *Turning Tool, Gouge*.

GOUGE BIT. See *Boring Tool, Bit, Gouge*.

GOUGE CHISEL. See *Anvil Tool, Gouge*.

GOUGE STONE. See *Sharpening Stone, Gouge*.

GRAB MAUL. See *Maul, Grab*.

GRAB SKIPPER. Also called CARTING GRAB SKIPPER. A logging tool used to pry a grab hook loose from a log. Also used to pry a log loose from the pile or from a wagon.

Grab Skipper

GRADE LEVEL. See *Level, Grade*.

GRAFTING FROE. Also called GRAFTING KNIFE. A tool used in grafting fruit trees. The long cutting edge makes the initial split in the receiving tree. The extended point is used to open the split for insertion of the new wood.

Grafting Froe

Grafting Froe

GRAFTING KNIFE. See *Grafting Froe*.

GRAILLE. A comb makers' tool similar to a single-cut file. Used to smooth and dress the sides of comb teeth. Length is 6 1/2 to 10 inches. There are 12 to 18 teeth per inch.

Graille

GRAIN CRADLE. A tool used to cut ripened wheat or other small grain. The wooden teeth catch the stalks as they are cut and allow them to be placed in a neat pile for tying. The mechanical reaper obsoleted this tool.

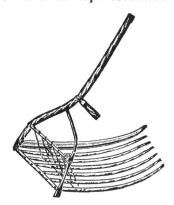

Grain Cradle

GRAIN SAMPLER. See *Prune Tester* and *Sampler, Grain*.

GRAIN SCOOP. Also called DULUTH GRAIN SCOOP. A scoop used to unload grain from a truck or railroad car. Size is 1/2 to 1 bushel. See also *Shovel, Scoop*.

Grain Scoop

GRAIN SCYTHE. See *Grain Cradle* and *Scythe*.

GRAIN SHOVEL. See *Shovel, Scoop*.

GRAIN SICKLE. A one-hand tool used to cut ripened grain. A handful of stalks is grasped with one hand and then cut off with the sickle. The grain sickle is much longer and more graceful than the common grass hook or corn knife.

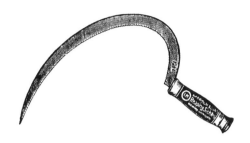

Grain Sickle

GRAIN TESTER. See *Prune Tester.*

GRAIN TRIER. See *Sampler, Grain.*

GRAINING BOARD. A curriers' tool. See *Raising Board.*

GRAINING COMB. See *Graining Tool.*

GRAINING ROLLER. See *Graining Tool.*

GRAINING TOOL. A tool used by a painter to simulate a wood grain. A base coat of paint is applied to the workpiece and allowed to dry. The hard-rubber grainer or the flexible comb is then drawn through or pressed into a second coat of wet paint to produce the desired pattern. The combs are generally made of steel; however, leather and rubber varieties have been noted.

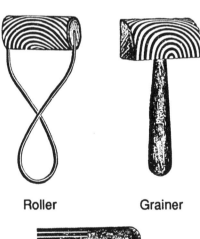

Roller   Grainer

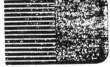

Comb

Graining Tool

GRANITE BUSH CHISEL. See *Chisel, Bush.*

GRANITE CARVERS' CALIPER. See *Caliper, Firm Joint.*

GRANITE CHISEL. See *Stone Cutters' Tool, Chisel.*

GRANITE CUTTERS' BUSH HAMMER. See *Hammer, Bush.*

GRANITE CUTTERS' HAND HAMMER. See *Hammer, Stone Cutters'.*

GRANITE CUTTERS' SCOTIA. See *Hammer, Scotia.*

GRANITE PEEN HAMMER. See *Axe, Stone.*

GRANITE TOOL TONGS. See *Tongs, Blacksmiths'.*

GRANITE TOOLS. See *Stone Cutting Tools.*

GRANITE WEDGE TONGS. See *Tongs, Blacksmiths'.*

GRANITOID TOOL. Granitoid was a form of concrete said to resemble granite. See *Cement Tool.*

GRAPE HOE. See *Hoe, Farm.*

GRAPE KNIFE. See *Knife, Grape.*

GRAPPLE. See *Hook, Grappling* and *Timber Grapple.*

GRAPPLING HOOK. See *Hook, Grappling.*

GRAPPLING IRON. See *Hook, Grappling.*

GRASS HOOK. A hand tool used for cutting grass and weeds in a confined area. A long-handled hook for use while standing upright was also available.

Grass Hook

GRASS SHEARS. See *Shears, Grass.*

GRAVEL SCOOP. See *Shovel, Round Point* and *Shovel, Scoop.*

GRAVEL SHOVEL. See *Shovel, Round Point* and *Shovel, Scoop.*

GRAVER. Also called ENGRAVING TOOL and GRAVING TOOL. A small hand tool used to carve or engrave a hard material such as silver or boxwood. Used extensively for engraving printing blocks and by jewelers. See also *Lining Tool.*

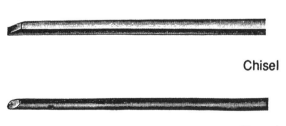

Chisel

Round

Graver

197

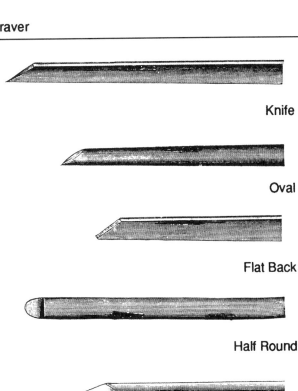

Knife

Oval

Flat Back

Half Round

Square, Diamond or Burin

Lozenge

Bent

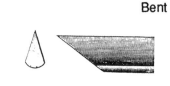

Tint Tool

Ring Tool

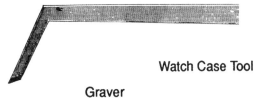

Watch Case Tool

Graver

GRAVER HANDLE. Graver handles are generally made very short to fit entirely within the palm of the hand. They are often flat on one side to allow the blade to lie almost flat on the workpiece. Several types of quickly removeable handles were available to allow use of one handle with two or more blades. Handles are made of hardwood or ivory.

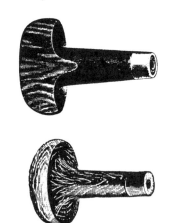

Graver Handle

GRAVER SHARPENER. A tool used to hold a graver at a fixed angle while sharpening or honing.

Graver Sharpener

GRAVING TOOL. See *Graver.*

GREASE BOX. A small wooden container intended for holding grease or beeswax. These containers are usually 2 to 3 inches wide and generally have a lid that is hinged on a nail. Some are intricately carved and have various types of locking lids. Grease or wax is used to lubricate a nail, tack or screw thereby reducing driving friction.

Grease Box

GREASE GUN. A device used to apply grease to a bearing through a pressure fitting. Primarily a farm machinery or automobile tool.

Grease Gun

GREASER. See *Spring Greaser*.

GREAT AMERICAN FILE. See *File, Cross Cut*.

GRECIAN OGEE. See *Plane, Moulding, Grecian Ogee*.

GRECIAN OVOLO. See *Plane, Moulding, Grecian Ovolo*.

GRIND STONE. Also called GRINDING WHEEL. A circular stone used for sharpening cutting tools. Many grind stones have a trough or well to allow the bottom of the stone to run in water for the purpose of cooling the workpiece. See also *Grinding Machine*.

GRIND STONE, FAMILY. Also called KITCHEN GRIND STONE. The wheel is 6 to 14 inches in diameter. The water trough is usually of cast iron.

Family Grind Stone

GRIND STONE, HAND. A bench-mounted grind stone popular in small workshops. These stones were made in a

variety of shapes and sizes. The illustrated tool is geared in order to attain a high wheel speed.

Hand Grind Stone

GRIND STONE, PEDAL. A grind stone operated with one or both feet. The wheel is 18 to 36 inches in diameter. A conical drip can suspended above the wheel provides cooling water to avoid overheating of the workpiece. Some of these machines have a curved sheet metal water trough below the wheel in place of the drip can. When the sheet metal rusted out, it was often replaced with a section of an automobile tire.

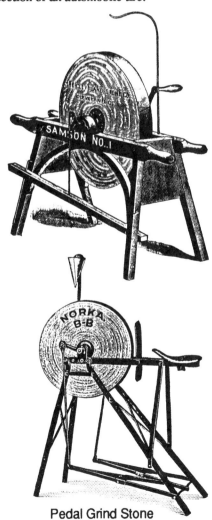

Pedal Grind Stone

GRIND STONE, SHIP. A compact grinding wheel suitable for carriage aboard a ship. Wheel is 8 to 18 inches in diameter.

Ship Grind Stone

GRIND STONE, SICKLE. A geared grinding wheel with a unique shape used for sharpening sickle bars for mowing machines or reapers.

Sickle Grind Stone

GRIND STONE TRUING DEVICE. A tool used to true or smooth a large grind stone. The device is clamped to the frame close to the stone and brought into contact with the stone by action of the hand adjustment wheel. As the grinding wheel is rotated, the high points are removed by the truing device.

Grind Stone Truing Device

GRINDING HOLDER. See *Chisel Grinder.*

GRINDING MACHINE. Also called GRIND STONE. A foot-powered machine used to turn a small grinding or polishing wheel at high speed.

Grinding Machine

GRINDING MILL. A hand-operated grinder intended for use in the home or for infrequent use in a shop. The Bone Mill was used to grind bones for use in fertilizer or for chicken feed. Bones were also used to make carbon black. The Coffee, Spice or Drug Mill was a grocery store or drug store tool. See also *Cider Mill.*

GRINDING WHEEL. See *Grind Stone.*

GRINDING WHEEL DRESSER. A tool used for trueing, shaping, dressing and removing glaze from a grinding wheel. The point of the dresser is held against the wheel as the wheel is being rotated.

Grist Mill

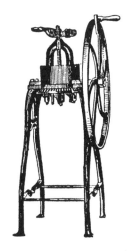

Bone Mill(Green)

Grinding Mill

Paint Mill

Grinding Wheel Dresser

Coffee, Spice or Drug Mill

GROMMET DIE. See *Grommet Set*.

GROMMET PUNCH. See *Punch, Grommet*.

GROMMET SET. Also called GROMMET DIE and SETTING DIE. A tool used to swage a grommet into a canvas or tarpaulin. Several sizes were available.

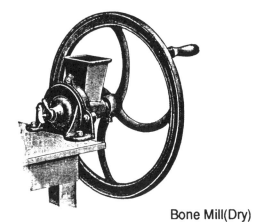

Bone Mill(Dry)

Grinding Mill

Grommet Set

GROOVER. See *Belt Groover; Cement Tool, Jointer; Floor Groover* and *Grooving Tool.*

GROOVING CHISEL. See *Chisel, Bent Grooving.*

GROOVING MACHINE. See *Tinsmiths' Machine, Grooving.*

GROOVING PLOW PLANE. See *Plane, Panel Plow.*

GROOVING TOOL. Also called HAND GROOVER. A tinners' hand tool used to groove sheet metal. Sizes to form grooves 3/32 to 19/32 inch wide were available.

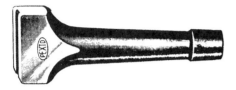

Grooving Tool

GRUB HOE. See *Hoe, Grub.*

GUANO HORN. A horn-shaped tube used for placing fertilizer in the hill with the seed when planting corn. Made of tin. Size of the illustrated tool is 30 inches long and about 5 1/2 inches in diameter at the large end.

Guano Horn

GUARDED CHISEL. See *Chisel, Guarded.*

GUARDED HATCHET. See *Hatched, Guarded.*

GULLETING FILE. See *File, Round.*

GUN STOCK SCRAPER. See *Scraper, Coach Makers'.*

GUN STOCK TOOL. A tool used for inlaying and ornamenting a gun stock. Length is 4 1/2 to 6 inches.

Shovel

Checkering or Bordering

Fluting

Gun Stock Tool

GUNSMITHS' SCREW DRIVER. See *Screw Driver, Gunsmiths'.*

GUNSMITHS' WRENCH. See *Wrench, Gunsmiths'.*

GUNTER'S RULE. See *Rule, Calculating.*

GUTTER ADZE. See *Adze, Gutter.*

GUTTER PLANE. See *Plane, Gutter.*

GUTTER TONGS. A tool used for working sheet metal. See *Tongs, Roofing.*

GUTTER TOOL. See *Cement Tool, Gutter.*

H

Tool names starting with the letter H including multiple listings of:

> HAMMER
> HATCHET
> HOE
> HOOK
> HORSE COLLAR TOOL

HACK. See *Turpentine Hacker*.

HACK SAW. See *Saw, Hack*.

HACKER. See *Turpentine Hacker*.

HACKING KNIFE. See *Knife, Chipping*.

HAFT. See *Awl Haft*.

HAIR PICKER. A machine used for combing out hair, moss or tow for use in padding such as in carriage seats.

Hair Picker

HAIR PINCER. See *Pinching Iron*.

HAIR SHEDDER. A semi-rigid rubbing tool used to remove loose hair from a horse.

Hair Shedder

HALF AXE. See *Axe, Campers'*.

HALF BACK SAW. See *Saw, Half Back*.

HALF CLAW HATCHET. See *Hatchet, Half Claw*.

HALF HATCHET. See *Hatchet, Half*.

HALF ROUND FILE. See *File, Half Round*.

HALF ROUND NOSE GOUGE. See *Chisel, Half Round Nose*.

HALF ROUND NOSE CHISEL. See *Chisel, Half Round Nose*.

HALFTONE COMB. See *Electrotype Finishers' Tool, Halftone Comb*.

HALFTONE RAKE. See *Electrotype Finishers' Tool, Halftone Comb*.

HALFTONE SOFTENING HAMMER. See *Hammer, Halftone Softening*.

HALVING PLANE. See *Plane, Halving*.

HAM STRINGER. A butchers' tool used for tying a boned ham. Length of blade is approximately 7 inches.

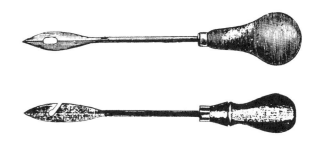

Ham Stringer

HAM TRIER. A round pointed instrument used to probe around the bone of a ham. Freshness was determined by the resultant odor or lack of same.

Ham Trier

HAME CLIP GOUGE. See *Leather Tool, Edger*.

HAMMER. A one-handed striking tool consisting of a solid head set crosswise on a handle. The term is also used to apply to a mechanical striking machine such as a power hammer or trip hammer.

HAMMER, ADVERTISING. See *Hammer, Bill Posters'*.

HAMMER, ADZE. A hammer with a poll similar to a nail hammer and a sharpened adze bit opposite the poll. The bit has a keyhole-shaped slot for use in pulling nails.

Adze Hammer

HAMMER, ANGLE PEEN. A hammer with a dull edge-peen formed at 45 degrees to the handle.

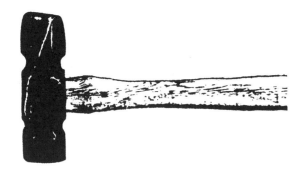

Angle Peen Hammer

HAMMER, BACKING. Also called BLANK HAMMER and BOOK BINDERS' HAMMER. A bookbinding tool used to round the back of a book during the binding process. The signatures are held in the backing press and pounded over toward the sides to form a rounded shape. Weight is 1 1/2 to 2 1/2 pounds. Length of handle is approximately 9 1/2 inches. The backing hammer is similar, but somewhat larger, than one variety of Shoe Makers' Hammer.

Backing Hammer

HAMMER, BALL PEEN. A general-purpose hammer with a semi-spherical peen. Used for riveting, forming and forging. Weight is 1 to 56 ounces.

HAMMER, BALL PEEN, AUTO. A ball peen hammer with a special metal handle intended for use as an automobile tire tool. Weight is 7 to 20 ounces not including the handle.

Machinists'

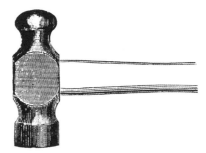

Engineers'

Ball Peen Hammer

Auto Ball Peen Hammer

HAMMER, BEATING. A book binders' tool used to flatten the pages and signatures of a book.

Beating Hammer

HAMMER, BELT. Also called CHISEL PEEN HAMMER. This hammer was offered as a belt makers' tool. The peen is apparently shaped like a rounded chisel.

Belt Hammer

HAMMER, BILL POSTERS'. Also called ADVERTISING HAMMER. A small hammer with a long jointed handle and a spring clip on the side. The clip will hold a card and a tack in such a way as to allow the card to be posted above the normal reach of the user. Handle length is 24 to 45 inches. Weight of the hammer head is 5 to 8 ounces.

Bill Posters' Hammer

HAMMER, BLACKSMITHS'. Also called BLACKSMITHS' CROSS PEEN HAMMER, BLACKSMITHS' HAND HAMMER, ENGINEERS' HAMMER, PLOW HAMMER and WEDGE PEEN HAMMER. A type of hammer favored by most blacksmiths for general forging work. Weight is 18 to 72 ounces. Normal weight is about 48 ounces. Handle length is 16 to 20 inches.

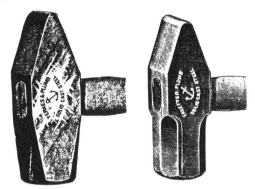

Blacksmiths' Hammer

HAMMER, BLACKSMITHS' CROSS PEEN. See *Hammer, Blacksmiths'*.

HAMMER, BLACKSMITHS' HAND. See *Hammer, Blacksmiths'*.

HAMMER, BLACKSMITHS' SHOULDER PEEN. See *Hammer, Shoulder Peen*.

HAMMER, BLANK. A book binders' tool. See *Hammer, Backing*.

HAMMER, BLOCK MAKERS' TRIMMING. See *Hammer, Pavers' Side*.

HAMMER, BLOCKING. See *Hammer, Electrotype Finishers'*.

HAMMER, BOILER MAKERS'. A large riveting or backing hammer. Weight is 2 1/2 to 6 pounds.

HAMMER, BOILER RIVETING. Also called BOILER MAKERS' RIVETING HAMMER and BOILER BUILDERS' RIVETING HAMMER. A medium weight riveting hammer. Weight is 24 to 48 ounces.

Button   Bevel Face

Boiler Makers' Hammer

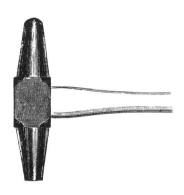

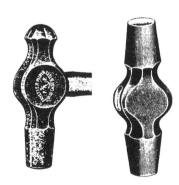

Boiler Riveting Hammer

HAMMER, BOILER SCALING. See *Hammer, Scaling*.

HAMMER, BOOK BINDERS'. See *Hammer, Backing*.

HAMMER, BOXING. Also called FRAMING HAMMER. A large nail hammer used by fruit packers to assemble boxes and by framing carpenters. Weight is approximately 30 ounces.

Boxing Hammer

HAMMER, BRAD. Also called CIGAR BOX HAMMER. A hammer used for driving small nails or brads. Weight is 2 to 6 ounces.

Brad Hammer

HAMMER, BRASS. See *Hammer, Soft Faced.*

HAMMER, BREAKING. See *Hammer, Bursting.*

HAMMER, BRICK LAYERS'. Also called BRICK HAMMER and MASONS' BRICK HAMMER. A hammer used to remove a portion of a brick. Weight is 16 to 48 ounces.

Adze Eye

Brick Layers' Hammer

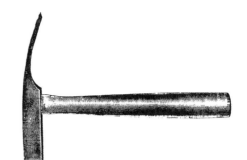

Boston Pattern

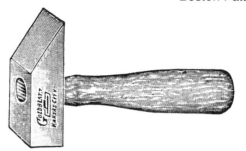

For Acid Brick

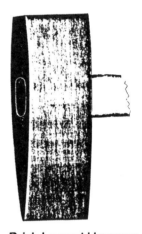

Brick Layers' Hammer

HAMMER, BRIDGE BUILDERS'. Also called SHIP RIVETING HAMMER. Weight is 4 to 5 pounds. This hammer is essentially the same as the Boiler Riveting Hammer except larger.

Bridge Builders' Hammer

HAMMER, BROOM MAKERS'. Also called BROOM POUNDER. A unique hammer used to compress the broom corn and tighten the wire as the corn is fastened to the handle. Length of the striking surface is approximately 5 inches.

Broom Makers' Hammer

HAMMER, BURSTING. Also called PAVERS' BOXING HAMMER, PAVERS' BREAKING HAMMER, PAVERS' BURSTING HAMMER, QUARRYMANS' BREAKING HAMMER, STONE BREAKING HAMMER and STONE CUTTERS' BREAKING HAMMER. A heavy hammer used for breaking stone. Weight is in excess of 6 pounds.

Bursting Hammer

HAMMER, BUSH. Also called CONCRETE BUSH HAMMER, GRANITE CUTTERS' BUSH HAMMER, MASONS' BUSH HAMMER, QUARRYMANS' BUSH HAMMER and STONE BUSH HAMMER. A hammer used for breaking stone and for removing projections to flatten a stone. Weight is 3 to 10 1/2 pounds. One variety of bush hammer is made of several leaves that can be disassembled for sharpening.

Bush Hammer

HAMMER, BUTTERFLY PEEN. See *Axe, Stone*.

HAMMER, CARD. A weaving mill tool used for tacking the carding to the roll. See also *Hammer, Saddlers'*.

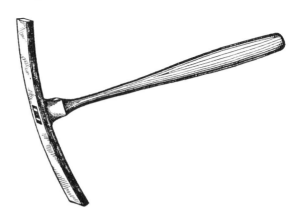

Card Hammer

HAMMER, CARPET. See *Hammer, Upholsterers'*.

HAMMER, CARPET LAYERS'. See *Hammer, Upholsterers*.

HAMMER, CARRIAGE IRONERS'. A hammer used for bending and shaping iron straps. The peen is rounded for use in riveting. Weight is 24 to 44 ounces.

Carriage Ironers' Hammer

HAMMER, CASE. A small hammer used to repair and smooth a watch case.

Case Hammer

HAMMER, CAULKING. A plumbers' hammer used for driving the tools when caulking water and gas pipes. Weight is 2 to 3 1/2 pounds.

Caulking Hammer

HAMMER, CHASING. A hammer used to drive a chasing tool when decorating thin metal. The rounded peen is used for forming or raising. Weight is 1 to 6 ounces. Handle length is approximately 9 1/2 inches.

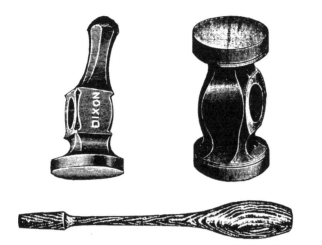

Typical Handle

Chasing Hammer

HAMMER, CHIPPING. A hammer used to chip paint or scale from metal. Weight is 12 to 50 ounces. See also *Hammer, Scaling.*

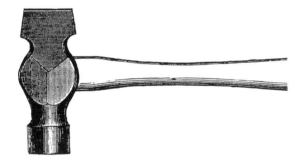

Machinists'

Chipping Hammer

HAMMER, CIGAR BOX. A small hammer used to drive the brad in a cigar box lid. See illustration under *Hammer, Brad.*

HAMMER, CIRCULAR CLAW. A nail hammer with a closed claw said to prevent breakage of the handle when drawing nails. Patented by Solomon Anderson in 1845.

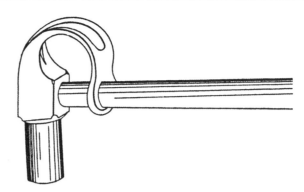

Circular Claw Hammer

HAMMER, CLAW. See *Hammer, Nail.*

HAMMER, COBBLERS'. See *Hammer, Shoe Makers'.*

HAMMER, COMBINATION. A tool serving the function of a hammer in combination with other tools. Illustration (a) shows a Household Combination Hammer. The hammer shown in illustration (b) is a fencing tool that will pull staples, pull nails, twist wire and serve as a wrench for square nuts.

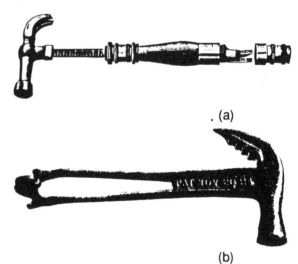

. (a)

(b)

Combination Hammer

HAMMER, COOPERS'. A straight-peen hammer described by one supplier as a large hammer with a straight face and no bevel. Weight is 2 to 6 1/2 pounds. The peen is used to flare a metal hoop in order to obtain a proper fit to a tapered barrel.

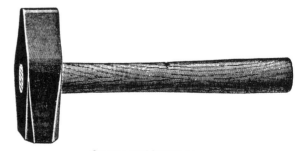

Coopers' Hammer

HAMMER, COPPER. See *Hammer, Soft Faced.*

HAMMER, COPPER TIPPED. See *Hammer, Soft Faced.*

HAMMER, COPPERING. A hammer with a wide convex face used to form and nail copper sheets to a large surface such as a ship or church steeple. Weight is 21 to 35 ounces. The wide face prevents excess dimpling of the copper as the nail is driven in tightly.

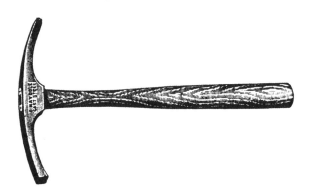

Coppering Hammer

HAMMER, COPPER WORKERS'. See *Hammer, Coppersmiths'.*

HAMMER, COPPERSMITHS'. Also called COPPER WORKERS' HAMMER. A forming tool used when working sheet copper. Weight is about 10 ounces.

Coppersmiths' Hammer

HAMMER, CORNICE. A tinsmiths' tool used for making sharp bends in sheet metal. Weight is 8 to 24 ounces.

Cornice Hammer

HAMMER, CRANDALL. Also called CRANDAL, CRANDALL and CRANDLE. A stone dressing tool made up of several sharpened spikes held together with a frame and wedge. Weight is 8 1/2 to 11 1/2 pounds.

HAMMER, CROSS PEEN. Also called MACHINISTS' CROSS PEEN HAMMER. A hammer with the peen at right angles with the handle. Weight is 2 ounces to 8 1/2 pounds. Useful for forming a bend in metal and for stretching a workpiece. Also used for riveting in a restricted area

where a ball peen is not suitable. See also *Hammer, Blacksmiths'.*

Crandall

Cross Peen Hammer

HAMMER, DENGEL. A hammer used for sharpening a scythe. Weight is about 20 ounces. These hammers are normally used with a very short handle in order to maintain precise control of the hammer stroke. Used with a dengel or scythe anvil. See *Anvil, Scythe.* One catalogue stated that a fresh hammered dengel edge would suffice for a full days mowing.

Dengel Hammer

HAMMER, DOUBLE CLAW. A hammer having two sets of claws. Weight is 15 to 21 ounces. The two pairs of claws are useful when attempting to pull nails of various lengths. Some double claw hammers have the second set of claws made as a separate piece.

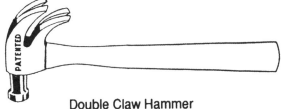

Double Claw Hammer

HAMMER, DOUBLE FACE. Also called DOUBLE FACED PLOW HAMMER and ENGINEERS' DOUBLE FACED HAMMER. A hammer having two identical faces. Weight is 20 to 64 ounces. Handle length is 16 to 20 inches. See also *Hammer, Sharpening*.

Double Face Hammer

HAMMER, DOUBLETREE PIN. Also called WAGON HAMMER. A small hammer, with a metal handle, that serves the dual function of a utility hammer and a double tree pin. The end of the handle is often shaped to a dull taper for use in prying out a linch pin.

Doubletree Pin Hammer

HAMMER, DRILL. See *Hammer, Striking*.

HAMMER, DRILL SHARPENING. See *Hammer, Sharpening*.

HAMMER, DRILLING. See *Hammer, Striking*.

HAMMER, DRIVING. See *Hammer, Farriers' Shoeing*.

HAMMER, ELECTROTYPE FINISHERS'. Also called BLOCKING HAMMER. A print shop tool.

Electrotype Finishers' Hammer

HAMMER, ENGINEERS'. See *Hammer, Blacksmiths'* and *Hammer, Double Face*.

HAMMER, ENGINEERS' BALL PEEN. See *Hammer, Ball Peen*.

HAMMER, FARRIERS' DRIVING. See *Hammer, Farriers' Shoeing*.

HAMMER, FARRIERS' FITTING. A farriers' hammer used for final fitting of the shoe prior to nailing it to the hoof. This fitting might include adjustment of the heel or of the general curvature of the shoe. After any adjustment, the shoe is flattened and the calks touched up as required. Weight is 24 to 48 ounces.

Farriers' Fitting Hammer

HAMMER, FARRIERS' NAIL. See *Hammer, Farriers' Shoeing*.

HAMMER, FARRIERS' ROUNDING. Also called MAUD S ROUNDING HAMMER. A farriers' hammer used for the basic forging work when forming a horse shoe from bar stock. Weight is 24 to 48 ounces. Some suppliers referred to this tool as a DOUBLE FACE TURNING HAMMER.

New York Pattern

Newark Pattern

Farriers' Rounding Hammer

HAMMER, FARRIERS' SHARPENING. A hammer used by a farrier when sharpening toe calks. These hammers have one smooth face and one serrated or ribbed face. The ribbed face, generally a cross peen, is used to pull the metal when forming or sharpening the calk. Weight is 24 to 44 ounces.

French or Cincinnati Pattern

Hellers' Round Poll

Plain Eye

Farriers' Sharpening Hammer

HAMMER, FARRIERS' SHOEING. Also called DRIVING HAMMER, FARRIERS' DRIVING HAMMER, FARRIERS' NAIL HAMMER and SHOEING HAMMER. The farriers' shoeing hammer, as the name implies, is the hammer used to drive the nails that fasten the shoe to the hoof. The claw is used to twist off the protruding end of the nail where it exits the side of the hoof. There are numerous patterns of shoeing hammers in addition to the homemade varieties. The primary difference between the patterns is the shape of the claws. Some representative examples are illustrated. Weight is 7 to 20 ounces.

Scotch Pattern

Farriers' Shoeing Hammer

HAMMER, FARRIERS' TURNING. A hammer used by some farriers for turning the iron bar to form a basic shoe. It was also used to flatten the shoe, turn the heel calks and to draw out the clips. Some references indicate that the TURNING and ROUNDING HAMMERS are the same item; however, they are shown separately in several dealer catalogues. It is assumed that turning and rounding hammers are different shaped tools used for essentially the same purposes. Weight is 28 to 52 ounces.

Boston or California Pattern

Clean Claw

Farriers' Shoeing Hammer

Farriers' Turning Hammer

Cats' Head Pattern

Farriers' Turning Hammer

HAMMER, FILE CUTTERS'. Also called FILE MAKERS' HAMMER. The hammer used when cutting the serrations in a file. Size is 2 ounces to 8 pounds. A different weight of hammer was used for each width of file. This hammer is almost identical to one variety of saw hammer. It is probable that many of the hammers now considered to be file cutters' tools were originally intended for tensioning of a circular saw. See *Hammer, Saw*.

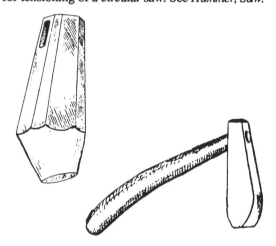

File Cutters' Hammer

HAMMER, FILE MAKERS'. See *Hammer, File Cutters'*.

HAMMER, FLOGGING. A boiler makers' or steel contractors' tool used to flatten uneven spots in a large metal plate or to drive a large cold chisel to cut off projections. Weight is 5 to 8 pounds. "Flogging" is an old term meaning to smooth out irregularities in metal.

Flogging Hammer

HAMMER, FLOOR LAYERS'. See *Hammer, Flooring*.

HAMMER, FLOORING. Also called FLOOR LAYERS' HAMMER. A heavy nail hammer with an extra heavy face. Weights up to 32 ounces were listed.

Flooring Hammer

HAMMER, FOOT POWER. Also called TRIP HAMMER. A mechanical striking machine in which the operator uses his foot as the source of power thus leaving both hands free to manipulate the workpiece. This tool is the forerunner of the power-operated trip hammer used by many blacksmiths for repetitive operations such as sharpening plow shares.

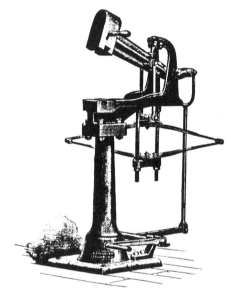

Foot Power Hammer

HAMMER, FORGING. A general-purpose forging hammer. Weight is 32 to 52 ounces. See also *Hammer, Blacksmiths'* and *Hammer, Farriers' Rounding*.

Forging Hammer

HAMMER, FRAMING. See *Hammer, Boxing.*

HAMMER, GLAZIERS'. A hammer used to drive a glaziers' point. The triangular head shown in illustration (a) is free to rotate such that it will always lie flat on the glass while in use . Illustration (b) shows a combination hammer, putty knife and scraper.

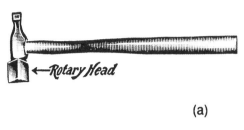

(a)

(b)

Glaziers' Hammer

HAMMER, GOLD BEATING. A hammer used to beat gold ribbon into gold leaf. Weight is 5 to 16 pounds. *Knight* states that the gold beater used four hammers in the following order; Flat or Enlarging Hammer, Commencing Hammer, Spreading Hammer and Finishing Hammer. The face of each hammer in the series is slightly more convex than that of the preceding one.

Gold Beating Hammer

HAMMER, GRANITE CUTTERS' SCOTIA. See *Hammer, Scotia.*

HAMMER, GRANITE CUTTERS' BUSH. See *Hammer, Bush.*

HAMMER, GRANITE PEEN. See *Axe, Stone.*

HAMMER, HALFTONE SOFTENING. A tool used in a press shop for softening the harsh border of a halftone. The face has a stippled pattern or sharp lines to match a standard halftone screen. Softening is accomplished by tapping the outline with the hammer.

Halftone Softening Hammer

HAMMER, HITCHING. A hammer that can be screwed into a tree or post and used for hitching a horse. This tool is also suitable for use as a regular hammer and as a snowball hammer.

Hitching Hammer

HAMMER, HOOP SET. A hammer used for setting or drawing barrel hoops or other light bands.

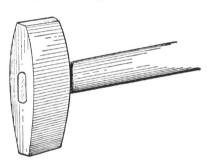

Hoop Set Hammer

HAMMER, HOUSEHOLD. See *Hammer, Ladies'.*

HAMMER, INSTRUMENT REPAIR. Also called DENT REMOVING HAMMER. A very small hammer used to remove the dents from a brass musical instrument. The largest of the illustrated hammers has a 1 1/8 inch diameter face.

Instrument Repair Hammer

HAMMER, JACK. A patented hammer with extra notches under the claws to facilitate pulling a long nail. A jack hammer with the sales tag attached is shown in the illustration.

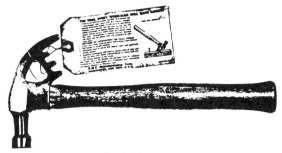

Jack Hammer

HAMMER, JEWELERS'. Also called STAKING HAMMER and WATCH MAKERS' HAMMER. A small hammer used by a jeweler for delicate repair and assembly tasks. Length of the hammer head is 1 3/4 to 3 inches. The illustrated types were each available in six sizes.

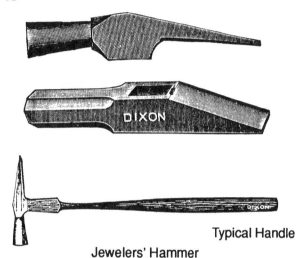

Typical Handle

Jewelers' Hammer

HAMMER, JOINERS. A nail hammer recommended for use by a finish carpenter or joiner. Weight is 4 to 24 ounces.

Joiners' Hammer

HAMMER, LADIES'. Also called HOUSEHOLD HAMMER. A small nail hammer intended for household tasks. Overall length is 10 1/2 to 11 inches. Weight is 7 to 10 ounces.

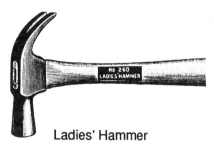

Ladies' Hammer

HAMMER, LATHERS'. A hammer used for nailing plaster lathe. Weight is 1 1/2 to 2 1/2 pounds. The peen is sharp enough to crease a lathe sufficiently for it to be broken off square.

Lathers' Hammer

HAMMER, LETTERERS'. See *Hammer, Stone Cutters'*.

HAMMER, LINCH PIN. See *Hammer, Doubletree Pin*.

HAMMER, LOG MARKING. See *Hammer, Marking*.

HAMMER, MACADAM. Also called MACADAMIZING HAMMER and NAPPAN KNOCKER. A hammer used to break up stone for use on a roadway. Weight is 1 to 2 pounds. "Macadamizing" is a process of building a roadbed by carefully placing and tamping layers of small stone. The name was derived from *John Loudon McAdam* who developed the procedure about the first quarter of the nineteenth century. See also *Hammer, Napping*.

Macadam Hammer

HAMMER, MACADAMIZING. See *Hammer, Macadam*.

HAMMER, MACHINISTS' CHIPPING. See *Hammer, Chipping*.

HAMMER, MACHINISTS'. See *Hammer, Ball Peen; Hammer, Cross Peen* and *Hammer, Straight Peen*.

HAMMER, MAGNETIC. See *Hammer, Tack*.

HAMMER, MARKING. Also called STAMP HAMMER. A hammer used for imprinting a mark on a log or other wooden item. Symbols or initials are raised in reverse on the peen of the hammer such that the proper mark is made by striking the workpiece.

HAMMER, MASONS'. See *Hammer, Stone*.

HAMMER, MASONS' BUSH. See *Hammer, Bush*.

Marking Hammer

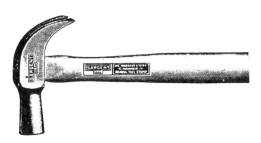

Plain Eye, Plain Face

HAMMER, MASONS' PINNING. Also called PINNING HAMMER. Weight is 2 to 5 1/2 pounds.

Masons' Pinning Hammer

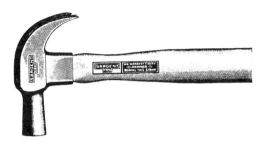

Adze Eye, Plain Face

HAMMER, MILL. A variety of stone hammer used for working mill stones. This hammer are similar and perhaps identical to one variety of Bush Hammer.

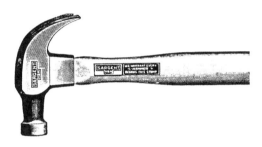

Bell Face

Facing

Home Made

Furrowing Hammer

Mill Hammer

HAMMER, MINERS' STRIKING. See *Hammer, Striking*.

HAMMER, NAIL. Also called CLAW HAMMER. A carpenters' tool especially adapted for use in driving and pulling nails. Weight is 4 to 28 ounces. See also *Hammer, Boxing; Hammer, Jack; Hammer, Joiners'; Hammer, Nail Holding; Hammer, Ripping* and *Hammer, Wrench.*

Wedge Plate Handle

Nail Hammer

Hollow Handle

Ball Type

Nail Holding Hammer

For Square Nails

Nail Hammer

HAMMER, NAIL HOLDING. A hammer that will hold a nail in position for starting with the initial blow of the hammer. Advertised by one supplier as suitable for use by a one-armed carpenter. The Hartford Pattern hammer was listed as being capable of holding any size of wire or cut nail.

Hartford Pattern

Slotted

Magnetic

Nail Holding Hammer

HAMMER, NAPPING. Also called MACADAM HAMMER and STONE HAMMER. A hammer used to break stone into small pieces for use in macadamizing a road. Weight is 3 to 6 pounds.

Napping Hammer

HAMMER, NON-SPARKING. A hammer made of non-ferrous material intended for use in areas where sparks are undesirable. Several sizes of Nail and Ball Peen Hammers made of a hard copper alloy have been noted.

HAMMER, PANEING. See *Hammer, Tinners' Paneing*.

HAMMER, PATTERN MAKERS'. A hammer used for driving small nails when assembling wooden patterns. Weight is about 5 ounces.

Pattern Makers' Hammer

HAMMER, PAVERS'. See *Hammer, Paving*.

HAMMER, PAVERS' BOXING. See *Hammer, Bursting*.

HAMMER, PAVERS' BREAKING. See *Hammer, Bursting*.

HAMMER, PAVERS' BURSTING. See *Hammer, Bursting*.

HAMMER, PAVERS' TRIMMING. Also called PAVERS' REAL HAMMER and PAVERS' SIDE HAMMER. A heavy hammer used for trimming paving blocks.

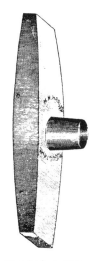

Side Hammer   Real Hammer

Pavers' Trimming Hammer

HAMMER, PAVING. Also called PAVERS' HAMMER and STONE PAVING HAMMER. A hammer used to seat and move large paving stones. Weight is 1 to 4 pounds.

Belgian Pattern

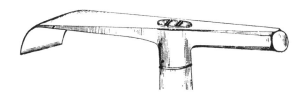

Boston Pattern

Cobble Pattern

Paving Hammer

Washington DC Pattern

Paving Hammer

HAMMER, PEEN. See *Axe, Stone*.

HAMMER, PERCUSSION. A medical tool used in neurological examination. Overall length is approximately 7 inches.

Percussion Hammer

HAMMER, PIANO. See *Piano Tool, Stringing Hammer* and *Piano Tool, Tuning Hammer*.

HAMMER, PINNING. See *Hammer, Masons' Pinning*.

HAMMER, PLANISHING. A small hammer, with a flat face, used to smooth and thin metal by pounding.

Planishing Hammer

HAMMER, PLOW. See *Hammer, Blacksmiths'* and *Hammer, Double Face*.

HAMMER, PLUGGING. A boiler makers' tool. Weight is approximately 2 1/2 pounds.

Plugging Hammer

HAMMER, PRIMITIVE. The illustrated hammer is of the type used by North American Eskimos and is the same general type found throughout the world. It can be reasonably assumed that the hammer is the oldest tool form used by man. However, there is a lack of general agreement as to when prehistoric man first fitted a handle to a hammer stone.

Primitive Hammer

HAMMER, PROSPECTING. A hammer used by a prospector for breaking rocks. Weight is 16 to 32 ounces.

Prospecting Hammer

HAMMER, QUARRYMANS' BREAKING. See *Hammer, Bursting.*

HAMMER, QUARRYMANS' FACE. See *Hammer, Stone.*

HAMMER, QUARRYMANS' HAND. See *Hammer, Stone Cutters'.*

HAMMER, QUARRYMANS' STRIKING. See *Hammer, Striking.*

HAMMER, RAISING. Also called BUMPING HAMMER. A tinners' tool used for raising light sheet metal. Weight is 1 to 5 pounds. "Raising" is a process of hammering unheated metal into a form or depression.

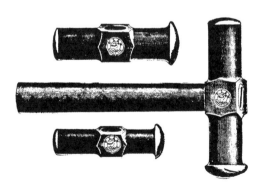

Raising Hammer

HAMMER, RAWHIDE. See *Mallet, Rawhide.*

HAMMER, RIPPING. Also called STRAIGHT-CLAW NAIL HAMMER. A nail hammer having a claw somewhat straighter than the claw of the common nail hammer. Said to be better for ripping up flooring and removing siding.

Ripping Hammer

HAMMER, RIVET SET. See *Anvil Tool, Rivet Set.*

HAMMER, RIVETING. A tinsmiths' tool. Weight is 1 to 64 ounces. See also *Hammer, Boiler Riveting* and *Hammer, Ship Riveting.*

Riveting Hammer

HAMMER, ROOFING. Also called SETTING HAMMER, TINNERS' ROOFING HAMMER, TINNERS' SET HAMMER and TINNERS' SETTING HAMMER. A hammer used to turn and close a lock when installing metal roofing. Also used to peen and close double seams and wire rims on metal ware. Weight is 6 to 24 ounces.

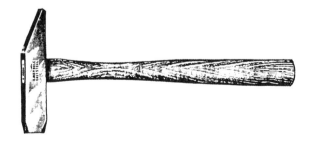

Roofing Hammer

HAMMER, ROUNDING. See *Hammer, Farriers' Rounding*.

HAMMER, SADDLERS'. A saddle makers' tool. Diameter of the hammer face is 1/4 to 5/8 inches. Five sizes were available. This tool is also listed by some suppliers as a TRIMMERS' HAMMER. Also called CARD HAMMER when used in a textile mill.

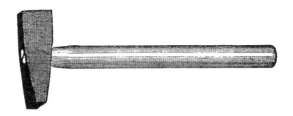

Cross Peen
Saw Hammer

HAMMER, SAW SETTING. A hammer used to set the teeth of cross cut and circular saws. The teeth are pounded or pried to the side to obtain the proper amount of set. Weight is 6 1/2 to 7 ounces.

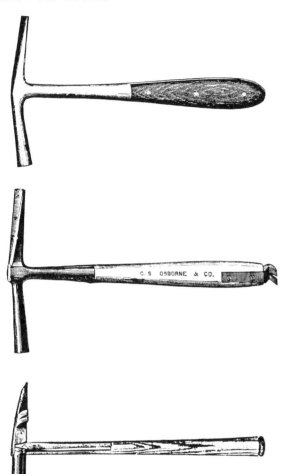

Saddlers' Hammer

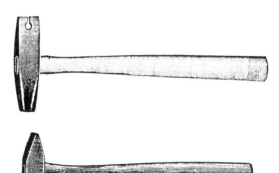

HAMMER, SAW. Also called SAW MAKERS' HAMMER. A hammer used to tension or true a circular saw blade or a large mill saw. The dog head hammer shown in the illustration is used primarily for tensioning a circular saw. The hammer with oblong faces is used to take out lumps and twists. Weight is 2 1/2 to 6 pounds.

Saw Setting Hammer

HAMMER, SAW SWAGING. Also called SWAGE BAR HAMMER. A hammer used with a swage bar to set the teeth of a large saw by hammering. Weight is 12 to 20 ounces.

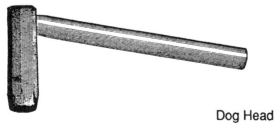

Dog Head
Saw Hammer

Saw Swaging Hammer

Saw Swaging Hammer

HAMMER, SCALING. Also called BOILER SCALING HAMMER. A hammer used for removing scale from a boiler. This type of hammer has a straight peen on one end and a cross peen on the other.

Scaling Hammer

HAMMER, SCOTCH. See *Skutch*.

HAMMER, SCOTIA. Also called GRANITE CUTTERS' SCOTIA HAMMER. Weight is approximately 4 pounds. The scotia is a stone cutters' tool similar to the Bush Hammer except thinner and with fewer cutting edges.

Scotia Hammer

HAMMER, SET. See *Anvil Tool, Set Hammer*.

HAMMER, SETTING. See *Hammer, Roofing*.

HAMMER, SHARPENING. Also called DRILL SHARPENING HAMMER. A forging hammer intended for sharpening rock drilling tools. Weight is 4 to 5 pounds. See also *Hammer, Farriers' Sharpening*.

Round Skew   Skew   Cross Peen
Sharpening Hammer

Double Faced

Sharpening Hammer

HAMMER, SHIP RIVETING. See *Hammer, Bridge Builders'*.

HAMMER, SHOE. See *Hammer, Shoe Makers'*.

HAMMER, SHOE FITTERS'. Used for smoothing or beating out wrinkles when lasting a boot or shoe. Also used for flattening a new seam.

Shoe Fitters' Hammer

HAMMER, SHOE MAKERS'. Also called COBBLERS' HAMMER, SHOE COBBLERS' HAMMER and SHOE HAMMER. This is the most common of the shoe makers' tools. Used for driving tacks and heel nails. Weight is 7 to 24 ounces. Length of handle is 9 to 10 inches.

Shoe Makers' Hammer

French Pattern

Shoe Makers' Hammer

HAMMER, SHOE MAKERS' BEATING OUT. Also called SHANK LEVELER. Used to beat thick sole leather to assure that it is compact and solid. Weight is about 20 ounces.

Beating Out Hammer

HAMMER, SHOE MAKERS' TOE. Also called TURN-SHOE HAMMER. A hammer used to round the leather for forming the toe of a shoe.

Shoe Makers' Toe Hammer

HAMMER, SHOEING. See *Hammer, Farriers' Shoeing*.

HAMMER, SHOULDER PEEN. Also called BLACKSMITHS' SHOULDER PEEN HAMMER. A forging hammer with a thin cross-peen. Weight is 32 to 48 ounces.

Shoulder Peen Hammer

HAMMER, SIDE. See *Hammer, Stone*.

HAMMER, SILVERSMITHS'. A forming hammer for thin metal. Weight of the illustrated tool is 3 to 44 ounces. The silversmith used a variety of chasing, planishing and forming hammers. One report indicates that an early practicing silversmith often owned in excess of 100 hammers.

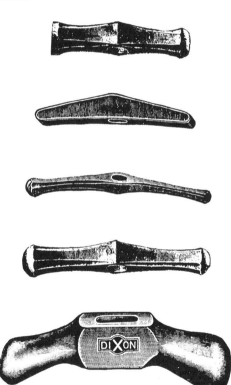

Silversmiths' Hammer

HAMMER, SLATERS'. A tool used for punching and trimming roofing slates. The slaters' hammer often has a leather filled handle said to reduce the shock on the hand. Weight is approximately 2 pounds.

HAMMER, SNOB. Also called SADDLERS' SNOB HAMMER. A saddlers' tool used to form leather around a curved surface. The face is slightly convex to avoid damage to the leather when pounding.

221

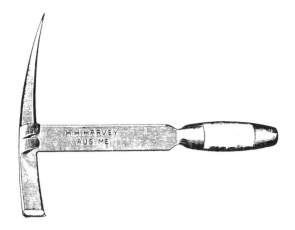

Slaters' Hammer

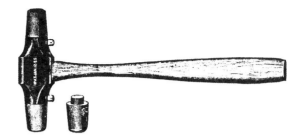

Randall's Patent

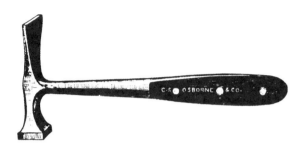

Snob Hammer

Soft Faced Hammer

HAMMER, SNOW BALL. Also called Snow Knocker. A hammer used to remove the built-up snow from the hoof cavity of a horse. These hammers were generally blacksmith made and are therefore of almost infinite variety. Most of them have one flat face and a blunt hook on the opposite side. They are generally equipped with a strap, ring or snap to allow them to be carried on the harness hame.

HAMMER, SPALLING. A heavy hammer used for rough dressing of stone. This tool is the same as the common Stone Hammer except that it is generally listed only in the larger sizes. Weight is 6 to 20 pounds. See illustration under *Hammer, Stone.*

HAMMER, SPIKING. See *Maul, Spike.*

HAMMER, STAKING. See *Hammer, Jewelers'.*

HAMMER, STAMP. See *Hammer, Marking.*

HAMMER, STAKING. See *Hammer, Jewelers'.*

HAMMER, STONE. Also called MASONS' HAMMER, MASONS' HAND HAMMER, QUARRYMANS' FACE HAMMER, STONE CUTTERS' FACE HAMMER and STONE MASONS' HAMMER. Used for breaking and dressing large blocks of stone. Weight is 2 1/2 to 14 pounds. See also *Hammer, Napping* and *Hammer, Spalling.*

Snow Ball Hammer

HAMMER, SOFT FACED. A hammer with a soft face used for striking finished metal work without marring. The face is made of soft metal such as babbitt, lead, copper or brass. Some examples are illustrated.

Soft Faced Hammer

Toothed

Stone Hammer

Single Face
or Peen Hammer

Double Face
or Side Hammer

Stone Hammer

The straps are intended to increase the strength of the handle.

Blacksmiths'

HAMMER, STONE BREAKING. See *Hammer, Bursting.*

HAMMER, STONE BUSH. See *Hammer, Bush.*

HAMMER, STONE CUTTERS'. Also called GRANITE CUTTERS' CHISELING HAMMER, GRANITE CUTTERS' HAND HAMMER, LETTERERS' HAMMER, QUARRYMANS' HAND HAMMER, STONE CUTTERS' HAND HAMMER and STONE CUTTERS' MASH HAMMER. Used to drive stone carving tools and wedges. Weight is 1 to 6 pounds.

Machinists'

Stone Cutters' Hammer

Plumbers'

Straight Peen Hammer

HAMMER, STONE CUTTERS' BREAKING. See *Hammer, Bursting.*

HAMMER, STONE CUTTERS' MASH. See *Hammer, Stone Cutters'.*

HAMMER, STONE CUTTERS' FACE. See *Hammer, Stone.*

HAMMER, STONE CUTTERS' PEEN. See *Axe, Stone.*

HAMMER, STONE PAVING. See *Hammer, Paving.*

HAMMER, STRAIGHT CLAW. See *Hammer, Ripping.*

HAMMER, STRAIGHT PEEN. A general-purpose hammer with an edge peen parallel with the handle. Useful for forming a bend in metal and for stretching a metal workpiece. Also used for riveting in a restricted area where a ball peen is not suitable.

HAMMER, STRAPPED. A hammer on which metallic straps extend over a portion of the handle. In some cases, the straps are forged as an integral part of the hammer head.

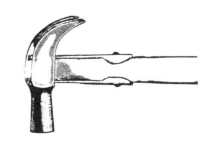

Strapped Hammer

HAMMER, STRIKING. Also called DRILL HAMMER, DRILLING HAMMER, MINERS' STRIKING HAMMER, QUARRYMANS' STRIKING HAMMER and STONE CUTTERS' DRILLING HAMMER. A hammer used for driving a star drill or other stone drilling tool. Weight is 2 to 14 pounds.

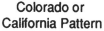

Colorado or California Pattern   Nevada Pattern

Striking Hammer

HAMMER, STRINGING. See *Piano Tool, Stringing Hammer*.

HAMMER, SWAGE. See *Hammer, Saw Swaging*.

HAMMER, SWAGE BAR. See *Hammer, Saw Swaging*.

HAMMER, TACK. A small hammer used for driving tacks and for other light tasks. Weight is about 5 ounces. Tack hammers were available in a wide variety of shapes and sizes. Some examples are illustrated.

Magnetic or Undertakers'

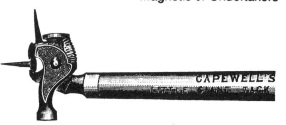

Combination

Tack Hammer

HAMMER, TILE LAYERS'. See *Hammer, Tile Setters'*.

HAMMER, TILE SETTERS'. Also called TILE LAYERS' HAMMER. Weight is 3 to 4 ounces.

Tile Setters' Hammer

HAMMER, TINNERS'. A tinsmiths' tool. See also *Hammer, Riveting* and *Hammer, Roofing*.

HAMMER, TINNERS' FLANGED. A hammer with a tapered flange extending in the same plane as the handle. The flange is used for lifting the locking edge of a sheet of roofing tin. Patented July 28, 1903.

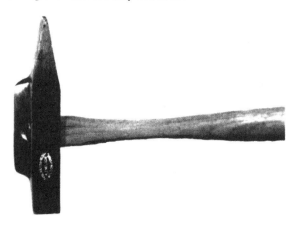

Tinners' Flanged Hammer

HAMMER, TINNERS' PANEING. Also called TINNERS' SETTING HAMMER. Weight is 5 to 28 ounces.

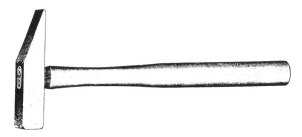

Tinners' Paneing Hammer

HAMMER, TINNERS' SETTING. See *Hammer, Tinners' Paneing*.

HAMMER, TOFFEE. A small hammer intended for breaking toffee. Overall length is 4 to 7 inches.

HAMMER, TOOTHED. See *Hammer, Stone*.

HAMMER, TRACK WALKERS'. A railroad workers' tool used to accomplish minor track repair.

Toffee Hammer

Claw Peen

Track Walkers' Hammer

HAMMER, TRIMMERS'. See *Hammer, Saddlers'*.

HAMMER, TRIP. See *Hammer, Foot Power*.

HAMMER, TUNING. See *Piano Tool, Tuning Hammer*.

HAMMER, TUNING PIN. A hammer used for setting a piano tuning pin. Weight is 2 to 4 1/2 ounces.

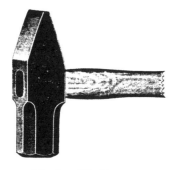

Tuning Pin Hammer

HAMMER, TURN-SHOE. See *Hammer, Shoe Makers' Toe*.

HAMMER, TURNING. See *Hammer, Farriers' Turning*.

HAMMER, UNDERTAKERS'. See *Hammer, Tack*.

HAMMER, UPHOLSTERERS'. Also called CARPET HAMMER and CARPET LAYERS' HAMMER. A hammer used by upholsterers and carpet layers for driving tacks. Size of the face is 3/16 to 7/8 inches. Handle length is 10 to 11 inches.

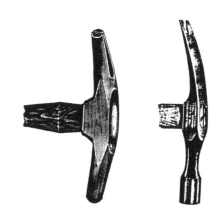

Upholsterers' Hammer

HAMMER, VENEER. A light hammer with a thin wide peen. Weight is 6 to 13 ounces. The wide peen is used to smooth the veneer and squeeze out excess glue.

Veneer Hammer

HAMMER, WAGON. See *Hammer, Doubletree Pin*.

HAMMER, WATCH MAKERS'. See *Hammer, Jewelers*.

HAMMER, WEDGE PEEN. See *Hammer, Blacksmiths'*.

HAMMER, WRENCH. A nail hammer having notches under the claw that will fit square nuts of various sizes. Intended for use by a framing carpenter to tighten the nuts on sill bolts.

HAMMER ATTACHMENT. A patented cutting edge that can be attached to a hammer and used similar to a Hand Adze. A set screw secures the device to a bell faced nail hammer. The cutting edge of the illustrated tool is 2 inches.

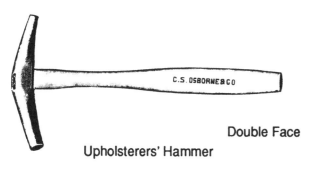

C.S. OSBORNE&CO

Double Face

Upholsterers' Hammer

Wrench Hammer

Hammer Attachment

HAMMER HEAD ADZE. See *Adze, Hammer Head*.

HAMMER HEAD BORING TOOL. A piano makers' tool. See *Boring Tool, Hammer Head*.

HAMMER HEAD CHISEL. See *Chisel, Plumbers'*.

HAMMER HEAD GOUGE. See *Gouge, Plumbers'*.

HAMMER IRON. See *Piano Tool, Hammer Iron*.

HAMMER MOULD. A casting mould used for making a lead hammer.

Hammer Mould

HAMMER-SHANK EXTRACTOR. See *Piano Tool, Hammer-Shank Extractor*.

HAMMER-SHANK ROLLER. See *Piano Tool, Hammer-Shank Roller*.

HAMMER-SHANK TONGS. See *Piano Tool, Hammer-Shank Tongs*.

HAMMER-SHANK TRIMMER. See *Piano Tool, Hammer-Shank Trimmer*.

HAMMER SPACER. See *Piano Tool, Hammer Spacer*.

HAND ADZE. See *Adze, Hand*.

HAND AXE. A small axe. Usually listed as a hatchet. See *Hatchet*.

HAND BEADER. See *Beading Tool, Wood*.

HAND BELLOWS. See *Bellows, Hand*.

HAND CART. See *Cart, Hand*.

HAND CORKER. See *Corker*.

HAND DRIFTING PICK. See *Pick, Poll*.

HAND DRILL. See *Boring Tool, Hand Drill*.

HAND FILE. See *File, Flat* and *File, Hand*.

HAND GAINING TOOL. A grooving tool for wood. See *Gaining Tool*.

HAND GRIND STONE. See *Grind Stone, Hand*.

HAND GROOVER. See *Grooving Tool*.

HAND HACK SAW. See *Saw, Metal Cutting*.

HAND PALLET. See *Bookbinding Tool, Hand Pallet*.

HAND PICK. See *Pick, Poll*.

HAND PULLER. Also called CLOCK HAND PULLER, GAUGE HAND PULLER and HAND REMOVER. A small press used to remove the hands from a gauge or clock.

Hand Puller

HAND PUNCH. See *Punch, Hand* and *Punch, Metal*.

HAND RAIL PLANE. See *Plane, Hand Rail*.

HAND REMOVER. See *Hand Puller*.

HAND RIMMER. A small hand tool used to remove burs from the edge of a hole and for similar tasks.

Hand Rimmer

HAND SAW. See *Saw, Hand*.

HAND SCREW. See *Clamp, Hand Screw* and *Clamp, Wooden*.

HAND SHEARS. See *Tinners' Snips*.

HAND SLICKER. See *Leather Tool, Slicker*.

HAND SPIKE. A logging tool similar to a Pike except that it has a 6 to 7 foot handle. Used to maneuver logs in a mill pond or sluice.

Hand Spike

HAND STAMP. See *Bookbinding Tool, Hand Stamp*.

HAND TONGS. See *Tongs, Hand* and *Tongs, Jewelers'*.

HAND TOOL. A tool intended for use without power other than that provided by the users' hands or feet. See also *Tool*.

HAND TRIMMER. See *Chisel, Electrotype Trimmer*.

HAND VISE. See *Vise, Hand*.

HANDLE. See *Awl Haft; Axe Handle; Boring Tool, Auger Handle; Chisel Handle* and *File Handle*.

HANDLE CLAMP. See *Clamp, Handle*.

HANDLED GIMLET. See *Boring Tool, Gimlet*.

HANDRAIL WRENCH. See *Wrench, Handrail*.

HARDIE. See *Anvil Tool, Hardie*.

HARDY. See *Anvil Tool, Hardie*. Hardy is a variation in spelling.

HARNESS AWL. See *Awl, Harness*.

HARNESS MAKERS' ANVIL. See *Anvil, Harness Makers'*.

HARNESS MAKERS' PRESS. See *Leather Tool, Harness Makers' Press*.

HARNESS MAKERS' TOOLS. See *Saddle and Harness Tools*.

HARROW TOOL. See *Anvil Tool, Harrow Tooth*.

HARROW TOOTH TOOL. See *Anvil Tool, Harrow Tooth*.

HARVESTER KNIFE. See *Knife, Maize*.

HAT BRIM CUTTER. A slitting knife used to cut the brim of a hat a given distance from the crown. The knife can be adjusted to cut a brim of any width. Adjustment screws also allow for varying the curvature of the fence.

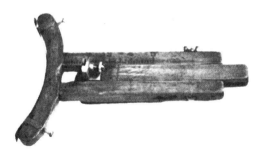

Hat Brim Cutter

HAT BRIM IRON. A curved pressing tool used for smoothing the brim of a hat. The illustrated tool has a flat surface about 4 inches long. The entire tool is made of brass.

Hat Brim Iron

HATCHET. A one-handed cutting tool with the cutting edge mounted parallel to the handle.

HATCHET, ADJUSTABLE. A hatchet on which the blade can be swiveled 90 degrees to serve as an adze. The blade is loosened by unscrewing the peen.

Adjustable Hatchet

HATCHET, AXE PATTERN. See *Axe, Hunters'*.

HATCHET, BARREL. See *Hatchet, Barreling* and *Hatchet, Box*.

HATCHET, BARRELING. Also called BARREL HATCHET, BOX HATCHET, COOPERS' HATCHET and PRODUCE HATCHET. Width of cut is 1 7/8 to 3 1/8 inches. Handle length is 10 to 14 inches. One supplier listed a small variety of this tool as a POCKET BARRELING HATCHET.

Barreling Hatchet

HATCHET, BENCH. See *Hatchet, Broad.*

HATCHET, BOX. Also called BARREL HATCHET, CALIFORNIA LATH HATCHET, FRUIT BOX HATCHET, LATH BOX HATCHET, PRODUCE DEALERS' HATCHET, PRODUCE HATCHET and PRODUCERS' HATCHET. A hatchet used by fruit and poultry packers for assembling wooden boxes. Width of cut is 2 to 2 1/8 inches. Handle length is 11 to 12 1/2 inches. See also *Hatchet, Barreling.*

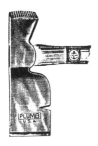

Lath Box

Box Hatchet

HATCHET, BOY SCOUT. See *Axe, Boy Scout.*

HATCHET, BRICK. See *Brick Cleaner.*

HATCHET, BROAD. Also called BENCH AXE and BENCH HATCHET. Width of cut is 4 to 9 inches. Handle length is 16 to 18 1/2 inches. Broad hatchets were available with either a single or a double bevel. See also *Hatchet, Linemans'.*

Western Pattern

Broad Hatchet

Broad Hatchet

HATCHET, CAMP. Also called BOYS' CAMP AXE. Width of cut is 3 1/4 to 3 1/2 inches. Handle length is approximately 14 inches.

Camp Hatchet

HATCHET, CAR BUILDERS'. See *Hatchet, Half.*

HATCHET, CLAW. Width of cut is 3 1/4 to 4 5/8 inches. Handle length is 12 1/2 to 14 inches. See also *Hatchet, Metal Handle.*

Claw Hatchet

HATCHET, COAL MINERS' TRACK. Width of cut is about 3 7/8 inches. Handle length is 18 to 19 inches.

Coal Miners' Track Hatchet

HATCHET, COOPERS'. See *Hatchet, Barreling*.

HATCHET, DERRICK. See *Hatchet, Rig Builders'*.

HATCHET, DOUBLE BIT. A hatchet shaped the same as a double bit axe. Width of cut is approximately 2 3/4 inches. Handle length is about 15 1/2 inches.

Double Bit Hatchet

HATCHET, ENGINEERS'. Width of cut is approximately 7 inches. Handle length is 16 1/2 inches.

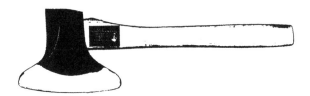

Engineers' Hatchet

HATCHET, FIREMANS'. A small variety of firemans' axe. Weight is about one pound.

Firemans' Hatchet

HATCHET, FLOORING. A heavy half hatchet used for laying wooden flooring. Width of cut is 3 3/4 to 4 3/4 inches. Handle length is 14 to 15 1/2 inches.

Firemans' Hatchet

Flooring Hatchet

HATCHET, FRUIT BOX. See *Hatchet, Box*.

HATCHET, GUARDED. Also called SAFETY AXE and SAFETY HATCHET. A hatchet with a metal guard that can be moved into place to cover the sharp edge thus allowing the tool to be carried and stored without injury to the carrier or damage to the cutting edge. The guard is lined with lead.

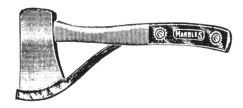

Guarded Hatchet

HATCHET, HALF. Also called CAR BUILDERS' HATCHET. Width of cut is 3 1/4 to 4 3/4 inches. Handle length is 12 to 15 inches.

HATCHET, HALF CLAW. A variety of Half Hatchet with a claw on the poll. Width of cut is 3 1/4 to 4 1/4 inches.

HATCHET, HUNTERS'. See *Axe, Hunters'*.

Car Builders' Pattern

HATCHET, ICE. A one-handed version of an Ice Axe. Width of cut is 2 1/4 to 3 inches and weight is about one pound. Also listed as a SOUTHERN PATTERN ICE AXE.

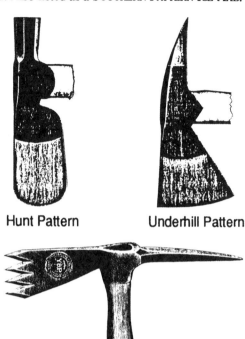

Hunt Pattern   Underhill Pattern

Tobacco Pattern

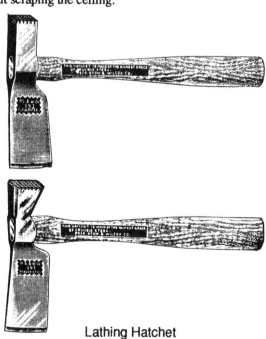

Ice Hatchet

HATCHET, LATH BOX. See *Hatchet, Box.*

HATCHET, LATHING. Also called PLASTERERS' HATCHET. A hatchet having a narrow bit and a ribbed or creased face. Width of cut is 2 to 3 1/2 inches. Handle length is 12 to 13 1/2 inches. The lathing hatchet is straight across the top to allow nailing the upper lathe on a wall without scraping the ceiling.

Half Hatchet

Half Claw Hatchet

Lathing Hatchet

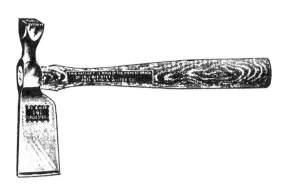

Lathing Hatchet

HATCHET, LINEMANS'. A small Broad Hatchet with a heavy poll. Width of cut is 3 to 4 1/2 inches.

Linemans' Hatchet

HATCHET, METAL HANDLE. A hatchet with a formed handle made entirely of metal. Width of cut is 3 1/2 inches. This variety of hatchet was also made in a Shingling Pattern.

Metal Handled Hatchet

HATCHET, OIL DERRICK. See *Hatchet, Rig Builders'*.

HATCHET, PACKERS'. See *Hatchet, Packing*.

HATCHET, PACKING. Also called PACKERS' HATCHET. A tool used for assembling wooden boxes or crates. Width of cut is 2 1/4 to 2 3/4 inches. Handle length is 11 to 13 inches.

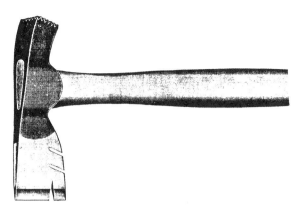

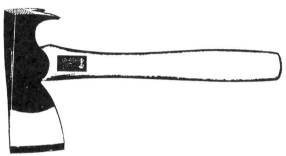

Packing Hatchet

HATCHET, PLASTERERS'. Weight is approximately 24 ounces. See also *Hatchet, Lathing*.

Plasterers' Hatchet

HATCHET, POCKET BARRELING. See *Hatchet, Barreling*.

HATCHET, PRODUCE. See *Hatchet, Box*.

HATCHET, PRODUCE DEALERS'. See *Hatchet, Box*.

HATCHET, PRODUCERS'. See *Hatchet, Box*.

HATCHET, PRUNING. Width of cut is 3 1/2 to 4 1/2 inches.

Pruning Hatchet

HATCHET, RIG BUILDERS'. Also called DERRICK HATCHET and OIL DERRICK HATCHET. A Half Hatchet, with a long handle, used in building wooden oil derricks. Width of cut is 3 to 4 inches. Handle length is 17 to 18 inches.

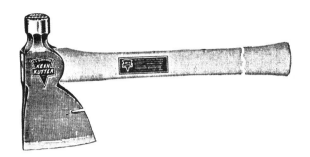

Rig Builders' Hatchet

HATCHET, SAFETY. See *Hatchet, Guarded*.

HATCHET, SCOUT. See *Axe, Boy Scout*.

HATCHET, SHINGLING. A hatchet intended for use in nailing wooden shingles. The cutting edge is useful for trimming a shingle to match a given space. See also *Hatchet, Metal Handle*.

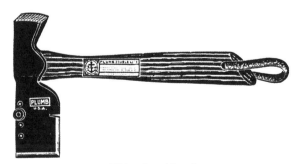

Shingling Hatchet

HATCHET, SPORTSMANS'. See *Axe, Hunters'*.

HATCHET, TOBACCO. A hatchet used for cutting tobacco stalks. Width of cut is 3 1/2 to 4 inches. See also *Hatchet, Half*.

Tobacco Hatchet

HATCHET, WAREHOUSE. A combination tool used to open and close wooden crates. Width of cut is approximately 3 7/8 inches.

Warehouse Hatchet

HATCHET BOLT. See *Soldering Iron*.

HATCHET CASE. See *Axe Sheath*.

HATCHET GAUGE. See *Shingle Gauge*.

HATCHET IRON. See *Soldering Iron*.

HATCHET SHEATH. See *Axe Sheath*.

HATCHET STAKE. See *Stake, Hatchet*.

HAWK. A plasterers' tool used for holding and carrying wet plaster. The tool consists of a 13 inch square of smooth wood or metal with a handle on the bottom. The illustrated Callous Preventer is a sponge rubber washer for use on the bottom of the wooden hawk.

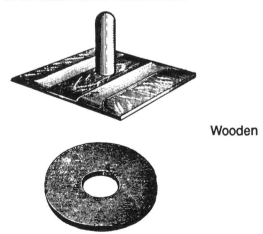

Wooden

Callous Preventer

Hawk

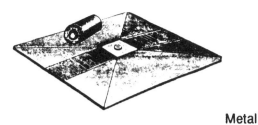

Metal

Hawk

HAWK BILL PLIERS. See *Pliers, Hawk Bill.*

HAWSING BEETLE. Also called **HAWSING MALLET.** A large and heavy version of a ship builders' Caulking Mallet. Usually made of live oak or white oak and equipped with iron rings.

Hawsing Beetle

HAWSING IRON. A caulking tool used for ship building and repair. Edge of the blade is 1/8 to 1/2 inch thick.

Hawsing Iron

HAWSING MALLET. See *Hawsing Beetle.*

HAY FORK. See *Fork, Hay.*

HAY HOOK. See *Hook, Bale.*

HAY KNIFE. See *Knife, Hay.*

HAY RAKE. See *Rake, Hay.*

HAY THIEF. A farm tool consisting of a long rod with two or more barbs. The hay thief can be pushed into a haystack and retrieved along with several stems of hay from inside the stack. The sample can then be examined for quality and condition.

Hay Thief

HAZEL HOE. See *Hoe, Farm.*

HEAD CUTTER. Also called **HEADING CUTTER.** A coopers' tool used to cut the head for a dry barrel. The illustrated tool is adjustable to cut heads from 8 to 21 inches in diameter.

Head Cutter

HEAD FLOAT. Also called **COOPERS' FLOAT** and **HEADING FLOAT.** A coopers' tool used for dressing the head of a barrel. Width of cutting edge is 4 to 4 1/2 inches.

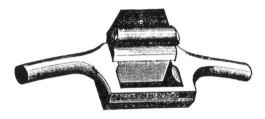

Head Float

HEAD KNIFE. See *Knife, Curriers'* and *Knife, Leather.*

HEADER. See *Barrel Header, Bolt Header* and *Nail Header.*

HEADER FORK. See *Fork, Header.*

HEADING CUTTER. See *Head Cutter.*

HEADING FLOAT. See *Head Float.*

HEADING KNIFE. See *Drawing Knife, Coopers'.*

HEADING MACHINE. See *Bolt Heading Machine.*

HEADING TOOL. See *Bolt Header* and *Nail Header.*

HEATER. See *Glue Pot* and *Paper Hangers' Stove.*

HEATING TONGS. See *Tongs, Heating.*

HEAVER. A sail makers' tool used primarily as a lever for tightening the wrapping when serving a rope. Length is approximately 7 inches. The dimpled end of the heaver can be used to push a needle through heavy sailcloth when use of a sewing palm is not convenient.

Heaver

HEDGE KNIFE. See *Knife, Hedge.*

HEDGE SHEARS. See *Shears, Hedge.*

HEEL BURNISHER. See *Shoe Makers' Tool, Burnisher.*

HEEL FORMER. See *Anvil Tool, Heel Former.*

HEEL KNIFE. See *Shoe Makers' Tool, Heel Knife.*

HEEL PLANE. See *Plane, Circular.*

HEEL PRYER. See *Shoe Makers' Tool, Heel Pryer.*

HEEL SHAVE. See *Shoe Makers' Tool, Heel Shave.*

HEIGHT MEASURE. An instrument used to determine the height of a tree or structure by sighting across the scaled leg to the top of the item to be measured. The illustrated device is calibrated from 15 to 75 feet. Patented November 1922.

Height Measure

HERMAPHRODITE CALIPER. A type of caliper. See *Caliper, Firm Joint.*

HEWING AXE. See *Axe, Hewing.*

HILLING HOE. See *Hoe, Farm.*

HITCHING HAMMER. See *Hammer, Hitching.*

HOBBLE. See *Cow Kickers.*

HOCK. See *Hawk.* Hock is a variation in spelling.

HOD. A carrying container for brick or mortar. Length is 22 to 24 inches. Both metal and wood varieties were available. A hod is often fitted with a handle several feet long.

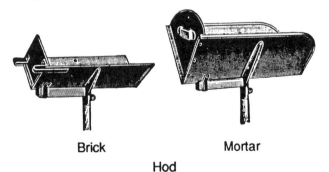

Brick   Mortar

Hod

HOE. A long-handled tool used to loosen soil, chop, mix and smooth. The cutting edge is set at a right angle to the handle.

HOE, ASPHALT PATCHING. A tool used to smooth asphalt or roofing tar when patching a damaged surface. Width is approximately 10 inches.

Asphalt Patching Hoe

HOE, BEET. See *Hoe, Farm.*

HOE, BOG. See *Hoe, Farm.*

HOE, CANE. See *Hoe, Farm.*

HOE, COTTON. See *Hoe, Farm.*

HOE, CRANBERRY. See *Hoe, Farm.*

HOE, CULTIVATING. See *Hoe, Farm.*

HOE, DIGGING. See *Hook, Potato.*

HOE, FARM. A field hoe used for planting, thinning, cultivating and weeding various farm crops. See also *Hoe, Planters'* and *Hoe, Scuffle.*

Beet Hoe (Thinning)

Beet Hoe (Weeding)

Cane Hoe   Cultivating Hoe

Cotton Hoe

Farm Hoe

Grape or Vineyard Hoe

Grape, Bog or Cranberry Hoe

Hazel Hoe   Hilling Hoe   Palmetto Hoe

Mattock Hoe

Strawberry Hoe

Warren Pattern Hoe

Farm Hoe

HOE, GARDEN. A hoe used in the garden for planting, thinning, cultivating and weeding. See also *Hoe, Scuffle*.

Planters' Hoe

Pull Hoe

Weeding Hoe

Garden Hoe

HOE, GRAPE. See *Hoe, Farm*.

HOE, GRUB. Also called MATTOCK HOE and SPROUTING HOE. A heavy hoe used in new ground for cutting roots and sprouts. Width is 3 1/2 to 5 1/2 inches. The cutting edge is made of high quality steel that will retain a keen edge. See also the Hazel Hoe illustration under *Hoe, Farm*.

Grub Hoe

Cuban or Rice

Planters' Hoe

HOE, HILLING. See *Hoe, Farm.*

HOE, MATTOCK. See *Hoe, Grub.*

HOE, MORTAR. A hoe used by a brick or stone mason to mix mortar. Width is approximately 10 inches. The holes allow escape of the water.

HOE, PULL. See *Hoe, Garden.*

HOE, RICE. See *Hoe, Planters'.*

HOE, SCUFFLE. Also called RAILROAD SCUFFLE HOE. A tool used for rapid cutting of small weeds. Width is 7 to 9 inches.

Mortar Hoe

Beet

HOE, PALMETTO. See *Hoe, Farm.*

HOE, PLANTERS'. Also called PLANTERS' EYE HOE. A farm tool used for planting field crop seedlings.

Garden

American

Railroad

Scuffle Hoe

HOE, SPROUTING. See *Hoe, Grub.*

HOE, STABLE. Also called PUSHING HOE. A scraping tool used for cleaning a horse stable. Width is approximately 10 inches.

English

Planters' Hoe

HOE, STRAWBERRY. See *Hoe, Farm.*

HOE, VINEYARD. See *Hoe, Farm.*

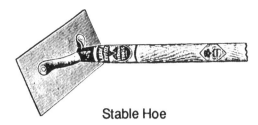

Stable Hoe

HOE, WEEDING. See *Hoe, Farm* and *Hoe, Garden.*

HOE DOWN. See *Hook, Hop.*

HOE RAKE. A combination hoe and digging rake.

Hoe Rake

HOE TROWEL. See *Trowel, Garden.*

HOG CATCHER. A long-handled catcher for swine. The illustrated item was listed with packing house tools but would also be useful as a farm tool. A hog is always caught by the front leg rather than the rear to avoid injury to the animal.

Hog Catcher

HOG HOLDER. A device used for holding a hog for ringing or snouting. See also *Tongs, Hog.*

Hog Holder

HOG MARKER. See *Ear Marker.*

HOG RINGER. A tool used to install a ring in the nose of a hog. Rings are used to prevent the hog from rooting up the grass in the pasture and to decrease the tendency to breach a fence. Rings are also placed in the ear as a method of marking.

Hog Ringer

HOG SCRAPER. See *Scraper, Hog.*

HOG SCRAPING KNIFE. See *Knife, Hog Scraping.*

HOG SNOOTER. See *Hog Snouter.*

HOG SNOUTER. Also called HOG SNOOTER and HOG TAMER. A device used to cut a notch in a hog's nose. The notch makes the nose tender and thereby reduces rooting and fence crawling. This device was sometimes equipped with interchangeable cutting lips for use in ear-marking of livestock.

Hog Snouter

HOG TAMER. See *Hog Snouter.*

HOG TONGS. See *Tongs, Hog.*

HOLD DOWN. See *Clamp, Bench.*

HOLD FAST. See *Clamp, Bench.*

HOLE CUTTER. Also called KNOCKOUT PUNCH. An adjustable device used to cut a hole in a thin workpiece. The tool shown in illustration (a) was intended for use in cutting the hole for installation of a panel clock. Illustration (b) was listed as a tool for cutting holes in a radio chassis.

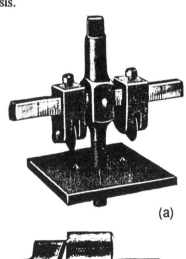

(a)

(b)

Hole Cutter

HOLE GAUGE. Also called TAPER GAUGE. A gauge used to determine the size and taper of a hole. The tool shown in illustration (b) was intended for use in gauging the orifice size of fire extinguishers in a factory or warehouse.

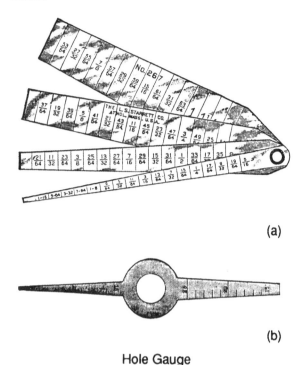

(a)

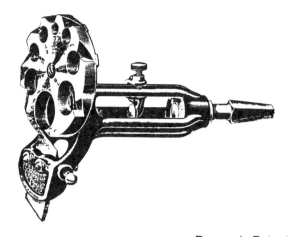

Bonney's Patent

(b)

Hole Gauge

HOLE SAW. See *Boring Tool, Bit, Barrel Saw* and *Boring Tool, Bit, Hole Saw.*

HOLLOW AUGER. Also called SPOKE AUGER and TENON CUTTER. A bit brace tool used to cut a round tenon such as required on a wagon spoke or chair rung. Inasmuch as spokes often needed replacement, the hollow auger was a common tool in repair shops as well as in wheelwright shops. They were made in a wide variety of shapes, sizes and patterns. Each type has a knife arrangement on the face for cutting the square shoulder and most types have an adjustable depth stop. One variety can be adjusted to cut a tapered tenon. See also *Bench, Spoke Tenoning; Hollow Auger Brace* and *Tenon Machine.* The adjustable types were also called EXPANSIVE HOLLOW AUGERS.

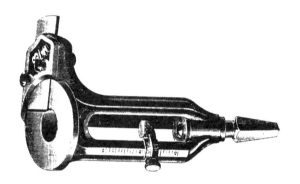

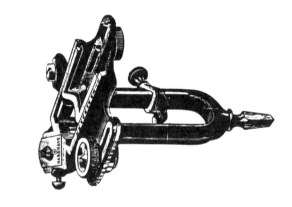

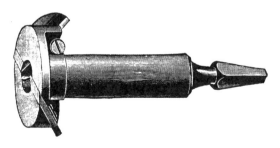

Ames' Patent

Hollow Auger

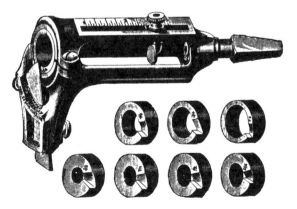

Hollow Auger

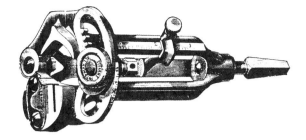

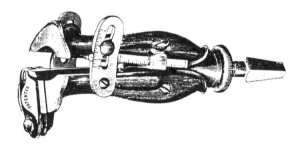

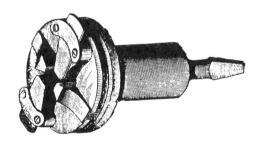

Taper Cutting

Hollow Auger

HOLLOW AUGER BRACE. A hollow auger permanently attached to a handle similar to a bit brace.

HOLLOW BEVEL AXE. A general type of axe head design in which the bit is beveled to remove weight without appreciable decrease of size or strength. See illustration under *Axe, Single Bit*.

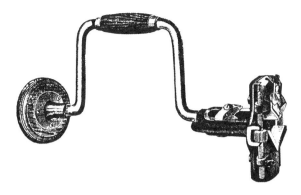

Hollow Auger Brace

HOLLOW HANDLE TOOL. See *Tool Handle*.

HOLLOW MANDREL. See *Mandrel, Stove Pipe*.

HOLLOW MANDREL STAKE. See *Mandrel, Stove Pipe*.

HOLLOW MILL SAW. See *Boring Tool, Bit, Hole Saw*.

HOLLOW PLANE. See *Plane, Moulding, Hollow and Round Pair*.

HOLLOW PLIERS. See *Pliers, Opticians'*.

HOLLOW PUNCH. A sheet metal tool. See *Punch, Hollow*.

HOLLOWING ADZE. See *Adze, Bowl*.

HOLLOWING KNIFE. See *Drawing Knife, Coppers'*.

HOLZAXT. See *Axe, Wedge*.

HOOF HOOK. See *Hook, Hoof*.

HOOF KNIFE. See *Knife, Farriers'*.

HOOF LEVELER. See *Foot Adjuster*.

HOOF NIPPERS. See *Nippers, Hoof*.

HOOF PARER. Also called HOOF PARING NIPPERS, HOOF PARING PINCERS and PARING NIPPERS. A farriers' tool used to shorten the hoof by paring the excess length. Handle length is 12 to 14 inches. A horse hoof continues to grow under the shoe and has to be trimmed at each shoeing. If the horse has went without shoes for a period prior to shoeing, the hoof might be worn off such that paring is not required or is required only for minor leveling. The hoof parer has only one cutting jaw thus avoiding an uneven surface in the center where two cutting jaws would normally meet.

Hoof Parer

HOOF PARING NIPPERS. See *Hoof Parer*.

HOOF PARING PINCERS. See *Hoof Parer*.

HOOF RASP. See *Rasp, Horse.*

HOOF PICK. See *Hook, Hoof.*

HOOF SHEARS. See *Hoof Trimmer.*

HOOF TESTER. A tool used to apply pressure to the inside and outside of a hoof to determine the presence and location of a sore spot. If a tender spot is found, extra care can be taken in trimming and nailing. The hoof tester is approximately 15 inches long.

Hoof Tester

HOOF TRIMMER. Also called HOOF PARER and HOOF SHEARS. A farriers' tool used for trimming thick parts of a hoof.

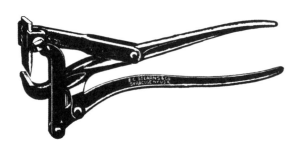

Hoof Trimmer

HOOK. A curved tool intended for use in catching, cutting, holding or lifting.

HOOK, BAG. A hook used in handling heavy jute bags. Use of this type of hook is now generally prohibited because of possible damage to the bags.

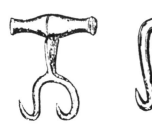

Bag Hook

HOOK, BALE. A hook used for handling bales of soft material such as hay and cotton. The cotton hook is made of heavier material and is usually longer than the hay hook.

HOOK, BENCH. See *Bench Hook, Bench Stop* and *Hook, Sail Makers'.*

Cotton Hook, Texas Pattern

Hay Hook

Bale Hook

HOOK, BILL. A knife, with a curved point, used to prune and cut shrubs. A similar tool with a long handle is generally called a bush hook. See *Hook, Bush.*

Bill Hook

HOOK, BOAT. A hook with a long handle used to maneuver a small boat up to the dock and hold it steady until tied up. See also *Pike.*

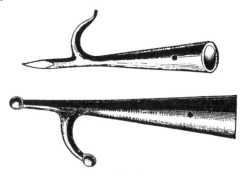

Boat Hook

HOOK, BOX. Also called CASE HOOK and FREIGHT HOOK. A hook used at one time to handle cardboard boxes. Similar to a Bale Hook but made of lighter material and usually shorter.

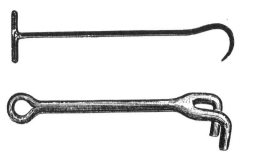

Devil's Claw

Chain Hook

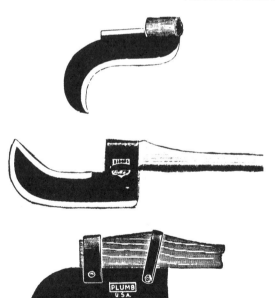

Box Hook

HOOK, BUSH. Also called HEDGE KNIFE. A tool used for cutting small brush and cleaning out fence rows. Most tools of this type were fitted with an axe-type handles.

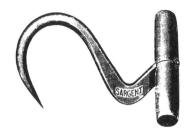

Humbolt Pattern

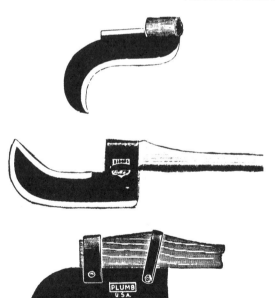

Bush Hook

HOOK, CAR. See *Hook, Ice*.

HOOK, CAR ICING. See *Hook, Ice*.

HOOK, CASE. See *Hook, Box*.

HOOK, CHAIN. Also called DEVIL'S CLAW. A tool used for handling heavy chain. Length is 20 to 28 inches.

HOOK, CLAM. A short-handled hook with 4 to 6 tines. Used for digging clams.

Clam Hook

HOOK, COTTON. See *Hook, Bale*.

HOOK, DIGGING. See *Hook, Potato*.

HOOK, FIRE. A firemans' tool. Handle is approximately 6 feet long.

Fire Hook

HOOK, FREIGHT. See *Hook, Box*.

HOOK, GRAPPLING. Also called GRAPPLING IRON. A tool used to snag and recover a submerged object. Available with 3, 4 or 5 hooks.

Grappling Hook

HOOK, GRASS. See *Grass Hook.*

HOOK, HAY. See *Hook, Bale.*

HOOK, HOE DOWN. See *Hook, Hop* and *Hook, Potato.*

HOOK, HOOF. Also called HOOF PICK. A blunt hook used by a teamster or farrier to remove stones and debris from the hoof of a horse.

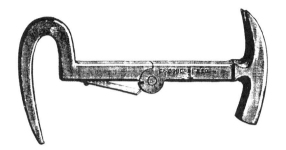

Jointed or Pocket Hook

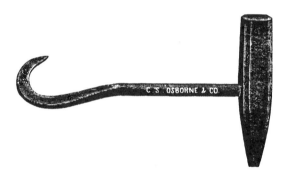

Hoof Hook

HOOK, HOP. Also called HOE DOWN HOOK. A strong hook similar to the Stone Hook except that the tines are blunt. A similar hook with longer tines was listed as a PHOSPHATE HOOK and PHOSPHATE DRAG HOOK.

Hop Hook

HOOK, ICE. Also called CAR HOOK, CAR ICING HOOK and ICING HOOK. A tool used to handle blocks of ice during the storage and shipping process. Handle length is up to 18 feet. Hooks used in railroad cars had 3 to 5 foot handles. See also *Fork, Elevator.*

Ice Hook

HOOK, LANDING. See *Landing Hook.*

HOOK, LAST. See *Shoe Makers' Tool, Last Hook.*

HOOK, LUG. See *Timber Grapple.*

HOOK, MANURE. See *Hook, Potato.*

HOOK, POT. A hook used to handle a heated container such as a plumbers' melting pot.

Pot Hook

HOOK, POTATO. Also called DIGGING HOE, DIGGING HOOK, HOE DOWN HOOK, MANURE HOOK and POTATO HOE. A tool used for digging potatoes and other root crops. This type of tool was also used for cleaning barns and stables and as a drag hook for mill refuse. See also *Hook, Hop.*

Potato Hook

HOOK, PRUNING. See *Hook, Bill; Hook, Bush* and *Knife, Pruning.*

HOOK, PULP. A hand hook used for handling processed wood pulp.

Pulp Hook

242

HOOK, RUBBING. See *Rubbing Hook.*

HOOK, SAIL MAKERS'. Also called SAIL MAKERS' BENCH HOOK. A hook used to apply a strain to a sail while it is being worked by the sail maker. The hook secures one end of the sail to the bench so that it can be pulled out straight. In other cases, the hook is fastened to the waist of the sail maker and acts as a third hand to hold the sail taut.

Sail Makers' Hook

HOOK, SHAVE. See *Shave Hook.*

HOOK, STONE. A strong hook intended for leveling a pile of gravel or small stones. The illustrated tool has 10 inch flat tines.

Stone Hook

HOOK, STRINGING. See *Piano Tool, Stringing.*

HOOK, TANNERS'. A hook used to remove a hide or skin from the tanners' pit. The hides were removed from the pit and replaced every day to assure that each part was equally exposed to the tanning ooze.

Tanners' Hook

HOOK, THATCHERS'. A thin hook used to gather the thatching material and hold it tightly for sewing.

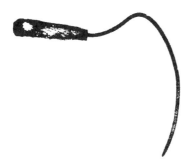

Thatchers' Hook

HOOK, TILE. A hook used for laying drainage tile without getting down into the ditch. Length of the handle is approximately 6 feet.

Tile Hook

HOOK, WEAVERS'. A textile mill tool.

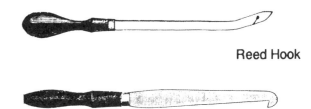

Reed Hook

Drawing-In Hook

Weavers' Hook

HOOK CHISEL. See *Chisel, Ice.*

HOOK END CLAMP. See *Clamp, Ship Carpenters'.*

HOOK JOINT PLANE. See *Plane, Case Makers'.*

HOOK TOOL. See *Turning Tool, Hook.*

HOOK TOOTH FILE. See *File, Hook Tooth.*

HOOKAROON. Also called HOOKEROON, HOOKAROON PICK and AXE HANDLE HOOKAROON. A tool used to maneuver small timbers such as pulp wood and cedar posts. Handle length is approximately 3 feet.

Hookaroon

HOOKAROON PICK. See *Hookaroon.*

HOOKEROON. See *Hookaroon.* Hookeroon is a variation in spelling.

HOOP. See *Truss Hoop.*

HOOP DOG. Also called HOOP LIFTER and LEVER HOOK. A device used as a lever to loosen the chime hoop on a barrel. Also used to press a bulged stave into place for starting the chime hoop over the end of the barrel. The wooden shaft is sometimes formed into the shape of a wedge and faced with metal.

Hoop Dog

Hoop Dog

HOOP DRIVER. Also called COOPERS' DRIVER and HOOP SET. A coopers' tool used to drive down and thereby tighten a barrel hoop. The hoop driver was held in position while being struck with a hammer or the cooper's adze. Some types of hoop drivers were fitted with short handles.

Iron Bound   Wooden

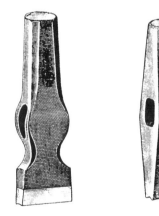

Nantucket

Socket Type

Hoop Driver

HOOP KNIFE. See *Drawing Knife, Coopers'*.

HOOP SET. See *Hoop Driver*.

HOOP SET HAMMER. See *Hammer, Hoop Set*.

HOOP TONGS. See *Tongs, Angle Jaw*.

HOP HOOK. See *Hook, Hop*.

HORIZONTAL BLACKSMITHS' DRILL. See *Boring Tool, Tire Drill*.

HORIZONTAL DRILL. See *Boring Tool, Tire Drill*.

HORN GROOVER. See *Tinsmiths' Machine, Grooving*.

HORN MALLET. See *Mallet, Horn*.

HORN PLANE. See *Plane, Horn*.

HORN TRIMMER. See *Leather Tool, Trimmer*.

HORSE. See *Bench, Shaving* and *Stitching Horse*.

HORSE BRUSH. See *Brush, Horse*.

HORSE CLIPPER. See *Clipper*.

HORSE COLLAR TOOL. A tool used for making harness collars for horses or mules. See also *Mallet, Horse Collar; Maul, Horse Collar* and *Sewing Palm*.

HORSE COLLAR TOOL, COLLAR BLOCK. A forming block for making a horse collar.

Collar Block

HORSE COLLAR TOOL, MEASURING YOKE. A gauge used to determine the correct size of collar to fit a particular horse.

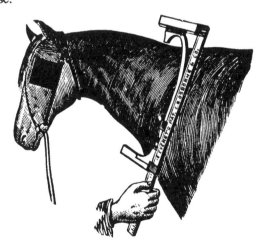

Measuring Yoke

HORSE COLLAR TOOL, STUFFING ROD. Also called STUFFING IRON. A tool used for hand stuffing a horse collar. Also suitable for use by harness makers, saddlers, trimmers and upholsterers.

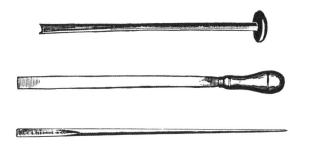

Stuffing Rod

HORSE COLLAR TOOL, WEDGE. A wooden wedge or driver used to form the leather around a horse collar block.

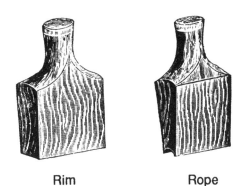

Rim   Rope

Horse Collar Wedge

HORSE MEASURE. See *Rule, Horse Measure*.

HORSE NAIL CLINCHER. See *Tongs, Clinch*.

HORSE RASP. See *Rasp, Horse*.

HORSE SHOE CALK SWAGE. See *Anvil Tool, Toe Calk Die*.

HORSE SHOE SLEDGE. See *Sledge, Turning*.

HORSE SHOEING KNIFE. See *Knife, Farriers'*.

HORSE SHOEING PINCERS. See *Pincers, Farriers'*.

HORSE SHOERS' ANVIL. See *Anvil, Farriers'*.

HORSE SHOERS' MACHINE. See *Vise, Farriers'*.

HORSE SHOERS' TONGS. See *Tongs, Farriers'*.

HORSE TOOTH FILE. See *File, Horse Tooth*.

HORSE TOOTH FLOAT. See *File, Horse Tooth*.

HORSE TOOTH RASP. See *File, Horse Tooth*.

HOT CHISEL. See *Anvil Tool, Hot Cutter*.

HOT CUTTER. See *Anvil Tool, Hot Cutter*.

HOT RASP. A farriers' tool. See *Rasp, Hot*.

HOT SET. See *Anvil Tool, Hot Cutter*.

HOUSE ADZE. See *Adze, Carpenters'*.

HOUSE AXE. See *Axe, House*.

HOUSE BAR. See *Bar, Ice*.

HOUSE CARPENTERS' ADZE. See *Adze, Carpenters'*.

HOUSEHOLD HAMMER. See *Hammer, Ladies*.

HOUSEHOLD SAW. See *Saw, Household*.

HOUSING SAW. See *Saw, Stair*.

HOWEL. A coopers' plane. See *Plane, Howel*.

HOWELING KNIFE. See *Jigger, Coopers'*.

HUB BORER. See *Hub Boxing Machine*.

HUB BOXING GAUGE. A tool used to gauge the location when setting a box in a wagon wheel hub. When installing a box, it generally has to be shimmed to center it properly in the hub. The illustrated gauge centers automatically in the box.

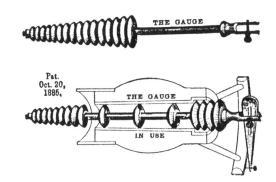

Hub Boxing Gauge

HUB BOXING MACHINE. Also called HUB BORER. A device used to drill the center hole in a wagon hub for insertion of the metal hub box. Illustration (a) shows the Silvers Patent Hub Boxing Machine attached to a hub for boring. It was advertised as being capable of cutting either a straight or a tapered hole. Illustration (b) shows a boxing machine that clamps to one end of the hub. This type of device reduces the possibility of splitting the hub while boring.

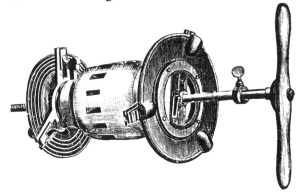

(a) Silver's Patent

Hub Boxing Machine

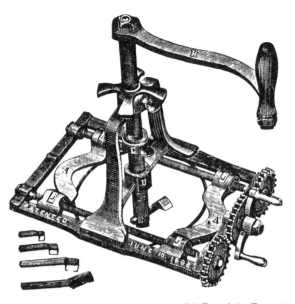

(b) Brecht's Patent

Hub Boxing Machine

HUB REAMER. See *Boring Tool, Hub Reamer.*

HUB WRENCH. See *Wrench, Axle Nut Holder; Wrench, Buggy* and *Wrench, Wagon.*

HUNTERS' AXE. See *Axe, Hunters'.*

HUNTERS' HATCHET. See *Axe, Hunters'.*

HUSKING HOOK. See *Corn Husker.*

HUSKING PEG. See *Corn Husker.*

HUSKING PIN. See *Corn Husker.*

HUSTLER. See *Turning Tool, Beading* and *Turning Tool, Hustler.*

HYDRAULIC JACK. See *Jack, Hydraulic.*

HYDROSTATIC LEVEL. See *Level, Hydrostatic.*

I

Tool names starting with the letter I. Included is a listing of tools used in the:
ICE INDUSTRY

ICE AUGER. See *Boring Tool, Ice Auger.*

ICE AWL. See *Ice Pick.*

ICE BREAKER. See *Fork, Splitting* and *Ice Shaver.*

ICE CHIPPER. Also called ICE SHAVER.

Ice Chipper

ICE CLEAVER. Length of blade is 20 inches.

Ice Cleaver

ICE CREEPERS. Sharp points with provisions for fastening to boots or shoes to facilitate walking on ice. See also *Boot Calk Tool.*

Ice Creepers

Ice Creepers

ICE MALLET. See *Mallet, Ice.*

ICE PACKING CHISEL. See *Chisel, Ice.*

ICE PICK. Also called ICE AWL. A sharp-pointed tool used for breaking blocks of ice and chipping small pieces. See also *Mallet, Ice.*

Ice Pick

ICE PICK SHEATH. A leather sheath used to allow an ice pick to be carried in a pocket without the danger of injury.

Ice Pick Sheath

ICE PLANE. Also called ICE SHAVE. A soda fountain or bar tool used to prepare ice for drinks.

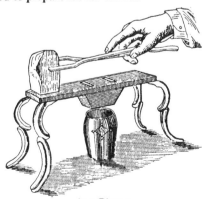

Ice Plane

Ice Plane

ICE PLOW. A hand operated plow often used for making the first line on an ice field and for finishing out the groove made by a horse drawn plow. An ice harvest tool.

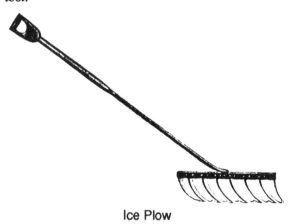

Ice Plow

ICE SHAVER. Also called FLOOR SHAVE, FLOOR SHAVER and ICE BREAKER. A tool used to reduce one surface of a large block of ice or for leveling a layer of ice in the ice house during the storage process. Length is 3 to 5 feet. See also *Ice Chipper.*

Block Shaver

Floor Shaver

Ice Shaver

ICE SPLITTING CHISEL. See Chisel, Ice.

ICE TOOLS. The special-purpose ice industry tools listed below can be found in normal alphabetical sequence. These tools may also have been used for other purposes.

> ADZE, ICE
> AXE, ICE
> BAR, ICE
> BORING TOOL, ICE AUGER
> CANT HOOK, ICE
> CHISEL, ICE
> FORK, ELEVATOR
> FORK, SPLITTING
> HATCHET, ICE
> HOOK, ICE
> ICE CLEAVER
> ICE CREEPERS
> ICE PICK
> ICE PICK SHEATH
> ICE PLOW
> ICE SHAVER
> MEASURING IRON
> SAW, ICE
> SCALES, ICE
> SCOOP NET
> SHOVEL, SCOOP
> SHOVEL, SIEVE
> TONGS, ICE

IN-SHAVE. Also called COOPERS' IN-SHAVE, COOPERS' SHAVE and ROUND SHAVE. A coopers' tool used for smoothing the inside of a barrel. See also *Scorper.*

In-Shave

INCLINOMETER. See *Level, Inclinometer.*

INDENTATION ROLLER. See *Cement Tool, Roller.*

INDIAN AXE. See *Axe, Indian.*

INK ERASER. Also called KNIFE ERASER and STEEL ERASER. A tool used by a draftsman or artist to remove overrun lines and small defects from an inked drawing. The steel tip is used as a scraper to remove the ink.

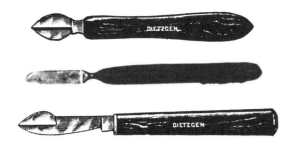

Ink Eraser

INK KNIFE. See *Knife, Ink*.

INKING ROLLER. See *Proofing Roller*.

INSIDE CALIPER. A caliper used to take an inside measurement. See *Caliper, Combination; Caliper, Double; Caliper, Firm Joint; Caliper, Self Registering* and *Caliper, Spring*.

INSIDE CEMENT TOOL. See *Cement Tool, Inside*.

INSIDE RULE. See *Rule, Extension* and *Rule, Slide*.

INSIDE SQUARE ANGLE TOOL. See *Cement Tool, Inside*.

INSTRUMENT MAKERS' PLANE. See *Plane, Violin*.

INSTRUMENT REPAIR HAMMER. See *Hammer, Instrument Repair*.

IRON. The cutting bit of a woodworking plane is commonly called the "Iron". The term is probably left over from the days of the wooden plane when only the cutter was made of metal. See also *Caulking Tool, Plumber; Caulking Tool, Ship; Chincing Iron; Hat Brim Iron; Piano Tool, Hammer Iron; Smoothing Iron* and *Soldering Iron*.

IRON SHEARS. See *Tinsmiths' Machine, Shears*.

ITALIAN GRAPE HOE. See *Hoe, Farm*.

IVORY CLAMP. See *Clamp, Ivory*.

IVORY FILE. See *File, Ivory*.

IVORY FLOAT. See *File, Ivory*.

IVORY RULE. See *Rule, Ivory*.

IVORY TURNING TOOL. See *Turning Tool, Metal*.

J

Tool names starting with the letter J, including multiple listings of:

JACK

JIGGER

Included also is a listing of tools used by the:

JEWELER

JACK. A device used for lifting or raising a heavy object a short distance and holding it in that position. Jack is also a combining term applied to other tools that accomplish rough work or are used for multiple tasks.

JACK, BUGGY. See *Jack, Wagon.*

JACK, CLAW. See *Jack, Lifting.*

JACK, COTTON. See *Jack, Lifting.*

JACK, FLOOR. See *Floor Jack.*

JACK, HYDRAULIC. A jack that uses liquid as a lifting medium. Hydraulic jacks were made in sizes up to 120 tons and in a wide variety of styles. The illustrated jack was offered for sale in 1887.

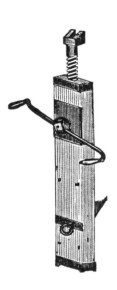
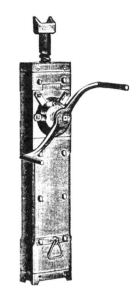

Claw Jack
or Timber Jack

Cotton Jack, Cotton Screw,
Sugar Jack or Sugar Screw

Hydraulic Jack

JACK, LIFTING. A type of wooden-frame jack that was listed under the general heading of lifting jacks as well as under several other names. The claw jack and the cotton jack were listed as having 24 to 48 inch screws. The planker jack has a 30 to 42 inch screw and the stone jack has a 36 to 42 inch screw.

JACK, LOGGING. A strong jack used for lifting and positioning logs.

JACK, PIPE FORCING. A tool used to drive a pipe underneath an obstacle such as a sidewalk. The jack is staked down in a trench and the lever is operated to apply endwise force to a pipe. The pipe is fitted with a sharp point to facilitate driving.

Planker Jack

Stone Jack

Lifting Jack

illustrations are representative of the many types of wagon jacks available. The light-weight types were sometimes listed as BUGGY JACKS.

Logging Jack

Badgley's Patent

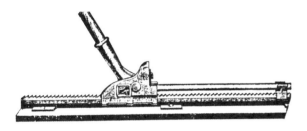

Pipe Forcing Jack

JACK, PLANKER. See *Jack, Lifting.*

JACK, STONE. See *Jack, Lifting.*

JACK, SUGAR. See *Jack, Lifting.*

JACK, TIMBER. See *Jack, Lifting.*

JACK, TRACK. A jack used to lift and support a railroad rail. Height is 24 inches.

Huson's Patent

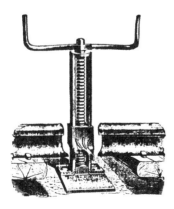

Track Jack

JACK, WAGON. A tool used for raising and supporting one end of a wagon or buggy axle. Jacking was necessary for repair and frequent greasing of the axles. The

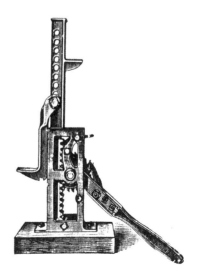

Wagon Jack

Buggy Jacks

Wagon Jack

JACK HAMMER. A type of nail hammer. See *Hammer, Jack.*

JACK PLANE. See *Plane, Jack.*

JACK RABBET. See *Plane, Rabbet.*

JACK SCREW. A tool used for general-purpose lifting. Jack screws are used extensively for leveling machinery and houses. Length of stand is up to 24 inches. The larger variety is also called LOCOMOTIVE JACK SCREW.

Jack Screw

JARVIS. Also called CARRIAGE MAKERS' JARVIS and WHEELERS' JARVIS. A scraping tool used for rounding up wagon wheel spokes and for other sharply curved surfaces.

Jarvis

JEDDING AXE. See *Cavel.*

JEWELERS' SNIPS. See *Shears, Jewelers'.*

JEWELERS' STAKE. See *Anvil, Jewelers'.*

JEWELERS' TOOLS. The special-purpose jewelers' tools listed below can be found in normal alphabetical sequence. These tools may also have been used for other purposes.

  ANVIL, JEWELERS'
  BENCH, JEWELERS'
  BENCH PIN
  BENDING BLOCK
  BORING TOOL, BENCH DRILL
  BORING TOOL, JEWELERS' STOCK
  BORING TOOL, LENS DRILL
  BRUSH, SWING
  BUFF
  BURNISHING TOOL, AGATE
  BURNISHING TOOL, BLOODSTONE
  BURNISHING TOOL, JEWELERS'
  CLAMP, RING
  DAPPING DIE
  FILING PLATE
  GRAVER
  GRAVER HANDLE
  GRAVER SHARPENER
  HAMMER, JEWELERS'
  KNIFE, JEWELERS'
  LATHE, JEWELERS'
  LATHE, POLISHING
  MALLET, JEWELERS'
  MANDREL, JEWELERS'
  MILGRAIN TOOL
  PLIERS, BOW
  PLIERS, RING
  PLIERS, RING SAW
  RING SIZER
  RING STAMP
  RING STICK
  SAW, HACK
  SAW, JEWELERS'
  SCREW DRIVER, WATCH MAKERS'

SETTING BUR
SHEARS, JEWELERS'
SHOVEL, DIAMOND
SHOVEL, TEMPERING
SOLDERING IRON
STONE SIZE GAUGE
TONGS, JEWELERS'
TWEEZERS
VISE, JEWELERS'
VISE, PIN

JIGGER. A catch-all word used to designate a tool similar to a standard tool.

JIGGER, COACH MAKERS'. A coach makers' routing tool that cuts on one or both sides rather than downward. See *Router, Carriage Makers'*.

JIGGER, COOPERS'. Also called HOWELING KNIFE. A tool used to cut the howel in a barrel. This tool was used by some coopers in place of a plane. The coopers' jigger normally has a two to three inch cutting edge but was listed with cutting edges up to 6 1/2 inches. Left hand and right hand varieties were available. The jigger was not widely used in the United States except as a repair tool for trimming a replaced stave.

Coopers' Jigger

JIGGER, SHOE MAKERS'. See *Shoe Makers' Tool, Jigger*.

JIM CROW. See *Rail Bender*.

JOINER SAW. See *Saw, Joiner*.

JOINERS' BENCH. See *Bench, Cabinet Makers'*.

JOINERS' CLAMP. See *Clamp, Bar*.

JOINERS' HAMMER. See *Hammer, Joiners'*.

JOINERS' TOOL CHEST. See *Tool Chest, Cabinet Makers'*.

JOINERS' TOOLS. See *Cabinet Makers' Tools*.

JOINT FILE. See *File, Joint*.

JOINT FILLER. A tuck pointers' tool used to apply mortar to the joint between bricks and to smooth off the excess.

Joint Filler

JOINT FORMER. See *Tuck Pointer*.

JOINT RAKER. A tool used for cleaning and removing excess mortar from the joint between bricks or stones.

Brick

Stone

Joint Raker

JOINT RUNNER. See *Lead Joint Runner*.

JOINT WIRE FILING PLATE. See *Filing Plate*.

JOINTER. See *Saw Jointer* and *Tuck Pointer*.

JOINTER GAUGE. Also called PLANE GAUGE. An adjustable guide for attachment to a jointer plane to facilitate cutting to a given angle. Jointer gauges were available for attachment to either wooden or metal planes.

Jointer Gauge

JOINTER PLANE. See *Plane, Coopers' Jointer* and *Plane, Jointer*.

JOIST TOOL. See *Boring Tool, Sill Borer*.

JORGENSEN CLAMP. See *Clamp, Hand Screw*.

JOURNAL GAUGE. A railroad tool listed also as a WORM JOURNAL COLLAR and JOURNAL FILLET GAUGE.

Journal Gauge

JUMPER. A coopers' tool consisting of a bent iron rod upset on one end. The upset end is entered into the bung hole of a barrel and used to tap and pry the head into place.

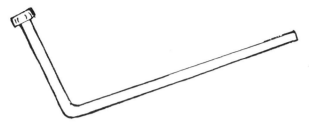

Jumper

JUMPING WEDGE. See *Wedge, Jumping.*

K

Tool names starting with the letter K, including a multiple listing of:
Knife

KACR KNIFE. See *Knife, Kacr.*

KALSOMINE BRUSH. See *Brush, Calcimine.* Kalsomine is a variation in spelling.

KEG BRUSH. See *Brush, Keg.*

KENT AXE. See *Axe, Broad, Ship Carpenters'* and *Axe, Kent.*

KEY LEAD BIT. See *Boring Tool, Bit, Key Lead.*

KEY LIFTING CHISEL. See *Chisel, Key Lifting.*

KEY PULLER. A device used to pull large shaft keys from heavy farm machinery.

Key Puller

KEY REAMER. See *Piano Tool, Key Reamer.*

KEY SEAT CLAMP. See *Clamp, Key Seat.*

KEY SEAT RULE. See *Rule, Key Seat.*

KEY SEAT RULE BLOCKS. See *Clamp, Key Seat.*

KEY SEATING CHISEL. See *Chisel, Key Seating.*

KEY SPACER. See *Piano Tool, Regulating.*

KEY WRENCH. See *Wrench, Key.*

KEYHOLE CALIPER. See *Caliper, Firm Joint* and *Caliper, Spring.*

KEYHOLE SAW. See *Saw, Keyhole* and *Saw, Pad.*

KEYWAY CUTTER. See *Chisel, Key Seating.*

KEYWAY SEATING CHISEL. See *Chisel, Key Seating.*

KILLING AXE. See *Axe, Pole.*

KIT SAW. See *Saw, Hand.*

KITCHEN GRIND STONE. See *Grind Stone, Family.*

KITCHEN SAW. See *Saw, Kitchen.*

KNEE ANVIL. See *Anvil, Knee* and *Anvil, Lap.*

KNIFE. A tool used for cutting with a slicing or drawing action. See also *Drawing Knife, Machete* and *Tobacco Spud.*

KNIFE, ASPARAGUS. Also called DANDELION CUTTER and WEED DIGGER. A knife used to cut asparagus shoots or weeds below the surface of the ground. See also *Chisel, Asparagus.*

Asparagus Knife

KNIFE, BALE TIE CUTTER. A knife used to cut the twine securing a bale of hay or fodder. Also used to cut the binder twine as a bundle of grain is fed to the separator.

Bale Tie Cutter

KNIFE, BANANA. A knife used in a grocery store for cutting bananas from the stalk.

Banana Knife

KNIFE, BAND. The illustrated knife has a 5 inch serrated cutting edge. This tool is probably another form of bale tie cutter.

Band Knife

KNIFE, BANDAGE. A medical tool used when removing a bandage. Usually made with an integral metal handle.

Bandage Knife

KNIFE, BEAM. See *Knife, Curriers'*.

KNIFE, BEET. Also called BEET TOPPING KNIFE. A farm tool used for removing the tops from sugar beets. Length of cutting edge is 9 to 12 inches.

Beet Knife

KNIFE, BEET TOPPING. See *Knife, Beet*.

KNIFE, BELT. See *Knife, Leather*.

KNIFE, BELT PUNCH. A pocket or clasp knife with a special curved blade for punching holes in a flat leather or webbed belt.

Belt Punch Knife

KNIFE, BLOCK. A knife that swivels on a hook or ring fastened to a heavy block. A long handle provides considerable leverage for easy paring and forming of wooden objects. The block knife is the primary tool used for shaping the outside of a wooden shoe. These knives were usually home made or made by the local blacksmith. Also used as a farm tool for such tasks as heading cane and chopping tubers.

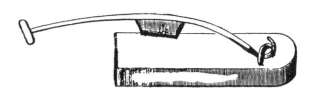

Block Knife

KNIFE, BONING. See *Knife, Butchers'*.

KNIFE, BOOK BINDERS'. A style of knife favored by book binders for paring and skiving leather, paper and boards.

German Pattern

French Pattern

Paring

Book Binders' Knife

KNIFE, BROOM CORN. Also called BROOM KNIFE. A knife used by a broom maker or broom corn harvester. Length of cutting edge is approximately 4 1/2 inches.

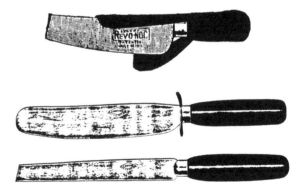

Broom Corn Knife

KNIFE, BUDDING. A rigid knife used to make the slit when budding a fruit tree. Budding is a form of tree grafting in which only a small twig is transferred to a rooted tree. Length of cutting edge is about 2 1/2 inches.

Budding Knife

KNIFE, BUTCHERS'. Any of the knives intended for slaughtering an animal for meat and for preparing the carcass for consumption.

General Purpose

Boning

Skinning

Sticking

Butchers' Knife

KNIFE, BUTTER. A knife used for preparing butter and cheese for packaging. Length of cutting edge is 5 to 12 inches.

Butter and Cheese

Butter Knife

KNIFE, CABLE SHEATH. See *Knife, Chipping.*

KNIFE, CANE. Also called SUGAR CANE KNIFE. A long knife used for cutting sugar cane or sorghum cane. Length of cutting edge is 11 to 14 1/2 inches.

Cane Knife

KNIFE, CAP MAKERS'. Length of blade is 5 1/2 inches. The knife is illustrated without a handle.

Cap Makers' Knife

KNIFE, CARVERS'. Also called SLOYD KNIFE and WOOD CARVERS' KNIFE. Any of a variety of knives favored by wood carvers.

Chip Carving

Chip Carving

Spear Point

Carvers' Knife

KNIFE, CHAMFER. A coopers' tool used to cut the chamfer on the inside lip of a barrel. Length of blade is 4 to 7 inches. Right and left hand varieties were available.

KNIFE, CHEESE. A knife used to cut cheese for packaging. Length of cutting edge is 6 to 14 inches.

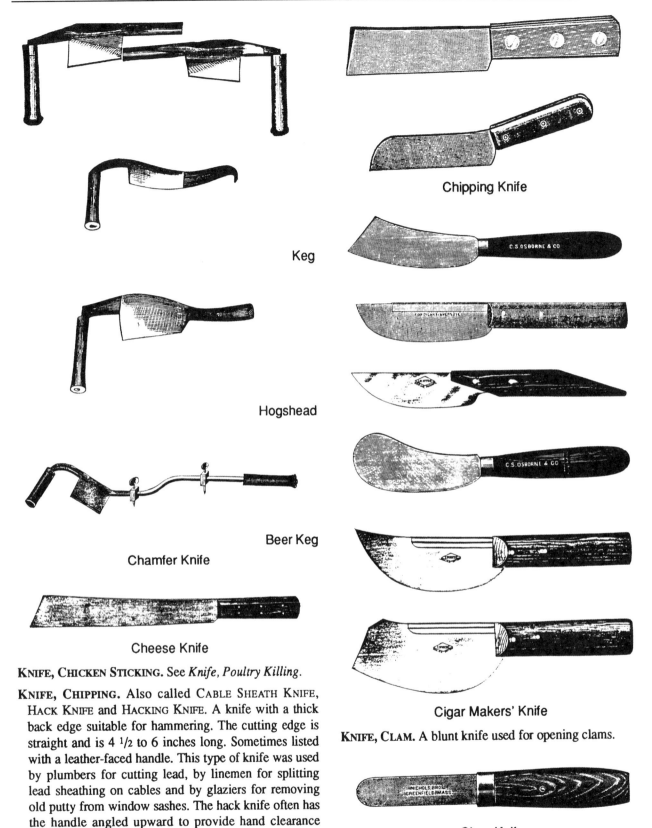

Keg

Hogshead

Beer Keg

Chamfer Knife

Cheese Knife

Chipping Knife

Cigar Makers' Knife

Clam Knife

KNIFE, CHICKEN STICKING. See *Knife, Poultry Killing*.

KNIFE, CHIPPING. Also called CABLE SHEATH KNIFE, HACK KNIFE and HACKING KNIFE. A knife with a thick back edge suitable for hammering. The cutting edge is straight and is 4 1/2 to 6 inches long. Sometimes listed with a leather-faced handle. This type of knife was used by plumbers for cutting lead, by linemen for splitting lead sheathing on cables and by glaziers for removing old putty from window sashes. The hack knife often has the handle angled upward to provide hand clearance when cutting on a flat surface.

KNIFE, CIGAR MAKERS'. Also called CIGAR KNIFE. A tool used for trimming tobacco leaves for rolling a cigar and for cutting the cigar to length.

KNIFE, CLAM. A blunt knife used for opening clams.

KNIFE, CLASP. Any knife in which the blade closes into the handle. A pocket knife. See *Knife, Bale Cutter* and *Knife, Belt Punch*.

258

KNIFE, CLOTH. Also called PATTERN MAKERS' KNIFE. A tailor shop tool. Overall length is about 7 inches. The illustrated tool has several interchangeable blades. See also *Knife, Extension Blade.*

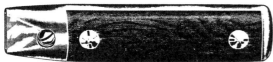

Cloth Knife

KNIFE, COMB MAKERS'. A knife used to scrape tortoise shell and horn comb blanks. Listed by one supplier as a SCRAPING KNIFE.

Comb Makers' Knife

KNIFE, CORING. A knife used for preparing fruit for canning or consumption. See also *Pitting Spoon.*

Open Hook

Closed Hook

Pear Knife

Coring Knife

KNIFE, CORK CUTTERS'. A very thin knife used to trim a square block of cork into the conventional round shape to fit a bottle. Length of the blade is about 6 inches.

Cork Cutters' Knife

KNIFE, CORN. Also called CORN CUTTER. A farm tool used for cutting corn stalks. The knife shown in illustration (c) is strapped to the users' leg and cuts with a downward motion of the foot.

Reversible Blade

Hook

(c) Foot Operated

Corn Knife

259

Straight or Hedge Type

Corn Knife

KNIFE, CORN TOPPING. A knife used for cutting the seed heads from kaffir corn. The tool shown in illustration (b) is a one-handed type. The grain head is grasped in the hand and the knife severs the stalk by a twist of the wrist.

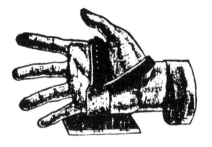

(b)

Corn Topping Knife

KNIFE, CORSET. Also called CROOKED CORSET KNIFE. Length of cutting edge is approximately 3 inches.

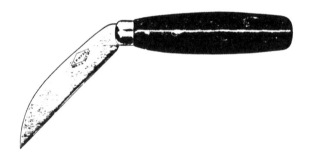

Corset Knife

KNIFE, COT SCARFER. Also called SCARFERS' KNIFE. A textile mill tool.

Cot Scarfer

KNIFE, COTTON SAMPLING. The cutting edge is 4 1/8 to 6 inches long.

Folding Handle

Cotton Sampling Knife

KNIFE, CROOKED. A small general-purpose knife used primarily in the Upper New England area. This type of knive is home made.

Crooked Knife

KNIFE, CURD. See *Curd Cutter*.

KNIFE, CURRIERS'. Also called BEAM KNIFE and HEAD KNIFE. A knife used to scrape hides during the leather finishing process. The curriers' knife is used as a wire edged scraper, with a pushing stroke, to thin and to even the thickness of a tanned hide. The process is called "Beaming".

Curriers' Knife

KNIFE, DITCH. Also called DITCH BANK BLADE. A tool used for cutting brush and large weeds especially along irrigation ditches. Length of blade is 19 to 21 inches. Similar in function to the Bush Hook.

Ditch Knife

KNIFE, DRAWING. See *Drawing Knife*.

KNIFE, ELECTROTYPE BUILDERS'. A smoothing tool for electrotype plates. Both left hand and right hand varieties were available.

Electrotype Builders' Knife

KNIFE, EXTENSION BLADE. A general-purpose knife with replaceable blades. Used in the garment industry for working cloth, rubber and leather. This knife is the same general type as the Cloth Knife.

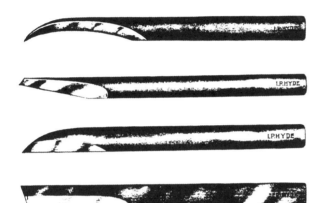

Leather

Rubber

Extension Blade Knife

KNIFE, FARRIERS'. Also called HOOF KNIFE, HORSE KNIFE and HORSE SHOEING KNIFE. A farriers' tool used to pare the hoof and to clean out the inside cavity. The blade is slightly curved over the cutting length. The end of the knife is sharply bent over to reduce the possibility of digging into the sensitive bottom of the hoof cavity. The curve can also be used as a scraper to clean out the hoof. Handles are made of bone, horn, iron or wood. A farriers' knife with a narrow blade was listed as a SEARCHER by several suppliers.

Pope's Iron Handle

Searcher

Farriers' Knife

KNIFE, FEATHER. A milliners' tool. Length of cutting edge is 2 1/2 to 2 7/8 inches. Available with either a rounded edge for curling or sharp edge for cutting.

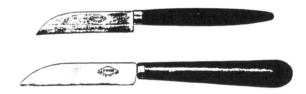

Feather Knife

KNIFE, FELT. A knife used to cut and skive small pieces of felt when making or repairing a piano. A piano makers' tool.

French Type

Tuners' Knife

Felt Knife

KNIFE, FISH. Any of several knives favored by fish butchers and processors.

Dressing

Heading

Scaling

Slicing or Bait

Splitter

Sticking or Throater

Fish Knife

KNIFE, FLESHING. A knife used by a tanner to scrape the inside surface of a hide and to trim off the tags. The concave side was used for scraping with the hide stretched over the curved beam. The convex side was sharpened as a cutting tool and used for trimming. Length of the blade is approximately 15 inches.

Fleshing Knife

KNIFE, FURRIERS'. A knife used by a furrier to cut and trim fur segments for assembly into a garment. The knife is used on the flesh side with a slicing action to avoid damage to the fur. Blade length is 5 to 6 inches The illustrated tool was listed as being trimmed with brass.

Furriers' Knife

KNIFE, GLAZIERS'. See *Knife, Putty.*

KNIFE, GOLD. A thin flexible tool similar to the Pallet Knife. Used by a book binder or gilder for dividing and handling sheets of gold leaf. The knife is thin on the edges but not sharp.

Gold Knife

KNIFE, GRAFTING. See *Grafting Froe.*

KNIFE, GRAPE. A knife used for picking grapes. Length of blade is approximately 3 inches.

Grape Knife

KNIFE, HACKING. See *Knife, Chipping.*

KNIFE, HARVESTER. See *Knife, Maize.*

KNIFE, HAY. A knife used to cut hay from a haystack. See also *Knife, Sod.*

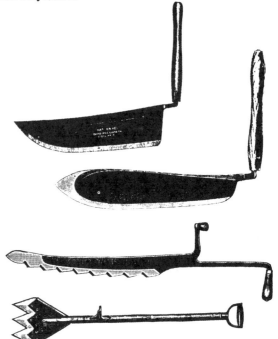

Hay Knife

KNIFE, HEAD. See *Knife, Curriers'* and *Knife, Leather*.

KNIFE, HEDGE. A knife used to trim and cut hedge rows. Similar in design and function to the machete and to one type of corn knife. See also *Hook, Bill* and *Hook, Bush*.

Hedge Knife

KNIFE, HEEL. See *Shoe Makers' Tool, Peg Cutter*.

KNIFE, HOG SCRAPING. Also called DANISH HOG SCRAPING KNIFE. A knife used for scraping the hair from a butchered hog. Length of cutting edge is about 7 inches.

Hog Scraping Knife

KNIFE, HOOF. See *Knife, Farriers'*.

KNIFE, INK. A knife used in a press room to spread the ink on the proof press. Length of blade is 6 to 10 inches.

Ink Knife

KNIFE, JEWELERS'. Also called JEWELERS' BENCH KNIFE. A general-purpose knife used in assembly and repair of jewelry. Length of cutting edge is about 2 inches.

Jewelers' Knife

KNIFE, KACR. A knife intended for use by a rabbi. The cutting edge is 17 to 20 inches.

Kacr Knife

KNIFE, LEATHER. A knife used in one of the leather working trades. There is a wide overlap of tools used by the saddle maker, harness maker, shoe maker and other leather-working craftsmen. Several of the illustrated knives were listed as being suitable for use in more than one craft.

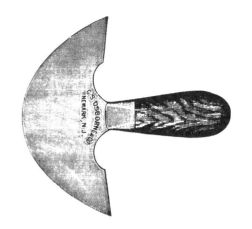

Round Knife

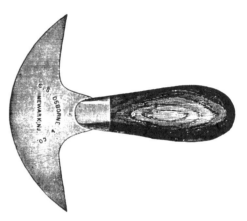

Head Knife

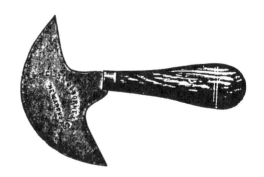

Head Knife, French Pattern

Head Knife

Leather Knife

Skiving Knife

R H Curved Lip

Button Knife

R H Straight Lip

Cap Knife

Sharp Curve

Hawk Bill

Skiving

McKay Stitcher

Square Point

Paring or Curved Square Point

Taper Point

Paris Curve

Wide Point or Belt Knife

Leather Knife

KNIFE, LETTUCE. Also called LETTUCE CUTTER. A farm tool used to harvest head lettuce. Overall length is approximately 14 inches.

Round Edge Heel

Lettuce Knife

KNIFE, LINOLEUM. See *Knife, Oil Cloth.*

Round Point

Leather Knife

KNIFE, MAIZE. Also called HARVESTER KNIFE. A knife used for cutting the heads from maize or kaffir corn. Length of cutting edge is approximately 2 1/2 inches.

Maize Knife

KNIFE, MOON. A circular knife, 8 to 12 inches in diameter, with a slight dish shape. Used by a currier for scraping, paring and trimming a finished hide. The knife was used by grasping it with one or both hands through the center hole. *Salaman* states that the moon knife has a wooden bar across the hole to serve as a handle.

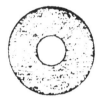

Moon Knife

KNIFE, NET MAKERS'. A knife that is worn on the finger like a ring. It is useful for repairmen of fishing nets and for other tasks requiring frequent cutting of twine or light cord. The illustrated tool was patented in 1912.

Net Makers' Knife

KNIFE, OIL CLOTH. Also called ROOFING KNIFE. A knife used for cutting oil cloth or other semi-rigid material such as tar paper or linoleum. Later catalogues list this tool as a LINOLEUM KNIFE.

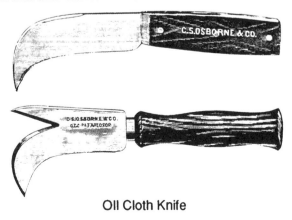

Oil Cloth Knife

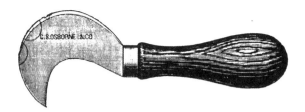

Oil Cloth Knife

KNIFE, ONE ARMED. Also called ONE ARMED MANS' KNIFE. Length is 8 1/2 to 9 1/2 inches overall. The back is ground to a cutting edge.

One Armed Knife

KNIFE, OPERATING. Also called SCALPEL. A medical tool used for surgical operations. This type of knife usually has an integral metal handle.

Operating Knife

KNIFE, OYSTER. A blunt tool used to open oysters. Length of blade is 2 1/2 to 5 inches.

Oyster Knife

KNIFE, PALLET. A tool with a thin flexible blade used by an artist or sign painter for mixing paint on a pallet. Length of blade is 2 1/2 to 6 inches. Similar to a spatula except generally smaller and more fragile.

Pallet Knife

KNIFE, PAPER HANGERS'. Length of blade is 3 to 3 1/2 inches.

265

Paper Hangers' Knife

KNIFE, PAPER HANGERS' CASING. Also called BASE KNIFE, BASE WHEEL, CASING WHEEL, CORNER KNIFE and WALL PAPER TRIMMER. A sharp wheel used for trimming wall paper along a base moulding or other straight edge.

Base Wheel

Casing Wheel

Casing Wheel

Casing Knife

KNIFE, PATTERN MAKERS'. See *Knife, Cloth.*

KNIFE, PEELING. A fruit peeling knife used by commercial canning factories. Length of blade is about 3 inches. Both right and left hand types were available. The illustrated knife is a Pomona Pattern. See also *Pitting Spoon.*

Peeling Knife

KNIFE, PEG. See *Turning Tool, Hook.*

KNIFE, PICKING. A basket makers' tool used for trimming the ends of the splits from a finished basket.

Picking Knife

KNIFE, PIG FOOT. A butcher shop device used to split a boiled pig foot.

Pig Foot Knife

KNIFE, PLASTER. A tool used by an orthopedic surgeon for removing a plaster cast.

Plaster Knife

KNIFE, PLASTERERS' TRIMMING. Length of blade is approximately 6 inches.

Plasterers' Trimming Knife

KNIFE, POULTRY KILLING. Also called CHICKEN STICKING KNIFE and TURKEY STICKING KNIFE. A knife used in a slaughter house to stick chickens or turkeys. One type appears to be similar in shape to an INK ERASER.

Poultry Killing Knife

KNIFE, PRUNING. Also called PRUNING HOOK. A curved knife used for pruning grapes and for similar tasks.

Pruning Knife

KNIFE, PUTTY. Also called GLAZIERS' KNIFE. A knife with a dull flexible blade used to apply putty to a window sash. Width of blade is 1 to 1 1/2 inches.

Putty Knife

KNIFE, RACE. See *Timber Scribe.*

KNIFE, RASE. See *Timber Scribe.*

KNIFE, ROOFING. See *Knife, Oil Cloth.*

KNIFE, ROPE. Length of blade is 3 inches.

Rope Knife

KNIFE, ROUND. See *Knife, Leather.*

KNIFE, RUBBER. A knife used for working sheet rubber during manufacture of rubber goods. Some of the shapes illustrated appear to be identical to leather knives. See also *Knife, Extension Blade.*

Bead Trimming

Bent V Trimming

Rubber Knife

Bevel Point

Double Edge Square

Half Round Point

Mill

Point

Tire Repairing

Tire Repairing

Turnover

Rubber Knife

KNIFE, SEED POTATO. A knife used for cutting potatoes for planting. Seed potatoes are cut such that each segment has one eye and a generous wedge of the heart of the potato.

Seed Potato Knife

KNIFE, SHOE MAKERS'. See *Knife, Leather.*

KNIFE, SHOE MAKERS' WELT. A knife used to trim and smooth the top of the welt on a shoe or boot after stitching.

Shoe Makers' Welt Knife

KNIFE, SILVER PLATERS'. Overall length is approximately 11 inches.

Silver Platers' Knife

KNIFE, SLOYD. See *Knife, Carvers'*.

KNIFE, SOD. A knife used for cutting thick sod. Also suitable for use as a hay knife. The tool is shown without a handle.

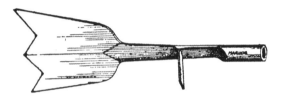

Sod Knife

KNIFE, SOLE. See *Sole Knife*.

KNIFE, STRAW. See *Feed Cutter*.

KNIFE, TOBACCO. Length of blade is approximately 4 inches.

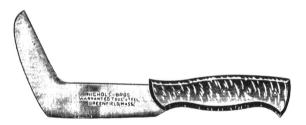

Carolina Pattern

Kentucky Pattern

Tobacco Knife

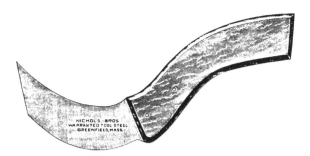

Richmond Pattern

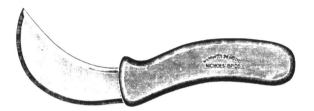

Virginia Pattern

Tobacco Knife

KNIFE, TOE. See *Toe Knife*.

KNIFE, TRUNK. A shape of knife favored by a trunk maker or trimmer. Probably the same as the WIDE POINT LEATHER KNIFE. See *Knife, Leather*.

Trunk Knife

KNIFE, TURKEY STICKING. See *Knife, Poultry Killing*.

KNIFE, UNCAPPING. A knife used by a bee keeper. The knife is flat on the bottom and the top is beveled toward the edges. Both edges are thin but not sharp. The knife is heated and used to melt a layer of honeycomb wax thus releasing the honey. The illustrated tool is hollow and has provisions for connection of an external source of steam for heating. Other types are heated by insertion into hot water.

Uncapping Knife

KNIFE, UNHAIRING. A tanners' tool similar to a fleshing knife but sharpened on the concave side only. This tool is pushed over the hide to scrape and shave off the hair. The blade is curved to match the curvature of the tanners' beam.

Unhairing Knife

KNIFE, UPHOLSTERERS'. Length of blade is 2 3/4 to 4 1/2 inches. Square Point and Round Point Leather Knives were also listed by some suppliers as upholsterers' knives. See *Knife, Leather*.

Half Round Point

Trimmer Point

Upholsterers' Knife

KNIFE, WALL PAPER. See *Knife, Paper Hangers'*.

KNIFE, WELT. See *Knife, Shoe Makers' Welt*.

KNIFE, WILLOW. A basket makers' tool used for harvesting the willow withies for use as basket material. A specialized form of BILL HOOK.

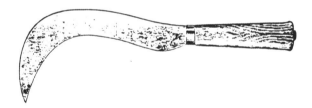

Willow Knife

KNIFE CLEANER. A machine used to clean and polish knives. The knife blade is entered into a hole in the periphery of the machine and polished by two counter-rotating disks driven by the hand crank.

KNIFE ERASER. See *Ink Eraser*.

KNIFE FILE. See *File, Knife*.

KNITTING NEEDLE GAUGE. A gauge with holes graduated in standard knitting needle and crochet hook sizes.

Knitting Needle Gauge

KNOCKOUT PUNCH. See *Hole Cutter*.

KNUCKLE JOINT PLANE. See *Plane, Knuckle Joint*.

KNURL HOLDER. Also called KNURL WHEEL and MILLING WHEEL. A handle for holding interchangeable knurling cutters. Several patterns of cutters were available.

Knurl Holder

KNURL WHEEL. See *Knurl Holder*.

L

Tool names starting with the letter L, including multiple listings of:
LADLE
LATHE
LEATHER MACHINE
LEATHER TOOL
LEVEL

Included also is a listing of tools used for:
LOGGING (LUMBERING)

LACE CUTTER. Also called LACE LEATHER CUTTER. A tool used to cut boot laces and other narrow strips of thin leather. It will cut strips from 3/16 to 3/4 inches wide. The illustrated tool is the Elliot Patent granted May 3, 1880.

Lace Cutter

LACE CUTTER, COMBINATION. A combined lace cutter, awl and belt punch.

Combination Lace Cutter

LACE LEATHER CUTTER. See *Lace Cutter*.

LACE PUNCH. See *Punch, Lace*.

LACING AWL. See *Awl, Lacing*.

LACING NEEDLE. A needle, with a large eye, for use in lacing with leather strips.

LACING PLIERS. See *Pliers, Lacing*.

LADIES HAMMER. See *Hammer, Ladies*.

LADLE. A dipper or carrier used for handling hot liquid.

LADLE, FOUNDRY. A ladle used in a foundry for transporting large quantities of molten metal.

Bull Ladle

Sulky Ladle

Foundry Ladle

LADLE, MELTING. Also called BABBITT LADLE and PLUMBERS' LADLE. An iron ladle, with one or two pouring lips, suitable for use with molten metal. Sizes from 2 1/2 to 14 inches in diameter were available.

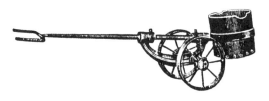

Melting Ladle

LADLE, PITCH. A pitch container used by a roofer to fill seams and cracks.

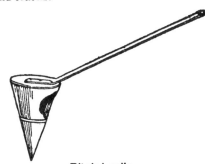

Pitch Ladle

LAG SCREW WRENCH. See *Wrench, Lag Screw.*

LAMBS TONGUE. See *Plane, Moulding, Reverse Ogee.*

LAND CHAIN. See *Surveyors' Chain.*

LANDING HOOK. A logging tool with the combined features of a cant hook and a pinch bar. Used for breaking landings and rollways.

Landing Hook

LANDSLIDE HOLDER. See *Anvil Tool, Plow Iron.*

LANTERN. A portable outdoor light with a protective globe. The illustrated devices are common-type kerosene lanterns.

Dashboard or Driving

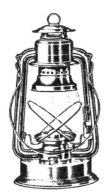

Farm or
General Purpose

Lantern

LANTERN CHISEL. See *Chisel, Lantern.*

LAP ANVIL. See *Anvil, Lap.*

LAP IRON. See *Anvil, Lap.*

LAP SKIVER. See *Leather Machine, Lap Skiver.*

LAP TRIMMER. See *Leather Tool, Trimmer.*

LARD PRESS. See *Wine Press.*

LARD SPADE. See *Butter Packer.*

LARD TROWEL. See *Trowel, Butter.*

LAST. See *Shoe Makers' Tool, Last.*

LAST BLOCK AXE. See *Axe, Last Block.*

LAST BLOCK CHIPPING AXE. See *Axe, Last Block.*

LAST HOOK. See Shoe *Makers' Tool, Last Hook.*

LAST MAKERS' RASP. See *Rasp, Last Makers'.*

LASTING PINCERS. See *Pincers, Lasting.*

LASTING PLIERS. See *Pincers, Lasting.*

LATH BOX HATCHET. See *Hatchet, Box.*

LATHE. A machine capable of rotating a workpiece about a horizontal axis. Used when shaping a cylindrical item.

LATHE, FOOT POWERED. A treadle or pedal operated lathe. Both wood-cutting and metal-cutting varieties were available.

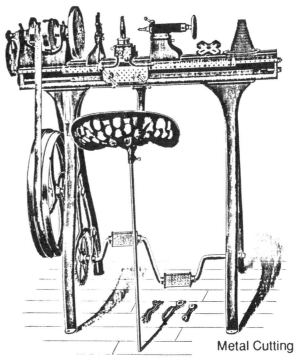

Metal Cutting

Foot Powered Lathe

LATHE, JEWELERS'. A small lathe normally powered by a foot power wheel or with a treadle.

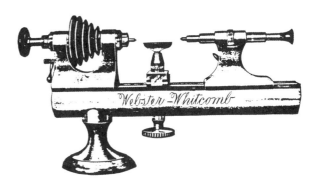

Jewelers' Lathe

Wood Cutting

Foot Powered Lathe

LATHE, POLISHING. A treadle-powered spindle used by a jeweler for polishing and buffing.

Polishing Lathe

LATHE, SPRING POLE. A lathe in which the treadle is returned by tension in a bent pole. Pressing the treadle rotates the work in one direction and the spring pole returns it to the original position. Cutting is accomplished only on the treadle stroke.

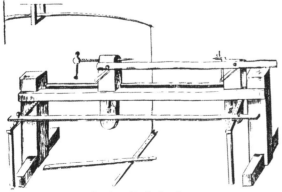

Spring Pole Lathe

LATHE ANVIL. See *Anvil, Lathe.*

LATHE CHISEL. See *Turning Tool, Chisel.*

LATHE DOG WRENCH. See *Wrench, Lathe Dog.*

LATHE FILE. See *File, Lathe.*

LATHE TOOL. See *Metal Spinning Tool* and *Turning Tool.*

LATHE TOOL TONGS. See *Tongs, Blacksmiths'.*

LATHE WHEEL. See *Foot Power Wheel.*

LATHERS' HAMMER. See *Hammer, Lathers'.*

LATHERS' NIPPERS. See *Nippers, Tinners' Cutting.*

LATHERS' TOOL CASE. See *Tool Case, Lathers'.*

LATHING HATCHET. See *Hatchet, Lathing.*

LAWN EDGE TRIMMER. A device used to trim grass along a sidewalk or driveway.

Lawn Edge Trimmer

LAWN MOWER. A grass-cutting machine with rotating blades driven from one wheel.

Lawn Mower

LAWN MOWER SHARPENER. A device used to sharpen a reel-type lawn mower. It consists of a segment of file clamped into a handle. Both types illustrated have a guide to help maintain the proper angle of the file.

Lawn Mower Sharpener

Lawn Mower Sharpener

LAWN ROLLER. A heavy iron roller used to compact and flatten a lawn after seeding. Weight of the illustrated type of roller is 175 to 565 pounds when filled with water.

Lawn Roller

LAWN SPUD. See *Weed Digger*.

LAWN TOOLS. See *Garden and Lawn Tools*.

LAYER CREASER. See *Leather Tool, Creaser*.

LEAD BEATER. See *Dresser*.

LEAD DRESSER. See *Dresser*.

LEAD FILE. See *File, Babbitt*.

LEAD FLOAT. See *File, Babbitt*.

LEAD JOINT RUNNER. Also called JOINT RUNNER. A device used to direct molten lead around the periphery of an iron pipe joint. The lead is poured into the funnel pointed out by the arrow in the illustration.

Lead Joint Runner

LEAD PIPE PLIERS. See *Pliers, Lead Pipe*.

LEAD PLANE. See *Plane, Shoot Board, Lead*.

LEAD TYPE PLANE. See *Plane, Shoot Board, Lead*.

LEAF RAKE. See *Rake, Leaf*.

LEAF TOOL. See *Plasterers' Ornamental Tools*.

LEATHER FILLET PLANE. See *Plane, Leather Fillet*.

LEATHER MACHINE. A machine used in one of the leather working trades such as harness maker, saddle maker or shoe maker.

LEATHER MACHINE, CREASING. A machine used for continuous creasing of straps up to 1 3/4 inches wide. Generally used for making a small decorative crease along each edge of a strap. The straps were sometimes dampened before being creased. Several patterns of rollers were available.

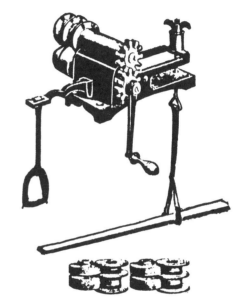

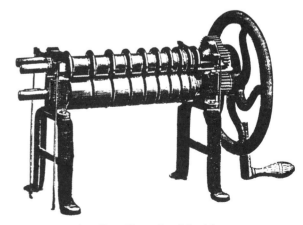

Leather Creasing Machine

LEATHER MACHINE, EMBOSSING. Also called SADDLE EMBOSSING MACHINE. A machine used for continuous embossing of straps up 1 3/4 inches wide. Several patterns of rollers were available.

273

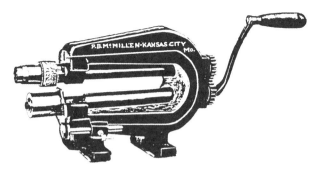

Embossing Machine

LEATHER MACHINE, LAP SKIVER. A machine used to taper a wide strap of leather for lap joining. The illustrated tool is a Dixon's Patent.

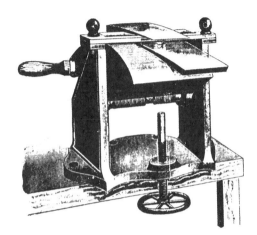

Lap Skiver

LEATHER MACHINE, LOOP PRESS. A press used for embossing a leather box loop.

Loop Press Die

Loop Press

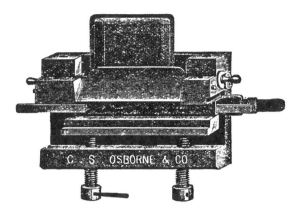

Loop Press

LEATHER MACHINE, PINKING. A machine used for making a scalloped edge on leather or felt. Small machines of this general type were sold for home use in pinking cloth and felt.

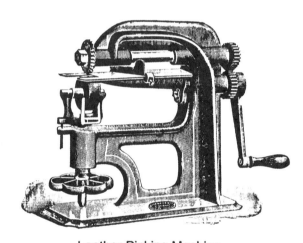

Leather Pinking Machine

LEATHER MACHINE, SKIRT CHANNELING. A saddle makers' tool.

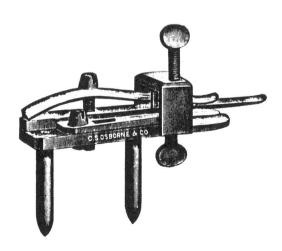

Skirt Channeling Machine

LEATHER MACHINE, SPLITTING. Also called SPLITTER, SPLITTING KNIFE and SPLITTING MACHINE. An adjustable device used to pare strips of leather to a given thickness.

Leather Splitter

LEATHER MACHINE, TRACE TRIMMER. A machine designed to trim a trace to the proper width and to bevel both edges.

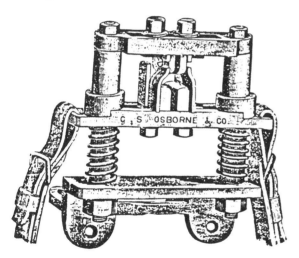

Trace Trimmer

LEATHER TOOL. A hand tool used for trimming, cutting, embossing or smoothing leather. There is considerable overlap in the use and names of tools used by the different leather-working trades. See listings under *Book Binders' Tools, Saddle and Harness Tools* and *Shoe Makers' Tools.* See also *Belt Groover.*

LEATHER TOOL, BAG FRAME STUFFER. A tool used to insert the leather into a handbag or carpet bag frame.

Bag Frame Stuffer

LEATHER TOOL, BAG PUNCH. A punch used to make an elongated buckle tongue hole in leather. Sizes were available to cut a hole 1/4 to 1 1/2 inches long.

Bag Punch

LEATHER TOOL, BAG PUNCH GAUGE. A tool used to determine the size of a bag punch required to make a given size of hole.

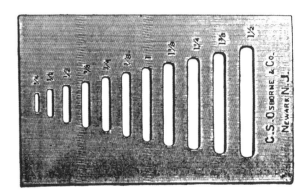

Bag Punch Gauge

LEATHER TOOL, BEADER. A leather embossing tool. Available in several patterns to make 2, 3 or 4 lines.

Beader

LEATHER TOOL, BEADER CHUCK. A handled chuck made to hold interchangeable beader stubs or an embossing wheel carriage stub.

Beader Chuck

LEATHER TOOL, BEVELER. Also called HAND PUSH BEVELER.

Beveler

LEATHER TOOL, BEVELING MACHINE. Also called ROLL BEVELING MACHINE. A device used to bevel a heavy leather strap.

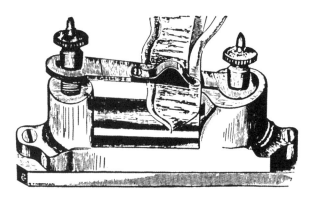

Beveling Machine

LEATHER TOOL, BLEEDER. A pointed knife intended to make a short slit in leather to accommodate lacing or knotting. Width is 1/2 to 5/8 inches.

Bleeder

LEATHER TOOL, BOUNCER. A leather tool used to smooth and burnish large curved surfaces such as parts of a saddle. The bouncer can also be used in a light hammering mode to round the edges of a stuffed section. Usually made of lignum vitae or dogwood. Overall length is approximately 5 inches.

Bouncer

LEATHER TOOL, BOX LOOP EDGER. A tool used for finishing the top edges and corners of a box loop.

Box Loop Edger

LEATHER TOOL, BUCKLE TONGUE PUNCH. A plier-like device used to make an elongated hole for a buckle tongue. See also *Leather Tool, Bag Punch.*

Buckle Tongue Punch

LEATHER TOOL, CARVING. Also called SADDLERS' CARVING TOOL. Width is 1/32 to 1/2 inch.

Leather Carving Tool

LEATHER TOOL, CHAMFER. A tool used to chamfer the edge of heavy leather. The tool is pulled along the edge of the workpiece and an adjustable knife removes a portion of the edge.

Leather Chamfer Tool

LEATHER TOOL, CHANNELER. Also called EDGE CHANNELER. A tool used to cut a slit or channel in the edge of a heavy leather workpiece. Stitching is placed in the channel and the upper lip is then glued down to form an invisible seam.

Boston Pattern

Eureka Pattern

Channeler

Hall's Patent

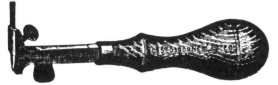

Gig Saddle Skirt

Stevens' Patent

Channeler

LEATHER TOOL, CHECKING. A tool used for making background checks on leather. See *Leather Tool, Creaser.*

LEATHER TOOL, CLAW. See *Tack Claw.*

LEATHER TOOL, CLIP. See *Trimmers' Clip.*

LEATHER TOOL, COMPASS. See *Compass, Leather.*

LEATHER TOOL, CONCHO CUTTER. Also called ROSETTE CUTTER. A hollow punch that cuts a rounded shape with scalloped or pinked edges. Diameter is 1/2 to 2 inches.

Concho Cutter

LEATHER TOOL, COUNTERSINK. Also called PATENT LEATHER COUNTERSINK. A form of creaser.

Countersink

LEATHER TOOL, CREASER. An embossing tool used to make a groove in leather. The creaser is normally used for decorative purposes but can also be used for marking a pattern or cutoff. The leather is dampened prior to use of the creaser and sometimes the tool is heated for use. See also *Leather Tool, Countersink; Leather Tool, Modeling; Leather Tool, Spreading* and *Leather Tool, Tickler.*

Bevel or Single Layer

Double Layer

End Loop

Iron End

Loop

Mexican Cutting, Single
Leather Creaser

277

Mexican Cutting, Double

Screw Type

Screw Type, Layer

Welcher's Patent

Wooden

Leather Creaser

LEATHER TOOL, CROWN SPLITTER. A leather slitting knife that can be mounted on a bench.

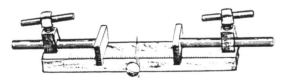

Crown Splitter

LEATHER TOOL, CUTTING DIE. Also called PATTERN DIE. A hollow cutting punch formed in the shape of a functional element such as part of a shoe or harness. The die is positioned on the leather and struck with a leather maul. A cutting die used by a shoe maker was called a DINK at one time and the process of cutting out parts was called "Dinking". A heavy block of wood, called a Dinking Board, was used as a base for the cutting action.

Cutting Die

LEATHER TOOL, DRAWING PLATE. A tool used for rounding boot laces and similar items. Large workpieces were worked with a Rounder. See *Leather Tool, Rounder.*

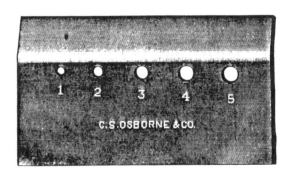

Drawing Plate

LEATHER TOOL, EDGER. Also called EDGE TOOL. A tool used for removing sharp edges from new straps and similar items of heavy leather. The type with the cutting edge enclosed in a hole was also called ROUND TRIMMER.

Bissonette

Crotch

Leather Edger

278

English Type

French Type

Hame Clip Gouge

Safety Edger

Skirt Edger

Leather Edger

LEATHER TOOL, EMBOSSING WHEEL CARRIAGE. A handle that will accept several interchangeable embossing wheels. The wheels were used to impress a continuous design on a leather workpiece.

Embossing Wheel Carriage

LEATHER TOOL, FINISHING WHEEL. See *Leather Tool, Overstitch Wheel.*

LEATHER TOOL, HAND SLICKER. See *Leather Tool, Slicker.*

LEATHER TOOL, HARNESS MAKERS' PRESS. A press used to set a sharp bend in a leather strap. This type of press could also be used with embossing dies to decorate small leather workpieces.

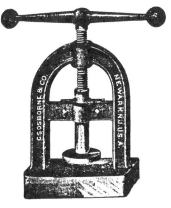

Harness Makers' Press

LEATHER TOOL, KNIFE. See *Knife, Leather.*

LEATHER TOOL, LOOP STICK. A straight wooden or steel stick about 12 inches long and 3/8 to 1 1/4 inches wide. Used as a mold or pattern to form a strap loop. Usually made of hardwood such as hickory or boxwood.

Loop Stick

LEATHER TOOL, MODELING. A tool used for working small leather objects such as key ring covers and wallets.

Broad Surface Tool

Deer Foot

Double Ball

Drawing Tool

Lining Tool

Spade Point

Leather Modeling Tool

LEATHER TOOL, OVERSTITCH WHEEL. Also called FINISHING WHEEL. A tool used to set the completed stitches in leather and to smooth the seam. The spaces between the points of the overstitch wheel are rounded as shown in the illustration and the points are blunt rather than being sharp.

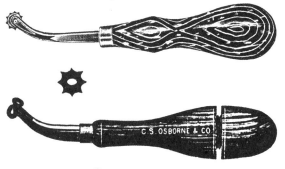

Overstitch Wheel

LEATHER TOOL, PINKING IRON. A cutting punch with a scalloped border. Tools that will cut two and three portions of an arc were also available. Size is 3/8 to 2 inches.

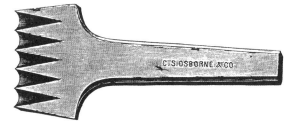

Pinking Iron

LEATHER TOOL, PRICKING IRON. A leather tool used to mark off stitch positions.

Pricking Iron

LEATHER TOOL, PRICKING WHEEL. Also called MARKING WHEEL. A wheel used to mark off stitch positions. The points of the pricking wheel are sharp and intended to pierce the surface of the leather. The spaces between the points are sharp notches rather than being rounded as in the overstitch wheel.

Pricking Wheel

LEATHER TOOL, PRICKING WHEEL CARRIAGE. A handle that will accept several interchangeable pricking wheels.

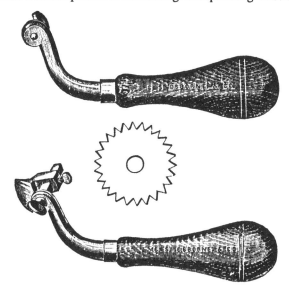

Pricking Wheel Carriage

LEATHER TOOL, ROSETTE CUTTER. See *Leather Tool, Concho Cutter.*

LEATHER TOOL, ROUND PUNCH GAUGE. A tool used to determine the proper size of round punch to use for a given application.

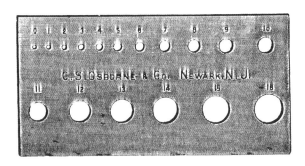

Round Punch Gauge

LEATHER TOOL, ROUNDER. Also called REIN ROUNDER. A tool used to form flat leather straps into a round shape. Dampening leather, with sizing added, is pulled through the proper hole in the rounder to force it into a cylindrical shape. Two or more holes of descending size may be used to complete the rounding process. Rounded leather was often used as bridle reins. See also *Leather Tool, Drawing Plate.*

Rounder

LEATHER TOOL, SCALLOPING WHEEL. A two-handed cutting wheel that will produce a scalloped edge on leather.

Scalloping Wheel

LEATHER TOOL, SINKING. A heavy creaser used to make wide grooves.

Sinking Tool

LEATHER TOOL, SLICKER. Also called HAND SLICKER. A tool with a smooth rounded edge used for slicking, smoothing and stretching leather. Also used to rub in tallow or sizing. One type of slicker consists of a piece of glass set in a wooden or leather handle.

Wooden

Glass

Slicker

LEATHER TOOL, SPREADING. Also called MEXICAN SPREADING TOOL. A heavy beveled creaser.

Spreading Tool

LEATHER TOOL, STAMP. Also called SADDLE STAMP. A steel embossing tool used to make a decorative design on leather. These tools were made in a large variety of sizes and shapes. Some examples are illustrated.

Leather Stamp

LEATHER TOOL, STAR STITCHER PUNCH. A tool used to make the holes for a star stitch design on leather.

Star Stitcher Punch

LEATHER TOOL, STIPPLING. Also called BACKGROUND TOOL. A tool used to make the background design for a decorative pattern on leather.

Stippling Tool

LEATHER TOOL, STITCH MARKER. See *Leather Tool, Pricking Iron* and *Shoe Makers' Tool, Clamming Marker.*

LEATHER TOOL, STRAP END PUNCH. A tool used to finish the end of a strap. Width is 1/4 to 1 1/2 inches.

Strap End Punch

English Type

Strap End Punch

LEATHER TOOL, STRAP HOLDER. A clamp for holding one end of a leather strap while performing some function such as edging.

Strap Holder

LEATHER TOOL, SWIVEL CUTTER. Also called SWIVEL TOP CUTTER.

Swivel Cutter

LEATHER TOOL, TACK CLAW. See *Tack Claw.*

LEATHER TOOL, TICKLER. A blunt tool used primarily for decoration of leather. Essentially the same as a creaser. The single tickler can also be used as a marking tool.

Bevel

Double

Tickler

Single

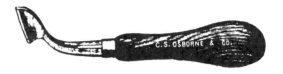

Saddlers' Bevel

Tickler

LEATHER TOOL, TRACE PUNCH. A punch that cuts a triangular shaped hole. Used at the end of a buggy trace to allow connection to a trace hook. Sizes were available to cut holes 5/8 to 1 1/2 inches long.

Trace Punch

LEATHER TOOL, TRACE PUNCH GAUGE. A tool used to determine the proper size of trace punch to use for a given application.

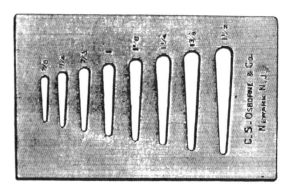

Trace Punch Gauge

LEATHER TOOL, TRACING WHEEL. See *Tracing Wheel.*

LEATHER TOOL, TRIMMER. Leather tools used to trim, smooth and bevel the edges of various workpieces. See also *Leather Tool, Edger.*

Binding

Leather Trimmer

Binding with Guide

Gig Saddlers'

Horn

Lap

Pad

Rein

Ring

Turnback

V Horn

Leather Trimmer

LEATHER TOOL, V. A leather carving tool with a V shaped cutting edge.

V Tool

LEG VISE. See *Vise, Post.*

LEMON SQUEEZER. An elaborate tool used for the simple task of extracting the juice from a lemon. Probably intended for a commercial application such as a soda fountain.

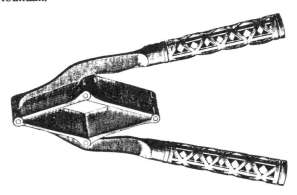

Lemon Squeezer

LENS DRILL. See *Boring Tool, Lens Drill.*

LETTER PRESS. See *Copying Press.*

LETTERERS' HAMMER. See *Hammer, Stone Cutters'.*

LETTERING PALLET. See *Bookbinding Tool, Lettering Pallet.*

LETTUCE CUTTER. See *Knife, Lettuce.*

LETTUCE KNIFE. See *Knife, Lettuce.*

LEVEL. A device for indicating a horizontal line or establishing the position of a surface with reference to the horizontal.

LEVEL, ALUMINUM. A spirit level made of aluminum. Aluminum was used for making levels as early as 1906. See *Level, Carpenters* and *Level, Masons.*

LEVEL, BENCH. See *Level, Straight Edge.*

LEVEL, BIT AND SQUARE. A small spirit level intended to be clamped to a boring bit or a carpenters' square.

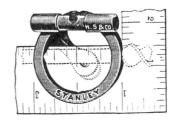

Bit and Square Level

283

LEVEL, BRASS BOUND. A wooden level with both ends and each corner of the sides edged in brass. See *Level, Carpenters'*.

LEVEL, CAMERA. See *Level, Cross Test*.

LEVEL, CARPENTERS'. A spirit level, usually having one or more plumb glasses, intended for use by a carpenter. The carpenters' level is generally made of wood but aluminum is also used. Cherry is the wood most often used; however, mahogany, rosewood, beech and pine have also been noted. Length is generally 10 to 30 inches. See also *Level, Electric*.

Plain Ends

Brass Corners

Brass Ends

Brass Bound

Carpenters' Level

LEVEL, CIRCULAR. A small spirit level, with a circular vial, that will indicate in any horizontal plane. This type of device was often used for leveling clocks.

Circular Level

LEVEL, COMBINATION. Also called CROSS TEST LEVEL. A spirit level and square combination. Several varieties of these combination tools were available.

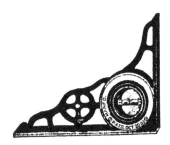

Combination Level

LEVEL, CROSS TEST. Also called CAMERA LEVEL. A device used for leveling an object in two planes. Each leg of the illustrated tool is 2 3/4 inches long. See also *Level, Combination*.

Cross Test Level

LEVEL, ELECTRIC. A carpenters' spirit level with a built-in electric light for viewing the level glass. Used in mine and tunnel construction work. Length is 18 to 30 inches.

Electric Level

LEVEL, ELECTRICIANS'. A non-magnetic level used by an electrician. Length is 8 to 16 inches. The illustrated level is made of bronze.

Electricians' Level

LEVEL, GRADE. Also called RAILROAD LEVEL. A level intended for use in laying out the grade for road and railroad construction. Sighting apertures are included to allow it to be used as a transit.

Grade Level

Inclinometer Level

LEVEL, HYDROSTATIC. Also called SHAFTING LEVEL and WATER LEVEL. A level that uses water as an indicating medium. This device consists of two hollow stands connected by a length of tubing. It is used for leveling machinery and structures and can be used for leveling points separated by long distances or obstructions. Twenty five feet of tube was provided with the illustrated level.

LEVEL, LINE. A small light-weight level intended for use while suspended on a heavy cord. Length is approximately 3 inches.

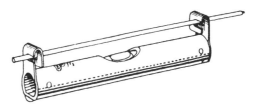

Line Level

Hydrostatic Level

LEVEL, INCLINOMETER. A level with a moveable bubble vial such that the bubble can be centered with the level resting on either a flat or inclined surface. The vial holder is generally scaled to indicate the degree of inclination. Inclinometer levels of both cast iron and wood were available. The metal varieties were also listed as MACHINISTS' LEVELS. See also *Level, Plumb Bob; Level, Plumbers'* and *Level, Pocket*.

LEVEL, MACHINISTS'. A precision iron level used when installing machinery. Length is usually from 4 to 12 inches. See also *Level, Inclinometer.*

Machinists' Level

LEVEL, MASONS'. A long spirit level with one or more plumb glasses. This type of level was usually made of wood but aluminum was also used to reduce weight. Cherry, mahogany and pine are the woods most often used. The masons' level often has provisions for hanging a plumb bob as shown in the illustration. A small plumb bob is suspended from a notch in one end of the level. A precise vertical is indicated when the bob is centered in the aperture at the other end of the level. Length is 36 to 48 inches.

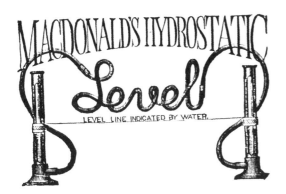

Inclinometer Level

Masons' Level

LEVEL, METALLIC. A general-purpose level made of iron or aluminum. This type of level was listed as being suitable for use by machinists, plumbers, steam fitters and for general construction. Sizes are 6 to 24 inches.

Metallic Level

LEVEL, MILLWRIGHTS'. A large cast iron level used when setting and smoothing the bottom grinding stone in a mill. Length is 3 to 4 feet. Weight of the 4 foot level is approximately 60 pounds. During the smoothing process, the milled bottom of the level is coated with chalk and rubbed across the stone. Bits of the chalk are transferred to each high point on the stone.

Millwrights' Level

LEVEL, PAPER HANGERS'. A level intended to be used in conjunction with a paper hangers' straight edge.

Paper Hangers' Level

LEVEL, PENDULUM. A level consisting of a weighted pointer that is free to rotate about a pivot. The pointer seeks a vertical position that can be scaled to indicate either a vertical or horizontal position of the base. The illustrated tool was patented March 19, 1889.

Pendulum Level

LEVEL, PLUMB BOB. An ancient form of leveling device in which a plumb bob or pendulum is used as the indicator. This type of tool was generally obsoleted by the spirit level. The plumb bob holder on the Pittsburgh Level can be swiveled to allow the level to be used as an inclinometer. See also *Level, Masons'*.

Pittsburgh Novelty Co.

Plumb Bob Level

LEVEL, PLUMBERS'. A metal level, with an adjustable level glass holder, scaled to indicate pitch in inches per foot. Used to install sewer pipe and for similar tasks. Length of the illustrated tool is 10 to 15 inches. See also *Level, Radial*.

Plumbers' Level

LEVEL, POCKET. A level of a convenient size for carrying in the pocket. Some pocket-size levels have provisions for attachment to a straight edge such as a carpenter's square.

Pocket Level

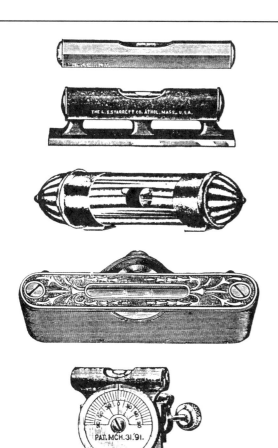

Pocket Level

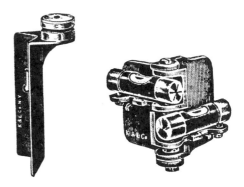

Rod Level

LEVEL, STRAIGHT EDGE. Also called BENCH LEVEL. A small level intended for attachment to a straight edge such as a carpenter's square. See also *Level, Pocket.*

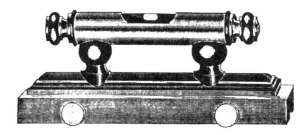

Straight Edge Level

LEVEL, TORPEDO. A small general-purpose spirit level that is tapered on both ends. Length is 9 to 10 inches.

Torpedo Level

LEVEL, TRACK. A spirit level long enough to span both rails of a railroad track. The stepped notches on the illustrated level are intended to facilitate measuring track pitch on a curve.

Track Level

LEVEL, WATER. See *Level, Hydrostatic.*

LEVEL, WEIGHTED WHEEL. A level in which a weighted wheel on a pivot is used to indicate the vertical. The illustrated tool has a scale that indicates pitch in 1/2 inches to the foot and the number of degrees that the base is inclined from the horizontal.

Weighted Wheel Level

LEVEL, RAILROAD. See *Level, Grade* and *Level, Track.*

LEVEL, RADIAL. A level on which one vial can be adjusted. The pointer is free to move about 1 1/2 inches which results in rotation of the attached bubble vial. The device is probably intended for use in construction of a sewer system or gravity feed water system. The moveable vial assembly was patented in 1905. It appears to have been incorporated into a standard brass-bound level.

Radial Level

LEVEL, ROD. A surveyors' tool used to assure accurate alignment of the leveling rod. The levels can be attached to the rod or carried separately.

LEVEL, SHAFTING. See *Level, Hydrostatic.*

LEVEL, SPIRIT. A common level having a sealed glass tube containing a liquid and a bubble. When the bubble travels to the center of the arched tube, the tube is horizontal. Early level glasses were filled with grain alcohol to inhibit freezing; hence the term "Spirit" level.

LEVEL SIGHTS. Sights suitable for attachment to a level such that the level can be used as a transit. Sights were available for attachment to either wooden or metal levels.

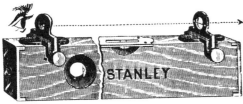

Level Sights

LEVELER. See *Foot Adjuster* and *Plane, Leveling*.

LEVELING BLOCK. Also called TABLE BLOCK. A black-smiths' tool consisting of a metal block with one side machined smooth and hardened. Size is 12 to 80 inches long and 1 5/8 to 5 inches thick. The leveling block was generally mounted on a low stand for use.

Leveling Block

LEVELING PLANE. See *Plane, Leveling*.

LEVELING STAND. A swivel stand that can be used with a spirit level and level sights to serve as a survey transit.

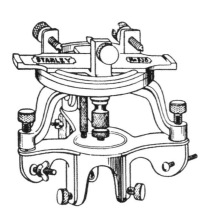

Leveling Stand

LEVER CLAMP. See *Shoe Makers' Tool, Lever Clamp*.

LEVER DOG. See *Hoop Dog*.

LIFTER. See *Moulders' Hand Tool* and *Pan Lifter*.

LIGHTNING FILE. See *File, Cant Saw*.

LINCH PIN HAMMER. See *Hammer, Doubletree Pin*.

LINE BAR. See *Bar, Crow*.

LINE LEVEL. See *Level, Line*.

LINE ROLLER. See *Cement Tool, Roller*.

LINE TRACER. An edge tool used for making lines on a stone carving. A granite or marble cutters' tool.

Line Tracer

LINEMANS' DRAWING KNIFE. See *Drawing Knife, Linemans'*.

LINEMANS' HATCHET. See *Hatchet, Linemans'*.

LINEN PROVER. See *Pick Counter*.

LINING BAR. See *Bar, Crow*.

LINING GAUGE. See *Electrotype Finishers' Tool, Lining Gauge*.

LINING TOOL. Also called MULTIPLE GOUGE. A print shop tool with multiple cutting edges for making shallow parallel lines. Used on a metal plate or wood cut. Lines on the tool are spaced to match standard halftone screens.

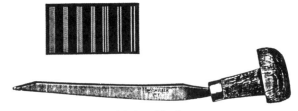

Lining Tool

LINING UP PUNCH. See *Punch, Taper*.

LINK TONGS. See *Tongs, Chain*.

LINOLEUM KNIFE. See *Knife, Oil Cloth*.

LIP BIT. See *Boring Tool, Bit, Shell*.

LIP TONGS. See *Tongs, Blacksmiths'*.

LIPPED ADZE. See *Adze, Ship Carpenters' Lipped*.

LIQUOR THIEF. A device used for taking a sample of liquid. This type of device was available in glass, copper or tin. Called a PIPETTE when used in a laboratory.

Liquor Thief

LOBSTER CLAW. See *Clamp, Rope*.

LOCK, AUTO TIRE. A lock that will clamp around the rim and tire of an automobile wheel to prevent theft. It can also be used as a restraining device when the car is parked on a downgrade.

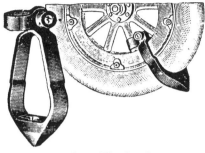

Auto Tire Lock

LOCK MORTISING MACHINE. A device used to cut the mortise in a door for installation of a lock. Two holes are drilled for the ends of the mortise; the machine cuts out the wood between the holes. Advertised as being capable of cutting a clean mortise of any width in three minutes.

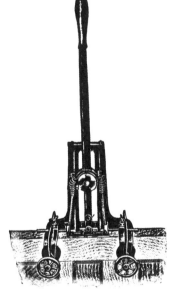

Lock Mortising Machine

LOCK PICKS. Tools used to open tool box locks, inside door locks and similar fasteners.

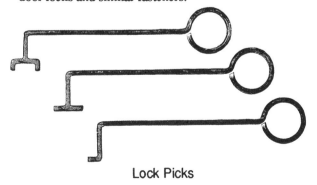

Lock Picks

LOCK SCREW DRIVER. See *Screw Driver, Locksmiths'*.

LOCK MORTISING CHISEL. See *Chisel, Lock Mortising*.

LOCK MORTISING TOOL. See *Chisel, Lock Mortising*.

LOCK STITCH AWL. See *Awl, Lock Stitch*.

LOCKSMITHS' SCREW DRIVER. See *Screw Driver, Locksmiths'*.

LOCOMOTIVE COAL PICK. See *Pick, Poll*.

LOCOMOTIVE JACK SCREW. See *Jack Screw*.

LOG CALIPER. See *Caliper, Log*.

LOG DOG. See *Logging Dog*.

LOG MARKING HAMMER. See *Hammer, Marking*.

LOG MEASURE. See *Rule, Log Measure*.

LOG RULE. See *Rule, Log Measure*.

LOGGING DOG. Also called LOG DOG, RAFTING DOG and TIMBER DOG. A heavy iron spike or hook used in binding logs together to form a float or raft.

Chain Dog

Eye Dog   Ring Dog

Logging Dog

LOGGING TOOLS. Also called LUMBERING TOOLS and TIMBER TOOLS. The special-purpose logging tools listed below can be found in normal alphabetical sequence. These tools may also have been used for other purposes.

  AXE, DOUBLE BIT
  AXE, MARKING
  AXE, SINGLE BIT
  BAR, TIMBER
  BORING TOOL, RAFTING AUGER
  CALIPER, LOG

CALIPER, WALKING WHEEL
CANT HOOK
CRAYON, LUMBER
GRAB SKIPPER
HAMMER, MARKING
HAND SPIKE
HOOK, PULP
HOOKAROON
JACK, LOGGING
LANDING HOOK
LOGGING DOG
MAUL, GRAB
MARKING WHEEL
PEAVEY
PENCIL, LUMBER
PICKAROON
PIKE
RING DOG
RULE, BOARD MEASURE
RULE, BOARD STICK
RULE, LOG MEASURE
SAW, CROSSCUT
SAW GUMMER
SAW SET
SAW SET BLOCK
SAW SET GAUGE
STARTING LEVER
TIMBER GRAPPLE
TIMBER SCRIBE
WEDGE, EXPLODING
WEDGE, LOGGING

LONG JOINTER. See *Plane, Coopers' Jointer.*
LONG KNIFE. See *Clog Makers' Tools.*
LONG NOSE PLIERS. See *Pliers, Long Nose.*
LONG PLANE. See *Plane, Coopers' Jointer.*
LONG STICK. See *Shoe Makers' Tool, Long Stick.*
LOOM DUSTER. See *Brush, Loom Duster.*
LOOP CREASER. See *Leather Tool, Creaser.*
LOOP PRESS. See *Leather Machine, Loop Press.*
LOOP STICK. See *Leather Tool, Loop Stick.*

LOPPING AXE. A light axe used to trim small branches from a log. See *Axe, Chopping.*
LOW ANGLE PLANE. See *Plane, Low Angle.*
LUG HOOK. See *Timber Grapple.*
LUMBER CRAYON. See *Crayon, Lumber.*
LUMBER DOG. See *Logging Dog.*
LUMBER GAUGE. A gauge for measuring the thickness of a board. These tools were often used as give-a-way advertising pieces by lumber yards and mills. Generally made of brass and often nickel plated.

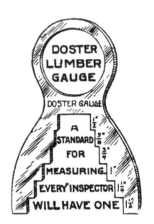

Lumber Gauge

LUMBER PENCIL. See *Pencil, Lumber.*
LUMBER RULE. See *Rule, Board Measure; Rule, Board Stick* and *Rule, Log Measure.*
LUMBERING TOOLS. See *Logging Tools.*
LUMBERMANS' APRON. See *Apron, Blacksmiths'.*
LUMBERMANS' STAMPING WHEEL. See *Marking Wheel.*
LUTING TROWEL. See *Trowel, Gas.*

M

Tool names starting with the letter M including multiple listings of:

MALLET
MANDREL
MAUL

Included also is a listing of tools used by the:

MOULDER

MACADAM HAMMER. See *Hammer, Macadam* and *Hammer, Napping.*

MACADAMIZING HAMMER. See *Hammer, Macadam.*

MACARONI TOOL. See *Carving Tool, Macaroni.*

MACHETE. A long heavy knife used for cutting vines and underbrush. Also used for cutting sugar cane.

Machete

MACHINE BIT. See *Boring Tool, Bit, Machine.*

MACHINE PUNCH. See *Punch, Hand.*

MACHINE STANDARD. See *Tinsmiths' Machine Standard.*

MACHINE WRENCH. See *Wrench, S.*

MACHINISTS' BALL PEEN HAMMER. See *Hammer, Ball Peen.*

MACHINISTS' CHIPPING HAMMER. See *Hammer, Chipping.*

MACHINISTS' CLAMP. See *Clamp, C* and *Clamp, Parallel.*

MACHINISTS' FORGE. See *Forge, Tool Makers'.*

MACHINISTS' HAMMER. See *Hammer, Ball Peen; Hammer, Chipping; Hammer, Cross Peen* and *Hammer, Straight Peen.*

MACHINISTS' LEVEL. See *Level, Inclinometer* and *Level, Machinists'.*

MACHINISTS' SCRAPER. See *Scraper, Bearing.*

MACHINISTS' VISE. See *Vise, Bench.*

MACHINISTS' WRENCH. See *Wrench, S.*

MAGNETIC HAMMER. See *Hammer, Tack.*

MAGNETO FILE. See *File, Magneto.*

MAINSPRING GAUGE. A watch or clock makers' tool used for measuring the width and thickness of a mainspring.

Mainspring Gauge

MAINSPRING WINDER. A clock makers' tool used to wind a mainspring. The tool is clamped in a vise while in use.

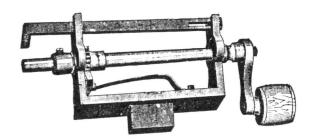

Mainspring Winder

MAIZE KNIFE. See *Knife, Maize.*

MALLET. A one-handed striking tool with a large head made of non-marring material such as wood or rubber. A mallet is generally used for driving another tool or for striking a surface without marring.

MALLET, AUTOMOBILE. See *Mallet, Rubber.*

MALLET, BOSSING. A hard wooden mallet used by a plumber for forming lead sheet. Usually made of boxwood or lignum vitae.

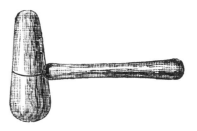

Bossing Mallet

MALLET, CARVERS'. A mallet used for driving a carving chisel. Made of hardwood such as beech, dogwood, hickory or lignum vitae. The carvers' mallet used with large chisels sometimes has the faces banded with metal to reduce fraying.

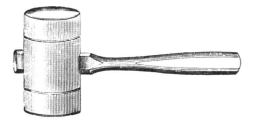

Banded

Carvers' Mallet

MALLET, CAULKING. A banded mallet, with a long wooden head, used for driving ship caulking tools. Usually made of a hard wood such as boxwood, black mesquite or live oak.

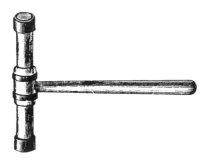

Caulking Mallet

MALLET, CHISEL. Also called CARPENTERS' MALLET, MORTISE MALLET and SQUARE MALLET. A heavy mallet favored for use in driving wood chisels. The chisel mallet is made of lignum vitae or other durable wood.

Chisel Mallet

MALLET, COPPERSMITHS'. A small wooden mallet used in forming copper. The face is 2 to 4 inches in diameter.

Coppersmiths' Mallet

MALLET, FIBRE. A general-purpose mallet with the head made of fibre secured with metal bands. Size is 5 to 24 ounces.

Fibre Mallet

MALLET, FROE. See *Froe Club.*

MALLET, HAWSING. See *Hawsing Beetle.*

MALLET, HORN. A mallet made of a solid horn tip. One reference indicates that this type of mallet was used in silversmithing. The illustrated tool is made of buffalo horn.

Horn Mallet

MALLET, HORSE COLLAR. A mallet used to form leather around the block when making a horse collar.

Round

Horse Collar Mallet

292

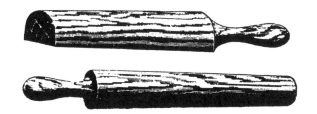

Breaking

Blocking

Iron

Horse Collar Mallet

MALLET, ICE. Also called ICE PICK. A wooden mallet with an iron spike used to chip ice.

French Style

Ice Mallet

MALLET, JEWELERS'. A small general-purpose mallet, made of wood or rawhide, intended for use by a jeweler or for other light striking tasks. Size of the face is 1 to 2 inches. See also illustration under *Mallet, Rawhide.*

MALLET, MORTISE. See *Mallet, Chisel.*

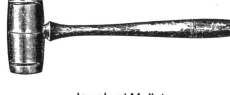

Jewelers' Mallet

MALLET, ORTHOPEDIC. A medical tool used in bone surgery. Overall length is 7 to 9 inches. Made of metal including the handle. One variety was listed as having a brass head.

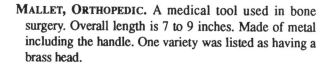

Orthopedic Mallet

MALLET, RAISING. A mallet used for raising thin metal over a contoured form. The face of the mallet is shaped to the desired contour by the user. Made of dogwood or other durable hardwood.

Raising Mallet

293

MALLET, RAWHIDE. Also called RAWHIDE HAMMER and RAWHIDE MAUL. A general-purpose mallet with the striking surface made of rawhide. The rawhide provides a tough and resilient surface especially suited for working metal without marring the surface. Weight is 1 1/2 to 24 ounces.

Solid

Faced

Rawhide Mallet

MALLET, RING. Also called BOUND MALLET. A mallet with metal or rawhide rings used as reinforcement for each face. The rings reduce fraying of the faces and thereby increase the life of the tool. See also *Mallet, Carvers'* and *Mallet, Fibre.*

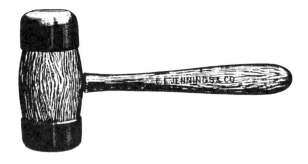

Ring Mallet

MALLET, ROUND. A general-purpose wooden mallet. Diameter of the face is 2 to 4 1/2 inches.

Round Mallet

MALLET, RUBBER. Also called AUTOMOBILE MALLET. A mallet with the head made of rubber or with a rubber face. Used in woodworking factories and for working light castings. The rubber mallet is also widely used in garages and service stations for such tasks as installing hub caps.

Faced

Rubber Mallet

MALLET, SADDLERS'. An iron mallet with wood inserts. Weight is 4 to 8 pounds.

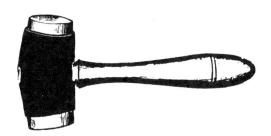

Saddlers' Mallet

MALLET, SCULPTORS'. See *Mallet, Stone Masons'.*

MALLET, SERVING. A mallet-shaped tool used to tighten and hold the winding when serving a rope. Diameter of the face is 2 1/2 to 3 inches. The serving yarn is looped around the handle of the tool such that the handle can be used as a lever to tighten the wrap.

Serving Mallet

MALLET, SOCKET. A mallet with a metal body and replaceable faces. Face is 2 to 4 inches in diameter. See also *Mallet, Rawhide* and *Mallet, Saddlers'.*

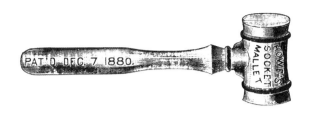

Socket Mallet

MALLET, STONE CUTTERS'. See *Mallet, Stone Masons'*.

MALLET, STONE MASONS'. Also called SCULPTORS' MALLET and STONE CUTTERS' MALLET. A heavy mallet used to drive stone masons' or sculptors' tools. Made of oak, hickory or maple. Weight is 2 to 8 pounds. Sizes up to 8 inches across have been noted.

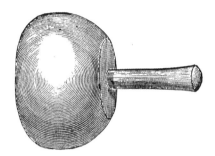

Stone Masons' Mallet

MALLET, TINNERS'. A small mallet used by a tinner when forming metal over a stake. Diameter is approximately 2 inches. Usually made of hickory.

Tinners' Mallet

MALLET, UPHOLSTERERS'. A heavy wooden mallet used to beat upholstery padding into a smooth contour. Similar in function to the Round Horse Collar Mallet.

Upholsterers' Mallet

MALT RAKE. See *Rake, Malt*.

MANDREL. A curved piece of metal on which a workpiece is positioned for hammering or shaping. A mandrel has a circular or curved work surface as opposed to an Anvil which normally has a flat work surface. See also *Eaves Trough Closing Form*.

MANDREL, BLACKSMITHS'. See *Cone*.

MANDREL, BRACELET. See *Mandrel, Jewelers'*.

MANDREL, HOLLOW. See *Mandrel, Stovepipe*.

MANDREL, JEWELERS'. A small mandrel used by a jeweler for straightening or smoothing a metal workpiece.

Bracelet

Ring

Hexagon

Square

Jewelers' Mandrel

MANDREL, RING. See *Mandrel, Jewelers'*.

MANDREL, STOVE PIPE. Also called HOLLOW MANDREL, HOLLOW MANDREL STAKE and STOVE PIPE ANVIL. A long mandrel, rounded on the top edge, that is used for assembling a section of stove pipe. Lengths up to 5 feet overall were listed. The mandrel was attached to a bench such that a section of pipe could be slipped over the rounded portion. These devices were standard hardware store fixtures when stove pipe was sold in large quantities and assembled in the store. Weight is 60 to 108 pounds.

Stove Pipe Mandrel

MANDREL, THIMBLE. See *Stake, Thimble*.

MANDREL STAKE. See *Stake, Mandrel*.

MANE COMB. Also called MANE DRAG. A coarse comb used to groom horses.

Mane Comb

MANUAL TRAINING BENCH. See *Bench, Manual Training*.

MANUAL TRAINING RULE. See *Rule, Manual Training*.

MANURE FORK. See *Fork, Shaving*.

MANURE HOOK. See *Hook, Potato*.

MARBLE BIT. See *Boring Tool, Bit, Marble*.

MARBLE CUTTERS' FILE. See *File, Marble Cutters'*.

MARBLE DRILL. See *Boring Tool, Bit, Marble*.

MARBLE FILE. See *File, Marble Cutters'*.

MARBLE TOOLS. See *Stone Cutting Tools*.

MARGIN TROWEL. A plasterers' tool. See *Trowel, Margin*.

MARKER. See *Carving Tool, Marker; Clapboard Marker; Ear Marker; Tile Marker* and *Tire Marker*.

MARKING AWL. See *Awl, Scratch*.

MARKING AXE. See *Axe, Marking*.

MARKING BRUSH. See *Brush, Marking*.

MARKING GAUGE. A gauge used for scribing a line parallel with the edge of a workpiece. The tool was generally used with a pushing motion. Beechwood was the most common material used; however, rosewood, boxwood, ebony and steel gauges are frequently noted. A large variety of these tools were available. Some examples are illustrated. See also *Panel Gauge*.

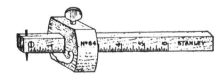

Common Type

Marking Gauge

Metal

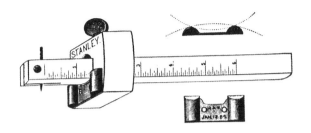

For Curved Edges

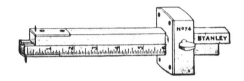

Double

For Ovals or Circles

Three Segment or Triple

Wheelwrights' or Coach Makers'
Marking Gauge

MARKING HAMMER. See *Hammer, Marking.*

MARKING IRON. See *Timber Scribe.*

MARKING POT. A container for stencil paint and the associated brush.

Marking Pot

MARKING SET. Also called STEEL STAMP. A set of individual steel letters or numbers used for stamping wood or metal. Size is 1/8 to 1/2 inches.

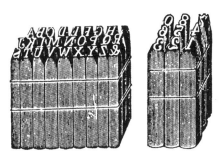

Marking Set

MARKING STAMP. A stamp used to put a name, date or other information on wood or wet concrete. See also *Axe, Marking* and *Hammer, Marking.*

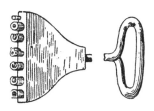

Burning

Cement

Marking Stamp

MARKING STICK. A stick with provisions for holding a lumber crayon in the end. Length of handle is up to 36 inches.

Marking Stick

MARKING WHEEL. Also called LUMBERMANS' STAMPING WHEEL. A stamping device having several faces. Used for stamping logs, planks or ties. The tool was available with either sharp or dull symbols for use on side or end grain respectively. See also *Leather Tool, Pricking Wheel.*

Marking Wheel

MARLIN SPIKE. A round pointed tool, made of steel, used to separate the strands when splicing a rope. Length is 6 to 24 inches. A common length is 12 inches. *See also Fid.*

For Manila Rope

For Wire Rope

Sail Makers'

Marlin Spike

MASH HAMMER. See *Hammer, Stone Cutters'.*

MASONS' BEADING TOOL. See *Tuck Pointer.*

MASONS' BRICK HAMMER. See *Hammer, Brick.*

MASONS' BUSH HAMMER. See *Hammer, Bush.*

MASONS' HAMMER. See *Hammer, Bush; Hammer, Masons' Pinning* and *Hammer, Stone.*

MASONS' LEVEL. See *Level, Masons'.*

MASONS' RIPPER. See *Ripper, Carpenters' Staging.*

MASONS' TROWEL. See *Trowel, Brick.*

MATCH PLANE. See *Plane, Match.*

MATCH STRIKER. A patented device intended to provide a rough surface for striking a common kitchen match. The illustrated tool consists of a curved piece of tin punctured from the inside such that the outer surface is rough. The spring is used to secure the device to the steering wheel or column of an automobile. A similar device was available for fastening to the dashboard of a Model A.

Match Striker

MATTING TOOL. See *Carving Tool, Marker.*

MATTOCK. A two-handed tool with a narrow axe-type blade on one side and a grub hoe on the other. Used for cutting underbrush, vines and tree roots. Similar in function to the Grub Hoe.

Mattock

MATTOCK, ASPHALT. A tool used to trim out a section of asphalt road or driveway. Width of cut is approximately 2 3/4 inches.

Asphalt Mattock

MATTOCK-AXE. See *Axe Mattock.*

MATTOCK HOE. See *Hoe, Grub.*

MAUD S ROUNDING HAMMER. See *Hammer, Farriers' Rounding.*

MAUL. A heavy striking tool generally intended for use with both hands. The maul is used for driving posts and for similar tasks. See *Sledge* for striking tools used for forging. See also *Beetle* and *Hawsing Beetle.*

MAUL, BASKET MAKERS'. Also called BEATING IRON and RAPPING IRON. A small striking tool used to tighten and flatten the basket weave by pounding. The hole at the end is said to be used for straightening a split or rod.

Basket Makers' Maul

MAUL, BOILER MAKERS'. A hickory maul, with a dome shaped face, used for bending and forming boiler plates. Size is 3 to 9 inches in diameter.

Boiler Makers' Maul

MAUL, CHIME. A coopers tool used to to drive down the chime hoop (end hoop) of a barrel. Made of hickory or solid metal. Weights up to 10 1/2 pounds were listed.

Wooden

Iron

Chime Maul

MAUL, COAL. See *Sledge, Coal.*

MAUL, GRAB. A heavy maul used to set and remove a grab hook from a log.

Grab Maul

MAUL, HORSE COLLAR. A tool used for bending heavy leather around the collar block when making a horse collar. Larger and heavier than the Horse Collar Mallet.

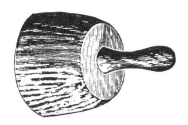

Horse Collar Maul

MAUL, POST. A maul used for driving wooden posts or stakes. Usually made of cast iron but mauls having wooden faces were also occasionally listed as post mauls. Weight is 10 to 21 pounds.

Bell Faced

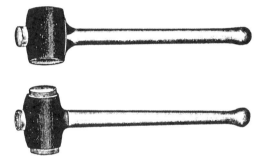

Post Maul

MAUL, RAILROAD. See *Maul, Spike.*

MAUL, RAILROAD TOP. See *Maul, Ship.*

MAUL, RAWHIDE. Also called rawhide mallet. A maul used primarily by leather workers for striking cutting dies and punches. Weight is 3 to 12 pounds. The maul face consists of leather rings compressed between two metal washers.

Rawhide Maul

MAUL, SEWER. An iron-bound wooden maul used to drive sheet pilings. Weight is 16 to 22 pounds.

Sewer Maul

MAUL, SHIP. Also called RAILROAD TOP MAUL and TOP MAUL. Weight is 4 to 8 pounds.

Ship Maul

MAUL, SPIKE. Also called RAILROAD MAUL, SPIKING HAMMER and TRACK MAUL. A maul used for driving railroad spikes. Weight is 5 to 12 pounds.

Pittsburgh Pattern

Spike Maul

MAUL, TIMBER. See *Sledge, Double Face.*

MAUL, TOP. See *Maul, Ship.*

MAUL, TRACK. See *Maul, Spike.*

MAUL, WOOD CHOPPERS'. A maul used to drive a metal wedge for splitting a log. The tapered peen is used to help open the split created by the wedge. Weight is 5 to 9 pounds.

Oregon   Straight Bit   Truckee

Wood Choppers' Maul

MAULING AXE. See *Axe, Single Bit,* rafting pattern.

MEASURING IRON. An ice harvest tool used to measure the thickness of ice through a small hole in the surface of the ice field.

Measuring Iron

MEASURING PUMP AUGER. See *Boring Tool, Measuring Pump Auger.*

MEASURING STICK. See *Rule, Measuring Stick.*

MEASURING WHEEL. See *Tire Measuring Wheel.*

MEASURING YOKE. See *Horse Collar Tool, Measuring Yoke.*

MEAT CLEAVER. See *Cleaver.*

MEAT CUTTER. A butcher shop machine used to cut and mix meat. The illustrated machine will cut 15 to 20 pounds in 8 minutes. The literature states that cut meat will absorb more water than ground meat and thus improve the profit margin.

Meat Cutter

MEAT POLE. A 5 to 6 foot pole used in a meat packing house to hook a carcass onto the overhead track carriage. Also used to push and pull the carriage along the track.

Meat Pole

MEAT POUNDER. See *Steak Grieth* and *Steak Pounder.*

MEETING RAIL PLANE. See *Plane, Meeting Rail.*

MELTING LADLE. See *Ladle, Melting.*

MELTING POT. See *Solder Pot.*

MENS' COLLICE. See *Shoe Makers' Tool, Collice.*

METAL BENDER. See *Bending Machine.*

METAL CAN BURNISHER. A canning factory tool used for cleaning or burnishing a filled can prior to installing the label. The cup contains a steel-wool collar.

Metal Can Burnisher

METAL CRAYON. A crayon for marking on metal. See *Crayon, Metal.*

METAL CUTTING HAND SAW. See *Saw, Metal Cutting.*

METAL CUTTING SAW. See *Saw, Hack* and *Saw, Metal Cutting.*

METAL DRILL. See *Boring Tool, Bit, Flat* and *Boring Tool, Bit, Twist Drill.*

METAL PUNCH. See *Punch, Metal.*

METAL SHEARS. See *Tinsmiths' Machine, Shears.*

METAL SPINNING TOOL. Also called LATHE TOOL and SPINNING TOOL. A lathe tool used for forming soft metal such as aluminum. Each tool, except the cutoff, consists of a metal shaft with a smooth rounded end. It is used to push and smooth the rotating sheet metal against a wood or metal form.

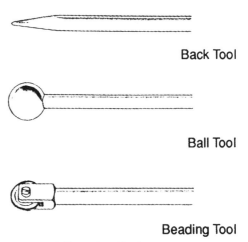

Back Tool

Ball Tool

Beading Tool

Metal Spinning Tool

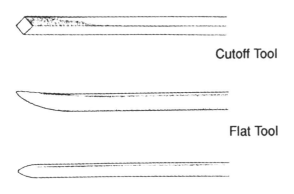

Cutoff Tool

Flat Tool

Round Point

Metal Spinning Tool

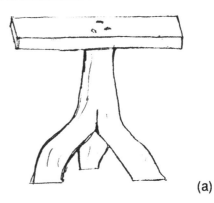

(a)

(b)

Milking Stool

METAL TURNING TOOL. See *Turning Tool, Metal.*

METAL WOOD CHISEL. See *Chisel, Plumbers'.*

METAL WORKERS' CRAYON. See *Crayon, Metal.*

METALLIC LEVEL. See *Level, Metallic.*

METER STICK. See *Rule, Meter.*

METRIC RULE. See *Rule, Metric.*

MEXICAN CUTTING CREASER. See *Leather Tool, Creaser.*

MEXICAN SPREADING TOOL. See *Leather Tool, Spreading.*

MILGRAIN TOOL. A tool used to make a continuous chain or rope design on soft metal jewelry. The tool consists of a miniature steel wheel with a sharp cut design.

Holder

Milgrain Tool

MILKING STOOL. A stool used when milking a cow by hand. The tool shown in illustration (a) is a typical home made device fashioned from the fork of a small tree with a board nailed across the top. The illustration (b) stool has two slots for attaching leather straps. The straps are buckled about the hips of the milker allowing the stool to be carried from cow to cow without use of the hands.

MILL BILL. See *Pick, Mill.*

MILL FILE. See *File, Mill.*

MILL HAMMER. See *Hammer, Mill.*

MILL HOOK. See *Cant Hook.*

MILL PICK. See *Pick, Mill.*

MILL REFUSE RAKE. See *Rake, Pine Needle.*

MILLINERS' PLIERS. See *Pliers, Pincer.*

MILLING WHEEL. See *Knurl Holder.*

MILLWRIGHTS AUGER. A long T-handled auger. See *Boring Tool, Millwrights' Auger.*

MILLWRIGHTS' CHISEL. A long chisel. See *Chisel, Millwrights'.*

MILLWRIGHTS' GOUGE. A long gouge. See *Gouge, Millwrights'.*

MINERS' AXE. See *Axe, Coal Miners'.*

MINERS' BLASTING TOOLS. See *Coal Miners' Blasting Tools.*

MINERS' LAMP. See *Carbide Lamp.*

MINERS' LIGHT. See *Carbide Lamp.*

MINERS' PICK. See *Pick, Miners'.*

MINERS' PIT LAMP. See *Carbide Lamp.*

MINERS' SLEDGE. See *Sledge, Coal.*

MINERS' STRIKING HAMMER. See *Hammer, Striking.*

MINERS' TRACK HATCHET. See *Hatchet, Coal Miners' Track.*

MINERS' WEDGE. See *Wedge, Coal*.

MINIM. A small blacksmith anvil. See *Anvil, Blacksmiths'*.

MITER. A 45 degree joint or angle. The term is often used as a modifying word in conjunction with any tool intended to work a 45 degree angle.

MITER BLOCK. See *Miter Jack*.

MITER BOX. A device for holding a saw at a fixed angle to the workpiece. Used primarily for making 45 degree corner cuts. The more elaborate miter boxes are adjustable to allow a cut to be made at any angle. See also *Miter Jack* and *Miter Machine*.

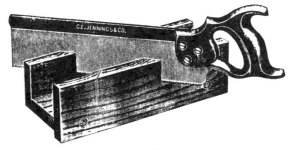

Miter Box

MITER BOX SAW. See *Saw, Miter Box*.

MITER CLAMP. See *Clamp, Miter*.

MITER CUTTER. See *Miter Trimmer*.

MITER JACK. Also called MITER BLOCK and MITER BOX. A clamp with a 45 degree face used for planing and smoothing a miter cut.

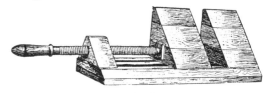

Miter Jack

MITER MACHINE. Also called PICTURE FRAME MACHINE. A device used to hold and cut picture framing stock. Also useful for holding the stock for glueing.

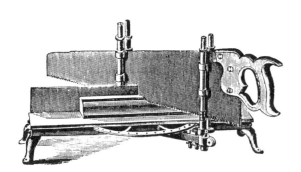

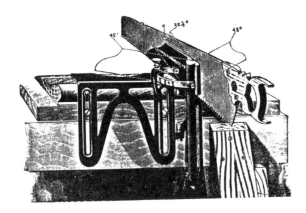

Seavey's Patent

Miter Machine

MITER PLANE. See *Plane, Miter*.

MITER PLANER. A type of shoot board intended for planing light stock at any angle.

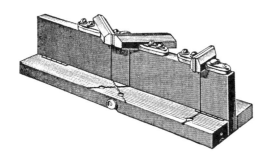

Folding

Miter Box

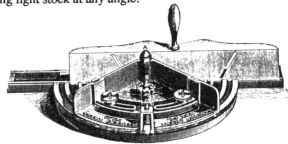

Miter Planer

MITER ROD. A leveling tool used by a plasterer or mason. Length is 4 to 24 inches.

Miter Rod

MITER SAW. See *Saw, Miter Box.*

MITER SQUARE. See *Square, Miter.*

MITER TEMPLATE. A template used for marking or cutting of narrow stock such as window sash or picture frame material.

Miter Template

MITER TRIMMER. Also called MITER CUTTER and WOOD TRIMMER. A lever-operated knife used for precision trimming of mouldings, picture frame corners and similar miter cuts. The shearing action of the cutting knife will trim a moulding smoother than a normal saw cut.

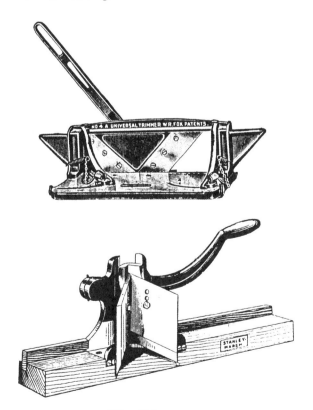

Miter Trimmer

MITER VISE. See *Vise, Picture Frame.*

MITRE. See *Miter.* Mitre is a variation in spelling that was widely used in early trade catalogues.

MODELING TOOL. A tool used for shaping a clay model. Tools made of both wood and wire were available. Length is 5 to 11 inches. See also Leather Tool, Modeling.

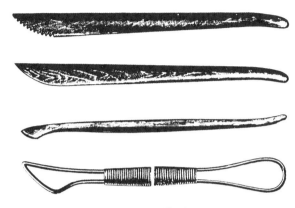

Modeling Tool

MOLASSES AUGER. A auger used to extract molasses from a barrel in cold weather. The auger is inserted into the tap hole in the barrel. A gate over the opening at the bottom of the auger prevents dripping. The illustrated tool is made entirely of brass. This is probably the same tool that was listed elsewhere as a SPOUT AUGER. Also used for removing heavy grease from a barrel.

Molasses Auger

MOLDING. See *Moulding.* Molding is a variation in spelling.

MONKEY WRENCH. See *Wrench, Screw.*

MORTAR AND PESTLE. A device used for pulverizing a small quantity of semi-solid material. Used primarily in a drug store for preparing medications.

Mortar and Pestle

MORTAR HOE. See *Hoe, Mortar.*

MORTISE BIT. See *Boring Tool, Bit, Mortise*.

MORTISE MALLET. See *Mallet, Chisel*.

MORTISER. See *Butt Gauge Mortiser, Butt Mortiser* and *Passer Drill*.

MORTISING AXE. See *Axe, Post*.

MORTISING CHISEL. See *Chisel, Mortising*.

MORTISING CHISEL AXE. See *Axe, Mortising Chisel*.

MORTISING GAUGE. A device used for simultaneously scribing two lines parallel to the edge of a workpiece. Useful for quickly scribing the outlines of a mortise.

Common Type

Metal

Twist Lock

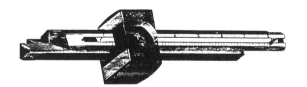

Scholl's Patent 4 Bar
Mortising Gauge

MORTISING MACHINE. A foot-operated machine used to clean out a mortise. The machine removes the wood left in the corners and along the edges of the mortise when the center is bored out. The workpiece is placed on the machine table and the cutting tool is driven straight down by action of the operator's foot on a lever. A set of chisels from 1/4 to 1 inch wide were furnished with the illustrated machine.

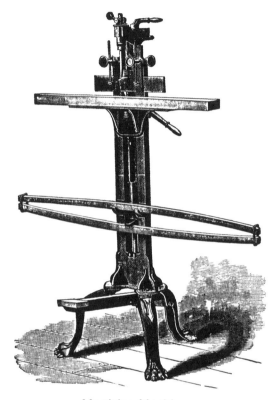

Mortising Machine

MOTHER PLANE. See *Plane, Mother*.

MOTTLING BRUSH. See *Brush, Mottling*.

MOULDERS' DUSTER. See *Brush, Brick Layers' Dust*.

MOULDERS' HAND TOOL. The illustrated hand tools are used in conjunction with plaster or sand casting and in shaping built-up plaster mouldings. See also *Plasterers' Ornamental Tools*.

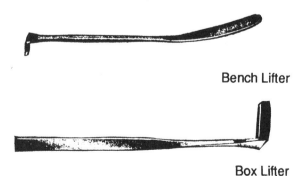

Bench Lifter

Box Lifter

Moulders' Hand Tool

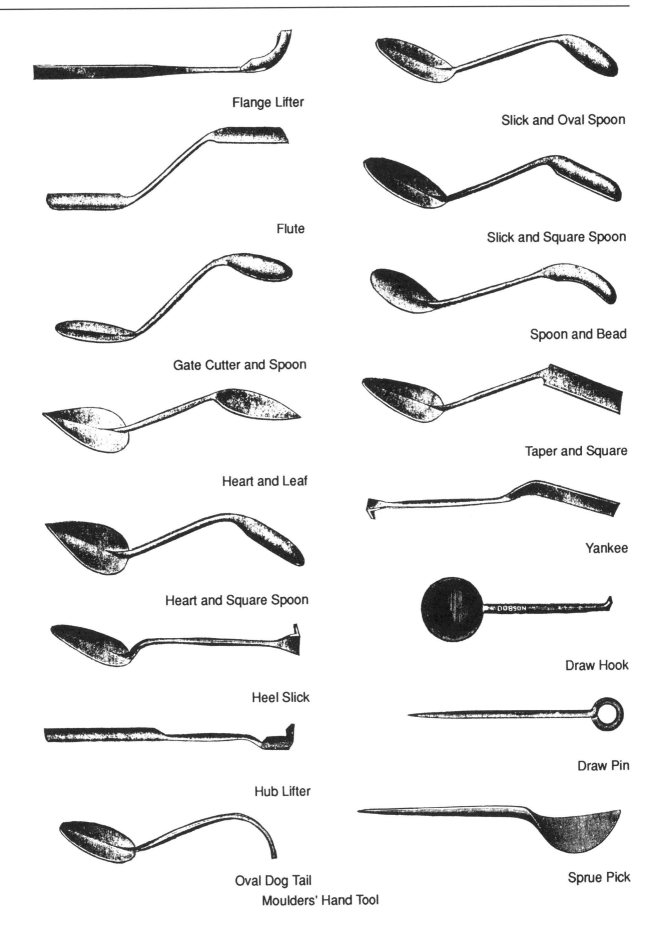

Flange Lifter

Slick and Oval Spoon

Flute

Slick and Square Spoon

Gate Cutter and Spoon

Spoon and Bead

Heart and Leaf

Taper and Square

Heart and Square Spoon

Yankee

Heel Slick

Draw Hook

Hub Lifter

Draw Pin

Oval Dog Tail

Sprue Pick

Moulders' Hand Tool

Button Slick

Egg Slick

Half Round Corner Slick

Inside Corner Slick

Pipe Slick

Square Corner Slick

Moulders' Hand Tool

MOULDERS' SIEVE. See *Riddle*.

MOULDERS' TOOLS. The special-purpose sand casters' tools listed below can be found in normal alphabetical sequence. These tools may also have been used for other purposes.

BELLOWS, MOULDERS'
BRUSH, BRICK LAYERS' DUST
BRUSH, MOULDERS'
CLAMP, FLASK
DUSTER
FIRE TOOLS, FURNACE
FLASK
MOULDERS' HAND TOOL
MOULDING MACHINE
PICK, MOULDING
RAMMER, BENCH
RIDDLE
SAND SCREEN
TROWEL, MOULDERS'

MOULDING FORMER. Also called CONTOUR MARKER. A tool consisting of many loosely-held metal strips that can be adjusted and locked in any position relative to each other. When the loose strips are pressed against a moulding, the exact contour of the moulding is produced in reverse.

MOULDING MACHINE. A machine used to compact sand in a mould rather than use a hand rammer. Said to save 25 to 50 percent of the cost of a sand casting.

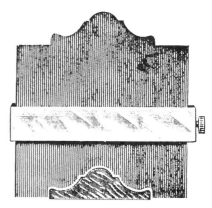

Moulding Former

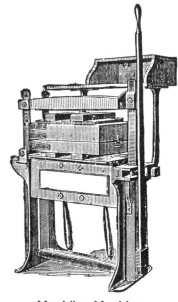

Moulding Machine

MOULDING PICK. See *Pick, Moulding*.

MOULDING PLANE. See *Plane, Moulding*.

MOULDING SCRAPER. See *Scraper, Moulding*.

MOULDING TOOL, CARRIAGE MAKERS'. A tool used to strike a moulding along a curved workpiece. The cut is made as the tool is drawn toward the user. Two cutting edges are often provided to allow working from either direction.

Carriage Makers' Moulding Tool

MOVING FILLETSTER. See *Plane, Filletster*.

MULTIPLE GOUGE. See *Lining Tool*.

N

Tool names starting with the letter N including a multiple listing of:

NIPPERS

NAIL APRON. See *Apron, Nail.*

NAIL BAR. See *Bar, Wrecking.*

NAIL CLAW. Also called NAIL RAKE. A tool used in a hardware store to draw nails from the bulk bin. Advertised by one supplier as being ideal for cultivating a flower bed.

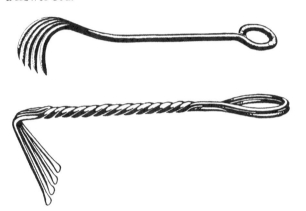

Nail Claw

NAIL CLINCHER. See *Tongs, Clinch.*

NAIL CUTTING NIPPERS. See *Nippers, Hoof.*

NAIL CUTTING PINCERS. See *Nippers, Hoof.*

NAIL CUTTING SAW. See *Saw, Metal Cutting.*

NAIL GIMLET. See *Boring Tool, Gimlet.*

NAIL GRAB. Also called NAIL GRIP. A tool used in a hardware store to pick up nails from the bulk bin.

Nail Grab

NAIL GRIP. See *Nail Grab.*

NAIL HAMMER. See *Hammer, Nail.*

NAIL HEADER. A blacksmiths' tool used for forming the head on a section of nail rod. The nail hole in the header is either round or square. Those with round holes may have been intended for making rivets or clout nails rather than common nails. The hole is always made larger at the bottom of the tool to avoid having the nail stick in the hole. The rod is slightly splayed on one end or upset to avoid having the nail drop completely through the hole. The thickened end is hammered against the header to form the nail head.

Nail Header

NAIL HOLDER. A cast iron tool that will grasp and hold a 6 penny or larger wire nail. The tool is hinged at one end and has a groove at the other end that will firmly hold a nail. The illustrated tool is marked *Williams Nail Holder and Guide.*

Nail Holder

NAIL HOLDER AND SET. A Nail Set with a spring-loaded lever that will grasp and hold a small nail or brad for starting.

Nail Holder and Set

NAIL HOLDING HAMMER. See *Hammer, Nail Holding.*

NAIL MAKERS' ANVIL. See *Anvil, Nail Makers'.*

NAIL PULLER. A tool used to grasp a nail and provide leverage for extraction. Length is 15 to 18 inches. One type of puller has a telescoping handle that extends to provide additional leverage.

Pelican

Nail Puller

Nail Puller

NAIL PUNCH. See *Anvil Tool, Nail Punch* and *Pritchel*.

NAIL SET. A small punch used for driving a finishing nail below the surface of the wood. The point is often cupped to aid in keeping the tool centered on the nail. See also *Nail Holder and Set*.

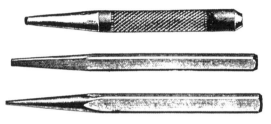

Nail Set

NAILING MACHINE. A machine used for driving small nails such as used in shingling. The illustrated tool will drive 3 penny nails. The advertisement stated that nails can driven at the rate of 125 per minute.

Nailing Machine

NAPPAN KNOCKER. See *Hammer, Macadam*.

NAPPING HAMMER. See *Hammer, Napping*.

NASAL SAW. See *Saw, Nasal*.

NAVY CALIPER. See *Caliper, Navy*.

NEEDLE. A small slender sewing tool with an eye at one end for insertion of either a thread, cord or thong. See also *Etching Tool*.

NEEDLE BAR. See *Bar, Ice*.

NEEDLE CASE STAKE. See *Stake, Needle Case*.

NEEDLE FILE. See *File, Needle*.

NEEDLE NOSE PLIERS. See *Pliers, Long Nose*.

NETTING NEEDLE. A tool used in making and repairing fishing nets. A length of string is wound on the needle allowing it to be easily passed through a loop when forming a knot. Length is up to 9 1/2 inches.

Netting Needle

NEWSPAPER POLE. A wooden pole used in a library or reading room for storing a newspaper. The newspaper is inserted into a long slit in the pole. The pole serves as a hanger for the paper and as a carrying handle.

Newspaper Pole

NIPPERS. A cutting tool with opposed jaws on one end. The jaws are generally set at right angles to the handle.

NIPPERS, BAND. A book binders' tool used for forming up the leather to the bands on the spine of a book. The nippers are used to press the leather tightly against the bands so that the paste will properly adhere. The process is called "Nipping Up".

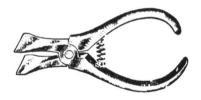

Band Nippers

NIPPERS, BLACKSMITHS'. Length is 12 to 14 inches. The blacksmiths' nippers are similar or identical to Hoof Nippers but were listed separately by some suppliers.

Blacksmiths' Nippers

NIPPERS, CHAMPAGNE. A tool used to trim the cork-retaining wire of a wine bottle. Length is 5 to 6 inches.

Champagne Nippers

NIPPERS, CUTTING. See *Nippers, Tinners' Cutting* and *Nippers, Wire*.

NIPPERS, END CUTTING. Also called END CUTTING PLIERS. Short nippers that cut only on the end at right angles to the handle. Usually made to work with one hand.

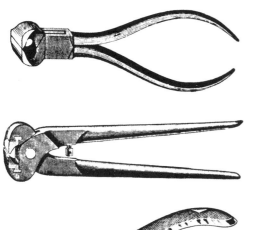

Open Throat

End Cutting Nippers

NIPPERS, FARRIERS'. Nippers intended for cutting clinches and leveling nail heads. Length is 12 to 14 inches.

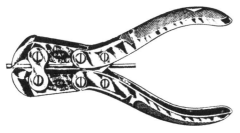

Nail Head

Clinch

Farriers' Nippers

NIPPERS, FARRIERS' CUTTING. See *Nippers, Hoof*.

NIPPERS, HOOF. Also called BLACKSMITHS' NIPPERS, FARRIERS' NAIL CUTTING NIPPERS, FARRIERS' NAIL CUTTING PINCERS, NAIL CUTTING NIPPERS and NAIL NIPPERS. Nippers used for cutting the excess length from the horse shoe nail prior to clinching. Length is 12 to 14 inches. This tool was also used for trimming the hoof; however, most farriers used the Hoof Parer or Hoof Trimmer for this purpose.

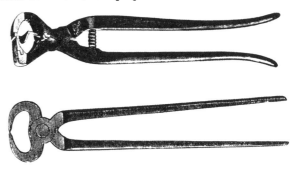

Hoof Nippers

NIPPERS, HOOF PARING. See *Hoof Parer*.

NIPPERS, LATHERS'. See *Nippers, Tinners' Cutting*.

NIPPERS, NAIL. See *Nippers, Hoof*.

NIPPERS, NAIL CUTTING. See *Nippers, Hoof*.

NIPPERS, PEG. A shoe makers' tool used for cutting the excess length from a shoe peg.

Peg Nippers

NIPPERS, SHOE TACK. Curved nippers used to clip off shoe tacks that protrude inside the shoe. Length is approximately 12 inches.

Shoe Tack Nippers

NIPPERS, SIDE. Also called SIDE CUTTING PLIERS. Small nippers that cut on the side of the jaws rather than the front. Length is 4 1/2 to 8 inches. See also *Nippers, Champagne*.

NIPPERS, SUGAR. A tool used to break off a lump of sugar from the loaf. Overall length is 7 to 9 1/2 inches.

Wall Tile

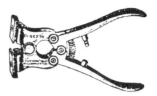

Tile Nippers

Side Nippers

Tinners' Cutting Nippers

Sugar Nippers

NIPPERS, WALL TILE. See *Nippers, Tile*.

NIPPERS, THREAD. A textile mill tool used for picking and clipping loose threads from finished cloth.

NIPPERS, WIRE. Also called CUTTING NIPPERS. Nippers intended for cutting small wire. Length is about 4 inches. The illustrated tool has a cutting slot on the side as well as on the end.

Knife Type

Point Type

Wire Nippers

NIPPLE WRENCH. See *Wrench, Gunsmiths'* and *Wrench, Nipple*.

NON-SPARKING HAMMER. See *Hammer, Non-Sparking*.

NOSE AUGER. See *Boring Tool, Bit, Nose* and *Boring Tool, Nose Auger*.

NOSE BIT. See *Boring Tool, Bit, Nose*.

NOSING AUGER. See *Boring Tool, Bit, Nose* and *Boring Tool, Nose Auger*.

Shear Type

Thread Nippers

NOSING MOULDING PLANE. See *Plane, Moulding, Nosing*.

NIPPERS, TILE. Also called WALL TILE NIPPERS. A nibbling tool used to break small pieces from a tile. Length is 5 1/2 to 10 inches.

NOSING PLANE. See *Plane, Nosing*.

NOTARIAL PRESS. See *Seal Press*.

NIPPERS, TINNERS' CUTTING. Also called CUTTING NIPPERS and LATHERS' NIPPERS. Length is 6 to 16 inches.

NOTCHING CHISEL. A stair builders' tool. See *Chisel, Notching*.

NURL WHEEL. See *Knurl Wheel*. Nurl is an improper variation in spelling.

NUT AUGER. See *Boring Tool, Nut Auger*.

NUT PLIERS. See *Pliers, Nut*.

NUT RUNNER. See *Wrench, Socket*.

NUT SWAGE. See *Anvil Tool, Swage*.

NUT WRENCH. See *Wrench* and *Wrench, Socket*.

NUT AND WASHER GAUGE. A tool used to measure diameter and thickness of nuts and washers. See also *Taper Gauge*.

Nut and Washer Gauge

O

Tool names starting with the letter O.

OAR PLANE. See *Plane, Oar*.

ODD JOBS TOOL. See *Combination Tool, Odd Jobs*.

OFFSET CHISEL. See *Chisel, Bent* and *Chisel, Offset*.

OFFSET GOUGE. See *Gouge, Bent*.

OFFSET SCREW DRIVER. See *Screw Driver, Offset*.

OGEE. See *Plane, Moulding, Grecian Ogee; Plane, Moulding, Reverse Ogee; Plane, Moulding, Roman Ogee* and *Plane, Moulding, Roman Reverse Ogee*.

OIL CAN. See *Oiler* and *Pocket Oiler*.

OIL CLOTH KNIFE. See *Knife, Oil Cloth*.

OIL CLOTH VISE. See *Vise, Carpet*.

OIL DERRICK HATCHET. See *Hatchet, Rig Builders'*.

OIL FILLER. A large container with a pour spout used to fill other cans and to fill drip oilers. Sizes up to 4 quarts were available.

Oil Filler

OIL GAUGER. See *Plumb Bob, Oil Gaugers'*.

OIL STONE. A type of sharpening stone. Oil is used on some sharpening stones to float off the metal particles removed from the piece being sharpened. See *Sharpening Stone*.

OIL SYRINGE. A device used for oiling engine bearings, shafting and automobile parts.

Oil Syringe

OIL TROUGH. See *Wheel Oiler*.

OILER. Also called **OIL CAN.** A can used to hold and apply lubricating oil. Oilers were made in almost unlimited variety from the small sewing machine oilers to the giant cans used in locomotive shops. The large vessel shown in the Engineers' Set is an Oil Filler Can. See also *Pocket Oiler* and *Wheel Oiler*.

Kaye's Patent

Non-Tip

Engineers' Oiler Set

Oiler

OILFIELD ANVIL. See *Anvil, Oilfield*.

OLD MAN. See *Boring Tool, Drilling Post*.

OLD WOMANS' TOOTH. See *Router*.

ONE ARMED KNIFE. See *Knife, One Armed*.

ONE ARMED MANS' KNIFE. See *Knife, One Armed*.

OPEN END WRENCH. See *Wrench, Open End.*

OPERATING KNIFE. See *Knife, Operating.*

OPTICAL RIVETING ANVIL. See *Anvil, Optical Riveting.*

OPTICIANS' PLIERS. See *Pliers, Opticians'.*

ORANGE CLIPPERS. A fruit growers' tool use to clip oranges and other citrus fruit.

Orange Clipper

ORE PICK. See *Pick, Ore.*

ORGAN BUILDERS' BRACE. See *Screw Driver Brace.*

ORGAN TUNERS' CONE. Also called PIPE MAKERS' CONE and VOICERS' CONE. A cone used to flare or reduce the diameter of a metal organ pipe thus changing the pitch of the pipe. Made of cast brass or bronze.

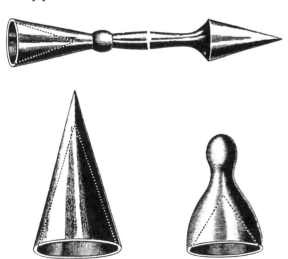

Organ Tuners' Cone

ORNAMENTAL PLASTERERS' TOOL. See *Plasterers' Ornamental Tools.*

ORTHOPEDIC BIT BRACE. See *Boring Tool, Bit Brace, Orthopedic.*

ORTHOPEDIC DRILL. See *Boring Tool, Bit Brace, Orthopedic.*

ORTHOPEDIC MALLET. See *Mallet, Orthopedic.*

ORTHOPEDIC SAW. See *Saw, Bone.*

OSTRAGAL. See *Plane, Moulding, Astragal.* Ostragal is an incorrect variation in spelling.

OSTRIGAL. See *Plane, Moulding, Astragal.* Ostrigil is an incorrect variation in spelling.

OUTSIDE CALIPER. See *Caliper, Combination; Caliper, Double; Caliper, Firm Joint; Caliper, Self Registering* and *Caliper, Spring.*

OUTSIDE SQUARE ANGLE TOOL. See *Cement Tool, Outside.*

OUTSIDE TOOL. See *Cement Tool, Outside.*

OVAL FILE. See *File, Crossing.*

OVAL SCRAPER. See *Scraper, Moulding.*

OVALO. See *Plane, Moulding, Quarter Round.* Ovalo is a variation in spelling of Ovolo.

OVERSTITCH WHEEL. See *Leather Tool, Overstitch Wheel.*

OVOLO MOULDING PLANE. See *Plane, Moulding, Quarter Round.*

OYSTER KNIFE. See *Knife, Oyster.*

P

Tool names starting with the letter P including multiple
  listings of:
    PENCIL
    PIANO TOOL
    PICK
    PINCERS
    PLANE
    PLANE, MOULDING
    PLANE, SHOOT BOARD
    PLIERS
    PUNCH

Included also are listings of tools used by the:
    PATTERN MAKER
    PIANO MAKER (PIANO TUNER)
    PLASTERER
    PLUMBER

PACKERS' HATCHET. See *Hatchet, Packing.*

PACKING CHISEL. See *Caulking Tool, Plumbers'* and
Chisel, Ice.

PACKING HATCHET. See *Hatchet, Packing.*

PACKING TOOLS. Tools used for removing old packing
from bearings and stuffing boxes on engines and pumps.
Made of hardened steel.

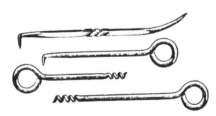

Packing Tools

PAD AWL. See *Awl, Seat.*

PAD SAW. See *Saw, Pad.*

PAD SCREW PLIERS. See *Pliers, Pad Screw.*

PAD TRIMMER. See *Leather Tool, Trimmer.*

PAINT BURNER. A gasoline torch used to loosen old paint.
This burner was listed with carriage painters' tools and
supplies.

PAINT BRUSH. See *Brush, Paint; Brush, Sash* and *Brush,
Striping.*

PAINT MILL. See *Grinding Mill.*

1891

Paint Burner

PAINT MIXER. A wall-mounted device with a spiral shaft
used to stir a container of paint. The illustrated device
was patented in 1893.

Paint Mixer

PAINT PRESS. A wall-mounted device for dispensing
semi-liquid paint.

PAINT SCRAPER. See *Scraper, Wall.*

PAINTERS' DUST BRUSH. See *Brush, Painters' Dust.*

PALLET. See *Bookbinding Tool, Hand Pallet* and
Bookbinding Tool, Lettering Pallet.

PALLET KNIFE. See *Knife, Pallet.*

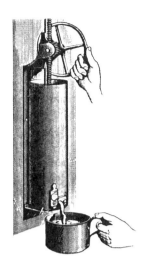

Paint Press

PALM. See *Sewing Palm*.

PALMETTO HOE. See *Hoe, Farm*.

PAN LIFTER. A kitchen tool used for lifting a hot pan from the stove.

Pan Lifter

PANEING HAMMER. See *Hammer, Tinners' Paneing*.

PANEL GAUGE. A marking tool used for scribing a line parallel with the edge of a large workpiece such as a panel. Length is 18 to 24 inches.

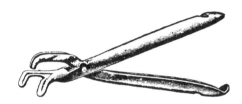

Panel Gauge

PANEL PLANE. See *Plane, Raising*.

PANEL PLOW. See *Plane, Panel Plow*.

PANEL ROUTER. See *Router, Carriage Makers'*.

PANEL SAW. See *Saw, Hand* and *Saw, Panel*.

PAPER CUTTER. A draftsmans' tool for cutting drawings, blueprints and Bristol Board. It cuts while being slid along a straight edge.

PAPER GAUGE. A print shop tool used to separate an approximate number of sheets of paper from the stack. The small foot can be adjusted by loosening the threaded handle.

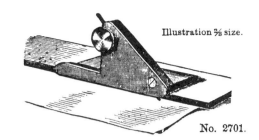

Illustration ⅜ size.

No. 2701.

Paper Cutter

Paper Gauge

PAPER HANGERS' BRUSH. See *Brush, Paper Hangers'*.

PAPER HANGERS' CASING KNIFE. See *Knife, Paper Hangers' Casing*.

PAPER HANGERS' CUTTER. See *Knife, Paper Hangers' Casing*.

PAPER HANGERS' KNIFE. See *Knife, Paper Hangers'*.

PAPER HANGERS' LEVEL. See *Level, Paper Hangers'*.

PAPER HANGERS' ROLLER. A roller used to smooth and seat wall paper. The smoothing roller is often covered with soft material such as felt or flannel. The seam roller has a hard surface made of wood, bone, metal or ivory.

Seam Roller

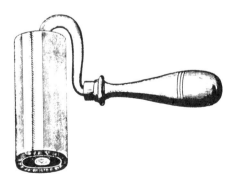

Smoothing Roller

Paper Hangers' Roller

PAPER HANGERS' SHEARS. See *Shears, Paper Hangers'*.

PAPER HANGERS' STOVE. A small heater intended for heating a container of wall paper paste. The illustrated stove uses alcohol as fuel.

Paper Hangers' Stove

PAPER HANGERS' TRIMMER. A tool used to trim a long straight length of wall paper. The trimmer shown in illustration (b) is used with a special grooved straight edge.

Length or Base Trimmer

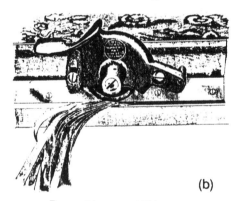

(b)

Paper Hangers' Trimmer

PAPER MILL TONGS. See *Tongs, Paper Mill*.

PARALLEL BAR. See *Rule, Parallel*.

PARALLEL CLAMP. See *Clamp, Parallel*.

PARALLEL DIVIDERS. See *Dividers, Parallel*.

PARALLEL PLIERS. See *Pliers, Parallel*.

PARALLEL RULE. See *Rule, Parallel*.

PARING CHISEL. See *Chisel, Paring*.

PARING GOUGE. See *Gouge, Paring*.

PARING KNIFE. See *Drawing Knife, Coopers'* and *Knife, Leather*.

PARING NIPPERS. See *Hoof Parer*.

PARTING TOOL. See *Carving Tool, Parting* and *Turning Tool, Parting*.

PASSER DRILL. A rare tool that was used to clean out an irregular mortise such as might be used for the escutcheon plate on the handle of a try square. The tool was rotated inside of a shallow template. The spring action of the legs of the tool allowed the cutting tips to circumscribe the template opening thus making a narrow groove. The wood inside the groove was then removed with a chisel or graver. The illustrated tool was probably held with some type of rotating knob that is not shown.

Passer Drill

PASTE BRUSH. See *Brush, Paper Hangers'*.

PATENT LEATHER COUNTERSINK. See *Leather Tool, Countersink*.

PATTERN DIE. See *Leather Tool, Cutting Die*.

PATTERN MAKERS' TOOLS: The special-purpose pattern makers' tools listed below can be found in normal alphabetical sequence. These tools may also have been used for other purposes.

  CHISEL, BENT
  CHISEL, PARING
  FILLET TOOL
  GOUGE, BENT
  GOUGE, PARING
  HAMMER, PATTERN MAKERS'
  KNIFE, CLOTH
  PLANE, COREBOX
  PLANE, LEATHER FILLET
  PLANE, PATTERN MAKERS'
  RULE, SHRINKAGE
  SAW, PATTERN MAKERS'
  SPOKE SHAVE, DOUBLE
  SPOKE SHAVE, PATTERN MAKERS'
  VISE, PATTERN MAKERS'
  VISE, UNIVERSAL

PATTERN TRACER. See *Tracing Wheel*.

PAVEMENT CHISEL. See *Chisel, Wall Joint*.

PAVERS' BAR. See *Bar, Flagging*.

PAVERS' BOXING HAMMER. See *Hammer, Bursting*.

PAVERS' BREAKING HAMMER. See *Hammer, Bursting*.

PAVERS' BURSTING HAMMER. See *Hammer, Bursting*.

PAVERS' BURSTING SLEDGE. See *Sledge, Bursting*.

PAVERS' HAMMER. See *Hammer, Paving*.

PAVERS' REAL HAMMER. See *Hammer, Pavers' Trimming*.

PAVERS' SIDE HAMMER. See *Hammer, Pavers' Trimming.*

PAVERS' TRIMMING HAMMER. See *Hammer, Pavers' Trimming.*

PAVERS' WEDGE. See *Wedge, Pavers'.*

PAVING HAMMER. See *Hammer, Paving.*

PEAT SPADE. See *Spade.*

PEAVEY. Also called CANT DOG, DRIVING HOOK and SOCKET PEAVEY. A pointed tool with a swinging hook used to move logs and other heavy timbers such as railroad ties. The stock is 2 1/4 to 6 feet long and is usually made of hickory or maple. This tool was invented by Joseph Peavey about 1860.

Log

Tie

Peavey

PEDAL GRIND STONE. See *Grind Stone, Pedal.*

PEELING IRON. See *Bark Spud.*

PEELING KNIFE. See *Drawing Knife, Shingle.*

PEEN HAMMER. See *Axe, Stone.*

PEEN HAMMER TONGS. See *Tongs, Blacksmiths'.*

PEG AWL. See *Awl, Peg.*

PEG BREAK. See *Shoe Makers' Tool, Peg Break.*

PEG CUTTER. See *Shoe Makers' Tool, Peg Cutter.*

PEG FLOAT. See *Shoe Makers' Tool, Peg Break.*

PEG KNIFE. See *Turning Tool, Hook.*

PEG NIPPERS. See *Nippers, Peg.*

PEG WHEEL. See *Shoe Makers' Tool, Peg Wheel.*

PEIN. See *Peen.* Pein is a variation in spelling.

PENCIL. A marking instrument consisting of a slender shaft containing a core of marking material such as graphite.

PENCIL, CARPENTERS'. A pencil with a heavy flat core suitable for marking on wood. Length is 7 to 12 inches.

Carpenters' Pencil

PENCIL, ENGRAVERS'. A pencil with a 1/8 inch square india stone in the center. Some have a fine stone in one end and a coarse stone in the other.

Engravers' Pencil

PENCIL, LUMBER. A pencil intended for marking on rough lumber. Similar to the Carpenters' Pencil except shorter and with a heavier core. Length is approximately 4 3/4 inches.

Lumber Pencil

PENCIL CLASP. Also called PENCIL HOLDER. A small clamp used to fasten a common round pencil to a compass or trammel point.

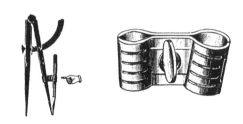

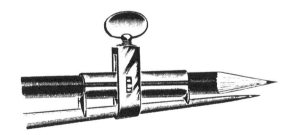

Pencil Clasp

PENCIL COMPASS. See *Compass, Pencil.*

PENCIL DIVIDERS. See *Compass, Pencil.*

PENCIL HOLDER. See *Pencil Clasp.*

PENDULUM LEVEL. See *Level, Pendulum.*

PENDULUM PLIERS. See *Pliers, Pendulum.*

PENE. See *Peen.* Pene is a variation in spelling.

317

PERCUSSION HAMMER. See *Hammer, Percussion*.

PERFECT HANDLE TOOL. A type of handle applied to various hand tools in which the metal extends full length and breadth of the tool handle. Wooden grips are solidly riveted to the metal. Some examples are illustrated.

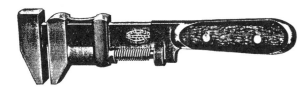

Perfect Handle Tools

PERFLING TOOL. See *Purfling Tool*. Perfling is an incorrect spelling.

PERFORATOR. See *Pouncing Wheel*.

PEWTER MOULD. A casting mould for pewter. Simple pewter pieces were made by pouring molten metal into two-piece brass or iron moulds. Smoke was sometimes applied to the mould as a parting agent. An excellent example of a spoon mould is illustrated.

Pewter Mould

PEWTERERS' BURNISHER. See *Burnishing Tool, Silversmiths'*.

PG MOULDING PLANE. See *Plane, Moulding, PG*.

PHOSPHATE DRAG. See *Hook, Hop*.

PHOSPHATE HOOK. See *Hook, Hop*.

PIANO MAKERS' CLAMP. See *Clamp, Cabinet Makers'*.

PIANO MAKERS' EDGE PLANE. See *Plane, Edge*.

PIANO MAKERS' TOOLS. The special-purpose piano makers' tools listed below can be found in normal alphabetical sequence. These tools may also have used for other purposes. Also included in this listing are piano tuning and repair tools.

  BELLOWS, PIANO
  BORING TOOL, BIT, KEY LEAD
  BORING TOOL, BOW DRILL
  BORING TOOL, HAMMER HEAD
  CHISEL, PIANO MAKERS'
  CLAMP, CABINET MAKERS'
  CLAMP, IVORY
  FILE, IVORY
  HAMMER, TUNING PIN
  KNIFE, FELT
  PIANO TOOL, BRIDLE TAPE INSERTER
  PIANO TOOL, BUTT FELT INSERTER
  PIANO TOOL, FELT PICKER
  PIANO TOOL, FELT SCISSORS
  PIANO TOOL, FELT SPADE
  PIANO TOOL, HAMMER IRON
  PIANO TOOL, HAMMER-SHANK BURNING LAMP
  PIANO TOOL, HAMMER-SHANK EXTRACTOR
  PIANO TOOL, HAMMER-SHANK ROLLER
  PIANO TOOL, HAMMER-SHANK TONGS
  PIANO TOOL, HAMMER-SHANK TRIMMER
  PIANO TOOL, HAMMER SPACER
  PIANO TOOL, KEY REAMER
  PIANO TOOL, PIN SETTER
  PIANO TOOL, REGULATING
  PIANO TOOL, REGULATING SCREW EXTRACTOR
  PIANO TOOL, STRINGING
  PIANO TOOL, STRINGING HAMMER
  PIANO TOOL, TUNING HAMMER
  PIANO TOOL, TUNING PIN EXTRACTOR
  PIANO TOOL, TUNING PIN GAUGE
  PIANO TOOL, TUNING WEDGE
  PIANO TOOL, VOICING PLIERS
  PLANE, EDGE
  PLANE, CARRIAGE MAKERS'
  PLIERS, PIANO TUNERS'
  SCREW DRIVER, PIANO
  SCREW DRIVER BIT
  SCREW HOLDER
  WRENCH, BALL BOLT

PIANO TOOL. A tool used to make, repair or tune a piano.

PIANO TOOL, BRIDLE TAPE INSERTER. A tool used to insert and attach a bridle ribbon or tape.

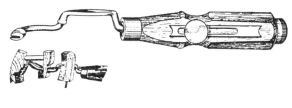

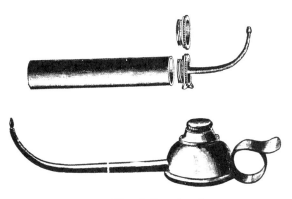

Bridle Tape Inserter

PIANO TOOL, BUTT FELT INSERTER. An extension arm used to insert a felt pad in a location not readily accessible to the hand.

Butt Felt Inserter

PIANO TOOL, FELT PICKER. A tool used to roughen the felt on the hammer to obtain a softer tone.

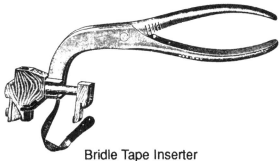

Felt Picker

PIANO TOOL, FELT SCISSORS. A uniquely shaped scissors used for cutting small pieces of felt.

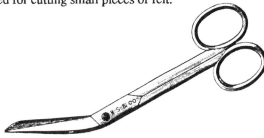

Felt Scissors

PIANO TOOL, FELT SPADE. A combination scraper-chisel used to remove old felt and glue. Width is approximately 2 1/2 inches.

Felt Spade

PIANO TOOL, HAMMER IRON. Also called HAMMER SMOOTHING TOOL. A tool used for ironing the felt on a piano hammer after the hammer has been filed. The hammer iron is heated during use. The illustrated tool is made of copper.

Hammer Iron

PIANO TOOL, HAMMER-SHANK BURNING LAMP. A piano repairmans' tool.

Hammer-Shank Burning Lamp

PIANO TOOL, HAMMER-SHANK EXTRACTOR. A clamp-like device used to pull or push a damaged hammer-shank from a hammer.

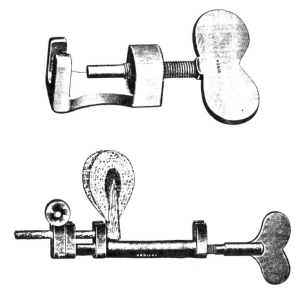

Hammer-Shank Extractor

PIANO TOOL, HAMMER-SHANK ROLLER. A tool used to rough up a hammer shank leaving a knurled or serrated surface suitable for glueing.

PIANO TOOL, HAMMER-SHANK TONGS. Length is 10 to 11 inches.

Hammer-Shank Roller

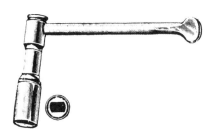

Pin Setter

PIANO TOOL, REGULATING. Piano makers' adjustment tools.

Action Regulator

Action Regulator

Hammer-Shank Tongs

PIANO TOOL, HAMMER-SHANK TRIMMER. A tool used to remove the old glue from a hammer-shank for re-installation. It can also be used to reduce the diameter of a hammer-shank.

Action Spring Regulator

Action Spring Regulator

Hammer-Shank Trimmer

PIANO TOOL, HAMMER SPACER. A gauge used in piano repair.

Damper Spring Regulator

Damper Wire Regulator

Hammer Spacer

PIANO TOOL, KEY REAMER. A piano makers' reaming tool.

Key Spacer

Key Spacer

Key Reamer

PIANO TOOL, PIN SETTER. A tool used to hold a pin in position and to provide a surface for driving with a hammer.

Regulating Screw Driver

Piano Regulating Tool

Rocker Screw Driver

Spoon Bender

Piano Regulating Tool

For Upright Pianos

PIANO TOOL, REGULATING SCREW EXTRACTOR. A tool used to remove a broken or damaged regulating screw. Length is about 6 inches.

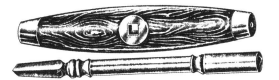

Piano Stringing Hammer

Regulating Screw Extractor

PIANO TOOL, STRINGING. Tools used when installing a new piano wire.

String Lifter

Piano Tuning Hammer

PIANO TOOL, TUNING PIN EXTRACTOR. A T handled wrench for removing a tuning pin. Length is approximately 6 inches.

String Lifter

String Spacer

Stringing Hook

Piano Stringing Tool

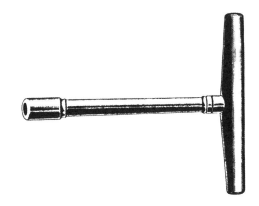

Tuning Pin Extractor

PIANO TOOL, TUNING PIN GAUGE. A gauge used for selecting the proper size of tuning pin when repairing a piano.

PIANO TOOL, STRINGING HAMMER. Also called TUNING HAMMER. A piano tuners' wrench.

PIANO TOOL, TUNING HAMMER. A piano tuners' wrench with interchangeable heads. The double head has one square and one oblong hole. The extra head has a star-shaped hole.

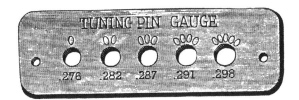

Tuning Pin Gauge

PIANO TOOL, TUNING WEDGE. A small wedge generally made of flexible hard rubber. Rubber wedges were available with and without a wire handle. Padded wooden wedges were also available.

Hard Rubber

Leather Covered

Piano Tuning Wedge

PIANO TOOL, VOICING PLIERS. A pliers-like device that pierces 9 holes in the hammer felt with one action. Holes in the felt will result in a softer tone.

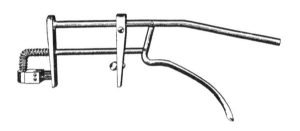

Voicing Pliers

PICK. A heavy metal striking tool with a pointed or chisel end fixed at right angles to a handle. Used for loosening dirt, shale or rock. The suppliers were not always consistent in their nomenclature of several types of picks. The names for Contractors', Dirt, Drifting, Railroad and Surface Picks were often used interchangeably in two or more catalogues of the same time period. The illustrations shown are representative of the general types of picks.

PICK, BOILER. A small pick used to remove scale from a boiler. Weight is 3/4 to 3 pounds. This is a large version of the scaling hammer.

Boiler Pick

PICK, BUNG. A tool used to pry the bung from a barrel.

Bung Pick

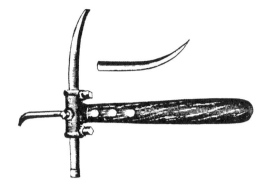

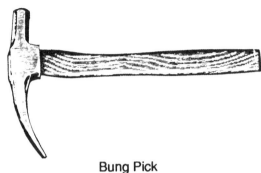

Bung Pick

PICK, BURR STONE. See *Pick, Mill.*

PICK, CLAY. See *Pick, Railroad.*

PICK, COAL. Also called MINING PICK. A slender pick used in coal mines. Weight is 1 1/2 to 5 pounds.

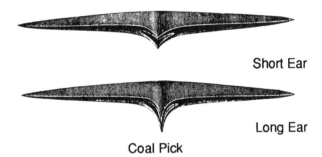

Short Ear

Long Ear

Coal Pick

PICK, CONTRACTORS'. A large pick with a point on both ends. Weight is 7 to 10 pounds.

Contractors' Pick

PICK, CUPOLA. A hand pick used to chip slag and scale from a melting furnace.

Cupola Pick

322

PICK, CUTTING. A sharp pick used for breaking up layers of rock or hardpan. Also used in coal mining. Weight is 2 1/2 to 3 pounds.

Cutting Pick

PICK, DIRT. Same as Railroad Pick except that some suppliers' indicated that a dirt pick has shorter bits.

Dirt Pick

PICK, DRIFTING. A general-purpose pick used for digging in soil having loose rock and hardpan. Weight is 3 to 4 1/2 pounds. The drifting pick, as defined by most suppliers, has a narrow eye.

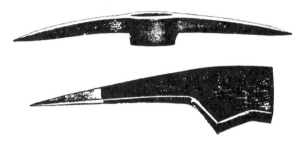

Drifting Pick

PICK, FIREMANS' WALL. See *Pick, Poll*.

PICK, FURROWING. See *Pick, Mill*.

PICK, HAND. See *Pick, Poll*.

PICK, LOCOMOTIVE COAL. See *Pick, Poll*.

PICK, MILL. Also called BURR STONE PICK, FURROWING PICK and MILL BILL. A pick used to cut the furrows in a grist mill or burr stone. Weight is 1 1/2 to 4 pounds. Width of cut is 1 1/8 to 1 3/4 inches.

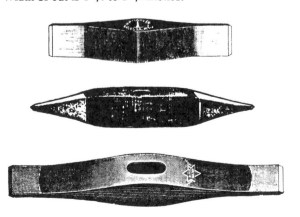

Mill Pick

Mill Pick

PICK, MINERS'. Weight is 2 1/2 to 6 pounds. See also *Pick, Coal*.

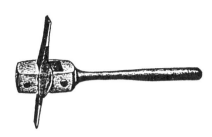

Eyeless

Strapped

Miners' Pick

PICK, MOULDING. Width is approximately 1 1/2 inches.

Moulding Pick

PICK, ORE. A miners' tool. Weight is 5 to 10 pounds.

Ore Pick

PICK, POLL. Also called FIREMANS' WALL PICK, HAND DRIFTING PICK, HAND PICK and LOCOMOTIVE COAL PICK. A one-handed pick with a hammer head on one side. Weight is 3 1/2 to 7 pounds.

Poll Pick

PICK, PROSPECTING. A one-handed pick used by prospectors. Weight is 1 to 2 pounds.

Walking Stick Type

Prospecting Pick

PICK, QUARRY. See *Pick, Stone*.

PICK, RAILROAD. Also called CLAY PICK and DIRT PICK. A pick, with a wide and deep eye, that has one pointed and one chisel bit. The large eye was listed by some suppliers as a Railroad Eye.

Railroad Pick

PICK, RAILROAD STAMPING. See *Pick, Tamping*.

PICK, STONE. Also called QUARRY PICK. A pick used to quarry stone. Weight is 3 to 17 pounds.

Soft Stone

Stone Pick

PICK, SURFACE. A pick similar to the Contractors' Pick except that one side has a chisel edge rather than a point. Weight is 4 to 7 pounds.

Surface Pick

PICK, TAMPING. Also called RAILROAD STAMPING PICK and RAILROAD TAMPING PICK. A Railroad Pick with a blunt end that can be used for tamping loose dirt or gravel. Weight is 6 to 9 pounds.

Tamping Pick

PICK, TIE. A tool for removing old railroad ties. Weight is about 26 ounces.

Tie Pick

PICK, WRECKING. A pick used for prying and lifting. Similar to the Poll Pick except that the wrecking pick has a railroad eye for greater strength. Weight is approximately 5 pounds.

Wrecking Pick

PICK COUNTER. Also called LINEN PROVER, LINEN TESTER and THREAD COUNTER. A textile mill tool used when counting the number of threads per inch of cloth. The aperture at the base of the illustrated glass-type counter is exactly one inch square.

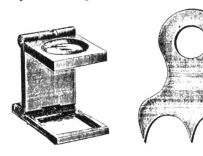

Pick Counter

PICK MATTOCK. A combination tool with a pick bit on one side and a mattock on the other. Width of cut of the mattock bit is 1 1/2 to 5 inches. Weight is 3 to 6 pounds.

Pick Mattock

PICK POLE. See *Pike*.

PICK TONGS. See *Tongs, Blacksmiths'*.

PICKAROON. Also called PICKEROON. A short-handled tool used to work railroad ties, pulp wood or mill refuse. Length of the handle is 2 to 4 feet. A tool similar to the hatchet head type, with a 1 1/2 to 2 foot handle, was listed as a LUMBER SORTERS' PICKAROON.

Hatchet Head

Pickaroon

PICKEROON. See *Pickaroon*. Pickeroon is a variation in spelling.

PICKING KNIFE. See *Knife, Picking*.

PICK-UP TONGS. See *Tongs, Blacksmiths'*.

PICTURE FRAME VISE. See *Vise, Picture Frame*.

PICTURE FRAMING MACHINE. See *Miter Machine*.

PIG FORCEPS. See *Forceps, Pig*.

PIG FOOT KNIFE. See *Knife, Pig Foot*.

PIKE. Also called PICK POLE and PIKE POLE. A pointed tool with a long wooden handle used to work logs in the mill pond and for river driving. Length of the handle is 4 1/2 to 20 feet. The hook type was also listed as a BOAT HOOK. See also *Pole Support*.

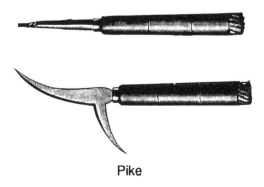

Pike

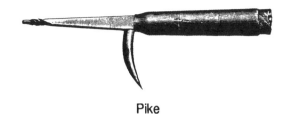

Pike

PIKE POLE. See *Pike*.

PILASTER. See *Plane, Moulding*.

PILL MACHINE. Also called PILL ROLLER. A device used in an apothecary shop to make pills. The ingredient mixture is formed into a long roll on the flat portion of the board. Pills are then formed by pressing the roll across the corrugated part of the board. The individual pills are rolled within the corrugations until round.

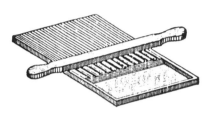

Pill Machine

PILL ROLLER. See *Pill Machine*.

PILLAR FILE. See *File, Pillar*.

PIN PLIERS. See *Pliers, Long Nose*.

PIN PUNCH. See *Punch, Pin*.

PIN SETTER. See *Piano Tool, Pin Setter*.

PIN VISE. See *Vise, Pin*.

PINCER PLIERS. See *Pliers, Pincer*.

PINCER WRENCH. See *Wrench, Pincer*.

PINCERS. A tool having two handles and two opposed grasping jaws working around a pivot. Pincers are intended primarily to grasp and hold rather than to cut. See also *Pliers*.

PINCERS, BLACKSMITHS'. See *Pincers' Farriers'*.

PINCERS, BULLDOG. A shoe makers' tool used for stretching and forming the leather down over the side of the shoe last. This tool was listed as a shank laster in one catalogue.

Bulldog Pincers

325

PINCERS, CARPENTERS'. Also called SHOE MAKERS' PINCERS. A tool used to pull nails and roofing tacks. Length is 6 to 12 inches. A small tool of this type was sometimes listed as a coopers' tool.

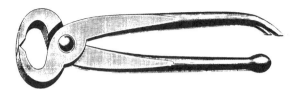

Carpenters' Pincers

PINCERS, FARRIERS'. Also called BLACKSMITHS' SHOEING PINCERS, HORSE SHOEING PINCERS and SHOEING PINCERS. Pincers intended for use in removing a horse shoe. The pincer is clasped under the shoe and twisted in a prying motion to separate the shoe from the hoof. The farriers' pincers can also be used for pulling a broken nail. Length is 10 to 16 inches. Also listed as BLACKSMITHS' PINCERS; however, one supplier listed blacksmiths' pincers as being shorter than the farriers' pincers.

Blacksmiths' Type

Larson's Pattern

Farriers' Pincers

PINCERS, FARRIERS' NAIL CUTTING. See *Nippers, Hoof.*

PINCERS, HOOF PARING. See *Hoof Parer.*

PINCERS, LASTING. Also called LASTING PLIERS and SHOE MAKERS' PINCERS. A shoe makers' tool used to stretch leather over a shoe last or form. The square extension on the pincers is used as a fulcrum for stretching and as a hammer for tacking. Length is about 8 inches.

Laufenberger's Patent

Timmons' Patent

Lasting Pincers

PINCERS, SADDLERS'. See *Pincers, Tacking.*

PINCERS, SHOEING. See *Pincers, Farriers'.*

PINCERS, SHOE MAKERS'. See *Pincers, Shoe Makers'* and *Pincers, Lasting.*

PINCERS, TACKING. Also called TACKING PLIERS and SADDLERS' PINCERS. A leather workers tool used for straining leather over a wooden form. Length is approximately 8 inches.

Tacking Pincers

PINCERS, TANNERS'. A pincers used for grasping a hide for stretching. Length is approximately 10 inches.

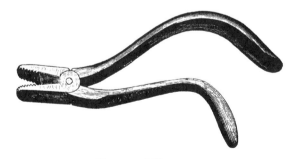

Tanners' Pincers

PINCH BAR. See *Bar, Crow.*

PINCH COCK. See *Clamp, Tubing.*

PINCH DOG. A tapered spike used to force two pieces of wood together and hold them while the glue is drying. As the pinch dog is driven into the ends of two pieces of wood, the pieces are pressed together. Width between the points is 3/4 to 4 inches.

Pinch Dog

PINCHING IRON. Also called HAIR DRYING AND PINCHING COMB and HAIR PINCERS. A tool used to remove the curl from a strand of hair. The tool is pinched over a small lock of dampened hair and the hair is then pulled through the iron. It can also be used to set a ringlet curl in a lock of hair. The working end consists of two flat surfaces approximately one inch in diameter. The tool is heated during use.

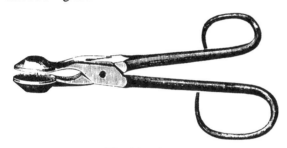

Pinching Iron

PINE NEEDLE RAKE. See *Rake, Pine Needle*.

PINKING IRON. See *Leather Tool, Pinking Iron*.

PINKING MACHINE. See *Leather Machine, Pinking*.

PINKING AND SCALLOPING MACHINE. A machine used for pinking and scalloping cloth, felt and paper. Similar to the Leather Pinking Machine except that the machine used for working leather is much heavier and stronger.

Pinking and Scalloping Machine

PINNING HAMMER. See *Hammer, Masons' Pinning*.

PIPE BENDING IRON. See *Bending Iron*.

PIPE BENDING MACHINE. A machine used to bend thin-wall pipe or conduit.

Pipe Bending Machine

PIPE BENDING PIN. See *Bending Iron*.

PIPE BENDING SPRING. See *Bending Spring*.

PIPE BIT. See *Boring Tool, Bit, Pipe*.

PIPE CLAMP. A cabinet makers' tool. See *Clamp, Pipe*.

PIPE CRIMPER. See *Tinsmiths' Machine, Crimping* and *Tinsmiths' Machine, Stove Pipe Crimper*.

PIPE CUTTER. A tool used for cutting metal pipe. Sizes were available to cut pipes up to 12 inches in diameter.

Barnes' Patent

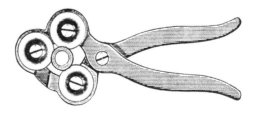

Conner's Patent (Lead Pipe)

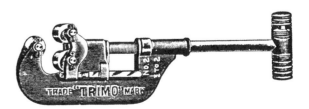

Pipe Cutter

Miller's Patent
Pipe Cutter

PIPE DIE. See *Pipe Threader* and *Tap and Die*.

PIPE DRILL. See *Boring Tool, Bit, Pipe* and Bri*ck Drill*.

PIPE FITTERS' TOOL CHEST. See *Tool Chest, Pipe Fitters'*.

PIPE FORCING JACK. See *Jack, Pipe Forcing*.

PIPE FORMING MACHINE. See *Tinsmiths' Machine, Pipe Former*.

PIPE GRIPS. See *Vise Jaws*.

PIPE MAKERS' CONE. See *Organ Tuners' Cone*.

PIPE REAMER. See *Boring Tool, Pipe Reamer*.

PIPE SLICK. See *Moulders' Hand Tool*.

PIPE TAP. See *Pipe Threader* and *Tap and Die*.

PIPE THREADER. A tool used to cut threads on metal pipe. It usually consists of one handle and several interchangeable cutting dies.

Pipe Threader

PIPE TONGS. See *Tongs, Pipe*.

PIPE VISE. See *Vise, Pipe*.

PIPE WRENCH. See *Wrench, Pipe*.

PIPE YARNING TOOL. See *Caulking Tool, Plumbers'*.

PIPETTE. See *Liquor Thief*.

PIPPIN FILE. See *File, Pippin*.

PISTOL ROUTER. See *Router, Carriage Makers'*.

PIT SAW. See *Saw, Pit*.

PIT SAW FILE. See *File, Pit Saw*.

PITCH ADJUSTER. A device used to elevate one end of a spirit level. A reading can be taken from the elevation slide to determine pitch of the level relative to the base. The illustrated tool is intended to be clamped to a standard 1 3/8 inch wooden level. A similar tool was available for attachment to a metal level.

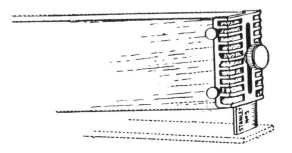

Pitch Adjuster

PITCH FORK. See *Fork, Bundle* and Fork, *Hay*.

PITCH GAUGE. See *Thread Gauge*.

PITCH LADLE. See *Ladle, Pitch*.

PITCH MOP. A tool used to spread coal tar pitch on eaves troughs, overhangs and other curved surfaces.

Pitch Mop

PITCHING CHISEL. See *Stone Cutters' Tool, Pitching*.

PITCHING TOOL. See *Stone Cutters' Tool, Pitching*.

PITTING SPOON. Also called PEELING AND CORING KNIFE. A spoon-shaped knife used for pitting, coring and peeling fruit. Minor variations of the tool were offered for use on peaches, strawberries and tomatoes.

Pitting Spoon

PIVOT FILE. See *File, Watch Makers'*.

PLANE. A hand tool consisting of a flat-bottomed stock with a cutting iron held in a fixed position relative to the bottom of the stock. The purpose of a plane is to shave small pieces from the surface of a workpiece thus smoothing the workpiece or reducing it to the desired thickness.

PLANE, ALUMINUM. Several types of woodworking planes were made of aluminum starting in the 1920s. These planes were advertised as being light weight and easy to handle. The aluminum planes varied little, if any, in appearance from the cast iron planes having the same function.

PLANE, AMATEURS'. A small plane intended for general purpose household tasks. The iron and knob assembly of the illustrated tool can be removed as a unit and used as a chisel.

Amateurs' Plane

PLANE, ANGLE. See *Plane, Chamfer.*

PLANE, BACK CHECK. See *Plane, Sash Filletster.*

PLANE, BACK FILLETSTER. See *Plane, Sash Filletster.*

PLANE, BADGER. Also called CARPENTERS' BADGER. A flat-bottomed plane with a skewed iron that runs out at the lower right hand corner of the plane body. Used for cutting the tapered edge of a panel or for making a wide rabbet.

Badger Plane

PLANE, BANDING. A long rabbet plane used for cutting a flat bottomed groove in a convex surface. Similar to a handled or jack rabbet except that the two side spurs contact the workpiece immediately ahead of the main iron. See illustration under *Plane, Rabbet.*

PLANE, BASKET SHAVE. A plane used to smooth and pare down a willow split previously made with another tool. The plane is held in a vise or clamp and the split is passed through between the iron and the sole thus reducing it to a fixed thickness.

Basket Shave Plane

PLANE, BEADING. A metal plane with several interchangeable beading irons. Late models of this plane were also used for light plow and filletster work. It was then listed as a LIGHT COMBINATION PLANE. See also *Plane, Car Beading; Plane, Moulding, Center Bead; Plane, Moulding, Side Bead* and *Plane, Moulding, Torus Bead.*

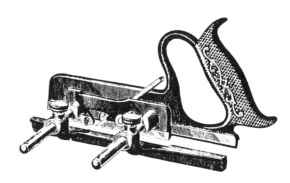

Beading Plane

PLANE, BELT MAKERS'. A metal plane used to scarf or trim the ends of a flat leather belt for end joining. See also *Spoke Shave, Carriage Makers' Panel.*

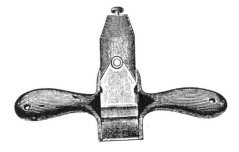

Belt Makers' Plane

PLANE, BENCH. A term given to the family of flat-bottomed planes used for general shaping and smoothing of a workpiece. See *Plane, Fore; Plane, Jack; Plane, Jointer* and *Plane, Smooth.*

PLANE, BEVELING. A plane that will cut a bevel on both sides of a workpiece with one pass. The illustrated tool was patented by M. B. Tidey July 4, 1854.

PLANE, BLOCK. A small metal plane, with a low cutting angle, used for trimming across the grain on the end of a workpiece. The name was derived from the term "Blocking In" which meant trimming the piece to an exact length to fit a given space. Length is 3 1/2 to 10 inches. The term "Block Plane" was used for metal or wood bottom planes only. Wooden planes used for the same purpose were called MITER PLANES or MITRE PLANES by the makers. See also *Plane, Knuckle Joint*.

Handled

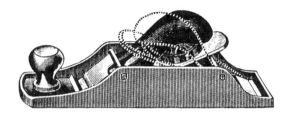

Double End

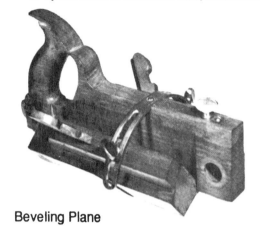

Beveling Plane

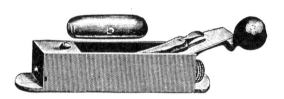

Wood Bottom

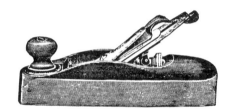

Cabinet Makers'

Block Plane

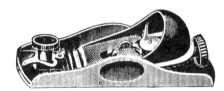

Low Angle

PLANE, BOOK BINDERS' PLOW. A plane used to trim the collected pages of a book. The book is clamped in a press for trimming. The plane is moved back and forth in a groove that is part of or attached to the press.

School or Steel Block

Book Binders' Plow

Bullnose

Block Plane

PLANE, BULL. A German Pattern smooth plane with a horn was listed by one plane maker as a bull plane. See illustration under *Plane, Smooth*.

330

PLANE, BULLNOSE. A plane in which the cutting edge is close to or forms the leading edge of the tool.

PLANE, BULLNOSE BLOCK. See *Plane, Block.*

PLANE, BULLNOSE RABBET. A Rabbet Plane with the cutting edge close to the front.

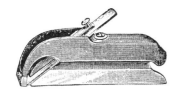

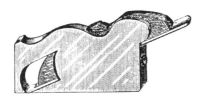

Bullnose Rabbet

PLANE, BUTCHER BLOCK. A plane intended for use in squaring and smoothing a meat cutters' block. This plane has the iron set at a very low angle to facilitate cutting the end grain on a maple block.

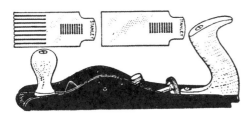

Butcher Block Plane

PLANE, CABINET OGEE. See *Plane, Moulding, Cabinet Ogee.*

PLANE, CABINET MAKERS'. Bench planes with the irons set at a large angle to the workpiece were sometimes listed as cabinet makers' planes. These planes were intended to be used for finish work only and would cut a very small shaving.

PLANE, CABINET MAKERS' EDGE. See *Plane, Edge.*

PLANE, CAPPING. See *Plane, Hand Rail.*

PLANE, CAR BEADING. A special beading plane with a metal face used for beading the paneling boards of railway cars.

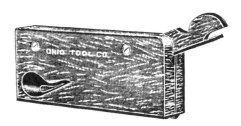

Car Beading Plane

PLANE, CARD. A textile mill tool used to smooth the card clothing and the doffer in a carding machine.

Card Plane

PLANE, CARRIAGE MAKERS'. A family of small planes, 5 to 6 1/2 inches long, favored by carriage makers. The short planes were adaptable for use on the small and curved workpieces characteristic of carriage building. The smooth and circle face planes were also listed as PIANO MAKERS' PLANES.

Circle Face or Circular

Smooth

Rabbet

Carriage Makers' Plane

T Rabbet

Circular Rabbet

Metal T Rabbet

Carriage Makers' Plane

PLANE, CARRIAGE MAKERS' PLOW. ALSO CALLED COACH MAKERS' PLOW. A grooving tool used in the carriage building trade. The tools shown in illustration (a) are a matched pair of French style plows. Illustration (b) is a typical German type carriage makers' plow.

(a)

Carriage Makers' Plow

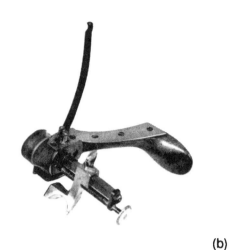

(b)

Carriage Makers' Plow

PLANE, CASE MAKERS'. Also called AIRTIGHT PLANE and HOOK JOINT PLANE. The plane used to cut the groove for fitting a dustproof cabinet door. The matching surface is cut with a Cock Bead Moulding Plane.

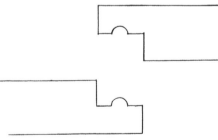

Case Makers' Plane

PLANE, CASEMENT. Casement is a name infrequently applied to a plane used for making a casing or quarter round moulding. See *Plane, Moulding, Quarter Round*.

PLANE, CHAMFER. Also called ANGLE PLANE. A plane used to chamfer the corner of a long workpiece. An optional beading attachment was available to fit the illustrated metal plane.

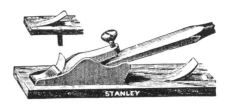

Chisel Gauge

PLANE, CHUTE BOARD. See *Plane, Shoot Board*. Chute is a variation in spelling.

PLANE, CIGAR LIGHTER. See *Plane, Spill*.

PLANE, CIRCLE FACE. See *Plane, Carriage Makers'* and *Plane, Circular*.

Double Chamfer

PLANE, CIRCULAR. A metal plane with a flexible steel sole or a wooden plane with a convex sole. The flexible sole of the metal plane can be adjusted to work on either convex or concave surfaces of various radii. See also *Plane, Carriage Makers'* and *Plane, Rounding*. The wooden circular plane is also called CIRCLE FACE PLANE, COMPASS PLANE and HEEL PLANE.

Chamfer Plane

PLANE, CHARIOT. A small plane with the front hand-grip curved up and back like the front of a sleigh or chariot.

Chariot Plane

PLANE, CHISEL GAUGE. Also called BLIND NAIL PLANE and BLIND NAIL TOOL. A tool used in conjunction with a quarter inch chisel to lift a sliver of wood from the surface of the workpiece. A nail is driven in the resulting recess and the sliver is then glued back in place to hide the nail.

Circular Plane

PLANE, COACH MAKERS'. See *Plane, Carriage Makers'*.

PLANE, COCK BEAD. See *Plane, Moulding, Cock Bead*.

PLANE, COFFIN SHAPED. See *Plane, Smooth*.

PLANE, COMBINATION. A metal plane with several interchangeable irons capable of making a variety of cuts. See also *Plane, Beading*.

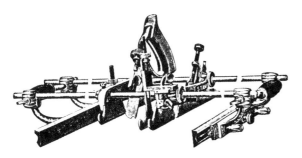

Stanley No. 55 or Universal

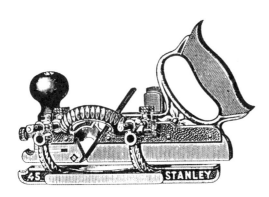

Stanley No. 45

Combination Plane

PLANE, COMBINATION TONGUE & GROOVE. See *Plane, Match*.

PLANE, COMPASS. See *Plane, Carriage Makers'* and *Plane, Circular*.

PLANE, COOPERS'. A unique plane used in making barrels or other coopered containers. See *Plane, Coopers' Jointer; Plane, Croze; Plane, Howel; Plane, Leveling* and *Plane, Rounding*.

PLANE, COOPERS' JOINTER. Also called COOPERS' LONG JOINTER and COOPERS' LONG PLANE. A large plane used for dressing and shaping the edges of a stave for a coopered vessel. The coopers jointer remains stationary while the workpiece is drawn over the cutting edge. It is generally equipped with two legs to support one end higher than the other. Available with either one or two irons. Length is 3 to 6 feet. Home made planes up to 8 feet long have been noted.

PLANE, COPING. Also called SASH COPING PLANE. A plane used to undercut the bottom and top rails of a window sash or frame. See also *Plane, Double Coping*.

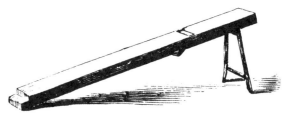

Coopers' Jointer

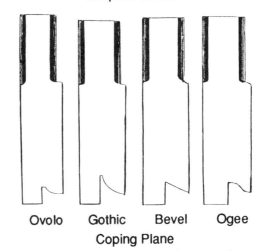

Ovolo   Gothic   Bevel   Ogee

Coping Plane

PLANE, COREBOX. A pattern makers' tool used to make a large semi-circular groove in a workpiece.

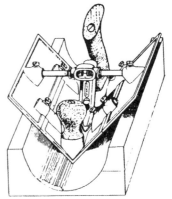

Corebox Plane

PLANE, CORNER ROUNDING. A metal plane used to round the corner of a long workpiece such as a baseboard or shelf.

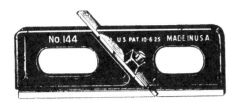

Corner Rounding Plane

PLANE, CROWN MOULDING. See *Plane, Moulding, Cornice.* "Crown Moulding Plane" is a term mistakenly used by many collectors when referring to any moulding plane wider than two inches. The wide moulding used at the juncture of floor and ceiling in a large room was sometimes called the crown moulding. The name Crown Moulding Plane was derived from the usage of a wide plane to make such a moulding. The term was not used by the plane makers and is grossly over-used by collectors and tool dealers. Only a small percentage of the wide moulding planes will cut a moulding suitable for use as a crown or cornice board.

PLANE, CROZE. Also called CROWS and CROWS STOCK. A coopers' tool used to cut the groove in the inside lip of a barrel. The croze groove provides a seat for the barrel head. An adjustable croze, such as the beer hogshead croze shown below, is sometimes listed as a SHIFTING CROZE.

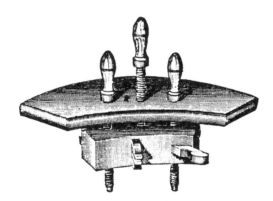

Beer Hogshead

Salt Barrel

Croze

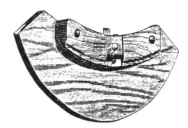

Lance

V Type

Lance Croze Iron   V Croze Iron

Croze Plane

PLANE, DADO. Also called CUT AND THRUST and RAGLET. A plane used to cut a flat-bottomed groove of a given width. It is especially adapted for cutting across the grain. The vertical side cutters and the skewed main iron allows the plane to cut cleanly across the grain. Size is 1/8 to 1 inch.

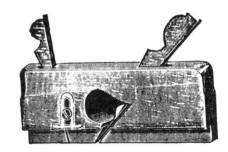

Dado Plane

PLANE, DOOR. A plane used to cut both sides of a paneled door stile with one pass of the plane. The groove in the center of the stile is used as a guide. Available in a bevel or ogee pattern.

Door Plane

PLANE, DOOR TRIM. A plane made especially for routing out mortises for butts, face plates and escutcheons.

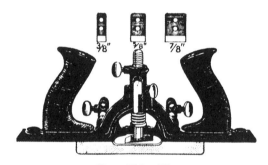

Door Trim Plane

PLANE, DOUBLE BEAD. See *Plane, Moulding, Reeding*.

PLANE, DOUBLE COPING. Also called SASH DOUBLE COPING PLANE. A coping plane with an extended fence. The fence side is the same size as the main body.

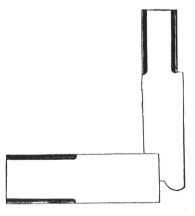

Double Coping Plane

PLANE, DOUBLE END BLOCK. See *Plane, Block.*

PLANE, DOUBLE END MATCH. See *Plane, Match.*

PLANE, DOUBLE RAZEE. A bench plane with both the front and the rear of the main body cut away. The term "Double Razee" is used for descriptive purposes and was not used in the supplier literature. The lower tote was said by one supplier to provide better control when using the plane.

Double Razee Plane

PLANE, DOVETAIL. A unique plane intended for cutting both sides of a dovetail. Patented in 1910.

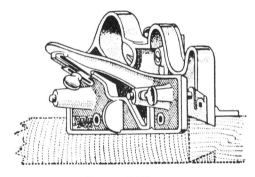

Dovetail Plane

PLANE, DUTCH. A plasterers' tool. See *Dutch Plane.*

PLANE, EDGE. Also called CABINET MAKERS' EDGE PLANE and PIANO MAKERS' EDGE PLANE. A bullnose plane used for precision smoothing and trimming in a confined area. See also *Shoe Makers' Tool, Edge Shave.*

Edge Plane

PLANE, EDGE TRIMMING. Also called EDGE TRIMMING BLOCK PLANE. A plane used to do minor trimming on the square edge of a workpiece. The illustrated plane can be used on boards up to 7/8 inches thick. Length is approximately 6 inches.

Edge Trimming Plane

PLANE, FANCY. Some suppliers referred to wooden planes other than bench and moulding planes as "Fancy Planes". This general category included the panel plows, dados and filletsters.

PLANE, FIBRE BOARD. A plane used to bevel, slit or groove composition board or fibre board.

Beveler

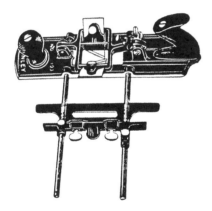

Fibre Board Plane

PLANE, FILLETSTER. A Rabbet Plane with an adjustable fence. See also *Sash Filletster.*

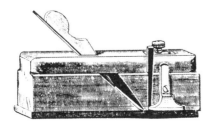

Filletster

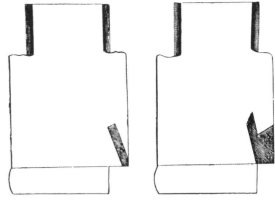

Single Box   Shoulder Box

Screw Arm

Filletster

PLANE, FILLISTER. See *Plane, Filletster.* Fillister is a variation in spelling.

PLANE, FLOOR. A plane used to smooth a large surface such as a bowling alley, floor or deck. The wooden variety of floor plane is 32 to 40 inches long. This type of wooden plane was listed by some suppliers as a TANK BUILDERS' JOINTER.

Floor Plane

Floor Plane

PLANE, FLUTING. A plane that will cut a small semi-circular groove. Used for making decorative cuts on columns, porch posts and similar items.

Fluting Plane

PLANE, FORE. A bench plane slightly longer than a jack plane and shorter than a jointer. It is said to be called a fore plane because it is used before the jointer. Length is 18 to 22 inches.

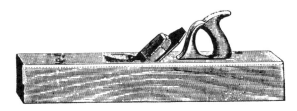

Wooden

Wood Bottom

Fore Plane

Metal

Fore Plane

PLANE, FORKSTAFF. Any plane in which the cutting edge has a concave cross section is occasionally listed as a forkstaff. See *Plane, Moulding, Hollow and Round Pair; Plane, Oar* and *Plane, Spar.*

PLANE, FURRING. A plane used for preliminary smoothing of rough sawed lumber. The sole is relieved to provide minimum friction on a rough surface.

Furring Plane

PLANE, GROOVING PLOW. See *Plane, Panel Plow.*

PLANE, GUTTER. A plane with a convex bottom used for hollowing out gutters, troughs and similar long workpieces. Many gutter planes are home made or made by reworking wooden jack planes.

Gutter Plane

PLANE, HALVING. A special-purpose rabbet plane intended to cut away one half of a standard one inch board for use as lap siding. The bottom extension serves as a fence and the notch at the top provides a stop.

Halving Plane

PLANE, HAND RAIL. Also called CAPPING PLANE and STAIR RAIL PLANE. A plane used to cut the curved surface of a stair rail. These planes were generally sold in pairs.

Wood Bottom

Hand Rail Plane

Metal

PLANE, HEEL. See *Plane, Circular.*

PLANE, HORN. Also called GERMAN PATTERN PLANE. A plane with a horn-shaped hand grip at the front. This type of plane was produced in the United States but apparently was not popular with American craftsmen. See illustrations under *Plane, Jack* and *Plane, Smooth.*

PLANE, HOWEL. A coopers' tool used to cut the shallow groove at the end of the barrel into which the deeper croze groove is cut.

Box Makers'

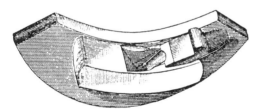

Howel

Horn or German Pattern

Jack Plane

PLANE, JACK. A general-purpose bench plane used for surfacing and rough edge planing. Length is 14 to 18 inches. The iron of the jack plane was often ground to a slightly convex shape to allow fast removal of excess stock from the workpiece. However, there is no available evidence to indicate that the irons were ground to the convex shape by the plane makers or sellers. See also *Plane, Double Razee* and *Plane, Razee.*

PLANE, JACK RABBET. See *Plane, Rabbet.*

PLANE, JOINTER. A long plane used for making the final cut for edge joining. Length is 22 to 32 inches. See also *Plane, Coopers' Jointer; Plane, Double Razee; Plane, Floor* and *Plane, Razee.*

Wooden

Jack Plane

Wooden

Jointer Plane

Wood Bottom

Metal

Jointer Plane

PLANE, KNUCKLE JOINT. A block plane with a unique lever cap that loosens by lifting the rear of the cap. Length is 6 to 7 inches.

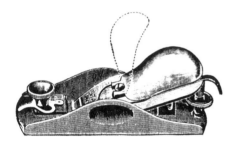

Knuckle Joint Plane

PLANE, LEAD TYPE. See *Plane, Shoot Board, Lead.*

PLANE, LEATHER FILLET. A pattern makers' plane that will cut a V shaped shaving from thick leather. The shaving is used as a fillet in a casting pattern.

Leather Fillet Plane

PLANE, LEVELING. Also called COOPERS' LEVELER, COOPERS' LEVELING PLANE, LEVELER and TOPPING PLANE. A curved plane used by a cooper to level the end of a barrel after assembly. Made of beech, birch or applewood. Several sizes were available for use on the various sizes of coopered containers.

Leveling Plane

PLANE, LONG. See *Plane, Coopers' Jointer.*

PLANE, LONG JOINTER. See *Plane, Coopers' Jointer.*

PLANE, LOW ANGLE. Also called LOW ANGLE JACK PLANE. A metal plane having the iron set at a low angle to the workpiece. Used for trimming cross grain. See also *Plane, Block* and *Plane, Edge.*

Low Angle Plane

PLANE, MATCH. A plane used to cut one or both sides of a matching tongue and groove. Some planes would cut both the tongue and the groove. The tools that would cut only one side were usually sold in matching pairs.

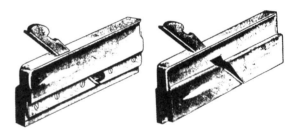

Board Match

Double End

Match Plane

Moving or Moving Plank

Double Handle

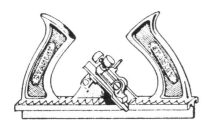

Double End

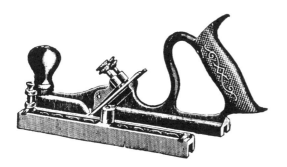

Swinging Fence

Double Side

Match Plane

PLANE, MEETING RAIL. The plane used to make the stepped cut where the two sashes of a double hung window seat together.

Meeting Rail Plane

PLANE, MITER. A low-angle wooden plane used for cutting across the end grain of a workpiece. Often listed as a MITRE PLANE. This plane is the wooden equivalent of the metal Block Plane.

Miter Plane

PLANE, MOTHER. A tool used by a plane maker to cut the bottom of a moulding plane. The surface contour is the reverse of the plane being manufactured.

PLANE, MOULDING. A plane with a contoured bottom used to cut any of the many shapes of moulding. Moulding Tool is a more appropriate name inasmuch as "Plane" is a misnomer when applied to any tool that cuts a curved surface. However, the makers and sellers of these tools generally listed them as planes. Even when they were called moulding tools by the suppliers, they were usually shown under the general heading of planes. The names applied to some of the moulding tools by the sellers sometimes referred to the suggested usage of the resulting moulding rather than the shape of the contour. Names such as ARCHITRAVE, BED MOULDING, BAND MOULDING, BASE MOULDING, BASE AND BAND and PILASTER are typical of the usage names.

341

Inasmuch as more than one shape was suitable for a given usage, shape names provide a more positive identification and are used here-in where possible.

The unofficial standard size of American moulding planes is 9 1/2 inches long and 3 1/2 inches deep. Some of the early planes are slightly longer than the standard and home made types are apt to be any length. Wide moulding planes were sometimes made with a rear tote for ease of usage. These handled moulding planes are up to 16 inches long. The use of beechwood for making moulding planes was almost universal in America. A few early planes made of birch have been noted and an occasional plane of rosewood is seen. Planes made of other types of wood are almost certain to be home made. Isolated examples of cherry, pine, oak, and mahogany have been noted.

PLANE, MOULDING, ARCHITRAVE. See *Plane, Moulding.*

PLANE, MOULDING, ASTRAGAL. A moulding plane that cuts a salient bead with an extended lip.

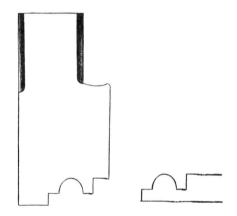

Astragal Moulding Plane

PLANE, MOULDING, BAND. See *Plane, Moulding.*

PLANE, MOULDING, BASE. See *Plane, Moulding.*

PLANE, MOULDING, BASE AND BAND. See *Plane, Moulding.*

PLANE, MOULDING, BEAD. A plane that makes a moulding having a small outward projecting section of semicircular contour. See *Plane, Beading; Plane, Moulding, Astragal; Plane, Moulding, Center Bead; Plane, Moulding, Cock Bead; Plane, Moulding, Side Bead* and *Plane, Moulding, Torus Bead.*

PLANE, MOULDING, BED. See *Plane, Moulding.*

PLANE, MOULDING, BOLECTION. Also called BELECTION MOULDING PLANE and BILECTION MOULDING PLANE. A bolection moulding profile is illustrated. See also *Plane, Moulding, Nosing.*

PLANE, MOULDING, CABINET OGEE. Also called CABINET MAKERS' OGEE and CORNICE OGEE. A wide moulding plane that cuts a low profile ogee was listed by some suppliers as a cabinet ogee.

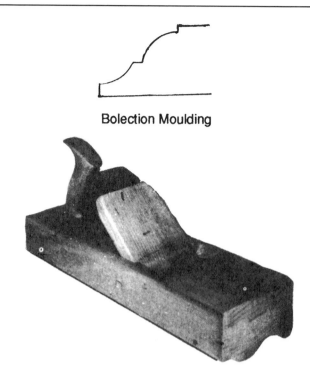

Bolection Moulding

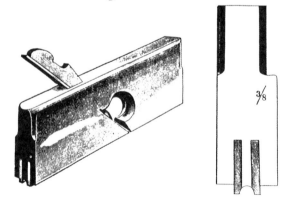

Cabinet Ogee

PLANE, MOULDING, CASING. See *Plane, Moulding, Quarter Round.*

PLANE, MOULDING, CENTER BEAD. Also called SINGLE BEAD REEDING PLANE. A moulding plane that forms a bead with a quirk on each side. Often used to decorate the center of a ceiling board.

Center Bead

PLANE, MOULDING, CLUSTER BEAD. A moulding tool that will cut a cluster of three partial beads.

PLANE, MOULDING, COCK BEAD. A tool that cuts away the workpiece on both sides leaving a bead extending from the surface.

PLANE, MOULDING, COMPLEX. Any moulding plane that cuts a contour comprised of a combination of two or more of the standard shapes. A plane having any desired shape could be special-ordered from several of the major suppliers.

Cluster Bead

Cock Bead

PLANE, MOULDING, CORNICE. A wide moulding plane used to make a cornice board for a large room such as a ballroom. These planes are often provided in pairs.

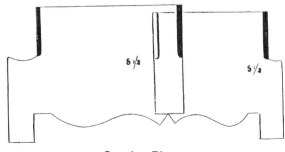

Cornice Plane

Cornice Moulding

PLANE, MOULDING, COVE. Also called CAVETTO, COVETTO, SCOTIA and STAIR COVE MOULDING PLANE. A moulding plane that will make a simple concave cut.

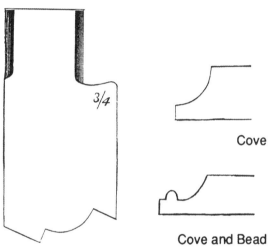

3/4

Cove

Cove and Bead

Cove Moulding Plane

PLANE, MOULDING, COVER JOINT. This type of moulding was used to cover the unsightly joint between two elements of a flat surface. An example of usage is at the intersection of two bookcases.

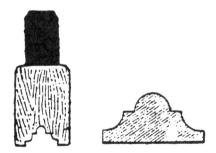

Cover Joint Moulding Plane

PLANE, MOULDING, COVETTO. See *Plane, Moulding, Cove.*

PLANE, MOULDING, CROWN. See *Plane, Moulding, Cornice*

PLANE, MOULDING, CYMA. See Plane, Moulding, Ogee and *Plane, Moulding, Reverse Ogee.*

PLANE, MOULDING, DOOR. The illustration shows a profile of a moulding made with a door moulding plane.

Door Moulding

PLANE, MOULDING, GOTHIC BEAD. A moulding tool that will cut a bead shaped in the form of a gothic arch.

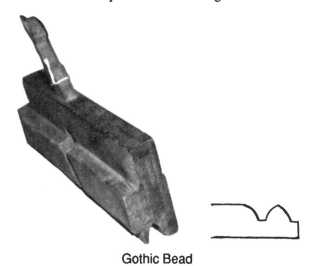

Gothic Bead

PLANE, MOULDING, GRECIAN OGEE. Also called QUIRK MOULDING PLANE and QUIRK OGEE. A moulding tool that will cut an ogee curve with a quirk.

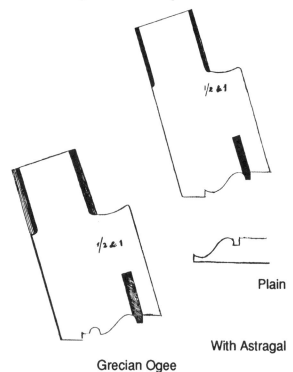

Plain

With Astragal

Grecian Ogee

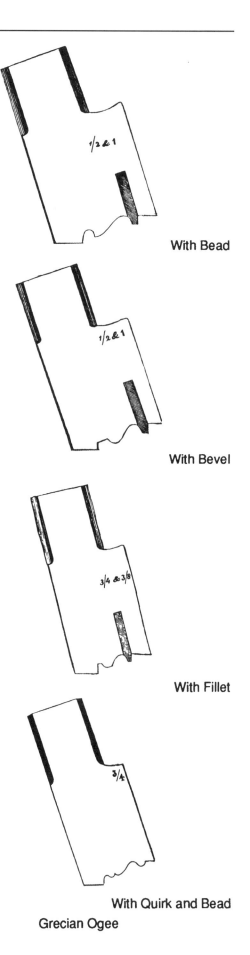

With Bead

With Bevel

With Fillet

With Quirk and Bead

Grecian Ogee

344

PLANE, MOULDING, GRECIAN OVOLO. Also called QUIRK OVOLO. A moulding tool that will cut an ovolo curve with a quirk.

Grecian Ovolo

With Astragal

With Square or Fillet
Grecian Ovolo

PLANE, MOULDING, HOLLOW. See *Plane, Moulding, Hollow and Round Pair.*

PLANE, MOULDING, HOLLOW AND ROUND PAIR. Planes used to produce shallow hollow or round surfaces. Also used in conjunction with other moulding planes to produce a complex moulding shape. Twenty four sizes were listed by some suppliers. Widths up to 2 inches were available. These plane were usually sold in pairs or in sets of nine pairs.

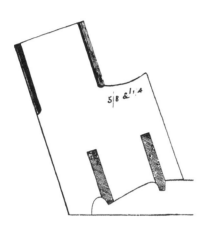

With Bead

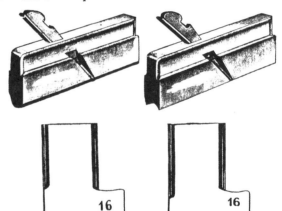

Round   Hollow

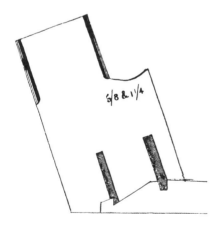

With Bevel or Fillet

With Square

Grecian Ovolo

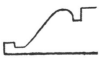

Side Round

Hollow and Round Pair

345

PLANE, MOULDING, NOSING. Also called BOLECTION and TORUS BEAD AND COVE. A plane that will cut a complex moulding consisting of a quirked bead and a shallow cove.

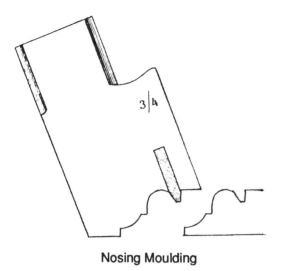

Nosing Moulding

PLANE, MOULDING, OGEE. Also called PLAIN OGEE and COMMON OGEE MOULDING PLANE. A moulding tool that cuts an ogee curve without a quirk.

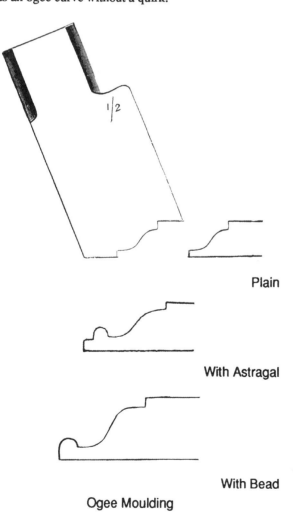

Plain

With Astragal

With Bead

Ogee Moulding

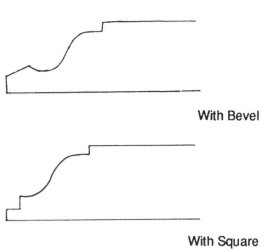

With Bevel

With Square

Ogee Moulding

PLANE, MOULDING, OVOLO. See *Plane, Moulding, Quarter Round.*

PLANE, MOULDING, PILASTER. See *Plane, Moulding.*

PLANE, MOULDING, PG. A moulding profile of a PG moulding plane is illustrated.

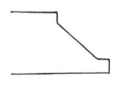

PG Moulding

PLANE, MOULDING, QUARTER ROUND. Also called CASING MOULDING PLANE. A plane used to made the common quarter round used at the juncture of floor and wall.

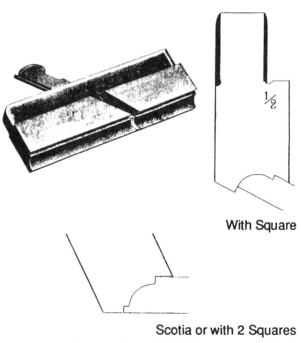

With Square

Scotia or with 2 Squares

Quarter Round Moulding

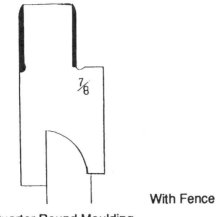

7/8

With Fence

Quarter Round Moulding

PLANE, MOULDING, QUIRK. See *Plane, Moulding, Grecian Ogee.*

PLANE, MOULDING, QUIRK OGEE. See *Plane, Moulding, Grecian Ogee.*

PLANE, MOULDING, REEDING. Also called CLUSTER BEAD MOULDING PLANE. A plane that will cut two or more beads with one pass. Reeding planes that would cut 2, 3, 4 and 5 beads were available.

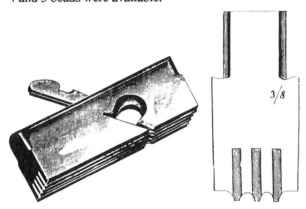

3/8

Double or Two Bead

Reeding Plane

PLANE, MOULDING, REVERSE OGEE. Also called BACK OGEE and LAMBS TONGUE. A tool that will cut a common ogee formed in reverse.

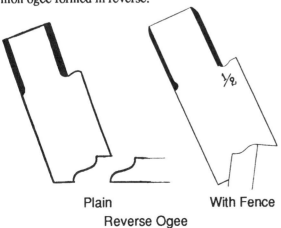

Plain

1/2

With Fence

Reverse Ogee

Flat

With Astragal

With Bead

With Bead and Square

With Double or Two Squares

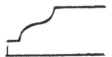

With Square or Fillet

Flat with Square

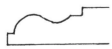

Flat with Two Squares

Reverse Ogee

PLANE, MOULDING, ROMAN OGEE. Similar to the common ogee except that the Roman type curve is generally more abrupt. The illustrated tool is intended to work the edge of a board.

Roman Ogee

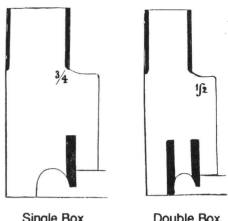

Single Box   Double Box

PLANE, MOULDING, ROMAN REVERSE OGEE. A reverse ogee having abrupt curves.

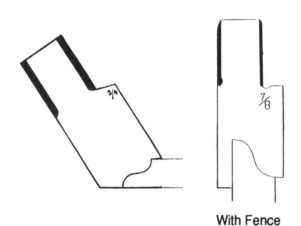

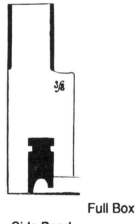

Full Box

Side Bead

With Fence

Roman Reverse Ogee

PLANE, MOULDING, ROUND. See *Plane, Moulding, Hollow and Round Pair.*

PLANE, MOULDING, SCOTIA. See *Plane, Moulding, Cove.*

PLANE, MOULDING, SIDE BEAD. A plane used to cut a bead along the side of a workpiece. This type of tool was commonly used on ceiling boards. The illustrations show application of various types of boxwood inserts. These inserts were often used as wear strips on side beads and other types of moulding planes to increase the useful life of the tool. Boxwood is one of the hardest woods known.

PLANE, MOULDING, SNIPE BILL. A tool used to clean out or deepen a cut made with another plane. Usually sold in right and left pairs.

PLANE, MOULDING, TORUS BEAD. Similar to the side bead moulding plane except that the torus bead has an extended lip.

PLANE, MOULDING, TORUS BEAD AND COVE. See *Plane, Moulding, Nosing.*

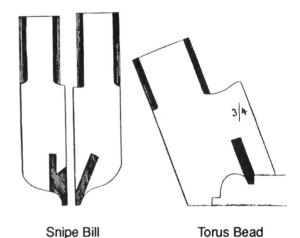

Snipe Bill   Torus Bead

PLANE, MOVING FILLETSTER. See *Plane, Filletster.* Occasionally a maker or dealer referred to a filletster as a moving filletster. The term is redundant inasmuch as all filletsters have a moveable fence.

PLANE, NOSING. Also called STEP NOSING PLANE and STEP PLANE. A plane used to cut the half-circle curve at the front edge of a stair tread. Sizes to cut a curve from

348

3/4 to 2 inches across were available. This type of plane could be procured with either one or two irons. Handled varieties were also listed.

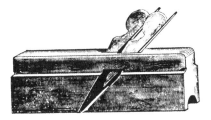

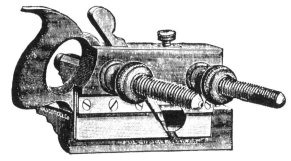

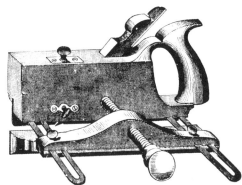

Nosing Plane

PLANE, OAR. A short plane, with a hollow bottom, used to round a curved object such as a boat oar.

Oar Plane

PLANE, PANEL. See *Plane, Raising.*

PLANE, PANEL PLOW. Also called GROOVING PLOW PLANE, PLOUGH PLANE and PLOW PLANE. An adjustable plane used to cut the stile groove for installation of paneling. This tool was generally sold with a set of 6 or 8 irons of different widths.

Panel Plow

PLANE, PANEL PLOW, CARRIAGE MAKERS'. A panel plow with a short skate adapted for plowing a groove along a shallow curve. The illustrated tool is shown with three interchangeable fence shoes having different amounts of curvature. This type of plow is usually smaller than the common panel plow. The body of the illustrated plane is 5 1/4 inches long.

Slide Arm

Panel Plow

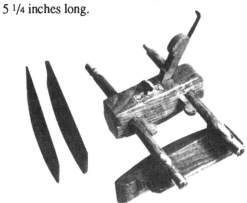

Carriage Makers' Panel Plow

PLANE, PANEL PLOW, CURVED. A special-purpose plow used to cut a panel groove in a curved stile. The curvature of the fence can be adjusted to match the curve of the workpiece. A short skate allows the plane to follow a curve without binding.

Curved Panel Plow

PLANE, PATTERN MAKERS'. A wooden plane having two or more detachable bottoms with different degrees of lateral curvature. The illustrated plane has five sets of bottoms and irons for working curves from 4 to 26 inches in diameter.

Pattern Makers' Plane

PLANE, PIANO MAKERS'. See *Plane, Carriage Makers'*.

PLANE, PLOW. See *Plane, Panel Plow*.

PLANE, PUMP. A plane that will cut a semi-circular groove 1 to 1 1/2 inches in diameter. Two such workpieces were fastened together to form a section of well pump or pipe.

Pump Plane

PLANE, RABBET. A flat-bottomed plane with the iron running out at the bottom on both sides. See also *Plane, Bullnose Rabbet* and *Plane, Carriage Makers'*.

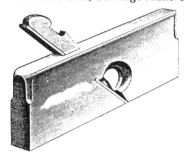

Wooden

Handled or Jack

Metal

Cabinet Makers'

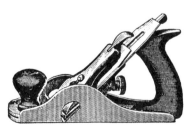

Carriage Makers'

Rabbet Plane

350

Bridge Builders'

Shoulder

Carriage Makers', Wooden

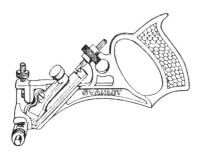

Curved

Rabbet Plane

PLANE, RABBET AND FILLETSTER. A rabbet plane with a detachable fence that allows the plane to be used as a filletster.

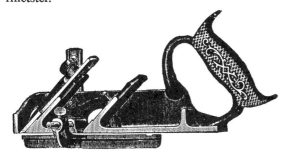

Rabbet and Filletster Plane

PLANE, RAISING. A plane used to taper the edges of a panel to fit the panel groove. This process was called "Raising a Panel". The raising plane has a flat bottom and often has a skewed iron. These planes were available with irons 2 1/2 to 4 inches wide. The narrow variety was sometimes listed as a PANEL PLANE.

Raising Jack

Screw Arm

Raising Plane

PLANE, RAZEE. Also called CARPENTERS' RAZEE PLANE and SHIP PLANE. A bench plane with the main body cut away in the rear. Razee planes are often home made and many are made of rare woods such as lignum vitae and rosewood.

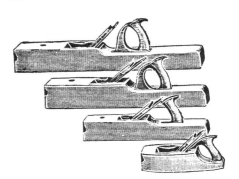

Razee Plane

PLANE, RIPPING. A plane used for ripping or slitting thin stock such as veneer. The illustrated plane cuts by use of a circular iron that rotates as the plane is moved

351

forward. This type of cutter is said to reduce the tendency to split the workpiece ahead of the plane iron.

Kinney's Patent

Ripping Plane

Single Iron

PLANE, ROUNDING. Also called COOPERS' ROUNDING PLANE. A plane with a concave bottom used to smooth the outside of a barrel or pulley. The illustrated iron plane has a bail such that it can be tied to an upright while being used to smooth a rotating workpiece. See also *Plane, Circular; Rounder* and *Witchet.*

Double Iron

Rounding Plane

PLANE, ROUTER. See *Router.*

PLANE, SASH. A window-sash makers' plane used to cut the inside moulding and the rabbet with one pass of the plane. The sash plane generally has two irons; however, single iron planes have been noted. Sash planes were offered in several patterns including bevel, ogee and bevel, bevel square, bolection, gothic and lambs tongue.

Thumbscrew Type

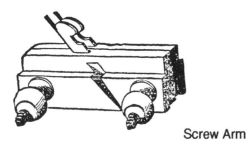

Screw Arm

Sash Plane

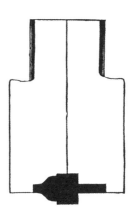

Ogee Pattern

Sash Plane

PLANE, SASH COPING. See *Plane, Coping.*

PLANE, SASH FILLETSTER. Also called BACK CHECK PLANE and BACK FILLETSTER. A filletster in which the iron runs out on the side adjacent to the fence.

Sash Filletster

PLANE, SCRAPER. A flat-bottomed scraper shaped like a plane. One variety was sold with an interchangeable toothing iron. See also *Scraper, Veneer.*

Tilt Handle

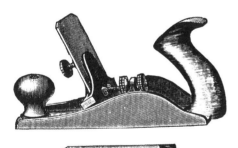

Scraper Plane

PLANE, SCRUB. A flat-bottomed plane with the iron ground to a pronounced convex shape. Used for rapid removal of excess stock from a workpiece. The scrub plane is generally narrower than the common smooth plane.

PLANE, SHELF RAIL. Also called BOOKCASE PLANE. A plane used to cut the notches in a bookcase side rail for insertion of shelves. A continuous series of triangular notches were often cut to allow the shelves to be placed in any position.

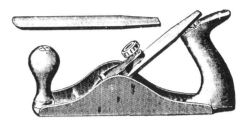

Scrub Plane

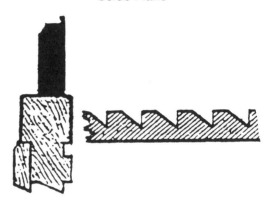

Shelf Rail Plane

PLANE, SHIP. See *Plane, Razee.*

PLANE, SHOOT BOARD. Also called CHUTE BOARD PLANE and SHUTE BOARD PLANE. A plane that runs in a fixed groove or against a side stop relative to the workpiece. Used for precise trimming.

PLANE, SHOOT BOARD, LEAD. A shoot board plane used in a print shop for squaring up blocked plates and for removing the rough edges from a plate after it has been through the saw. A bevel plane was available that could be used on the same board. The plane shown in illustration (b) is also called a TYPE HIGH PLANE. It can be used with either a cutting iron or with a rasp attached to the bottom.

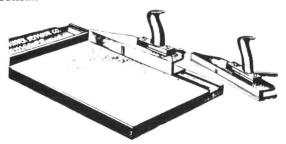

Shoot Board, Lead

(b)

Shoot Board, Lead

PLANE, SHOOT BOARD, WOOD. Also called PICTURE FRAME MITER PLANE and SHOOTING PLANE. A shoot board plane used extensively for trimming picture framing and mouldings. See also *Miter Planer*.

Amateurs'

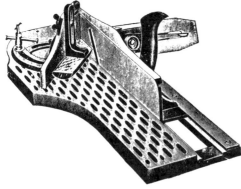

Shoot Board, Wood

PLANE, SHOULDER. A type of rabbet plane. See *Plane, Rabbet*.

PLANE, SIDE RABBET. A plane intended to trim the side of a rabbet. The iron cuts on the side of the plane only. Right and left hand planes were available. The wooden side rabbets were generally sold in pairs.

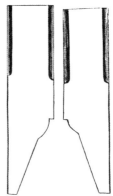

Side Rabbet

PLANE, SMOOTH. A bench plane used for surface smoothing and for cleanup around obstructions where a longer plane can not be maneuvered. Length is 7 to 10 1/2 inches. See also *Plane, Carriage Makers'; Plane, Double Razee* and *Plane, Razee*.

Wooden or Coffin Shaped
Smooth Plane

Handled or Razee

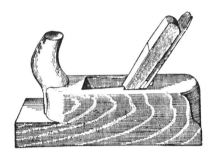

German Pattern or Bull

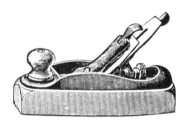

Wood Bottom

Handled Wood Bottom

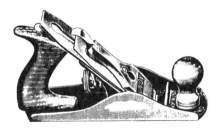

Metal

Smooth Plane

PLANE, SMOOTH, BOYS. A plane identical to the common wooden smooth plane except smaller. The boys plane is made both shorter and narrower than the common smooth plane in order to accommodate smaller hands. These planes were made to cut and should not be confused with toy planes. Length is 5 ½ to 7 inches. A common size has a 1 ½ inch iron. Both double and single iron types were available. See illustration under *Plane, Smooth.*

PLANE, SPAR. A plane with a concave bottom capable of working a curved surface of large diameter such as a spar.

Spar Plane

PLANE, SPILL. A plane used to pare a long thin shaving from a pine block. The shaving is used to transfer a flame from the fireplace to a cigar or to a candle. Most spill planes are home made. The illustrated plane is a commercial item marked CIGAR LIGHTER PLANE.

Spill Plane

PLANE, STAIR RAIL. See *Plane, Hand Rail.*

PLANE, STEP. See *Plane, Nosing.*

PLANE, STEREOTYPE. Listed as being suitable for planing a plate and gouging the open spaces. The front of the plane can be used to knock burrs from the plate.

Stereotype Plane

PLANE, T RABBET. See *Plane, Carriage Makers'*.

PLANE, TABLE. A matched pair of planes used to cut the edges of a dining room table including the matching edges where the drop leaf joins the top. Table planes are sometimes fitted with wide boxing strips to reduce the possibility of misfit due to wear of the plane surface.

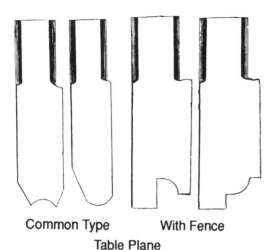

Common Type   With Fence
Table Plane

PLANE, TANK BUILDERS' JOINTER. See *Plane, Floor*.

PLANE, TONGUE AND GROOVE. See *Plane, Match*.

PLANE, TOOTH. See *Plane, Toothing*.

PLANE, TOOTHING. A plane having an iron with small teeth on the cutting edge. The iron is set high in order for the teeth to accomplish a scraping action on the workpiece. The illustrated plane has 26 teeth per inch. This type of plane was used by some craftsmen to prepare a surface for installation of veneer. A roughened surface was thought to be superior for accepting glue.

Toothing Plane

PLANE, TOPPING. See *Plane, Leveling*.

PLANE, TOY. A wooden plane made for inclusion in a toy tool box. These planes have soft irons that were never intended to be sharpened to a cutting edge. They do not have a makers' name and generally lack the chamfered edges and finished appearance of a working plane. Toys were made in the general shapes of smooth and jack planes. The toy jack plane is approximately 12 inches long.

Toy Plane

PLANE, TRYING. See *Plane, Fore*. The term "Trying Plane" was rarely, if ever, used by American tool makers'.

PLANE, TURNING. See *Witchet*.

PLANE, UNIVERSAL. See *Plane, Combination*.

PLANE, VIOLIN. Also called INSTRUMENT MAKERS' PLANE and THUMB PLANE. A very small plane used by an instrument maker. Length is 1 to 2 inches.

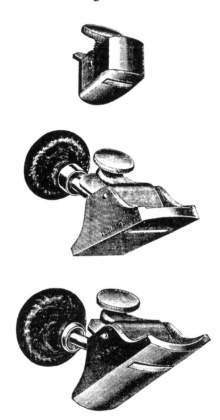

Violin Plane

PLANE, WASHBOARD. A plane used for cutting rounded grooves such as would be required for a washboard. The illustrated plane cuts one groove at a time and has a second bottom ridge that serve as a follower to assure equal spacing of the grooves.

PLANE, WEATHER STRIP. A plane made especially for installing one type of weather-stripping material.

Washboard Plane

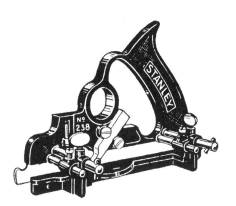

Special Dado

Edge Grooving

Meeting Rail

Weather Strip Plane

Special Grooving

Weather Strip Plane

PLANE, WHIP. A short coffin-shaped wooden plane with a steel face. Reported to have been used for making whip handles. *D..R. Barton* listed this plane but did not indicate a size. See illustration under *Plane, Smooth*.

PLANE, WOODEN. Any of a vast variety of planes with the body made entirely of wood. American wooden planes from commercial makers are generally made of beech but occasional examples of apple, birch, boxwood, ebony, lignum vitae and rosewood are noted. Home made varieties are apt to be made of any kind of wood. Most commercially made wooden planes have the makers name on the toe or front end. An owners stamp may appear at any point on the plane and often appears more that once.

PLANE GAUGE. See *Jointer Gauge*.

PLANE MAKERS' FLOAT. See *Float, Plane Makers'*.

PLANE SHAVE. See *Spoke Shave, Carriage Makers'*.

PLANER. Also called PROOF PLANER. A printers' tool used to press down the type before lockup. Usually made of hard maple. Size is approximately 3 by 8 inches.

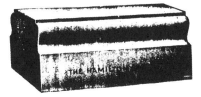

Planer

PLANER, HAND POWERED. A mechanical planer powered by a hand crank. Used for working metal.

PLANER KNIFE FILE. See *File, Planer Knife*.

PLANER TOOL TONGS. See *Tongs, Blacksmiths'*.

PLANISHING HAMMER. See *Hammer, Planishing*.

PLANK LEVER. See *Plank Puller*.

PLANK PULLER. Also called PILE PULLER and SHEATHING PULLER. A tool used to pull sewer or sheathing boards that have been driven into the ground. The slotted dog is hooked over a board and the pole is used as a pry bar. The pole is up to 12 feet long. The puller dog can be used without the lever when a hoisting mechanism is available.

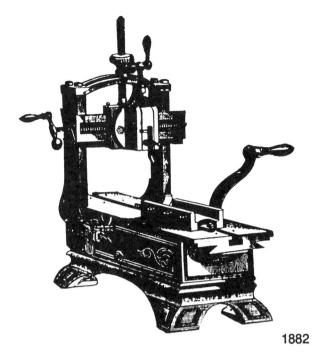

1882

Hand Powered Planer

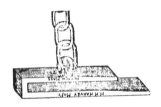

Puller Dog

Plank Lever

Plank Puller

PLANK SCREW CLAMP. See *Clamp, Plank Screw.*

PLANKER JACK. See *Jack, Lifting.*

PLANOMETER. See *Surface Plate.*

PLANTERS' HOE. See *Hoe, Planters'.*

PLASTER CARVING TOOL. See *Plasterers' Ornamental Tools.*

PLASTER KNIFE. A medical tool. See *Knife, Plaster.*

PLASTER SAW. See *Saw, Plaster.*

PLASTERERS' DARBY. See *Darby.*

PLASTERERS' FLOAT. See *Darby.*

PLASTERERS' ORNAMENTAL TOOLS. Also called PLAS-
TERERS' CARVING TOOLS and PLASTERERS' MITERING
TOOLS. Small tools used by the plasterer for carving,
smoothing and finishing ornamental work. These tools
are 1/4 to 1 inch wide.

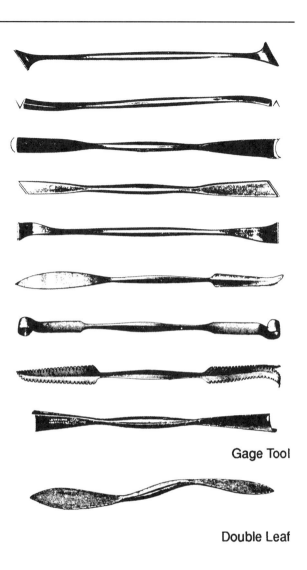

Gage Tool

Double Leaf

Leaf and Quirk

Leaf and Square

Trowel and Quirk

Trowel and Square

Plasterers' Ornamental Tools

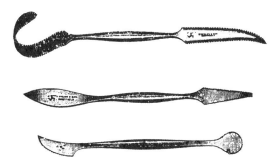

Scratch Tools

Plasterers' Ornamental Tools

PLASTERERS' PADDLE. See *Angle Paddle*.

PLASTERERS' TOOLS. The special-purpose plasterers' tools listed below can be found in normal alphabetical sequence. These tools may also have been used for other purposes.

ANGLE PADDLE
BRUSH, PLASTERERS' FINISHING
DARBY
DUTCH PLANE
FLOAT, PLASTERERS'
HATCHET, LATHING
HATCHET, PLASTERERS'
HAWK
KNIFE, PLASTERERS' TRIMMING
MITER ROD
PLASTERERS' ORNAMENTAL TOOLS
SAW, PLASTERERS'
SAND SCREEN
SQUARE, PLASTERERS' SET
SQUARE, PLASTERERS' STEEL
TOOL BAG
TOOL CASE, PLASTERERS'
TROWEL, CROSS JOINT
TROWEL, GAUGING
TROWEL, MARGIN
TROWEL, MUDDING
TROWEL, PLASTERERS' ANGLE
TROWEL, PLASTERERS' BROWNING
TROWEL, PLASTERERS' CORNER
TROWEL, PLASTERERS' FINISHING
TROWEL, POINTING

PLATE. See *Bench Plate*.

PLATE CLEANING BRUSH. See *Brush, Plate Cleaning*.

PLATE STAKE. See *Stake, Tray*.

PLATINUM FILE. See *File, Magneto*.

PLATINUM POINT FILE. See *File, Magneto*.

PLIERS. A one-handed tool, similar to Pincers, having two opposed jaws working around a pivot. Pliers are normally intended to grasp and hold rather than cut. Also called PLYERS in early catalogues. See also *Pincers*.

PLIERS, BATTERY. Pliers used for servicing a lead-acid battery.

Battery Pliers

PLIERS, BELL HANGERS'. Length is 5 to 6 inches. See also *Pliers, Bottlers'*.

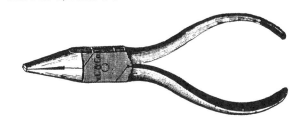

Bell Hangers' Pliers

PLIERS, BELT PUNCH. See *Punch, Belt*.

PLIERS, BOLT NUT. See *Pliers, Nut*.

PLIERS, BOTTLERS'. Also called BELL HANGERS' PLIERS and CHAMPAGNE PLIERS. A tool used to fasten the wire over the cork and neck of a wine bottle. Length is 4 to 8 inches.

Bottlers' Pliers

PLIERS, BOW. A jewelers' tool used to expand or remove a split ring.

Bow Pliers

PLIERS, BURNER. See *Pliers, Gas*.

PLIERS, BUTTON HOLE. See *Button Hole Cutter*.

PLIERS, CAP CRIMPING. A tool used to crimp a dynamite cap to the fuse. Also used to cut the fuse.

Cap Crimping Pliers

PLIERS, CARBON. An electricians' tool for replacing carbon rods in an arc light. This tool can be used to either grasp or cut the rod. It can also be used to file the points.

Carbon Pliers

PLIERS, CHAIN. Also called CHAIN NOSE PLIERS and SNIPE NOSE PLIERS. Length is 3 to 6 inches.

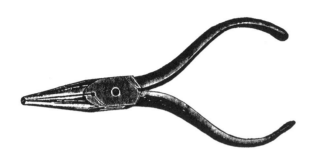

Chain Pliers

PLIERS, CHAIN NOSE. See *Pliers, Chain.*

PLIERS, CHAMPAGNE. See *Pliers, Bottlers'.*

PLIERS, COMBINATION. A combination pliers, wire cutter and screw driver.

Combination Pliers

PLIERS, COTTER PIN. A tool used to remove a cotter pin.

Cotter Pin Pliers

PLIERS, CUTTING. See *Pliers, Wire Cutting.*

PLIERS, DIAGONAL. Also called SIDE CUTTERS and SIDE CUTTING PLIERS. A general purpose wire cutting pliers.

Diagonal Pliers

PLIERS, DUCKBILL. See *Pliers, Stockinger.*

PLIERS, END CUTTING. See *Nippers, End Cutting.*

PLIERS, EXPANSION. A pliers with an adjustable throat.

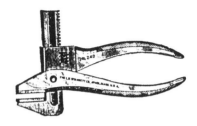

Expansion Pliers

PLIERS, FENCE. Also called STAPLE PULLER. A pliers used for pulling fence staples and cutting wire. This type of tool is generally flattened on one or both sides to serve as a hammer.

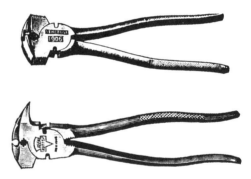

Fence Pliers

PLIERS, FLAT NOSE. Length is 3 to 8 inches.

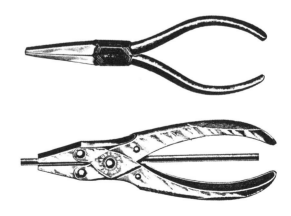

Flat Nose Pliers

PLIERS, FRAME OPENER. A leather workers' tool used when attaching the leather to a hand bag or carpet bag frame.

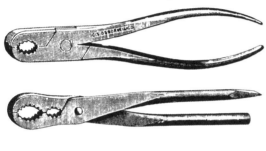

Frame Opener Pliers

PLIERS, FRONT CUTTING. See *Nippers, End Cutting*.

PLIERS, GAS. Also called BURNER PLIERS, GAS BURNER PLIERS and GAS PIPE PLIERS. Length is 5 to 24 inches.

Gas Pliers

PLIERS, GAS BURNER. See *Pliers, Gas*.

PLIERS, GAS PIPE. See *Pliers, Gas*.

PLIERS, GLASS. Pliers used to grasp the narrow edge of a sheet of glass in order to apply a steady pressure for breaking. Length is 6 to 10 inches. The jaws meet only at the outer ends.

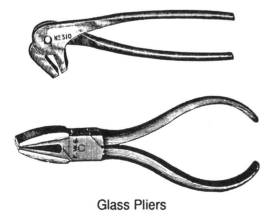

Glass Pliers

Glass Pliers

PLIERS, GLASS ROLLER. Length is 11 inches.

Glass Roller Pliers

PLIERS, HAWK BILL. A jewelers' tool. Overall length is 4 to 4 1/2 inches.

Hawk Bill Pliers

PLIERS, HOLLOW. See *Pliers, Opticians'*.

PLIERS, LACING. A tool used for pulling and tightening the thongs when installing leather lacing.

Lacing Pliers

PLIERS, LASTING. See *Pincers, Lasting*.

PLIERS, LEAD PIPE. Also called LEAD PIPE EXPANDING PLIERS. Pliers used for turning out a collar on a lead pipe or lead trap.

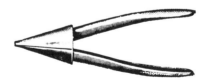

Lead Pipe Pliers

PLIERS, LEAD PIPE EXPANDING. See *Pliers, Lead Pipe*.

PLIERS, LONG NOSE. Also called NEEDLE NOSE PLIERS and PIN PLIERS. Length is 5 1/2 to 6 inches.

Long Nose Pliers

Long Nose Pliers

PLIERS, MILLINERS'. See *Pliers, Pincer.*

PLIERS, NEEDLE NOSE. See *Pliers, Long Nose.*

PLIERS, NUT. A tool shaped especially for grasping a nut or the head of a bolt. Length is 6 to 7 inches.

Nut Pliers

PLIERS, OPTICIANS. Pliers used to shape and adjust spectacles. Length is 4 to 6 inches.

Hollow Bending

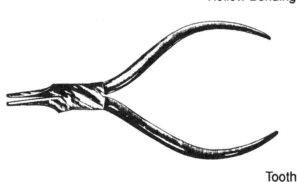

Tooth

Opticians' Pliers

PLIERS, PAD SCREW. Pliers used to tighten the retaining nut on a harness terret. These pliers engage small holes in the nut in the same manner as a spanner wrench.

Pad Screw Pliers

PLIERS, PARALLEL. Pliers in which the jaws remain parallel to each other as they are opened.

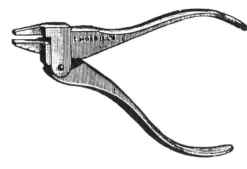

Morrill's Patent

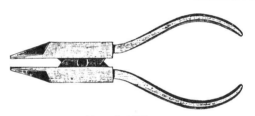

Parallel Pliers

PLIERS, PENDULUM. A tool used by a clock maker to adjust a pendulum. Length is 3 to 6 inches.

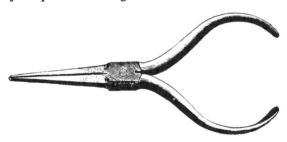

Pendulum Pliers

PLIERS, PIANO TUNERS'. Special-purpose pliers used by a piano tuner or repairman.

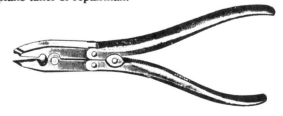

Action Regulating
Piano Tuners' Pliers

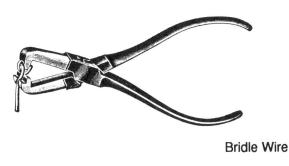

Bridle Wire

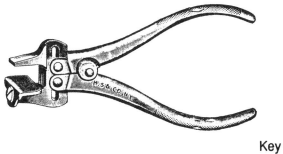

Key

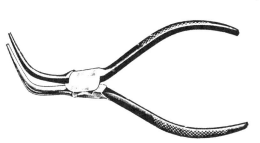

Valve

Piano Tuners' Pliers

PLIERS, PIN. See *Pliers, Long Nose.*

PLIERS, PINCER. Also called MILLINERS' PLIERS and SADDLERS' PLIERS. A tool, with sharply serrated jaws, used to grasp and pull leather or felt. Length is 5 to 8 inches.

Pincer Pliers

PLIERS, PUMP CHAIN. A tool used for opening and closing links of the unique chain used in water pumps.

Chain Pliers

PLIERS, RATTAN SPICING. A tool used to crimp a metal clip around a segment of rattan when making a splice or attachment.

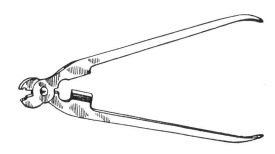

Rattan Splicing Pliers

PLIERS, REED. See *Pliers, Stockinger.*

PLIERS, RING. A jewelers' tool used for closing a split ring.

Ring Pliers

PLIERS, RING SAW. A jewelers' tool used to cut a ring.

Ring Saw Pliers

PLIERS, ROUND NOSE. Length is 3 to 8 inches. This type of pliers was available with a short or long nose.

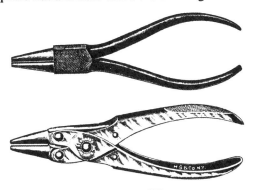

Round Nose Pliers

PLIERS, SADDLERS'. See *Pliers, Pincer.*

PLIERS, SIDE CUTTING. Length is 4 to 9 inches.

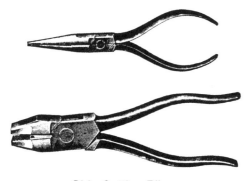

Side Cutting Pliers

PLIERS, SLIP JOINT. Also called COMBINATION PLIERS. A plier with an elongated hole at the pivot to allow the jaws to be adjusted to a wide or narrow grip. Length is 6 to 10 inches. Many of these pliers have a wire cutter at the rear of the jaws and some have one handle sharpened to serve as a screw driver.

Offset

Slip Joint Pliers

PLIERS, SLOT CUTTING. See *Pliers, Wire.*

PLIERS, SNIPE NOSE. See *Pliers, Chain.*

PLIERS, STOCKING. See *Pliers, Stockinger.*

PLIERS, STOCKINGER. Also called DUCK BILL PLIERS, REED PLIERS, STOCKING PLIERS, SWAN BILL PLIERS and WEAVERS' PLIERS. Pliers with long smooth jaws suitable for use in a textile mill and by a reed organ maker. Length is 3 to 9 inches.

Stockinger Pliers

PLIERS, SWAN BILL. See *Pliers, Stockinger.*

PLIERS, TACKING. See *Pincers, Tacking.*

PLIERS, TAXIDERMISTS'. A tool used by a taxidermist, furrier or tanner when stretching and tacking out skins. Length is approximately 10 inches.

Taxidermists' Pliers

PLIERS, TIRE. A tool used for spreading a cut in a rubber tire and holding it open for cleaning.

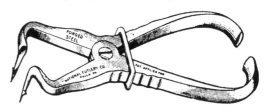

Tire Pliers

PLIERS, TIRE PLUG. Also called BICYCLE TIRE PLUG PLIERS. A tool used to insert a repair plug into a bicycle tire. Length is approximately 5 inches.

Tire Plug Pliers

PLIERS, TOOTH. See *Pliers, Opticians'.*

PLIERS, UMBRELLA. Pliers with a wide jaw used for stretching cloth over a frame. Length is 4 to 9 inches.

Umbrella Pliers

PLIERS, VISE. A pliers in which the jaws are capable of being locked in position. Length of the illustrated tool is approximately 6 ½ inches.

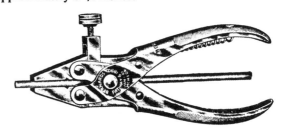

Vise Pliers

PLIERS, WATCH CASE JOINT. A watch makers' tool.

Watch Case Joint Pliers

PLIERS, WATCH HAND. A tool used to remove the hands from a watch or clock.

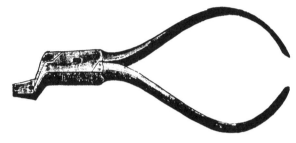

Watch Hand Pliers

PLIERS, WEAVERS'. See *Pliers, Stockinger.*

PLIERS, WEBBING. See *Webbing Stretcher.*

PLIERS, WIRE. Also called BUTTON'S PLIERS and SLOT CUTTING PLIERS. Pliers used for cutting and twisting wire. Length is 4 1/2 to 12 inches.

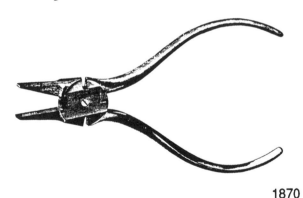

1870

Button's Patent

Wire Pliers

With Staple Hammer

Wire Pliers

PLIERS, WIRE CUTTING. Also called CUTTING PLIERS. Length is 4 1/2 to 7 1/2 inches.

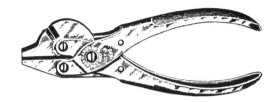

Bernard's Open Throat

Wire Cutting Pliers

PLIERS, WIRE SKINNING. An electricians' tool intended for stripping insulation from wire.

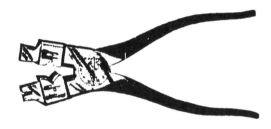

Wire Skinning Pliers

PLOUGH PLANE. See *Plane, Panel Plow.* Plough is a variation in spelling.

PLOW. See *Garden Plow, Ice Plow* and *Plane, Panel Plow.*

PLOW ANVIL. See *Anvil, Plow.*

PLOW BOLT HOLDER. A tool used to press the head of a plow bolt to prevent rotation as the nut is removed.

Plow Bolt Holder

PLOW CHISEL. See *Chisel, Plow.*

PLOW HAMMER. See *Hammer, Blacksmiths'* and *Hammer, Double Face.*

PLOW HOLDER. See *Anvil Tool, Plow Iron.*

PLOW IRON. See *Anvil Tool, Plow Iron.*

PLOW MAKERS' ANVIL. See *Anvil, Plow Makers'*.

PLOW PLANE. See *Plane, Book Binders' Plow; Plane, Carriage Makers' Plow* and *Plane, Panel Plow*.

PLOW POINT CLAMP. See *Clamp, Plow Point*.

PLOWSHARE TONGS. See *Tongs, Blacksmiths'*.

PLUG CUTTER. Also called CARRIAGE MAKERS' PLUG CUTTER. A bit used to cut a short plug commonly inserted into a counter-sunk hole to conceal the head of a wood screw. Sizes from 3/8 to 5/8 inches were available.

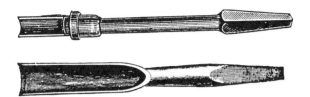

Plug Cutter

PLUG AND FEATHERS. A type of stone wedge. See *Wedge, Stone*.

PLUGGING CHISEL. See *Chisel, Plugging*.

PLUGGING HAMMER. See *Hammer, Plugging*.

PLUMB BOB. A conical weight used to show verticality when suspended on a line. Weights up to 4 ½ pounds have been noted. See also *Plummet*.

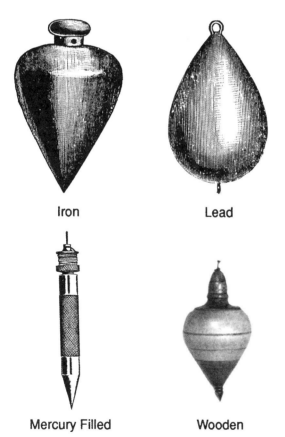

Iron   Lead

Mercury Filled   Wooden

Plumb Bob

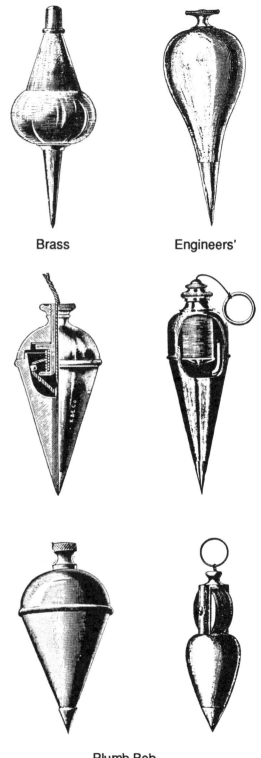

Brass   Engineers'

Plumb Bob

PLUMB BOB, OIL GAUGERS'. Also called TAPE LINE. A variety of plumb bob consisting of a weight on the end of a graduated steel tape. This device was used to measure the depth of crude oil in a storage tank.

PLUMB BOB LEVEL. See *Level, Plumb Bob*.

366

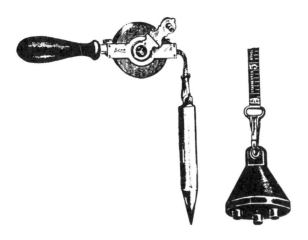

Oil Gaugers' Plumb Bob

PLUMBERS' TOOLS. The special-purpose plumbers' tools listed below can be found in normal alphabetical sequence. These tools may also have been used for other purposes.

BENDING IRON
BENDING SPRING
BOBBIN
BORING TOOL, BIT, PIPE
BORING TOOL, PIPE REAMER
BORING TOOL, TAP BORER
BOSSING STICK
CAULKING TOOL, PLUMBERS'
CHISEL, PLUMBERS'
DRESSER
DRIFT PLUG
DUMMY
FIRE POT
GOUGE, PLUMBERS'
HAMMER, CAULKING
HAMMER, STRAIGHT PEEN
HOOK, POT
KNIFE, CHIPPING
LADLE, MELTING
LEAD JOINT RUNNER
LEVEL, INCLINOMETER
LEVEL, PLUMBERS'
MALLET, BOSSING
PIPE THREADER
PLIERS, LEAD PIPE
SAW, PLUMBERS'
SCRAPER, TINNERS' ROOFING
SHAVE HOOK
SIDE EDGER
SOLDER POT
SOLDERING IRON
TOOL BAG, PLUMBERS'
TORCH, GASOLINE
TURN PIN
VISE, PIPE

WIPING CLOTH
WRENCH, BASIN
WRENCH, CROW'S FOOT
WRENCH, PIPE

PLUMMET. A miners' plumb bob with a lamp oil reservoir and wick in the top. The plumb is mounted in a gimbal. The illustrated tool is two inches in diameter.

Plummet

PLYERS. See *Pliers.*

POCKET BARRELING HATCHET. See *Hatchet, Barreling.*

POCKET CHISEL. See *Chisel, Pocket.*

POCKET LEVEL. See *Level, Pocket.*

POCKET OILER. An oiler small enough to be carried in the pocket. These oilers were often carried by sportsmen to lubricate guns and by bicycling enthusiasts. The pocket oiler was equipped with a tight cap to prevent leakage. Some said that the term "Pocket Oiler" meant that the cap or the oiler usually leaked and kept the pocket well oiled. See also *Oiler.*

Pocket Oiler

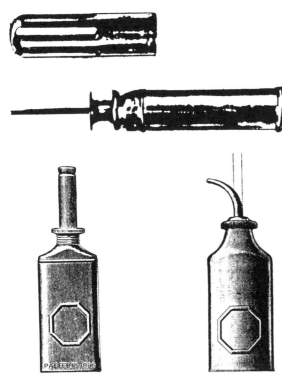

Jenny Pattern   Mule Pattern

Pole Support

Pocket Oiler

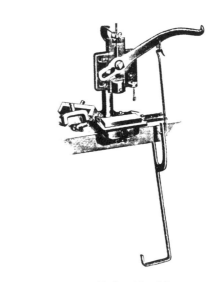

Polka Machine

POCKET RULE. See *Rule, Pocket.*

POCKET SCREW DRIVER. See *Screw Driver, Pocket.*

POCKET TOOL CHEST. See *Tool Handle.*

POCKET WRENCH. See *Wrench, Pocket.*

POD AUGER. See *Boring Tool, Pod Auger.*

POD BIT. See *Boring Tool, Bit, Gouge; Boring Tool, Bit, Shell* and *Boring Tool, Bit, Spoon.*

POINT. See *Electrotype Finishers' Tool, Point* and *Stone Cutters' Tool, Point.*

POINT DRIVER. See *Sash Point Driver.*

POINTED LIP TONGS. See *Tongs, Blacksmiths'.*

POINTING TROWEL. See *Trowel, Pointing.*

POKER. See *Fire Tools.*

POLE AXE. See *Axe, Pole.*

POLE COLLAR. See *Clamp, Measuring Bar.*

POLE SUPPORT. A linemans' tool used to support one end of a pole during up-ending. Length is 6 to 8 feet. A light version of the Mule Pattern support was available in lengths up to 20 feet. The long type was also listed as a GUARDED PIKE, PIKE and RAISING FORK.

POLISHER. See *Bookbinding Tool, Polisher.*

POLISHING LATHE. See *Lathe, Polishing.*

POLISHING MACHINE. See *Lathe, Polishing.*

POLKA MACHINE. A small press used by a comb maker for making jewelry blanks and for cutting out open work.

POLL AXE. See *Axe, Poll.*

POLL PICK. See *Pick, Poll.*

POMMEL. Also called ARM BOARD and RAISING BOARD. A curriers' tool, with a cork surface, used for final smoothing of finished leather. The pommel was used by placing the forearm through the loop and grasping the spike handle.

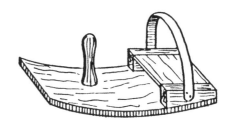

Pommel

POND ICE SAW. See *Saw, Ice*.

PONTY. See *Glass Blow Pipe*.

PONY DRAWING KNIFE. See *Drawing Knife, Pony*.

PONY SAW. See *Saw, Hand*.

POOL CUE BEVELER. A tool used to bevel a new pool cue tip. The cue is inserted through a lengthwise hole in the handle and rotated against the knurled steel cutter.

Pool Cue Beveler

POOL CUE CLAMP. See *Clamp, Pool Cue*.

PORK PACKERS' SAW. See *Saw, Pork Packers'*.

POST AUGER. See *Boring Tool, Post Auger*.

POST AXE. See *Axe, Post*.

POST COLLARS. See *Clamp, Mesuring Bar*.

POST DRILL. See *Boring Tool, Coal Miners'* and *Boring Tool, Post Drill*.

POST HOLE AUGER. See *Boring Tool, Post Hole Auger*.

POST HOLE DIGGER. A tool used for making a hole for setting fence posts. See also *Boring Tool, Post Hole Auger*.

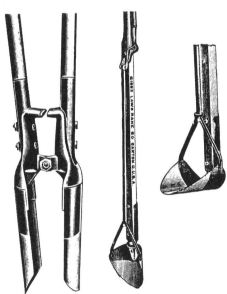

Post Hole Digger

POST HOLE SPOON. Also called TELEGRAPH POST SPOON and TELEGRAPH SPOON. A tool used to remove dirt from a deep post hole. Length of handle is 7 to 8 feet.

Post Hole Spoon

POST MAUL. See *Maul, Post*.

POST VISE. See *Vise, Post*.

POT. See *Glue Pot, Marking Pot* and *Solder Pot*.

POT HOOK. See *Hook, Pot*.

POTANCE FILE. See *File, Flat*.

POTATO FORK. See *Fork, Spading*.

POTATO HOE. See *Hook, Potato*.

POTATO HOOK. See *Hook, Potato*.

POTATO PLANTER. A device used to plant potatoes in loose soil. The planter is pushed into the soil and opened to allow a segment of potato to drop into the hole.

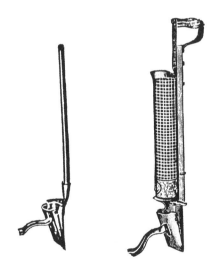

Potato Planter

POTATO SCOOP. See *Shovel, Scoop*.

POTATO SHOVEL. See *Shovel, Scoop*.

POULTRY KILLING KNIFE. See *Knife, Poultry Killing*.

POULTRY PUNCH. See *Punch, Poultry*.

POUNCING WHEEL. Also called PERFORATOR. A tailors' tool used to perforate a pattern. A fine powder is dusted through the perforations made by the wheel thus marking the material underneath. The steel wheel is 1/8 to 1/4 inch in diameter. See also *Tracing Wheel*.

Pouncing Wheel

POURING CAN. A tar can used for filling seams in wood or brick pavement. Capacity of the illustrated can is two gallons.

Pouring Can

POWDER GUN. See *Bedbug Gun* and *Bellows, Sulphur.*

POWER HAMMER. See *Hammer, Foot Power.*

PREACHER. A home made tool used to mark a drop siding board for cutoff. The preacher is placed astride the siding board and against the upright to provide a straight edge for marking. The illustrated tool is made of walnut.

Preacher

PRESS. See *Bookbinding Tool, Press; Copying Press; Veneer Press* and *Wheel Box Press.*

PRESS PALLET. See *Bookbinding Tool, Press Pallet.*

PRICK PUNCH. See *Punch, Prick.*

PRICKER. Also called SAIL MAKERS' PRICKER. A sail makers' tool used for making and enlarging holes for ropes. Also used for splaying the strands when working a small rope. Length is 8 to 10 ½ inches. The pricker is used for essentially the same purposes as a marlin spike. See also *Coal Miners' Blasting Tools.*

Pricker

PRICKING IRON. See *Leather Tool, Pricking Iron.*

PRICKING WHEEL. See *Leather Tool, Pricking Wheel.*

PRICKING WHEEL CARRIAGE. See *Leather Tool, Pricking Wheel Carriage.*

PRIMITIVE BIT BRACE. See *Boring Tool, Bit Brace, Primitive.*

PRIMITIVE RASP. See *Rasp, Primitive.*

PRINTERS' RULE. See *Rule, Printers'.*

PRITCHEL. Also called FORE PUNCH. A square-faced punch used by a farrier to punch out or enlarge the nail holes in a horse shoe. The shoulders of the pritchel are kept square so that a slug of metal is punched out rather than being pushed aside. The pritchel hole in the anvil allows the slug and the face of the pritchel to pass cleanly through the shoe. The pritchel is normally 10 to 12 inches long.

Pritchel

PRODUCE DEALERS' HATCHET. See *Hatchet, Box.*

PRODUCE HATCHET. See *Hatchet, Box.*

PRODUCERS' HATCHET. See *Hatchet, Box.*

PROOF PLANER. A printers' tool. The illustrated tool is made of maple with the face covered with felt.

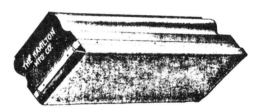

Proof Planer

PROOFING ROLLER. Also called INKING ROLLER. A printers' tool used to spread ink on the proof press. Length is 6 to 22 inches.

Proofing Roller

PROSPECTING HAMMER. See *Hammer, Prospecting.*

PROSPECTING PICK. See *Pick, Prospecting.*

PROTRACTOR SQUARE. See *Square, Protractor.*

PRUNE TESTER. A scale used to weigh a fixed volume of prunes. The weight is used as a measure of moisture content. The same device with a different scale is used in the wheat belt to measure grain. Several sizes of containers were available.

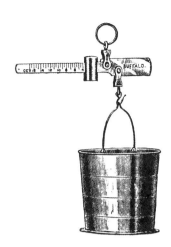

Prune Tester

PRUNING HATCHET. See *Hatchet, Pruning*.

PRUNING HOOK. See *Hook, Bill; Hook, Bush* and *Knife, Pruning*.

PRUNING KNIFE. See *Knife, Pruning*.

PRUNING SAW. See *Saw, Pruning*.

PRUNING SHEARS. See *Shears, Pruning*.

PUG. A short screw driver. See *Screw Driver, Pug*.

PULASKI. See *Axe Mattock*.

PULL HOE. See *Hoe, Garden*.

PULLER DOG. See *Plank Puller*.

PULLEY MORTISING BIT. See *Boring Tool, Bit, Mortise*.

PULLEY SET BLOCK. See *Sash Pulley Driver*.

PULP HOOK. See *Hook, Pulp*.

PUMP AUGER. See *Boring Tool, Pump Auger*.

PUMP CHAIN PLIERS. See *Pliers, Pump Chain*.

PUMP DRILL. See *Boring Tool, Pump Drill*.

PUMP LOG AUGER. See *Boring Tool, Pump Auger*.

PUMP PLANE. See *Plane, Pump*.

PUMP REAMER. See *Boring Tool, Pump Reamer*.

PUNCH. A short length of metal that is intended to be struck on one end and has the other end configured to perform an operation such a cutting, driving, embossing, perforating or spreading.

PUNCH, ARCH. See *Punch, Leather*.

PUNCH, BACKING OUT. A general-purpose punch used for driving out a pin or a rivet. Size is 5/8 to 7/8 inches in diameter. See also *Anvil Tool, Backing Out Punch*.

Backing Out Punch

PUNCH, BAG. See *Leather Tool, Bag Punch*.

PUNCH, BELL CENTERING. Also called BELL CENTERING TOOL. A tool used to locate and indent the center of a round shaft or rod.

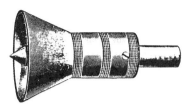

Bell Centering Punch

PUNCH, BELT. Also called BELT BORER. A tool used for cutting a round hole in a leather or web belt. See also *Belt Punch Knife* and *Punch, Leather*.

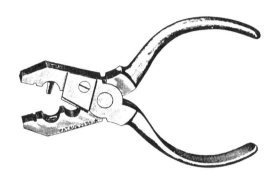

For Round Belts

Open Type

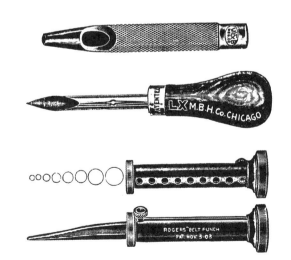

Belt Punch

PUNCH, BELT HOLE PROTECTOR. A tool used to punch the hole for insertion of a metal belt hole protector.

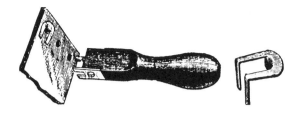

Belt Hole Protector Punch

PUNCH, BENDING. See *Bending Block.*

PUNCH, BLACKSMITHS'. See *Anvil Tool, Punch* and *Punch, Hand.*

PUNCH, BOBBING. See *Anvil Tool, Countersink.*

PUNCH, BRAD. Also called BRAD SETTER. A device used for nailing a moulding to the edge of a door panel.

Brad Punch

PUNCH, BUCKLE LOOP. A tool used to punch the holes for insertion of buckle loop prongs. This item was listed as a trimmers' tool especially suited for use when installing side curtains in a carriage.

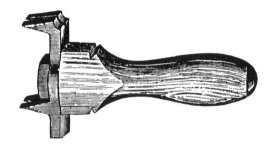

Buckle Loop Punch

PUNCH, BUCKLE TONGUE. See *Leather Tool, Buckle Tongue Punch.*

PUNCH, CARVERS'. See *Carving Tool, Marker.*

PUNCH, CENTER. A punch with a sharp point used to provide a dimple in the workpiece for starting a drill. Length is 3 to 12 inches. See also *Anvil Tool, Center Punch* and *Punch, Bell Centering.*

Center Punch

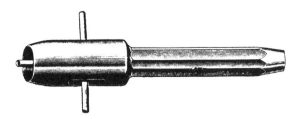

Center Punch

PUNCH, CENTERING. See *Punch, Bell Centering.*

PUNCH, CHAIN. A punch with a long straight shank. Used to drive the link pins from a machine chain.

Chain Punch

PUNCH, CHASING. See *Chasing Tool.*

PUNCH, CHICKEN. See *Punch, Poultry.*

PUNCH, CLEARANCE. See *Punch, Pin.*

PUNCH, CLOSING HOLE. See *Punch, Hole Closing.*

PUNCH, CONDUCTORS'. Also called TICKET PUNCH. A hand tool used to punch an identifying hole in a cardboard ticket.

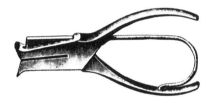

Conductors' Punch

PUNCH, COOPERS'. A small round punch used by a cooper to make the rivet holes in a metal barrel hoop. See illustration under *Punch, Hand.*

PUNCH, COPPERING. A tool used for punching the rivet or nail holes in copper plating.

Coppering Punch

PUNCH, CUTTING. See *Punch, Grommet.*

PUNCH, DRIFT. A tool used to force alignment of the holes in two workpieces. See also *Punch, Taper.*

Drift Punch

PUNCH, DRIVE. See *Punch, Leather* and *Punch, Pin.*

PUNCH, DRIVING. Listed by one supplier as a FINE DRIVING PUNCH. This tool appears to be the same as a narrow pin punch.

Driving Punch

PUNCH, EAR. See *Ear Marker.*

PUNCH, ELECTROTYPE FINISHERS'. A plate makers' tool. This punch was made in several sizes to match the different sizes of type.

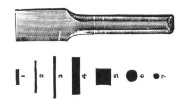

Straightening

Revising

Electrotype Finishers' Punch

PUNCH, EYELET. A tool used to punch the holes in leather or canvas for installation of pronged eyelets.

Eyelet Punch

PUNCH, FORE. See *Anvil Tool, Nail Punch* and *Pritchel.*

PUNCH, GROMMET. Also called CUTTING PUNCH. A tool used to cut the hole in a canvas for installation of a grommet. Available in round and oblong shapes and in several sizes.

Grommet Punch

PUNCH, HALFTONE SOFTENING. A tool used to soften the harsh borders of a halftone. These punches were used for precise work in corners and in areas not easily worked with a softening hammer. See *Hammer, Halftone Softening.*

Halftone Softening Punch

PUNCH, HAND. Also called BLACKSMITHS' PUNCH, MACHINE PUNCH, ROUND PUNCH and SQUARE PUNCH. A general-purpose steel punch. See also *Punch, Sheetmetal.*

Hand Punch

PUNCH, HOLE CLOSING. Also called CLOSING HOLE PUNCH and CLOCK HOLE CLOSING PUNCH. A tool used by a watch or clock maker for reducing the size of a worn hole in soft metal such as brass. The punch is centered at the original hole location and struck with a hammer. The metal is thereby swaged inward to reduce the size of the opening. The centering pin shown in the illustration is spring loaded.

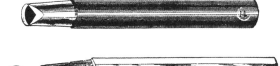

Hole Closing Punch

PUNCH, HOLLOW. Also called METAL PUNCH. A hollow punch used to cut a round hole in sheet metal. Sizes are 3/8 to 3 1/2 inches in diameter.

Hollow Punch

PUNCH, KNOCKOUT. See *Hole Cutter.*

PUNCH, LACE. Also called THONGING CHISEL. A punch used to pierce the holes in leather for lacing.

Lace Punch

PUNCH, LEATHER. A hollow punch used to cut a hole in leather. Round and oval types were available. See also *Belt Punch Knife; Punch, Belt* and *Punch, Lace.*

Arch

Round

Spring

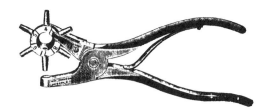

Revolving

Automatic or Spiral

Leather Punch

PUNCH, LINING UP. See *Punch, Taper.*

PUNCH, MACHINE. See *Punch, Hand.*

PUNCH, MARKING. A boiler makers' tool used to mark hole locations.

Marking Punch

PUNCH, METAL. Also called HAND METAL PUNCH and HAND PUNCH. A tool used to punch holes in sheet metal. See also *Punch, Hollow.*

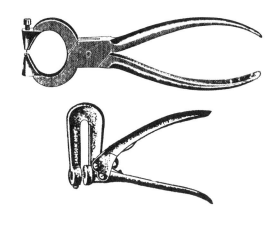

Hand

Screw

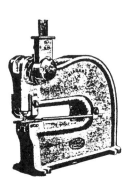

Lever

Metal Punch

PUNCH, NAIL. See *Anvil Tool, Nail Punch* and *Pritchel.*

PUNCH, NAIL SET. See *Nail Set.*

PUNCH, PIN. Also called CLEARANCE PUNCH, DRIVE PUNCH, RIVET PUNCH and SICKLE PUNCH. A straight punch used for clearing a hole. See also *Sickle Punch.*

Pin Punch

PUNCH, POULTRY. Also called CHICKEN PUNCH and TURKEY PUNCH. A punch used for marking poultry by making a hole in the web between the toes.

Poultry Punch

PUNCH, PRICK. Also called TINNERS' PRICK PUNCH. A tool used to make holes in sheet metal for insertion of sheet metal screws.

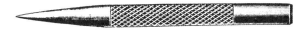

Prick Punch

PUNCH, RIVET. See *Punch, Pin.*

PUNCH, ROUND. See *Anvil Tool, Punch; Punch, Hand* and *Punch, Leather.*

PUNCH, SAW. Also called BUTCHER SAW PUNCH and SAW BLADE PUNCH. A tool used to punch the mounting holes in a saw blade such as for a butcher saw.

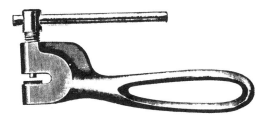

Saw Punch

PUNCH, SHEETMETAL. See *Punch, Hollow* and *Punch, Metal.*

PUNCH, SICKLE. See *Punch, Pin* and *Sickle Punch.*

PUNCH, SQUARE. See *Anvil Tool, Punch* and *Punch, Hand.*

PUNCH, STAR STITCHER. See *Leather Tool, Star Stitcher Punch.*

PUNCH, STOP. A tinsmiths' tool used to pierce sheet metal. The shoulder stops the punch thereby limiting the size of the hole. Sizes were available to match standard sheet-metal screws.

Stop Punch

PUNCH, STRAP END. See *Leather Tool, Strap End Punch.*

PUNCH, TAPER. Also called LINING-UP PUNCH. A punch with a constant taper. Used to force alignment of holes in two thin pieces of metal such as might be required when installing boiler plates.

Taper Punch

PUNCH, TICKET. See *Punch, Conductors'.*

PUNCH, TRACE. See *Leather Tool, Trace Punch.*

PUNCH, TRACK. A heavy punch used for making a hole in the web of a railroad rail. Weight is approximately 5 pounds.

Track Punch

PUNCH, VENEER. A hollow punch used for cutting out a damaged spot when repairing a veneered surface. The same punch is then used to cut a segment of new veneer for insertion into the hole. These tools are usually irregular in shape. An unsymmetrical shape is said to be less apparent to casual inspection. A common size is 1 1/2 by 3 inches.

Veneer Punch

PUNCH, WAD. A punch used to make shotgun shell wads. Same as a specific size of arch punch or round punch. See illustration under *Punch, Leather.*

PUNCH, WASHER. A cutting punch used to stamp out washers or small gaskets.

Washer Punch

PUNCHING BLOCK. See *Anvil Tool, Punching Block.*

PURFLING TOOL. Also called VIOLIN PURFLING TOOL. A tool used for making the small inlay groove around the edge of a musical instrument.

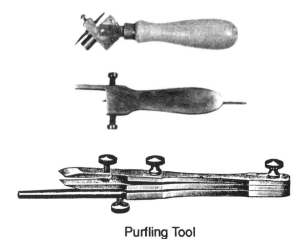

Purfling Tool

PUSH BRACE. See *Boring Tool, Push Drill.*

PUSH DRILL. See *Boring Tool, Push Drill.*

PUSH SCREW DRIVER. See *Screw Driver, Push.*

PUSHING HOE. See Hoe, Stable.

PUTTY CLOW. A tool used for removing old putty from a wooden window sash.

Putty Clow

PUTTY KNIFE. See *Knife, Putty.*

PUTTY SCRAPER. See *Scraper, Putty.*

Q

Tool names starting with the letter Q.

QUANNET. A coarse file used by a comb maker to smooth and reduce the thickness of horn blanks. The cut is 5 to 6 teeth per inch. Length is approximately 10 inches. *Knight* states that the teeth of a quannet are cut with a file rather than with a chisel.

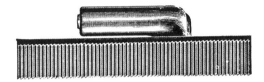

Quannet

QUARRY TOOLS. The term "Quarry" is used to indicate that the tool is intended for use in a stone or marble quarry. For instance, a quarry hammer and stone hammer listed in two different catalogues are often the same item. See listing under *Stone Quarry Tools.*

QUARTER AXE. See *Axe, House.*

QUARTER ROUND. See *Plane, Moulding, Quarter Round.*

QUICK CLAMP. See *Clamp, Quick.*

QUILL BIT. See *Boring Tool, Bit, Shell.*

QUILT CLAMP. See *Clamp, Quilting Frame.*

QUILTING FRAME CLAMP. See *Clamp, Quilting Frame.*

QUIRK OGEE. See *Plane, Moulding, Grecian Ogee.*

QUIRK MOULDING PLANE. See *Plane, Moulding, Grecian Ogee.*

QUIRT. See *Whip.*

QUOIN. A device used in a print shop to wedge a page of set type into the chase for printing. The key tightens and loosens the quoin.

Quoin Key

Quoin

R

Tool names starting with the letter R, including multiple listings of:

RAKE
RAMMER
RASP
ROUTER
RULE

Included also is a list of tools used in:

RAILROAD CONSTRUCTION

RABBET KNIFE. See *Drawing Knife, Carriage Body* and *Drawing Knife, Carriage Router.*

RABBET PLANE. See *Plane, Bullnose Rabbet; Plane, Carriage Makers'* and *Plane, Rabbet.*

RABBET SAW. See *Saw, Rabbet.*

RABBET AND FILLETSTER. See *Plane, Rabbet and Filletster.*

RACE KNIFE. See *Timber Scribe.*

RADIUS EDGER. See *Cement Tool, Edger.*

RADIUS GAUGE. See *Ball Gauge* and *Fillet Gauge.*

RADIUS TOOL. See *Cement Tool, Edger.*

RAFTER SQUARE. See *Square, Steel.*

RAFTING AUGER. See *Boring Tool, Rafting Auger.*

RAFTING AXE. See *Axe, Single Bit*, rafting pattern.

RAFTING DOG. See *Logging Dog.*

RAG SCYTHE. See *Scythe, Rag.*

RAGLET. See *Plane, Dado.*

RAIL BENDER. A device used to bend a railroad rail.

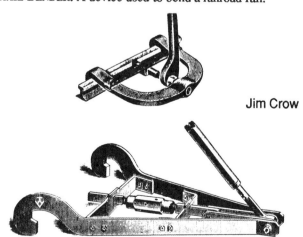

Jim Crow

Rail Bender

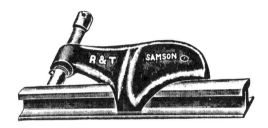

Rail Bender

RAIL TONGS. See *Tongs, Rail.*

RAIL WRENCH. See *Wrench, Handrail.*

RAILROAD CHALK CRAYON. See *Crayon, Chalk.*

RAILROAD CONSTRUCTION TOOLS. The special-purpose railroad construction tools listed below can be found in normal alphabetical sequence. These tools may also have been used for other purposes.

ADZE, DOUBLE BIT
ADZE, RAILROAD
ADZE, TIE
ANVIL TOOL, SIDE CHISEL
BAR, CLAW
BAR, CROW
BAR, SHACKLE
BORING TOOL, TRACK DRILL
CHISEL, TRACK
FORK, RAIL
JACK, TRACK
LEVEL, GRADE
LEVEL, TRACK
MAUL, SPIKE
MAUL, SHIP
PEAVEY
PICK, RAILROAD
PICK, TAMPING
PICK, TIE
RAIL BENDER
SAW, RAIL
SPIKE PULLER
TIE HOLDER
TONGS, RAIL
TONGS, TIE
TRACK GAUGE
WRENCH, TRACK

RAILROAD LEVEL. See *Level, Grade.*

RAILROAD LINE BAR. See *Bar, Crow.*

RAILROAD MAUL. See *Maul, Spike*.

RAILROAD SCUFFLE HOE. See *Hoe, Scuffle*.

RAILROAD TAMPING PICK. See *Pick, Tamping*.

RAILROAD TOP MAUL. See *Maul, Ship*.

RAILROAD TORCH. See *Torch*.

RAILROAD TRACK BROOM. See *Broom, Railroad Track*.

RAILROAD TRACK CHISEL. See *Chisel, Track*.

RAILROAD TRACK LEVEL. See *Level, Track*.

RAISING BOARD. Also called ARM BOARD, CRIPPLER and GRAINING BOARD. A curriers' tool used to give a granular appearance to a finished hide and to increase flexibility of the leather. The tool has a rough corrugated surface. During use, the currier places his forearm through the loop and grasps the spike handle.

Raising Board

RAISING FORK. See *Pole Support*.

RAISING HAMMER. See *Hammer, Raising*.

RAISING IRON. A coopers' tool used for prying off the end hoop and for removing the head of a barrel. The illustrated tool is 8 1/2 inches long.

Raising Iron

RAISING MALLET. See *Mallet, Raising*.

RAISING PLANE. See *Plane, Raising*.

RAISING TOOL. See *Electrotype Finisher' Tool, Raising*.

RAKE. A handled tool, with projecting prongs, intended to be pulled over a surface for smoothing or for the collection of loose material.

RAKE, ASPHALT. Also called TAR RAKE. A tool used for spreading asphalt or tar when repairing a road surface.

Asphalt Rake

RAKE, CURD. A rake used in a creamery for stirring and breaking curd. Width of the illustrated tool is 27 inches.

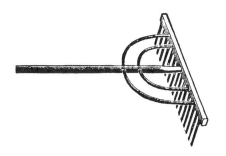

Curd Rake

RAKE, DANDELION. A rake used to pull dandelions from a lawn. Width is 16 to 23 inches. Guaranteed to kill dandelions.

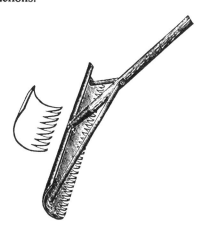

Dandelion Rake

RAKE, FIRE. A tool used for cleaning out a fire line when fighting a forest fire. The rake is comprised of several mowing machine cutting sections riveted to a bar. The sections are replaceable. Width of the illustrated tool is 8 inches.

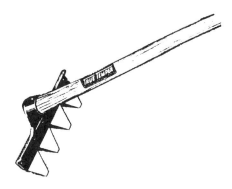

Fire Rake

RAKE, GARDEN. A garden tool used for smoothing a seedbed and for collection of debris.

RAKE, HAY. A large rake, with wooden teeth, used for gathering hay. Width of the illustrated rake is 27 inches.

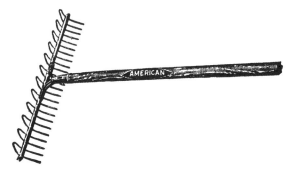

Garden Rake

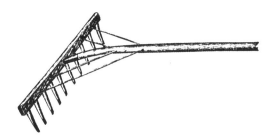

Hay Rake

RAKE, LEAF. Also called BROOM RAKE. A lawn tool used for gathering leaves or grass clippings. This tool has flexible steel tines.

Leaf Rake

RAKE, MALT. A rake used to stir malt on the kiln floor to hasten drying.

Malt Rake

RAKE, PINE NEEDLE. Also called MILL REFUSE RAKE. A large rake used for gathering pine needles and other heavy refuse.

Pine Needle Rake

RAKE, TWO-MAN. A two-handled rake used for leveling a pile of gravel or sand. Length of teeth is about 6 inches.

Two-Man Rake

RAMMER. A blunt tool used to tamp sand or stone. See also *Tamper*.

RAMMER, BENCH. Also called SAND RAMMER. A tool used for tamping sand into a casting mould. Diameter is 3 1/2 to 4 1/2 inches.

Rammer

RAMMER, SAND. Also called COBBLE RAMMER and RAMMER. A tool used by a stone paver for compacting and smoothing a cobblestone surface or sand base. Weight is 25 to 40 pounds.

Sand Base

Belguim Cobble

Sand Rammer

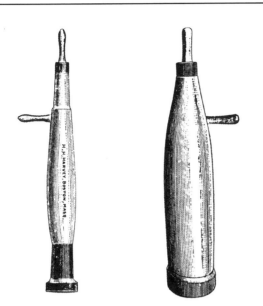

Bell Faced   Pavers' Wooden
Sand Rammer

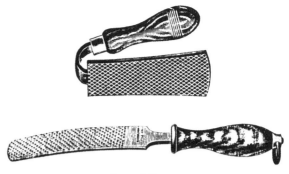

Bread Rasp

RASP, CABINET. See *Rasp, Wood.*

RASP, FELLOE. See *Rasp, Wood.*

RASP, HOOF. See *Rasp, Horse.*

RASP, HORSE. Also called HOOF RASP. A farriers' tool used to smooth the surface of the hoof after use of the hoof parer or hoof nipper. It was also used to flatten a small area below the exit point of each nail thus allowing a smoother and neater clinch. After the shoe is completely nailed and clinched, the rasp is sometimes used to smooth off the toe should it overhang the shoe. Horse rasps were offered in plain and tanged patterns plus some special varieties as illustrated. The standard patterns have punched teeth on one side and double cut file teeth on the other. The edges are single cut. Length is 10 to 20 inches.

RAMS HORN SCRAPER. See *Scraper, Rams Horn.*

RASE KNIFE. See *Timber Scribe.*

RASP. A hand tool with coarse cutting teeth on one or more sides. The teeth are formed by raising small bits of the base metal rather than by forming a series of continuous cuts as on a file. Rasp cuts are classified in accordance with the degree of roughness. They range in roughness from the horse rasp to the smooth cut. A comparison of cuts is shown in the illustration.

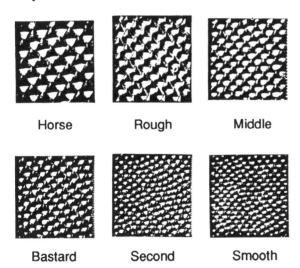

Horse   Rough   Middle

Bastard   Second   Smooth

Rasp Cut Comparison

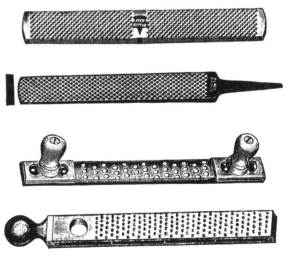

Horse Rasp

RASP, HORSE TOOTH. See *File, Horse Tooth.*

RASP, HOT. A farriers' tool used at the anvil to chamfer the edges of a hot horse shoe as a last step in the forging process. It is important that the shoe be relieved of sharp corners on the inside edge to reduce the chance of injury should a foot strike the other leg. Length is 14 to 16 inches. A hot rasp has a half-round shape and a tang handle.

RASP, BENT. A rasp that is formed such that the handle in not in a direct line with the cutting teeth.

RASP, BREAD. Also called BAKERS' RASP. A bakers' tool used to rasp off the burned or hard portions of a loaf of bread. More commonly used in England than in America.

Hot Rasp

RASP, LAST MAKERS'. A tool used for making wooden shoe lasts. The teeth are formed in curved rather than straight rows.

Last Makers' Rasp

RASP, LEAD. A small smoothing tool used for removing the excess lead when patching a hole or dent in an automobile body. It has a serrated surface essentially the same as that of a babbitt file.

Lead Rasp

RASP, PRIMITIVE. A home-made rasp said to have been made and used by an American Indian tribe. The illustrated tool was used for rasping out the center of a cane for use as a blow gun. A similar tool was made in a flat pattern to smooth arrow shafts. The cutting nibs were fashioned by simply punching holes in a thin piece of tin and then forming the tin into the desired shape. Information is from *The File in History* by *Henry Disston & Sons*.

Primitive Rasp

RASP, SADDLE TREE. A tanged half round rasp used in the manufacture of wooden saddle trees. The teeth are formed in slanted rather than straight rows.

Saddle Tree Rasp

RASP, SHOE. Also called SOLE RASP. A shoe makers' tool used to remove the overhang from a leather shoe sole or heel. The shoe rasp is generally second cut. Length is 6 to 14 inches.

Half Round

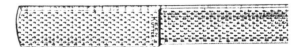

Flat

Oval or Bellied

Shoe Rasp

RASP, WOOD. A general-purpose rasp intended for use on wood. Length is 6 to 18 inches. A wood rasp has a tang handle. The flat variety is generally a bastard cut and is used by carriage makers and wheelwrights. The cabinet rasp is generally smooth cut.

Flat

Half Round

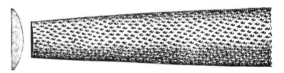

Half Round Cabinet

Round

Wood Rasp

RASP, WOOD CARVERS'. See *Riffler*.

RASP HANDLE. A detachable handle for use with a flat rasp.

Rasp Handle

RAT TAIL FILE. See *File, Round*.

RATCHET BRACE. See *Boring Tool, Ratchet*.

RATCHET CHAIN DRILL. See *Boring Tool, Chain Drill*.

RATCHET DRILL. See *Boring Tool, Ratchet*.

RATCHET DRILL BIT. See *Boring Tool, Bit, Ratchet*.

RATCHET EXTENSION. See *Boring Tool, Ratchet Extension*.

RATCHET FILE. See File, *Watch Makers'*.

RATCHET SCREW DRIVER. See *Screw Driver, Ratchet*.

RATCHET WRENCH. See *Wrench, Ratchet*.

RATTAN SPLICING PLIERS. See *Pliers, Rattan Splicing*.

RAWHIDE HAMMER. See *Mallet, Rawhide*.

RAWHIDE MALLET. See *Mallet, Rawhide*.

RAWHIDE MAUL. See *Mallet Rawhide* and *Maul, Rawhide*.

RAZEE PLANE. See *Plane, Razee*.

REAMER. See *Boring Tool, Bit, Broach; Boring Tool, Bit, Reamer; Boring Tool, Bone Reamer; Boring Tool, Hub Reamer; Boring Tool, Pipe Reamer* and *Hand Rimmer*.

REAMING IRON. A blunt chisel used for opening the seams between two planks of a ship for application of caulking material.

Reaming Iron

REAPER FILE. See *File, Reaper*.

REBATE. See *Plane, Rabbet*. Rebate is a term used in England. The name was not used by American plane makers and sellers.

RECIPROCATING DRILL. See *Boring Tool, Archimedes* and *Boring Tool, Push Drill*.

REED ORGAN SCRAPER. See *Scraper, Reed Organ*.

REED PLIERS. See *Pliers, Stockinger*.

REEDING PLANE. See *Plane, Moulding, Reeding*.

REIN ROUNDER. See *Leather Tool, Rounder*.

REGISTER CALIPER. See *Caliper, Self Registering*.

REGULATING NEEDLE. See *Upholsterers' Regulator*.

REGULATING TOOL. See *Piano Tool, Regulating*.

REGULATOR. See *Upholsterers' Regulator*.

REIN TRIMMER. See *Leather Tool, Trimmer*.

REVERSE OGEE. See *Plane, Moulding, Reverse Ogee*.

REVOLVING NAIL CUP. See *Tack and Rivet Holder*.

RIB SHAVE DRAWING KNIFE. See *Drawing Knife, Rib Shave*.

RICE HOE. See *Hoe, Planters'*.

RICE SAMPLER. See *Sampler, Grain*.

RICE SHOVEL. See *Shovel, Rice*.

RICE TRIER. See *Sampler, Grain*.

RIDDLE. Also called FOUNDRY RIDDLE, MINERS' RIDDLE, MOULDERS' RIDDLE and SIEVE. A round sieve used by a moulder to sift casting sand. Also used for sifting grain and coffee beans and by miners. Size is 14 to 20 inches in diameter.

Riddle

RIDING WHIP. See *Whip*.

RIFFLER FILE. See *Riffler*.

RIFFLER. Also called BOW FILE and RIFFLER FILE. A small curved tool with file serrations on a short section at one or both ends. Used for general-purpose smoothing of intricate shapes of wood and metal. Overall length is 6 to 9 inches. Those with very short cutting surfaces were often listed as die sinkers' tools. A riffler with a longer cutting surface, as illustrated, is generally listed as a silversmiths' tool. See also *File, Marble Cutters'*.

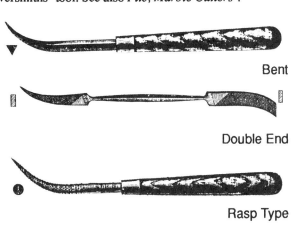

Bent

Double End

Rasp Type

Riffler

Die Sinkers

Silversmiths'

Riffler

RIFLE. See *Scythe Rifle.*

RIG BUILDERS' HATCHET. See *Hatchet, Rig Builders'.*

RIGGERS' SCREW. See *Clamp, Rope.*

RIM BIT. See *Boring Tool, Bit, Rim.*

RIM CLAMP. See *Clamp, Rim.*

RIM MACHINE. See *Tinsmiths' Machine, Rim.*

RIM WRENCH. See *Wrench, Automobile Rim* and *Wrench, Rim.*

RIMMER. See *Hand Rimmer* and *Reamer.* Rimmer an obsolete spelling of reamer.

RING AUGER. See *Boring Tool, Ring Auger.*

RING AWL. See *Awl, Scratch.*

RING BENDING BLOCK. A jewelers' tool. See *Bending Block.*

RING CLAMP. See *Clamp, Ring.*

RING DOG. A logging tool used to roll or start a log. It is used similar to a Cant Hook except that any stout pole can be used instead of a fixed handle. See also *Logging Dog.*

Ring Dog

RING GRAVER. See *Graver.*

RING HOLDER. See *Clamp, Ring.*

RING MALLET. See *Mallet, Ring.*

RING MANDREL. See *Mandrel, Jewelers'.*

RING PLIERS. See *Pliers, Ring.*

RING SAW PLIERS. See *Pliers, Ring Saw.*

RING SIZER. A jewelers' tool used to determine the proper size of ring to fit a given finger.

Ring Sizer

RING STAMP. A device used to stamp an initial or symbol on the inner surface of a ring.

Ring Stamp

RING STICK. A jewelers' gauge used to determine the size of a ring.

Ring Stick

RING TAP. See *Boring Tool, Tap Borer.*

RIP SAW. See *Saw, Rip.*

RIPPER. A tool used to tear up or disassemble.

RIPPER, CARPENTERS' STAGING. Also called Masons' Ripper. Length of the illustrated tool is 15 inches.

Carpenters' Staging Ripper

RIPPER, MASONS'. See *Ripper, Carpenters' Staging.*

RIPPER, SHINGLE. See *Ripper, Slaters'.*

RIPPER, SLATERS'. Also called SHINGLE RIPPER. A tool used to reach underneath a slate or shingle and cut a hidden nail. Used when removing a damaged shingle or slate from a finished roof. Overall length is 26 to 31 inches.

Slaters' Ripper

RIPPING BAR. See *Bar, Wrecking.*

RIPPING CHISEL. See *Chisel, Ripping.*

RIPPING HAMMER. See *Hammer, Ripping.*

RIPPING PLANE. See *Plane, Ripping.*

RIPPING TOOL. See *Upholsterers' Ripping Tool.*

RIVET BUSTER. A bridge or structural steel tool. Size of face is 1 1/2 inches square. See also *Anvil Tool, Side Chisel* and *Chisel, Rivet Buster.*

Rivet Buster

RIVET CLIPPER. See *Bolt Clipper.*

RIVET EXTRACTOR. A tool used to extract a split rivet from a flat belt.

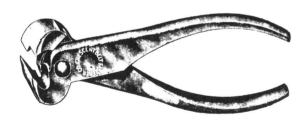

Rivet Extractor

RIVET FORGE. See *Forge, Rivet.*

RIVET HEADER. See *Nail Header* and *Rivet Set.*

RIVET HOLDER. A tool used to hold a belt rivet while driving.

Rivet Holder

RIVET PUNCH. See *Punch, Pin.*

RIVET SET. Also called RIVET HEADER. Used to upset the straight end of a rivet to form the head. The end has one or more half-round indentations. See also *Anvil Tool, Rivet Set.*

Rivet Set

RIVET SET HAMMER. See *Hammer, Rivet Set.*

RIVET SNAP. See *Anvil Tool, Rivet Set.*

RIVET TONGS. See *Tongs, Rivet.*

RIVETER. See *Riveting Machine.*

RIVETING ANVIL. See *Anvil, Curtain Fastener.*

RIVETING CLAMP. See *Clamp, Riveting.*

RIVETING DOLLY. A backup tool used when clinching a rivet.

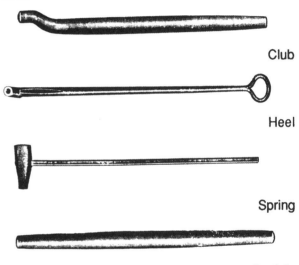

Club

Heel

Spring

Straight

Riveting Dolly

RIVETING HAMMER. See *Hammer, Boiler Riveting; Hammer, Bridge Builders'* and *Hammer, Riveting.*

RIVETING MACHINE. Also called RIVETER. A tool used to crimp soft copper rivets. This type of tool was used extensively for repair of harness.

Riveting Machine

ROACHING SHEARS. See *Shears, Horse.*

ROCK WEDGE. See *Wedge, Stone.*

ROD CUTTER. A device used to sever iron rods. The illustrated tool will cut rods up to 5/8 inches in diameter. Used primarily in blacksmith and welding shops.

Rod Cutter

ROLL BEVELING MACHINE. See *Leather Tool, Beveling Machine.*

ROLLER. See *Lawn Roller, Paper Hangers' Roller* and *Proofing Roller.*

ROLLING MILL. A machine used by a jewelry maker to reduce and form malleable metal into strips and other specific shapes.

Rolling Mill

ROLLING PARALLEL BAR. See *Rule, Parallel.*

ROMAN OGEE. See *Plane, Moulding, Roman Ogee.*

ROMAN REVERSE OGEE. See *Plane, Moulding, Roman Reverse Ogee.*

ROOF AUGER. See *Boring Tool, Roof Auger.*

ROOF BRUSH. See *Brush, Roof.*

ROOFING BRACKET. A device used by a roofer to provide a level platform on a slanted roof.

ROOFING CLEATER AND NAILER. A roofing tool used to fold a metal cleat and nail the cleat to the sheathing board. A nail is inserted into the side of the device before each operation.

Roofing Bracket

Cleater and Nailer

ROOFING DOUBLE SEAMER. Also called DOUBLE ROOFING SEAMER. A tool used for forming the seams of a tin roof after the edges have been turned with double seaming tongs.

Double Seamer

ROOFING HAMMER. See *Hammer, Roofing.*

ROOFING IRON. See *Smoothing Iron, Roofing.*

ROOFING KNIFE. See *Knife, Oil Cloth.*

ROOFING SEAMER. See *Roofing Double Seamer.*

ROOFING TONGS. See *Tongs, Double Seamer* and *Tongs, Roofing.*

ROPE CLAMP. See *Clamp, Fodder* and *Clamp, Rope.*

ROPE CLAMP ANVIL. See *Anvil, Rope Clamp.*

ROPE CUTTER. A hardware store tool used to cut a length of rope from the coil.

Rope Cutter

ROPE GAUGE. A set of semi-circular gauges from 1/2 to 1 inch in diameter and about .05 inches thick. It is assumed that these gauges are intended to measure a slot or groove, such as a pulley, for selection of the proper size of rope.

Rope Gauge

ROPE KNIFE. See *Knife, Rope*.

ROPE MACHINE. A machine used to make a rope from binder twine or other cord. The machine consists of three or four hooks which rotate in unison from a single handle. The metal spreader, shown in the illustration, serves the same purpose as a *Rope Top*.

Rope Machine

ROPE SHEARS. See *Shears, Horse*.

ROPE TOP. The tool used to tighten the twist when making a rope. The top is slid along the length of the strands during the twisting action to force the formation of a tight and constant spiral.

Rope Top

ROSETTE CUTTER. See *Leather Tool, Concho Cutter*.

ROTARY SHEARS. See *Tinsmiths' Machine, Circular Shears*.

ROULETTE. See *Electrotype Finishers' Tool, Roulette*.

ROUND. See *Plane, Moulding, Hollow* and *Round Pair*.

ROUND AWL. See *Awl, Seat*.

ROUND CORNER TROWEL. See *Cement Tool, Curbing*.

ROUND EDGE FILE. See *File, Joint*.

ROUND EYE PUNCH. See *Anvil Tool, Punch*.

ROUND FILE. See *File, Round*.

ROUND GULLETING FILE. See *File, Round*.

ROUND HEAD STAKE. See *Stake, Ball*.

ROUND JAW TONGS. See *Tongs, Blacksmiths'*.

ROUND KNIFE. See *Knife, Leather*.

ROUND MALLET. See *Mallet, Round*.

ROUND NOSE CHISEL. See *Chisel, Round Nose*.

ROUND NOSE PLIERS. See *Pliers, Round Nose*.

ROUND POINT. See *Stone Cutters' Tool, Round Point*.

ROUND PUNCH. See *Anvil Tool, Punch; Punch, Hand* and *Punch, Leather*.

ROUND PUNCH GAUGE. See *Leather Tool, Round Punch Gauge*.

ROUND SHAVE. A coopers' tool used to smooth the inside of a small coopered vessel such as a bucket or churn. See also *In-Shave* and *Turpentine Round Shave*.

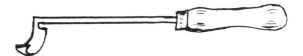

Round Shave

ROUND TRIMMER. See *Leather Tool, Edger*.

ROUNDER. Also called ROUND PLANE and ROUND SHAVE. A device used to round a tool handle or cut the tenon on a wagon spoke. See also *Leather Tool, Rounder*.

Rounder

ROUNDING HAMMER. See *Hammer, Farriers' Rounding*.

ROUNDING OFF FILE. See *File, Rounding Off*.

ROUNDING PLANE. See *Plane, Rounding* and *Witchet*.

ROUNDING TOOL. See *Cement Tool, Rounding*.

ROUTER. Also called ROUTER PLANE. A tool used to cut a flat-bottomed groove or pattern in a flat surface.

ROUTER, CABINET MAKERS'. A general-purpose router used for all types of woodworking. The Old Womans' Tooth, shown in the illustration, is often made from a section of a stair rail.

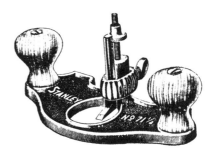

Closed Throat

Open Throat

Cabinet Makers' Router

D Type

ROUTER, CARRIAGE MAKERS'. Also called CARRIAGE MAKERS' PANEL ROUTER. A router used to cut a small groove parallel to a curved edge. Such grooves were often required for decorative inlay work on carriages.

Old Womans' Tooth

Panel

Panel

Plane Type

Single or Pistol

Cabinet Makers' Router

Jigger or Side

Carriage Makers' Router

Double

Carriage Makers' Router

ROUTER, FOOT POWER. See *Former*.

ROUTER PLANE. See *Router*.

ROW PLANTER. See *Garden Planter*.

RUBBER. See *Bookbinding Tool, Rubber* and *Seam Rubber*.

RUBBER KNIFE. See *Knife, Rubber*.

RUBBER MALLET. See *Mallet, Rubber*.

RUBBER POLICEMAN. A laboratory tool used to remove precipitate from the walls of a beaker. This tool is made of flexible rubber with a glass rod handle. Width of the illustrated tool is 7/16 inches.

Rubber Policeman

RUBBER TIRE CLAMP. See *Clamp, Rubber Tire*.

RUBBING BRICK. A block impregnated with carborundum grit and shaped in the form of a brick. Used for dressing marble, granite or concrete and for scouring castings. The brick holder has a four foot handle.

Plain

Fluted

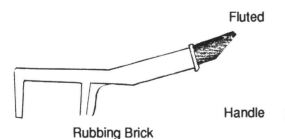

Handle

Rubbing Brick

RUBBING HOOK. The illustrated device was listed with leather tools. It is assumed to be a holding fixture for leather.

Rubbing Hook

RULE. Also called **RULER.** An instrument for making linear measurements. A rule is generally in the form of a rigid or semi-rigid strip with calibrations along one or more edges. See also *Horse Collar Tool, Measuring Yoke* and *Measuring Iron*.

RULE, ARCHITECTS'. Also called **DRAFTING RULE.** A folding rule, with drafting scales, that has the inside edges beveled to bring the scales closer to the work.

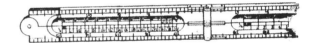

Architects'

RULE, BENCH. See *Rule, Manual Training*.

RULE, BLACKSMITHS'. A brass or steel rule intended for use by a blacksmith. A metal rule was necessary to avoid scorching or burning when used to measure a heated workpiece.

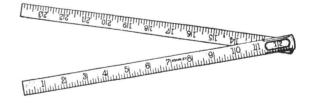

Folding

Hook

Blacksmiths' Rule

RULE, BLINDMANS'. A boxwood folding rule with extra-large numbers.

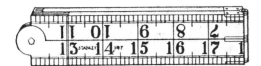

Blindmans' Rule

RULE, BOARD. See *Rule, Board Measure* and *Rule, Board Stick.*

RULE, BOARD MEASURE. A folding rule calibrated to read the number of board feet in a board of a given length. See also *Rule, Board Stick.*

Wooden

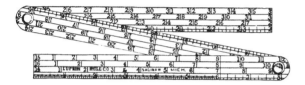

Steel

Board Measure Rule

RULE, BOARD STICK. A long rule calibrated to read the number of board feet in a board of given length. Usually made of hickory. Sometimes called BOARD RULE.

Flat

Round

Walking Cane

Board Stick Rule

RULE, BOXWOOD. Any flat or folding rule made of box-wood. Turkey boxwood was considered by some

suppliers to the best possible material for use in making rules. Most of the folding rules extant are made of box-wood.

RULE, BRASS BOUND. A rule that has a brass strip along each edge. A 4 or 6 fold rule that has brass along the outside edges only is said to be "Half Bound".

RULE, BUTTON GAUGE. A caliper rule marked in units called "Lines". The diameter of a button is generally measured in lines, each of which is equivalent to 1/40 of an inch.

Button Gauge

RULE, CALCULATING. Also called GUNTERS' RULE, GUNTERS' SLIDE RULE and SLIDE RULE. A rule having logarithm or trigonometric scales that can be used for making calculations.

Calculating Rule

RULE, CALIPER. A rule, with a sliding caliper, suitable for measuring round or irregular objects. See also *Rule, Button Gauge* and *Rule, Cordage.*

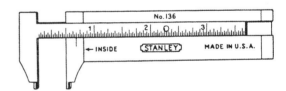

Inside-Outside

Two Fold

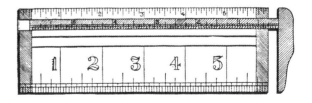

Spoke

Caliper Rule

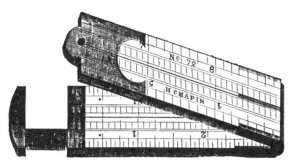

Four Fold

Caliper Rule

RULE, CIRCUMFERENCE. A rule that has scales calibrated in inches and pi times inches. The circumference of a circle can be read directly from the rule by scaling the diameter. Length is 1 to 4 feet. This type of rule is especially useful to tinners.

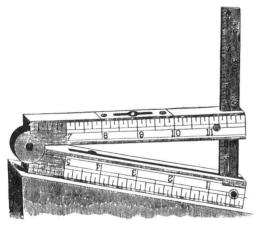

Circumference Rule

RULE, COMBINATION. An adjustable rule containing a level vial and a third leg. The illustrated rule can be used as a scale, bevel, T square, plumb or protractor.

Combination Rule

RULE, CORDAGE. A wide caliper rule used to measure the diameter of a rope.

Cordage Rule

RULE, CORK MEASURE. A rule used to select the proper cork for a standard bottle. A drug store tool.

Cork Measure

RULE, COTTON STAPLE. A rule intended for measuring the length of cotton fibres.

Cotton Staple Rule

RULE, CRUISERS' STICK. A timber cruisers' rule that has a hypsometer scale, a Biltmore scale and a board foot scale. The illustrated rule is one meter long. The hypsometer scale is used to determine height (length of the log) of a standing tree. The Biltmore scale will indicate the diameter of the tree. Both of these scales are used by sighting across the rule to a given point on the tree.

Cruisers' Stick

RULE, DESK. See *Rule, School.*

RULE, DRAFTING. A 12 inch rule with various scales intended for use in mechanical drawing. See also *Rule, Architects'*.

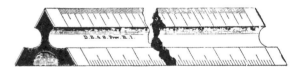

Wooden

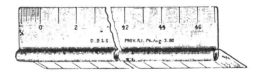

Metal

Drafting Rule

RULE, ENGINEERS'. A rule having a slide and tables for calculating weights and measures of common commodities.

Engineers' Rule

391

RULE, EXTENSION. An extendable rule used for measuring the inside of an opening such as a doorway or window well. The rule is calibrated to be read directly in the extended position.

Extension Rule

RULE, EYE GLASS. A rule used to select the proper frames and bows of eye glasses. The illustrated tool is scaled in inches and millimeters.

Eye Glass Rule

RULE, FOLDING. A hinged rule that can be folded endwise for convenience in storage.

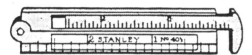

Two Fold

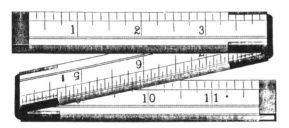

Three Fold

Four Fold

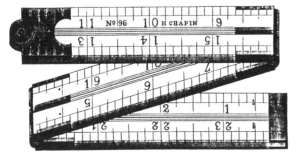

Six Fold

Folding Rule

RULE, FORWARDING STICK. A solid five foot rule used to measure cargo for rail or water shipment. One end is fitted with a T head for convenience in rapid measurement of large objects.

RULE, GAUGING ROD. A tool used to measure the amount of liquid in a barrel or cask.

Gauging Rod

RULE, GLASS CUTTERS'. A rigid rule used by a glass cutter for measurement and layout and as a straight edge. Length is 2 to 7 feet. The illustrated rule has a brass lip.

Glass Cutters' Rule

RULE, GUNTERS'. See *Rule, Calculating.*

RULE, GUNTERS' SLIDE. See *Rule, Calculating.*

RULE, HEM MEASURE. A short scale used by a seamstress to measure the amount of material to be turned up for a hem. The illustrated rule has a three inch scale and a moveable slide. It has a sterling silver handle.

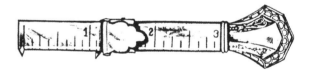

Hem Measure

RULE, HORSE MEASURE. A unique scale used to measure the size of a horse or mule. Size is specified as hands high at the withers. A hand is 4 inches. In order to attain a true vertical measurement, a cross bar with a level vial was often used. A telescoping or folding mechanism was sometimes incorporated to facilitate storage or to allow the rule to double as a walking cane.

RULE, INSIDE MEASURE. See *Rule, Extension* and *Rule, Slide.*

RULE, IVORY. A folding rule made of ivory rather than boxwood. German silver was generally used for the hinges and the binding on ivory rules. This variety of rule was bought for appearance rather than utility. Boxwood was considered by the makers to be a better material for the purpose and was less expensive. These rules were often used to occupy the top tray of a gentlemans' tool box or as a desk accessory. They also made excellent vest-pocket pieces.

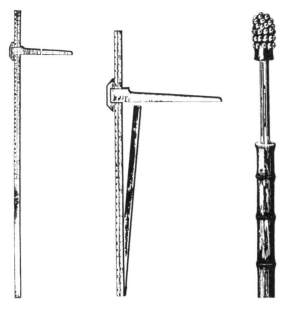

Folding   Walking Cane

Tape

Horse Measure

RULE, KEY SEAT. A tool used by a machinist as a straight edge to draw parallel lines on a round shaft. Length is 4 to 8 inches.

Key Seat Rule

RULE, LOG. See *Rule, Log Measure.*

RULE, LOG MEASURE. Also called LOG RULE and LOG STICK. A rule used to indicate the number of board feet of lumber in a log of a given length. The flat type is usually made of hickory. Length is 4 to 5 feet. See also *Rule, Spring Joint.*

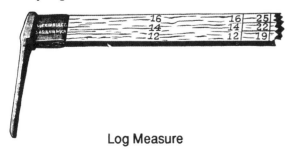

Log Measure

Log Measure

RULE, LOG STICK. See *Rule, Log Measure.*

RULE, MANUAL TRAINING. Also called BENCH RULE and MANUAL TRAINING BENCH RULE. A one or two foot rule used in high school and other manual training classes.

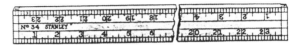

Manual Training Rule

RULE, MEASURING STICK. A three to six foot utility rule with standard graduations. The three foot rule is usually called a yard stick. The five foot stick was listed by one supplier as a WOOD MEASURE.

Measuring Stick

RULE, METER. Also called METER STICK. A rule that is one meter long and calibrated in the metric scale.

RULE, METER STICK. See *Rule, Meter.*

RULE, METRIC. Any rule that is marked with the metric scale.

RULE, PARALLEL. Also called PARALLEL BAR. A tool used by a draftsman or architect to construct a straight line parallel with another line. The rolling type rule has two knurled rollers that contact the table and cause the rule to move in a straight line. It was offered in 12 and 18 inch lengths. Length of the folding type is 6 to 24 inches.

Rolling

Folding

Parallel Rule

RULE, PATTERN MAKERS'. See *Rule, Shrinkage.*

RULE, POCKET. Any rule small enough to carry in the pocket. The rules that folded down to three inches were popular for pocket use. A small ivory or boxwood rule was often carried in a gentlemans' vest pocket.

RULE, PRINTERS'. A metal rule, usually made of brass, used by a printer or typesetter to measure a stick of type or a space. These rules are graduated in picas and inches. A pica is equivalent to 1/6 of an inch.

Printers' Rule

RULE, SADDLERS'. A 2 or 3 foot boxwood rule favored by leather workers. Both straight and one-fold varieties were available.

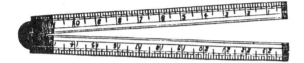

Saddlers' Rule

RULE, SCARF CUTTERS'. A rule used to lay out a long scarf. Width of the illustrated rule is 3 inches. One edge is made of brass to provide a durable surface for use as a straight edge.

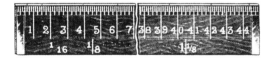

Scarf Cutters' Rule

RULE, SCHOOL. Also called DESK RULE and SCHOLARS RULE. A 12 inch utility rule with a beveled edge.

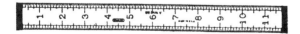

School Rule

RULE, SHIP CARPENTERS' BEVEL. A combined rule and bevel with either one or two tongues. The body of the rule is generally made of boxwood. The tongue is made of brass.

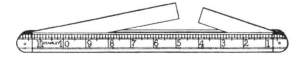

Ship Carpenters' Bevel

RULE, SHRINKAGE. Also called PATTERN MAKERS' RULE and PATTERN MAKERS' SHRINKAGE RULE. A rule that is slightly oversized for making casting patterns. Each pattern is made somewhat larger than the desired size of the casting to account for shrinkage of the metal as it cools. Several increments of size were available for measuring patterns intended for use with various metals.

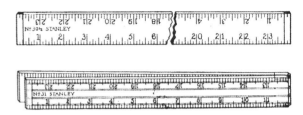

Shrinkage Rule

RULE, SLIDE. A rule that extends by sliding action of each jointed section. Available in lengths of 2 to 6 feet. This type of rule is ideal for measuring the inside of a door or window opening. See also *Rule, Calculating*.

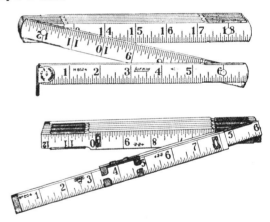

Slide Rule

RULE, SPRING JOINT. A rule that extends by folding around a flat swivel joint at the end of each section. Length is 3 to 8 feet. Made of aluminum, boxwood, maple or steel.

Extension Type

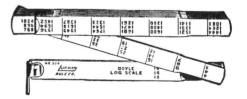

Log

Spring Joint Rule

RULE, STAVE. Also called HOOK STAVE RULE. A short rule used to measure the width of a barrel stave.

Stave Rule

RULE, STEAM VALVE. A rule used to measure the throat of a large steam valve. The illustrated rule has graduations of 1/80 of an inch.

Steam Valve Rule

RULE, TAILORS'. A rule used as a scale and layout tool when making a garment. These rules often are curved on one or both edges. The rule shown in illustration (c) is intended to measure from waistband to underarm. It was patented March 27, 1894.

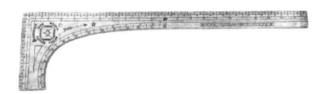

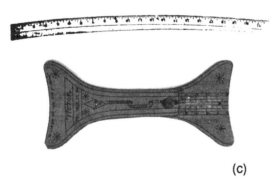

(c)

Tailors' Rule

RULE, WANTAGE ROD. A rule used to determine the amount of liquid required to fill a coopered container.

Wantage Rod

RULE, WOOD MEASURE. See *Rule, Measuring Stick*.

RULE, YARD STICK. A straight rule that is one yard long. Folding varieties were also available. The type shown in illustration (b) is intended to be attached to the inside of a store counter. See also *Rule, Measuring Stick*.

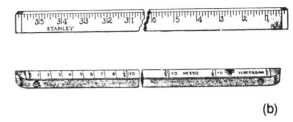

(b)

Yard Stick

RULE ATTACHMENT. Also called RULE GAUGE and RULE TOOL. A device used to convert a common rule into a square and miter. The tool clamps to a one inch rule by means of an eccentric, spring clip or set screw.

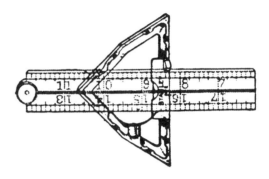

Three Angle Rule Tool

Campbell Tool

Rule Attachment

RULE CLAMP. See *Clamp, Rule*.

RULE GAUGE. A device that can be clamped to any standard folding rule to form a gauge or stop.

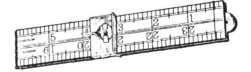

Rule Gauge

RULE AND HOLDER. A machinists' measuring tool comprised of short sections of steel rule intended to be grasped in the split chuck of a short holder. Used for measuring in a recess where a standard rule is not convenient.

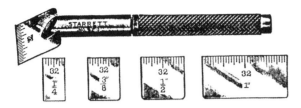

Rule and Holder

RULER. See *Rule*.

S

Tool names starting with the letter S including multiple listings of:

SAMPLER
SAW
SCALES
SCRAPER
SCREW DRIVER
SHARPENING STONE
SHEARS
SHOE MAKERS' TOOL
SHOVEL
SLEDGE
SPOKE SHAVE
SQUARE
STAKE

Included also are listings of tools used by the:

SADDLE AND HARNESS MAKER
SHIP BUILDER
SHOE MAKER
SLATER
STONE CUTTER
STONE MASON
STONE QUARRYMAN

S WRENCH. See *Wrench, S*.

SABOT MAKERS' AXE. See *Axe, Clog Makers'*.

SABOT MAKERS' TOOLS. See *Clog Makers' Tools*.

SADDLE. See *Anvil Tool, Saddle*.

SADDLE AND HARNESS TOOLS. There is considerable overlap of tools between the various leather working trades. Many of the saddle and harness makers' tools were also listed as TRIMMERS' TOOLS. See also *Book Binders' Tools* and *Shoe Tools*. The special-purpose saddle and harness tools listed below can be found in normal alphabetical sequence. These tools may also have been used for other purposes.

ANVIL, HARNESS MAKERS'
AWL, HARNESS
AWL, LACING
AWL, STRIP
AWL, THONG
AWL, SADDLERS' STRINGING
COMPASS, LEATHER
DRAW GAUGE
HAMMER, SADDLERS'
HAMMER, SNOB
HORSE COLLAR TOOL, STUFFING ROD

KNIFE, LEATHER
LACE CUTTER
LACE CUTTER, COMBINATION
LACING NEEDLE
LEATHER MACHINE, CREASING
LEATHER MACHINE, EMBOSSING
LEATHER MACHINE, LAP SKIVER
LEATHER MACHINE, LOOP PRESS
LEATHER MACHINE, SPLITTER
LEATHER MACHINE, SKIRT CHANNELING
LEATHER MACHINE, TRACE TRIMMER
LEATHER TOOL, BAG PUNCH
LEATHER TOOL, BAG PUNCH GAUGE
LEATHER TOOL, BEADER
LEATHER TOOL, BEADER CHUCK
LEATHER TOOL, BEVELER
LEATHER TOOL, BEVELING MACHINE
LEATHER TOOL, BLEEDER
LEATHER TOOL, BOUNCER
LEATHER TOOL, BOX LOOP EDGER
LEATHER TOOL, BUCKLE TONGUE PUNCH
LEATHER TOOL, CARVING
LEATHER TOOL, CHAMFER
LEATHER TOOL, CHANNELER
LEATHER TOOL, CONCHO CUTTER
LEATHER TOOL, COUNTERSINK
LEATHER TOOL, CREASER
LEATHER TOOL, CROWN SPLITTER
LEATHER TOOL, CUTTING DIE
LEATHER TOOL, DRAWING PLATE
LEATHER TOOL, EDGER
LEATHER TOOL, EMBOSSING WHEEL CARRIAGE
LEATHER TOOL, HARNESS MAKERS' PRESS
LEATHER TOOL, MODELING
LEATHER TOOL, OVERSTITCH WHEEL
LEATHER TOOL, PINKING IRON
LEATHER TOOL, PRICKING IRON
LEATHER TOOL, PRICKING WHEEL
LEATHER TOOL, PRICKING WHEEL CARRIAGE
LEATHER TOOL, ROUND PUNCH GAUGE
LEATHER TOOL, ROUNDER
LEATHER TOOL, SCALLOPING WHEEL
LEATHER TOOL, SINKING
LEATHER TOOL, SLICKER
LEATHER TOOL, SPREADING
LEATHER TOOL, STAMP
LEATHER TOOL, STAR STITCHER PUNCH
LEATHER TOOL, STIPPLING

LEATHER TOOL, STRAP END PUNCH
LEATHER TOOL, STRAP HOLDER
LEATHER TOOL, SWIVEL CUTTER
LEATHER TOOL, TICKLER
LEATHER TOOL, TRACE PUNCH
LEATHER TOOL, TRACE PUNCH GAUGE
LEATHER TOOL, TRIMMER
LEATHER TOOL, V
MALLET, SADDLERS'
MAUL, RAWHIDE
PINCERS, TACKING
PLIERS, LACING
PLIERS, SADDLERS'
PUNCH, BUCKLE LOOP
PUNCH, LACE
PUNCH, LEATHER
RASP, SADDLE TREE
RIVETING MACHINE
RUBBING HOOK
RULE, SADDLERS'
SHOE MAKERS' TOOL, LEVER CLAMP
SHOE MAKERS' TOOL, SLICK BONE
SPOKE SHAVE, SINGLE HANDLE
STRAINING JACK
TACK CLAW
TACK AND RIVET HOLDER
TRIMMERS' CLIP

SADDLE MAKERS' TOOLS. See *Saddle* and *Harness Tools.*

SADDLE STAMP. See *Leather Tool, Stamp.*

SADDLERS' AWL. See *Awl, Harness.*

SADDLERS' COMPASS. See *Compass, Leather.*

SADDLERS' TOOLS. See *Saddle* and *Harness Tools.*

SAFETY AXE. See *Hatchet, Guarded.*

SAFETY EDGER. See *Leather Tool, Edger.*

SAFETY FILE. See *File, Safety.*

SAFETY HATCHET. See *Hatchet, Guarded.*

SAFETY POCKET AXE. See *Hatchet, Guarded.*

SAIL CLOTH SLITTER. A right and left hand pair of heavy iron slitters capable of holding razor blade type cutters. The cutter extends below the flat surface of the tool such that it will cut as the tool is pushed across a workpiece.

Sail Cloth Slitter

SAIL MAKERS' BENCH HOOK. See *Hook, Sail Makers'.*

SAIL MAKERS' HOOK. See *Hook, Sail Makers'.*

SAIL MAKERS' PALM. See *Sewing Palm.*

SAIL MAKERS' PRICKER. See *Pricker.*

SAIL MAKERS' SEAM RUBBER. See *Seam Rubber.*

SAILORS' PALM. See *Sewing Palm.*

SAILORS' SEWING PALM. See *Sewing Palm.*

SALTPETRE TONGS. See *Tongs, Saltpetre.*

SAMPLER. A tool used to remove a sample from a bulk quantity of the specified material.

SAMPLER, BUTTER. See *Sampler, Cheese.*

SAMPLER, CEMENT. Also called FLOUR AUGER, SUGAR AUGER and SUGAR GIMLET. A tool used to take a sample from a barrel of cement, flour or sugar. An auger or gimlet point allows the tool to penetrate a barrel stave to reach the contents at any point. Length is 10 to 24 inches.

Cement Sampler

SAMPLER, CHEESE. Also called BUTTER SAMPLER, BUTTER TRIER, CHEESE SAMPLER, TALLOW SAMPLER and TALLOW TRIER. A tool used to take a sample from a wheel of cheese or a tub of butter. Also used for sampling tallow. Length is 4 to 36 inches.

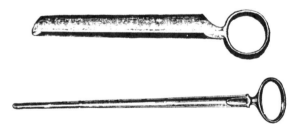

Cheese Sampler

SAMPLER, COFFEE. See *Sampler, Grain.*

SAMPLER, COTTON. Also called COTTON GIMLET. A barbed instrument used for pulling a sample of cotton from the inside of a bale. Length is 16 to 20 inches.

Cotton Sampler

Sampler, Grain. Also called COFFEE TRIER, GRAIN TRIER, GRAIN TRYER, RICE SAMPLER, RICE TRIER, SEED SAMPLER and SEED TRIER. The device shown in illustration (a) is used to take a sample of coffee, grain or seed from a burlap bag. Length is 4 to 12 inches. Illustration (b) sampler consists of two hollow tubes with overlapping holes. This device can be used to obtain a true sample of a truck or car lot of grain. Also used for beans, coffee and peanuts. Length is 4 to 5 feet. The tool shown in illustration (c) can be pushed into a bin, boxcar or elevator to sample grain at any depth. As the tool is withdrawn, the linked cap opens to accept the sample. The device was sold with 18 feet of extension handle.

Samson

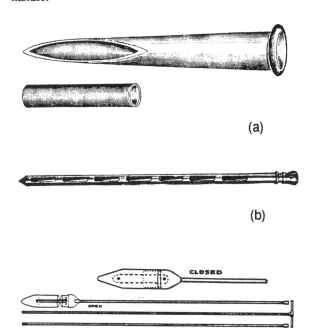

(a)

(b)

(c)

Grain Sampler

SAMPLER, RICE. See *Sampler, Grain.*

SAMPLER, SEED. See *Sampler, Grain.*

SAMPLER, SUGAR. See *Sampler, Cement.*

SAMPLER, TALLOW. See *Sampler, Cheese.*

SAMSON. A special-purpose wheelwrights' clamp used to draw two felloes of a wagon wheel together prior to nailing on a strake. The samson was hooked around a spoke on one side of the felloe joint and a nail head on the adjacent strake. The nuts of the samson were then tightened to draw the ends of the felloes together. The continuous wagon tire replaced strakes and eliminated the need for this tool.

SAND RAMMER. See *Rammer, Bench* and *Rammer, Sand.*

SAND SCREEN. A framed screen used to separate the large particles from sand. Used by brick masons, moulders and plasterers. See also *Riddle.*

Sand Screen

SAND SHOVEL. See *Shovel, Round Point.*

SANDPAPER. Sandpaper was made by early American craftsmen by spreading glue on heavy paper or cloth and then pressing sand into the glue. It was also offered commercially in some of the earliest American trade catalogues. The William H. Carr Catalogue of 1838 offered at least 6 different grits of sandpaper.

SANDPAPER BLOCK. A block covered with sandpaper. Size of the illustrated block is 2 1/2 by 4 inches.

1886

Sandpaper Block

SASH BRUSH. See *Brush, Sash.*

SASH COPING PLANE. See *Plane, Coping.*

SASH FILLETSTER. See *Plane, Sash Filletster.*

SASH PLANE. See *Plane, Sash.*

SASH POINT DRIVER. Also called DIAMOND POINT DRIVER and POINT DRIVER. A device used to drive glaziers' points into a window sash.

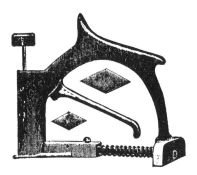

Sash Point Driver

SASH PULLEY DRIVER. Also called PULLEY SET BLOCK. A tool that is placed over the face of a sash cord pulley assembly when driving it into the mortise. The driver allows the pulley to be inserted squarely without damaging the pulley housing.

Sash Pulley Driver

SASH TOOL. See *Brush, Sash.*

SAUSAGE MEAT CHOPPER. See *Cleaver.*

SAW. A thin tool, usually iron or steel, with teeth formed along one or more edges. Used to cut rigid material such as wood or metal. The saw is one of the most ancient forms of tools. The sharp edges of shells and stones used by American Indians for cutting can be classified either as saws or as knives. Inasmuch as these crude tools are generally notched and are used in a reciprocating fashion, they meet all of the general criteria of a saw. It has been reported that steel saws were made commercially in the United States starting in 1806.

SAW, BACK. Also called TENON SAW. A saw with the back of the blade stiffened to reduce bending and wobble. Length is 8 to 24 inches.

Back Saw

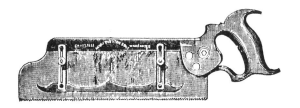

With Gauge

Back Saw

SAW, BAND. See *Saw, Foot and Hand Power.*

SAW, BEAD. A saw used for scoring window and door frames for insertion of weather stripping.

Bead Saw

SAW, BENCH. Also called BENCH HACK SAW. A bench-mounted cutoff saw for metal. See also *Saw, Joiner.*

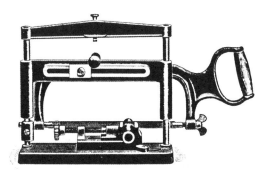

Bench Saw

SAW, BONE. A medical tool used in orthopedic surgery.

Bone Saw

SAW, BOTTOMING. A comb makers' tool used for rounding and evening the spaces between the teeth of a comb.

Bottoming Saw

SAW, BOW. See *Saw, Turning.*

400

SAW, BRACKET. A small frame saw with a deep throat used for cutting intricate curves in thin wood. Also called Buhl Saw, Fret Saw and Scroll Saw. The buhl saw is generally listed as having an especially deep throat and a very thin blade.

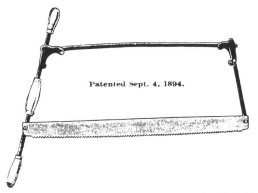

Jacobs' Patent

Saw Buck

Buck Saw

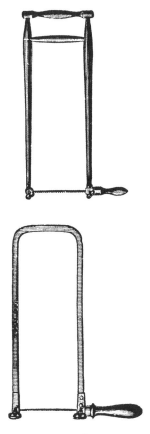

Bracket Saw

SAW, BUHL. See *Saw, Bracket.*

SAW, BUTCHER. A saw used by a butcher for cutting bones. Length is 18 to 36 inches.

Beef Splitting

Butcher Saw

SAW, BUCK. Also called FRAMED WOOD SAW and WOOD SAW. A one-man framed saw with coarse cross-cut teeth. Used primarily to cut firewood. The saw buck, as shown in the illustration, provides a means of holding a short log while sawing. The saw buck was listed by a few suppliers but was generally home made.

SAW, CABINET. A fine toothed saw used by a cabinet maker. The framed cabinet saw is similar to a Turning Saw except that the cabinet saw generally has a wider blade. The framed variety was also called COOPERS' SAW and FRAME SAW.

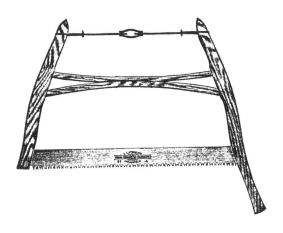

Buck Saw

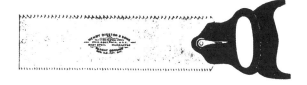

Cabinet Saw

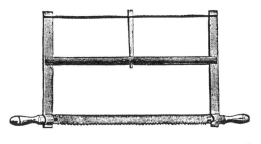

Framed

Cabinet Saw

SAW, CHAIN. A saw that is made flexible by use of jointed links. This type of saw can be used to cut through the back side of a workpiece that is inaccessible to other types of saws.

Chain Saw

SAW, CIRCULAR. See *Saw, Foot and Hand Powered.*

SAW, COMBINATION. A hand saw in which the back can be used as a scale or straight edge. The illustrated saw has a scratch awl and a spirit level incorporated into the handle.

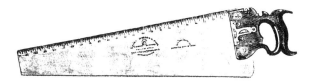

Combination Saw

SAW, COMPASS. Also called KEYHOLE SAW. A narrow saw that can be used to cut a shallow curve in thin stock. Length of the blade is 8 to 18 inches. See also *Saw, Pad.*

Compass Saw

SAW, COOPERS'. See *Saw, Cabinet* and *Saw, Turning.*

SAW, COPING. A rudimentary version of the Bracket Saw intended for occasional household or amateur use.

SAW, CROSS CUT. A long saw with coarse teeth intended for cutting green timber. The cross cut was originally used for cutting logs to length and for squaring up axe

butts. It was not until late in the nineteenth century that the cross cut came into general use for felling trees. Lengths up to 25 feet have been reported. See also *Saw, Hand.*

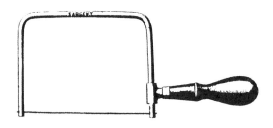

Coping Saw

One-Man

Two-Man

Virginia Pattern

Cross Cut Saw

SAW, DEHORNING. A saw used to cut the horns from cattle. Length of the blade is approximately 10 inches.

Dehorning Saw

SAW, DOCKING. Also called FRAMING SAW. A heavy hand saw, with coarse teeth, used for cutoff work around mills and yards and for large framing work. The illustrated tool has 4 1/2 teeth per inch.

402

Docking Saw

SAW, DOVETAIL. A small back saw used for cutting dovetails and for similar shallow work. Length of the blade is 6 to 12 inches. The dovetail saw has has extra-fine teeth (15 points per inch) with very little set.

Dovetail Saw

SAW, ELECTROTYPE FINISHERS'. Used for sawing projecting type or sections from the back of plates after corrections have been soldered in place. Note the offset handle. Blade of the illustrated saw is 3 ½ inches long.

Electrotype Finishers' Saw

SAW, FELLOE. Also called FRAME SAW. A saw used by a wheelwright to cut the curved felloe sections for making a wagon wheel.

Felloe Saw

SAW, FLOOR. Also called FLOORING SAW. A hand saw with teeth on the top front edge. Length of blade is 18 inches. The unique shape of this saw will allow a section of flooring to be cut out without making a starting hole for insertion of the saw blade. See also *Saw, Rabbet.*

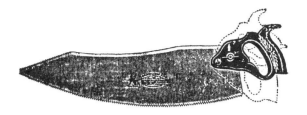

Floor Saw

SAW, FLOORING. See *Saw, Floor.*

SAW, FOOT AND HAND POWERED. A sawing machine powered by a hand crank or by the users feet. The illustrated rip saw was advertised by the supplier as being capable of ripping 6000 lineal feet of one inch pine in a 10 hour shift.

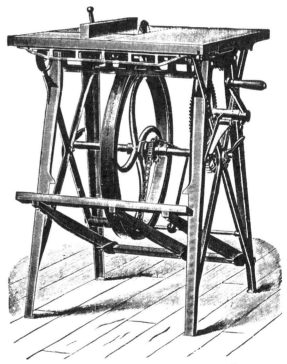

Crosscut

Foot and Hand Powered Saw

SAW, FRAME. See *Saw, Cabinet; Saw, Felloe* and *Saw, Turning.*

SAW, FRAMING. See *Saw, Docking.*

SAW, FRET. See *Saw, Bracket.*

SAW, FUTTOCK. A narrow two-man rip saw used in the ship building industry to cut timbers to a shallow curve. Used for the same general purpose as the longer Whip Saw. Width of the blade is 1 ½ to 4 ½ inches.

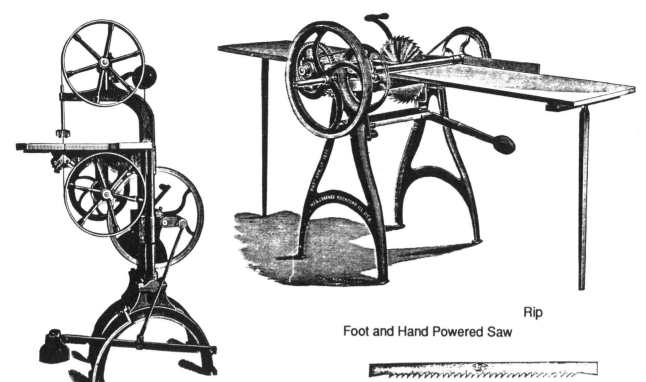

Band Saw

Rip

Foot and Hand Powered Saw

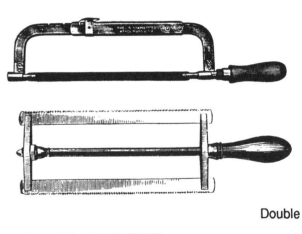

Futtock Saw

SAW, HACK. A saw intended for cutting metal. Length of blade is 6 to 20 inches except for the jewelers' saw which has a 5 inch blade. See also *Saw, Bench* and *Saw, Rail*.

Double

Jewelers'

For Car Bands

Scroll or Velocipede

Foot and Hand Powered Saw

Hack Saw

SAW, HALF BACK. Also called HALF BACK BENCH SAW. A saw with a portion of the blade stiffened at the back. Length of blade is 14 to 20 inches.

Half Back Saw

SAW, HAND. A one-handed saw used for general-purpose woodworking. This type of saws was often sub-divided into Cross Cut, Panel and Rip Saws. See also *Saw, Combination; Saw, Docking* and *Saw, Ship Carpenters'*. Cross Cut Saws have considerable set and are used for cutting across the grain of the wood. Blade length is 14 to 28 inches. A common length is 26 inches. Number of teeth per inch is 6 to 12. The early definition of a hand saw was a cross cut saw with a 26 inch blade. Panel Saws are the same as the cross cut except shorter. Many early catalogues referred to any cross cut hand saw under 24 inches as a Panel Saw. Blade length is 12 to 24 inches. Some suppliers referred to a small panel saw as a PONY SAW or KIT SAW.

Rip Saws are used for cutting with the grain of the wood. The teeth have little or no set. Blade length is 18 to 36 inches; a common length is 28 inches. Number of teeth per inch is 4 to 7. A short rip saw is sometimes called a SPLITTING SAW.

Many questions have been asked about the nib on the front end of a hand saw. The following statement regarding the nib is a quote from *The Saw In History*, copyright 1921 by *Henry Disston:* "It is of no practical use; merely serving to break the straight line of the back of the blade and is only ornamental".

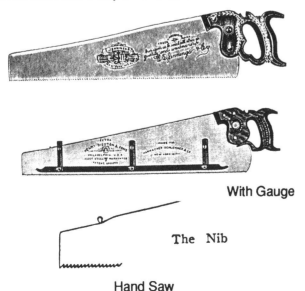

With Gauge

The Nib

Hand Saw

Timber

Hand Saw

SAW, HOUSEHOLD. A general-purpose hand operated saw. Length is 26 inches.

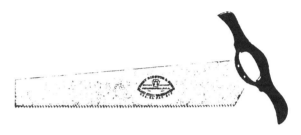

Household Saw

SAW, HOUSING. See *Saw, Stair.*

SAW, ICE. A saw used primarily by farmers and cattlemen for cutting holes in the ice to allow access to the water below the ice. In cold weather the ice must be cut twice a day to allow the livestock to reach the water. The hand ice saw is 24 to 36 inches long and the pond saw is up to 6 feet long. The crescent saw is an ice harvest tool used in the storage house to start the separation when an entire layer of blocks were frozen together. Teeth of the ice saw do not have any set.

Wagon or Hand

Pond

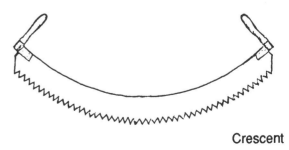

Crescent

Ice Saw

Hollow Back or One Hand
Ice Saw

SAW, JEWELERS'. A fine toothed saw used by a jeweler. Length of blade is 2 3/4 to 6 inches.

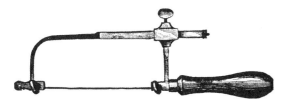

Jewelers' Saw

SAW, JOINER. Also called BENCH SAW. A cabinet makers' cross cut saw with extra fine teeth having very little set. Length of blade is approximately 17 inches.

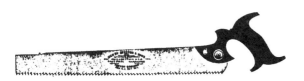

Joiner Saw

SAW, KEYHOLE. A narrow saw used for cutting small diameter holes. Length of blade is 10 to 12 inches. See also *Saw, Compass* and *Saw, Pad*.

Keyhole Saw

SAW, KIT. See *Saw, Hand*.

SAW, KITCHEN. A small version of the butchers' saw used in the home for cutting bones in meat. Length of the blade is 12 to 16 inches.

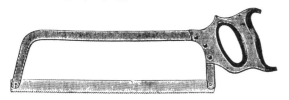

Kitchen Saw

SAW, METAL CUTTING. Also called HAND HACK SAW, METAL CUTTING HAND SAW and NAIL CUTTING SAW. A hand saw with small teeth tempered for cutting light metal. This type of saw is sometimes used by a carpenter when there is a possibility of striking a hidden nail. Length of blade is 18 to 26 inches.

Metal Cutting Saw

SAW, MITER BOX. Also called MITER SAW. A rigid saw intended for use in a miter box. Length of blade is 18 to 30 inches.

Miter Box Saw

SAW, NAIL CUTTING. See *Saw, Metal Cutting*.

SAW, NASAL. A surgical tool used for cutting bone and cartilage.

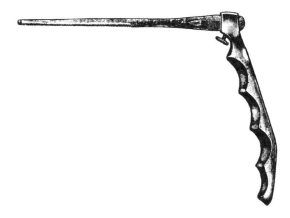

Nasal Saw

SAW, PAD. Also called KEYHOLE SAW. A type of narrow wood-cutting saw with interchangeable blades. Blade length is 6 to 13 inches. Blades of the pad saw are generally made to cut on the pull stoke.

Pad Saw

SAW, PANEL. A short variety of cross cut hand saw. See *Saw, Hand*.

Saw, Pattern Makers'. A saw intended for small accurate work in pattern or cabinet making. The illustrated saw has a 7 1/2 inch blade and 15 teeth per inch.

Pattern Makers' Saw

Saw, Pit. A saw intended for cutting boards or planks from a log. Length of a pit saw blade is 5 to 10 feet. The saw is so named because one man often stood in a pit to pull the saw on the down stroke. The pit saw is a primitive tool that was generally obsoleted by power driven saw mills. Inasmuch as water driven mills were operated for most of the American Colonial period, pit saws were used in America primarily for special purpose or short-run applications.

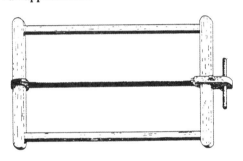

Framed

Open

Box

Tiller

Pit Saw

Saw, Plaster. A medical tool used to cut a plaster cast.

Plaster Saw

Saw, Plasterers'. A short hand saw with teeth on both sides. The coarse side is used for cutting plaster and the fine side is suitable for cutting wood. Length of blade is 14 to 18 inches. Also listed under linemans' tools as a Cablemans' Saw.

Plasterers' Saw

Saw, Plumbers'. A saw with fine teeth on one side that are suitable for cutting metal and coarse teeth on the other side. Length of blade is 12 to 18 inches.

Plumbers' Saw

Saw, Pony. See *Saw, Hand*.

Saw, Pork Packers'. A unique form of meat saw. Length of blade is 14 to 18 inches.

Pork Packers' Saw

Saw, Pruning. A saw used for cutting limbs and branches from a standing tree. Length of blade is 14 to 18 inches. Some types are equipped with 12 to 16 foot handles.

Saw, Rabbet. A saw used to cut a rabbet across the end grain of a workpiece. The tool shown in illustration (b) is also suitable for use as a Floor Saw or Stair Saw.

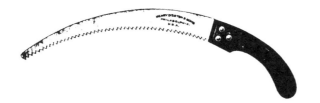

California Pattern

(b)

Rabbet Saw

Chisel Edged

With Hook

With Copper Handle

Pruning Saw

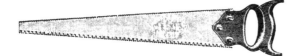

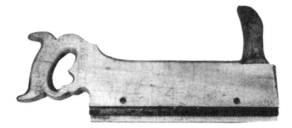

Rabbet Saw

SAW, RAIL. A large Hack Saw intended for use in cutting railroad rails. Length of blade is approximately 18 inches.

Rail Saw

SAW, RIP. A saw intended for cutting wood along the direction of the grain. See *Saw, Hand* and *Saw, Foot and Hand Powered.*

SAW, SCROLL. See *Saw, Bracket* and *Saw, Foot and Hand Powered.*

SAW, SHIP CARPENTERS'. Also called SHIP CARPENTERS' HAND SAW and SHIP CARPENTERS' RIP SAW. A saw similar to a Hand Saw but with a more pronounced taper of the blade. The ship carpenters' saw is narrow at the fore end. Length is 18 to 28 inches. Both cross cut and rip tooth varieties were available.

Ship Carpenters' Saw

SAW, SPLITTING. See *Saw, Hand.*

SAW, STAIR. Also called HOUSING SAW and STAIR BUILDERS' SAW. A saw used for cutting cross-grain notches of a given depth.

SAW, TENON. See *Saw, Back.*

Stair Saw

SAW, TURKISH. A small general-purpose wood saw with teeth that cut on the pull stroke. Length of blade is 12 to 16 inches. The tool was manufactured in America primarily for export.

Turkish Saw

SAW, TURNING. Also called BOW SAW, COOPERS' SAW, FRAME SAW and WEB SAW. A frame saw with a narrow blade used for cutting a curve. Length of blade is 10 to 36 inches. See also *Saw, Cabinet*.

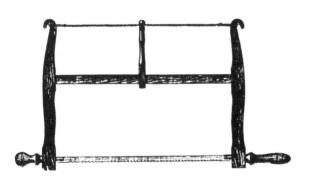

Turning Saw

SAW, VENEER. A saw used to cut veneer stock from a balk is shown in illustration (a). This type of saw has a heavy narrow frame and a wide blade. Width of the blade is 4 to 4 1/2 inches. The veneer saw shown in illustration (b) is a small hand tool used when applying and patching veneer.

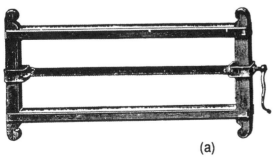

(a)

Veneer Saw

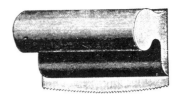

(b)

Veneer Saw

SAW, WEB. See *Saw, Turning*.

SAW, WHIP. Similar to an Open Pit Saw except that the blade is thin and flexible. Used by ship builders for cutting curved timbers. Length of blade is 5 to 7 1/2 feet. The whip saw is used with a box and tiller as shown under *Saw, Pit*.

Whip Saw

SAW, WOOD. See *Saw, Buck*.

SAW ANVIL. See *Anvil, Saw Makers'* and *Swage Bar*.

SAW BLADE PUNCH. See *Punch, Saw*.

SAW BUCK. See *Saw, Buck*.

SAW CLAMP. See *Vise, Saw*.

SAW FILE. See *File, Band Saw; File, Cant Saw; File, Cross Cut; File, Hook Tooth; File, Gin Saw* and *File, Taper*.

SAW FILE HOLDER. Also called SIDE FILE. A device used to hold and guide a side file for a circular or large band saw blade. A side file is used to remove any excess overhang of a tooth before sharpening.

Saw File Holder

SAW FILING GUIDE. A device used for holding the file at a fixed angle when filing a hand saw.

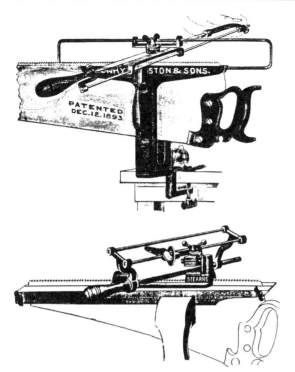

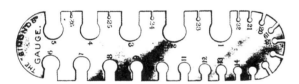

Saw Filing Guide

SAW FILING VISE. See *Vise, Saw*.

SAW GAUGE. A gauge used to determine the thickness of a saw blade. The number 1 thickness is .30 inches.

Saw Gauge

SAW GUMMER. A tool used to deepen the space between the teeth of a saw thus making the teeth longer. One type of gummer uses a punch action to remove the excess material. Later gummers use a grinding or milling action to accomplish the same purpose. When using the punch-type machine, it was recommended that alternate spaces be punched from opposite sides to reduce spring of the teeth.

1870

Saw Gummer

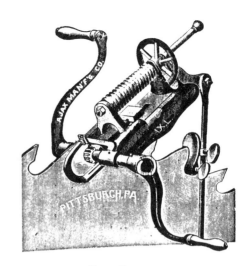

Saw Gummer

SAW HAMMER. See *Hammer, Saw; Hammer, Saw Setting* and *Hammer, Saw Swaging*.

SAW JOINTER. A device used to level the teeth of a saw prior to sharpening. A replaceable file or section of a file is used in the jointer. See also *Skate Sharpener*.

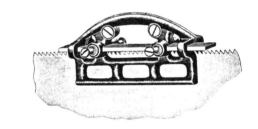

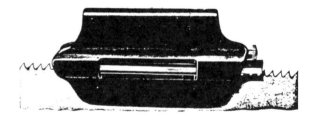

Saw Jointer

SAW JUMPER. See *Saw Swage*.

SAW MAKERS' ANVIL. See *Anvil, Saw Makers'*.

SAW MAKERS' HAMMER. See *Hammer, Saw*.

SAW PUNCH. See *Punch, Saw*.

SAW SCARF WEDGE. See *Wedge, Logging*.

SAW SET. A device used to bend the teeth of a cross cut saw. The teeth must be bent alternately to each side to widen the kerf and prevent binding. The bend is called "Set" and the tool used to impart the bend is called a SAW SET, SAW SETTER or SAW WREST. Some examples are illustrated.

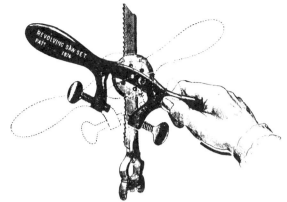

Disston's

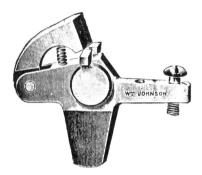

Aiken Hammer Type

Disston's

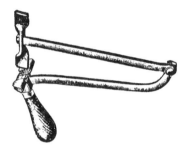

Bishop's Hammer Blow

French Type (Saw Wrest)

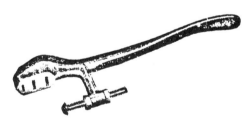

Buller

Foot Powered
Saw Set

1866 Patent
Saw Set

411

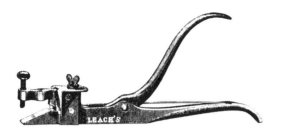

Leach's

Stillman's

Monarch

Saw Set

SAW SET BLOCK. A block used as a base for hammering and as a stop to gauge the proper amount of set to be hammered into a cross cut saw.

Morrill's

Saw Set Block

SAW SET GAUGE. A device used to gauge the amount of set in a saw.

Morins'

Saw Set Gauge

SAW SETTING HAMMER. See *Hammer, Saw, Setting.*

SAW SETTING MACHINE. A machine used for setting a band saw blade.

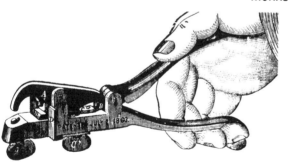

Nash's

Saw Set

Saw Setting Machine

SAW SETTING STAKE. See *Stake, Saw Setting.*

SAW STRAIGHT EDGE. See *Saw Tension Gauge.*

SAW SWAGE. Also called SAW JUMPER and UPSET. A tool used on large circular and mill saws to spread the points of teeth that have been reduced by wear and sharpening.

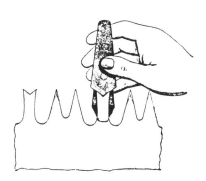

Raker Tooth Swage

For Circular Saw

Saw Swage

SAW SWAGING HAMMER. See *Hammer, Saw Swaging.*

SAW TENSION GAUGE. Also called SAW STRAIGHT EDGE. A gauge used to determine the flatness when tensioning a large circular saw or mill band saw. Length is 12 to 36 inches.

Saw Tension Gauge

SAW TOOTH GAUGE. A tool used to gauge and regulate the cleaner teeth on a cross cut saw. The gauge rests on two or more cutting teeth and indicates the proper length of the cleaner tooth.

Saw Tooth Gauge

SAW VISE. See *Vise, Circular Saw* and *Vise, Saw.*

SAW WEDGE. See *Wedge, Logging.*

SAW WREST. See *Saw Set.*

SAWDUST SCOOP. See *Shovel, Scoop.*

SAWING MACHINE. Also called FOLDING SAWING MACHINE. A one-man cross cut saw that is capable of felling and sectioning trees. The makers' brochure states that one man, using this machine, can cut 9 cords of wood in 10 hours.

Sawing Machine

SAX. See *Axe, Slaters'.*

SAXE. See *Axe, Slaters'.* Saxe is a variation of Sax.

SCALER. See *Fish Scaler.*

SCALES. A device for determining weight.

SCALES, ICE. Scales used by the door-to-door ice man when delivering ice. This type of scale was largely obsoleted when the common icebox was replaced by the refrigerator. These scales are widely called HIDE SCALES and BUFFALO HIDE SCALES in the midwest. Although they were probably used for a multitude of purposes, including the weighing of hides, catalogue entries list them only as ice scales.

SCALES, STEELYARD. Also called BEAM SCALES. A balance-type scale used for general-purpose weighing. Steelyard scales capable of handling weights up to 800 pounds were listed. This type of scale was widely used for weighing hay bales and cotton bales.

413

Ice Scales

Steelyard Scales

SCALING HAMMER. See *Hammer, Scaling.*

SCALLOPING MACHINE. See *Pinking and Scalloping Machine.*

SCALLOPING WHEEL. See *Leather Tool, Scalloping Wheel.*

SCALPEL. See *Knife, Operating.*

SCARF CUTTERS' RULE. See *Rule, Scarf Cutters'.*

SCARF WEDGE. See *Wedge, Logging.*

SCARFERS' KNIFE. See *Knife, Cot Scarfers'.*

SCHOLARS' RULE. See *Rule, School.*

School Rule. See *Rule, School.*

SCISSORS. See *Shears.*

SCISSORS SHARPENER. A device for sharpening household scissors. The scissors are worked with a cutting action across a small metal rod.

Scissors Sharpener

SCOOP. See *Gas Retort Scoop, Grain Scoop* and *Shovel, Scoop*

SCOOP NET. A handled net, made of welded steel links, used during the ice harvest to remove chips from the channel. The relative movement of the chain links during use served to reduce buildup of ice on the net. Diameter is approximately 15 inches.

Scoop Net

SCOOP SHOVEL. See *Shovel, Scoop.*

SCORER. See *Turpentine Hacker.*

SCORING AXE. See *Axe, Single Bit,* scoring pattern.

SCORP. See *Scorper.*

SCORPER. A one-handed tool used for hollowing out a shallow depression such as a chair seat. Usually called a chair makers' or bowl makers' tool. A similar tool, generally with a longer handle, was used by a cooper for smoothing the inside of a barrel or keg. See *In-Shave.*

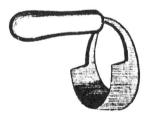

Scorper

SCOTCH HAMMER. See *Skutch.*

SCOTCH PATTERN ADZE. See *Adze, Hammer Head.*

SCOTIA. See *Plane, Moulding, Cove.*

SCOTIA HAMMER. See *Hammer, Scotia.*

SCOUT AXE. See *Axe, Boy Scout.*

SCOUT HATCHET. See *Axe, Boy Scout.*

SCRAPER. A tool, with a square edge, used to abrade the surface of the workpiece rather than to cut or shave. See also *Knife, Comb Makers'*.

SCRAPER, BEARING. Also called MACHINISTS' SCRAPER. A scraper used to clean open bearings and cylinder cavities. Overall length is 9 to 12 inches.

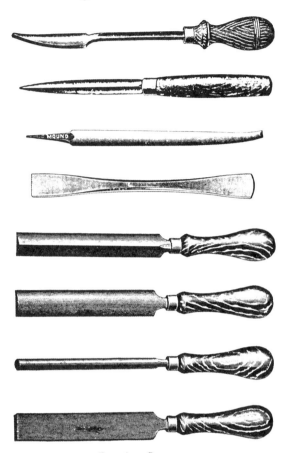

Bearing Scraper

SCRAPER, BEE HIVE. A scraper used by a bee keeper to clean hives and supers.

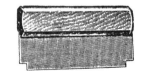

Frame

Section

Bee Hive Scraper

SCRAPER, BLOCK. See *Scraper, Butcher Block.*

SCRAPER, BOX. A scraper used to remove the markings from a wooden box or crate. See also *Scraper, Coopers'* and *Shave Hook.*

Box Scraper

SCRAPER, BUTCHER BLOCK. Also called BLOCK SCRAPER. A scraper used to clean and smooth the top of a butchers' block.

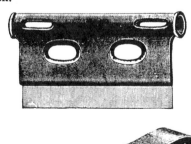

Butcher Block Scraper

SCRAPER, CABINET. Also called WOOD SCRAPER. A general purpose scraper used by cabinet makers and other craftsmen who work with wood. The edge is turned such that it removes a shaving much like that of a finely set plane. See also *Scraper, Rams Horn.*

Calendar Scraper

Or Glue Scraper

SCRAPER, CARBON. Also called **CYLINDER SCRAPER.** A tool used to remove carbon from the top cavity of an engine cylinder.

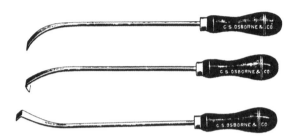

Carbon Scraper

SCRAPER, CARD. A weaving mill tool.

Card Scraper

SCRAPER, CHICKEN HOUSE. A scraper used for cleaning the floor and dropping boards of a chicken house. Also used for cleaning barn floors. Similar to a STABLE HOE.

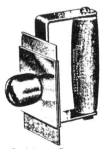

Cabinet Scraper

SCRAPER, CALENDER. A paper mill tool used to scrape off scabs and spots.

Chicken House Scraper

SCRAPER, COACH MAKERS'. Also called CABINET MAKERS' SCRAPER, GULL WING SCRAPER and GUN STOCK SCRAPER. A type of small two-handed scraper with the irons shaped in a variety of patterns. Gull wing handles are characteristic. Used for final finishing and shaping of small workpieces. The illustrated tools were used in a carriage makers' shop.

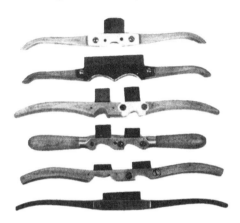

Coach Makers' Scraper

SCRAPER, COOPERS'. Also called BOX SCRAPER. A coopers' tool used to smooth a rough spot on a coopered container. Width is approximately 2 1/2 inches.

Coopers' Scraper

SCRAPER, CURVED. See *Scraper, Moulding*.

SCRAPER, CYLINDER. See *Scraper, Carbon*.

SCRAPER, DECK. See *Scraper, Ship*.

SCRAPER, ELECTROTYPE FINISHERS'. A steel scraper used for cleaning and revising plates. Length is 5 3/4 to 7 inches.

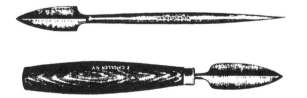

Electrotype Finishers' Scraper

SCRAPER, FLOOR. A scraper used for working a large surface such as a floor or bowling alley. The device shown in illustration (a) has a 6 inch blade and weighs 100 pounds. Illustration (b) shows a small hand-held tool having a replaceable canvas pad studded with stiff wire.

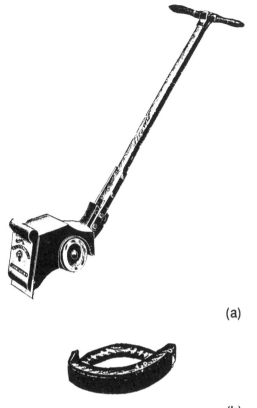

(a)

(b)

Floor Scraper

SCRAPER, FLUE. A tool used to clean the tubes and flues of a steam engine or other boiler.

Outside

Flue Scraper

SCRAPER, GLUE. See *Scraper, Cabinet*.

SCRAPER, HOG. A tool used to remove the hair from a hog carcass. The carcass is dipped in boiling water which loosens the hair sufficiently to allow ready removal by scraping.

417

Hog Scraper

SCRAPER, MACHINISTS'. See *Scraper, Bearing*.

SCRAPER, MOULDING. A tool used to scrape a curved surface such as a moulding.

Swan Neck or Oval

Moulding Scraper

SCRAPER, OVAL. See *Scraper, Moulding*.

SCRAPER, PLUMBERS'. See *Scraper, Tinners' Roofing* and *Shave Hook*.

SCRAPER, PUTTY. A putty knife that has a sharpened end for use in scraping old putty from a glass or sash.

Putty Scraper

SCRAPER, RAMS HORN. A type of two-handed wood scraper with graceful curved handles. This tool was listed by one supplier as a FLOOR SCRAPER.

Rams' Horn Scraper

SCRAPER, REED ORGAN. An tool used by an organ builder or repairman. Length is approximately 7 inches.

Reed Organ Scraper

SCRAPER, SHIP. Also called DECK SCRAPER. A shave hook with an 18 to 24 inch handle.

Ship Scraper

SCRAPER, SIDEWALK. Also called SIDEWALK CLEANER. A tool used to scrape ice from sidewalks and steps. Handle is approximately 4 1/2 feet long.

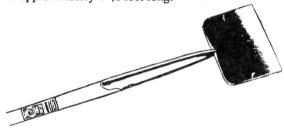

Sidewalk Scraper

SCRAPER, SKIN. A tool used by a taxidermist for cleaning and softening a dried skin. Length is 9 to 10 inches.

Skin Scraper

SCRAPER, TINNERS' ROOFING. Also called PLUMBERS' SCRAPER. Length is approximately 10 inches.

Tinners' Roofing Scraper

SCRAPER, TURPENTINE. A scraper used to remove the thickened rosin from the lower part of the slash on a turpentine tree. The illustrated tool is sharpened on both the forward and aft edges. Single-edge turpentine scrapers were also available.

Turpentine Scraper

SCRAPER, VENEER. Also called SCRAPER PLANE. A scraper used for finish work in preparation for installation of veneer. It is also suitable for general-purpose finish work on wood.

Veneer Scraper

SCRAPER, WALL. Also called PAINT SCRAPER. A tool used to remove wallpaper and dried paste. Also used to remove scaling paint from a flat surface. Width of blade is 3 to 4 inches. One variety can be fitted with a long handle.

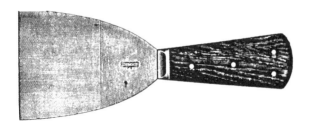

Wall Scraper

SCRAPER, WAX. A scraper used in the press room for smoothing off wax cases prior to moulding.

Wax Scraper

SCRAPER, WOOD. See *Scraper, Cabinet*.

SCRAPER PLANE. See *Plane, Scraper* and *Scraper, Veneer*.

SCRAPER STEEL. See *Burnishing Tool, Scraper*.

SCRATCH AWL. See *Awl, Scratch*.

SCRATCH BONE. See *Shoe Makers' Tool, Scratch Bone*.

SCRATCH BRUSH. See *Brush, Scratch* and *Brush, Wire*.

SCREEN. See *Riddle* and *Sand Screen*.

SCREW BOX. Also called SCREW CUTTER and WOOD SCREW CUTTER. A tap and matching die used for cutting the coarse threads and nuts for panel plow arms, vise screws and similar items. Sizes were available for cutting 1/4 to 2 inch diameter screws.

Wooden

Metal

Screw Box

SCREW CHASER. Also called THREAD CHASER. A hand-held lathe tool used for cleaning, cutting or straightening screw threads.

Screw Chaser

SCREW CLAMP. See *Clamp, Carriage Makers'*.

SCREW CUTTER. See *Screw Box*.

SCREW DRIVER. A tool used to tighten or loosen a screw.

SCREW DRIVER, ARCHIMEDES. Also called SPIRAL SCREW DRIVER. A screw driver in which the bit is attached to the end of a spiral shaft. The bit is caused to rotate by moving a nut or sleeve up and down the spiral. See also *Screw Driver, Bench*.

Archimedes Screw Driver

SCREW DRIVER, AUTOMATIC. See *Screw Driver, Push*.

SCREW DRIVER, BENCH. A screw driver mounted in a frame which can be attached to a work bench. Overall length of the illustrated tool is 17 1/2 inches.

Bench Screw Driver

SCREW DRIVER, CLOCK. Length of blade is 2 to 3 inches.

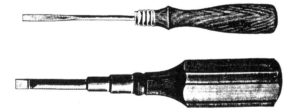

Clock Screw Driver

SCREW DRIVER, COMBINATION. A screw driver in which the handle can be swiveled to serve as a hammer.

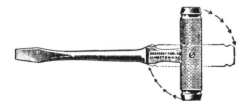

Combination Screw Driver

SCREW DRIVER, EYE GLASS. A very small screw driver used for repairing eye glasses. Overall length is approximately 2 1/2 inches. The blade of the illustrated tool can be concealed inside the handle while being carried on a watch chain or in the pocket.

Eye Glass Screw Driver

SCREW DRIVER, FLAT. A general-purpose screw driver with a flat handle. Length of blade is 1 1/2 to 12 inches.

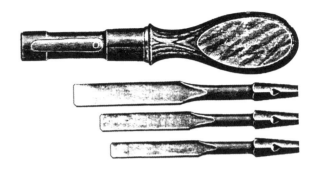

Clark's Patent

Flat Screw Driver

SCREW DRIVER, GUNSMITH. A short screw driver with a rigid blade.

Gunsmiths' Screw Driver

SCREW DRIVER, JEWELERS'. See *Screw Driver, Watch Makers'*.

SCREW DRIVER, LOCK NUT. A unique screw driver that will facilitate holding either a center screw or a special lock nut while the other one is being rotated. Used in telephone panel work and for typewriter repair.

Lock Nut Screw Driver

SCREW DRIVER, LOCKSMITHS'. Also called LOCK SCREW DRIVER. Length of blade is about 3 inches. The squares on the shank can be used to turn two sizes of door locks that have the knobs and shafts removed.

SCREW DRIVER, OFFSET. A screw driver with the handle offset 90 degrees from the blade. Length is 4 to 10 inches.

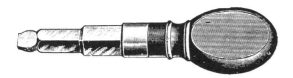

Locksmiths' Screw Driver

Offset Screw Driver

SCREW DRIVER, PERFECT HANDLE. See *Perfect Handle Tool.*

SCREW DRIVER, PIANO. Blade length is 2 to 12 inches.

Piano Screw Driver

SCREW DRIVER, PISTOL GRIP. A ratchet screw driver with the handle offset to increase leverage. The illustrated tool has three interchangeable blades. The blades are 12 inches long.

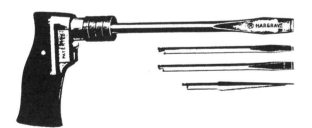

Pistol Grip Screw Driver

SCREW DRIVER, POCKET. A small screw driver with a means of withdrawing or covering the point while being carried in the pocket. Length is 3 to 4 inches.

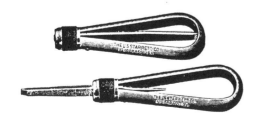

Pocket Screw Driver

Billings' Magazine
Pocket Screw Driver

SCREW DRIVER, PUG. A screw driver with a very short blade and handle. This type of tool later became known as a STUBBY SCREW DRIVER.

Pug

SCREW DRIVER, PUSH. Also called AUTOMATIC SCREW DRIVER and SPIRAL SCREW DRIVER. A spiral-shaft screw driver in which the point is made to rotate by pushing on the handle.

Push Screw Driver

SCREW DRIVER, RATCHET. A screw driver containing a mechanism that allows the point to be rotated in one direction only while moving the handle in a reciprocating fashion. See also *Screw Driver, Pistol Grip.*

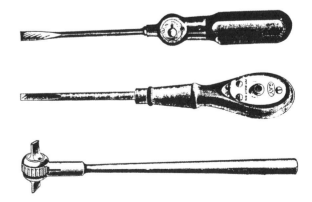

Ratchet Screw Driver

Ratchet Screw Driver

SCREW DRIVER, ROUND HANDLE. A common general-purpose screw driver with a round handle. Length of blade is 1 1/2 to 15 inches.

Round Handle Screw Driver

SCREW DRIVER, SCREW HOLDING. A screw driver with two clasps arranged to grasp and hold the head of a common wood screw. The illustrated device was patented August 11, 1873. See also *Screw Holder*.

Kolb's Patent

Screw Holding Screw Driver

SCREW DRIVER, SEWING MACHINE. A type of small screw driver that was often provided with the purchase of a sewing machine. These tools were made in a variety of patterns. Overall length is approximately 3 1/2 inches.

Sewing Machine Screw Driver

SCREW DRIVER, SPIRAL. See *Screw Driver, Archimedes* and *Screw Driver, Push*.

SCREW DRIVER, UNDERTAKERS'. Length of blade is approximately 2 inches.

Undertakers' Screw Driver

SCREW DRIVER, WATCH MAKERS'. Also called JEWELERS' SCREW DRIVER. A screw driver, with a very small point, intended for working on watches or jewelry.

Watch Makers' Screw Driver

SCREW DRIVER BIT. A bit brace tool used for driving and removing screws. Screw driver bits were available in a variety of sizes and patterns as shown in the illustrations. The reversible pattern has tapered shanks on each end that terminates in screw driver bits of different sizes.

Billiard

Capstan

Slotted

Reversible

With Holder

Adjustable

Screw Driver Bit

King's Self Centering

Screw Driver Bit

SCREW DRIVER BRACE. Also called COMBINATION BRACE and ORGAN BUILDERS' BRACE. A tool similar to a bit brace except that the chuck is intended to hold a screw driver blade.

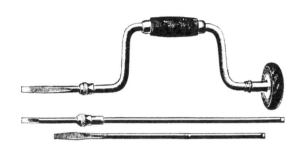

Screw Driver Brace

SCREW EXTRACTOR. Also called EASY OUT. A tapered pin with coarse left-hand threads used to remove a broken bolt or screw. A small hole is drilled in the broken stud and the screw extractor is pounded into the hole. Torque is then applied to the extractor in the proper direction to remove the stud. Sizes up to 2 $5/16$ inches in diameter were available.

Screw Extractor

SCREW EYE DRIVER. A ratchet-type driver used for rapid installation of screw eyes.

Screw Eye Driver

SCREW GAUGE. See *Thread Gauge* and *Wire Gauge.*

SCREW HEAD FILE. See *File, Screw Head.*

SCREW HOLDER. A device used to grasp a wood screw and start it in a position inaccessible to the hand. Listed as a piano makers' tool.

Screw Holder

SCREW PITCH GAUGE. See *Thread Gauge.*

SCREW PLATE. A tool used to cut, straighten or clean threads on a machine screw. See also *Tap and Die.*

Screw Plate

SCREW POINT GIMLET. See *Boring Tool, Gimlet.*

SCREW PRESS. See *Veneer Press.*

SCREW THREAD GAUGE. See *Thread Gauge.*

SCREW WRENCH. See *Wrench, Screw.*

SCRIBE. See *Awl, Scratch; Marking Gauge* and *Timber Scribe.*

SCRIBER. A compass with a tracing wheel on one leg. See also *Awl, Scratch* and *Marking Gauge.*

Scriber

SCROLL SAW. See *Saw, Bracket* and *Saw, Foot and Hand Powered.*

SCRUB PLANE. See *Plane, Scrub.*

SCUFFLE HOE. See *Hoe, Scuffle.*

SCULPTORS' MALLET. See *Mallet, Stone Masons'.*

SCUTCH. See *Skutch.* Scutch is a variation in spelling.

SCYTHE. A curved cutting blade set at 90 degrees to a long handle. Used for cutting grass, weeds or small brush. The handle is called a Snath. See also *Grain Cradle.*

Bush

Weed

Scythe

New England Pattern

Western Pattern

Scythe

SCYTHE, RAG. A paper-mill tool.

Rag Scythe

SCYTHE ANVIL. See *Anvil, Scythe.*

SCYTHE RIFLE. Also called RIFLE. An emery-coated strap or board intended for sharpening a scythe. These tools were advertised as having 2, 3 or 4 coats of grit.

Scythe Rifle

SCYTHE SNATH WRENCH. See *Wrench, Snath.*

SCYTHE STONE. See *Sharpening Stone, Scythe.*

SEAL PRESS. Also called NOTARIAL PRESS. A screw press intended to imprint a seal on a document.

Seal Press

SEAM RUBBER. Also called CREASER. A sail makers' tool used to flatten the seams and creases of a sail. Usually made of a durable material such as lignum vitae, horn or ivory.

Seam Rubber

SEAM SET. See *Shoe Makers' Tool, Seam Set.*

SEAMER. See *Roofing Double Seamer.*

SEAMING MACHINE. See *Tinsmiths' Machine, Double Seaming.*

SEARCHER. See *Knife, Farriers'.*

SEARING IRON. Also called FIRING IRON. A cauterizing iron used to seal an open wound. Listed as a Farriers' tool in one catalogue. The local farrier often served as a horse doctor when a veterinarian was not available in the area.

Searing Iron

SEAT AWL. See *Awl, Seat.*

SEAT SHAVE. See *Spoke Shave, Chair Makers'.*

SECOND CUT FILE. See *File, Second Cut.*

SECTOR. A mathematical rule marked with trigonometric scales and chords. Usually made of boxwood or ivory.

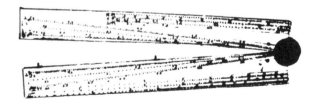

Sector

SEED CORN HANGER. A wire hanger with several spikes for suspending ears of seed corn for drying. The catalogue listing states that 100 of these hangers will provide seed for eighty acres of corn.

SEED POTATO KNIFE. See *Knife, Seed Potato.*

SEED SAMPLER. See *Sampler, Grain.*

SEED STRIPPER. A farm tool used for gathering seed from bluegrass or similar foliage crop.

SEED TRIER. See *Sampler, Grain.*

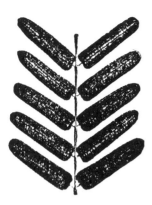

Seed Corn Hanger

Seed Stripper

SEEDER. A device used to sow grass seed. See also *Garden Planter*.

Rotary

Tin Horn

Seeder

SEGAR KNIFE. See *Knife, Cigar Makers'*. Segar is an improper variation of cigar.

SELF LOCKING CLAMP. See *Clamp, Quick*.

SELF REGISTERING CALIPER. See *Caliper, Self Registering*.

SEPARATING CHISEL. See *Chisel, Ice*.

SEPARATOR. See *Cream Separator*.

SERVING MALLET. See *Mallet, Serving*.

SERVING TOOL. Also called SIZER. A tool used to hold and compress the wraps when serving a rope. The serving cord is looped around the handle in such a manner that the tool can be used as a lever to tighten the wrap. "Serving" is a process of wrapping a rope or hawser with a lighter cord to reduce chafing.

Serving Tool

SET AUGER. See *Boring Tool, Set Auger*.

SET HAMMER. See *Anvil Tool, Set Hammer*.

SET SCREW WRENCH. See *Wrench, Set Screw*.

SETTING BAR. See *Bar, Setting*.

SETTING BUR. Also called BUR and BURR. A small rotary cutting tool used by a jeweler to enlarge or shape a metal setting.

Setting Bur

SETTING DIE. See *Grommet Die*.

SETTING DOWN MACHINE. See *Tinsmiths' Machine, Setting Down*.

SETTING HAMMER. See *Hammer, Roofing*.

SETTING PLATE. See *Tire Setting Plate*.

SEWER MAUL. See *Maul, Sewer*.

SEWER SHOVEL. See *Shovel, Brick*.

SEWER TROWEL. See *Trowel, Sewer*.

SEWING AWL. See *Awl, Sewing*.

SEWING FRAME. See *Bookbinding Tool, Press*.

SEWING KEY. A device used on the book binders' sewing press to hold the bottom end of the band in place for sewing. The key holds the band taut while allowing it to be moved to either side as may be required by the size of the book. When ribbons or tapes are used in place of cords, the key is shaped like the letter H. Made of wood or metal.

Sewing Key

SEWING MACHINE SCREW DRIVER. See *Screw Driver, Sewing Machine.*

SEWING PALM. Also called SAIL MAKERS' PALM and SAILORS' SEWING PALM. A tool used to press the needle when sewing heavy material such as leather or sail cloth.

Collar Palm

Sailors' Palm

Sewing Palm

SEWING PRESS. See *Bookbinding Tool, Press.*

SHACKLE BAR. See *Bar, Shackle.*

SHACKLE CLAMP. See *Clamp, Shackle.*

SHACKLE JACK. See *Thill Coupler.*

SHADBELLY FILE. See *File, Crossing.*

SHAFTING LEVEL. See *Level, Hydrostatic.*

SHANK BURNISHER. See *Shoe Makers' Tool, Shank Burnisher.*

SHANK CHISEL. See *Chisel, Tang.*

SHANK IRON. See *Shoe Makers' Tool, Shank Iron.*

SHANK LASTER. See *Shoe Makers' Tool, Shank Laster.*

SHANK LEVELER. See *Hammer, Shoe Makers' Beating Out.*

SHANK WHEEL. See *Shoe Makers' Tool, Cord Wheel.*

SHAPER. See *Former.*

SHARPENING HAMMER. See *Hammer, Farriers' Sharpening* and *Hammer, Sharpening.*

SHARPENING STAKE. See *Stake, Sharpening.*

SHARPENING STONE. Also called OIL STONE, SLIP, SLIP STONE and WHETSTONE. A small stone used for sharpening a cutting tool. The Arkansas Stone is generally considered to be the best variety of stone for use on very hard steel such as razors and gravers. The Soft Arkansas and Washita Stone are most often used for for sharpening woodworking tools. A stone in a fitted box is said to be "Mounted". See also *Grind Stone.*

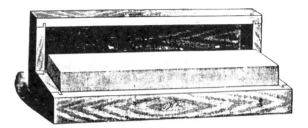

Mounted

Sharpening Stone

SHARPENING STONE, AXE. A small sharpening stone intended to be carried by the workman and used for quick touch-up of the axe without returning to the shop.

Axe Stone

SHARPENING STONE, CARVING TOOL. Also called CARVING TOOL SLIP. A sharpening stone with a unique shape suitable for sharpening a variety of carving tools. Length is 2 to 3 inches.

Carving Tool Stone

SHARPENING STONE, DISC. See *Disc Sharpener.*

SHARPENING STONE, GOUGE. Also called GOUGE SLIP. A tapered stone suitable for use on gouges of various sizes. Length is 6 to 9 inches.

Gouge Stone

Sharpening Stone, Horse Shoer's Knife. A sharpening stone shaped to fit the hook of a farriers' knife.

Horse Shoer's Knife Stone

Sharpening Stone, Scythe. A stone intended for sharpening a grain scythe or sickle. Length is approximately 10 inches. One type of scythe stone is carried in a belt sheath. Inasmuch as certain natural stones should be kept immersed in water, the sheath is made waterproof and can be filled with water each morning during use. The sheath shown in the illustration is made of iron. Many of these sheaths are home made and consist of a single piece of wood hollowed out to fit the stone.

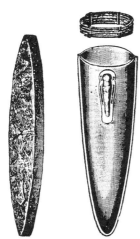

Scythe Stone

Shave. See also *Drawing Knife, Shingle; Shave Hook* and *Spoke Shave.*

Shave, Comb Makers'. A shave used by a comb maker to thin and shape a comb blank. Length of blade is about 10 inches.

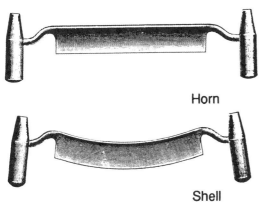

Horn

Shell

Comb Makers' Shave

Shave Hook. Also called **Plumbers' Scraper.** A tool used for de-burring inside the end of a lead pipe. Also used for brightening the surface of a lead pipe prior to soldering. See also *Box Scraper.*

Shave Hook

Shave-Up Knife. See *Drawing Knife, Coopers'.*

Shaving Bench. See *Bench, Shaving.*

Shaving Fork. See *Fork, Shaving.*

Shaving Horse. See *Bench, Shaving.*

Shear Tooth File. See *File, Shear Tooth.*

Shears. A tool comprised of two cutting edges that shear as they slide past each other around a pivot. See also *Bale Tie Snips* and *Tinsmiths' Machine, Shears.*

Shears, Bankers'. See *Shears, Desk* and *Shears, Paper Hangers'.*

Shears, Belting. A heavy shears with teeth on one cutting edge. Intended to cut asbestos, belting, packing material, leather or rubber. Overall length is 8 1/2 to 11 inches.

Belting Shears

Shears, Bench. A large shears intended for use by a tinsmith. The common type, shown in illustrations (a) and (b), have one handle bent down to fit into a bench plate thus allowing the shears to be operated with one hand. This type of bench shears was available with cutting jaws up to 12 inches long. Overall length is 25 to 46 inches. The type shown in illustration (c) has provisions for bolting to a work bench.

(a)

Bench Shears

427

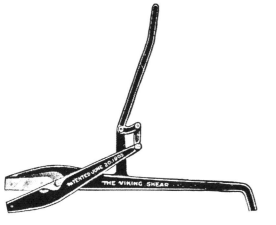

(b) Compound

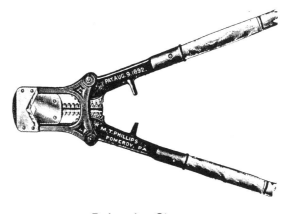

Dehorning Shears

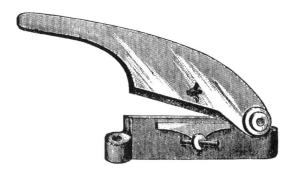

(c)

Bench Shears

Desk Shears

SHEARS, GRAPE. A farm tool used to pick grapes. Overall length is about 7 inches.

Grape Shears

SHEARS, BORDER. A lawn tool used to trim around a flower bed or walkway. Length of cutting edge is approximately 10 inches.

SHEARS, GRASS. Similar in appearance to sheep shears. Length of blade is approximately 5 1/2 inches. Grass shears often have the handles offset to allow trimming along a flat surface.

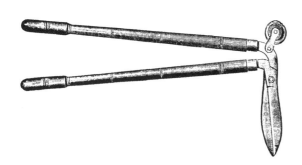

Border Shears

Grass Shears

SHEARS, CARPET. See *Shears, Upholsterers'*.

SHEARS, DEHORNING. A farm tool used to cut the horns from cattle. Overall length is 34 to 37 inches.

SHEARS, HEDGE. A two-handed shears used for trimming a shaped hedge.

SHEARS, DESK. Also called BANKERS' SHEARS and EDITORS' SHEARS. Long shears intended for use in cutting paper. Useful for trimming documents, drawings and maps. See also *Shears, Paper Hangers'*.

Hedge Shears

SHEARS, EDITORS'. See *Shears, Desk*.

SHEARS, HOOF. See *Hoof Trimmers*.

SHEARS, HORSE. Also called ROACHING SHEARS and ROPE SHEARS. A heavy shears used to trim the mane of a horse or mule. Length of cutting edge is 4 1/2 to 7 1/2 inches. These shears have a slight bow in the cutting edge.

Horse Shears

SHEARS, JEWELERS'. Also called JEWELERS' SNIPS and SILVERSMITHS' SHEARS. A small metal-cutting shears used for jewelry work and similar tasks. Overall length is 5 to 12 inches.

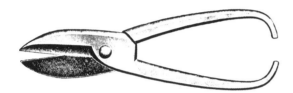

Jewelers' Shears

SHEARS, METAL. A blacksmiths' machine used to cut bar iron or rods. The illustrated tool will cut mild steel bars or strips up to 3/8 inches thick.

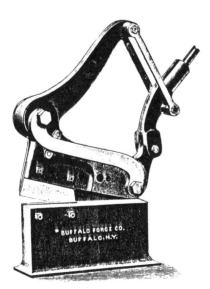

Metal Shears

SHEARS, PAPER HANGERS'. Also called BANKERS' SHEARS. Overall length is 10 to 16 inches.

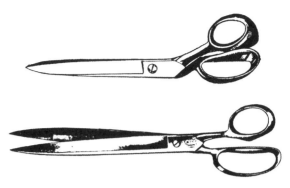

Paper Hangers' Shears

SHEARS, PRUNING. A shears used for general-purpose pruning of shrubs, trees and vines.

Pruning Shears

SHEARS, ROACHING. See *Shears, Horse.*

SHEARS, SHEEP. A shears used to clip the wool from a sheep or goat. Length of blades are 3 1/2 to 8 inches.

Sheep Shears

SHEARS, SILVERSMITHS'. See *Shears, Jewelers'.*

SHEARS, TAILORS'. See *Shears, Upholsterers'.*

SHEARS, TIN. See *Tinners' Snips.*

SHEARS, UPHOLSTERERS'. Also called CARPET SHEARS and TAILORS' SHEARS. A heavy shears intended for cutting thick material. Overall length is 10 to 16 1/2 inches.

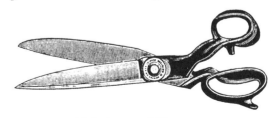

Upholsterers' Shears

SHEARS, WEAVERS'. A small hand shear used in a textile mill. Overall length is about 5 1/4 inches. Similar in appearance to Sheep Shears but much smaller.

Weavers' Shears

SHEARS GAUGE. A metal guide that can be attached to a pair of shears or scissors to facilitate cutting goods on the bias. The sliding clip can be set at any distance from the shears to serve as a guide for cutting strips of the desired width. The tool was patented November 30, !875.

Shears Gauge

SHEATHING PULLER. See *Plank Puller.*

SHEEP SHEARS. See *Shears, Sheep.*

SHEET METAL GAUGE. A tool used to gauge the thickness of a metal sheet.

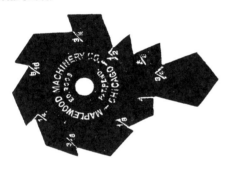

Sheet Metal Gauge

SHEET METAL PUNCH. See *Punch, Hollow; Punch, Metal* and *Punch, Stop.*

SHEFFIELD BIT BRACE. See *Boring Tool, Bit Brace, Sheffield.*

SHELF PICKER. A grocery store tool used to lift a can or box from a high shelf. The curved prongs will close about an object when the hand grip is rotated. Length is about 5 feet.

Shelf Picker

SHELF RAIL PLANE. See *Plane, Shelf Rail.*

SHELL AUGER. See *Boring Tool, Bit, Shell.*

SHELL BIT. See *Boring Tool, Bit, Shell.*

SHELL EXTRACTOR. A small tool used to pull a shell case from a rifle or shotgun.

Shell Extractor

SHEPHERDS' CROOK. A device used to catch and hold a sheep. Length of handle is normally 8 to 10 feet.

Shepards' Crook

SHIFTING CROZE. See *Plane, Croze.*

SHINGLE GAUGE. Also called HATCHET GAUGE and SHINGLING GAUGE. A device intended to be secured to the back edge of a shingling hatchet to gauge the amount of spread between courses of shingles. Size of the illustrated gauge is 3/4 of an inch in diameter.

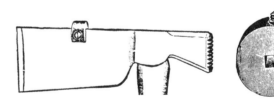

Shingle Gauge

SHINGLE KNIFE. See *Drawing Knife, Shingle.*

SHINGLE RIPPER. See *Ripper, Slaters'.*

SHINGLE SHAVE. See *Drawing Knife, Shingle.*

SHINGLING HATCHET. See *Hatchet, Shingling.*

SHIP ADZE. See *Adze, Ship Carpenters'.*

SHIP AUGER. See *Boring Tool, Bit, Ship* and *Boring Tool, Ship Auger.*

SHIP AUGER BIT. See *Boring Tool, Bit, Ship.*

SHIP AUGER CAR BIT. See *Boring Tool, Bit, Ship Auger Car.*

SHIP AXE. See *Axe, Broad, Ship Carpenters'*.

SHIP BIT. See *Boring Tool, Bit, Ship*.

SHIP BUILDERS' TOOLS. The special-purpose ship builders' tools listed below can be found in normal alphabetical sequence. These tools may also have been used for other purposes.

  ADZE, HAMMER HEAD
  ADZE, SHIP CARPENTERS'
  ADZE, SHIP CARPENTERS' LIPPED
  AWL, SCRATCH
  AXE, BROAD, SHIP CARPENTERS'
  BORING TOOL, BIT, SHIP
  BORING TOOL, BOOM AUGER
  BORING TOOL, SHIP AUGER
  BORING TOOL, TREENAIL AUGER
  BRUSH, SHIP SEAM
  CAULKING TOOL, SHIP
  CHISEL, DECK
  CHISEL, SLICE
  CLAMP, PLANK SCREW
  CLAMP, SHIP CARPENTERS'
  HAMMER, BRIDGE BUILDERS'
  HAWSING BEETLE
  HAWSING IRON
  MAUL, SHIP
  PLANE, RAZEE
  PLANE, SPAR
  RULE, SHIP CARPENTERS' BEVEL
  SAW, FUTTOCK
  SAW, SHIP CARPENTERS'
  SAW, WHIP
  SCRAPER, SHIP
  SPIKE START

SHIP CARPENTERS' AUGER. See *Boring Tool, Ship Auger*.

SHIP CARPENTERS' AXE. See *Axe, Broad, Ship Carpenters'*.

SHIP CARPENTERS' BEVEL. See *Rule, Ship Carpenters' Bevel*.

SHIP CARPENTERS' BROAD AXE. See *Axe, Broad, Ship Carpenters'*.

SHIP CARPENTERS' CHISEL. See *Chisel, Deck*.

SHIP CARPENTERS' CLAMP. See *Clamp, Ship Carpenters'*.

SHIP CARPENTERS' SAW. See *Saw, Ship Carpenters'*.

SHIP CAULKING TOOL. See *Caulking Tool, Ship*.

SHIP CLAMP SCREW. See *Clamp, Ship Carpenters'*.

SHIP GRIND STONE. See *Grind Stone, Ship*.

SHIP MAUL. See *Maul, Ship*.

SHIP PATTERN BROAD AXE. See *Axe, Broad, Ship Carpenters'*.

SHIP PLANE. See *Plane, Razee*.

SHIP RIVETING HAMMER. See *Hammer, Bridge Builders'*.

SHIP SCRAPER. See *Scraper, Ship*.

SHIP SEAM BRUSH. See *Brush, Ship Seam*.

SHIP TREENAIL AUGER. See *Boring Tool, Treenail*.

SHOE COBBLERS' TOOL. See *Shoe Tools*.

SHOE FITTERS' TOOL. See *Shoe Tools*.

SHOE JACK. A shoe makers' last attached to a ball swivel such that it can be adjusted to any convenient position.

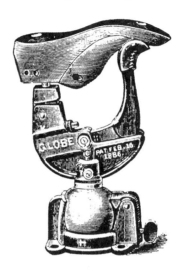

Shoe Jack

SHOE LACE TIPPER. A tool used to crimp a tip on a shoe lace. A shoe shop tool.

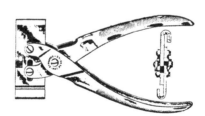

Shoe Lace Tipper

SHOE MAKERS' MACHINE. A hand-operated machine used to make or repair shoes.

SHOE MAKERS' MACHINE, SKIVER. A machine used to taper a half sole before installation.

Skiving Machine

SHOE MAKERS' MACHINE, SOLE CUTTER. Also called SOLE TRIMMER. A device used to trim around the sole after it is attached to the upper.

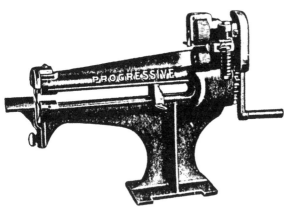

Sole Cutter

SHOE MAKERS' MACHINE, WELT ROLLER. A machine that will flatten and firm up the welt thus allowing neat stitching.

Welt Roller

SHOE MAKERS' TOOL. A hand tool used for making or repairing a leather shoe for the human foot.

SHOE MAKERS' TOOL, BOTTOM WHEEL. Also called CORD WHEEL and SHANK WHEEL. A tool used for making a small decorative design across the sole of a shoe or along a channel.

Bottom Wheel

SHOE MAKERS' TOOL, BOX WHEEL. A tool used to make a decorative design around the edge of the sole where it joins the heel.

Box Wheel

SHOE MAKERS' TOOL, BUFFER STEEL. A small steel used to turn the edges of the various scrapers and scraping knives used by the leather worker. This is essentially the same tool as the Finger Steel used by the currier.

Buffer Steel

SHOE MAKERS' TOOL, BURNISHER. Also called HEEL BURNISHER and HEEL SLICKER. A burnishing or slicking tool used on shoe heels or the edges of thick soles. Also used to smooth and distribute wax. These tools are often heated for use. See also *Shoe Makers' Tool, Shank Burnisher.*

Plain

Shoulder

Burnisher

Corrugated

Burnisher

SHOE MAKERS' TOOL, CHANNEL CUTTER. A cutting tool used to make a slit in the edge of a leather workpiece. Stitching is placed in the slit to provide a neat appearance or to avoid wear on the stitch loops.

Channel Cutter

SHOE MAKERS' TOOL, CHANNEL GOUGE. A cutting tool that removes a thin bead of leather to provide a groove for recessing of stitches. This allows the stitches to be placed below the surface to reduce wear on the stitch loops.

Channel Gouge

SHOE MAKERS' TOOL, CHANNEL OPENER. A wedge-shaped tool used to spread the channel slit for ease of stitching.

Channel Opener

SHOE MAKERS' TOOL, CLAMMING MARKER. Also called STITCH MARKER. A tool used to mark stitch locations on leather.

Clamming Marker

SHOE MAKERS' TOOL, COLLICE. Also called COLLICE IRON and MENS' COLLICE. One of the many types of burnishers used on the edge of a shoe sole. The collice sets and seals the edge of the sole and the small chamfer at the edge.

Single

Double

Adjustable

Collice

SHOE MAKERS' TOOL, CORD WHEEL. See *Shoe Makers' Tool, Bottom Wheel*.

SHOE MAKERS' TOOL, CRIMPING SCREW. A device used to stretch the leather down over the toe of a last to form the proper curve and to remove the wrinkles.

Crimping Screw

SHOE MAKERS' TOOL, EDGE PLANE. See *Shoe Makers' Tool, Edge Shave*.

SHOE MAKERS' TOOL, EDGE SHAVE. Also called EDGE PLAIN and EDGE PLANE. A cutting tool used to trim the edge of the sole. The base is short and slightly convex to allow the shave to be used in the concave section at the waist of the sole.

Edge Plane

Edge Shave

SHOE MAKERS' TOOL, FUDGE WHEEL. A tool used to mark the welt to give the appearance of having been hand stitched. It is used after the actual stitches have been set and waxed.

Fudge Wheel

SHOE MAKERS' TOOL, HEEL KNIFE. See *Shoe Makers' Tool, Peg Cutter.*

SHOE MAKERS' TOOL, HEEL PRYER. A tool used as a pry bar to remove a heel or sole from a shoe.

Heel Pryer

SHOE MAKERS' TOOL, HEEL SHAVE. A two-handed tool used to trim the heel of a boot or shoe. Several different curvatures were available. This device is often mistaken for a woodworking tool.

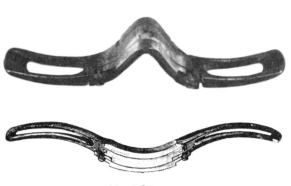

Heel Shave

SHOE MAKERS' TOOL, JIGGER. The jigger is used to make a small crease or shoulder around the welt. It it also used to set the stitches and burnish the surface. Wax or gum is then rubbed into the crease made by the jigger.

Shoe Makers' Jigger

SHOE MAKERS' TOOL, LAST. A metal holder or backing stake made to fit the inside of a shoe. Used primarily during repair.

Bench Last   Floor Last

Combination

Shoe Makers' Last

Lap

Shoe Makers' Last

SHOE MAKERS' TOOL, LAST HOOK. A hook used to remove the wooden form or last from the completed shoe.

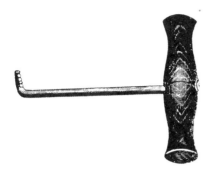

Last Hook

SHOE MAKERS' TOOL, LEVER CLAMP. A clamp intended to hold two pieces of leather in position while stitching. Used by a shoe maker, harness maker or other leather worker. Usually held between the knees while being used.

Lever Clamp

SHOE MAKERS' TOOL, LONG STICK. A hardwood stick, usually oval in cross section, used to polish the shank or upper of a boot or shoe. The Colted Long Stick has a piece of sandstone or sharpening stone embedded in one side for use in scouring rough spots on the leather.

Colted

Long Stick

SHOE MAKERS' TOOL, PEG BREAK. Also called PEG FLOAT. A tool used to smooth off the ends of the wooden pegs used to secure the heel.

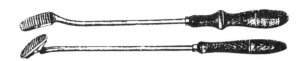

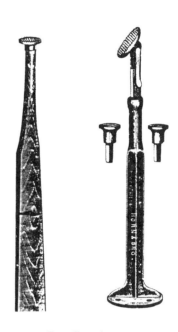

Peg Break

SHOE MAKERS' TOOL, PEG CUTTER. Also called HEEL KNIFE, YANKEE CUTTER and YANKEE PEG CUTTER. A cutting tool with a short blade at right angles to the handle. Used to trim the excess length from shoe pegs inside the shoe. Overall length is up to 15 inches.

Closed

Hook

Peg Cutter

SHOE MAKERS' TOOL, PEG WHEEL. A sharp-pointed wheel used to mark the locations for driving pegs. The illustrated tool is adjustable with reference to the stem which serves as a fence or guide.

435

Peg Wheel

SHOE MAKERS' TOOL, RAHN BREAK. A knurled tool used for smoothing and leveling the edge of the sole immediately above the heel. This tool is used in preparation for use of the box wheel.

Rahn Break

SHOE MAKERS' TOOL, RAHN FILE. A coarse file used for leveling the top of the sole above the heel.

Rahn File

SHOE MAKERS' TOOL, SCRATCH BONE. This tool was probably used for cleaning excess wax or gum from the welt before final finishing with a burnisher and fudge wheel.

Scratch Bone

SHOE MAKERS' TOOL, SEAM SET. One of several tools used to rub gum, wax or soap into a new seam thus setting and hardening the stitches. The tool is heated for use. The illustrated device was listed by one supplier as a WELT SET.

Seam Set

SHOE MAKERS' TOOL, SHANK BURNISHER. A smooth steel tool used as a burnisher for the shank and tops of riding boots.

Shank Burnisher

SHOE MAKERS' TOOL, SHANK IRON. A burnishing and setting tool used on the welt along the instep or narrow part of the shoe.

Single

Double

Shank Iron

SHOE MAKERS' TOOL, SHANK LASTER. A device used to stretch the upper of a boot over the last into the hollow of the shank. See also *Pincers, Bulldog*.

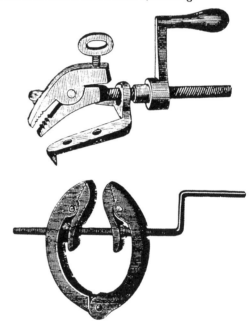

Shank Laster

SHOE MAKERS' TOOL, SHANK LEVELER. See *Hammer, Shoe Makers' Beating Out*.

SHOE MAKERS' TOOL, SHOULDER IRON. This tool is another of the edge irons used to burnish and set the edge of the sole. Used primarily on the front part of the shoe.

Single

Shoulder Iron

Double

Shoulder Iron

SHOE MAKERS' TOOL, SHOULDER STICK. A wooden tool used as an alternate to the shoulder iron. See *Shoe Makers' Tool, Shoulder Iron.*

Shoulder Stick

SHOE MAKERS' TOOL, SLICK BONE. A piece of bone used to smooth new stitches and to burnish the edges of a thick straps. Used by harness makers in some cases but more often listed as a shoe makers' tool. These tools were generally home made but were offered as standard catalogue items by several suppliers.

Slick Bone

SHOE MAKERS' TOOL, SOLE GAUGE. A tool used to measure the thickness of shoe soles and taps. The tool is graduated in 48ths of an inch and figured to show irons and half irons from sizes 2 thru 12.

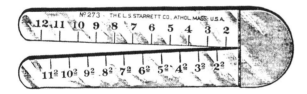

Sole Gauge

SHOE MAKERS' TOOL, STITCH CUTTER. A tool used to cut the stitches on top of the welt thus allowing a sole to be quickly removed.

Stitch Cutter

SHOE MAKERS' TOOL, STITCH DIVIDER. Used to press the welt beside each stitch thus helping to set and even the stitches. This process makes the stitches appear to be bolder and more precise. The stitch divider was probably used as an alternate process to the fudge wheel.

Stitch Divider

SHOE MAKERS' TOOL, STITCH MARKER. See *Shoe Makers' Tool, Clamming Marker.*

SHOE MAKERS' TOOL, STITCH WHEEL. A marking wheel with sharp points. Used to lay out stitch locations.

Stitch Wheel

SHOE MAKERS' TOOL, TOP CHANNEL SET. The top channel set is used to close and burnish the channel after the stitching is complete. Glue or paste is applied to prevent the channel from opening when the leather is bent.

Top Channel Set

SHOE MAKERS' TOOL, TURNING BONE. This tool is listed in an American shoe tool catalogue but size and usage is not known. *Salaman* states that a 9 to 12 inch tool of similar appearance, called a TURNING IRON or TURNING STICK, is used to keep the toe in shape as one variety of shoe is turned inside out after assembly.

Turning Bone

SHOE MAKERS' TOOL, WELT GROOVER. This tool was probably used to make a recess in the welt prior to stitching.

Welt Groover

SHOE MAKERS' TOOL, WELT MILL. A block used as a thickness gauge for making a welt. A straight knife is placed across one of the notches on the mill and a strip of leather is pulled through the slot against the cutting edge.

Welt Mill

SHOE MAKERS' TOOL, WELT TRIMMER. A cutting tool used to trim the outer edge of a welt after stitching. Used with a pushing action similar to the shoe makers' welt knife.

Welt Trimmer

SHOE SPREADER. A farriers' tool used to spread the ends of a horse shoe. The shoe can be spread with this tool after it has been partially nailed to the hoof.

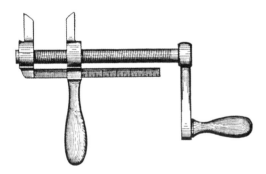

Shoe Spreader

SHOE STRETCHER. A device that will stretch a local spot in a leather shoe. Useful for relieving the pressure and abrasion on a corn or bunion.

Chicago Pattern
Shoe Stretcher

Shoe Stretcher

SHOE TOOLS. Also called COBBLERS' TOOLS, CORDWAINERS' TOOLS, SHOE COBBLERS' TOOLS, SHOE FITTERS' TOOLS and SHOE MAKERS' TOOLS. There is considerable overlap between tools of the various leather working trades. See also *Book Binders' Tools* and *Saddle and Harness Tools*. The special-purpose shoe makers' tools listed below can be found in normal alphabetical sequence. These tools may also have been used for other purposes.

  ANVIL, KNEE
  AWL, PEG
  AWL, SEAT
  AWL, SEWING
  AWL, STRIP
  AWL HAFT
  BUTTON FASTENER
  BUTTON HOLE CUTTER
  BUTTON MACHINE
  EYELET REMOVER
  HAMMER, SHOE FITTERS'
  HAMMER, SHOE MAKERS'
  HAMMER, SHOE MAKERS' BEATING OUT
  HAMMER, SHOE MAKERS' TOE
  KNIFE, LEATHER
  KNIFE, SHOE MAKERS' WELT
  LEATHER TOOL, CUTTING DIE
  NIPPERS, PEG
  NIPPERS, SHOE TACK
  PINCERS, BULLDOG
  PINCERS, LASTING
  PINCERS, TACKING
  RASP, SHOE
  SHOE LACE TIPPER
  SHOE MAKERS' MACHINE, SKIVER
  SHOE MAKERS' MACHINE, SOLE CUTTER
  SHOE MAKERS' MACHINE, WELT ROLLER
  SHOE MAKERS' TOOL, BOTTOM WHEEL
  SHOE MAKERS' TOOL, BOX WHEEL
  SHOE MAKERS' TOOL, BUFFER STEEL
  SHOE MAKERS' TOOL, BURNISHER
  SHOE MAKERS' TOOL, CHANNEL CUTTER
  SHOE MAKERS' TOOL, CHANNEL GOUGE
  SHOE MAKERS' TOOL, CHANNEL OPENER
  SHOE MAKERS' TOOL, CLAMMING MARKER
  SHOE MAKERS' TOOL, COLLICE
  SHOE MAKERS' TOOL, CORD WHEEL
  SHOE MAKERS' TOOL, EDGE SHAVE
  SHOE MAKERS' TOOL, FUDGE WHEEL
  SHOE MAKERS' TOOL, HEEL PRYER

SHOE MAKERS' TOOL, HEEL SHAVE
SHOE MAKERS' TOOL, JIGGER
SHOE MAKERS' TOOL, LAST
SHOE MAKERS' TOOL, LAST HOOK
SHOE MAKERS' TOOL, LEVER CLAMP
SHOE MAKERS' TOOL, LONG STICK
SHOE MAKERS' TOOL, PEG BREAK
SHOE MAKERS' TOOL, PEG CUTTER
SHOE MAKERS' TOOL, PEG WHEEL
SHOE MAKERS' TOOL, RAHN BREAK
SHOE MAKERS' TOOL, RAHN FILE
SHOE MAKERS' TOOL, SCRATCH BONE
SHOE MAKERS' TOOL, SEAM SET
SHOE MAKERS' TOOL, SHANK BURNISHER
SHOE MAKERS' TOOL, SHANK IRON
SHOE MAKERS' TOOL, SHANK LASTER
SHOE MAKERS' TOOL, SHOULDER IRON
SHOE MAKERS' TOOL, SHOULDER STICK
SHOE MAKERS' TOOL, SLICK BONE
SHOE MAKERS' TOOL, SOLE GAUGE
SHOE MAKERS' TOOL, STITCH DIVIDER
SHOE MAKERS' TOOL, STITCH WHEEL
SHOE MAKERS' TOOL, TOP CHANNEL SET
SHOE MAKERS' TOOL, TURNING BONE
SHOE MAKERS' TOOL, WELT GROOVER
SHOE MAKERS' TOOL, WELT MILL
SHOE MAKERS' TOOL, WELT TRIMMER
TACK CLAW
TACK PULLER
TACK AND RIVET HOLDER
TURNING TOOL, HOOK

SHOEING FRAME. See *Shoeing Rack*.

SHOEING HAMMER. See *Hammer, Farriers' Shoeing*.

SHOEING KNIFE. See *Knife, Farriers'*.

SHOEING PINCERS. See *Pincers, Farriers'*.

SHOEING RACK. Also called SHOEING FRAME and SHOEING STOCK. A farriers' mechanism used when shoeing a mean or untrained animal. The general approach of the shoeing rack is to support the animal on a sling such that all four feet are removed from the floor. Each foot can then be separately secured while it is being trimmed and nailed. Most horses readily accept shoeing without use of the rack; however, the rack was often necessary for shoeing oxen. In a shop where a rack was not available, it was sometimes necessary to throw and hog-tie a mean or flighty animal during the shoeing process. The illustrated mechanism is a Barkus Pattern Rack.

SHOEING STOCK. See *Shoeing Rack*.

SHOEING TONGS. See *Tongs, Farriers'*.

SHOOT BOARD. See *Plane, Shoot Board*.

SHOOTING PLANE. See *Plane, Shoot Board*.

SHOP APRON. See *Apron, Shop*.

Shoeing Rack

SHOULDER IRON. See *Shoe Makers' Tool, Shoulder Iron*.

SHOULDER PEEN HAMMER. See *Hammer, Shoulder Peen*.

SHOULDER PLANE. See *Plane, Rabbet*.

SHOULDER STICK. See *Shoe Makers' Tool, Shoulder Stick*.

SHOULDERED AWL. See *Awl, Brad* and *Awl, Peg*.

SHOVEL. A handled tool with a broad hollowed-out blade used to lift or move loose material.

SHOVEL, BRICK. Also called SEWER SHOVEL. A shovel developed especially for handling the heavy blue clay used for making bricks. Size of the blade is approximately 8 3/4 by 9 inches.

Brick Shovel

SHOVEL, COAL. See *Shovel, Scoop*.

SHOVEL, COAL MINERS'. A shovel with a short handle. Suitable for use in a narrow or cramped space. The illustrated tool has a 17 1/2 inch handle.

Coal Miners' Shovel

SHOVEL, DIAMOND. A tool used in a jewelry store for handling diamonds and other precious stones.

Diamond Shovel

SHOVEL, RICE. A shovel used to dig and clean out ditches in a rice field. The holes allow the water to drain off thus lightening the task.

Rice Shovel

SHOVEL, ROUND POINT. A shovel used for handling dirt or gravel.

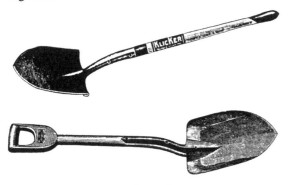

Round Point Shovel

SHOVEL, SCOOP. A large shovel with characteristics suitable for the intended task. See illustrations.

Ash Pan

Breaking Down (Soft Coal)

Scoop Shovel

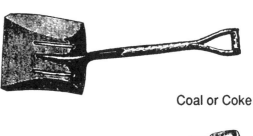

Coal or Coke

Coke

Furnace or Firing

Grain or Sawdust

Gravel or Sand

Moulders' or Square Point

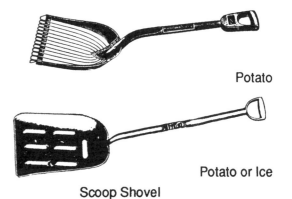

Potato

Potato or Ice

Scoop Shovel

440

SHOVEL, SEWER. See *Shovel, Brick.*

SHOVEL, SIEVE. A tool used during the ice harvest to clean the channel of ice chips and other bits of debris. The illustrated shovel is 14 inches wide.

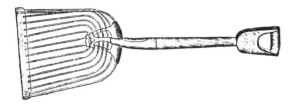

Sieve Shovel

SHOVEL, SQUARE POINT. See *Shovel, Scoop.*

SHOVEL, TEMPERING. A shovel used by a jeweler to hold small workpieces while being heated for tempering.

Tempering Shovel

SHOVEL, TRUCK. A wheeled shovel used to unload grain or coal from a boxcar into a truck or wagon. Capacity of the illustrated shovel is 2 1/2 bushels.

Truck Shovel

SHRINK RULE. See *Rule, Shrinkage.*

SHRINKAGE RULE. See *Rule, Shrinkage.*

SHRINKER. See *Tire Shrinker.*

SHUFFLE HOE. See *Hoe, Scuffle.* Shuffle is an incorrect variation in spelling.

SHUTE BOARD. See *Plane, Shoot Board.* Shute is a variation in spelling.

SICKLE. See *Grain Sickle.*

SICKLE GRIND STONE. See *Grind Stone, Sickle.*

SICKLE PUNCH. A small punch used to remove the rivets from from the sickle bar of a mowing or reaping machine. The used cutting section is hit with a hammer in a direction to shear the two rivets and remove the section. The punch is then used to remove the remaining ends of the rivets. See illustration under *Punch, Pin.*

SIDE AXE. See *Axe, Side.*

SIDE BEAD. See *Plane, Moulding, Side Bead.*

SIDE CHISEL. See *Anvil Tool, Side Chisel* and *Chisel, Rivet Buster.*

SIDE CUTTERS. See *Pliers, Diagonal* and *Pliers, Side Cutting.*

SIDE CUTTING PLIERS. See *Pliers, Diagonal* and *Pliers, Side Cutting.*

SIDE EDGER. A plumbers' tool used for bending and creasing sheet lead. It is suitable for pressing and for light pounding. Usually made of lignum vitae or dogwood.

Side Edger

SIDE FILE. See *Saw File Holder.*

SIDE HAMMER. See *Hammer, Stone.*

SIDE NIPPERS. See *Nippers, Side.*

SIDE RABBET PLANE. See *Plane, Side Rabbet.*

SIDE SET. See *Anvil Tool, Side Chisel.*

SIDEWALK CLEANER. See *Scraper, Sidewalk.*

SIDEWALK CREASER. See *Cement Tool, Jointer.*

SIDEWALK EDGER. See *Turf Edger.*

SIDEWALK GROOVER. See *Cement Tool, Driveway Groover* and *Cement Tool, Jointer.*

SIDEWALK ROLLER. See *Cement Tool, Roller.*

SIDEWALK SCRAPER. See *Scraper, Sidewalk.*

SIDEWALK SOCKET CHISEL. See *Chisel, Ice.*

SIDEWALK TAMPER. See *Tamper.*

SIDING GAUGE. See *Clapboard Gauge.*

SIDING MARKER. See *Clapboard Marker.*

SIEVE. See *Riddle.*

SIEVE SHOVEL. See *Shovel, Scoop* and *Shovel, Sieve.*

SILAGE FORK. See *Fork, Coal.*

SILL BORER. See *Boring Tool, Sill Borer.*

SILO FORK. See *Fork, Coal.*

SILVER PLATERS' KNIFE. See *Knife, Silver Platers'.*

SILVERSMITHS' BRUSH. See *Brush, Silversmiths'.*

SILVERSMITHS' BURNISHER. See *Burnishing Tool, Agate; Burnishing Tool, Bloodstone* and *Burnishing Tool, Silversmiths'*.

SILVERSMITHS' HAMMER. See *Hammer, Silversmiths'*.

SILVERSMITHS' SHEARS. See *Shears, Jewelers'*.

SILVERSMITHS' STAKE. See *Stake, Silversmiths'*.

SINGEING LAMP. An alcohol or gas burning device used to singe the hair on a horse as an alternative to clipping. The head is approximately 3 1/2 inches wide. The illustrated tool is made of brass.

Singeing Lamp

SINGLE BIT AXE. See *Axe, Single Bit*.

SINGLE PICKUP TONGS. See *Tongs, Blacksmiths'*.

SINGLE TWIST AUGER. See *Boring Tool, Ship Auger*.

SINKING TOOL. See *Leather Tool, Sinking*.

SIZE STICK. A shoe store tool used to determine the proper shoe size to fit a given foot.

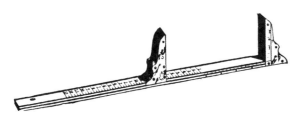

Size Stick

SIZER. See *Serving Tool* and *Turning Tool, Sizer*.

SKATE SHARPENER. A pocket-sized sharpening tool consisting of a short piece of file held rigidly between two side guides. Used to sharpen and burnish the runners of ice skates. It can also be used as a lawn mower sharpener and as a saw jointer.

Skate Sharpener

SKETCH PAD. A drawing pad used by a surveyor or field engineer. A strap on the back allows the pad to be carried on the arm while leaving both hands free. The illustrated tool has a long strip of paper contained on two rolls such that it can be advanced across the face of the pad. A compass is built-in at the top.

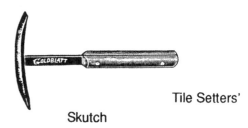

Sketch Pad

SKETZ. See *Skutch*. Sketz is a variation in spelling.

SKEW. See *Turning Tool, Chisel*.

SKEWER. See *Upholsterers' Skewer*.

SKIMMER. A tool used in the type-setting room to skim the surface impurities from the tank or pot of molten lead. Size is 7 to 9 inches in diameter. See also *Sorghum Skimmer*.

Skimmer

SKIN SCRAPER. See *Scraper, Skin*.

SKINNING GAMBREL. See *Gambrel*.

SKINNING KNIFE. See *Knife, Butchers'*.

SKIRT CHANNELING MACHINE. See *Leather Machine, Skirt Channeling*.

SKIRT EDGER. See *Leather Tool, Edger*.

SKIVER. See *Knife, Leather* and *Shoe Makers' Machine, Skiver*.

SKUTCH. Also called BRICK AXE, BRICK LAYERS' SKUTCH, BRICK SKUTCH and SCOTCH HAMMER. A brick masons' tool used to cut or trim a brick. Weight of the brick layers' skutch is 16 to 42 ounces. The illustrated tile setters' skutch weighs 9 ounces.

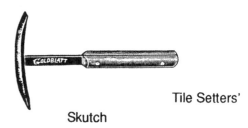

Tile Setters'
Skutch

Skutch

SLASHING MACHINE. A lever-operated knife used by a comb maker for cutting horn into comb blanks. The illustrated machine has a 14 inch cutter.

Slashing Machine

SLATE CLEAVER. See *Axe, Slaters'*.

SLATE CUTTERS' TRIMMER. See *Axe, Slaters'*.

SLATE TRIMMER. See *Axe, Slaters'*.

SLATERS' TOOLS. The special-purpose slaters' tools listed below can be found in normal alphabetical sequence. These tools may also have been used for other purposes.
AXE, SLATERS'
HAMMER, SLATERS'
RIPPER, SLATERS'
STAKE, SLATE CUTTER

SLEDGE. A two-handed striking tool with the head set at right angles to the handle. A sledge is made of steel and is intended for striking dense material such as an iron forging or a metal stake.

SLEDGE, BLACKSMITHS'. A common type of sledge favored by blacksmiths. Weight is 3 to 24 pounds. See also *Sledge, Double Faced*.

SLEDGE, BURSTING. Also called PAVERS' BURSTING SLEDGE and STONE SLEDGE. A stone-quarry tool used for breaking a large slab of rock.

SLEDGE, COAL. Also called COAL MAUL and COAL MINERS' SLEDGE. Used for driving wedges to break out coal. Weight is 3 to 10 pounds.

Straight Peen   Cross Peen
Blacksmiths' Sledge

Bursting Sledge

Coal Sledge

SLEDGE, COAL MINERS'. See *Sledge, Coal*.

SLEDGE, CROSS PEEN. See *Sledge, Blacksmiths'*.

SLEDGE, DOUBLE FACE. Also called STONE MASONS' SLEDGE and TIMBER MAUL. A common type of general-purpose sledge offered by many suppliers of blacksmithing tools. Weight is 4 to 40 pounds.

SLEDGE, FARMERS'. A sledge with a sharpened straight peen on one side. Used for general-purpose sledge work and for opening the split on a log.

Blacksmiths'   Nevada Pattern

Double Face Sledge

Straight Peen Sledge

SLEDGE, TURNING. Also called FARRIERS' SLEDGE, FARRIERS' TURNING SLEDGE, HORSE SHOE SLEDGE and HORSE SHOERS' SLEDGE. A sledge used in turning the iron bar to form a basic horse shoe. Weight is 5 to 12 pounds.

Farmers' Sledge

SLEDGE, FARRIERS'. See *Sledge, Turning.*

SLEDGE, STONE. A general-purpose stone quarry tool. Weight is 4 to 24 pounds. One supplier referred to a stone axe as a DOUBLE EDGE STONE SLEDGE. See also *Axe, Stone* and *Sledge, Bursting.*

Turning Sledge

SLEDGE AXE. See *Axe, Wedge.*

SLEEPER AXE. See *Axe, Sleeper.*

SLEEVE DRIVER. See *Wrench, Sleeve.*

SLEEVE WRENCH. See *Wrench, Sleeve.*

SLICE BAR. See *Fire Tools, Furnace.*

SLICE CHISEL. See *Chisel, Slice.*

SLICE GOUGE. See *Gouge, Slice.*

SLICK. A wide chisel-shaped tool.

SLICK, CARPENTERS. A 2 1/2 to 4 inch wide chisel having a long handle with a knob on the end. The slick is intended to be pushed to accomplish the cutting action rather than being struck with a mallet. Used for shaping the joints for beam construction and for similar tasks.

SLICK, CLAPBOARD. A light slick used for making clapboards. This tool is intended for splitting rather than cutting and therefore does not have a keen cutting edge. The crossbar or D handle facilitates the twisting motion required for completing the split.

Stone Sledge

SLEDGE, STRAIGHT PEEN. Also called BLACKSMITHS' STRAIGHT PEEN SLEDGE and HUBBARD PATTERN SLEDGE. Weight is 3 to 20 pounds.

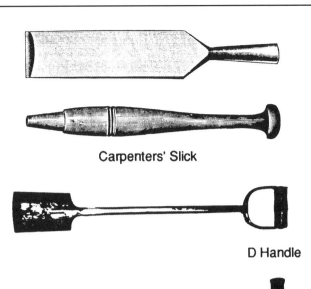

Carpenters' Slick

D Handle

T or Cross Bar Handle

Clapboard Slick

Slick Bone. See *Shoe Makers' Tool, Slick Bone*.

Slicker. See *Curriers' Slicker* and *Leather Tool, Slicker*.

Slide Arm Plow. See *Plane, Panel Plow*.

Slide Rule. See *Rule, Calculating* and *Rule, Slide*.

Sliding T Bevel. Also called Bevel. A tool used to transfer an angle and as a straight edge to mark a given angle for multiple cuts. Length is 6 to 14 inches. The tool can be set and locked at any angle.

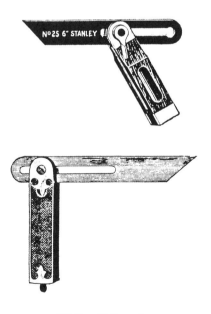

Sliding T Bevel

Sliding Tongs. See *Tongs, Jewelers'*.

Slim Taper File. See *File, Taper*.

Slip. See *Sharpening Stone*.

Slip Joint Pliers. See *Pliers, Slip Joint*.

Slip Stone. See *Sharpening Stone*.

Slitting File. See *File, Slitting*.

Slitting Gauge. Also called Cutting Gauge. A tool with a knife-like cutter used for cutting wide strips of veneer parallel with the edge of the cutting board. Length is 17 to 24 inches.

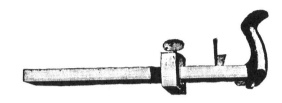

Slitting Gauge

Slot Cutting Pliers. See *Pliers, Wire*.

Sloyd Knife. See *Knife, Carvers'*.

Smasher. See *Electrotype Finishers' Tool, Smasher*.

Smoker. See *Bee Smoker*.

Smooth Plane. See *Plane, Smooth*.

Smoother. See *Plane, Smooth*.

Smoothing Brush. See *Brush, Paper Hangers'*.

Smoothing Iron, Hatters'. The illustrated tools are gas-heated hatters' smoothing irons. Similar irons were made for other trades and for household use. The household irons were generally heated by placing them on the surface of the kitchen stove. See also *Hat Brim Iron*.

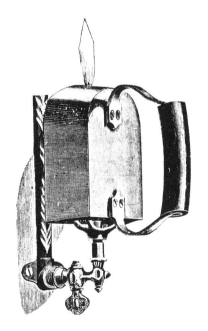

Hatters' Iron

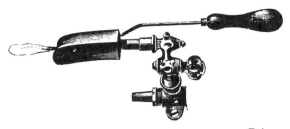

Brim

Hatters' Iron

SMOOTHING IRON, ROOFING. A long-handled tool used to smooth asphalt or roofing tar on a curved surface. Weight is 40 to 50 pounds.

Roofing Iron

SNAP FASTENER ANVIL. See *Anvil, Curtain Fastener*.

SNARLING IRON. See *Stake, Silversmiths'*.

SNATH. A curved handle for a scythe or grain cradle. A snath, as defined by the tool dealers, includes the hardware for attaching the scythe blade.

Snath

SNATH WRENCH. See *Wrench, Snath*.

SNIPE BILL. See *Plane, Moulding, Snipe Bill*.

SNIPE NOSE PLIERS. See *Pliers, Chain*.

SNIPS. See *Bale Tie Snips* and *Tinners Snips*.

SNOB HAMMER. A saddlers' tool. See *Hammer, Snob*.

SNOW BALL HAMMER. See *Hammer, Snow Ball*.

SNOW FENCE MACHINE. A device used to twist wires around upright slats to form a snow fence. Each of the seven wheels are intended to twist a pair of wires. All of the wheels turn in unison from a single crank.

SNOW KNOCKER. See *Hammer, Snow Ball*.

SOAPSTONE MARKER. See *Crayon, Metal*.

SOCKET CHISEL. See *Chisel, Socket*.

SOCKET FRAMING CHISEL. See *Chisel, Framing*.

SOCKET MALLET. See *Mallet, Socket*.

SOCKET PEAVEY. See *Peavey*.

Snow Fence Machine

SOCKET SET SCREW WRENCH. See *Wrench, Socket Set Screw*.

SOCKET WRENCH. See *Wrench, Socket*.

SOD KNIFE. See *Knife, Sod*.

SOD LIFTER. A tool used to remove sections of grass sod for replanting. The illustrated tool has a 9 inch blade.

Sod Lifter

SOFT FACED HAMMER. See *Hammer, Soft Faced*.

SOLDERING COPPER. See *Soldering Iron*.

SOLDER POT. Also called **MELTING POT.** A cast iron pot used as a container for melting lead or solder. A plumbers' or tinners' tool. Size of the pot is 4 to 13 1/2 inches in diameter at the top.

Solder Pot

SOLDERING IRON. Also called **SOLDERING COPPER.** A blunt metal tool that is heated and used to melt and smooth solder. Usually consists of a shaped copper slug formed on the end of an iron handle.

Hatchet Iron or Hatchet Bolt

Jewelers'

Plumbers' Round Iron

Self Heating

Soldering Iron

SOLDERING STOVE. A bench-mounted stove used for heating a soldering iron. The illustrated stove uses gas for fuel.

Soldering Stove

SOLE CUTTER. See *Shoe Makers' Machine, Sole Cutter.*

SOLE GAUGE. See *Shoe Makers' Tool, Sole Gauge.*

SOLE KNIFE. A knife with a small curved blade used to trim the inside of a horses hoof. It cuts by being struck with a hammer. The sole knife is used on coarse work that is too tough or too hard to trim with the common farriers' knife. It is similar in appearance to the Buffer but has a slightly curved blade and a keen cutting edge.

Sole Knife

SOLE RASP. See *Rasp, Shoe.*

SOLID CENTER BIT. See *Boring Tool, Bit, Irwin Pattern.*

SORGHUM SKIMMER. A scoop used to skim off the residue as cane juice is boiled to make sorghum molasses. The handle is approximately 24 inches long. Width of the illustrated skimmer is 5 inches.

Sorghum Skimmer

SOW. See *Anvil Tool, Sow.*

SPADE. A digging and separating tool capable of cutting action as it is pushed into the work. See also *Butter Packer.*

Concrete

Dirt

Draining

Hedge

Post

Spade

Iowa Pattern

Post Hole

Tiling

Bog or Peat

Spade

SPADING FORK. See *Fork, Garden* and *Fork, Spading*.

SPALDING HAMMER. See *Hammer, Spalling*. Spalding is an incorrect variation in spelling.

SPALLING HAMMER. See *Hammer, Spalling*.

SPANISH PATTERN ADZE. See *Adze, Spanish Round Eye*.

SPANISH PATTERN AXE. See *Axe, Single Bit*, Spanish pattern.

SPANNER. See *Wrench, Spanner*.

SPAR PLANE. See *Plane, Spar*.

SPATULA. A tool with a thin flexible blade used for lifting, mixing or spreading a soft substance such as paint. See also *Knife, Pallet*.

Spatula

SPATULA, TAR. A wooden tool used to smooth and distribute hot tar on a flat surface such as a roof or driveway.

Tar Spatula

SPAULING HAMMER. See *Hammer, Spalling*. Spauling is an incorrect variation in spelling.

SPEAR POINT. See *Turning Tool, Spear Point*.

SPEED INDICATOR. A device used to determine the speed of a rotating shaft. The dial indicates RPM when the point is pressed against the end of a shaft. The illustrated tool was patented September 12, 1876.

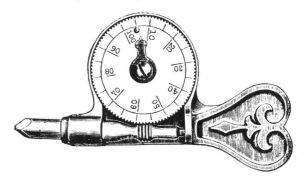

Speed Indicator

SPHEROMETER. A gauge for measuring the curvature of a lens, mirror or other curved surface. The illustrated tool is approximately 2 inches in diameter. It is calibrated in millimeters.

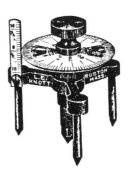

Spherometer

SPICE MILL. See *Grinding Mill*.

SPIKE. See *Hand Spike*.

SPIKE GIMLET. See *Boring Tool, Gimlet*.

SPIKE MAUL. See *Maul, Spike*.

SPIKE PULLER. A tool used to pull railroad spikes. The spike puller is used between switch rails and in other congested spaces not accessible to a claw bar. The claw of the spike puller is placed under the head of the spike and a claw bar is then attached above the top of the rail.

Spike Puller

SPIKE START. A ship builders' tool.

SPIKE TAMPER. A tool used for aerating a lawn. Reversing the head allows the tool to be used as a sand tamper.

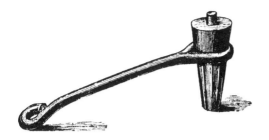

Spike Start

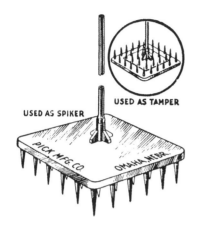

Spike Tamper

SPIKING HAMMER. See *Maul, Spike.*

SPILL PLANE. See *Plane, Spill.*

SPINNING TOOL. See *Metal Spinning Tool.*

SPIRAL SCREW DRIVER. See *Screw Driver, Archimedes* and *Screw Driver, Push.*

SPIRAL DRILL. See *Boring Tool, Archimedes Drill* and *Boring Tool, Push Drill.*

SPIRIT LEVEL. See *Level, Spirit.*

SPLICING CLAMP. Also called SPLICING TOOL. A linemans' tool used for splicing wire. The several holes allow use with different sizes of wire.

Splicing Clamp

SPLICING TOOL. See *Splicing Clamp.*

SPLITTER. Also called COOPERS' SPLITTER. A coopers' tool used to split a white oak sapling for making wooden barrel hoops. The splitter is made of solid iron. A similar tool used by a basket maker is called a CLEAVE. See also *Leather Machine, Splitting* and *Stone Cutters' Tool, Splitter.*

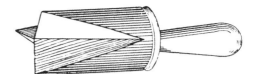

Splitter

SPLITTING BAR. See *Bar, Ice* and *Fork, Splitting.*

SPLITTING CHISEL. See *Anvil Tool, Hot Cutter; Chisel, Ice; Stone Cutters' Tool, Splitter* and *Stone Cutters' Tool, Splitting Chisel.*

SPLITTING FORK. See *Fork, Splitting.*

SPLITTING KNIFE. See *Leather Machine, Splitting.*

SPLITTING MACHINE. See *Leather Machine, Splitting.*

SPLITTING SAW. See *Saw, Hand.*

SPOKE AUGER. See *Hollow Auger.*

SPOKE AUGER MACHINE. See *Tenoning Machine.*

SPOKE BENCH. See *Bench, Spoke.*

SPOKE CALIPER. See *Rule, Caliper.*

SPOKE DOG. A device used to pull a spoke into the proper position to enter the hole in the felloe. The hook is looped over the troublesome spoke and the handle is used as a lever against a solid spoke.

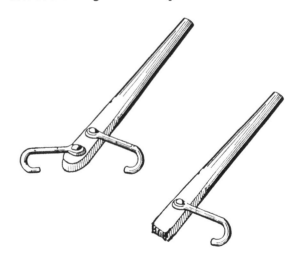

Spoke Dog

SPOKE EXTRACTOR. A machine used to pull a spoke from a wagon hub. A damaged spoke is quite difficult to remove from a solid hub. This device was an attempt to solve that problem.

SPOKE POINTER. Also called SPOKE TRIMMER. A tool used to taper the end of a wagon spoke so that the hollow auger can be started. The pointer automatically centers on a square or round spoke. These devices were made in a variety of types and sizes. One type has an adjustable shank that serves as a depth stop. Inasmuch as they were used frequently during wheel repair, spoke pointers were standard items in blacksmith shops as well as in wheelwright shops.

Spoke Extractor   Spoke Pointer

SPOKE SHAVE. Also called DRAW SHAVE. A small two-handed tool used for shaping a wagon or buggy spoke. It is generally used with a pushing stroke. The spoke shave was listed as a wheelwrights' tool but was such a handy gadget that most woodworkers owned one or more. These tools were made in almost countless sizes, shapes and qualities. Some general types are illustrated.

SPOKE SHAVE, CARRIAGE MAKERS'. Also called Coach Makers' Spoke Shave. A light-weight shave with long handles.

Carriage Makers' Spoke Shave

SPOKE SHAVE, CARRIAGE MAKERS' PANEL. A flat-bottomed shave with the handles curved upward to allow hand clearance on a flat surface. The tool shown in illustration (a) was also listed as a BELT MAKERS' SHAVE and as a BOX SCRAPER. The tool shown in illustration (b) was patented as a SHOE MAKERS' SHAVE intended to smooth the end grain of a shoe makers' cutting block. Available catalogue listings did not mention the shoe maker application.

(a)

Carriage Makers' Panel Shave

(b)

Carriage Makers' Panel Shave

SPOKE SHAVE, CHAIR MAKERS'. A shave that will cut a shallow concave surface such as might be required for a chair seat.

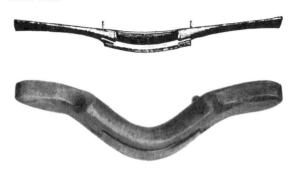

Chair Makers' Spoke Shave

SPOKE SHAVE, CHAMFER. Also called CHAMFERING SHAVE. A patented shave used to chamfer a long workpiece.

Chamfer Shave

SPOKE SHAVE, CIRCULAR. A small shave intended for use as a finishing tool on a curved surface. Used to remove very fine shavings.

Circular Spoke Shave

SPOKE SHAVE, COOPERS'. Also called COOPERS' SHAVE. A heavy-duty shave used for smoothing the outside of a barrel. Length is approximately 18 inches.

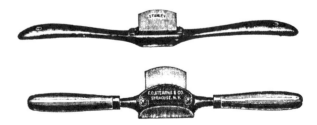

Coopers' Spoke Shave

SPOKE SHAVE, DOUBLE IRON. A shave with two cutting irons. Illustration (a) is a common type double shave having one straight and one concave iron. Illustration (B) shows a shave intended for use in a restricted area. The metal protector clip can be installed over either blade making the tool adaptable for either right or left hand work. Overall length of this shave is 3 ¹/₂ inches.

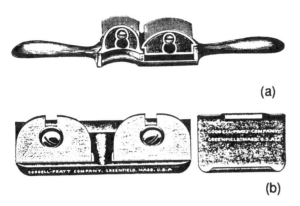

(a)

(b)

Double Iron Spoke Shave

SPOKE SHAVE, GENERAL PURPOSE. Some examples of the many varieties of general-purpose shaves are illustrated.

Wooden

Metal

Concave

Convex

Spoke Shave

SPOKE SHAVE, PATTERN MAKERS'. A wooden shave with a short blade and bottom. Intended for precision trimming.

Pattern Makers' Spoke Shave

SPOKE SHAVE, SINGLE HANDLE. A spoke shave used by a saddle maker to trim around the horn of a saddle tree.

Single Handle Spoke Shave

SPOKE TENON MACHINE. See *Tenoning Machine.*

SPOKE TENONER. See *Bench, Spoke.*

SPOKE TRIMMER. See *Spoke Pointer.*

SPOKE WRENCH. A bicycle wrench. See *Wrench, Nipple.*

SPOON. A tool used to remove the dust and debris from a hole drilled in stone. Length is 12 to 84 inches. See also *Post Hole Spoon.*

Spoon

SPOON AUGER. See *Boring Tool, Spoon Auger* and *Clog Makers' Tools.*

SPOON BIT. See *Boring Tool, Bit, Spoon.*

SPOON MOULD. See *Pewter Mould.*

SPOON STAKE. See *Stake, Spoon.*

SPORTSMANS' AXE. See *Axe, Hunters'.*

SPORTSMANS' HATCHET. See *Axe, Hunters'.*

SPOUT ADZE. See *Adze, Gutter.*

SPOUT AUGER. See *Molasses Auger.*

SPRAYER. A farm or garden device used for spreading liquid insect poison.

Pail Sprayer

Sprayer

Hand
Sprayer

SPREADING TOOL. See *Leather Tool, Spreading.*

SPRIG BIT. See *Boring Tool, Bit, Gimlet.*

SPRIG GIMLET. See *Boring Tool, Bit, Gimlet* and *Boring Tool, Gimlet.*

SPRING. See *Bending Spring.*

SPRING CALIPER. See *Caliper, Spring.*

SPRING GREASER. Also called SPRING LEAF LUBRICATOR, SPRING LEAF SPREADER and SPRING LUBRICATOR. A device used to spread the leaves of a spring for application of grease or oil. Used for maintenance of buggies, spring wagons and early automobiles. The devices shown in illustrations (a) and (b) have cup grease containers to allow insertion of grease directly through the hollow wedge point of the tool.

(a)

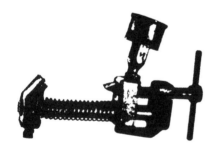

(b)

Spring Greaser

Spring Greaser

SPRING JOINT RULE. See *Rule, Spring Joint.*

SPRING LATCH BRACE. See *Boring Tool, Bit Brace, Spring Latch.*

SPRING LEAF SPREADER. See *Spring Greaser.*

SPRING LUBRICATOR. See *Spring Greaser.*

SPRING POLE LATHE. See *Lathe, Spring Pole.*

SPRING PUNCH. See *Punch, Leather.*

SPRING SWAGE. See *Anvil Tool, Swage.*

SPRING TONGS. See *Tongs, Spring.*

SPRING WINDER. A tool used for winding a small spring. The illustrated tool can be used in a lathe or with a bench vise.

Spring Winder

SPROUTING HOE. See *Hoe, Grub.*

SPRUE PICK. See *Moulders' Hand Tool.*

SPUD. See *Bark Spud* and *Weed Digger.*

SQUARE. A two-legged straight edge with one leg set at 90 degrees to the other. Used primarily to facilitate scribing a cutoff mark at 90 degrees relative to an adjacent side of the workpiece. Several fixed and adjustable angle straight-edge tools were also called squares by the suppliers. See also *Framing Tool* and *Triangular Mitre.*

SQUARE, BELT. A try square used for marking the ends of a flat belt. The illustrated square is 12 inches long.

SQUARE, BRIDGE BUILDERS'. A large square having a slotted leg three inches wide.

SQUARE, CARPENTERS'. See *Square, Steel.*

Belt Square

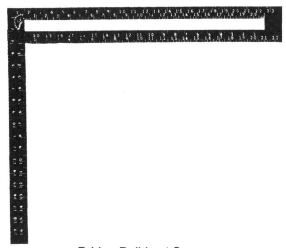

Bridge Builders' Square

SQUARE, CENTER. A square with one leg offset such that it can be used to locate the center of a circular object.

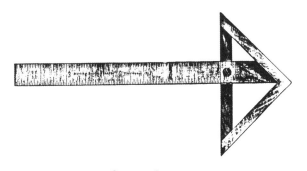

Center Square

SQUARE, COMBINATION. Numerous types of squares were made in combination with other tools. Some examples are illustrated. See also *Rule Attachment*.

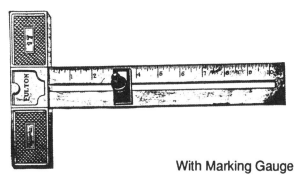

With Marking Gauge

Combination Square

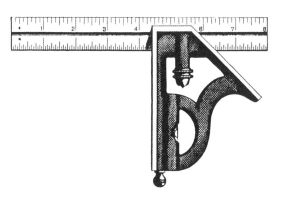

With Bevel and Level

With Bevel and Bevel Square

Combination Square

SQUARE, FRAMING. See *Square, Steel*.

SQUARE, GLASS CUTTERS'. A large square used by a glass cutter as a straight edge and for measuring. Length of the longest leg is 3 to 4 feet.

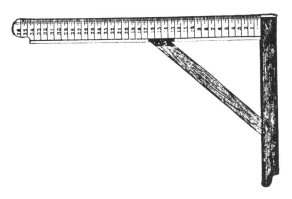

Glass Cutters' Square

SQUARE, MITER. A scaling tool with the blade or handle fixed at 45 degrees. See also *Triangular Mitre*.

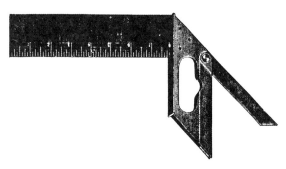

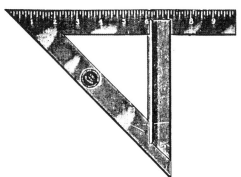

Miter Square

SQUARE, PLASTERERS'. A small metal square similar to a Steel Square except that it is marked in simple 1/8 inch graduations on the outside edges only. Size is 6 to 12 inches.

SQUARE, PLASTERERS' SET. A square and miter tool used by a plasterer when cutting and setting decorative mouldings. Size of the illustrated tool is 4 1/2 to 8 1/2 inches high.

Plasterers' Set Square

SQUARE, PROTRACTOR. This square was modestly advertised as follows: "This device prevents all possible errors in securing accurate dimensions and avoids the necessity of using complicated figures, rules or tables.

All difficulties in obtaining proper lengths for hip and jack rafters, the constructing of towers and all complicated shapes of buildings is obviated by the use of the ABC Protractor Square".

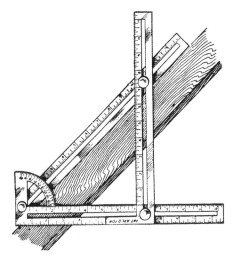

Protractor Square

SQUARE, RAFTER. See *Square, Steel*.

SQUARE, STEEL. Also called CARPENTERS' SQUARE, FRAMING SQUARE and RAFTER SQUARE. A large square used by a carpenter to lay out framing and rafters. Also used as a straight edge and squaring tool by the general woodworker.

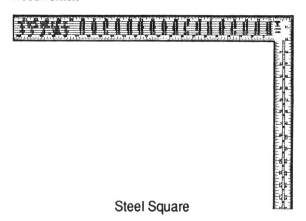

Steel Square

SQUARE, TAILORS'. A wooden square, usually with brass corner plates, used by a tailor. The long side of the illustrated tool is 21 1/2 inches.

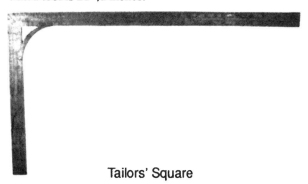

Tailors' Square

SQUARE, TAKE-DOWN. A steel square that is jointed at the corner such that it can be taken apart for storage.

Take-Down Square

SQUARE, TRY. A small square used as a straight edge when squaring the end of a board. The try square is also used to check a workpiece for squareness as it is being planed or sanded. Length of the scaled leg is 2 to 26 inches. The name is a hold-over from when each board was planed by hand and a tool was needed to try it for squareness during the planing process. The perforations in the blade of one type of try square allow it to be used with a pencil or scribe to serve as a marking gauge.

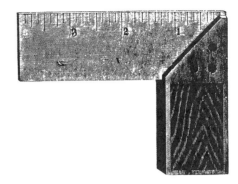

Try and Miter Combination

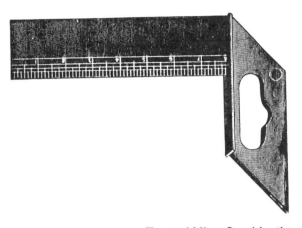

Try and Miter Combination

Wood Handle

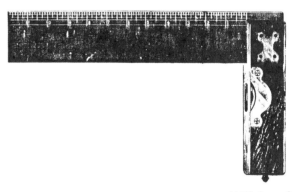

With Level

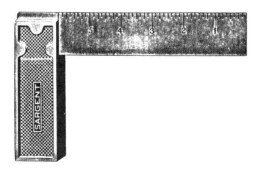

Steel Handle

Try Square

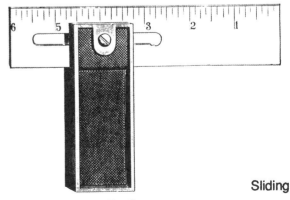

Sliding

Try Square

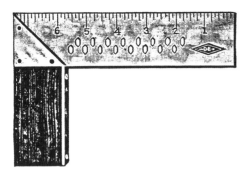

Perforated

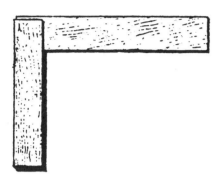

Wooden

Try Square

SQUARE, UNIVERSAL. A patented all-purpose square, mitre and straight edge.

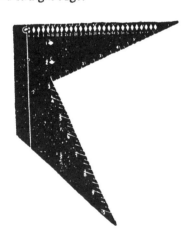

Universal Square

SQUARE CHISEL. See *Anvil Tool, Square Chisel*.

SQUARE EDGER. See *Cement Tool, Outside*.

SQUARE EDGE FILE. See *File, Joint*.

SQUARE FILE. See *File, Square*.

SQUARE HOLE BIT. See *Boring Tool, Bit, Square Hole*.

SQUARE MALLET. See *Mallet, Chisel*.

SQUARE PUNCH. See *Anvil Tool, Punch* and *Punch, Hand*.

SQUARE STAKE. See *Stake, Coppersmiths'* and *Stake, Sharpening*.

SQUARING SHEARS. See *Tinsmiths' Machine, Shears*.

STABBING AWL. See *Awl, Seat*.

STABLE BROOM. See *Broom, Stable*.

STABLE FORK. See *Fork, Stable*.

STABLE HOE. See *Hoe, Stable*.

STAGE SCREW. A device used by stage hands as a handle to pull stage curtains and props.

Stage Screw

STAIR BUILDERS' GAUGE. A gauge that can be attached to a steel square to lay out a stairway at any pitch or angle. Length is 18 to 28 inches.

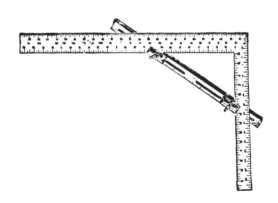

Stair Builders' Gauge

STAIR BUILDERS' SAW. See *Saw, Stair*.

STAIR COVE. See *Plane, Moulding, Cove*.

STAIR GAUGE. Also called **STAIR GAUGE FIXTURE.** A pair of stops that can be fastened to the legs of a steel square. These stops are used when marking the cuts for building a stair.

Stair Gauge

Stair Gauge

STAIR GAUGE FIXTURE. *See Stair Gauge.*

STAIR RAIL PLANE. See *Plane, Hand Rail.*

STAIR SAW. See *Saw, Stair.*

STAKE. A metal block used as a base for forming sheet metal by hammering.

STAKE, BALL. Also called BULLET STAKE and ROUND HEAD STAKE. A tinsmiths' stake with a rounded head. Diameter of head is 2 to 6 inches. Weight is 7 to 28 pounds.

Ball Stake

STAKE, BATHTUB. A stake used to form the curved rim on a bathtub.

Bathtub Stake

STAKE, BEAKHORN. A stake having a solid beak similar to the horn of a blacksmiths' anvil. Weight is 27 to 50 pounds.

STAKE, BEVEL EDGE SQUARE. Weight is 13 to 16 pounds.

STAKE, BICK IRON. See *Anvil, Coopers'.*

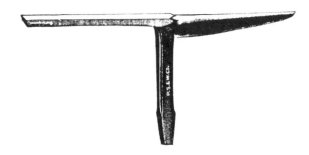

Beakhorn Stake

Bevel Edge Square Stake

STAKE, BLOWHORN. A stake with a wide tapered surface that can be used to shape objects such as funnels and the sides of dish pans. Weight is 14 to 19 pounds.

Blowhorn Stake

STAKE, BOTTOM. A stake used for forming the inside corners of a square pan or similar container. Length is 1 to 4 inches.

Bottom Stake

STAKE, BULLET. See *Stake, Ball.*

STAKE, CANDLE MOULD. A stake used to form candle moulds and other cylindrical shapes of small diameter. Length of the small end is approximately 18 inches. Weight is 6 1/2 to 7 1/2 pounds.

Candle Mould Stake

STAKE, CASE. See *Stake, Watch Case*.

STAKE, CONDUCTOR. A stake used for locking the seams of a metal pipe or conduit. Weight is 25 to 28 pounds.

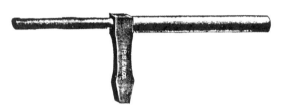

Conductor Stake

STAKE, COPPERSMITHS'. Also called COPPERSMITHS' SQUARE STAKE and SQUARE STAKE. Size of face is approximately 2 1/2 by 4 1/2 inches. Weight is 11 to 14 pounds.

Coppersmiths' Stake

STAKE, CREASING. A stake used to make creases for wire and stiffening. Weight is 12 to 12 1/2 pounds.

Creasing Stake

STAKE, CREASING HORN. A combination stake having both a creasing surface and a horn. Weight is approximately 12 pounds.

Creasing Horn Stake

STAKE, DOUBLE SEAM. Also called DOUBLE SEAMING STAKE. Total weight of the stake and the interchangeable heads is about 100 pounds.

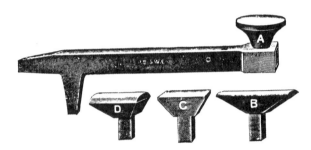

Double Seam Stake

STAKE, HATCHET. A stake used in making a sharp crease or bend in a long workpiece. Weight is 3 to 16 pounds.

Hatchet Stake

STAKE, HOLLOW MANDREL. See *Mandrel, Stove Pipe*.

STAKE, JEWELERS'. See *Anvil, Jewelers'*.

STAKE, MANDREL. Also called SOLID MANDREL STAKE. Weight is 43 to 86 pounds.

Mandrel Stake

Sharpening Stake

STAKE, NEEDLE CASE. A stake with a very small diameter extension. Used for making needle cases, small cylinders and spouts. The small end is 8 to 10 1/2 inches long. Weight is approximately 4 pounds.

Snarling Iron

Needle Case Stake

STAKE, PLATE. See *Stake, Tray*.

STAKE, ROUND HEAD. See *Stake, Ball*.

STAKE, SAW SETTING. A fixture used for holding a circular saw while setting.

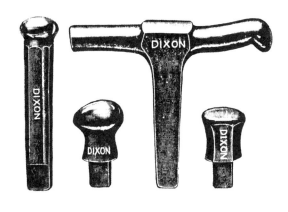

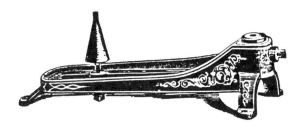

Saw Setting Stake

STAKE, SHARPENING. Also called SQUARE STAKE. A square or rectangular stake with a 1 3/4 to 5 1/2 inch face. Weight is 3 to 16 pounds.

STAKE, SILVERSMITHS'. A family of small stakes used by silversmiths and copper workers.

STAKE, SLATE CUTTER. Also called SLATERS' STAKE. A stake used for cleaving a roofing slate. Length is 16 to 24 inches.

STAKE, SPOON. A stake used by a silversmith for straightening or repairing a spoon. Three sizes were available.

Silversmiths' Stake

Slate Cutter Stake

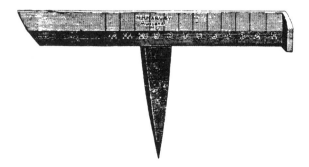

Slate Cutter Stake

Spoon Stake

STAKE, SOLID MANDREL. See *Stake, Mandrel.*

STAKE, SQUARE. See *Stake, Sharpening.*

STAKE, TEA KETTLE. Weight is 45 to 75 pounds.

Tea Kettle Stake

STAKE, THIMBLE. Also called THIMBLE MANDREL. A stake used for straightening a thimble.

Thimble Stake

STAKE, TRAY. Also called PLATE STAKE. A stake used for forming and planishing a tray or plate. This stake is intended for use in a bench vise.

Tray Stake

STAKE, WATCH CASE. Also called CASE STAKE. A stake used by a jeweler for straightening and repairing the case of a pocket watch.

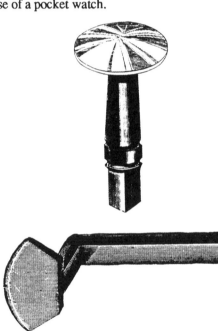

Watch Case Stake

STAKE PUNCH. A heavy iron tool used to make a starting hole for a stake or a sharpened fence post. Overall length is about 5 feet.

460

Stake Punch

STAKING HAMMER. See *Hammer, Jewelers'*.

STAMP. See *Leather Tool, Stamp*.

STAMP AXE. See *Axe, Marking*.

STAMP HAMMER. See *Hammer, Marking*.

STANDARD. See *Tinsmiths' Machine Standard*.

STANDING PRESS. See *Copying Press*.

STAPLE PULLER. A tool used as a lever for removing fence staples. Length is 9 to 10 inches. See also *Pliers, Fence*.

Staple Puller

STAR DRILL. Also called BRICK DRILL, MASONS' STAR DRILL and STONE DRILL. A tool used to make a hole in brick or stone. The tool is struck with a hammer or sledge and rotated a partial turn between blows. Size is 1/4 to 1 1/2 inches in diameter.

Star Drill

STAR STITCHER PUNCH. See *Leather Tool, Star Stitcher Punch*.

STARTING BAR. See *Bar, Car Starting*.

STARTING CHISEL. See *Bar, Ice*.

STARTING LEVER. A logging tool used to start a log roll. Usually equipped with a 5 or 6 foot handle.

Starting Lever

STAVE AXE. See *Axe, Stave*.

STAVE FROE. See *Froe*.

STAVE KNIFE. See *Drawing Knife, Coopers'*.

STAVE MAKERS' DRAWING KNIFE. See *Drawing Knife, Stave Makers'*.

STAVE SAW FILE. See *File, Stave Saw*.

STAVE RULE. See *Rule, Stave*.

STAVE WEDGE. See *Wedge, Stave*.

STEADY. An English clog makers' last used when nailing the irons to the bottom of the clog. Generally held between the knees during use. The illustrated tool is 27 inches tall.

Steady

STEAK GREITH. Also called MEAT TENDERER and STEAK GREATH. A kitchen tool used to tenderize meat by pounding and cutting.

Steak Greith

STEAK POUNDER. A kitchen tool used to tenderize meat by pounding. Overall length is about 11 inches.

Steak Pounder

STEAM FITTERS' CLAMP. See *Clamp, C*.

STEAM VALVE RULE. See *Rule, Steam Valve*.

STEEL ERASER. See *Ink Eraser*.

STEEL FIGURES. See *Marking Set*.

STEEL LETTERS. See *Marking Set*.

STEEL SQUARE. See *Square, Steel*.

STEEL STAMP. See *Marking Set* and *Ring Stamp*.

STEEL WOOD CHISEL. See *Chisel, Plumbers'*.

STEELYARD SCALES. See *Scales, Steelyard*.

STENCIL BRUSH. See *Brush, Stencil*.

STEP FINISHING TOOL. See *Cement Tool, Outside*.

STEP NOSING PLANE. See *Plane, Nosing*.

STEP PLANE. See *Plane, Nosing*.

STEP TOOL. See *Cement Tool, Step*.

STEREOTYPE PLANE. See *Plane, Stereotype*.

STICKING KNIFE. See *Knife, Butchers'* and *Knife, Poultry Killing*.

STIPPLING BRUSH. See *Brush, Stippling*.

STIPPLING TOOL. See *Leather Tool, Stippling*.

STIRRUP ADZE. See *Adze, Hand*.

STITCH CUTTER. See *Shoe Makers' Tool, Stitch Cutter*.

STITCH DIVIDER. See *Shoe Makers' Tool, Stitch Divider*.

STITCH MARKER. See *Shoe Makers Tool, Clamming Marker*.

STITCH WHEEL. See *Shoe Makers' Tool, Stitch Wheel*.

STITCHING FRAME. See *Bookbinding Tool, Press*.

STITCHING HORSE. A seat with an attached clamp used for holding leather for sewing or lacing.

Stitching Horse

STOCK AND DIE. See *Tap and Die*.

STOCK MARKER. See *Ear Marker*.

STOCKING PLIERS. See *Pliers, Stockinger*.

STOCKINGER PLIERS. See *Pliers, Stockinger*.

STONE BREAKING HAMMER. See *Hammer, Bursting*.

STONE BUSH HAMMER. See *Hammer, Bush*.

STONE CHISEL. See *Stone Cutters' Tool, Chisel*.

STONE CUTTERS' BREAKING HAMMER. See *Hammer, Bursting*.

STONE CUTTERS' FACE HAMMER. See *Hammer, Stone*.

STONE CUTTERS' MASH HAMMER. See *Hammer, Stone Cutters'*.

STONE CUTTERS' TOOL. Also called GRANITE TOOL and MARBLE TOOL. Any of a family of small tools used to carve and letter in stone. These tools have two general types of heads. See illustration.

Hammer Head

Mallet Head

Stone Cutters' Tool

STONE CUTTERS' TOOL, CHISEL. Also called DROVE, GRANITE CHISEL and TOOLER. Width is 3/8 to 5 inches. The 2 inch size is often called a BOASTING CHISEL and the 3 1/2 inch size is sometimes listed as a BROAD TOOL.

Stone Chisel

STONE CUTTERS' TOOL, DROVE. See *Stone Cutters' Tool, Chisel*.

STONE CUTTERS' TOOL, FROSTING. A background tool used for working stone or marble. Size is 5/16 to 5/8 inches square.

Frosting Tool

STONE CUTTERS' TOOL, PITCHING. Also called PITCHING CHISEL. A stone working tool that cuts with a square shoulder rather than a sharp edge. A pitching tool is used to trim and dress large blocks of stone. Width is 3/4 to 3 inches.

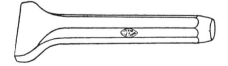

Pitching Tool

STONE CUTTERS' TOOL, POINT. Also called CARVING CHISEL and CARVING POINT. A lettering and carving tool for stone or marble.

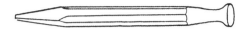

Point

STONE CUTTERS' TOOL, ROUND POINT. Also called MOULDING TOOL. A carving tool for stone.

Round Point

STONE CUTTERS' TOOL, SPLITTER. A separating chisel. Width of point is 3/8 to 3/4 inches.

Splitter

STONE CUTTERS' TOOL, SPLITTING CHISEL. A handled tool used for squaring up blocks of stone. Width of the cutting edge is 1 3/4 to 2 1/8 inches. Similar to the Blacksmiths' Hot Cutter.

Splitting Chisel

STONE CUTTERS' TOOL, TOOTH CHISEL. Width is 3/8 to 3 1/4 inches.

Granite

Marble

Tooth Chisel

Soft Stone

Tooth Chisel

STONE CUTTING TOOLS. Also called GRANITE TOOLS and MARBLE TOOLS. The special-purpose stone cutting tools listed below can be found in normal alphabetical sequence. These tools may also have been used for other purposes. See also *Stone Masons' Tools* and *Stone Quarry Tools*.

    AXE, STONE
    BULL SETT
    CALIPER, FIRM JOINT
    CHISEL, BUSH
    DRIFT PIN
    FILE, MARBLE CUTTERS'
    HAMMER, BURSTING
    HAMMER, BUSH
    HAMMER, CRANDALL
    HAMMER, SCOTIA
    HAMMER, STONE
    HAMMER, STONE CUTTERS'
    HAMMER, STRIKING
    LINE TRACER
    MALLET, STONE MASONS'
    RUBBING BRICK
    STONE CUTTERS' TOOL, CHISEL
    STONE CUTTERS' TOOL, FROSTING
    STONE CUTTERS' TOOL, PITCHING
    STONE CUTTERS' TOOL, POINT
    STONE CUTTERS' TOOL, ROUND POINT
    STONE CUTTERS' TOOL, SPLITTER
    STONE CUTTERS' TOOL, SPLITTING CHISEL
    STONE CUTTERS' TOOL, TOOTH CHISEL

STONE DRILL. A drill that makes a hole in stone by impact. The ball-type drill shown in the illustration is 7 feet long. The hand drill is intended to be struck with a hammer. See also *Star Drill*.

Ball Drill

Hand Drill

Stone Drill

STONE FORK. See *Fork, Stone.*

STONE GAUGE. See *Stone Size Gauge.*

STONE HAMMER. See *Hammer, Napping* and *Hammer, Stone.*

STONE HOOK. See *Hook, Stone.*

STONE JACK. See *Jack, Lifting.*

STONE JOINT RAKER. See *Joint Raker.*

STONE MASONS' TOOLS. The special-purpose stone masons' tools listed below can be found in normal alphabetical sequence. These tools may also have been used for other purposes. Many of these tools are also suitable for use by a brick mason.

  AXE, STONE
  BAR, SETTING
  CALIPER, FIRM JOINT
  CAVEL
  HAMMER, MASONS' PINNING
  HAMMER, STONE CUTTERS'
  HOD
  JACK, LIFTING
  JOINT RAKER
  LEVEL, MASONS'
  MALLET, STONE MASONS'
  PLUMB BOB
  TOOL BAG
  TROWEL
  TUCK POINTER

STONE PAVING HAMMER. See *Hammer, Paving.*

STONE QUARRY TOOLS. The special-purpose stone quarry tools listed below can be found in normal alphabetical sequence. These tools may also have used for other purposes. See also *Stone Cutting Tools.*

  AXE, STONE
  JACK, LIFTING
  HAMMER, BURSTING
  HAMMER, BUSH
  HAMMER, STONE
  HAMMER, STONE CUTTERS'
  HAMMER, STRIKING
  PICK, STONE
  SLEDGE, BURSTING
  SLEDGE, DOUBLE FACED
  SLEDGE, STONE
  STAR DRILL
  STONE DRILL
  WEDGE, JUMPING
  WEDGE, STONE

STONE SETTER. A press used by a comb maker to set small stones or brilliants into a heated comb blank.

STONE SIZE GAUGE. Also called DIAMOND GAUGE and STONE GAUGE. A jewelers' tool used to determine the approximate size of a precious stone. The illustrated tools are graduated in millimeters and carats.

Stone Setter

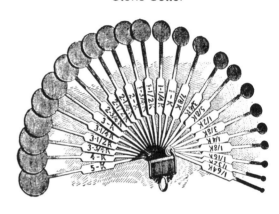

Stone Size Gauge

STONE SLEDGE. See *Axe, Stone* and *Sledge, Stone.*

STOP PUNCH. See *Punch, Stop.*

STORAGE BATTERY BIT. See *Boring Tool, Bit, Storage Battery.*

STOVE PIPE ANVIL. See *Mandrel, Stove Pipe.*

STOVE PIPE CRIMPER. See *Tinsmiths' Machine, Stove Pipe Crimper.*

STOVE PIPE FORMER. See *Tinsmiths' Machine, Pipe Former.*

STOVE PIPE MANDREL. See *Mandrel, Stove Pipe.*

STRAIGHT CLAW HAMMER. See *Hammer, Ripping.*

STRAIGHT FLUTED TONGS. See *Tongs, Blacksmiths'*.

STRAIGHT LIP TONGS. See *Tongs, Blacksmiths'*.

STRAIGHT PEEN HAMMER. See *Hammer, Straight Peen*.

STRAIGHT PEEN SLEDGE. See *Sledge, Blacksmiths'; Sledge Farmers'; Sledge, Stone* and *Sledge, Straight Peen*.

STRAINING FORK. See *Carpet Stretcher*.

STRAINING JACK. A mechanical device used to stretch webbing or leather. A pawl maintains the tension while the material is being tacked or sewed. A saddle makers' tool.

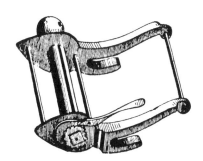

Straining Jack

STRAP END PUNCH. See *Leather Tool, Strap End Punch*.

STRAP HOLDER. See *Leather Tool, Strap Holder*.

STRAP WRENCH. See *Wrench, Strap*.

STRAPPED HAMMER. See *Hammer, Strapped*.

STRAW AND HAY CUTTER. A farm tool used to chop coarse fodder for livestock consumption or bedding. See also *Feed Cutter*.

Daniel's Patent

Straw and Hay Cutter

STRAW KNIFE. See *Knife, Straw*.

STRAWBERRY HOE. See *Hoe, Farm*.

STREET BROOM. See *Broom, Street*.

STRETCHER. See *Carpet Stretcher*.

STRETCHING IRON. See *Curriers' Slicker*.

STRICKLE. See *Card Strickle*.

STRIKE. A brickyard tool used to strike off the excess clay above the brick mold. A strike is also used to smooth off the excess from a container of grain or similar produce to obtain a precise measurement of volume.

Strike

STRIKING HAMMER. See *Hammer, Striking*.

STRIKING SLEDGE. See *Sledge, Double Face*.

STRIKING UNDER BAR. See *Bar, Ice*.

STRINGING AWL. See *Awl, Saddlers' Stringing*.

STRINGING HAMMER. See *Piano Tool, Stringing Hammer*.

STRINGING TOOL. See *Piano Tool, Stringing*.

STRIP AWL. See *Awl, Strip*.

STRIPING BRUSH. See *Brush, Striping*.

STRIPING WHEEL. A painters' tool used for making stripes or border designs. Wheels were available to make stripes up to 5/8 inches wide.

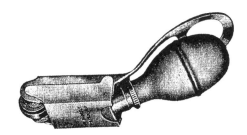

Striping Wheel

STRUCTURAL WRENCH. See *Wrench, Construction*.

STUCCO BRUSH. See *Brush, Stucco Dash*.

STUCCO DASH BRUSH. See *Brush, Stucco Dash*.

STUFFING FORCEPS. See *Forceps, Taxidermists'*.

STUFFING IRON. See *Horse Collar Tool, Stuffing Rod*.

STUFFING ROD. See *Horse Collar Tool, Stuffing Rod*.

SUEDE BRUSH. See *Brush, Suede*.

SUGAR AUGER. See *Sampler, Cement*.

SUGAR CANE KNIFE. See *Knife, Cane*.

SUGAR DEVIL. See *Fruit Auger*.

SUGAR GIMLET. See *Sampler, Cement*.

SUGAR JACK. See *Jack, Lifting*.

SUGAR NIPPERS. See *Nippers, Sugar.*

SUGAR SAMPLER. See *Sampler, Cement.*

SUGAR SCREW. See *Jack, Lifting.*

SUGAR TREE BIT. A boring bit with a short twist. See *Boring Tool, Bit, Sugar Tree.*

SULKY LADLE. See *Ladle, Foundry.*

SULPHUR BELLOWS. See *Bellows, Sulphur.*

SUMMER BAR. See *Bar, Ice.*

SUN PLANE. See *Plane, Leveling.* The curved coopers' plane used for leveling the top of a barrel is incorrectly called a sun plane by some collectors. There is no available evidence to indicate that American makers or dealers referred to this tool as a sun plane. The trade catalogues referred to it as a LEVELING PLANE and occasionally as a TOPPING PLANE.

SURFACE PICK. See *Pick, Surface.*

SURFACE PLATE. Also called PLANOMETER. A rigid metal plate used to check the surface flatness of a workpiece. The face of the surface plate is ground to a precision finish. Length is 12 to 68 inches. When in use, the surface of the plate is coated with a thin dye. The dye transfers to the surface of the workpiece to indicate each high spot.

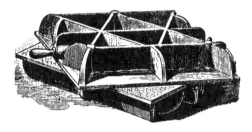

Surface Plate

SURVEYORS' CHAIN. Also called LAND CHAIN. A chain of known length used in land measure. These tools were available in lengths of one to four poles. A pole is the same as a rod or 16 1/2 feet.

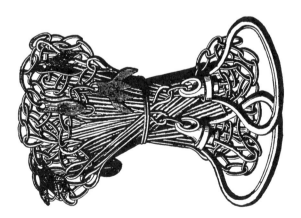

Surveyors' Chain

SWAGE. See *Anvil Tool, Channel Swage; Anvil Tool, Swage* and *Saw Swage.*

SWAGE BAR. Also called SAW ANVIL. A backing bar used by a saw maker or repairman. Size is 1 1/2 to 2 inches across the large end and approximately 5 inches long. The end is machined to specific tapers on two or more edges to use in gauging the amount of set in a saw.

Swage Bar

SWAGE BAR HAMMER. See *Hammer, Saw Swaging.*

SWAGE BLOCK. An iron block having various indentations and holes intended for use in forming hot metal. Weight is 100 to 675 pounds. The block could be procured with a low stand as illustrated. See also *Bending Block.*

Swage Block

SWAGING HAMMER. See *Hammer, Saw Swaging.*

SWAMPING AXE. See *Axe, Double Bit,* swamping pattern.

SWAN BILL PLIERS. See *Pliers, Stockinger.*

SWARM CATCHER. A wire-cloth basket used to catch a swarm of bees that has clustered on a tree or building. The illustrated tool has a 12 foot handle.

Swarm Catcher

SWEAT SCRAPER. A tool used to remove the sweat from a horse. Overall length of the wooden scraper is approximately 18 inches.

Wooden

Sweat Scraper

SWEDGE. A tinners' tool used for creasing or for forming a square corner.

Creasing

Square Pan

Swedge

SWING BRUSH. See *Brush, Swing.*

SWINGING MONKEY. A heavy iron ram suspended from the ceiling of a blacksmith shop or boiler assembly area. The monkey is pulled back from the vertical by use of the chain handle and released. As it swings forward, it strikes the workpiece with considerable force. A similar mechanism provides a striking action by letting the ram or monkey drop on the workpiece.

Swinging Monkey

SWITCH BROOM. See *Broom, Switch.*

SWIVEL CUTTER. See *Leather Tool, Swivel Cutter.*

SWIVEL JAW TONGS. See *Tongs, Blacksmiths'.*

SWIVEL TOP CUTTER. See *Leather Tool, Swivel Cutter.*

SYRINGE. See *Oil Syringe.*

T

Tool names starting with the letter T, including multiple listings of:

TAPE
TONGS
TOOL BOX
TOOL CHEST
TROWEL
TURNING TOOL

Included also are listings of tools used by the:

TANNER
TAXIDERMIST
TINSMITH
TURPENTINE HARVESTER

T BEVEL. See *Sliding T Bevel.*

T RABBET. See *Plane, Carriage Makers'.*

TABLE PLANE. See *Plane, Table.*

TACK CLAW. Also called CLAW and CLAW TOOL. A tool used to pull tacks and small nails. Length is 7 to 8 inches.

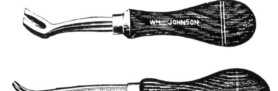

Tack Claw

TACK HAMMER. See *Hammer, Tack.*

TACK LIFTER. A simple tool used for inserting and extracting thumb tacks.

Tack Lifter

TACK PULLER. A device for removing tacks and staples.

Shoe or Saw Tooth

Tack Puller

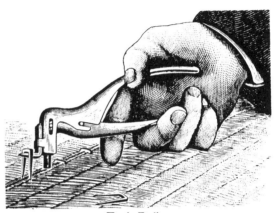

Tack Puller

TACK AND RIVET HOLDER. Also called REVOLVING NAIL CUP. A rotating cast iron bin used by shoe makers and harness makers for handy storage of tacks or rivets.

Tack and Rivet Holder

TACKING PINCERS. See *Pincers, Tacking.*

TACKING PLIERS. See *Pincers, Tacking.*

TACKLE BLOCK. A set of pulleys arranged to provide a mechanical advantage. Used for stretching fence wire, lifting heavy objects and for similar tasks.

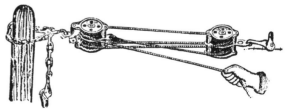

Tackle Block

TAIL SCREW. See *Vise, Tail*.

TAIL SQUARER. A shears used to square the brush of a horse tail. All of the tail hairs are gathered inside the circle of the tool and sheared with one movement of the cutter.

Tail Squarer

TAIL VISE. See *Vise, Tail*.

TAILORS' RULE. See *Rule, Tailors'*.

TAILORS' SHEARS. See *Shears, Upholsterers'*.

TAILORS' SQUARE. See *Square, Tailors'*.

TAKE-DOWN SQUARE. See *Square, Take-Down*.

TALLOW POT. A container for holding tallow. Capacity is 1 to 4 quarts. Tallow was used as a lubricant for low-speed bearings.

Tallow Pot

TALLOW SAMPLER. See *Sampler, Cheese*.

TALLOW TRIER. See *Sampler, Cheese*.

TALLY REGISTER. A hand counter used to tally livestock, car loading and for similar tasks. The read-out dial increases by one digit each time the thumb tab is pressed.

TAMPER. Also called RAMMER and SIDEWALK TAMPER. A tool used to tamp asphalt, concrete, dirt or sand. Weight is 7 to 35 pounds. See also *Rammer, Sand* and *Spike Tamper*.

TAMPING BAR. See *Bar, Tamping*.

TANBARK FORK. See *Fork, Coal*.

Tally Register

Cement   Dirt

Tamper

TANG CHISEL. See *Chisel, Tang*.

TANK BUILDERS' JOINTER. See *Plane, Floor*.

TANNERS' BEAM. A curved bench or platform over which a tanner places a hide for scraping.

Tanners' Beam

TANNERS' PIN. A metal scraper or smoother, with a triangular cross section, used to rub a hide after tanning to bring the bloom to the surface. Overall length of the illustrated tool is 27 inches.

Tanners' Pin

469

TANNERS' TOOLS. The special-purpose tanners' tools listed below can be found in normal alphabetical sequence. These tools may also have been used for other purposes.

BRUSH, TANNERS' BLACKING
FORK, COAL
HOOK, TANNERS'
KNIFE, FLESHING
KNIFE, UNHAIRING
PINCERS, TANNERS'
TANNERS' BEAM
TANNERS' PIN

TAP BORER. See *Boring Tool, Tap Borer.*

TAP TONGS. See *Tongs, Band Jaw.*

TAP WRENCH. See *Wrench, Tap.*

TAP AND DIE. Also called BOLT DIE, BOLT TAP, PIPE DIE, SCREW PLATE and STOCK AND DIE. Tools used to cut the threads for bolts and nuts. See also *Screw Box.*

Bit Brace

Blacksmiths'

Gunsmiths'

Machinists' Bottoming

Machinists' Plug

Machinists' Taper

Tap and Die

Pump Rod

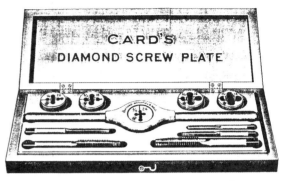

Screw Plate

Tap and Die

TAPE. A flexible strip calibrated for lineal measurement along one or more edges.

TAPE, CLOTH. Also called TAPE, TAPE LINE and TAPE MEASURE. A tape made of cloth or canvas. Spring-wind cloth tapes were generally 6 or 8 feet long. The crank-wind types were available up to 100 feet in length. The better quality cloth tapes were listed as having hard leather cases made of ass skin.

Crank Wind

Spring Wind

Upholsterers'

Cloth Tape

470

TAPE, STEEL. Also called TAPE RULE. A coiled tape made of steel.

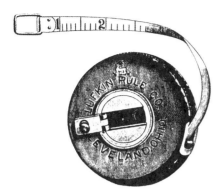

Crank Wind

Spring Wind

Farrand's Patent

Steel Tape

TAPE, UPHOLSTERERS'. See *Tape, Cloth.*

TAPE HOOK. A hook made for attachment to the end of a standard steel tape. The purpose of the hook is to secure one end of the tape while taking an outside measurement.

Tape Hook

TAPE LINE. See *Plumb Bob, Oil Gauger* and *Tape, Cloth.*

TAPE MEASURE. See *Tape, Cloth.*

TAPE RULE. See *Tape, Steel.*

TAPER BIT. See *Boring Tool, Bit, Taper.*

TAPER FILE. See *File, Taper.*

TAPER GAUGE. A tapered steel gauge used to measure a small diameter. The inside taper was also listed as a TEST TUBE GAUGE for laboratory work. The illustrated tools are graduated in millimeters. See also *Hole Gauge* and *Nut and Washer Gauge.*

Inside

Outside

Taper Gauge

TAPER MANDREL. A blacksmith tool. See *Cone.*

TAPER PIN REAMER. See *Boring Tool, Bit, Reamer.*

TAPER PUNCH. See *Punch, Taper.*

TAPPET WRENCH. See *Wrench, Check Nut.*

TAR RAKE. See *Rake, Asphalt.*

TAR SPATULA. See *Spatula, Tar.*

TAXIDERMISTS' TOOLS. The special-purpose taxidermists' tools listed below can be found in normal alphabetical sequence. These tools may also have been used for other purposes.

FORCEPS, TAXIDERMISTS'
KNIFE, CURRIERS'
KNIFE, FLESHING
PLIERS, TAXIDERMISTS'
SCRAPER, SKIN

TEA KETTLE STAKE. See *Stake, Tea Kettle.*

TEASEL. Also called FULLERS' TEASEL and TEASLE. A natural bur used for raising the nap on woolen cloth. The flower pod or bur of the teasel plant is covered with hooked spines. Diameter is 1 to 3 1/2 inches.

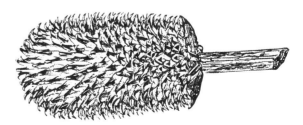

Teasel

TELEGRAPH SPOON. See *Post Hole Spoon.*

TELEPHONE POLE SUPPORT. See *Pole Support.*

TEMPERATURE PROBE. A brass cylinder containing a thermometer. Used to measure the internal temperature of bulk grain. A threaded rod is attached to the blunt end and used to insert the probe into a bin or car of grain. The illustrated probe is approximately 17 inches long.

Temperature Probe

TEMPERING SHOVEL. See *Shovel, Tempering.*

TENON CUTTER. See *Hollow Auger, Hollow Auger Brace, Tenoning Machine* and *Turning Tool, Tenoner.*

TENON SAW. See *Saw, Back.*

TENONER. See *Turning Tool, Tenoner.*

TENONING MACHINE. A hand-operated machine used to make a tenon. Illustration (a) shows a general-purpose machine for cutting rectangular tenons. Illustration (b) shows a machine comprised of a hollow auger, a handle and means for clamping a wagon spoke. The clamp holds the spoke squarely in line with the hollow auger thus assuring a straight cut. Also called SPOKE AUGER MACHINE and SPOKE TENON MACHINE.

(b)

Tenoning Machine

TERMINAL CLAMP PLIERS. See *Pliers, Battery.*

TERMINAL CLAMP TOOL. See *Battery Clamp Tool.*

TEST TUBE CLAMP. See *Clamp, Test Tube.*

TESTER. See *Prune Tester.*

TESTING NEEDLES. See *Gold Testing Needles.*

TEXTILE WRENCH. See *Wrench, Textile.*

THATCHERS' HOOK. See *Hook, Thatchers'.*

THATCHERS' NEEDLE. A device used for gathering and tying thatch.

Thatchers' Needle

THILL COUPLER. Also called SHACKLE JACK. A tool used by carriage makers and livery men to couple the thills to a buggy when rubber inserts are being used as anti-rattlers.

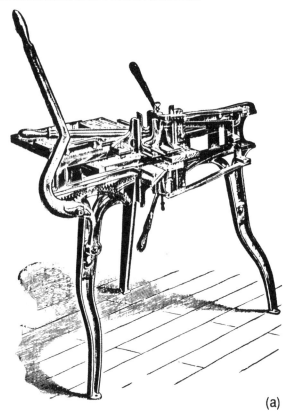

(a)

Tenoning Machine

Stone's Patent

Thill Coupler

Thill Coupler

THIMBLE. A device used on the finger or thumb to press a needle through cloth or leather. The upholsterer and trimmer often used an open-end thimble as shown in the illustration.

Thimble

THIMBLE MANDREL. See *Stake, Thimble*.

THIMBLE STAKE. See *Stake, Thimble*.

THONG AWL. See *Awl, Belt* and *Awl, Thong*.

THONGING CHISEL. See *Punch, Lace*.

THREAD CHASER. See *Screw Chaser*.

THREAD COUNTER. See *Pick Counter*.

THREAD GAUGE. Also called SCREW GAUGE, SCREW PITCH GAUGE and SCREW THREAD GAUGE. A tool used to determine the number of threads per unit length of a bolt, screw or nut.

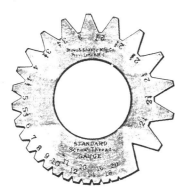

Thread Gauge

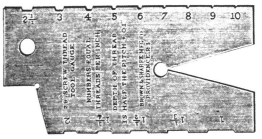

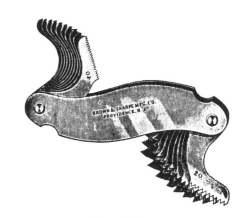

Thread Gauge

THREAD NIPPERS. See *Nippers, Thread*.

THREE ANGLE RULE TOOL. See *Rule Attachment*.

THREE-QUARTER AXE. See *Axe, Coal Miners'*.

THREE SQUARE FILE. See *File, Three Square*.

THRESHING FLAIL. See *Flail*.

THUMB COT. See *Thumb Stall*.

THUMB PLANE. See *Plane, Violin*.

THUMB SCREW BRACE. See *Boring Tool, Bit Brace, Thumb Screw*.

THUMB STALL. Also called THUMB COT. A guard used to protect the thumb and help provide a positive grip while husking corn. Illustration (a) shows a flexible wire thumb stall worn over a mitten.

TICKET PUNCH. See *Punch, Conductors'*.

TICKLER. See *Leather Tool, Tickler*.

Clark's Patent

(a)

Thumb Stall

Tie Adze. See *Adze, Tie.*

Tie Holder. A railroad tool used to hold a tie up against the rail while spiking. Two sizes were available.

Tie Holder

Tie Makers' Wedge. See *Wedge, Tie.*

Tie Peavey. See *Peavey.*

Tie Pick. See *Pick, Tie.*

Tie Tongs. See *Tongs, Tie.*

Tie Wedge. See *Wedge, Tie.*

Tight Barrel Croze. See *Plane, Croze.*

Tight Barrel Howel. See *Plane, Howel.*

Tile Drain Cleaner. See *Drain Cleaner.*

Tile Hook. See *Hook, Tile.*

Tile Layers' Hammer. See *Hammer, Tile Setters'.*

Tile Marker. A tool used for marking imitation tile.

Tile Marker

Tile Nippers. See *Nippers, Tile.*

Tile Setters' Hammer. See *Hammer, Tile Setters'.*

Tile Setters' Trowel. See *Trowel, Gauging* and *Trowel, Tile Setters'.*

Tiling Spade. See *Spade.*

Timber Bar. See *Bar, Timber.*

Timber Carrier. See *Timber Grapple.*

Timber Crayon. See *Crayon, Lumber.*

Timber Cruisers' Axe. A small double bit axe. See *Axe, Double Bit.*

Timber Dog. See *Logging Dog.*

Timber Drawing Knife. See *Drawing Knife, Timber.*

Timber Grapple. Also called Carrying Hook, Lug Hook and Timber Carrier. A two-man tool used for lifting ties, telephone poles and similar timbers. Length of the cross bar is 40 to 60 inches.

Timber Grapple

Timber Groover. See *Timber Scribe.*

Timber Jack. See *Jack, Lifting.*

Timber Maul. See *Sledge, Double Face.*

Timber Scribe. Also called Gaugers' Marking Iron, Marking Iron, Race Knife, Rase Knife and Timber Groover. A tool used to cut an identification mark in the end of a log or plank.

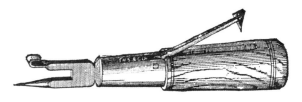

Timber Scribe

Timber Scribe

TIMBER SHAVE. See *Drawing Knife, Timber.*

TIMBER TOOLS. See *Logging Tools.*

TIMBERERS' AXE. See *Axe, Coal Miners'.*

TIN HORN. See *Seeder.*

TIN PIPE FORMER. See *Tinsmiths' Machine, Pipe Former.*

TIN ROOF CUTTER. A tool used to slit a sheet of roofing tin either before or after installation.

Tin Roof Cutter

TIN SNIPS. See *Tinners' Snips.*

TINNERS' AWL. See *Awl, Tinners'.*

TINNERS' BRAKE. See *Tinsmiths' Machine, Brake.*

TINNERS' CUTTING NIPPERS. See *Nippers, Tinners' Cutting.*

TINNERS' GROOVING TOOL. See *Grooving Tool.*

TINNERS' MALLET. See *Mallet, Tinners'.*

TINNERS' SNIPS. Also called HAND SHEARS and TIN SNIPS. A hand tool used for cutting sheet metal. Overall length is 7 to 15 3/4 inches. The hawk bill snips are especially suited to cutting around sharp corners without bending the metal.

For Curves

Hawk Bill

Tinners' Snips

Tinners' Snips

TINNERS' MACHINE. A hand-operated machine for bending, cutting, rolling or crimping sheet metal.

TINSMITHS' MACHINE, BEADING. A roller mechanism used by a tinsmith to make a bead in sheet metal. Beads are used for stiffening and joining as well as for ornamentation.

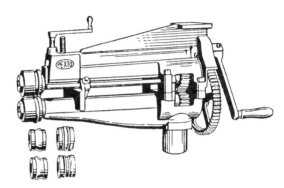

Beading Machine

TINSMITHS' MACHINE, BOSS FORMER. A device used to form a handle brace for a sheet metal container.

Boss Former

TINSMITHS' MACHINE, BRAKE. Also called CORNICE BRAKE. A machine for bending sheet metal. Forms were available to allow the machine to make circular as well as angular bends. Unlike the Folding Machine, the brake has an open throat and can be used to bend the workpiece at any point. A built-in clamp is used to hold a large sheet of metal in position while the bend is being formed.

Tinners' Brake

TINSMITHS' MACHINE, BURRING. A machine used for creasing the rim of a cover for a pail or boiler. Also used for preparing circular edges of vessels for double seaming.

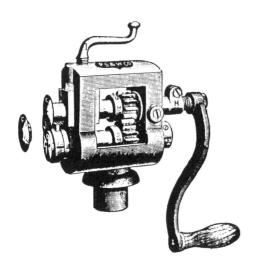

Burring Machine

TINSMITHS' MACHINE, CIRCULAR SHEARS. Also called ROTARY SHEARS. A machine that will cut a ring or circular plate from sheet metal without cutting through the outer edge. It will also cut an irregular curve when used without the locking arm.

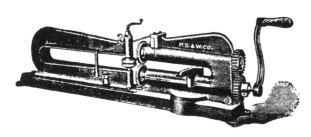

Circular Shears

TINSMITHS' MACHINE, CRIMPING. A machine used to crimp the bottom into a cylinder to form a can.

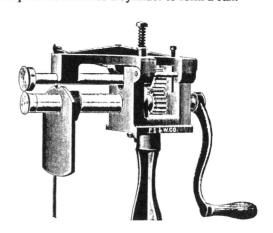

Crimping Machine

TINSMITHS' MACHINE, DOUBLE SEAMING. The double seaming machine follows the Setting Down Machine and bends the sealed joint back against the side of the workpiece. The seam is progressively tightened by multiple passes through the machine.

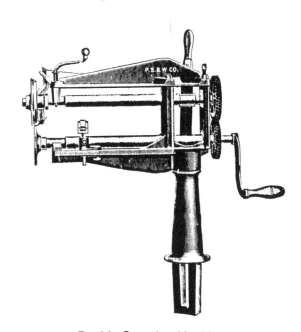

Double Seaming Machine

TINSMITHS' MACHINE, ELBOW EDGING. A machine used to form a square lip on the end of a cylindrical workpiece.

TINSMITHS' MACHINE, FOLDING. A machine used to fold the edge of a workpiece to form a lock or a groove for wire. Various models were available to bend sheets up to 85 inches wide. The illustrated machine will turn locks from 1/8 to 1 inch. BAR FOLDING, PIPE FOLDING and SHEET IRON FOLDING MACHINES are variations of this general type of device.

Elbow Edging Machine

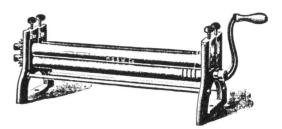

Pipe Former

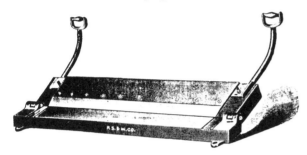

Folding Machine

Rim Machine

TINSMITHS' MACHINE, GROOVING. Also called HORN GROOVER. This device follows the Folding Machine to lock the seams together. It can be used on a flat or cylindrical workpiece.

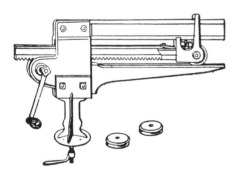

Grooving Machine

TINSMITHS' MACHINE, PIPE FORMER. Also called FORMING MACHINE and STOVE PIPE FORMER. A device, consisting of three round rollers, used to form sheet metal into a cylinder. Primary applications are making stovepipe, ducts and conduits. It can also be used to form small cylinders such as coffee pots and tin cans.

TINSMITHS' MACHINE, RIM. A crimping tool for flat or cylindrical work.

TINSMITHS' MACHINE, SETTING DOWN. This machine follows the Burring Machine and crimps the edge of the bottom section into the flange of the body of the container.

Setting Down Machine

TINSMITHS' MACHINE, SHEARS. Also called BENCH SHEARS, IRON SHEARS, METAL SHEARS and SQUARING SHEARS. A machine used for cutting sheet metal along a straight line. See also *Shears, Bench*.

TINSMITHS' MACHINE, STOVE PIPE CRIMPER. Also called PIPE CRIMPER. A machine used to crimp the end of a stove pipe section to allow insertion into the adjoining section. This machine is often combined with a beader that creates a swell in the pipe adjacent to the crimp.

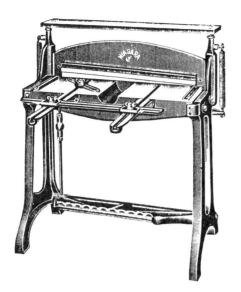

Tinsmiths' Shears

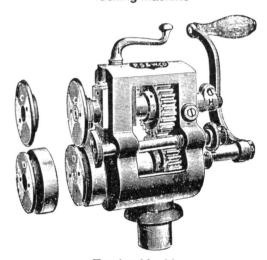

Tucking Machine

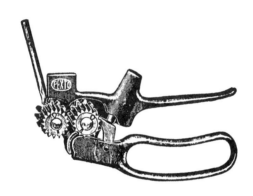

Turning Machine

TINSMITHS' MACHINE, WIRING. This machine rolls the metal tightly around the wire after the Turning Machine has formed a seat and the wire has been inserted. The workpiece is run through the machine several times as necessary to form a tight roll.

Stove Pipe Crimper

TINSMITHS' MACHINE, TUCKING. A machine used by the manufacturers of metal cans. It is intended for contracting or expanding the top or bottom edges of can bodies.

TINSMITHS' MACHINE, TURNING. A machine used to turn a circular or curved edge to receive a wire. The workpiece is run through the machine several times to achieve a tight bend on a small diameter curve.

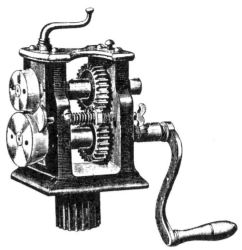

Wiring Machine

478

TINSMITHS' MACHINE STANDARD. Also called STANDARD. A fixture used for mounting a tinsmiths' machine. The machine standard is clamped to the workbench and serves as a single mount for one or more of the hand-operated machines.

Tinsmiths' Machine Standard

TINSMITHS' TOOLS. The special-purpose tinsmiths' tools listed below can be found in normal alphabetical sequence. These tools may also have been used for other purposes.

AWL, TINNERS'
BENCH PLATE
BOILER EXPANDER
CHISEL, LANTERN
CHISEL, WIRE
EAVES TROUGH CLOSING FORM
GROOVING TOOL
HAMMER, RAISING
HAMMER, RIVETING
HAMMER, ROOFING
HAMMER, TINNERS' FLANGED
HAMMER, TINNERS' PANEING
MALLET, TINNERS'
NIPPERS. TINNERS' CUTTING
PUNCH, HOLLOW
PUNCH, METAL
PUNCH, PRICK
PUNCH, STOP
RULE, CIRCUMFERENCE
SCRAPER, TINNERS' ROOFING
SHEARS, BENCH
SHEET METAL GAUGE
SOLDER POT
SOLDERING IRON
SOLDERING STOVE
STAKE, BALL
STAKE, BATH TUB
STAKE, BEAKHORN
STAKE, BEVEL EDGE SQUARE

STAKE, BLOWHORN
STAKE, BOTTOM
STAKE, CANDLE MOULD
STAKE, CONDUCTOR
STAKE, CREASING
STAKE, CREASING HORN
STAKE, DOUBLE SEAM
STAKE, HATCHET
STAKE, MANDREL
STAKE, NEEDLE CASE
STAKE, TEA KETTLE
SWEDGE
TINNERS' SNIPS
TINSMITHS' MACHINE, BEADING
TINSMITHS' MACHINE, BRAKE
TINSMITHS' MACHINE, BURRING
TINSMITHS' MACHINE, CIRCULAR SHEARS
TINSMITHS' MACHINE, CRIMPING
TINSMITHS' MACHINE, DOUBLE SEAMING
TINSMITHS' MACHINE, ELBOW EDGING
TINSMITHS' MACHINE, FOLDING
TINSMITHS' MACHINE, GROOVING
TINSMITHS' MACHINE, PIPE FORMER
TINSMITHS' MACHINE, RIM
TINSMITHS' MACHINE, SETTING DOWN
TINSMITHS' MACHINE, SHEARS
TINSMITHS' MACHINE, STOVE PIPE CRIMPER
TINSMITHS' MACHINE, TUCKING
TINSMITHS' MACHINE, TURNING
TINSMITHS' MACHINE, WIRING
TINSMITHS' MACHINE STANDARD
TONGS, ROOFING

TIRE BENDER. A device for bending the iron strap when making a new wagon or buggy tire. Imparting a uniform circular bend to a new tire without a bender is very difficult and extremely time consuming. The commercial benders consist of three rollers with one roller adjustable to control the degree of bend. In practice, the iron was generally run through the machine several times to obtain the correct amount of bend such that the ends would meet easily for welding. Benders were available in several sizes to suit the type of work anticipated. Sizes range from those suitable for use on a buggy tire up to those that will bend a 6 inch bar 1 1/4 inches thick. The large benders have a two-speed gear drive and some are designed to be power driven through a line shaft.

TIRE BOLT CLAMP. See *Tire Bolt Holder.*

TIRE BOLT HOLDER. Also called TIRE BOLT CLAMP. A tool used to hold the flush head of a tire bolt while removing the nut. The nut and end of the bolt were usually painted or rusty and therefore difficult to loosen. Illustration (a) shows one type of commercially made clamp. Illustration (b) shows a home made device that will accomplish the same task.

Tire Bender

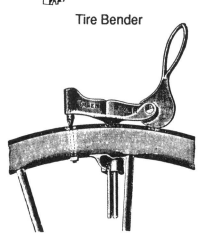

(a)

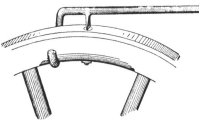

(b)

Tire Bolt Holder

Tire Bolter and Cutter. A device used to tighten the nuts on a wagon wheel bolt and to cut off the excess bolt length.

Tire Bolter and Cutter

Tire Channel Swage. See *Anvil Tool, Channel Swage*.

Tire Clamp. This type of clamp is used when installing a solid rubber tire on a buggy wheel. The clamp pushes the rubber back and holds it securely while the internal metal wires are being brazed or riveted together.

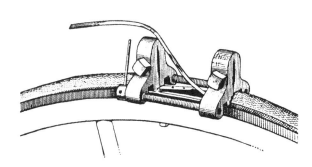

Tire Clamp

Tire Dog. A tool used to start a heated tire down over the rim of the wheel. After the tire is started with the tire dog, it can be driven down with a sledge or hand hammer.

Tire Dog

Tire Drill. See *Boring Tool, Tire Drill*.

Tire Gauge. See *Tire Measuring Wheel*.

Tire Heater. A special-purpose fire container used for heating a wagon or buggy tire. A metal wagon tire is expanded by heating before installation to assist in obtaining a tight fit to the wheel.

Tire Marker. A device used to mark a new tire for drilling to match an existing bolt hole in the felloe. The tire marker pin is placed in the old bolt hole from the inside and the center punch plunger is struck with a hammer.

Tire Heater

Wooden

Tire Marker

Tire Measuring Wheel

TIRE MEASURING WHEEL. Also called TIRE GAUGE, TIRE WHEEL and TRAVELER. A tool used to measure the length of flat strap required for making a new wagon tire. The wheel is measured by rolling the measuring wheel around the outside surface and counting the revolutions. The process is then repeated on a straight length of wagon tire iron. An additional amount is added to account for bending and welding. Most of the commercially made tire wheels are calibrated in inches and are equipped with a moveable pointer. The pointer can be set to the number of inches required in addition to complete revolutions. The home made measuring wheels generally have but one scribe line to mark the starting point of the measurement. Common commercial wheels are 24 inches in diameter and are made of either iron or brass. Home made varieties made of iron or wood are common.

TIRE PLIERS. See *Pliers, Tire.*

TIRE PLUG PLIERS. See *Pliers, Tire Plug.*

TIRE PULLER. Also called TIRE REMOVER. A device used to remove a tire from a wagon wheel. It can also be used for trueing a tire after installation. See also *Tongs, Tire Puller.*

Tire Puller

481

TIRE REMOVER. See *Tire Puller*.

TIRE SET. See *Anvil Tool, Tire Set*.

TIRE SETTER. A mechanism that consists of a tire setting plate in combination with a cooling tub. The tire is installed using the plate as a base for hammering. The plate and tire are then quickly lowered into a tub of water for cooling.

Tire Setter

TIRE SETTING PLATE. A metal plate 5 to 6 feet in diameter used by a wheelwright to provide a solid base for installing a tire on a wheel. These plates were available either flat or slightly dished. Weight is about 400 pounds.

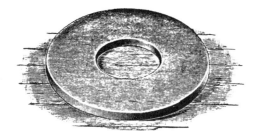

Tire Setting Plate

TIRE SHRINKER. Also called TIRE UPSETTER. A device used in blacksmith and wheelwright shops to decrease the diameter of a wagon or buggy tire. As the wheel ages, the wood parts tend to shrink and settle together resulting in the tire becoming loose. If the tire is only slightly loose, it can be easily tightened by shrinking. The tire shrinker grasps the heated tire at two points several inches apart and pushes the two points closer together. If too much shrinkage is attempted at one point on the tire, the metal will buckle or thicken to unusable proportions. The amount of shrinkage desired and possible with one heat is largely a matter of judgement. Shrinkers were available in various sizes from buggy tire size up to those capable of shrinking a 6 inch wide

tire. Some makers boasted that their machines were strong enough to shrink a cold tire.

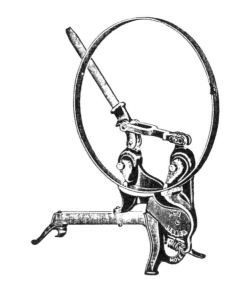

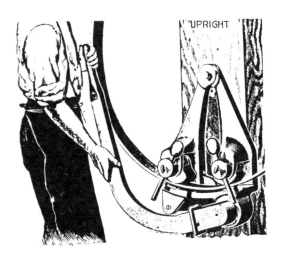

Tire Shrinker

TIRE SWAGE. See *Anvil Tool, Channel Swage.*

TIRE UPSETTER. A shop-made device used to decrease the diameter of a wagon tire. A heated tire is dented inward and clamped into the upsetter with wedges. The dent can then be hammered down resulting in a decrease in length. See also *Tire Shrinker.*

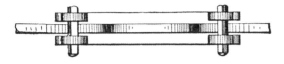
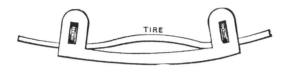

Tire Upsetter

TIRE WHEEL. See *Tire Measuring Wheel.*

TOBACCO HATCHET. See *Hatchet, Half* and *Hatchet, Tobacco.*

TOBACCO KNIFE. See *Knife, Tobacco.*

TOBACCO SPEAR. A metal spear approximately 6 inches long with a cavity in the end to fit a 1/2 by 1 1/2 inch lath. The spear is used as a needle to penetrate the stalk of a tobacco plant and string it on the lath. When the lath is full, the spear is removed and the lath is hung on a wagon for transfer to the shed and for subsequent storage. The lathe is exactly 48 inches long in order to fit on a standard wagon rack and on the drying rack in the storage shed. Spears are made of iron, brass or aluminum. Early varieties were forged iron. The illustrated spear is cast brass.

Tobacco Spear

TOBACCO SPUD. A knife used to cut tobacco stalks in the field. The cutting edge is about 4 inches wide and beveled on both sides. Overall length of the tool is approximately 12 inches.

Tobacco Spud

TOE CALK DIE. See *Anvil Tool, Toe Calk Die.*

TOE HARDIE. See *Anvil Tool, Hardie.*

TOE HARDY. See *Anvil Tool, Hardie.*

TOE KNIFE. A farriers' tool used to trim the portion of the hoof that overhangs the front of a new shoe. The knife is placed on the hoof and struck with a hammer.

Toe Knife

TOMMY AXE. See *Axe, Tommy.*

TONGS. A tool used for manipulating an object that cannot be readily grasped with the hands.

TONGS, ANGLE JAW. Also called HOOP TONGS. Tongs used to handle thin strips of metal. A tool of this general type was used to handle metal barrel hoops when the hoop was heated prior to installation.

Angle Jaw Tongs

TONGS, ANTI-RATTLER. A special tool used to install Ladds' anti-rattlers on a buggy.

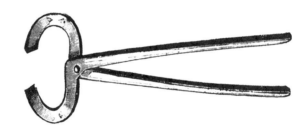

Anti-Rattler Tongs

TONGS, BAND JAW. Also called BAND TONGS, CLEVIS TONGS, DIE MAKERS' REAMER TONGS and TAP TONGS. Length is 14 to 30 inches.

Band Jaw Tongs

TONGS, BAR. See *Tongs, Blacksmiths'.*

TONGS, BENT. See *Tongs, Blacksmiths'.*

TONGS, BLACKSMITHS'. Tongs used in the general blacksmith shop. The blacksmith works on a wide variety of items and has numerous pairs of tongs to handle the various shapes of metal. Blacksmiths' tongs are from 14 to 30 inches long and made to hold an object of a given thickness. In addition to the examples shown below, most smiths made tongs to suit their own purposes and hand grip. It is not uncommon for a general blacksmith shop to have 25 or more pairs of tongs.

Lathe Tool or Granite Wedge

Bent

Lip or Peen Hammer

Bolt, Tool or Curved Lip

Pick

Crotch

Planer Tool

Double Pick-Up

Double Pick-Up

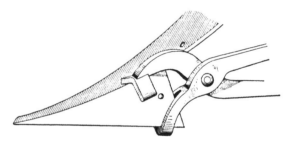

Plowshare

Gad or Die Makers' Gad

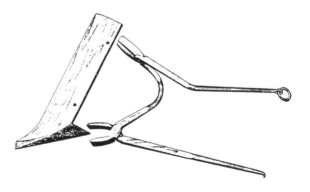

Granite Tool or Bolt

Plowshare

Pointed Lip

Lathe Tool or Bar

Blacksmiths' Tongs

Blacksmiths' Tongs

Round Jaw

Single Pick-Up

Straight Fluted

Straight Lip

Straight Lip

Swivel Jaw

V

Blacksmiths' Tongs

TONGS, BOLT. See *Tongs, Blacksmiths'*.

TONGS, BRAZING. A tool used when brazing a band saw blade. See also *Vise, Band Saw Brazing*.

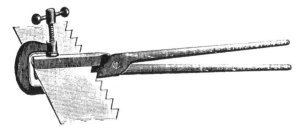

Brazing Tongs

TONGS, BRICK. Also called BRICK HANDLING TONGS. A tool used to grasp and carry a quantity of bricks.

Brick Tongs

TONGS, BUTTER. A tool used in a creamery for cutting and lifting slabs of butter.

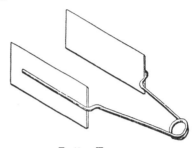

Butter Tongs

TONGS, CAN. A tool for handling a hot tin can. Used in a canning factory.

Can Tongs

TONGS, CHAIN. Also called LINK TONGS. Used for forging or repairing a log chain. The short lip allows a link of chain to held firmly. See also *Wrench, Chain Pipe*.

Chain Tongs

TONGS, CLEVIS. See *Tongs, Band Jaw*.

TONGS, CLINCH. Also called HORSE NAIL CLINCHER. Special tongs used by a farrier to clinch a nail after it is cut or twisted off to the correct length. One jaw rests on the shoe and the other jaw pulls the nail end down toward the shoe. Length is approximately 14 inches. Use of clinch tongs provide a more uniform appearance of the clinches and is somewhat faster than clinching the nails with a hammer. One supplier listed them as being useful on colts and nervous animals. Many farriers did not use clinch tongs and as a result, they are not as common as most farriers' tools.

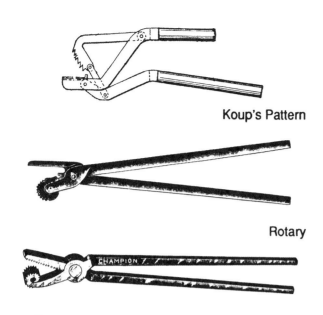

Koup's Pattern

Rotary

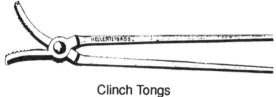

Clinch Tongs

TONGS, CLINKER. A tool used to remove clinkers from the firebox of a stove or furnace. Length is approximately 42 inches.

Clinker Tongs

TONGS, COAL. A tool used for adding coal to the fireplace. These tongs were available in several sizes.

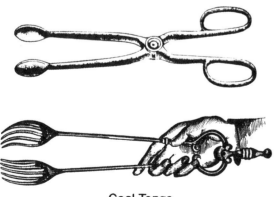

Coal Tongs

TONGS, COMB MAKERS'. Specialized tongs used to handle heated comb blanks. Overall length is 12 to 18 inches.

TONGS, COPPER. A laboratory tool similar to a large pair of tweezers. Length is approximately 9 inches.

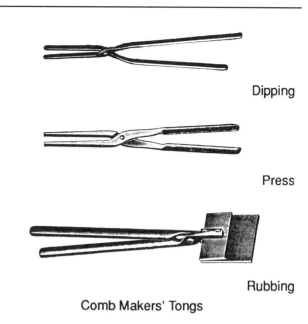

Dipping

Press

Rubbing

Comb Makers' Tongs

Copper Tongs

TONGS, CROTCH. See *Tongs, Blacksmiths'*.

TONGS, CRUCIBLE. Also called BENT CRUCIBLE TONGS. Length is 12 to 20 inches.

Crucible Tongs

TONGS, CURVED LIP. See *Tongs, Blacksmiths'*.

TONGS, DOUBLE PICKUP. See *Tongs, Blacksmiths'*.

TONGS, DOUBLE SEAMER. Also called DOUBLE ROOFING TONGS. A roofing tool used to start the double seam when two sections of metal roofing are to be joined.

Double Seamer Tongs

TONGS, DRAG. See *Tongs, Ice*.

TONGS, DRAW. Also called DRAWING PLIERS. Tongs used for grasping a wire and pulling it through a draw plate. Length is 8 to 12 inches.

Draw Tongs

TONGS, EDGING-UP. See *Tongs, Ice*.

TONGS, FARRIERS'. Also called FORGING TONGS, HORSE SHOERS' FORGE TONGS and HORSE SHOERS' TONGS. A tool used by the farrier to handle and manipulate a heated horse shoe. The hollow in the jaw of one type of farriers' tongs can be used as a spoon to apply welding flux when installing a toe calk. The tongs are 10 to 17 inches long.

Farriers' Tongs

TONGS, FORGING. See *Tongs, Blacksmiths'* and *Tongs, Farriers'*.

TONGS, GAD. See *Tongs, Blacksmiths'*.

TONGS, GLASS. Tongs used to extract pieces of broken glass from a cavity.

Glass Tongs

TONGS, GLASS BLOWERS'. Tongs suitable for grasping a glass rod or stem.

Glass Blowers' Tongs

TONGS, GRANITE WEDGE. See *Tongs, Blacksmiths'*.

TONGS, GUTTER. See *Tongs, Roofing*.

TONGS, HAMMER-SHANK. See *Piano Tool, Hammer-Shank Tongs*.

TONGS, HAND. A watch makers' tool used to hold a watch hand while enlarging the hole. The hand is grasped in the tongs with the hole coincident with one of the holes in the tongs. A broach is then used to ream the hole to the desired size. The illustrated tool has 9 sizes of holes. See also *Tongs, Jewelers'*.

Hand Tongs

TONGS, HEATING. A laboratory tool used for holding a small object in the flame of a burner. Length is 14 to 24 inches.

Heating Tongs

TONGS, HOG. Also called HOG HOLDER. A tool used for holding a hog while ear marking or inserting nose rings. Overall length is approximately 14 inches.

Hog Tongs

TONGS, HOOP. See *Tongs, Angle Jaw*.

TONGS, HORSE SHOERS'. See *Tongs, Farriers'*.

TONGS, ICE. A tool used for handling blocks of ice.

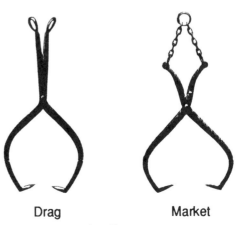

Drag   Market

Ice Tongs

Boston Pattern

Link

Paper Mill Tongs

Edging Up

Household

Ice Tongs

TONGS, JEWELERS'. Also called HAND TONGS and SLIDING TONGS. Locking tongs used for holding a small object for filing, forming or soldering. Length is 4 to 6 inches.

Jewelers' Tongs

TONGS, LATHE TOOL. See *Tongs, Blacksmiths'*.

TONGS, LINK. See *Tongs, Chain*.

TONGS, LIP. See *Tongs, Blacksmiths'*.

TONGS, PAPER MILL. Also called STOCK TONGS. Large tongs used for lifting paper stock from the vat. Width of opening of the illustrated tool is 18 inches.

TONGS, PEEN HAMMER. See *Tongs, Blacksmiths'*.

TONGS, PICK. See *Tongs, Blacksmiths'*.

TONGS, PICK-UP. See *Tongs, Blacksmiths'*.

TONGS, PIPE. A type of wrench used to grasp a pipe or round rod. This type of tongs were made in sizes suitable for use on pipes from 1/8 to 7 inches in diameter.

Jarecki's Patent

Pipe Tongs

TONGS, PLANER TOOL. See *Tongs, Blacksmiths'*.

TONGS, PLOWSHARE. See *Tongs, Blacksmiths'*.

TONGS, POINTED LIP. See *Tongs, Blacksmiths'*.

TONGS, RAIL. Also called TRACK TONGS. Two-man tongs used for handling a railroad rail. Weight is 15 to 20 pounds.

Rail Tongs

TONGS, RIVET. Tongs used for handling hot rivets. Used in steel construction work such as bridge building. Length is 18 to 30 inches.

Rivet Tongs

TONGS, ROOFING. Tongs used to draw two sections of roofing together before cleating. Some types of roofing tongs can be adjusted to turn locks of different widths. Length of blade is 14 to 18 inches.

Clamp Tongs

Gutter

Adjustable

Roofing Tongs

TONGS, ROUND JAW. See *Tongs, Blacksmiths'*.

TONGS, SALTPETRE. A tool used to insert capsules of saltpetre into a ham or slab of bacon. Saltpetre was used as a curing agent for meat.

Saltpetre Tongs

TONGS, SINGLE PICKUP. See *Tongs, Blacksmiths'*.

TONGS, SLIDING. See *Tongs, Jewelers'*.

TONGS, SPRING. A general-purpose laboratory tool. Length is 18 to 30 inches.

Spring Tongs

TONGS, STOCK. See *Tongs, Paper Mill*.

TONGS, STRAIGHT FLUTED. See *Tongs, Blacksmiths'*.

TONGS, STRAIGHT LIP. See *Tongs, Blacksmiths'*.

TONGS, SWIVEL JAW. See *Tongs, Blacksmiths'*.

TONGS, TAP. See *Tongs, Band Jaw*.

TONGS, TIE. Two-man tongs used for handling a railroad tie.

Tie Tongs

TONGS, TIRE PULLER. A tool used to remove a tire from a wagon or buggy wheel. Length is 20 to 30 inches.

Tire Puller Tongs

TONGS, TOOL. See *Tongs, Blacksmiths'*.

TONGS, TRACK. See *Tongs, Rail*.

TONGS, V. See *Tongs, Blacksmiths'*.

TONGS, WELL PIPE. Tongs used when lowering pipe into a well. These tongs will grasp a pipe and prevent endwise movement as well as rotation.

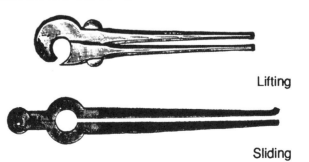

Lifting

Sliding

Well Pipe Tongs

TONGUE BRACE TEMPLATE. A pattern used when making side braces for a wagon tongue. Made of rigid sheet steel. The template is adjustable by loosening three wing nuts.

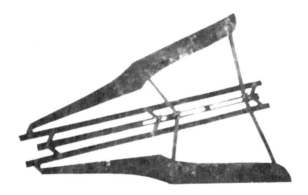

Tongue Brace Template

TONGUE AND GROOVE PLANE. See *Plane, Match.*

TOOL. For the purpose of this volume, a tool is any device or implement used in the hand or worked by hand to aid in the performance of a task. Generally, skill and dexterity of the workman are required to use a tool to accomplish the desired task. A tool has been defined as an extension of the hand.

TOOL BAG. Also called LINEMANS' TOOL BAG, MASONS' TOOL BAG and PLASTERERS TOOL BAG. A canvas bag used to store and carry tools. Length is 14 to 24 inches. The illustrated bag has a leather bottom.

Tool Bag

TOOL BAG, PLUMBERS'. Length is 12 to 24 inches. Made of carpet material and leather.

Plumbers' Tool Bag

TOOL BASKET. A canvas container intended for use in transporting tools when they were to be carried to the job. The tool basket is significantly lighter in weight than the common carpenters tool chest.

Tool Basket

TOOL BOX. A box used to transport tools to the job. The term is usually used to refer to an small open box. See also *Tool Chest.*

TOOL BOX, BEE KEEPERS. A box intended to be used by a bee keeper while working with the hive. The flat top is used as a hive seat. The center compartment provides space for hive records and queen cages.

Bee Keepers' Tool Box

TOOL BOX, FARRIERS'. A small portable tool box used by a farrier to transport shoeing tools. Farrier boxes are generally home made and therefore of almost infinite variety, however all boxes has several features in common. Each box is made to be easily moved, each has two or more compartments for different size nails and each has an open tray for the various tools used during the actual work on the hoof. The shoeing box does not contain the tools for turning and fitting the shoe. Illustration (b) shows a commercial box built with rollers on the bottom for easy movement on a hard-surface floor. The box is constantly moved by the farrier so that it remains within reach as he works on each foot of the horse.

TOOL CABINET. A small box intended to house tools for home use. The cabinet is generally portable and also suitable for hanging on the wall. Several makers offered this type of box complete with tools.

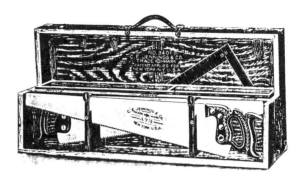

Carpenters' Tool Case

(b)

Farriers' Tool Box

Lathers' Tool Case

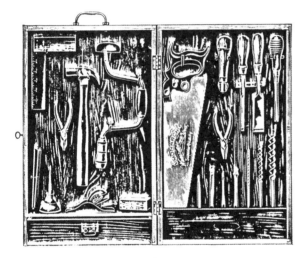

Tool Cabinet

Plasterers' Tool Case

TOOL CASE. A tool storage container small enough to be carried in one hand. See also *Tool Box.*

TOOL CASE, CARPENTERS'. Also called HOUSE FRAMERS' SHOULDER CHEST. A tool case intended to house and carry the basic tools of the framing carpenter. Length is 25 to 32 inches.

TOOL CASE, LATHERS'. A wooden case covered with metal. Length is 15 to 21 inches. This case was listed as being the correct size to hold all of the tools of a lather.

TOOL CASE, PLASTERERS'. A wooden case covered with metal. Length is 20 to 24 inches. Advertised as being just the right size to hold the tools of a plasterer.

TOOL CHEST. A covered chest or box used by a craftsman to store and transport his tools.

TOOL CHEST, CABINET MAKERS'. A large chest having several drawers and compartments to house the many small tools of the cabinet maker. These boxes are often decorated inside with hardwood and inlays.

TOOL CHEST, CARPENTERS'. Also called CARPENTERS' TOOL BOX. A wooden box intended to hold the tools of the general framing carpenter. It usually includes two or more trays for small objects and slots for storage of hand saws.

TOOL CHEST, PIPE FITTERS'. A long narrow chest suitable for storage of a pipe fitters' tools. Length is 39 to 45 inches.

TOOL HANDLE. Also called HOLLOW TOOL HANDLE, POCKET TOOL CHEST and TOOL HOLDER. A handymans' tool consisting of a small holder with several interchangeable tools stored inside the hollow handle.

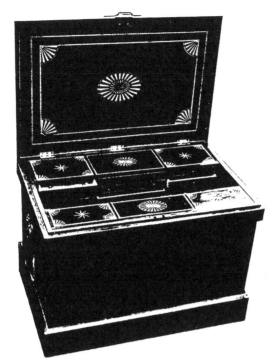

Cabinet Makers' Tool Chest

Carpenters' Tool Chest

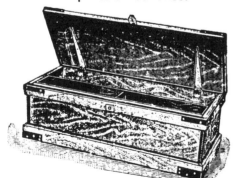

Pipe Fitters' Tool Chest

Iron

Wood

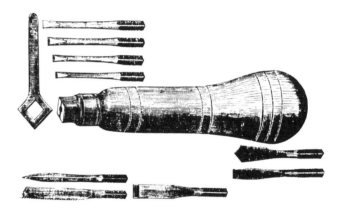

Tool Handle

TOOL HOLDER. See *Tool Handle.*

TOOL MAKERS' CLAMP. See *Clamp, Tool Makers'.*

TOOL MAKERS' FORGE. See *Forge, Tool Makers'.*

TOOL POST WRENCH. See *Wrench, Tool Post.*

TOOL TONGS. See *Tongs, Blacksmiths'.*

TOOLER. See *Stone Cutters' Tool, Chisel.*

TOOTH AXE. See *Axe, Stone.*

TOOTH CHISEL. See *Stone Cutters' Tool, Tooth Chisel.*

TOOTH FILE. See *File, Horse Tooth.*

TOOTH PLANE. See *Plane, Toothing.*

TOOTH PLIERS. See *Pliers, Opticians'.*

TOOTH POINTING FILE. See *File, Tooth Pointing.*

TOOTH PULLER. A weaving mill tool. See *Card Tooth Puller.*

TOOTHED HAMMER. See *Hammer, Stone.*

TOOTHING PLANE. See *Plane, Toothing.*

TOP CHANNEL SET. See *Shoe Makers' Tool, Top Channel Set.*

TOP MAUL. See *Maul, Ship*.

TOP TOOL. See *Anvil Tools*.

TOPPING FILE. See *File, Topping*.

TOPPING PLANE. A coopers' tool. See *Plane, Leveling*.

TORCH. A portable burner that provides a flame for light or heat.

Locomotive   Pyramid Lamp

Railroad Yard or Shop

Miners'

Torch

TORCH, ALCOHOL. A portable heating and soldering torch used by plumbers, steam fitters, laboratory technicians and general handymen. One of the varieties has a blow pipe, as can be seen in the illustration.

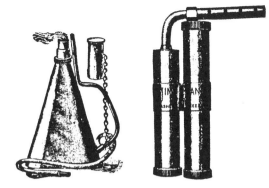

Alcohol Torch

TORCH, BRAZING. A gasoline torch with double gas jets that will provide a very hot flame. This torch is suitable for all brazing work but was recommended specifically for brazing the ends of the wire that is used to hold solid rubber tires in place. The ends of the wires were held together with a special tire clamp and brazed into brass-lined sleeves.

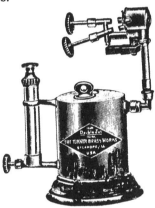

Brazing Torch

TORCH, GASOLINE. Also called BLAST TORCH, BLOW TORCH and HOT BLAST TORCH. A torch, with an integral air pump, capable of providing a very hot flame. The type of torch shown in illustration (a) is favored by plumbers and repairmen requiring use of a soldering iron. It has a hook and support on top especially designed for holding a common soldering iron above the flame.

(a)

Gasoline Torch

493

(b) Laboratory Type

Gasoline Torch

TORCH, SOLDERING. A gasoline torch used for small soldering jobs and for similar light tasks.

Soldering Torch

TORPEDO LEVEL. See *Level, Torpedo.*

TORUS BEAD. See *Plane, Moulding, Torus Bead.*

TORUS BEAD AND COVE. See *Plane, Moulding, Nosing.*

TOY PLANE. See *Plane, Toy.*

TRACE PUNCH. See *Leather Tool, Trace Punch.*

TRACE PUNCH GAUGE. See *Leather Tool, Trace Punch Gauge.*

TRACING WHEEL. Also called COPYING WHEEL and PATTERN TRACER. A tool, with a sharp pointed wheel, that can be used to transfer a design from a pattern to the workpiece. The wheel penetrates the pattern and marks the material underneath. Suitable for use by scroll saw workers, leather workers and similar craftsmen. See also *Pouncing Wheel.*

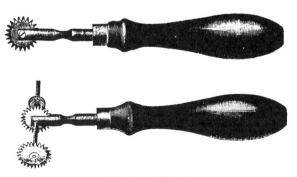

Tracing Wheel

TRACK ADZE. See *Adze, Railroad.*

TRACK CHISEL. See *Chisel, Track.*

TRACK DRILL. See *Boring Tool, Track Drill.*

TRACK GAUGE. A gauge used to indicate the proper distance between the rails when building or repairing a railroad track.

Huntington

Wooden

Track Gauge

TRACK HATCHET. See *Hatchet, Coal Miners' Track.*

TRACK JACK. See *Jack, Track.*

TRACK LEVEL. See *Level, Track.*

TRACK MAUL. See *Maul, Spike.*

TRACK PUNCH. See *Punch, Track.*

TRACK TONGS. See *Tongs, Rail.*

TRACK WALKERS' HAMMER. See *Hammer, Track Walkers'.*

TRACK WRENCH. See *Wrench, Track.*

TRADE AXE. See *Axe, Trade.*

TRAMMEL POINTS. Also called BEAM COMPASS. A pair of metal points used to scribe a circle or arc. The points have provisions for attachment along a bar to allow scribing an arc of any size.

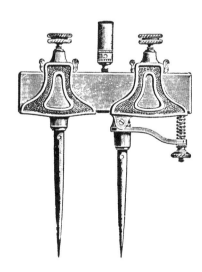

Cook's Adjustable

Trammel Points

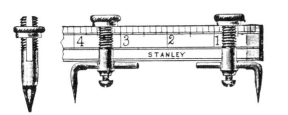

For Rule

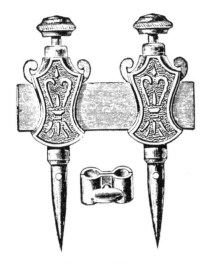

Trammel Points

TRANSPLANTER. A tool used for transplanting tobacco or garden plants. The trigger mechanism spreads the cone, after insertion into loose soil, and releases the plant.

Transplanter

TRANSPLANTING HOE TROWEL. See *Trowel, Garden.*

TRANSPLANTING TROWEL. See *Trowel, Garden.*

TRAP CLAMP. See *Clamp, Trap.*

TRAP SETTER. See *Clamp, Trap.*

TRAVELER. See *Tire Measuring Wheel.*

TRAY STAKE. See *Stake, Tray.*

TREENAIL AUGER. See *Boring Tool, Treenail Auger.*

TREPHINE. See *Boring Tool, Cranial.*

TRESTLE CLAMP. See *Clamp Horse.*

TRI SQUARE. See *Square, Try.*

TRIANGULAR MITRE. A type of miter square intended for use as a woodworking tool.

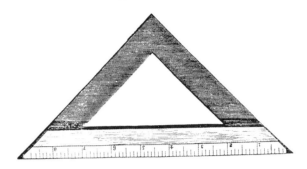

Triangular Mitre

TRIMMER. See *Hoof Trimmer; Knife, Paper Hangers' Casing* and *Leather Tool, Trimmer.*

TRIMMERS' CLIP. A tool used to hold leather or upholstery material while stitching. Length is 3 to 4 inches. Essentially a large clothes pin.

Trimmers' Clip

TRIMMERS' HAMMER. See *Hammer, Saddlers'.*

TRIMMERS' TOOLS. See *Saddle and Harness Tools.* The primary task of a trimmer was to install the leather upholstery in a carriage. Some suppliers' catalogues offered wide listings of trimmers' tools which consisted of essentially of the same items shown elsewhere as saddle makers' and harness makers' tools.

TRIP HAMMER. See *Hammer, Foot Power.*

TROCAR. Also called BULL PUNCH and BULL TROCAR. A veterinarians' tool used to punch bloated cattle. The trocar is pushed into the side of the bloated animal and removed leaving the hollow metal insert in place. The excess gas then escapes through the insert. The trocar can also be used to make the hole for ringing a bull.

Trocar

TROWEL. A tool used to apply and smooth loose or plastic material such as plaster or cement. Also any tool shaped like a trowel. See also Cement Tool, Gutter.

TROWEL, BRICK. Also called BRICK LAYERS' TROWEL, BRICK MASONS' TROWEL and MASONS' TROWEL. Length is 6 to 14 inches.

Boston Pattern

London Pattern

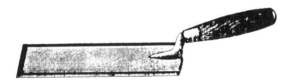

Philadelphia Pattern

Brick Trowel

TROWEL, BULB. See *Trowel, Garden.*

TROWEL, BUTTER. Also called LARD TROWEL. A trowel used to pack lard or butter into a tub or other container. Length of blade is 6 to 8 inches.

Butter Trowel

TROWEL, CEMENT. Same as a plasterers' finishing trowel except larger. Cement trowels were listed with blades up to 16 inches long. See illustration under *Trowel, Plasterers' Finishing.*

TROWEL, COKE. Blade is approximately 9 inches long.

Coke Trowel

TROWEL, CORNER. See *Cement Tool, Inside* and *Trowel, Plasterers' Corner.*

TROWEL, CROSS JOINT. Also called PLASTERERS' CROSS JOINT TROWEL. Length is 3 1/2 to 6 inches.

Cross Joint Trowel

TROWEL, FINISHING. See *Trowel, Moulders'* and *Trowel, Plasterers' Finishing.*

TROWEL, GARDEN. A tool used for transplanting seedlings in the garden.

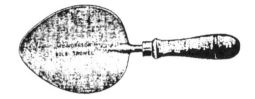

Bulb

Hoe

Transplanting

Garden Trowel

TROWEL, GAS. Also called LUTING TROWEL. A trowel used in a brick factory for packing the mold and smoothing the top surface of a brick.

Gas Trowel

TROWEL, GAUGING. Also called PLASTERERS' GAUGING TROWEL and TILE SETTERS' TROWEL. Length is 6 to 10 inches.

Gauging Trowel

TROWEL, HOE. See *Trowel, Garden.*

TROWEL, LARD. See *Trowel, Butter.*

TROWEL, LUTING. See *Trowel*, Gas.

TROWEL, MARGIN. Also called PLASTERERS' MARGIN TROWEL. Length is about 5 inches.

Margin Trowel

TROWEL, MOULDERS'. A moulders' smoothing tool. Length of blade is 3 to 7 inches.

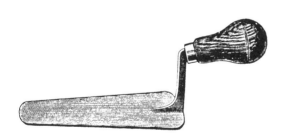

Finishing

Square

Moulders' Trowel

Heart

Moulders' Trowel

TROWEL, MUDDING. A plasterers' tool slightly larger than the moulders' tool of the same shape. Length of blade is 8 to 10 inches.

Mudding Trowel

TROWEL, PLASTERERS'. Any of the several types of trowels used by the plasterer. See *Plasterers' Tools.*

TROWEL, PLASTERERS' ANGLE. Also called ANGLE TROWEL and TWITCHER. Length is approximately 4 1/2 inches. A type of CORNER TROWEL.

Plasterers' Angle Trowel

TROWEL, PLASTERERS' BROWNING. Same as PLASTERERS' FINISHING TROWEL except that the browning trowel is made of heavy material. This trowel is used for first coat work. See illustration under *Trowel, Plasterers' Finishing.*

TROWEL, PLASTERERS' CORNER. A trowel intended for smoothing and flattening new plaster at the intersection of two walls.

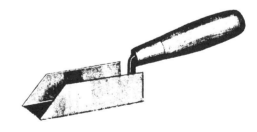

Plasterers' Corner Trowel

TROWEL, PLASTERERS' FINISHING. Also called FINISHING TROWEL. A tool used for finishing of a flat surface. Length is 10 to 13 inches. See also *Trowel, Cement* and *Trowel, Plasterers' Browning.*

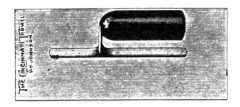

Finishing Trowel

TROWEL, POINTING. Length of blade is 4 to 7 inches.

Brick Layers'

Plasterers'

Pointing Trowel

TROWEL, SEWER. A trowel designed specifically for cement work in the Chicago water tunnel. Length of blade is 12 inches.

Sewer Trowel

TROWEL, TILE SETTERS'. A tool intended for spreading the mortar when setting tiles. Length of blade is approximately 7 1/2 inches. See also *Trowel, Gauging.*

Tile Setters' Trowel

TROWEL, TRANSPLANTING. See *Trowel, Garden.*

TRUCK SHOVEL. See *Shovel, Truck.*

TRUNK KNIFE. See *Knife, Trunk.*

TRUSS HOOP. A temporary hoop used by a cooper when assembling a barrel. Stout over-sized hoops are used to progressively form the staves into the final shape of the barrel. These hoops were sold in sets of six for use with a given size of barrel. The set consisted of two each head, quarter and bilge hoops. Usually made of hickory.

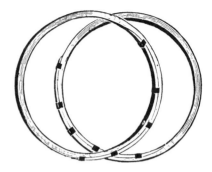

Truss Hoop

TRYING PLANE. See *Plane, Fore.* Trying Plane is name widely used in England for a bench plane of intermediate length. The term was not used by American plane makers and sellers.

TRY SQUARE. See *Square, Try.*

TUBE BEADING TOOL. See *Beading Tool, Boiler.*

TUBE BRUSH. See *Brush, Tube.*

TUBE EXPANDER. A tool used when fitting the steam boiler tubes in a fire box.

Tube Expander

TUBING CLAMP. See *Clamp, Tubing.*

TUCK POINTER. Also called BRICK JOINTER, JOINT FORMER, MASONS' BEADING TOOL, TUCK POINTERS' JOINT FILLER and TUCK POINTERS' JOINTER. A tool used to apply a coat of finish mortar to the exposed joints between bricks or stones. Length of blade is approximately 5 inches. Tools were available to make concave, convex or flat joints. A common type makes a convex shape and was often called a BEADING TOOL.

Tuck Pointer

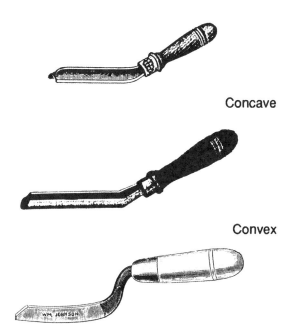

Concave

Convex

Tuck Pointer

TUCK POINTERS' BRUSH. See *Brush, Acid.*

TUCK POINTERS' JOINTER. See *Tuck Pointer.*

TUCKING MACHINE. See *Tinsmiths' Machine, Tucking.*

TUMBLER FILE. See *File, Tumbler.*

TUNING HAMMER. See *Piano Tool, Tuning Hammer.*

TUNING PIN GAUGE. See *Piano Tool, Tuning Pin Gauge.*

TUNING PIN HAMMER. See *Hammer, Tuning Pin.*

TUNING WEDGE. See *Piano Tool, Tuning Wedge.*

TURF EDGER. Also called SIDEWALK EDGER. A tool used to trim lawn turf along a sidewalk or driveway. See also *Lawn Edge Trimmer.*

Turf Edger

TURKEY PUNCH. See *Punch, Poultry.*

TURKEY STICKING KNIFE. See *Knife, Poultry Killing.*

TURKISH SAW. See *Saw, Turkish.*

TURN PIN. A plumbers' tool used for expanding or flaring the end of a lead pipe. Usually made of a hardwood such as maple or dogwood.

TURN-SHOE HAMMER. See *Hammer, Shoe Makers' Toe.*

TURNING BONE. See *Shoe Makers' Tool, Turning Bone.*

TURNING GAUGE. Also called WOOD TURNERS' GAUGE. A notched gauge graduated in 16ths of an inch.

Turn Pin

Turning Gauge

TURNING HAMMER. See *Hammer, Farriers' Turning.*

TURNING MACHINE. See *Tinsmiths' Machine, Turning.*

TURNING PLANE. See *Witchet.*

TURNING SAW. See *Saw, Turning.*

TURNING SLEDGE. See *Sledge, Turning.*

TURNING STEEL. See *Burnishing Tool, Scraper* and *Finger Steel.*

TURNING TOOL. Also called LATHE TOOL. A tool used with a turning lathe for cutting or scraping material from a rotating workpiece. The tools shown are for cutting wood except as noted. See also *Metal Spinning Tool.*

TURNING TOOL, ASTRAGAL. Also called ASTRAGAL TOOL and BEAD TOOL. A turning tool with a concave cutting edge that cuts a bead and step. The term was also loosely used to refer to any of a variety of turning tools that form a bead.

Astragal Tool

TURNING TOOL, BEADING. Also called HUSTLER BEADER. Width is 1/8 to 1 inch.

Beading Tool

TURNING TOOL, BEVEL. A skewed turning chisel that is beveled on one side only. Used for forming sharp grooves and tapers. Both right and left hand varieties were available. See illustration under *Turning Tool, Chisel.*

TURNING TOOL, CHISEL. Also called LATHE CHISEL, SKEW and SKEW CHISEL. A flat turning tool on which the cutting edge is slanted with respect to the handle and beveled on both sides. Width is 1/8 to 2 1/2 inches. This type of tool is widely used for cutting-in on shoulders and for straight cylindrical work. It was also used for stock cut-off before the parting tool became popular.

Turning Chisel

TURNING TOOL, DOWEL. A lathe tool used for turning round rods for dowels or pins. The illustrated tool has several interchangeable cutters to allow making dowels of different sizes.

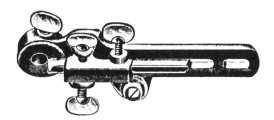

Dowel Tool

TURNING TOOL, GOUGE. A turning tool with a convex cutting edge. The edge is beveled on the outside only. Width is 1/8 to 2 1/2 inches. This is the primary cutting tool of the wood turner. It especially useful for removal of excess stock and for cutting hollows.

Turning Gouge

TURNING TOOL, HOOK. Also called BOTTOM TOOL and PEG KNIFE. A curved tool used for shallow face-plate turning. Right and left hand tools are illustrated. A similar tool is used by a shoe maker as a peg cutter.

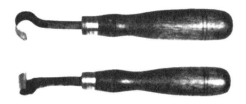

Hook Tool

TURNING TOOL, HUSTLER. Width is 1/8 to 1 inch. A tool used for rapid cutting-in on a square or rough workpiece.

Hustler

TURNING TOOL, METAL. A hand-held tool used for turning soft metal, ivory, bone, hard rubber and hardwoods. Overall length is 10 to 12 inches. Names of the tools are as follows: a. Square Point, b. Skew Point, c. Round Point, d. Spear Point, e. Square Groover, f. Inside Tool, Bent Tool or Broad, g. Side Tool, h. Cut Off Tool.

Metal Turning Tool

TURNING TOOL, PARTING. A tool used for stock cut off. Size is 1/2 to 3/4 inches. The parting tool was listed in catalogues as early as 1888; however, it was not generally offered with other turning tools until about 1920.

Parting Tool

TURNING TOOL, ROUND POINT. Also called ROUND NOSE. A scraping tool used for cleaning up a hollow or cove. Width is 1/4 to 1 1/2 inches.

Round Point

TURNING TOOL, SIZER. Also called CALIPER CHISEL. A scraping tool used for finishing a straight cylinder. The sizer can be used with a square nose tool or a hustler.

Sizer

TURNING TOOL, SKEW. See *Turning Tool, Chisel*.

TURNING TOOL, SPEAR POINT. Also called DIAMOND POINT. Width is 1/4 to 1/2 inch.

Spear Point

TURNING TOOL, SQUARE NOSE. Also called FLAT NOSE and SQUARE POINT. A scraping tool used for finishing a straight cylindrical shape.

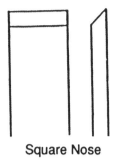

Square Nose

TURNING TOOL, TENONER. A tool used to cut uniform tenons on a series of workpieces.

Screw Type   V Type

Tenoner

TURNING TOOL, TOOTH. A skewed turning tool with a rounded shoulder said to be suitable for turning gear teeth. Width of the illustrated tool is 1 1/2 inches.

Tooth Turning Tool

TURPENTINE DIPPER. A tool used to dip the raw sap from the box (cavity) cut into a turpentine tree to collect the sap run.

Turpentine Dipper

Turpentine Dipper

TURPENTINE HACKER. Also called TURPENTINE SCORER. A tool used to slash the bark from a pine tree to allow the sap to flow. The hacker often has an iron weight on the end of the handle to provide additional momentum as the tool is pulled downward for the cut.

Open

Closed

Turpentine Hacker

501

TURPENTINE PULLER. See *Turpentine Round Shave*.

TURPENTINE ROUND SHAVE. Also called TURPENTINE PULLER. This tool is used for the same purpose as the Turpentine Hacker.

Turpentine Round Shave

TURPENTINE SCORER. See *Turpentine Hacker*.

TURPENTINE TOOLS. The special-purpose turpentine harvesting tools listed below can be found in normal alphabetical sequence. These tools may also have been used for other purposes.

AXE, BROAD, TURPENTINE
AXE, SINGLE BIT, TURPENTINE PATTERN
AXE, SINGLE BIT, BOXING TURPENTINE PATTERN
SCRAPER, TURPENTINE
TURPENTINE DIPPER
TURPENTINE HACKER
TURPENTINE ROUND SHAVE

TUYERE IRON. Also called TWEER IRON. A blast-air inlet and air connection to the bottom of a blacksmiths' forge. The tuyere generally has a grate or damper which can be used to regulate the flow of air.

Duck Nest Type

Tuyere Iron

TWEEZERS. A tool used by a jeweler to grasp and hold small parts. Also used by watch makers and for other tasks requiring the handling of small items.

Disc

Locking

Tweezers

Pointed

Pointed

Tweezers

TWIBIL. See *Twybil*. Twibil is a variation in spelling.

TWIST DRILL. See *Boring Tool, Bit, Twist Drill*.

TWIST DRILL GAUGE. See *Wire Gauge*.

TWIST GIMLET. See *Boring Tool, Gimlet*.

TWITCH. A device used for pinching the upper lip of a horse. Squeezing the lip causes enough pain to quiet a mean or flighty animal and allow the shoeing or doctoring to continue. Illustration (c) shows a patented twitch that can be tightened with the threaded cross-bar on the end. It was made by the *One Man Twitch Company* of Grand Island, NE. The patent date is February 26, 1918.

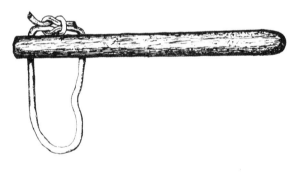

(c)

Twitch

TWITCHER. See *Trowel, Plasterers' Angle*.

TWO-MAN RAKE. See *Rake, Two-Man*.

TWYBIL. Also called *Twibil*. A mortising tool used with a pressing or a short chopping motion.

Twybil

TYPE HIGH GAUGE. See *Electrotype Finishers' Tool, Type High Gauge*.

TYPE HIGH PLANE. See *Plane, Shoot Board, Lead*.

U

Tool names starting with the letter U.

Included is a listing of tools used by the:
UPHOLSTERER

UMBRELLA PLIERS. See *Pliers, Umbrella*.

UNCAPPING KNIFE. See *Knife, Uncapping*.

UNDERTAKERS' HAMMER. One variety of tack hammer was listed as being made especially for use by an undertaker. See *Hammer, Tack*.

UNDERTAKERS' SCREW DRIVER. See *Screw Driver, Undertakers'*.

UNIVERSAL PLANE. One type of large combination plane was advertised as a universal plane. See *Plane, Combination*.

UNIVERSAL SQUARE. See *Square, Universal*.

UNIVERSAL VISE. See *Vise, Universal*.

UNHAIRING KNIFE. See *Knife, Unhairing*.

UPHOLSTERERS' AWL. See *Awl, Carpet* and *Awl, Seat*.

UPHOLSTERERS' PIN. See *Upholsterers' Skewer*.

UPHOLSTERERS' REGULATOR. Also called REGULATING NEEDLE. A tool used to adjust the position of the stuffing as required to provide a smooth contour in an irregular surface such as the arm of a chair. Length is 6 to 12 inches.

Upholsterers' Regulator

UPHOLSTERERS' RIPPING TOOL. A tool used to remove old upholstery material. Overall length of the illustrated tool is 8 1/4 inches.

Upholsterers' Ripping Tool

UPHOLSTERERS' SKEWER. Also called UPHOLSTERERS' PIN. A long pin used to hold one edge of the material in place while the other edge is being tacked. Length is 3 to 3 1/2 inches.

Upholsterers' Skewer

UPHOLSTERERS' TOOLS. The special-purpose upholsterers' tools listed below can be found in normal alphabetical sequence. These tools may also have been used for other purposes.
AWL, CARPET
AWL, SEAT
CARPET STRETCHER
HAMMER, UPHOLSTERERS'
KNIFE, UPHOLSTERERS'
MALLET, UPHOLSTERERS'
SHEARS, UPHOLSTERERS'
TAPE, CLOTH
THIMBLE
TRIMMERS' CLIP
UPHOLSTERERS' REGULATOR
UPHOLSTERERS' RIPPING TOOL
UPHOLSTERERS' SKEWER
WEBBING STRETCHER

UPHOLSTERY STRETCHER. See *Carpet Stretcher*.

UPRIGHT DRILL. See *Boring Tool, Post Drill*.

UPSET. See *Saw Swage*.

UPSETTER. See *Tire Shrinker* and *Tire Upsetter*.

UTILITY WRENCH. See *Wrench, Farmers'*.

V

Tool names starting with the letter V, including a multiple listing of:

VISE

V TONGS. See *Tongs, Blacksmiths'*.

V TOOL. See *Leather Tool, V.*

VALVE LIFTER. This tool was originally sold as a automobile valve lifter. However, it has been reported to be an excellent tool for twisting barb wire. It is listed as a fence tool in some current publications.

Valve Lifter

VARNISH BRUSH. See *Brush, Varnish*.

VARNISH POT. A varnish container with provisions for suspending a brush inside the pot. Leaving the brush submerged in the varnish is one method of preventing it from drying out.

Varnish Pot

VEGETABLE FORK. See *Fork, Vegetable*.

VEGETABLE SCOOP. See *Fork, Vegetable*.

VEIL. See *Bee Veil*.

VEINER. See *Carving Tool, Veiner*.

VEINING TOOL. See *Carving Tool, Veiner*.

VELOCIPEDE. A type of saw with a seat and foot pedals. See *Saw, Foot and Hand Powered*.

VENEER HAMMER. See *Hammer, Veneer*.

VENEER PRESS. Also called SCREW PRESS. A screw-operated press used to hold veneer in place while the glue is drying.

Veneer Press

VENEER PUNCH. See *Punch, Veneer*.

VENEER SAW. See *Saw, Veneer*.

VENEER SCRAPER. See *Scraper, Veneer*.

VICE. See *Vise*. Vice is a variation in spelling.

VINEYARD HOE. A type of agricultural hoe. See *Hoe, Farm*.

VIOLIN CLAMP. See *Clamp, Violin*.

VIOLIN PLANE. See *Plane, Violin*.

VIOLIN POST SETTER AND REGULATOR. A violin makers' tool used for setting the sound post. Overall length is approximately 9 inches.

Violin Post Setter and Regulator

VIOLIN PURFLING TOOL. See *Purfling Tool*.

VISE. A device used for holding a workpiece securely in the desired position while performing work with another tool.

VISE, BAND SAW BRAZING. A vise used to hold the two ends of a bandsaw blade in position for brazing. The tongs are heated and then applied to the joint to be brazed. Sometimes the jaws are pressed shut with a C clamp to assure good heat transfer.

Vise and Tongs

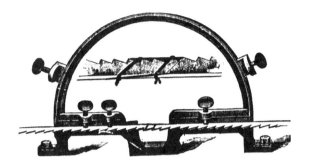

Band Saw Brazing Vise

VISE, BAND SAW FILING. Also called BAND SAW VISE. A vise used for holding a flexible saw blade in place for filing. The illustrated tool has adjustable take-up wheels in addition to a clamp.

Wright's Patent

Band Saw Filing Vise

VISE, BENCH. Also called MACHINISTS' VISE. A metalworkers' vise intended to be attached to the top of a workbench. Width of jaws is 2 to 8 1/2 inches. The illustrated vise has provisions to allow swiveling in two directions.

Bench Vise

VISE, BLACKSMITHS'. See *Vise, Post.*

VISE, BROOM MAKERS'. Also called BROOM MAKERS' PRESS and BROOM PRESS. A vise used by a broom maker to hold a flat broom in place for sewing. The jaws are approximately 10 inches wide.

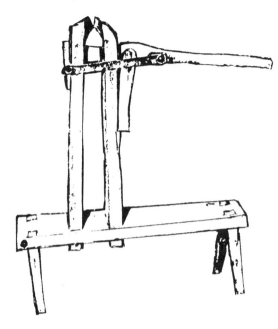

Broom Makers' Vise

VISE, CARPET. Also called OIL CLOTH VISE. A tool used to stretch carpet, fabric or oil cloth. It consists of a long spike which serves as a lever to exert a pulling force on a pair of attached webbing pliers.

Carpet Vise

VISE, CHAIN. A double-acting post vise in which the jaws remain parallel as the vise is opened and closed. See illustration under *Vise, Post.*

VISE, CIRCULAR SAW. A vise used to hold a circular saw for filing. The illustrated tool has provisions for tilting the saw blade toward the back of the bench.

VISE, COACH MAKERS'. Also called WOOD WORKERS' VISE. A vise with 3 1/2 to 4 1/2 inch jaws extending well above the adjustment screw. The extended jaws are assumed to have been used when sawing and trimming curved workpieces. This tool was also listed as being suitable for use by pattern makers and for all wood workers.

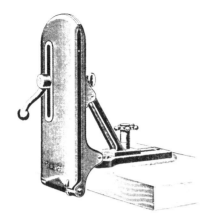

Circular Saw Vise

Coach Makers' Vise

VISE, COMBINATION. A vise intended to serve two or more functions. The illustrated tool has both regular and pipe jaws. See also *Anvil, Combination.*

Combination Vise

VISE, COOPERS'. A device used to pull the head of a barrel into place. The vise is screwed into the barrel head and used to pull the head upward into the croze groove.

Coopers' Vise

VISE, DRILL. A vise with long flat jaws intended for holding a workpiece in place on a drill press or milling machine table.

Drill Vise

VISE, DRILL PRESS. See *Vise, Drill.*

VISE, FARMERS'. A light-weight vise with 2 to 4 1/2 inch jaws intended for holding either metal or wood.

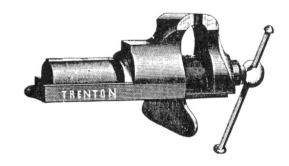

Farmers' Vise

VISE, FARRIERS'. Also called FOOT VISE, HORSE SHOERS' MACHINE and SHOEING VISE. A foot-operated vise intended for use by a farrier when making and fitting horse shoes. This type of vise was generally free-standing and was heavy enough to allow final forging to be done directly on the vise rather than on the anvil. Each of the illustrated examples is equipped with calk dies. The vise shown in illustration (a) also has a set of of bolt heading dies that could be inserted in place of the calk dies.

VISE, HAND. A vise intended to be held in the hand while in use. Overall length is 3 to 5 inches. Useful for holding small items while filing, grinding or soldering.

VISE, JEWELERS'. A very small bench-mounted vise.

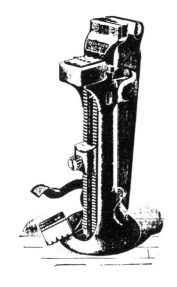

(a)

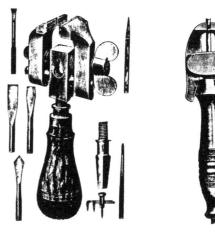

Hand Vise

(b)

Farriers' Vise

Jewelers' Vise

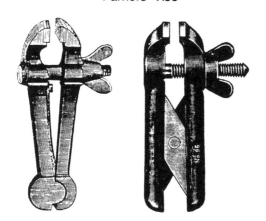

Hand Vise

VISE, LEG. See *Vise, Post.*

VISE, MACHINISTS'. See *Vise, Bench.*

VISE, MITER. See *Vise, Picture Frame.*

VISE, OIL CLOTH. See *Vise, Carpet.*

VISE, PATTERN MAKERS'. A vise intended to grip a finely finished pattern without marring. The face of each jaw is lined with leather to reduce the possibility of damage to the workpiece. See also *Vise, Coach Makers'* and *Vise, Universal.*

VISE, PICTURE FRAME. Also called MITER VISE. A clamping device used to hold two parts of a picture frame in position for nailing or glueing.

Pattern Makers' Vise

VISE, PIPE. A vise used by a plumber to hold a pipe during cutting or threading.

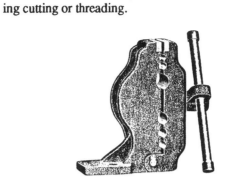

Copper Pipe

Picture Frame Vise

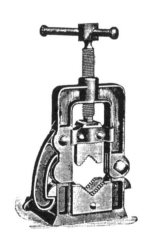

VISE, PIN. A small hand vise used primarily by jewelers. Suitable for holding a small file, broach or bur. Length is 3 to 5 inches.

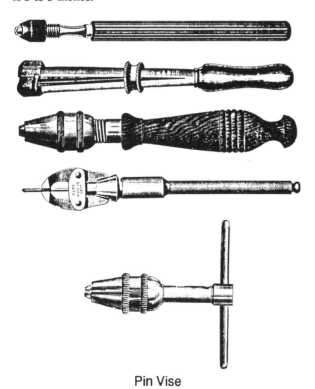

Pin Vise

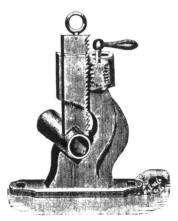

Pipe Vise

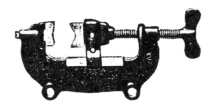

Pipe Vise

VISE, POST. Also called BLACKSMITHS' LEG VISE, BOX VISE and LEG VISE. A rugged vise favored by blacksmiths. This type of vise, when securely mounted, can survive the twisting and hammering of both hot and cold metal often required during blacksmith work. Length of jaws is 3 to 8 ½ inches. Weights of 25 to 200 pounds have been noted. A post vise with the tops of the jaws flattened for use in forging was called a FARRIERS' VISE by one supplier. The flat top could be used to form the heel calk on a shoe.

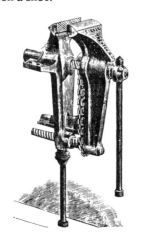

Post Vise

VISE, SAW. Also called SAW CLAMP and SAW FILING VISE. A light vise with 9 to 15 inch jaws used to hold a saw while being sharpened or set. See also *Vise, Circular Saw.*

VISE, TAIL. Also called TAIL SCREW. A vise intended for use on the end of a cabinet makers' bench. The tail vise is used to clamp a long workpiece along the front edge of the bench using a bench stop at the opposite end of the workpiece. A wooden screw and nut were used to construct a tail vise for older benches. See *Bench Screw.*

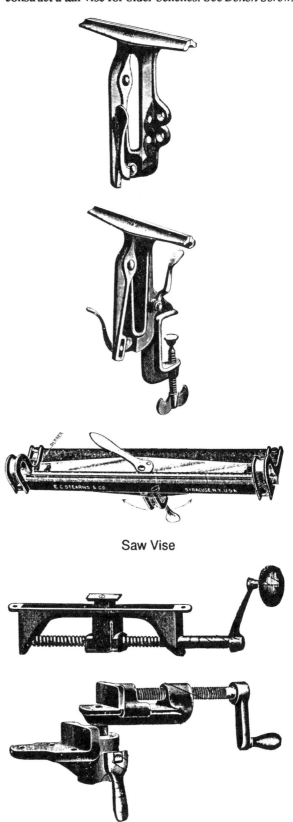

Saw Vise

Tail Vise

510

VISE, UNIVERSAL. Also called PATTERN MAKERS' VISE. A vise with two pairs of jaws for grasping either wood or metal. The illustrated device can be rotated such that either side or either end is toward the top. The jaws can also be adjusted to close at an angle.

Universal Vise

VISE, WHEEL. A clock makers' tool used to grasp and hold a small wheel.

Rose's Patent

Wheel Vise

VISE, WOOD CARVERS'. A rudimentary vise suitable for holding a small workpiece for carving. The lower extension can be clamped in a bench vise, secured to table with a C clamp or held between the knees. Width of the jaws is approximately 6 inches.

Wood Carvers' Vise

VISE, WOOD. See *Clamp, Wooden.*

VISE, WOOD WORKERS'. A vise with wide flat jaws intended for use in gripping wood. The jaws are often lined with hardwood to reduce marring of the workpiece. Jaws are up to 10 inches wide. See also *Vise, Coach Makers'.*

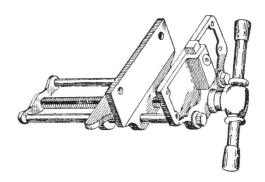

Wood Workers' Vise

VISE CUTTING TOOL. An attachment that fits between the jaws of a vise and allows the normal tightening of the vise to be used as the pressure for cutting metal. This tool was advertised as being ideal for trimming excess length from a bolt.

Vise Cutting Tool

VISE JAW CAP. A pair of caps used to cover the rough jaws of a bench vise to reduce marring of a finished workpiece. Made of copper or bronze.

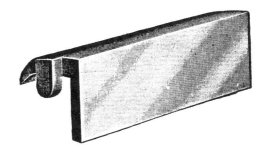

Vise Jaw Cap

VISE JAWS. Detachable jaws that allow a common bench vise to firmly grip a pipe or round bar.

511

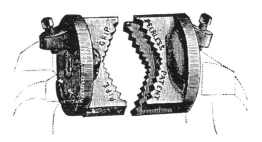

Vise Jaws

VISE PLIERS. See *Pliers, Vise*.

VOICERS' CONE. See *Organ Tuners' Cone*.

W

Tool names starting with the letter W, including multiple
listings of:
WEDGE
WRENCH

Included also is a listing of tools used by the:
WATCH AND CLOCK REPAIRMAN
WHEELWRIGHT

WAD CUTTER. See *Punch, Wad.*

WAD PUNCH. See *Punch, Wad.*

WAGON DRAG. See *Drag Shoe.*

WAGON Hammer. See *Hammer, Doubletree Pin.*

WAGON ICE SAW. A type of ice saw. See *Saw, Ice.*

WAGON JACK. See *Jack, Wagon.*

WAGON MAKERS' DRAWING KNIFE. See *Drawing Knife,
Wagon Makers'.*

WAGON MAKERS' FILE. See *File, Wagon Makers'.*

WAGON MAKERS' KNIFE. See *Drawing Knife, Carriage
Router* and *Drawing Knife, Wagon Makers'.*

WAGON TIRE CLAMP. See *Clamp, Wagon Tire.*

WAGON WRENCH. See *Wrench, Wagon.*

WALL BRUSH. A type of paint brush. See *Brush, Paint.*

WALL JOINT CHISEL. See *Chisel, Wall Joint.*

WALL PAPER CART. See *Cart, Wall Paper.*

WALL PAPER KNIFE. See *Knife, Paper Hangers'.*

WALL PAPER ROLLER. See *Paper Hangers' Roller.*

WALL PAPER TRIMMER. See *Paper Hangers' Trimmer.*

WALL PAPER TRUCK. See *Cart, Wall Paper.*

WALL SCRAPER. See *Scraper, Wall.*

WALL TILE NIPPERS. See *Nippers, Tile.*

WANTAGE ROD. See *Rule, Wantage Rod.*

WARDING FILE. See *File, Warding.*

WAREHOUSE BROOM. See *Broom, Warehouse.*

WAREHOUSE HATCHET. See *Hatchet, Warehouse.*

WASHBOARD PLANE. See *Plane, Washboard.*

WASHER CUTTER. Also called CIRCLE CUTTER, FLY
CUTTER and GASKET CUTTER. A tool used for cutting
annular disks or washers from felt, leather or similar
material.

WASHER GAUGE. See *Nut and Washer Gauge.*

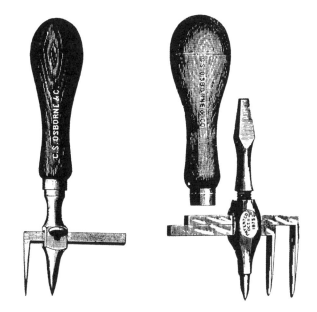

Single   Double

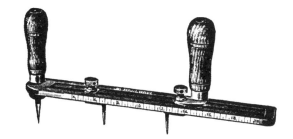

Washer Cutter

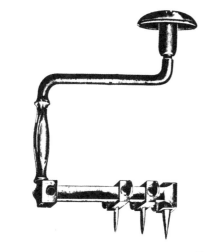

Brace Type

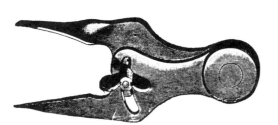

Hagerty's

Washer Cutter

WASHER PUNCH. See *Punch, Washer.*

WATCH CASE BEZEL TOOL. See *Bezel Tool.*

WATCH CASE CHUCK. See *Clamp, Watch Case.*

WATCH CASE JOINT PLIERS. See *Pliers, Watch Case Joint.*

WATCH CASE OPENER. See *Case Opener.*

WATCH CASE STAKE. See *Stake, Watch Case.*

WATCH FILE. See *File, Escapement.*

WATCH RACK. A watch makers' shop fixture used for storing pocket watches that are in the shop for repair. Each watch was hung on a numbered hook until picked up by the owner. The illustrated rack will support 48 watches.

Watch Rack

WATCH MAKERS' FILE. See *File, Escapement* and *File, Watch Makers'.*

WATCH AND CLOCK REPAIR TOOLS. The special-purpose watch and clock repair tools listed below can be found in normal alphabetical sequence. These tools may also have been used for other purposes.

BENCH, WATCH MAKERS'
BEZEL TOOL
BRUSH, SCRATCH
BRUSH, WATCH
CASE OPENER
CLAMP, WATCH CASE
CLOCK KEY
DAPPING DIE
FILE, EQUALING
FILE, ESCAPEMENT
FILE, JOINT
FILE, WATCH MAKERS'
HAMMER, CASE

HAMMER, JEWELERS'
HAND PULLER
MAINSPRING GAUGE
MAINSPRING WINDER
PLIERS, WATCH CASE JOINT
PLIERS, WATCH HAND
PUNCH, HOLE CLOSING
SCREW DRIVER, WATCH MAKERS'
TONGS, HAND
VISE, WHEEL
WATCH RACK
WIRE BENDER
WRENCH, SLEEVE

WATER LEVEL. See *Level, Hydrostatic*.

WATER YOKE. See *Yoke*.

WAX SCRAPER. See *Scraper, Wax*.

WAXING IRON. See *Fillet Tool*.

WEATHER BOARD MARKER. See *Clapboard Marker*.

WEATHER STRIP PLANE. See *Plane, Weather Strip*.

WEAVERS' APRON. See *Apron, Weavers'*.

WEAVERS' BELT. A textile workers' belt used to hold the shears in position for quick access. The belt also serves to assure that the workmans' clothing does not extend forward when he bends over the machine.

Weavers' Belt

WEAVERS' COMB. A textile mill tool.

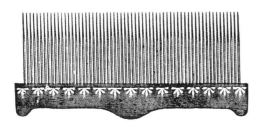

Weavers' Comb

WEAVERS' HOOK. See *Hook, Weavers'*.

WEAVERS' PLIERS. See *Pliers, Stockinger*.

WEAVERS' SHEARS. See *Shears, Weavers'*.

WEB SAW. See *Saw, Turning*.

WEBBING PLIERS. See *Webbing Stretcher*.

WEBBING STRETCHER. Also called WEBBING PLIERS. A tool used for grasping and stretching canvas, upholstery material or webbing. The jaws are 2 1/2 to 3 1/2 inches wide. See also *Carpet Stretcher*.

Webbing Stretcher

WEDGE. A tapered piece of solid material, usually iron or wood, used to split a rigid substance such as a log or to widen a seam between two blocks. See also *Horse Collar Tool, Wedge*.

WEDGE, COAL. Also called COAL MINERS' WEDGE. WEIGHT is 1 3/4 to 3 pounds.

Anthracite   Indiana Pattern   Missouri Pattern
Coal Wedge

WEDGE, EXPLODING. A wedge in which exploding gunpowder is used to complete the separating action. Up to two ounces of blasting powder can be used per explosion. Length of the wedge is approximately 13 inches. The cap shown in the illustration is used to protect the head of the wedge while being driven with a sledge.

Exploding Wedge

WEDGE, FROST. A long wedge used for breaking frozen ground. Length of the illustrated tool is 15 1/2 inches.

Frost Wedge

WEDGE, JUMPING. A wedge having a rapid increase in slope toward the top. Used for splitting out layers of stone.

Jumping Wedge

WEDGE, LOGGING. Also called FALLING WEDGE, SAW SCARF WEDGE, SAW WEDGE and SAWING DOWN WEDGE. A tool used to spread the kerf when sawing a large log or standing tree thus avoiding binding of the saw. Weight is 1 1/2 to 5 pounds. One type of saw wedge has a hole for attachment of a streamer to avoid loss of the wedge in deep snow.

Bolt Pattern

California Saw Scarf

Logging Wedge

WEDGE, PAVERS'. A tool used to separate two stones as they are being laid on a flat surface. Length is approximately two feet.

Or Pavers' Opening
Pavers' Wedge

WEDGE, PIANO TUNING. See *Piano Tool, Tuning Wedge.*

WEDGE, ROCK. See *Wedge, Stone.*

WEDGE, SAW. See *Wedge, Logging.*

WEDGE, SAW SCARF. See *Wedge, Logging.*

WEDGE, STAVE. A wide wedge used for splitting out barrel staves. Weight is 3 to 5 pounds.

Stave Wedge

WEDGE, STONE. A wedge used to break out layers of stone in a quarry. The sleeved-type stone wedge, shown in the illustration, is 2 1/2 to 8 inches long. This type wedge is sometimes called PLUG AND FEATHERS. Weight of the solid-type wedge is 2 to 8 pounds. See also *Drift Pin.*

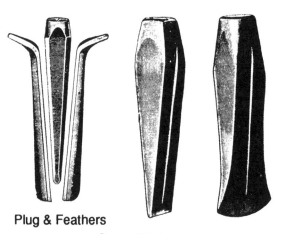

Plug & Feathers
Stone Wedge

WEDGE, TIE. Also called TIE MAKERS' WEDGE and WOOD CHOPPERS' WEDGE. A long thin wedge used for splitting out railroad ties. Weight is 3 to 8 pounds.

Tie Wedge

WEDGE, TUNING. See *Piano Tool, Tuning Wedge*.

WEDGE, WOOD SPLITTING. Also called WOOD CHOPPERS' WEDGE. A general-purpose wedge used when making fire wood, fence rails and posts. Weight is 2 to 10 pounds. See also *Wedge, Logging*.

Axe Pattern   Beetle Head or Wooden

Falling   Lake Superior   Oregon

Wood Splitting Wedge

Truckee   California or Truckee Flared

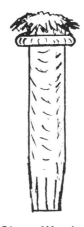

Glut or Wooden   Standard Pattern

Combination

Wood Splitting Wedge

WEDGE AXE. See *Axe, Wedge*.

WEDGE MAKER. A bench-mounted device that will make a wooden axe handle or hammer handle wedge with one motion of the lever. The wedge is cut as a scrap of wood is forced against a fixed blade.

Wedge Maker

WEDGE PEEN HAMMER. See *Hammer, Blacksmiths'*.

WEED DIGGER. Also called LAWN SPUD. A long-handled tool for removing isolated weeds from a lawn. Width is about 1 ½ inches. See also *Dandelion Digger* and *Knife, Asparagus*.

Weed Digger

WEED SCYTHE. A scythe with a short blade. See *Scythe*.

WEEDER. A garden tool used for cutting weeds below the surface of the ground.

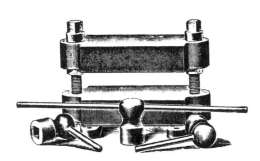

Weeder

WEEDING FORK. See *Fork, Garden*.

WELDING DIE. See *Anvil Tool, Toe Calk Die*.

WELDING PRESS. A comb makers' device used to weld tortoise shell. Size of the working surface is 7 by 11 inches. Both top and bottom plates are heated by circulating steam. Pieces of tortoise shell will combine if adequate heat and pressure are applied.

Welding Press

WELL AUGER. See *Boring Tool, Earth Auger* and *Boring Tool, Post Hole Auger*.

WELL PIPE TONGS. See *Tongs, Well Pipe*.

WELT GROOVER. See *Shoe Makers' Tool, Welt Groover*.

WELT KNIFE. See *Knife, Shoe Makers' Welt*.

WELT MILL. See *Shoe Makers' Tool, Welt Mill*.

WELT ROLLER. See *Shoe Makers' Machine, Welt Roller*.

WELT TRIMMER. See *Shoe Makers' Tool, Welt Trimmer*.

WHEEL BARROW. A small vehicle having a single wheel and one or two handles at the rear for pushing. See also *Barrel Truck* and *Cart*.

Brick

Garden

Mortar

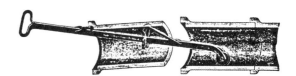

Pipe

Railroad or Canal

Wheel Barrow

Sawdust or Stable

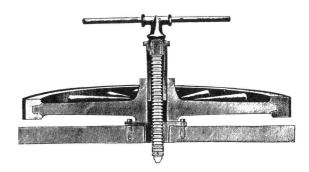

Wheel Box Press

Stave or Bark

Wheel Gauge

WHEEL HOLDER. A device used to hold a wagon wheel in a rigid position for assembly or repair.

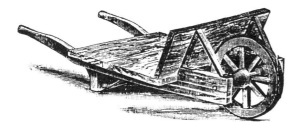

Stone

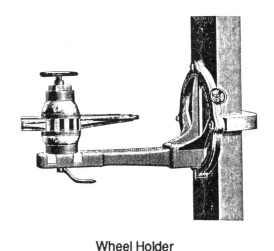

Wheel Holder

Three Wheel or Sidewalk
Wheel Barrow

WHEEL BENCH. See *Wheel Stand.*

WHEEL BLOCK. See *Wheel Stand.*

WHEEL BOX PRESS. Also called BOX PRESS. A tool made specifically for pressing a metal axle box into or out of a wagon wheel hub. These presses were listed in three sizes and each size had several interchangeable collars.

WHEEL GAUGE. A tool used to gauge the thickness of a solid rubber tire. The illustrated tool is Curran's Patent granted February 16, 1904.

WHEEL HORSE. See *Wheel Stand.*

WHEEL OILER. Also called FELLOE OILER and OIL TROUGH. A curved trough that can be filled with linseed oil and used for soaking wagon wheel felloes. Generally made of cast iron. Oilers were made in several sizes to accommodate wheels of various widths. One supplier listed a model with a built-in kerosene heater.

Wooden felloes must be kept saturated with oil to avoid shrinkage in dry weather and decay in wet weather. If they are allowed to dry out, shrinkage of the felloes and spoke tenons will result in a loose tire. Under severe conditions, the tire could come off and the wheel would then collapse. A quick, but temporary fix, for this dry weather shrinkage is to drive the wagon into the nearest pond or creek and leave it a few hours to soak up moisture.

Wheel Oiler

WHEEL PULLER. Also called GEAR PULLER. A tool used to pull a gear, pulley or wheel from an exposed shaft. A center screw and two hooks are used to apply equal pressure to both sides of the wheel.

Wheel Puller

WHEEL STAND. Also called WHEEL BENCH, WHEEL BLOCK, WHEEL HORSE and WHEEL STOOL. A bench or stand used to support a wooden wagon wheel for assembly or repair. The center screw is generally anchored to the floor of the shop to assure rigidity of the wheel.

Wheel Stand

Wheel Stand

WHEEL STOOL. See *Wheel Stand.*

WHEEL VISE. A clock makers' tool. See *Vise, Wheel.*

WHEEL WRENCH. See *Wrench, Wheel.*

WHEELERS' AXE. See *Axe, Bearded.*

WHEELWRIGHTS' TOOLS. Also called WHEELERS' TOOLS. Making a wooden wheel was a highly specialized craft. Obtaining the proper proportions of the various parts and the proper amount of dish was largely a matter of judgement and experience. The task was made even more difficult because only the toughest woods were used. The spokes and felloes were generally made of oak. The hub was made of elm or of the best quality oak if elm was not available. The tires and bands were often made and installed by a workman specializing in iron work. However, the wood and iron portions had to complement each other to produce a satisfactory wheel. Many of the common tools of the general wood worker and the general blacksmith were also used in the wheelwright shop. The special-purpose wheelwrights' tools listed below can be found in normal alphabetical sequence. These tools may also have been used for other purposes.

ANVIL TOOL, CHANNEL SWAGE
ANVIL TOOL, TIRE SET
AWL, SCRATCH
AXE, BEARDED
AXLE CUTTER
AXLE GAUGE
AXLE SETTER
BAND SETTER
BENCH, SPOKE
BORING TOOL, HUB REAMER
BORING TOOL, TIRE DRILL

Bung Burner
Clamp, Rim
Clamp, Wagon Tire
Cone
Fore Auger
Hollow Auger
Hollow Auger Brace
Hub Boxing Gauge
Hub Boxing Machine
Jarvis
Marking Gauge
Rasp, Felloe
Rounder
Rule, Caliper
Samson
Saw, Felloe
Spoke Dog
Spoke Extractor
Spoke Pointer
Spoke Shave
Tenoning Machine
Tire Bender
Tire Bolt Holder
Tire Bolter and Cutter
Tire Clamp
Tire Dog
Tire Heater
Tire Marker
Tire Measuring Wheel
Tire Puller
Tire Setter
Tire Setting Plate
Tire Shrinker
Tire Upsetter
Tongs, Tire Puller
Turning Tool, Tenoner
Vise, Post
Wheel Box Press
Wheel Gauge
Wheel Holder
Wheel Oiler
Wheel Stand
Wrench, Buggy
Wrench, Rim
Wrench, Wagon

Whetstone. See *Sharpening Stone*.

Whey Knife. See *Curd Cutter*.

Whimble Brace. See *Boring Tool, Bit Brace, Wimble*. Whimble is an incorrect spelling that was occasionally used in catalogues.

Whip. A flexible instrument used to strike a horse thereby urging it to more speed or exertion. See illustrations on the following page.

Whip Saw. See *Saw, Whip*.

Whist Broom. See *Broom, Whist*.

White Wash Brush. See *Brush, White Wash*.

Wick Cleaner. A special tool used to clean and trim the wick of an Aladdin lamp.

Wick Cleaner

Willow Brake. Also called Brake, Willow Peeler and Willow Stripper. An iron fork used to remove the bark from willow withies. The brake consists of two iron straps welded together at the bottom and formed such that the tops are held together with spring pressure. The spike at the bottom is embedded firmly in a stump or block during use. A green withe is pulled through the fork of the brake thus splitting the bark. Continued passes through the fork strips the bark or loosens it so that it can be easily removed with the hands.

Willow Brake

Willow Knife. See *Knife, Willow*.

Wimble Brace. See *Boring Tool, Bit Brace, Wimble*.

Winding Sticks. Also called Boning Sticks and Winking Sticks. Two flat sticks approximately 15 inches long that are used to determine if a board has any twist (wind). One stick is placed across the board at each end. Any twist in the board can be easily seen by sighting along the ends of the sticks. These sticks are often made of hardwood and ornamented with inlays.

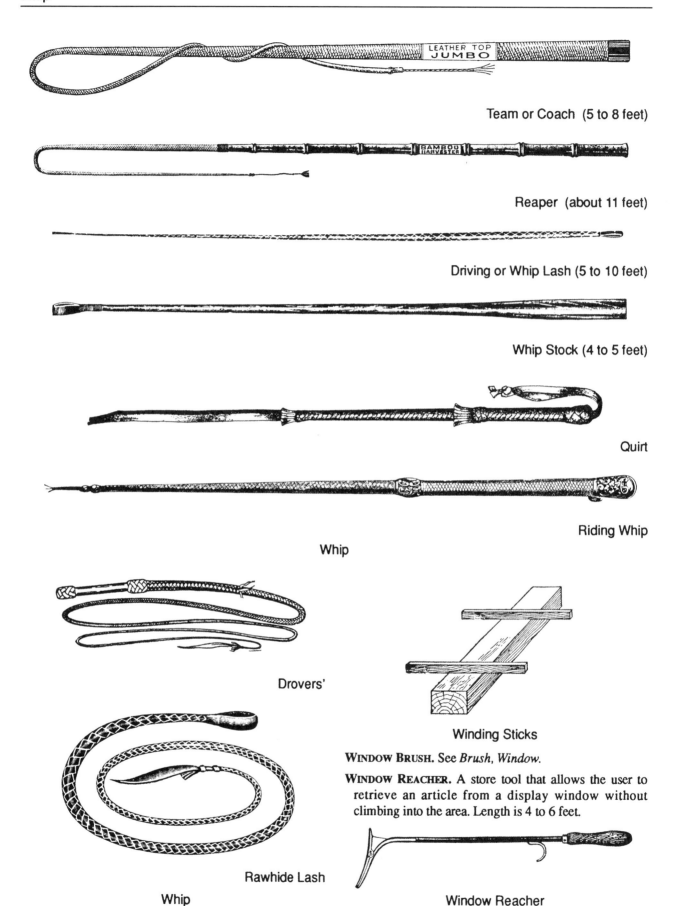

Team or Coach (5 to 8 feet)

Reaper (about 11 feet)

Driving or Whip Lash (5 to 10 feet)

Whip Stock (4 to 5 feet)

Quirt

Riding Whip

Whip

Drovers'

Winding Sticks

WINDOW BRUSH. See *Brush, Window.*

WINDOW REACHER. A store tool that allows the user to retrieve an article from a display window without climbing into the area. Length is 4 to 6 feet.

Rawhide Lash

Whip

Window Reacher

WINE PRESS. A screw press used to extract the juice from grapes for making wine. Also used for extracting juice from other fruit and as a lard press. Height is 36 to 48 inches.

Wine Press

WING CALIPER. See *Caliper, Wing.*

WING COMPASS. See *Compass, Wing.*

WING DIVIDER. See *Compass, Wing* and *Divider.*

WINKING STICKS. See *Winding Sticks.*

WIPING CLOTH. A cloth pad about 4 inches square used to smooth semi-molten lead or solder when joining two lead pipes. The pad is made of several layers of heavy cloth such as ticking.

Wiping Cloth

WIRE BENDER. A clock repair tool.

Wire Bender

WIRE BRUSH. See *Brush, Wire.*

WIRE CHISEL. See *Chisel, Wire.*

WIRE COILER. A device used to make kinks in straight fence wire. The device can be pulled along the wire by one man. The illustrated coiler was patented March 15, 1898.

WIRE CRIMPER. A tool used to crimp fence wire thus making the wire tighter. Overall length of the illustrated tool is 18 inches.

Wire Coiler

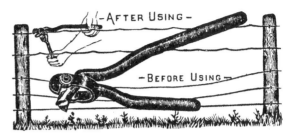

Wire Crimper

WIRE CUTTER AND STRIPPER. Also called WIRE PEELER and WIRE SKINNER. An electricians' tool used to cut and strip wire. One notch is used to cut the wire and the other notch cuts the insulation.

Wire Cutter and Stripper

WIRE CUTTERS. A linemans' tool. See also *Barbed Wire Cutter.*

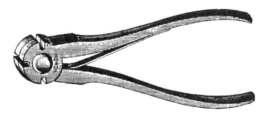

Wire Cutters

WIRE CUTTING PLIERS. See *Pliers, Wire Cutting.*

WIRE FENCE SPLICER. See *Wire Splicing Tool.*

WIRE GAUGE. Also called DRILL GAUGE and SCREW GAUGE. A gauge used to determine the size of a screw, twist drill or wire.

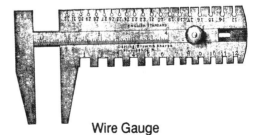

Wire Gauge

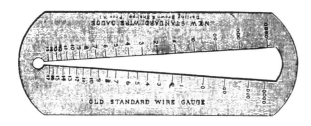

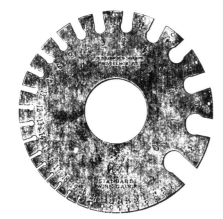

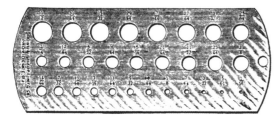

Wire Gauge

WIRE NIPPERS. See *Nippers, Wire*.

WIRE PEELER. See *Wire Cutter and Stripper*.

WIRE PLIERS. See *Pliers, Wire*.

WIRE SKINNER. See *Wire Cutter and Stripper*.

WIRE SPINDLE. A broom makers' device that holds a coil of wire and allows it to unwind as needed. Most of these spindles were home made and were generally crude. The illustrated tool is shown with a coil of wire in place.

Wire Spindle

WIRE SPLICING TOOL. A simple tool used to make the twist when splicing a fence or telephone wire.

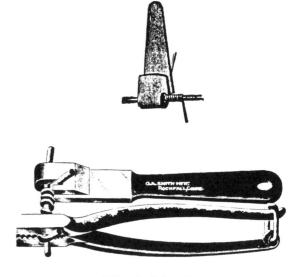

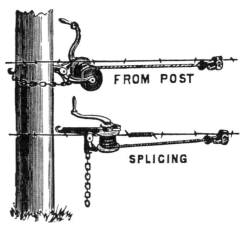

Wire Splicing Tool

WIRE STRETCHER. A fence-building and repair tool used to stretch barbed wire. The tool shown in illustration (b) was recommended for tightening guy wires.

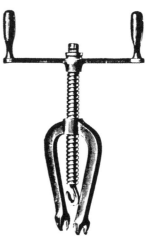

(b)

Wire Stretcher

WIRE THREADER. A device capable of threading wire or small rods. Intended to be clamped in a vise during use.

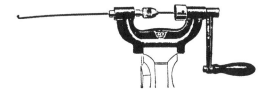

Wire Threader

WIRE TWISTER. A tool used to twist double-loop tie wires. The hook is placed through the end loops of both wires and caused to rotate, thus twisting the wires together. These wires were used to tie sacks, cables, bundles of pipe and similar items.

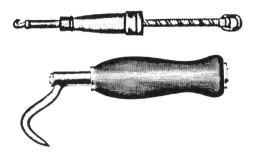

Wire Twister

WIRING MACHINE. See *Tinsmiths' Machine, Wiring.*

WITCHET. Also called ROUNDING PLANE and TURNING PLANE. A tool used to shave a square strip into a round rod. Often used for making tool handles. Many of these tools are home made and sometimes very crude. See also *Plane, Rounding* and *Rounder.*

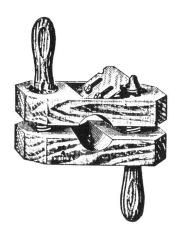

Witchet

WOOD CARVERS' FILE. See *Riffler.*

WOOD CARVERS' RASP. See *Riffler.*

WOOD CARVERS' TOOLS. See *Carvers' Tools.*

WOOD CHISEL. See *Chisel.*

WOOD CHOPPERS' MAUL. See *Maul, Wood Choppers'.*

WOOD CHOPPERS' WEDGE. See *Wedge, Wood Splitting.*

WOOD FILE. A woodworking tool. See *File, Wood.*

WOOD FLOAT. See *Float, Wood.*

WOOD RASP. See *Rasp, Wood.*

WOOD SAW. See *Saw, Buck.*

WOOD SCRAPER. See *Scraper, Cabinet.*

WOOD SPLITTING WEDGE. See *Wedge, Wood Splitting.*

WOOD TRIMMER. See *Miter Trimmer.*

WOOD TURNING TOOL. See *Turning Tool.*

WOOD VISE. See *Clamp, Wooden* and *Vise, Wood Workers'.*

WOOD WORKERS' FLOAT. See *Float, Wood.*

WOOD WORKERS' VISE. See *Vise, Wood Workers'.*

WOODEN CLAMP. See *Clamp, Wooden.*

WOOL COMB. A coarse comb used to straighten wool for spinning. The illustrated tool is a home-made device with flat tines. Two tines are missing.

Wool Comb

WOODEN SHOE TOOL. See *Clog Makers' Tools.*

WRECKING BAR. See *Bar, Wrecking.*

WRECKING CHISEL. See *Chisel, Wrecking.*

WRECKING PICK. See *Pick, Wrecking.*

WRENCH. A tool used to apply radial leverage for the purpose of tightening or loosening a threaded nut or bolt. See also *Piano Tool, Stringing Hammer* and *Piano Tool, Tuning Hammer.*

WRENCH, ADJUSTABLE. A wrench in which the size of the jaw opening is adjustable to fit nuts of several different sizes. Hundreds of varieties of adjustable wrenches were marketed in America. A sample of those wrenches are illustrated here and under other sub-headings of wrenches.

Adjustable Wrench

Barwick's Patent

Hill's Patent

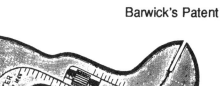

Baxter's Patent

Self Adjusting

Adjustable Wrench

WRENCH, ADJUSTABLE S. Length is 4 to 14 inches.

Baxter's Diagonal

Chaueffeur's Universal

Adjustable S Wrench

Angle or Crescent

WRENCH, AGRICULTURAL. Also called AGRICULTURAL MONKEY WRENCH. Length is 6 to 15 inches. This wrench is the same as one type of screw wrench except that the agricultural wrench is lighter in construction.

Angle or Crescent

Agricultural Wrench

WRENCH, ALLEN. See *Wrench, Socket Set Screw.*

WRENCH, ALLIGATOR. A general-purpose wrench having a V shaped mouth with notches on one side. The notches were intended to grip square nuts of various sizes.

Rapid Transit

Adjustable Wrench

Alligator Wrench

526

Boynton's Adjustable

Elgin Adjustable

Handy

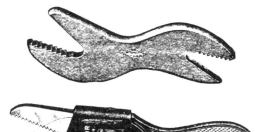

Alligator Wrench

WRENCH, ANGLE. See *Wrench, Adjustable.*

WRENCH, AUTO TOOL. A multi-purpose wrench made for occasional use on early automobiles.

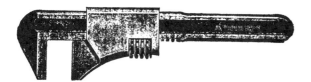

Auto Tool Wrench

WRENCH, AUTOMOBILE. An adjustable wrench of the type that was provided with many early automobiles.

Automobile Wrench

WRENCH, AUTOMOBILE RIM. A special tool used for removing nuts from demountable automobile wheel rims.

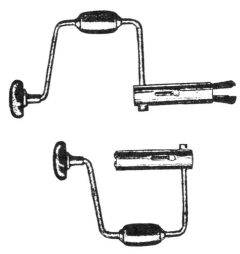

Automobile Rim Wrench

WRENCH, AXLE. A special wrench intended for use on Collinge buggy axles.

Axle Wrench

WRENCH, AXLE NUT HOLDER. Also called BUGGY WRENCH. A device used to hold a buggy axle nut such that it will screw on squarely and not damage the threads.

Axle Nut Holder

527

WRENCH, BALL BOLT. A special tool made to grasp the square shoulders of a ball bolt. A piano repairmans' tool.

Ball Bolt Wrench

WRENCH, BASIN. A plumbers' tool.

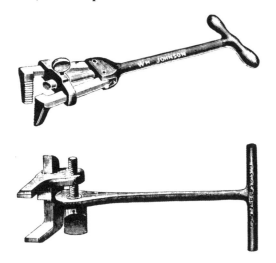

Basin Wrench

WRENCH, BATTERY. A box wrench, with a deep throat, especially adapted to remove and install battery terminal nuts.

Battery Wrench

WRENCH, BED KEY. Also called BED BOLT WRENCH and BEDSTEAD WRENCH. A wrench used to assemble the rails to the headboard of a bed.

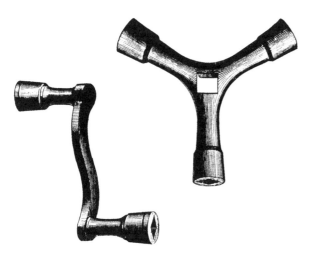

Bed Key

Gray's Ratchet

Bed Key

WRENCH, BICYCLE. A small wrench intended for inclusion in a bicycle tool kit. Length is 5 1/2 to 6 inches.

Bicycle Wrench

WRENCH, BIT. Also called AUGER BIT HANDLE. A cross bar with a hole made to fit the tapered shank of a bit brace tool. One supplier listed this tool specifically for use with a reamer.

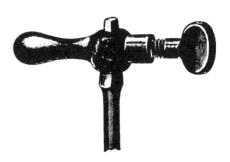

Bit Wrench

528

WRENCH, BIT BRACE. One type of socket wrench. See *Wrench, Socket*.

WRENCH, BOILER MAKERS'. See *Wrench, Combination*.

WRENCH, BOOT CALK. See *Boot Calk Tool*.

WRENCH, BOX. A wrench with the end completely enclosed. See also *Wrench, Battery* and *Wrench, Tool Post*.

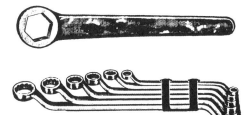

Box Wrench

WRENCH, BUGGY. Also called CARRIAGE WRENCH. A wrench used to loosen or tighten the axle nuts on a buggy or other light vehicle. The illustrations are representative of the many types available. Sizes from 3/4 inches to 1 1/2 inches were listed. Length is 7 to 12 inches. The Stafford's patent wrench is unique in that it retains the nut with the aid of a rubber band.

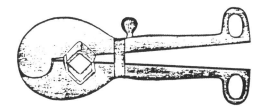

Stafford's Patent

Holdfast

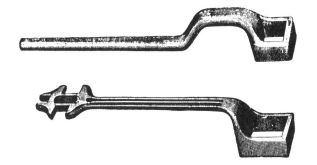

Buggy Wrench

Buggy Wrench

WRENCH, BUSH. A tool used for inserting a self tapping bush into the bung hole of a beer keg. The tapered wrench grasps the inside of the bush sleeve and allows the bush to be rotated.

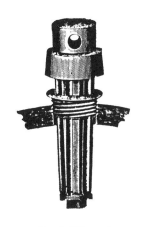

Bush Wrench

WRENCH, CAP SCREW. See *Wrench, Set Screw*.

WRENCH, CAR. See *Wrench, S*.

WRENCH, CARRIAGE. See *Wrench, Buggy*.

WRENCH, CARRIAGE KNOB. A bit brace tool intended for installing carriage curtain knobs. Essentially a special-purpose socket wrench.

Carriage Knob Wrench

WRENCH, CASING. A type of strap wrench used to assemble thin-wall well casing. Webbing is used as a gripping surface to avoid scratching the surface of the casing and to reduce the possibility of crushing.

WRENCH, CHAIN PIPE. Also called CHAIN TONGS. An adjustable pipe wrench that uses a chain to grasp the pipe thus allowing one tool to fit a wide range of pipe sizes. Chain pipe wrenches with handles up to 7 feet long were listed.

529

Casing Wrench

Chain Pipe Wrench

WRENCH, CHECK NUT. Also called TAPPET WRENCH. An open-end wrench that is extra thin to facilitate grasping the inner nut of a check nut pair.

Check Nut Wrench

WRENCH, COMBINATION. Also called ENGINEERS' WRENCH and NUT & PIPE WRENCH. An adjustable wrench that will grip both square nuts and pipe. Length is 8 to 18 inches.

Acme

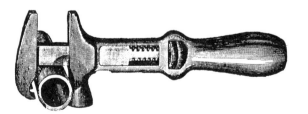

Boardman's Patent

Combination Wrench

Bemis and Call

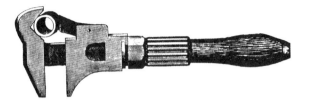

Donohue's Patent

Rouse's Patent

Webster's Patent

Combination Wrench

WRENCH, CONSTRUCTION. Also called BOILER MAKERS' WRENCH, CAR BUILDERS' WRENCH, FITTING UP WRENCH and STRUCTURAL WRENCH. A steel workers' tool. Size is 1/2 to 1 11/16 inches. Both straight and offset types were available. The tapered handle can be used as a lever to line up the holes in two members to be joined.

Construction Wrench

WRENCH, CRANK. A combination wrench that can serve as a bit brace. Some wrenches of this general type have a removable handle that can be used as a screw driver.

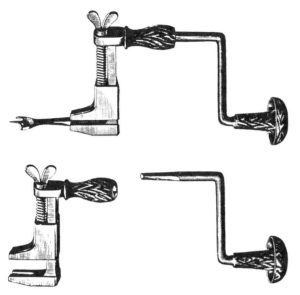

Crank Wrench

WRENCH, CRESCENT. See *Wrench, Adjustable. Crescent* is a trade name often used to designate a type of adjustable wrench.

WRENCH, CROSS RIM. A wrench used on the nuts on the inside edge of a carriage wheel felloe.

Cross Rim Wrench

WRENCH, CROW'S FOOT. A wrench that can be used on a nut recessed inside a deep cavity. Generally listed as a plumbers' tool. Sizes up to 2 inches have been noted.

Crow's Foot Wrench

WRENCH, CYLINDER. A special wrench used to tighten or loosen the cylinder teeth nuts on a grain separator.

WRENCH, DOOR SPRING. A special wrench used to tighten the built-in spring in a screen door check hinge.

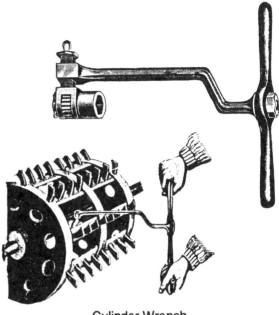

Cylinder Wrench

Door Spring Wrench

WRENCH, END. A wrench that is open on one or both ends. See *Wrench, Open End.*

WRENCH, ENGINEERS'. Several types of wrenches were listed by various suppliers as Engineers' Wrenches. See *Wrench, Combination; Wrench, Adjustable* and *Wrench, Open End.*

WRENCH, FARMERS'. Also called UTILITY WRENCH. An inexpensive wrench intended for occasional use. This type wrench was often furnished with new farm machines.

Farmers' Wrench

WRENCH, FLANGE. A type of spanner wrench used on the outside circumference of a wheel or pulley.

Flange Wrench

WRENCH, FURNITURE HANDLE. A cast iron socket-type wrench used for removing the nuts inside of a dresser drawer.

Furniture Handle Wrench

WRENCH, GIRDLE. Also called GIRDLE PIPE WRENCH. A type of pipe wrench with a wide gripping area that reduces the possibility of crushing the pipe.

Girdle Wrench

WRENCH, GUNSMITHS'. Also called NIPPLE WRENCH. A tool used to remove the nipple from a muzzle loading gun.

Gunsmiths' Wrench

WRENCH, HANDRAIL. Also called RAIL WRENCH. A stair builders' tool.

Handrail Wrench

WRENCH, HUB. See *Wrench, Buggy* and *Wrench, Wagon*.

WRENCH, KEY. An adjustable wrench in which the adjustment is fixed with a metal wedge. Length is 28 to 48 inches.

Key

Key and Screw

Key Wrench

WRENCH, LAG SCREW. A wrench used on a square-headed lag screw. The tool shown in illustration (a) was listed as a linemans' wrench.

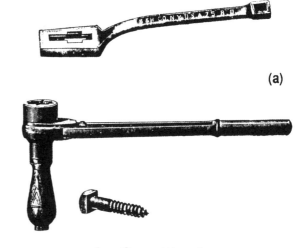

(a)

Lag Screw Wrench

WRENCH, LATHE DOG. A wrench with multiple holes to fit various sizes of lathe dog set screws. The illustrated tool will fit 3/8 to 3/4 inch posts.

Lathe Dog Wrench

WRENCH, MACHINE. See *Wrench, S.*

WRENCH, MONKEY. See *Wrench, Agricultural* and *Wrench, Screw.*

WRENCH, NIPPLE. Also called SPOKE TIGHTENER and SPOKE WRENCH. A tool used for tightening the spokes of a bicycle wheel. See also *Wrench, Gunsmiths'.*

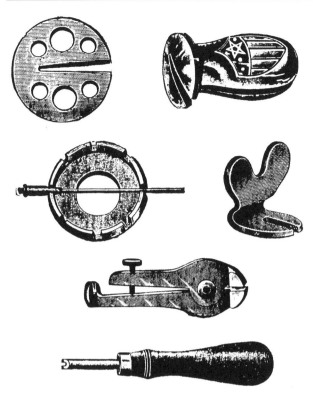

Nipple Wrench

WRENCH, NUT. See *Wrench, Socket*.

WRENCH, OPEN END. Also called ENGINEERS' WRENCH. A fixed size wrench that is open on one or both ends. Size is 1/16 to 7 5/8 inches. A thin variety of this wrench was sometimes listed separately as a CHECK NUT WRENCH. A thick type was often called a SET SCREW WRENCH. The name "Open End" is a descriptive term that was not used in early catalogues but gradually came into use in the 20th century. See also *Wrench, Check Nut; Wrench, S* and *Wrench, Set Screw*.

Open End Wrench

WRENCH, PINCER. A patented adjustable wrench with a lever-type handle.

Ripley's Patent

Pincer Wrench

WRENCH, PIPE. An adjustable wrench intended to grasp a cylindrical object such as a pipe or rod. Length is 6 to 48 inches. Pipe wrenches were made in a vast variety of types and sizes. Some typical examples are illustrated. See also *Tongs, Pipe; Wrench, Chain Pipe; Wrench, Girdle* and *Wrench, Strap*.

Bonner's Patent

Brosnihan's Patent

Bullard

Curtis

Eureka

Giles' Patent

Pipe Wrench

Merrick's Patent

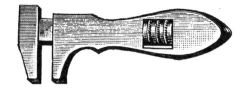

Bellamy

Pocket Wrench

Phillips' Patent

WRENCH, RATCHET. A wrench having a mechanism that will allow effective repeated motion in one direction with a reciprocating motion of the handle.

Reed's

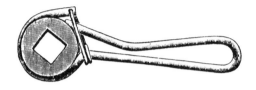

Stillson

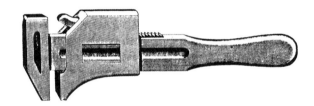

Wakefield

Ratchet Wrench

WRENCH, RIM. Also called TIRE BOLT WRENCH. A wrench intended for use on the nuts located on the inside of a wagon wheel felloe. One type of rim wrench has interchangeable sockets for use on three sizes of bolts. See also *Wrench, Automobile Rim* and *Wrench, Cross Rim*.

Wright's

Pipe Wrench

WRENCH, POCKET. An adjustable wrench small enough to carry in the pocket. Length is 3 to 4 1/2 inches.

Gem

Pocket Wrench

Rim Wench

534

Klopp's

Rim Wrench

Coe's Patent

WRENCH, S. A general-purpose open end wrench with a pronounced double curve. A light version of this wrench was listed by some suppliers as a CAR WRENCH. The heavier type was often called MACHINE WRENCH. Size is 1/4 to 2 $^7/_{16}$ inches.

Diamond

S Wrench

Hewet's Patent

Screw Wrench

WRENCH, SCREW. Also called MONKEY WRENCH. Length is 4 $^1/_2$ to 21 inches.

WRENCH, SET SCREW. Also called Cap Screw Wrench and Machine Wrench. An extra thick open-end wrench intended for tightening set screws. Sizes of these wrenches are 3/16 to 1 $^{13}/_{16}$ inches.

Acme

Set Screw Wrench

WRENCH, SLEEVE. Also called BENCH KEY and SLEEVE DRIVER. A wrench used by a watch maker to tighten and loosen the stem sleeve in a watch.

Bemis and Call

Briggs' Patent

Screw Wrench

Sleeve Wrench

Sleeve Wrench

With Ratchet Handle

WRENCH, SNATH. Also called SCYTHE SNATH WRENCH. A small special-purpose wrench made to fit the nuts on a snath.

Socket Wrench

Snath Wrench

WRENCH, SOCKET. Also called NUT RUNNER and NUT WRENCH. A type of wrench that fits over the entire nut thus providing an even torque and the largest possible gripping surface.

WRENCH, SOCKET SET SCREW. Also called ALLEN'S HOLLOW SOCKET WRENCH. A wrench that fits into a hole in the end of the screw. This type of wrench is now known as an ALLEN WRENCH.

Adjustable Brace Wrench

Socket Set Screw Wrench

WRENCH, SPANNER. A wrench that engages a notch or hole in the nut or wheel to be turned. Used on objects of large diameter and on couplings where a smooth outer surface is desirable.

Adjustable Brace Wrench

Face Spanner

Brace Wrench

Pin Spanner

Rim Spanner

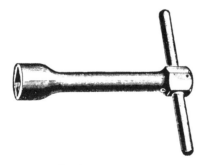

Spanner Wrench

WRENCH, SPOKE. See *Wrench, Nipple.*

WRENCH, STILLSON. See *Wrench, Pipe. Stillson* is a trade name often used to designate a certain variety of pipe wrench.

Socket Wrench

WRENCH, STRAP. A type of pipe wrench that uses a woven strap to grip the pipe. Used primarily on pipes with polished surfaces. Sizes were made to fit pipes up to 3 inches in diameter. See also *Wrench, Casing*.

Strap Wrench

WRENCH, STRUCTURAL. See *Wrench, Construction*.

WRENCH, TAP. A wrench intended for turning thread-cutting taps. Length of the cross handle is 5 to 24 inches.

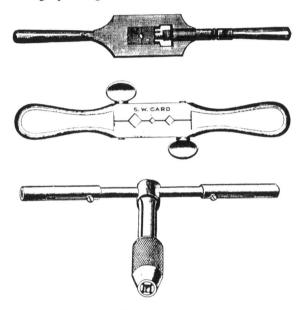

Tap Wrench

WRENCH, TAPPET. See *Wrench, Check Nut*.

WRENCH, TEXTILE. Also called TEXTILE MACHINE WRENCH. An open-end wrench with the openings at an angle of 22 1/2 degrees to the shank. Sizes of textile wrenches are 5/16 to 1 7/16 inches.

Textile Wrench

WRENCH, TOOL POST. An extra-thick wrench similar to the cap screw wrench. Size is 9/16 to 1 inch.

Tool Post Wrench

WRENCH, TOP PROP. A wrench intended for working the nuts on a buggy top standard.

Top Prop Wrench

WRENCH, TRACK. Also called RAILROAD TRACK WRENCH. Length is 22 to 36 inches.

Track Wrench

WRENCH, UTILITY. See *Wrench, Farmers'*.

WRENCH, WAGON. A wrench used to loosen and tighten the axle nuts on a wagon. Sizes from 1 1/2 to 2 3/4 inches were listed. Retaining nuts for wagon wheels require frequent removal for greasing the axles. The wagon wrench was often stowed in a loop fastened to the side of the wagon box or used as a double tree pin. In either case, the wrench was handy for use when needed.

Wagon Wrench

WRENCH, WHEEL. A patented device used to remove the axle nuts from a buggy or wagon.

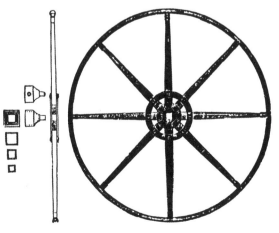

Wheel Wrench

537

WRENCH HAMMER. See *Hammer, Wrench.*

WRENCH JAW. Also called PIPE ATTACHMENT. A detachable device that will adapt a screw wrench for use on a pipe or rod.

Wrench Jaw

WREST. A slotted saw set in which a saw tooth is bent by applying leverage to the extended handle. See *Saw Set.*

Tool names starting with the letter Y.

YANKEE AXE. A specific pattern of axe. See *Axe, Broad, yankee pattern; Axe, Double Bit, yankee pattern* and *Axe, Single Bit, yankee pattern.*

YANKEE CUTTER. See *Shoe Makers' Tool, Peg Cutter.*

YANKEE SCREW DRIVER. A trade name of a push-type screw driver. See *Screw Driver, Push.*

YARD STICK. See *Rule, Yard Stick.*

YARNING CHISEL. See *Caulking Tool, Plumbers'.*

YARNING IRON. See *Caulking Tool, Plumbers'.*

YOKE. Also called WATER YOKE. A connecting cross-bar shaped to fit the neck and shoulders of the user. It allows the weight of two buckets of water or equivalent to be supported by the back and shoulders rather than by the arms. Intended for use on a farm for carrying water. Length of the illustrated yoke is 40 inches.

Yoke

Tool names starting with the letter Z.

ZAX. See *Axe, Slaters'.*

TOOL IDENTIFICATION

Proper identification of an old hand tool is often a challenge even to those who profess to be experts in the field. To the person with an average knowledge of the trades, identification of a common tool of 100 years ago could be an impossible task. It is hoped that this volume can be used by collectors, museum cataloguers, restoration personnel and antique enthusiasts in general to eliminate some of the problems associated with tool identification and proper nomenclature.

Some general guidelines and procedures for identifying a tool are listed below:

● **Check for patent dates and patent numbers on the tool.**

A patent number and usually any patent date can be quickly traced by reference to patent indices and gazettes. Many schools and libraries have patent documents on file. Once the patent number is obtained, a copy of the patent application can be obtained from the Commissioner of Patents and Trademarks in Washington, D.C.

● **Consider whether or not the item is complete.**

The tool in question may be only part of a larger device or perhaps an attachment to a machine. It may also be a common type item with some vital part missing that alters the appearance. Mounting holes or attachment points are clues. If a tool has a part missing, it is seldom worth cataloguing even if it can be identified.

● **Consider the purpose of the tool.**

Most tools can readily be assigned by inspection to one of eleven broad categories. These categories are:

    1. Boring Tool. Any tool used to make a hole by rotary motion.
        Boring Tool, Bit
        Boring Tool, Bit Brace
    2. Striking Tool. Any tool used to accomplish a forcing action by impact.
        Beetle
        Hammer
        Mallet
        Maul
        Rammer
        Sledge
        Tamper
    3. Cutting Tool. Any tool with a sharp cutting edge.
        Impact Type
          Adze
          Axe
          Hatchet
          Mattock
        Pull Type
          Draw Gauge

      Drawing Knife
      Knife
      Router
      Spoke Shave
     Pushing or Driving Type
      Carving Tool
      Chisel
      Gouge
      Knife
      Plane
      Slick
      Spoke Shave
     Toothed Type
      Saw

4. Measuring Tool. Any tool used to gauge or scale a dimension.
      Caliper
      Dividers
      Gauge
      Rule
      Scales
      Tape

5. Marking Tool. Any tool used to mark or scribe
      Crayon
      Marking Gauge
      Mortising Gauge
      Pencil
      Scribe
      Trammel Points

6. Holding Tool. Any tool used to hold a workpiece temporarily in position.
      Clamp
      Vise

7. Guiding or Testing Tool. Any tool used to determine or describe a parameter.
      Bevel
      Gauge
      Square

8. Sharpening Tool. Any tool used to sharpen a cutting edge.
      File
      Grindstone
      Sharpening Stone

9. Abrading Tool. Any tool used to reduce a workpiece by removing surface particles.
      Rasp
      Riffler
      Scraper

10. Supporting Tool. Any tool used as a backup or support for a workpiece.
      Anvil
      Leveling Block
      Mandrel
      Stake

11. Spreading or Piercing Tool. Any tool used to widen a perforation or rift.
    Awl
    Punch
    Wedge

If a tool can be assigned to one of the above categories, the identification task consists merely of reviewing the multiple illustrations in that group to find the specific tool. Note that sometimes a size or other factor is given to augment the illustration. For instance, the likely usage of a tool may depend upon size or weight. In many cases, the illustrated tool will have more than one usage.

● **Consider what trade used the tool.**

If the tool can be identified to a specific craft such as jeweler or farrier, review of the list of tools for that craft may lead to an identification. Listings of special-purpose tools used in several crafts are included in normal alphabetical sequence. The crafts represented are also listed in the front of the dictionary and in the beginning paragraph under each letter.

● **Consider what the tool will not do.**

It is sometimes necessary to rule out possible identifications by negative reasoning. For instance, a very small hammer would not be a blacksmiths' tool even though it is the proper shape.

● **Guess at the usage.**

The process of identification can often be shortened by intelligent guessing. The appearance of a tool generally reveals the intended usage. For instance, an item that looks like a hammer is indeed a hammer in the vast majority of the cases. If not found in the hammer section, a quick review of the above category list would suggest looking at the mallet illustrations.

Should the quest for identification prove unsuccessful, be consoled by the knowledge that even a panel of experts doesn't have a very good average. What-Is-It sessions are program events at many tool association meetings. These sessions seldom result in satisfactory identification of more than fifty percent of the items submitted for consideration. It is probable that an illustration of the unidentified tool resides in this book and that it will show up unexpectedly while you are looking for another item.

BIBLIOGRAPHY

Sellens, Alvin *The Stanley Plane, A History and Descriptive Inventory*. Augusta, KS: Alvin Sellens, 1975.

Sellens, Alvin *Stanley Folding Rules, A History and Descriptive Inventory*. Augusta, KS: Alvin Sellens, 1984.

Sellens, Alvin *Woodworking Planes, A Descriptive Register of Wooden Planes*. Augusta, KS: Alvin Sellens, 1978.

Adkins, E. C. & Co. Inc. *Text Book of Adkins Silver Steel Saws*. Indianapolis, Ind: E. C. Adkins & Co. Inc., 1927.

Adkins, E. C. & Co. Inc. *Saw Sense*. Indianapolis, Ind: E. C. Adkins & Co. Inc.

The Amateur Mechanic's Workshop. London: Trubner and Co., Seventh Edition 1888.

American Builder (Periodical). Chicago, Illinois: September, 1920.

American Carpenter and Builder (Periodical). Chicago, Illinois: September, 1912.

Audels Carpenters and Builders Guide. New York: Theo Audel & Co., 1923.

Audels Plumbers and Steam Fitters Guide. New York: Theo Audel & Co., 1925.

The Chronicle of The Early American Industries Association. Issues from 1933 to 1989. The Early American Industries Association.

Collins and Company. *One Hundred Years*. (A brochure). 1926.

The Cooper and His Work. Early Trades and Crafts Society, Second Printing 1972.

Diderot, Denis. *A Diderot Pictorial Encyclopedia of Trades and Industry* (Selected Plates). New York: Dover Publications, Inc., 1959.

Diehl, Edith. *Book Binding, Its Background and Technique (Two Volumes Bound in One)*. New York: Dover Publications, Inc., 1980.

Disston, Henry & Sons, Inc. *Lumberman Handbook*. Philadelphia, PA: Henry Disston & Sons, Inc. 1907.

Disston, Henry & Sons, Inc. *The File in History*. Philadelphia, PA: Henry Disston & Sons, Inc., Second Edition 1921.

Disston, Henry & Sons, Inc. *The Saw in History*. Philadelphia, PA: Henry Disston & Sons, Inc., Ninth Edition 1926.

Farnham, Alexander. *Tool Collectors Handbook*. Stockton, New Jersey: Alexander Farnham, 1970.

Gorlin, Jack. *Files*. Early Trades and Crafts Society, 1977.

Hasluck, Paul N. *Domestic Jobbing, The Repair of Household Articles*. New York: Funk and Wagnalls Company.

Hibbard, Spencer, Bartlett & Co. *The Marvel Cyclopedia*. Chicago: Hibbard, Spencer, Bartlett & Co., 1893.

Hjorth, Herman. *Principles of Woodworking*. The Bruce Publishing Company, 1930.

Holmstrom and Holford. *American Blacksmithing*. Sears, Roebuck & Company, 1916.

Kauffman, Henry J. *American Axes*. Brattleboro, VT: The Stephen Greene Press, 1972.

Kilby, K. *The Shire Album 28, The Village Cooper*. Aylesbury, Bucks, UK: Shire Publications, Ltd. 1977.

Kilby, Kenneth. *The Cooper and His Trade*. London: John Baker, Ltd., 1971.

Kline, John B. *Tobacco Farming and Cigar Making Tools*. No publisher listed. 1975.

Knight, Edward H. *Knight's American Mechanical Dictionary*. New York: J. B. Ford and Company, 1874.

Knight, Edward H. *The Practical Dictionary of Mechanics* (Supplementary Volume). Boston: Houghton, Mifflin & Co., Circa 1884.

Manual of Blacksmithing. Chicago, IL: Gerlotte Publishing Co., 1902.

Mercer, Henry C. *Ancient Carpenters' Tools*. Doylestown, PA: The Bucks County Historical Society, Fourth Edition 1968.

Nicholson File Company *A Treatise on Files and Rasps*. Providence, RI: Nicholson File Company, 1878. Reprinted by the Early American Industries Association, 1983.

Richardson, M. T. *Practical Blacksmithing Volume III*. New York: M.T. Richardson, 1890.

Richardson, M. T. *Practical Blacksmithing Volume IV*. New York: M. T. Richardson, 1891.

Richardson, M. T. *Practical Carriage Building*. New York: M. T. Richardson Co., 1892. Reprinted by The Early American Industries Association, 1981.

Roberts, Kenneth D. *Wooden Planes in 19th Century America*. Fitzwilliam, NH: Ken Roberts Publishing Company, 1975.

Salaman, R. A. *Dictionary of Leather Working Tools, c 1700-1950 and the tools of allied trades*. New York: Macmillan Publishing Company, 1986.

Salaman, R. A. *Dictionary of Tools used in the woodworking and allied trades, c 1700-1970*. New York: Charles Scribner's Sons, 1975.

Seymour, John *The Forgotten Crafts*. New York: A. Knoof, 1984.

Sloan, Eric *A Museum of Early American Tools*. New York: Funk and Wagnalls, 1964.

Smith, H. R. Bradley *Blacksmiths' and Farriers' Tools at Shelburne Museum*. Shelburne, VT: The Shelburne Museum, Inc., 1966.

Smith, Joseph *Smith's Key to the Various Manufactories of Sheffield*. Edited by John S. Kebabian. The Early American Industries Association, 1975.

Smith, Roger K. *Patented Transitional & Metallic Planes in America, 1827-1927*. Lancaster, MA: The North Village Publishing Co. , 1981.

Tomlinson, Charles *Illustrations of Trades. London:* Society for Promoting Christian Knowledge, 1860. Reprinted by The Early American Industries Association, 1972.

Tool Collectors' Picture Book, Second, Sixth and Seventh Volume. Early Trades and Crafts Society, 1972, 1974 and 1975 respectively.

Tunis, Edwin *Colonial Craftsmen*. Cleveland, Ohio: World Publishing Company, 1972.

Welsh, Peter C. *Woodworking Tools 1600-1900*. Washington, DC: Smithsonian Institution, 1966.

Weygers, Alexander G. *The Modern Blacksmith*. New York: Van Nostrand Reinhold Company, 1974.

Wildung, Frank H. *Woodworking Tools at Shelburne Museum*. Shelburne, VT: The Shelburne Museum, 1957.

Wyatt, E. M. *Common Woodworking Tools - I*. Industrial Arts and Vocational Education (Periodical), October, 1934.

Wyatt, Edwin M. *Common Woodworking Tools, Their History*. Milwaukee, Wis: The Bruce Publishing Company, 1936.

Wyke, John. *A Catalogue of Tools for Watch and Clock Makers*. The Henry Francis du Pont Winterthur Museum, 1978.

The Young Mechanic New York: G. P. Putnam's Sons, 1871.

Plus more than 200 trade catalogues and many brochures. The trade literature used was primarily from American Companies.